BASEBALL'S BEST

BEST The Hall of Fame Gallery

Martin Appel and Burt Goldblatt

Updated 1980 Edition

BASEBALL'S BEST

The Hall of Fame Gallery

Martin Appel and Burt Goldblatt

McGraw-Hill Book Company

New York   St. Louis   San Francisco   Auckland   Bogotá   Düsseldorf
Johannesburg   London   Madrid   Mexico   Montreal   New Delhi   Panama
Paris   São Paulo   Singapore   Sydney   Tokyo   Toronto

Facing title page: *Baseball*
Commissioner Bowie Kuhn
presides over the induction
ceremonies on the steps of the
Baseball Hall of Fame Library
at Cooperstown, N.Y., in 1974

Library of Congress Cataloging in Publication Data
Appel, Martin.
  Baseball's best.

  1. Baseball players—United States—Biography.
2. Cooperstown, N.Y. National Baseball Hall of Fame and
Museum.   I. Goldblatt, Burt, joint author.   II. Title.
GV865.A1A66   1980   796.357′092′2 [B]   80-12628
ISBN 0-07-002148-1

234567890   HDHD   8987654321

The editors for this book were Robert A. Rosenbaum and Patricia A. Allen,
the designer was Burt Goldblatt, and the production supervisor was Frank P.
Bellantoni. It was set in Optima by University Graphics, Inc.

Printed and bound by Halliday Lithograph Corporation.

Contents

Preface

To any American, a sports fan or not, "Hall of Fame" implies the Baseball Hall of Fame in Cooperstown, New York. Although Cooperstown isn't even located near a highway, millions of people have been drawn there since it became the home of the Hall of Fame in 1939—attracted by the magical powers that have put people in the role of spectator at baseball parks for more than a century.

Cooperstown probably wasn't the "Birthplace of Baseball," nor was General Abner Doubleday the inventor. But the quaint New York town is such a perfect setting for our national pastime that no one seems to mind the inconvenience of reaching it.

It was Ford Frick who really fathered the idea of a Hall of Fame. He borrowed the notion from New York University's Hall of Fame for Great Americans. Commissioner Landis was not enthusiastic about the concept, but today it's hard to find a sport that does not have a Hall of Fame of its own.

The first five electees were Ty Cobb, Honus Wagner, Babe Ruth, Walter Johnson, and Christy Mathewson. It might have been well to leave it at that; admittedly, not all the members who were chosen subsequently meet the standards set by those men. Many claim that at the rate of six new inductees each year, the population has grown too large. That may well be. But some 10,000 men have played major league baseball, and hundreds of thousands minor league ball. So, having 150 to 200 enshrined, including umpires and executives, is not really out of line.

There have been three methods of entrance into the Hall of Fame since the first election in 1936. Seemingly the most prestigious is election by the Baseball Writers' Association of America. This is an annual election, in which members vote on players with a minimum of 10 seasons of major league play, who have been retired for no less than 5 nor more than 20 years. Players in that category are eligible for election 15 times, and must be named on 75 percent of all ballots cast to be selected for membership.

A 12-man Committee on Baseball Veterans selected from players no longer eligible to be considered by the writers, and also chose executives and umpires. The committee was composed of writers, players, and executives, and also required 75 percent approval by its membership.

Between 1971 and 1977, a seven-man committee selected nine Negro League players for full induction before disbanding. This was an effort to welcome into the Hall of Fame great players who were denied the right to compete in the major leagues during the long period of an unwritten "color ban" in organized baseball.

In 1978, the Committee on Baseball Veterans was expanded to 18 members, and given the power to include Negro League players among its selections.

For the purposes of the biographies in this book, all men are treated equally, without regard to method of induction. This is the authors' way of seeing the Hall of Fame as the great equalizer—the highest and final achievement any man in baseball might reach.

Some figures, such as Babe Ruth, Joe DiMaggio, and Casey Stengel, have been covered more fully in previously published biographies. But many in this book are observed in detail for the first time, particularly the nineteenth-century players.

A note about statistics: They tend to vary from record book to record book, particularly when one deals with nineteenth-century players. Since most players were elected on the basis of records compiled by Spink Publications, we decided to honor those records, augmented by modern updated data provided by the *Baseball Encyclopedia.*

Great baseball writers whose works were invaluable in the research of this book include Lee Allen, Bob Broeg, Warren Brown, Frank Graham, Harold Kaese, Fred Lieb, Robert Peterson, Shirley Povich, Joe Reichler, Lawrence Ritter, Harold Rosenthal, Harold Seymour, Robert Smith, and Roy Stockton.

The authors would like to acknowledge the interest and help extended by the following people: Hall-of-Famers "Cool Papa" Bell and Buck Leonard who contributed a number of rare pictures, Pat Collins of the Aetna Life and Casualty Company, photographer Jeff Morey, the staffs of the New York Public Library, including the Newspaper Library and its director, Richard Hill who extended a helping hand in allowing us to copy some of the rare notebooks of Hall-of-Famer Harry Wright, Monte Irvin, of the Baseball Commissioner's office who made some rare photographic material available to the authors, and to Leslie Goldblatt for help in production.

The authors also wish to thank the following for their assistance: Bob Fishel, Phil Pepe, Red Foley, Ken Smith, Jack Redding, Pat Gitt, Stan Gedzelman, Fern Turkowitz, Eva Carey, the public relations staffs of the major league baseball teams, and especially Cliff Kachline, historian of the Baseball Hall of Fame.

We are particularly grateful to Clark Luke of Hollywood, Florida, for use of several rare photos contained in his remarkable collection of baseball memorabilia. Mr. Luke has very generously contributed his extensive collections to the Baseball Hall of Fame.

Martin Appel

Burt Goldblatt

Grover Cleveland Alexander (1887-1950)

The amazing career of Grover Cleveland Alexander was marked by 373 victories in the National League and a long battle against alcoholism and epilepsy. The contrast between success and failure made "Ol' Pete" one of the more dramatic characters in the first half-century of major league baseball.

Grover was born on a farm in St. Paul, Nebraska. One of thirteen children, twelve of them boys, he was named after the President of the United States, but as a child he was nicknamed "Dode."

Dode early showed the makings of a successful pitcher, hunting fowl with rocks and amazing his parents with his aim. The same precision control characterized his entire baseball career, during which he led the league in strikeouts six times and seldom walked more than one-third of his strikeout total.

At age 19, Grover lost a job as a telephone lineman by repeatedly showing up late for work because of baseball games. Shortly thereafter, he left home and traveled to Central City, where he pitched semi-pro ball for $50 a month. At a county fair in Butwell, Nebraska, Grover was discovered by the Galesburg club in the Illinois-Missouri League. Now 22, he signed his first professional contract for $100 a month.

Alex had a record of 15–8 for Galesburg, striking out 198 batters and walking only 42. But he suffered a serious injury when, running toward second base, he was hit squarely on the head by the throw to first, knocking him unconscious for 56 hours.

The injury left Alex with double vision, and the Galesburg manager, in a rather underhanded deal, quickly sold him to Indianapolis. With Alex's first practice pitch for the team, he broke the ribs of his new manager and alerted Indianapolis to the swindle. His career, which actually had 21 years to go, seemed over, and Grover was surprised when Indianapolis managed to peddle his contract to Syracuse in the New York State League for the 1910 season.

It came out later that his contract had been given to Syracuse free, and Indianapolis soon regretted its hasty generosity. Prior to the start of the 1910 season, Grover's double vision cleared up. Anyone who doubted the miracle had only to look at his 1910 record—a league-leading 29 victories and only 14 defeats in 43 games. The performance earned Alex a promotion to the majors when the Philadelphia Phillies drafted him. Syracuse netted $750 from the transaction. Alex's salary would be $250 a month with the Phillies.

Grover Alexander pitched a record-tying 373 victories during his National League career, including, in 1915, the only World Series game ever won by the Philadelphia Phillies. (Opposite page) Rookie Alexander pitching for the Phillies in 1911 when he won 28 games, including seven shutouts, four of them consecutive.

In 1911 Grover Cleveland Alexander had one of the finest rookie seasons ever recorded. He led the National League with 28 victories, including seven shutouts (four of them consecutive). He pitched 367 innings and had 31 complete games, both high for the league. The Phillies finished the season in fourth place.

Alexander's years in Philadelphia were the happiest and most stable of his career. In six of the seven years he played for the Phillies, he either tied or led the league in innings pitched, missing only in 1913. Alex led the league or tied for leadership in victories five times, including three consecutive seasons in which he won 30 or more games—1915 (31–10), 1916 (33–12), and 1917 (30–13). He posted five strikeout titles and gained three earned run average titles, including a spectacular 1.22 in 1915, a National League record that stood until 1969 when Bob Gibson of the Cardinals bettered it. As a member of the Phils, Alex led the league in complete games five times, with a high of 38 in 1916. He won five shutout crowns, including a record 16 in 1916. Alex pitched four one-hitters in 1915, a record for a single season. (Alexander never had a no-hitter in the big leagues.) On both September 23, 1916, and September 3, 1917, he pitched two complete-game victories in a doubleheader. Alex led the Phillies to the 1915 pennant, and then pitched their only victory in a five-game loss to Boston in the World Series. That win, in the opening game of the Series on October 8, is the only World Series victory ever recorded by the Philadelphia Phillies, who appeared again only in the 1950 classic, which they lost in four consecutive games to the Yankees. Alex scattered eight hits in winning, 3–1, over Ernie Shore in this historic game in Phillie history.

By the time the 1917 season closed, Alexander, at age 30, had won 190 games. With the United States in World War I, the Phillies decided to trade Alexander to the Cubs, thinking that he would soon be drafted. On November 11, 1917, the Cubs gave Philadelphia $60,000, pitcher Mike Prendergast, and catcher Pickles Dilhoefer in exchange for Alex and his long-time friend, catcher Bill Killefer. Killefer had been Alexander's catcher since Alex's rookie season and remained his receiver through 1921, when he became manager of the Cubs.

After pitching only three games for the Cubs in 1918, Alexander went to France as a member of the 89th Infantry Division. William Wrigley, the Cubs' owner, agreed to pay Alex's bride, Aimee, $500 a month in his absence.

Aimee came to be an important part of Alex's life, which was about to take a big

turn. Twice they married and twice they divorced, but always they remained close. Alexander simply became a difficult man to live with after the war.

In France Alexander lost the hearing in one ear as the result of shelling, and he experienced the first signs of epilepsy. Doctors never agreed on the exact cause of the illness, but they felt that the combination of the war and his illness drove him to alcoholism.

Alexander returned to the Cubs the following spring, won 16 of 27 decisions, and captured the league's ERA title with 1.72. He had another big year in 1920 with a 27–14 record, leading the league in victories and winning the circuit's strikeout and ERA crowns—his fifth straight ERA title, discounting the war-shortened 1918 season. But liquor was beginning to take its toll, and Alexander's ERA (under 2.00 for five straight years) rose to 3.39 in 1920 when he had a mediocre 15–13 record. A slowdown could be expected at age 33, but the turnabout was sudden, and it was well known in the league that Alexander was drinking excessively.

Various baseball people thought that Alexander was at his best on the mound when suffering from a hangover, but he never again led the league in any category. Alex managed to win 22 games for the Cubs in 1923, and in the Chicago city series, at the close of the 1925 season, he pitched a 19-inning game against the White Sox that darkness ended in a 2–2 tie. It was after that season that Alexander first entered a sanitarium.

On May 22, 1926, Cub admirers of Alexander staged an "Alexander Day" and gave him a $5500 car. The Braves spoiled the occasion by beating Alex, 7–1. This marked his last appearance for the Cubs. He subsequently came up with arm trouble and got into further difficulty with manager Joe McCarthy over drinking—and he was then waived to St. Louis. In his Cardinal debut on June 27, ironically, he beat the Cubs in 10 innings, 3–2, with a four-hitter.

The move to St. Louis set the stage for the most dramatic moment of Alexander's career. Rogers Hornsby managed the team into the World Series, and Alexander won nine games for the Cards. In the World Series against the Yankees, Alexander beat New York, 6–2, in the second game, then stopped the Yankees, 10–2, in game six. His work apparently done, Alexander celebrated that night, believing he had seen his last duty in the Series.

But game seven, on October 10 at Yankee Stadium, provided Alex with his finest hour. The Cardinals led, 3–2, in the seventh inning. The bases were loaded, two men were out, and Hornsby decided to relieve Jesse Haines. Meanwhile, Alexander had been napping in the bullpen, nursing a hangover. Still, Hornsby called for the 39-year-old righthander, and Ol' Pete (a nickname given by Killefer some years before) walked slowly to the mound. He faced the dangerous Yankee rookie, Tony Lazzeri, and with no place to put him, proceeded to strike him out on four pitches. It is probably the most remembered strikeout in World Series history. Many forget that Alexander, with two innings still to go, retired the side in order in the eighth and got the first two batters in the ninth before walking Babe Ruth. As Bob Meusel stood at the plate with a chance to win it for New York, Ruth, amazingly, attempted to steal second, and Bob O'Farrell threw him out. The Series was over, and Alexander was the star.

Alex came back in 1927 to win 21 games, his ninth and last season in the 20-victory circle, and then had a 16–9 record for the pennant-winning Cards of 1928. There were no heroics this time, as the Yankees avenged themselves by rocking Alexander for 11 earned runs in his two appearances while taking the Series in four games.

The 1929 season was a difficult one for Alexander. He spent part of it in a sanitarium, another part under suspension by manager Bill McKechnie, and most of it attempting to break Christy Mathewson's National League record of 372 victories. Finally, late in the season, he won No. 373, pitching five scoreless relief innings against the Phillies. Ironically, several years later, a statistical error was discovered in Mathewson's career, and he was given an additional victory, tying Alexander.

On December 11, 1929, the Cards traded Alexander back to the Phillies, for whom he pitched nine games in 1930 without a victory. After his release in June Alex pitched for Dallas in the Texas League, notching a 1–2 record in five appearances. That ended Alexander's professional career.

The remainder of his life was a sad one. Alex pitched for the barnstorming House of David team, and later appeared in a sideshow in Times Square in New York. Living on small pensions from both the government and the Cardinals, Alexander sank deeper into alcoholism, had additional problems with epilepsy, was hospitalized for cancer, and had an ear removed. One bright moment came in 1938 when he was elected to the Hall of Fame.

While his wife remained in Long Beach, California, Alexander returned to St. Paul, Nebraska, in 1950. On November 4, at the age of 63, he died in a rented room.

GROVER CLEVELAND ALEXANDER

Philadelphia (N.L.) 1911–1917
Chicago (N.L.) 1918–1926
St. Louis (N.L.) 1926–1929
Philadelphia (N.L.) 1930

G	IP	W	L	Pct.	H	R	ER	SO	BB	ERA
696	5189	373	208	.642	4868	1851	1372	2198	951	2.56

Alexander (second from left) gives some tips on handling the mound job to rookie pitchers at the Chicago Cubs spring training camp in 1934. He had pitched his last game in the majors four years earlier. Ill and an alcoholic, Alex enjoyed few bright moments after his pitching career ended.

Cap Anson (1852-1922)

Cap Anson was probably baseball's most prominent figure in the nineteenth century, helping shape the game from its early stages. He spent a record 27 seasons in the major leagues. At the time of his death he was known as "The Grand Old Man of Baseball."

Adrian Constantine Anson was born on April 17, 1852, in Marshalltown, Iowa. He was descended from British stock, the first Ansons having come to America in the seventeenth century. His pioneering parents had first settled in the towns of Adrian and Constantine, Michigan, hence his first and middle names. Later, Adrian's father built the first log cabin in Marshalltown, and Adrian became the first white child born there.

Baseball was just beginning to develop widely accepted rules when Anson was a youngster. Town teams sprung up in the 1860s, and the large Anson family made up the entire Marshalltown team. Even Cap's father played when the team was formed in 1866. Two years later, they faced the Rockford, Illinois team run by Albert Spalding. Spalding was impressed by 16-year-old Anson and made a note to remember him.

Adrian's father wrote a letter to the Chicago team recommending his son, but the letter was ignored. Adrian entered Notre Dame in 1870, but left after a year when he received an offer from Spalding to join the Rockford team of the National Association at a salary of $65 a month. His position on the team, also known as Forest City, was catcher. The club finished last among the Association's nine teams, and it folded after the season. Anson then signed with the Athletics of Philadelphia for $1250 a year. In Philadelphia Adrian was known as "Baby" Anson, and also the "Marshalltown Infant," because of his youth.

Spalding, now pitching for Boston, struck up a friendship with Anson during his four years with Philadelphia. When the National League was formed in 1876, Spalding persuaded Anson to quit Philadelphia and join the strong team being assembled in Chicago. The money was good, and although he had just married a Philadelphia girl, Anson decided to make the move. He was already in Chicago when the Athletics made a counteroffer. Having committed himself to the White Stockings, he reluctantly decided to stay. It took some coaxing from his new teammates to get Anson into the proper spirit despite his decision.

While in Chicago Anson developed into an outstanding hitter. Only twice in 22 seasons did he bat under .300, and he was the first player to reach 3000 career hits. Holding his bat with a split grip, Anson was basically a line-drive hitter. But he could also hit for power. On August 5 and 6, 1884, Anson hit five home runs in two consecutive games. The feat was not duplicated until 41 years later.

Anson's 20 visits to the .300 club constituted a record; he also set records for hitting six doubles in two consecutive games and for scoring six runs in one game. He established many standards which stood until broken by Honus Wagner and Ty Cobb. Hitting was certainly his strongest point, for he was never an accomplished fielder. Anson played every position during his career, beginning as a third baseman, but spending most of his time at first base, where he stood close to the bag, covered little ground, and reacted slowly. In 1884 he made 58 errors at first base, a record that has endured through modern times.

Anson first won a batting title in 1879 with an average of .407. He won three additional titles in his career, batting .399 in 1881, .421 in 1887 (when walks counted as hits), and .344 in 1888.

In 1876, the National League's first season, Chicago easily finished first, with Anson hitting .343 in 66 games. After the team finished fifth in 1877, Spalding retired to the front office. Bob Ferguson became captain and manager for the 1878 season, but was succeeded as captain by Anson the following year. Thus the source of his nickname "Cap." The following season Anson became co-manager with Ferguson, and in 1880 he became manager.

Anson was a strong disciplinarian. Having once spent a night in jail for drunkenness, he had sworn off alcohol and tobacco, and therefore refused to let his players indulge. There was an automatic $100 fine for drinking beer, a difficult rule to place on a team in the 1880s. Anson used room checks at night, seldom looking at the fun side of baseball. He clashed frequently with free-spirited King Kelly, a Chicago star.

Anson himself was often fined by the league president for his running battles with umpires, opponents, and even fans. His language on the field was frequently vile, but he did add a feeling of excitement to the game which prompted the fans to cheer and clap. Rival fans called him "Crybaby" Anson, but everyone appreciated his dedication to the game. Anson would accept only the best hotels for his team, and he would proudly march his players onto the field in single file for each game. During play, he would incite his team with shouts of "Come on fellows, play the game!" A player seeking a day off due to a slight injury had no chance with Anson, to whom manliness was essential.

As a strategist, Cap was one of the first to employ the hit-and-run play, but he called the bunt a "baby act." Another Anson innovation was the practice of having fielders back up other fielders on

Anson, the first player to reach 3000 career hits, holds a National League record for hitting .300 or better in 20 seasons. In 1884, he set another enduring record for 58 errors at first base in one season.

throws. He used signals on the field and was the originator of platoon baseball. Anson also set his pitching staff up on a rotation of sorts. He was among the first to take a team south for spring training, bringing the White Stockings to Hot Springs, Arkansas, in 1885. Although a strong believer in rigid conditioning (he permitted no player to be overweight), Anson became skeptical of the benefits of spring training, seeing the return to a cold climate as harmful.

When a game was in progress, Anson was the boss. He even tossed Spalding, the club owner, off the field for trying to suggest a play. And it was not beyond Cap to use his fists to make a point to one of his players.

Anson was largely responsible for the banning of blacks from organized baseball. In his autobiography, the first written by a baseball figure (*A Ball Player's Career,* published in 1900), Anson referred to a black mascot who accompanied an American team on a world tour in 1874 as "a no account nigger," in addition to other slurs. In 1883 Anson refused to take the field in an exhibition game at Toledo when Moses Fleetwood Walker, a black catcher, was on the opposing team. He backed down when threatened with forfeiture of the gate receipts. But in 1887, when John Montgomery Ward tried to sign George Stovey, a black, for the Giants, Anson went into a tirade and virtually forbade the signing. His position in the game was so prestigious that his actions set a precedent in baseball unbroken until Jackie Robinson signed with the Dodger organization in 1946.

Anson won five pennants with Chicago—in 1880, 1881, 1882, 1885, and 1886. In the latter two seasons, he faced Charles Comiskey's St. Louis Browns (American Association) in a postseason playoff. Cap's team earned a tie in 1885 (when Comiskey took his team off the field in the deciding game) and lost in six games in 1886.

Anson's old stars were fading by 1888, but Cap stayed on, earning the nickname "Pop" with his youthful team, now called the Colts. Later they would be called the Broncos. Anson never won another pennant, but he continued as player-manager until the age of 45, despite taunts from the crowd. One day he showed himself to be a good sport by donning grey whiskers in response to the fans.

Anson was part-owner of the Chicago club, but he never saw the books or made much money. He had a successful billiard parlor in Chicago during his career, but it provided little income thereafter. Although Anson had a 10-year contract to manage Chicago, he ran into trouble in 1891 when

Jim Hart took over the club presidency from Spalding. Anson, a few years earlier, had failed to contribute to a gift of cufflinks for Hart, then Chicago road secretary, during the 1874 world tour. Hart never forgot it, and when he became president, he asked Anson to sign a new contract, taking one year off the remaining six. After the 1897 season Hart asked Anson to resign, and when Anson refused, Hart fired him. The Chicago fans were so shocked that their club became known as the Orphans. Not until 1900 were they renamed the Cubs.

In 1898 Anson tried to raise $150,000 to buy the team from Spalding, but he could not obtain the money. Instead, he went to New York to manage the Giants, but his tenure lasted only from June 11 to July 6 due to a disagreement with Giant owner Andrew Freedman.

Chicago fans, having heard of a testimonial for an English athlete that raised $150,000, arranged for a $50,000 testimonial for Anson. Insulted by the charity, Cap rejected the offer, refusing also to take a pension from Chicago. When his billiard business collapsed, he entered vaudeville, performing a skit with his two daughters that was written by Ring Lardner. Anson served one term as city clerk in Chicago but lost a bid for reelection.

Anson, who spent considerable time on the golf course, remained a highly respected elder statesman of baseball. Even when he was over 50 he organized a semipro team called "Anson's Colts." The team toured the country, and Anson played first base.

Anson was still in vaudeville in 1921 at the age of 69. On April 14, 1922, he died in Chicago. His funeral was one of the largest ever given an American athlete.

ADRIAN CONSTANTINE ANSON

Rockford (N.A.) 1871
Philadelphia (N.A.) 1872–1875
Chicago (N.L.) 1876–1897

G	AB	R	H	2B	3B	HR	RBI	Avg.
2253	9084	1712	3081	530	129	92	1715	.339

Luke Appling (b.1909)

Luke Appling was a fixture at shortstop for the Chicago White Sox from 1931 to 1949, compiling a lifetime batting average of .310 at a position not usually manned by strong hitters. He was eventually selected as the "greatest White Sox player" of all time.

Lucius Benjamin Appling, Jr., was born on April 2, 1909, in High Point, North Carolina. There were three boys and three girls in the family. The youngest brother, Horace, had a tryout with the White Sox but quit after one season in the minors.

The Applings moved to Atlanta, Georgia, while Luke was still a boy. At Fulton High School Luke became an All-City shortstop under coach Byrd Hope, although he stood only 5'2" and weighed 102 pounds. During summers, Luke played semipro ball in a church-run league near LaGrange, Georgia.

After high school, Luke enrolled in Oglethorpe College as a business major. His weight had reached 155 pounds and he was able to participate in football as well as baseball, playing quarterback, halfback, fullback, and defensive linebacker for his college football team, while continuing to star at shortstop under coach Frank Anderson.

In the final game of his sophomore season, Luke belted four home runs before the watchful eye of Rell J. Spiller, business manager of the Atlanta Crackers of the Southern Association. Spiller offered Appling a contract to play professional ball, and Luke accepted, leaving Oglethorpe after two years.

Although Atlanta was a high minor league club, Luke was 21 years old and ready for the fast company. He quickly became the best shortstop in the league, batting .326 in 104 games with 75 runs batted in. The 5'11" righthanded-hitting youngster had some trouble in the field, however, leading the league with 42 errors.

Recognized at once as a top prospect, Luke quickly became the object of bidding by major league teams. The Chicago Cubs, run by Bill Veeck, Sr., almost bought his contract, but when they hesitated, Spiller turned to the Cubs' rivals, the White Sox. White Sox owner Charles Comiskey had a husband and wife scouting team, Mr. and Mrs. Roy Largent, and upon their recommendation Comiskey paid $20,000 for Appling and sent Atlanta an outfielder named Poco Taitt. It was the last major purchase for Comiskey, who died a year later.

In his first major league game, Luke had a single in four times at bat. He played six games in all that September, and was hitting .308 when he broke a finger on a high pop and was out for the remainder of the season.

Luke Appling, named the "greatest White Sox player" of all time, was a shining star on a mediocre team for most of 20 years. One of a fairly rare breed, a hard-hitting shortstop, Appling made seven All-Star teams in his career but never played in a World Series.

It was merely the start of a career of injuries for Appling, some real, some perhaps imagined. Luke always seemed to be on the trainer's table, receiving treatment for one ailment or another. Soon he was called "Ol' Aches and Pains," a nickname which stayed with him throughout his career. Luke may have been somewhat of a hypochondriac, but he was always good-humored about it.

Reporting to 1931 spring training in good shape, Luke easily won the regular shortstop job on the White Sox. It was not a very good club. In fact, when Luke was first purchased by Chicago, he assumed it to be the Cubs and was disappointed to discover himself bound for the second-division White Sox.

Not that Luke helped the Sox much in his rookie season. On opening day, he was hit on the elbow by a batting-practice pitch and promptly went into a 0–28 slump. His fielding was horrendous, and the fans started calling him "Kid Boots." The whole season was a disaster, with Luke hitting .232 in 96 games and committing 43 errors. The Sox finished last.

There was some improvement in 1932 when Lew Fonseca became manager. The team moved up to seventh, and Appling boosted his average to .274. Fonseca's presence meant a great deal to Luke, for Fonseca and coach Jimmy Austin worked Appling until he became a good shortstop. The arrival of Jimmy Dykes in 1933 to play third base gave yet another boost to Appling's education. Luke and Jimmy spent four years together in the White Sox infield, forming one of the strongest left sides in the business.

The 1933 season proved to be one of Luke's finest. He played 151 games and batted .322, the first of 9 consecutive seasons (15 in all) in which he topped the .300 mark. Appling had excellent bat control and was famous for his ability to foul off pitches until he got one to his liking.

In 1934 the two best shortstops in the league were probably Appling and Washington's Joe Cronin, but their clubs finished seventh and eighth, respectively. Appling was hampered for much of the season by a bad ankle, which he injured on a slide. The ankle continued to bother Luke for much of his career, but he continued to play despite this complaint.

After batting .303 in 1934 and .307 in 1935, Luke had his greatest season in 1936. He batted .388, the highest average compiled by a shortstop in the twentieth century—a mark not even Honus Wagner

They called him "Ol' Aches and Pains," because he was almost as famous for his injuries and ailments as for his playing, but Luke Appling's fans loved him. Here, youngsters give him a rousing greeting on Appling Day in 1947. He had starred for the White Sox since 1930 and would be with the team for three more years.

could reach. In beating out Earl Averill for the batting title, Appling became the first White Sox player to win a batting championship. When the American League celebrated its seventy-fifth anniversary in 1975, Luke remained the only White Sox player to have captured a batting title.

Appling's .388 included a 27-game hitting streak, a White Sox record. He pounded out 204 hits, drove in 128 runs, and scored 111 times. Luke made the All-Star team for the first of seven times. (He was also named in 1939, 1940, 1941, 1943, 1946, and 1947, compiling a lifetime All-Star average of .444.)

After hitting .317 in 1937, Luke suffered the most serious injury of his career during spring training in 1938. In a March 27 game against the Cubs, he fractured his leg trying to stop a slide when a foul ball was hit. He missed half the season and lost much of his speed and range. Neverthe-

less, he returned to hit .303 in 81 games, maintaining his string of consecutive .300 seasons. In 1939 he raised his batting average to .314.

Luke almost won his second batting title in 1940, losing to Joe DiMaggio .352 to .348. Two years later, he had perhaps his healthiest season but batted only .262. That led to considerable ribbing by writers and fans about Luke's need to be injured to play well. In fact, in 1943, a year in which he suffered from the flu, pulled muscles, indigestion, conjunctivitis, and a spiked knee, Luke hit .328 and won his second batting title.

During World War II, the league was without its biggest stars. On December 18, 1943, Appling too was inducted into the

Army. There was some question as to his age (one season, the White Sox listed his birthdate as "April 2, A.D." in their press guide), and Luke saw no action other than playing for the Army team at Lawson General Hospital in Georgia. He spent almost two years in the service and was released in September 1945, in time to play the final 18 games of the season and to bat .362.

Luke maintained batting averages above .300 in the postwar years, but the White Sox never rose above mediocrity and Luke never participated in a World Series. He finally called it a career after the 1950 season, surpassing Rabbit Maranville for the most games played at shortstop. (Eventually, Luis Aparicio passed Appling.)

Luke married Faye Dodd in 1932. They had two daughters and a son, and made their home in the Atlanta area.

Appling launched a minor-league managing career with Memphis of the Southern Association from 1951 to 1953, earning Minor League Manager of the Year honors in 1952. He managed Richmond of the International League in 1954 and 1955, Memphis in 1959, and pennant-winning Indianapolis of the American Association in 1962.

Luke was a coach with the Tigers in 1960. When his manager, Jimmy Dykes, was traded for Cleveland's manager, Joe Gordon, Luke went along, making him one of only two coaches ever traded (Detroit got JoJo White). Appling coached for the Indians through 1961, for Baltimore in 1963, and for Kansas City from 1964 to 1967. He was elected to the Hall of Fame in his first year with the Athletics. Owner Charles O. Finley also hired Gabby Hartnett in 1965 to give the club two Hall of Fame coaches on the lines.

When Alvin Dark was fired as Kansas City manager during the 1967 season, Appling took over his duties, winning 10 and losing 30. The team moved to Oakland in 1968 and Appling served as a scout through the 1969 season. He coached for the White Sox in 1970 and 1971, and served as a hitting instructor for the Twins in 1973 and the Braves in 1974.

LUCIUS BENJAMIN APPLING, JR.

Chicago (A.L.) 1930–1950

G	AB	R	H	2B	3B	HR	RBI	Avg.
2422	8857	1319	2749	440	102	45	1116	.310

Appling at bat. When the American League celebrated its seventy-fifth anniversary in 1975, Appling was still the only White Sox ever to have won a batting title, which he captured in 1936 with an average of .388 and again in 1943 with a .328 average.

Earl Averill (b.1903)

A hard-hitting center fielder for the Cleveland Indians for more than 10 years, Earl Averill became one of the most popular players in the city's history. Known throughout his playing career as the "Earl of Snohomish," Howard Earl Averill was born in Snohomish, Washington, on May 21, 1903. For as long as he could remember, he went by his middle name only. His father, a logger, died when Earl was only 18 months old. That left Earl's mother and grandmother to rear the family on a small ranch in Snohomish.

Earl was an athletic youngster, but the only opportunity he had to play ball was on his school team. His presence at home was needed to help with farm chores. Earl hurt his arm playing high school ball during his freshman year. Soon thereafter he quit school to take a job in a greenhouse. This was followed by employment in virtually any place where work was available—from construction camps to sawmills. Manual labor never quite restored Earl's arm strength, and although he became a fine outfielder, he was always considered to have a poor throwing arm.

Averill played semipro ball for the Anaconda, Montana team in the Butte Mines League. Subsequently, he played in central Washington, where he was spotted by former minor league player Tealey Raymond, operator of a local cigar store. Raymond had friends playing for San Francisco of the Pacific Coast League, and he interested them in the promising 23-year-old Averill. At this time Earl was married to Gladys Loette Hyatt, was rearing a family, and was playing baseball on the side for some extra money. But he would not be getting a late start with San Francisco, for this was a highly regarded minor league club, and few first-year players ever began there. Averill signed a contract for $300 a month.

Averill played 188 games in his debut season in the Coast League, collected 236 hits, pounded 23 homers, and batted .348. As he had played winter ball up and down the California coast, the heavy schedule did not seem to bother him. A line-drive hitter with power to right and right-center, Earl was recognized at once as a good prospect.

Averill continued to be observed by big league scouts in 1927 when he batted .324, with 20 home runs and 116 runs batted in, for San Francisco. In 1928 he was flanked in the outfield by Bob Johnson and Smead Jolley, both major league prospects in their own right. That year business manager Billy Evans of Cleveland went to San Francisco to look over Jolley. What he saw was Earl Averill enjoying a sensational season. Earl hit .354 that year, with 178 runs scored, 173 runs batted in, and 36 home

Earl Averill, Cleveland batting star from 1929 to 1939. When Averill was inducted into the Hall of Fame in 1975, he issued a statement urging a change in the selection rules so that "all of those who deserve to be there while they are still living are so honored."

runs in 189 games. Evans paid an incredible $50,000 for Averill's contract, taking the 5'9½" slugger home with him. Earl realized about $1000 from the transaction as a personal bonus.

"Averill is younger than Jolley, and more of a pull hitter," explained Evans. "He's perfect for our short right field wall." Still, the skeptics had to be shown.

Earl had a good spring training with Cleveland and was in center field on opening day of the 1929 season. His first time up, he caught hold of an 0–2 pitch from Detroit's Earl Whitehill and belted it into the seats for a home run. Earl was only the third player to homer in his first at bat in the major leagues, and the first in 23 years. And as if that was not enough, he homered again the next day, connecting off George Uhle.

The fans took to Earl at once. Although Tris Speaker had been gone from Cleveland for two seasons, his job in center field had not really been filled until Earl came along. Averill built up his weight to a stocky 172 and used one of the heaviest bats in baseball, a 44-ouncer. His strong wrists were his greatest asset.

Averill hit .330 in his rookie season and led the league's outfielders in putouts with 388. He hit 18 homers, an all-time Cleveland record at that point, and drove in 97 runs. The following year he increased his average to .339, his homers to 19, and his RBIs to 119. The Indians, managed by Roger Peckinpaugh, finished fourth in 1930 despite a .304 team batting average. Late in the season, Averill enjoyed his finest day in a baseball uniform. Facing Washington on September 17, the Earl of Snohomish belted four home runs in five official at bats during a double header. Three of the homers came consecutively in the first game, and in the nightcap, as Averill related years later, he saved the victory by getting away with a trapped ball in center. Although it actually took a short bounce, the umpire ruled an out. Averill claimed it was the only time he ever did it successfully.

In 1931 Earl hit 32 home runs, a career high which he duplicated in 1932. He drove in 267 runs in those two seasons, and the respect with which he was held was perhaps most reflected when the Red Sox pitchers issued him five consecutive walks on August 29, 1932.

Averill was selected to play in the first All-Star game, staged in Chicago in 1933. As a pinch-hitter in the eighth inning, he singled against Carl Hubbell of the Giants. Averill went on to play in five All-Star games altogether, hitting a collective .267.

Earl's most impressive performance in exhibition play occurred after the 1934 season when he accompanied Babe Ruth and many other stars on a trip to the Far East. In the Philippines, while the fans were awaiting Ruth's appearance at the plate, Averill hit one of the longest home runs ever recorded. Those who witnessed this first baseball game in the Philippines still speak of the Averill blast.

The 1935 season was an injury-ridden year for "The Rock," as some journalists called him. For the first time in his career, Earl failed to bat .300, settling for a .288 season with only 79 runs batted in. On June 26, while testing some firecrackers for the forthcoming Independence Day, Averill held one too long and it exploded in his hand, burning his thumb and two fingers. He missed two weeks of action.

Returning to face Washington and his favorite pitcher, Bobo Newsom, Averill selected a fastball and lined it back at Newsom's knee, fracturing the pitcher's leg. Two years later, in the All-Star game in Washington, Earl lined a ball right back at Dizzy Dean, fracturing the big toe on the pitcher's left foot. Although he recovered sufficiently to throw Averill out, Dean was forced to the sidelines. He tried to return to action too soon, and hurt his arm. Dean was never the same pitcher again.

On June 30, 1937, Earl was hitting .325 and the Indians were scheduled to play a home game. Earl reported to the park, got into his uniform, and headed for the field. Suddenly, his legs became paralyzed momentarily. Taken to a hospital and fully x-rayed, Averill was discovered to have a lifelong malformation of the lower portion of his spine. Earl had to change his hitting style and become an all-fields hitter to compensate for the sudden discovery. His average fell to .299, following a .378 showing the year before. His power was gone, and so too, apparently, was his trading value.

Cleveland fans threw a gala "Earl Averill Day" in 1938, presenting their hero with a Cadillac and other gifts. He enjoyed something of a comeback that year, hitting .330, but he had only 14 homers.

On June 14, 1939, he was traded to Detroit, amid the cries of the Cleveland faithful, for pitcher Harry Eisenstat and cash. Reduced to a part-time player, Earl hit .264 in 1939, and then batted .280 with two homers for the pennant-winning Tigers in 1940. He appeared in his only World Series that fall, going hitless in three pinch-hitting attempts.

Averill poses for a photograph in Yankee Stadium. He had made his mark in the field as a rookie by leading the league's outfielders in putouts, with 388.

Released by the Tigers, Earl signed with the Boston Braves in 1941. After only eight games he was demoted to Seattle of the Pacific Coast League, where he finished his career with a .247 average. His career total of 238 home runs was thirteenth on the all-time list at the time of his retirement.

Earl and his wife settled in Snohomish, where they reared four sons. One of them, Earl Douglas Averill, played in the major leagues from 1956 to 1963 as an outfielder, infielder, and catcher for the Indians, Cubs, White Sox, Angels, and Phillies. He had little success at bat.

The senior Averill operated a greenhouse with his brother Forrest in Snohomish until he sold his half-interest in 1949 and opened a motel. Earl managed the motel until his retirement in 1970.

In 1975 Earl was selected for inclusion in the Hall of Fame by the Committee on Veterans after a long campaign by friends and relatives. At the induction ceremonies in Cooperstown, Earl distributed a prepared release expressing his displeasure with the method of selection.

"My disagreement with how the Hall of Fame elections are held, and who is elected, is not based on bitterness that I had to wait 34 years after my retirement," Earl said, "but it is based on the fact that statistics alone are not enough to gain a player admittance into the Hall of Fame. . . . I urge the changing of the rules before it is too late, so that all of those who deserve to be there while they are still living are so honored."

Averill had instructed his family to decline his selection had it come posthumously.

HOWARD EARL AVERILL

Cleveland 1929–1939
Detroit 1939–1940
Boston (N.L.) 1941

G	AB	R	H	2B	3B	HR	RBI	Avg.
1669	6359	1224	2020	401	128	238	1165	.318

The "Earl of Snohomish" swings his mighty 44-ounce bat. Earl Averill slammed his way into the big time when he belted the ball into the stands for a homer his first time at bat in the majors.

Home Run Baker (1886-1963)

"Home Run" Baker never hit more than 12 home runs in a single season, and his career total of 93 is dwarfed by the totals of modern players. But in the dead ball era—also the age of spitballs, shine balls, and heavy bats—he surpassed all others in the art of hitting a ball over a fence.

John Franklin Baker was born on March 13, 1886, on a farm in Trappe, Maryland. His ancestry dated back well before the American Revolution, and Trappe was the only home he ever knew. Baker knew little of professional baseball even though he spent time playing ball on unused farm land with boyhood friends. Eventually some local leagues were formed, and Baker played a form of organized ball, usually serving as the team's pitcher.

A Baltimore resident, Buck Herzog, later a journeyman third baseman in the National League, was the first to recognize potential in young Baker. Herzog was playing for the semipro Ridgely, Maryland, team in 1906, and he traveled to Trappe to get Baker to join his club. Baker gained experience at Ridgely and earned a tryout with Jack Dunn's Baltimore Orioles of the Eastern League for the 1907 season.

It was not much of a tryout, however. Baker played 5 games at third base, had 2 singles in 15 times at bat, and committed 2 errors. Dunn released Baker, calling him too clumsy.

Baker returned to semipro ball with the Cambridge, Maryland, team. In 1908 Buck Herzog moved up from the Reading, Pennsylvania, team (Tri-State League) to join the Giants. He recommended Baker as his successor at third base when he left.

Baker played in 119 games for Reading, hitting .299 with six home runs and led the league in putouts at third base. Connie Mack purchased him on August 28, 1908, despite the disinterest of every other club in the major leagues. Baker was now a member of the Philadelphia Athletics.

He played nine games for the Mackmen in 1908, hitting .290 in 31 times at bat. The following season Baker won the regular third-base job. On April 24, 1909, Baker came to bat in the first inning and hit his first grand slam home run.

Home runs were uncommon in those days, grand slams even more so. The feat was the talk of the baseball world for days. Baker went on to hit .305 that year, with 4 homers and a league-leading 19 triples.

Although not a graceful third baseman, Baker was aggressive and had good speed. He stole 38 bases in 1911, 40 in 1912, and 34 in 1913. Although not a giant

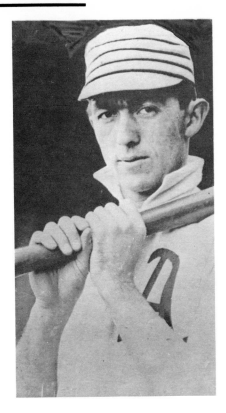

physically (he stood 5'11" and weighed 173), Baker was unafraid to challenge Ty Cobb in a celebrated spiking incident at third base in 1910. Cobb's spikes-high slide into Baker, for which he would always be remembered, forced the usually diplomatic Connie Mack to declare that "Cobb is the dirtiest player the game has ever known."

In 1910 Philadelphia captured its first pennant with Baker, winning 102 games and topping the second-place New York Highlanders by 14½ games. Baker hit only .283 that season, the only time in his first six seasons that he failed to reach .300, but he did lead the league in putouts. In the World Series victory over the Cubs, Baker hit .409, starring in his first Series game by hitting two doubles and a single.

In 1911 Baker hit .334, drove in 115 runs, and won his first home-run title with 9. The league record at that time was only 16. Home runs did not become a major part of the game until the appearance of Babe Ruth.

It was in the 1911 World Series that Baker reached his greatest fame and earned the nickname "Home Run." The Athletics were playing the Giants in the Series. John McGraw's two best pitchers, Christy Mathewson and Rube Marquard, had been hired by newspaper services to write daily columns during the Series.

Marquard started the second game and was involved in a 1–1 tie when Baker unloaded a two-run homer to right field in the sixth inning to win the game, 3–1. The next day, Mathewson's newspaper column criticized Marquard for pitching Baker "carelessly" in permitting him to hit the home run. Mathewson himself pitched that day, and he held a 1–0 lead in the ninth inning when Baker struck another home run to tie the score.

"I knew Matty wouldn't try to hit me, so I just waited for a good one," Baker said. In the eleventh inning, he contributed a single in the middle of a game-winning rally, and the Giants lost again. The following day, Marquard speculated in his own column that perhaps Mathewson had been "careless" in pitching to Baker.

Frank hit .375, scored 7 runs, had 5 runs batted in, and accumulated 9 hits as the A's won the Series in six games.

In 1912 Stuffy McInnis became the Athletics' first baseman, giving Connie Mack his "$100,000 Infield." Besides McInnis at first and Baker at third, Jack Barry was the shortstop and Eddie Collins the second baseman.

Philadelphia slipped to third place in 1912, but Baker led the American League in both home runs (10) and runs batted in (133), hitting a career high of .347. His 52-ounce bat also produced 40 doubles and 21 triples that season.

(Above) Baker tries vainly to stretch a triple into a home run. He is just dropping into his fall-away slide, hoping to get away from Cleveland catcher Easterly to score for the Athletics. But Easterly stands firmly at the plate. Roles are reversed (opposite page), where third baseman Baker reaches out to tag sliding Charlie Jamieson. (Opposite page, below) "Home Run" Baker completes his swing.

In 1913 the Athletics won another pennant. Baker captured his third straight home-run title that year with 12, and he again led the league with 126 RBIs. He hit .336 during the regular season and batted .450 in the Athletics' World Series victory over the Giants, accumulating nine hits for the third straight Series. One of his hits was a fifth-inning homer in the first game off Marquard.

Baker hit eight home runs in 1914, tying Detroit's Sam Crawford for the league lead, and batted .319 with 97 RBIs. Philadelphia won yet another pennant but lost the World Series to Boston in four games. Baker led the Athletics with a .250 mark in the Series.

Baker considered jumping to the Federal League in 1915 but could not make up his mind. When Connie Mack failed to offer him a raise, he decided to sit out the entire season and play semipro ball in Upland, Pennsylvania.

That year Colonel Jacob Ruppert and Captain Tillinghast L'Hommedieu Huston bought the New York Yankees. In attempting to beef up their club, they purchased Baker from Philadelphia on February 15, 1916, for a reported $35,000. Connie Mack had begun selling most of his stars that winter, and Baker, who had sat out the

1915 season, was an obvious candidate for sale.

Whereas he had been the cleanup hitter for the Athletics, Baker suddenly found himself the No. 7 hitter in the powerful Yankee lineup. His year out of the league apparently hurt, for he batted only .269 in 1916 and .283 in 1917.

In 1918 he topped .300 for the last time, hitting .306. In 1919 he hit .293 and won his seventh putout title at third base.

Upset by the illness and subsequent death of his first wife in 1920, and left with two daughters to care for, Baker sat out the 1920 season. Again he played some ball at Upland, but primarily he tended to his land in Trappe.

Baker returned to the Yankees in 1921, the year of their first pennant. Baker played in 94 games and hit .294 with nine homers; he then batted .250 against the Giants in the 1921 World Series. Joe Dugan replaced him as the regular third baseman in 1922, and Baker saw action in only 69 games, hitting .278. He made his final World Series appearance as a pinch-hitter in 1922, finishing his 25-game Series career with a .363 batting average.

Baker remarried in 1922 and had two more children with Margaret Mitchell Baker. He invested most of his money in farmland around Trappe. Always a farmboy at heart, Baker was happy to devote the remainder of his life to his land. He also raised and trained hunting dogs as a sideline.

Baker returned briefly to baseball to manage Easton of the Eastern Shore League in 1924 and 1925. In Baker's first year as manager, one of his players was 16-year old Jimmie Foxx, whom he recommended to Connie Mack. Baker also served as president of the Easton club in 1941.

Frank expressed surprise when he was elected to the Hall of Fame in 1955, for he realized that his own home run accomplishments seemed minimal by modern standards.

Baker suffered a stroke in 1962, and a second one in 1963. He died on June 28, 1963, at the age of 77 on his farm in Trappe.

JOHN FRANKLIN BAKER

Philadelphia (A.L.) 1908–1914
New York (A.L.) 1916–1919, 1921–1922

G	AB	R	H	2B	3B	HR	RBI	Avg.
1575	5985	887	1838	313	103	93	1012	.307

Dave Bancroft (1892-1972)

Dave Bancroft combined team leadership with outstanding play at shortstop to help two clubs to pennants. But as is often the case with men who seem like "born leaders," Dave never made a successful major league manager.

David James Bancroft was born on April 20, 1892, in Sioux City, Iowa; his family was of English extraction. He played sandlot ball and was also a shortstop on his high school team. At the age of 17, Dave signed his first professional contract, joining the Duluth club of the Minnesota–Wisconsin League. Before the season was over, Dave had been transferred to Superior, where he compiled a .210 batting average. It was not an impressive debut, but he led the league in both putouts and assists.

Dave was a natural shortstop. He had quick reflexes, a strong arm, and good range to both his right and left. Dave could also go back for the ball as well as he charged it. At 5'9½" and 160 pounds, he seemed perfectly cast for a long career at short. In fact, of the 1913 games in which he appeared during his major league career, Dave played only 19 at other positions.

Bancroft remained at Superior in 1910, leading the league in games played and putouts. He improved his average 57 points, to .267, but was still at Superior as the 1911 season opened.

Again his average improved, this time to .273. Dave was a switch-hitter in an era when few players were, and although he had little power (only 32 career home runs), he could hit to all fields and was a capable hit-and-run man. Little more was ever asked from shortstops.

After three seasons with Superior, Bancroft moved to Portland in the Class AA Pacific Coast League in 1912. Dave proved his durability that season, playing in 166 games, but he batted only .212. In 1913 he was demoted to Portland of the Class B Northwestern League, and hit .244. Bancroft returned to the Double-A Portland team in 1914, hitting .277 in 177 games and leading the league in putouts.

During his minor league days, "Banny" had a habit of verbally admiring pitches that got by him for third strikes. "Beauty," he would say as the ball sailed past, which earned him the nickname "Beauty Bancroft."

Despite his assets in the field, Dave committed many errors. In part, this accounted for his delay in reaching the big leagues. In his six full seasons in the minors, Dave averaged more than 50 errors a year. Even in the majors he maintained a high average, leading the league three times with totals of 60 or better.

The 1914 Philadelphia Phillies had finished sixth in the National League with a 74–80 record. The shortstop, Jack Martin, was as unknown as most of the other players on the team. For the 1915 season, Pat Moran was hired as manager. Ambitious to remake the club into a contender, Moran in one of his first acts purchased Bancroft from Portland and installed him as the club's regular shortstop.

Dave played all 153 games on the Phillies' schedule in 1915, hit a creditable .254 with a surprising seven home runs (a career high), and helped the Philadelphia club to its first pennant. Moran publicly credited Bancroft with providing the difference even though Grover Cleveland Alexander compiled 31 victories and outfielder Gavvy Cravath led the league with 24 home runs. In the World Series against Boston, Dave batted .294 as the Phillies went down to defeat in five games.

Although the Phillies did not win another pennant during his stay there, Dave was considered the club's defensive leader and one of the best infielders in the league.

The blue-eyed beauty hit .212 in 1916 as the Phillies finished second, and .243 in 1917 when Philadelphia again was runner-up. In 1918 Dave led the league in putouts, assists, and errors, handling 892 chances. But unfortunately the Phils dropped to sixth. Moran was fired as manager, and the club hit bottom in 1919, winning only 47 games. Dave, however, had his best season to date with a .272 average.

Dave started the 1920 season in Philadelphia, but on June 8 he was dealt to the New York Giants for shortstop Art Fletcher and pitcher Wilbur Hubbell. Giant manager John McGraw had long admired this fine, No. 2 hitter with the good bat control from either side of the plate. Fletcher had been adequate at short for McGraw, but he was not a star; whenever McGraw had a chance to obtain a player of note, he did.

On his first day with the Giants, catcher Pancho Snyder asked Dave if he would care to familiarize himself with the team's signals. "Won't be necessary," Dave told Snyder. "I knew them all when I was with Philadelphia!"

That was the kind of thinking player McGraw liked, and he named Dave team captain in his first season with the club. On the field Dave developed into McGraw's cutoff man, throwing out many runners on relays from the outfield, a rather new art at the time. At bat Dave suddenly blossomed into a .300 hitter. It turned out to be one of the Giants' finest trades.

New York placed second in 1920 as Dave batted .299, and again he led in putouts and assists. On June 28 he tied a record with six singles in one game. In 1921 Dave found himself part of a fine infield, with George Kelly, Frankie Frisch,

(Above) Bancroft, Braves' player-manager, lies unconscious in a 1927 game after sliding home into the fist of Pirate catcher Earl Smith, in upper left corner wearing chest protector. Bad blood between the two began a few years before when Smith, playing for the Braves, was fined $500 by Bancroft for throwing a chair out of a hotel room window. (Below) Bancroft has a safer trip to first as fellow Hall-of-Famer Bill Terry waits for a fumbled ball.

A much younger Bancroft batted cross-handed for the Phillies. Bancroft was to blossom as a hitter later, when he moved to the Giants and began to bat over .300.

and Johnny Rawlings surrounding him. Rawlings was later replaced by another fine third baseman, Heinie Groh. The 1921 Giants won 94 games and their first of four straight pennants. Dave batted .318, with 47 extra-base hits and 67 runs batted in. Although he batted only .152 in the World Series, the Giants beat the Yankees, and Beauty was the toast of New York's National League fans.

In 1922 the Giants captured another World Championship, again besting the Yankees in the Series. That year Dave really outdid himself, batting .321 with 209 hits, 41 of which were doubles. He was third in the league in hits, and for the third year in a row he scored more than 100 runs. Dave led the league in putouts and assists, and set a major league record by accepting 984 chances in the field.

The Giants made it three consecutive pennants in 1923. Dave hit .304 in 107 games—his third straight season over .300 (plus a .299 season in 1920). This time the Yankees won the World Series in six games. Dave played in his last Series that year and had only two singles, winding up with a .172 career Series average.

In the opinion of all who knew him, including McGraw, Dave was an ideal managerial type. Since the Giants had young Travis Jackson coming along at shortstop, and with Bancroft now 31 years old, McGraw arranged for him to become manager of the Boston Braves. In November 1923 he was traded to Boston with Casey Stengel and Bill Cunningham for Joe Oeschger and Billy Southworth. At Boston, he succeeded Fred Mitchell as manager.

But things did not fare well in 1924 for Bancroft and the Braves. Third baseman Tony Boeckel died in an automobile accident in February. Rube Marquard had an appendectomy, which limited him to six games and one victory. In late June Bancroft himself was hit in the stomach by a pitch, and on July 1 he required the removal of his appendix. It limited Dave's playing time to 79 games.

Early in the season, Bancroft had imposed $500 fines on Earl Smith and Jess Barnes for throwing a chair out of their hotel window in Philadelphia. Dave returned the money to Barnes when he discovered Smith to have been the guilty party. The relationship between Bancroft and Smith became a great problem. To solve it, Smith was dealt to Pittsburgh.

The sum of these unfortunate circumstances resulted in the Braves losing 100 games and finishing last. It was a difficult season for the rookie manager.

Dave hit .319 in 1925 as the Braves improved to fifth. But in 1926, when Dave batted .311, they fell to seventh. They remained seventh in 1927 when Bancroft batted .243.

Bancroft and Smith had a rematch of sorts that year. Smith, catching for Pittsburgh, was still demanding the return of his $500. His chance for retaliation came when Bancroft slid home in a game against the Pirates. Smith belted Banny on the jaw during the play and knocked his former manager unconscious. Dave sued Smith for $15,000, but Smith never accompanied the team to Boston to be served with the warrant.

At the end of the 1927 season, Judge Emil Fuchs of the Braves told Dave to try to make a deal for himself. He made a good one, selling himself to Brooklyn for $30,000. Dave managed to keep $20,000, for there was still a year remaining on his Boston managing contract. His $40,000 salary thus made him the highest paid Dodger in history to that point (the club was actually called the Robins in those days), and Dave was made an unofficial assistant manager to Wilbert Robinson.

Bancroft played in Brooklyn for two years, hitting .247 and .277. When he was released after the 1929 season, McGraw signed him as a player-coach for the Giants. In 10 games with the Giants in 1930, Dave collected only one hit. Two years later, when McGraw quit, Bancroft was considered a candidate to replace him, but McGraw selected Bill Terry.

Dave was a coach until Terry took over. In 1933 he managed Minneapolis of the American Association to a second-place finish. In 1936 he piloted Sioux City, becoming quite a hero in his birthplace. His final managerial effort came in 1947 with the St. Cloud team of the Northern League.

Dave and his wife, Edna, celebrated their sixtieth wedding anniversary in 1970, and the following year he was inducted into the Hall of Fame.

Dave died in Superior, Wisconsin, on October 9, 1972, at the age of 81.

DAVID JAMES BANCROFT

Philadelphia 1915–1920
New York (N.L.) 1920–1923, 1930
Boston (N.L.) 1924–1927
Brooklyn 1928–1929

G	AB	R	H	2B	3B	HR	RBI	Avg.
1913	7182	1048	2004	320	77	32	579	.279

Ed Barrow (1868-1953)

Ed Barrow is best remembered as one of the principal builders of the New York Yankees, but his career in professional baseball began 27 years before the first Yankee pennant.

Edward Grant Barrow was born on May 10, 1868, on a farm near Springfield, Illinois. His father was a farmer and a Union soldier, and Ed was named after General Grant. There were four boys in the family.

Ed had a much-traveled youth, as the family moved by covered wagon in search of more productive farmland. When Ed was still a baby, the family moved to Holden, Missouri, and in 1870 they shifted to Nebraska City, Nebraska. In 1876 it was off to a spread near Council Bluffs, Iowa. Finally, in 1879, Ed's father gave up farming and the family settled in Des Moines.

The four Barrow brothers played sandlot ball, and all developed an interest in boxing. Ed fought numerous bare-knuckle bouts. Once he was scheduled to fight an exhibition with Jim Corbett, but plans fell through at the last minute. Barrow looked more fit for boxing than for baseball, as he tended to be stocky and slow afoot. His bushy eyebrows gave him a ferocious look at times.

Any desire Ed had to play ball ended at the age of 18. He developed a sore arm pitching in the rain and seldom wore a baseball uniform again. When Ed later managed, he always wore street clothes and a straw hat.

Ed left high school in his sophomore year when his father's poor health forced him to get a job. He became a mailing clerk with the Des Moines *Daily News*. In time he was elevated to "city circulator," where he supervised all the newsboys. Ed also became manager and business director of the town team, the Elms. It was his first experience with the business aspect of baseball.

By 1889 Ed was head of the mailing department for the new paper in town, the Des Moines *Blade*. But when the newspaper plant burned down, he shifted to the Des Moines *Leader* as mailing clerk. Shortly thereafter Ed became the circulation and advertising manager at a salary of $30 a week. He also reported all sports news for the paper and hired young Fred Clarke as a carrier boy. Clarke played for Barrow's company team, the Stars, and later went on to play for and manage the Pittsburgh Pirates. Barrow always listed Clarke as his first discovery.

Ed and a brother left home soon thereafter and headed for Pittsburgh, armed with a new soapsuds invention that they hoped would make them rich. But their careers as soap salesmen were total failures, and they found themselves stranded in Pittsburgh. Ed then acquired a job as a clerk in a hotel.

Barrow's first contact in organized baseball occurred in 1894 when he struck up a close friendship with Harry Stevens, the enterprising young concessionaire who held scorecard and refreshment rights to the Pittsburgh ballpark. Stevens made Barrow a partner and Ed managed the concessions in the Pirates' park. That fall, Pittsburgh sportswriter George Moreland organized the Interstate League. Barrow, Stevens, and Al Buckenberger each invested $100 to gain the rights to the Wheeling, West Virginia franchise.

Barrow became manager of the Wheeling team. One of the players he signed was Zane Grey, later a famous western writer. Wheeling finished first when the league closed operations in July, but Barrow kept the club intact and entered it into the Iron and Oil League, finishing first in that league as well.

In 1896 Barrow ended his partnership with Stevens and purchased the Paterson, New Jersey, club in the Atlantic League. There he signed Honus Wagner at a salary of $125 per month, $25 higher than the league's limit. Barrow used Wagner at first, third, and in the outfield. At midseason in 1897, Barrow sold Wagner to Louisville of the National League for $2100. Barrow always considered Wagner the greatest player of all time.

On July 4, 1896, Barrow's team played what may have been the first night game in organized baseball history under makeshift lights in Wilmington, Delaware. Wagner played in that game.

Following the 1896 season, Barrow was elected president of the Atlantic League at a salary of $4000 a year. He served through the 1899 season and experimented with such stunts as the hiring of Lizzie Arlington, a female pitcher, for several clubs and the using of John L. Sullivan, Jim Jeffries, and Jim Corbett as umpires. Barrow spent his winters as a fight promoter, and he maintained a small interest in the theater business. The Atlantic League folded after the 1899 season.

In 1900 Ed purchased a one-quarter interest in the Toronto club of the Eastern League. He served as manager and had Nick Altrock on his team in 1901. But in 1901 Barrow lost 14 of his players to the new American League.

After winning the Eastern League pennant in 1902, Barrow was named manager of the Detroit Tigers in 1903 by club president Sam Angus. Barrow received $2500 worth of stock and a $5000 salary. It was his first taste of the major leagues. Ed made a forceful impression by throwing a bucket of water on a jeering fan one day, an act for which he wound up in jail.

Frank Navin bought the Tigers in 1904, and disagreements between Barrow and the new owner resulted in Ed's resignation in late July. In 1905, as manager of the Indianapolis club, Barrow turned down a chance to purchase Ty Cobb for $500. It was one of his few serious mistakes. In 1906 the Toronto club finished last and Ed quit baseball, going into the hotel business in Toronto for three years.

Barrow returned to Montreal in 1910 as manager of a team that featured Chick Gandil. The following winter Ed was elected president of the Eastern League. In 1912 he restored the league's original name, the International League (the same name in use today). During his tenure as league president, he developed a reputation for strongly backing umpires, ruling conservatively, and taking a hard line toward rule breakers. In 1912, at the age of 43, Barrow married Fannie Elizabeth Taylor of Toronto.

In 1917 Ed's salary was $7500. When club owners decided to cut his pay to $2500 in 1918, he quit. Harry Frazee, owner of the Red Sox, hired Barrow at once as Boston manager, and Ed promptly won the 1918 World Championship. He managed the Red Sox to a sixth-place finish in 1919 and to fifth place in 1920. In the latter year Frazee sold Babe Ruth to the Yankees after Barrow had converted Babe from a great pitcher to a great outfielder. The conversion was a slow ordeal, for Barrow resisted efforts to deprive him of a top pitcher. But eventually, under pressure from team captain Harry Hooper, and from Ruth himself, Ed yielded and moved Babe to the outfield.

Ed came across another fine player, Pie Traynor, in 1920. But he loaned Traynor to Portsmouth on a gentleman's agreement, and H. P. Dawson, the Portsmouth owner, promptly sold Pie to the Pirates.

After the 1920 season, Frazee recommended Barrow to Yankee owners Jacob Ruppert and Til' Huston following the death of Yankee business manager Harry Sparrow. Barrow joined the Yankees on October 29, 1920, and immediately told Ruppert, "If you ran your brewery along the lines of this ballclub, you'd go broke in no time."

With Barrow in the job, the role of business manager evolved into what is now known as the general manager position. Barrow took full charge of the major-league baseball operation, hiring Paul Krichell as his chief scout, and watching the Yankees grow into the greatest dynasty in professional sports history. The Yankees won pennants in 1921 and 1922 as co-tenants of the Polo Grounds. In 1923 Ruppert opened magnificent Yankee Stadium across the Harlem River, the first three-tiered stadium in the country. With Huston gone, Ruppert vested full confidence in Barrow. The Yankees won six pennants in Barrow's first eight years as business manager.

Babe Ruth was the only person who ever called Barrow "Eddie." The Yankee business manager was an imposing figure whose favorite expression was "proceed at once," and who commanded the title of "Mr. Barrow." But sportswriters, following the lead of W. O. McGeehan, began calling him "Cousin Egbert" and "Cousin Ed." Barrow became somewhat fond of the name.

Ed opposed night baseball almost as much as he opposed ladies smoking in his ballparks, but eventually he gave in to both. Barrow was also an early opponent

of the farm system developed by Branch Rickey in St. Louis. But in 1932 Ruppert hired George Weiss to establish one, and the Yankees soon had one of baseball's best minor league organizations.

After the death of manager Miller Huggins in 1929, the team continued to win pennants under new manager Joe McCarthy, capturing five flags in the 1930s. Ruppert died on January 13, 1939, and when his brother George declined the club presidency, Barrow was elected to the office on January 17.

The Yankees again won pennants in 1939, 1941, 1942, and 1943. In January 1945 the team of Dan Topping, Del Webb, and Larry MacPhail bought the club from Ruppert's heirs for $3 million. Barrow and MacPhail did not have the great personality clashes some suggested, but the free-thinking MacPhail and the conservative Barrow did not see eye-to-eye on the future of the Yankees. Ed became chairman of the board, seldom visiting the team's Manhattan offices, and in 1947 he resigned.

Among Barrow's many innovations were the placing of numbers on the backs of player's uniforms (with the 1929 Yankees), permitting fans to keep foul balls hit into the seats (with the 1918 Red Sox), and painting distances on outfield fences (with the 1923 Yankees).

After severing ties with the Yankees, Barrow and his wife retired to their home in Port Chester, New York. On May 13, 1950, "Ed Barrow Day" was celebrated in Yankee Stadium. One of the outfield plaques behind the famed Stadium monuments was then dedicated to Barrow.

In September 1953, Barrow was elected to the Hall of Fame. He died on December 15 that year at the age of 85.

More familiar in street clothes and straw hat, Barrow, then managing Montreal's Eastern League team, donned a uniform for spring training in Columbia, South Carolina, in 1910. Thirty-three years later (far right) Barrow was at home in the office of president of the Yankees.

Jake Beckley (1867-1918)

Jake Beckley played more games at first base than any man in baseball history, yet he was virtually unknown at the time he was elected to the Hall of Fame, 53 years after his death.

Jacob Peter Beckley was born in Hannibal, Missouri, on August 4, 1867. While a well-known and popular figure in Hannibal's past, Beckley never achieved the fame of Mark Twain, who moved to Hannibal in 1839 at age four.

Jake spent his childhood on the banks of the Mississippi River. His first job was with the Burlington Machine Shop in Hannibal. He spent his free time playing ball while his two sisters helped out at home.

In his teens, Jake played semipro ball with the team in Hannibal; a teammate, Bob Hart, preceded him into professional ball. Hart was playing for Leavenworth of the Western League in 1886 when the team was short of manpower. He told his manager about the lefthanded second baseman named Beckley back home, and the club sent for Jake.

Arriving to play on a Sunday before a good home crowd, Jake broke in with three hits, including a home run. He was at once a hero on the team. Shifted to first base the next season, Jake went on to play a record 2368 games in the major leagues at first. His longevity enabled him to set a record for career putouts as well.

In his first season with Leavenworth, at the age of 18, Jake batted .341. He opened the following season, 1887, even hotter. In midseason Leavenworth sold him to Lincoln, also of the Western League. Jake wound up hitting .401 for the season with 211 hits. This fine showing enabled Lincoln to sell Jake to the St. Louis Whites of the Western Association.

St. Louis had another baseball team, the Browns, and the Whites were strictly a minor league team. But Beckley helped draw many fans early in the 1888 season. He had spent the winter playing in Stockton, California, and had made big leaguers aware of him.

The Whites quickly turned Jake to profit. After playing only 34 games in St. Louis, he was sold to Pittsburgh of the National League for $4000, a considerable sum in those days.

Jake was a handsome figure, standing 6'1" and weighing 180 pounds. He had a dashing handlebar mustache and a genuine aura of excitement about him. He immediately made his presence felt in Pittsburgh's lineup by batting .343, only one point lower than league champion Cap Anson of Chicago. Pud Galvin, a future Hall of Famer, was a pitcher on that club. Another member of the team was Billy Sunday, the center fielder soon to turn evangelist.

In 1889, Jake's first full season in the big leagues, he batted .301 to lead the club's regulars. He also earned the nickname "Eagle Eye" for his ability to hit the ball well and often. In later years the name remained with him, but it was qualified to "Old Eagle Eye."

Jake may have had an eagle eye at the plate but, unfortunately, he had an eagle's arm in the field. Although balls hit or thrown to him were not particularly bothersome, he did not have a great deal of throwing ability.

In one famous play late in his career, Jake fielded a bunt by Pittsburgh's Tommy Leach and threw the ball 10 feet over the pitcher's head at first and into right field. He chased the ball down himself while Leach tore around the bases. When he recovered it, Tommy was approaching third, and Jake, knowing better than to attempt another throw, headed for home. So did Leach, and the two staged a footrace from opposite fields in the battle for home. Jake won, sliding hard into the plate ahead of Tommy and breaking two of the baserunner's ribs in the mighty crash. Jake himself was uninjured.

There was the famous incident in 1904 when Roger Bresnahan hit a disputed triple. Furious over the umpire's decision, Jake grabbed the ball from the ump's hands and flung it against the screen behind home. Unfortunately, time had not been called and Bresnahan walked home with the run.

That was not Jake's only embarrassing play. He was considered to be pretty successful with the hidden ball trick, somehow hiding it under the base when the runner was unaware. The play worked well when Beckley reached down for the ball, he lifted the wrong corner of the base. Wagner made it to second.

But the fans loved Jake, and he was not above coming up with funny plays to amuse them. He was a good bunter, and he learned to flip his bat and grab the fat part, then bunt the ball with the handle, a play which delighted the crowds. Casey Stengel, as a youngster, remembered seeing Jake do it. But when Casey tried it in the minors, he was fined.

"Chickazoola!" Beckley would holler when he was hot and eager to swing the bat. Thirteen times he batted over .300, but he never played for a pennant winner.

After only a year and a half with Pittsburgh's National League Club, Jake joined eight teammates in 1890 in jumping to the Pittsburgh club of the newly formed Players' League. Manager Ned Hanlon led the jump, which promised Jake a $3800 contract. Beckley was doubtful about the move at first, claiming he would remain a National Leaguer. But finally he jumped, telling the baseball world "I'm only in this game for the money anyway."

The Players' League folded after one year. Beckley and six teammates, including manager Hanlon, then returned to the Pirates.

In 1891 Jake married Molly Murphy of Hannibal, but she died seven months later after a long illness. Jake remarried many years later.

Beckley batted as high as 345 (in 1894) for Pittsburgh. But in July of 1896 he was traded to the New York Giants for Harry Davis, also a first baseman.

With the Giants, Jake hit only .268 for the season. Obviously, New York was disappointed in him, and he opened the 1897 season platooning with Willie Clark. After batting only .250 in 17 games, he was released by New York and then signed with Cincinnati.

Jake found his "eagle eye" again with the Reds. On September 26, 1897, he hit three home runs in one game. The feat was not duplicated until 1922 when Ken Williams did it. Jake finished the season with a .325 average.

After dropping to .299 in 1898, Jake batted .333 in 1899, putting together hitting streaks of 25 and 18 games. Cincinnati was managed by Buck Ewing then. Despite the presence of such stars as Sam Crawford, Kid Elberfeld, Harry Steinfeldt, Bid McPhee, Tommy Corcoran, and Noodles Hahn, the club finished sixth.

In 1900 Jake hit .343, but the Reds fin-ished seventh. After a last-place finish in 1901, Reds' president John T. Brush promised Jake that he would be traded to Brooklyn if Cincinnati could land Joe Kelley for the 1902 season. Kelley finally jumped his American League club in July to join the Reds, but Joe was past his prime and was used only in a utility role. Beckley, despite his protests, remained with Cincinnati.

In 1904 Jake was sold to the Cardinals. He was one of only three players still wearing handlebar mustaches, the others being Monte Cross of the Athletics and John Titus of the Phillies. Beckley was a colorful addition to St. Louis, but the team, managed by Kid Nichols, finished fifth. Jake's continual presence on second division teams did not enhance his prestige within the game.

Beckley remained with the Cardinals through the 1907 season, winding up his career with a .309 batting average and 23,696 putouts.

In the winter of 1907–1908, Jake moved from Hannibal to Kansas City, where he was named manager of the Kansas City Blues of the American Association. He remained there for two seasons, hitting .270 and .280, but was fired late in 1909 and replaced by Danny Shay.

In 1910 Jake was the player-manager for Bartlesville of the Western Association. When he was fired as manager during the season, Jake moved to Topeka of the Western League, where he played first base.

In 1911 Jake closed out his professional career in his old home town—as first baseman for the Hannibal Cannibals of the Central Association. At age 44, he played 98 games and batted .282.

Retiring to Kansas City, Jake continued to appear in amateur and semipro games. He opened a grain business. Once, ordering a delivery from a firm in Cincinnati, he received a telegram that read: "We can't find you in Dun and Bradstreet." Beckley wired back, "Try Spalding Baseball Guide for any of the last twenty years."

Jake died on June 25, 1918, in Kansas City; he was buried in Hannibal. In 1971 Jake was named to the Hall of Fame.

JACOB PETER BECKLEY

Pittsburgh (N.L.) 1888–1889, 1891–1896
Pittsburgh (P.L.) 1890
New York (N.L.) 1896–1897
Cincinnati (N.L.) 1897–1903
St. Louis (N.L.) 1904–1907

G	AB	R	H	2B	3B	HR	RBI	Avg.
2373	9476	1601	2930	455	246	87	1575	.309

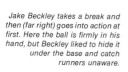

Jake Beckley takes a break and then (far right) goes into action at first. Here the ball is firmly in his hand, but Beckley liked to hide it under the base and catch runners unaware.

Cool Papa Bell (b. 1903)

One of the fastest men ever to play baseball, James "Cool Papa" Bell was one of many black stars forced to limit their careers to the Negro Leagues. Bell's playing years ended in 1950, three years after Jackie Robinson broke the color line and became the first black to play organized baseball in this century.

James Thomas Bell was born on May 17, 1903, in Starkville, Mississippi. Growing up with four brothers and a sister, he attended elementary school in Starkville. Because there was no local high school and only limited employment possibilities existed there, James and his brothers left home and moved to St. Louis. James found work in a packing house, played sandlot baseball, and managed to get two years of high school.

In 1922, at the age of 19, Bell was offered his first professional baseball contract—with the St. Louis Stars of the Negro National League. Fast afoot, bright, and well mannered, he became a favorite in his adopted home town. He remained with the Stars until 1932.

In Bell's first professional season, his manager, Frank Duncan, cautioned him against being nervous. Bell replied, "Back home, I played before crowds that sometimes reached a thousand people!" "He's a cool one, isn't he?" said a teammate. "Yeah," replied Duncan, "a real cool papa."

In 1932 Bell began the season with a team known as the Detroit Wolves, a "farm club" of the legendary Homestead Grays of the Negro National League. The club was disbanded within a few months, but five of the more talented players, including Bell, were transferred to the Grays.

The arrangement proved less than satisfactory. The Grays were overloaded with players, and by season's end Bell had moved on to the Kansas City Monarchs. With the Depression settling over the country, Bell was earning $250 a month as a switch-hitting center fielder.

In 1933 Bell moved on again, this time to the Pittsburgh Crawfords, where he remained for four seasons. The lure of additional money sent Bell south of the border after his stay in Pittsburgh, and he played in the Dominican Republic in 1937 and in Mexico from 1938 to 1941. It was in Mexico that he earned his top baseball salary—$450 a month.

Foreign territory became quite familiar to the well-traveled Bell, who spent 21 winters playing ball in Cuba and Mexico.

Back in the United States following his four-year stint in Mexico, Bell played for the Chicago American Giants in 1942 and the Homestead Grays from 1943 to 1946.

He then served as player-manager of the Detroit Senators, an independent team, in 1947 and the Kansas City Stars, a farm team of the Monarchs, from 1948 to 1950. On the Grays he was teamed with the legendary catcher Josh Gibson, the greatest power hitter in the Negro Leagues.

"There were many times," recalled Bell, "that I'd play a very shallow centerfield, and Gibson and me would pick runners off second base. He'd give me a signal, I'd run in from center, and we'd nail the base runner."

Accurate records were not kept in the Negro Leagues, but Bell is said to have batted over .400 several times. He is credited with a .437 average for Torreon and Veracruz in 1940, one of his Mexican seasons. Even at age 43, playing part-time for Homestead, he is reputed to have hit over .400.

But speed was Bell's finest trait. In 1933, playing a schedule of about 200 games, he was credited with 175 stolen bases. The record in the major leagues is 118, set by Lou Brock in 1974. Bell reportedly was clocked at 12 seconds running the bases; 13.2 seconds is considered the major league record, set by Evar Swanson of Cincinnati in the 1930s.

Satchel Paige, who preceded Bell into the Hall of Fame, liked to tell fables about Bell's speed. "I once saw Bell hit a ground ball," said Paige, "and then be declared out because he was hit by his own batted ball while sliding into second base!" Again, Paige claimed, "Bell could turn out the light and jump in bed before the room got dark."

Although travel was difficult and Negro teams often were barred from restaurants and hotels, Bell always had pleasant memories of his career. He never thought about playing in the major leagues because "it just wasn't anything to consider—we had our own league."

Bell's competition against white players was limited to occasional exhibition games. In one such game in 1948 he embarrassed Cleveland Indian pitcher Bob Lemon by scoring from first base on a bunt.

Bell's only offer to play in the major leagues came in 1951, after he had closed his baseball career by managing a farm team of the Kansas City Monarchs for three seasons. The St. Louis Browns made Bell an offer to play for them, but Cool Papa, then 48, knew he could not play at his best anymore.

Bell did do part-time scouting for the Browns with the understanding that he would receive a bonus if any player recommended by him reached the majors. When the Browns moved to Baltimore in 1954, he was released as a scout.

(Above) Bell slides into third base at Griffith Stadium in 1943. His baserunning speed was legendary. In an exhibition game against the Cleveland Indians in 1948, he scored from first base on a bunt. (Below) Switch-hitter Bell takes a left-handed stance.

Bell took credit for helping to develop some of the young black players who went to the majors. One of them, Jackie Robinson, was playing shortstop for Kansas City, and there were rumors that Robinson might be bound for organized baseball. But William Dismukes, secretary of the Monarchs, knew Robinson would not make it as a shortstop. So in a 1945 game against Homestead, Bell, at Dismukes' request, proved the point to Jackie. Although 42 years old, Bell was still at his 145-pound playing weight, and still had marvelous bat control. He proceeded to slap two ground balls to Robinson's right, beating them both out for hits.

"Jackie," Bell said after the game, "you just don't have the range to be a shortstop. Try first, second, or third." Robinson made the major leagues two years later—as a first baseman. He later played second and third base.

Bell was also enthused about the prospects of a young shortstop named Ernie Banks, but the Kansas City Monarchs were not interested. It was a source of pride with Bell that Banks eventually turned out to be one of the great Chicago Cubs of all time. Bell also "discovered" Elston Howard while managing the Kansas City farm team.

After his playing days, the Negro Leagues disbanded and Bell faded into obscurity. He returned to his home in St. Louis with his wife, Clarabelle. There he worked as a night watchman at City Hall until his retirement in 1970.

In 1971 a panel of seven men was created to elect members of the Negro Leagues to the Hall of Fame. Satchel Paige was the first, followed by Josh Gibson, Buck Leonard, and Monte Irvin.

Bell's election to the Hall of Fame was made on February 13, 1974, and he was flown to New York for the announcement. Tall, handsome, and proud at 70, no longer "the black Ty Cobb," Bell had earned baseball immortality in his own right.

JAMES THOMAS BELL

Negro Leagues 1922–1936, 1942–1947
No records available

From sandlot player to superstar, the saga of Yogi Berra is pictured here and on the following page. (At left) Berra is third from left, center row, in a team shot of the Stag Jrs. A.C. of St. Louis' YMCA League. Front row left, is Joe Garagiola. (Below) Sixteen-year-old Yogi steals home in the western section Legion baseball playoff of 1942, over the protests of opposing catcher, Gene Mauch, another future major leaguer. Yogi's team, the Stockhams, lost the sectionals.

Berra dives at Dodger runner Carl Furillo in a 1953 World Series game (above), but Furillo makes it home on time. At Right: Three years later there are joyous bearhugs between Berra and Don Larsen, who had just pitched a perfect World Series game.

and Yogi settled in New Jersey and went into partnership with a bowling business—a financially sound move during the bowling boom of the mid-1950s. Berra's luckiest business venture was his investment in, and endorsement of, a new chocolate drink called Yoo-Hoo. It made him a rich man.

On the field, Berra seemed to improve every year. He played in his first of 15 All-Star games in 1949 (he had been selected for the American League squad in 1948 but did not play). In 1948 Berra batted .305, the first of three times he exceeded the .300 mark. In 1949 he hit 20 home runs, a mark he bettered in each of the next nine years. Twice Berra hit 30 home runs, an American League record for catchers. On defense, he led American League catchers in putouts eight times, in assists three times, and in fielding percentage three times. From 1957 to 1959 he went 148 consecutive games without an error. Five times Berra drove in more than 100 runs in a single season. And in 1951, 1954, and 1955, he won Most Valuable Player awards. No player has ever won more.

As a Yankee player from 1947 to 1963, Berra appeared in a record 14 World Series. missing only in 1948, 1954, and 1959. He holds Series records for games played (75), times at bat (259), hits (71), and most times on the winning team (10). In 1947 Berra hit the first pinch-hit home run in World Series history, and in the 1956 Series he belted a grand-slam home run. That was the Series in which pitcher Don Larson credited Yogi with calling his perfect game "perfectly."

In 1964 the Yankees elevated Ralph Houk to general manager and named Berra manager of the club. The move was dictated in part by competition from New York's two-year-old National League expansion team, the Mets. The Mets were managed by Casey Stengel and, despite hapless playing, they attracted multitudes of fans. Berra found himself under double pressure. He was expected to follow in the Yankee tradition of pennant-winning managers—Miller Huggins, Joe McCarthy, Casey Stengel, and Ralph Houk—while moving up directly from the players' ranks to manage his former teammates. It was not an easy season for Berra. Only a late-season comeback enabled the Yankees to capture their fifth straight pennant. They went on to play seven games in the World Series against St. Louis before losing the championship. To everyone's surprise, the Yankees then fired Berra and signed the Cardinals' manager, Johnny Keane. The Yankees said Yogi was not managerial

timber, but the 1964 pennant proved to be the last of their dynasty.

Rather than take a front-office job with the Yankees, Yogi became a coach for Stengel's Mets in 1965, appearing briefly as a player. When Casey retired the following year and was succeeded by Wes Westrum and later by Gil Hodges, it seemed that Berra's managing days were past. But Hodges died suddenly before the start of the 1972 season, and the Mets named Berra their fourth manager.

The Mets finished third that year. Berra found managing easier because he was no longer working with former teammates. In 1973, with the team counted out as late as August, Berra led the Mets to their second pennant. In the World Series, they lost the championship to Oakland in seven games. He joined Joe McCarthy and Alvin Dark as the only managers to win pennants in both leagues.

Yogi's career as Met manager came to a sudden end in August 1975. It followed a dispute with management over the reinstatement of Cleon Jones, an outfielder suspended by Berra for his lack of hustle. Jones was released after an unusually strong stand by Berra, but within days, Yogi too was unemployed. As irony would have it, Yogi then returned to the Yankees as a coach for the 1976 season.

Physically, Yogi never looked like a ball-player, standing only 5'8" and weighing 190 pounds. But players and fans alike came to respect his professional commitment and his deep understanding of the game. Players would say, "Listen to Yogi—he's never wrong." Berra reached his greatest heights in 1972 when the Yankees retired his famed No. 8 uniform. That year the Baseball Writers Association elected him to the Hall of Fame.

LAWRENCE PETER BERRA

New York (A.L.) 1946–1963
New York (N.L.) 1965

G	AB	R	H	2B	3B	HR	RBI	Avg.
2120	7555	1175	2150	321	49	358	1430	.285

A pop foul by Jerry Lumpe of the Kansas City A's falls easily into Berra's mit during a September 21, 1963 game at Yankee Stadium. The A's won that game, but the Yankees won the pennant. The following year, Berra moved up to manager of the Yanks.

Jim Bottomley (1900-1959)

Jim Bottomley was one of the first products of a minor league farm system, and he came to reward the St. Louis Cardinals by helping them to four National League pennants.

James Leroy Bottomley was born in Oglesby, Illinois, on April 23, 1900. As a boy he assisted his family financially by working on a grocery truck and helping a blacksmith during his after-school hours. Sundays were devoted to baseball. By the time he was 19, Jim was earning $7.50 a day playing for the Witt, Illinois, semipro team. The Bottomleys by then had moved to Nokomis, Illinois—the town that Jim came to consider his home and which would one day hang signs proclaiming, "Welcome to Nokomis, Home of Jim Bottomley."

In a big Labor Day game in 1919, Jim belted two home runs and three triples. A local fan wrote to the St. Louis Cardinals scout Charlie Barrett concerning Bottomley's play, and Barrett traveled to Witt to observe Jim. He liked what he saw, offered Jim a Cardinal contract, and turned him into a professional first baseman.

Jim began his minor league career in 1920 with Sioux City of the Western League, but after collecting only 1 hit in 14 times at bat, he was sent to Mitchell of the South Dakota League. There, the 6'0", 175-pound, lefthanded-hitting Bottomley batted .312 and tied for the league lead with 97 games played. He also topped the league's first basemen in fielding percentage. Mitchell finished in first place that season.

In 1921 Jim was assigned to Houston, the team Branch Rickey had purchased two years earlier as the basis for the Cardinals' farm system. Jim batted only .227 with 4 homers and 62 runs batted in in 130 games, and he led the league's first basemen with 27 errors. He no longer seemed destined for the major leagues, and in 1922 the Cardinals assigned him to Syracuse in the International League.

Jack Fournier, a former Cub, had been the regular St. Louis first baseman since 1920, but in 1922 he was beginning to slip. His average dropped almost 50 points, and the Cards began to search for a replacement. They found it in Jim, who was hitting .348 for Syracuse, with 14 homers and 94 runs batted in. On August 18, 1922, Jim made his major league debut, participating in a 14-inning game against the Phillies in which he handled 17 chances and got a base hit. Bottomley went on to bat .325 in 37 games for the Cardinals, and when the season came to a close, Fournier was traded to Brooklyn.

Bottomley had a great spring training in 1923, removing all doubts about his abilities. In his first full season in the major

leagues, he batted .371 in 134 games. The figure was second in the league, 13 points behind teammate Rogers Hornsby, but 20 points higher than Fournier, who was third. The .371 was also a career high for Jim, who went on to register averages over .300 in 9 of his first 10 big-league seasons, missing only with a .299 mark in 1926.

In 1924 Rickey's Cardinals finished sixth, but Bottomley hit .316 with 14 home runs and 111 runs batted in. On September 16 of that season, Jim enjoyed one of the finest days ever experienced by a baseball player.

Playing against Wilbert Robinson's Brooklyn Robins, Jim singled home two runs in the first inning. In the second, he drove in another run with a double. In the fourth inning, Jim belted a grand-slam home run off Art Decatur. He also reached Decatur for a two-run homer in the sixth. In the seventh inning, he singled home two runs, and in the ninth, Jim had his sixth hit—another single and another RBI. For the game, won by St. Louis 17–3, Jim drove in 12 runs, breaking Robinson's record of 11 set on June 10, 1892. The event was not widely heralded at the time, but it has become one of the longest-standing records in the books.

Jim had another 6-for-6 day in 1931, making him one of only five players to perform the feat twice. But that September day in 1924 was certainly the apex of his career.

In 1925 Jim hit .367 with 21 homers, 128 RBIs, and league-leading figures in hits (227), doubles (44), and games played (153). Hornsby succeeded Rickey as manager early in the season, and the Cardinals rose to fourth. Bottomley again placed second to Hornsby in hitting, but this time Rogers bettered him by 36 points.

The Cardinals won the 1926 National League pennant. Jim's contribution was a league-leading 120 RBIs and 40 doubles. It was the one year he failed to bat .300, but his run production was so high that no one seemed to notice.

Jim had his only good World Series in 1926, batting .345 against Yankee pitching with 10 hits in 7 games. In the remaining 17 Series games in which he participated, Bottomley managed only 8 hits.

Jim was very popular with the St. Louis fans by now. He had a confident cockiness about him and an easy-going manner on the field. With his well-tailored uniform and his cap tilted slightly to one side, he was a special favorite of Ladies' Day audiences.

In 1927 Sunny Jim had a .303 average

Although the highlights of his career were for St. Louis, Bottomley played three years for the Cincinnati Redlegs. His batting and infield style look classic here, but by this time he was beginning to be plagued by arthritis of the spine.

with 19 homers and 124 RBIs, but the Cardinals finished second to the Pirates. St. Louis recaptured the flag the following season under manager Bill McKechnie. Jim had his best all-around season, hitting .325, leading the league with 20 triples and 136 runs batted in, and tying Hack Wilson for the home run championship with 31. For his efforts, he received the National League's Most Valuable Player award, worth $1,000.

In the 1928 World Series, Jim managed only 2 singles and a homer in 14 times at bat as the Yankees eliminated the Cardinals in four games. Jim's home run, off Waite Hoyt in the opening game, was the only Cardinal run that day.

Bottomley almost duplicated his 1928 season in 1929, hitting .314 with 29 homers and 137 RBIs. But no championships, titles, or awards came that year as the Cards dropped to fourth place. At one point, Jim belted seven homers over a five-game stretch, a National League record unequaled until Johnny Bench tied it in 1972. One of Bottomley's home runs struck a fan squarely in the face, and the fan filed a lawsuit against Jim. The case never went to court, however, for Bottomley was able to convince the fan's attorney that "there is no malice in any of my home runs."

In 1930 the Cardinals were grooming a farmhand named Rip Collins as a first baseman, and Rip was reportedly ready to take over from Jim. But Bottomley got hot, kept his job, and hit .304 with 97 RBIs as the Cardinals won another pennant. Jim suffered through a horrible World Series, however, managing only 1 hit in 22 times at bat for an .045 average. But the Cardinals defeated the Athletics in six games to capture the World Championship.

The 1931 season was Jim's first encounter with injuries. He suffered a hip injury on May 7, sidelining him for several games. On May 30 he was hit on the head by a pitch and subsequently sat out several more games. Late in June, Bottomley was benched in favor of Rip Collins. However, when Collins was injured on August 1, Bottomley returned to regular duty. Soon after his restoration to the lineup, Bottomley collected 12 hits in four games, and he finished the season closer to a batting title than he had ever been. His roommate, Chick Hafey, batted .3489 to capture the title. Bill Terry of the Giants hit .3486, and Bottomley finished third at .3482. One more hit would have won it for him.

Frankie Frisch considered Bottomley the best clutch hitter he ever saw. Using a choked grip on the bat, Jim hit .296 in 1932, his final year in a Cardinal uniform. By now, Collins was ready to replace Bottomley, just as Jim had replaced Fournier

in 1922. On December 17, 1932, the Cards traded Jim to Cincinnati for pitcher Owen Carroll and outfielder Estel Crabtree. Two months later, before spring training began, Jim married Betty Browner.

Bottomley spent three seasons with the Redlegs during which the club finished last twice and sixth once. He began to be troubled by arthritis of the spine, and by 1935 his average had fallen to .258 with just 1 homer and 49 RBIs. On March 21, 1936, Bottomley was traded to the St. Louis Browns for infielder Johnny Burnett. Hornsby was his manager on the seventh-place Browns, and Jim had somewhat of a revival at the plate, hitting .298 in his first American League season. St. Louis fans were so happy to have him back in town that they staged a "Jim Bottomley Day" on August 15.

On July 22, 1937, Hornsby was fired as the Browns' manager, and Bottomley was named as his replacement. Jim did not fare much better than Rogers. The team won only 21 of the 79 remaining games under his leadership, finishing last. Jim played his final 65 major league games that year, hitting .239.

Gabby Street became the third former Cardinal in succession to manage the Browns when he replaced Bottomley for the 1938 season. Jim went to Syracuse, from where the Cardinals had purchased him in 1922. There he served as manager of the Chiefs. He also played seven games and had 1 hit in 14 at bats.

After the 1938 season, Jim retired from baseball and returned to his farm near Sullivan, Missouri. Earlier in his career he had spent winters as a policeman in Nokomis, but now he considered himself a farmer.

Bottomley returned to baseball as a scout for the Cubs in 1957, and he was named manager of their Pulaski farm team in the Appalachian League that year. But on opening day, Jim suffered a heart attack and retired from the game for good.

On December 11, 1959, Jim had another heart attack in a parking lot in St. Louis and died at the age of 59. He was elected to the Hall of Fame in 1974.

JAMES LEROY BOTTOMLEY

St. Louis (N.L.) 1922–1932
Cincinnati 1933–1935
St. Louis (A.L.) 1936–1937

G	AB	R	H	2B	3B	HR	RBI	Avg.
1991	7471	1177	2313	465	151	219	1422	.310

Lou Boudreau (b. 1917)

One of the most popular players in the history of the Indians, Lou Boudreau brought Cleveland a pennant as both manager and Most Valuable Player in 1948.

Louis Boudreau was born in Harvey, Illinois, on July 17, 1917. Although his surname was French, he also had German blood, and his maternal grandmother was Jewish.

Louis Boudreau, Sr., was a machinist and a semipro baseball player who instilled a love of the game in his sons. Al Boudreau, the younger son, was a catcher, but the elder Lou wanted Lou, Jr., to be an infielder. He bought Lou an infielder's glove and made him a third baseman. Lou kept the glove until it wore out after a few seasons in the major leagues.

At Thornton High School, Lou was an outstanding basketball player and was named captain in his sophomore year. Three times he was chosen All-State. Lou also starred at third base for the Thornton baseball team.

Passed up by the Chicago White Sox, Lou accepted a scholarship to the University of Illinois in 1936. It was not a full scholarship, however, and Lou helped work his way through college as a waiter and dishwasher in his fraternity house and as a clerk at the Illinois Athletic Association. As a college sophomore, Lou was named captain of the basketball team. On the diamond, he proved to be a great infielder for the Illinois team. Majoring in physical education, Lou aspired to become a basketball coach upon graduation.

Lou's parents separated in 1937, and his mother required additional financial assistance. Fortunately, the Cleveland Indians came calling at an opportune time. Scout Harold Ireland signed Lou to a contract that provided $100 a month for his mother while Lou was in school, a $1000 bonus, and an additional $2500 bonus after Lou had played 60 major league games. Lou accepted the arrangement, but in February 1938, the Western Conference declared him to be a professional and thus ineligible for college athletics.

Lou joined the Indians' Cedar Rapids farm team in the summer of 1938, batting .290 in 60 games as a third baseman. He also played one game with the Indians before returning to school, where he earned his bachelor of arts degree the following year.

In 1938 Lou married Della Elizabeth DeRuiter. They had three children. One of Lou's daughters married Detroit pitching star Denny McLain.

With school behind him, Lou opened the 1939 season with Buffalo in the International League, playing shortstop and batting .331 with 17 home runs in 115 games. On August 7, he and second baseman Ray

Mack were called up by the Indians. Although an ankle injury reduced Lou's speed, he compensated with a fine knowledge of hitters. As he had demonstrated by captaining teams in his sophomore years in high school and college, Lou was a natural leader. Even the veterans on the Indians looked to this 22-year-old rookie with respect.

In Lou's first full season as a regular, 1940, he made the All-Star team for the first of seven times. He led the American League in fielding percentage, a feat he accomplished eight times in all. Lou also drove in 101 runs and hit .295, despite playing the final two weeks with an inflamed appendix and peritonitis.

Roger Peckinpaugh became the Cleveland manager the following season, and Lou batted .257 with a league-leading 45 doubles. But the Indians were below .500 and finished in a tie for fourth. Peckinpaugh moved up to the front office after the season, leaving the managing job open.

One of the first to apply for the position was Boudreau himself. He informed Indian president Alva Bradley of his ambition, and at the urging of stockholder George Martin, Bradley gave Lou the job. At 24, Lou was the youngest manager ever appointed to open a season. Peckinpaugh himself had been 23 when he managed the New York Yankees for the final three weeks of the 1914 season.

Boudreau handled his new responsibility well. He no longer roomed with his buddy Ray Mack, and, in fact, Lou had little contact with the players off the field, spending his time with his coaches instead. He was a strong manager whose authority was never questioned, and his marked self-confidence carried over to the players.

Lou made the All-Star team for the third time in 1942, hitting a home run his first time up. But for the season, the Indians posted a record identical to the previous year, 75–79, and finished in fourth place.

The fans loved Lou and were extremely patient with him. Although tending toward the heavy side, he was graceful and a joy to watch at shortstop. Five times he led the league in double plays, including a record 134 in 1944. Boudreau set a fielding percentage record of .978 that year, and broke it in 1947 with .982. He led the league in putouts four times, and his lifetime .973 percentage is an all-time record for shortstops. Lou was not a power hitter, but he hit the ball hard and led the league in doubles three times.

The Indians finished third in 1943, fifth in 1944, and fifth again in 1945. Boudreau had a fine season in 1944, leading the American League with a .327 batting average. A fractured ankle suffered in mid-August cut his playing time to 97 games in 1945. Boudreau compiled a .306 batting average that year.

Bill Veeck took over as president of the Indians in the middle of the 1946 season, but the club finished sixth, 18 games under .500. Despite an improvement to fourth in 1947, Veeck decided the Indians had given the ''Boy Manager'' opportunity enough. At the end of the season, Veeck attempted to trade Lou to the St. Louis Browns in a multiplayer deal.

Cleveland fans were outraged. Veeck, who had leaked the possibility of a trade to the newspapers, was besieged with irate letters. The Cleveland newspapers ran polls in which more than 90 percent of the fans declared their desire to stay with Boudreau. Veeck was taken off the hook when the Browns finally nullified the transaction.

As the expression goes, the best deals are often the ones you do not make. With Boudreau at the helm in 1948, Cleveland enjoyed its finest season. Attendance reached 2,620,627 at Municipal Stadium as the Indians found themselves locked in a great pennant race. On August 8, with three teams percentage points apart, Cleveland swept a double header from the Yankees before 73,484 Indian fans. An ailing Boudreau came off the bench to deliver a crucial two-run, pinch-hit single in the opening game.

The regular season ended with the Indians and Red Sox tied for first, the first pennant deadlock in American League history. A toss of a coin awarded the playoff game to Fenway Park. Boudreau surprised the experts by naming rookie Gene Bearden, a lefthander, as the starter on only one day of rest. With Boudreau himself belting two homers and two singles, the Indians won the game, 8–3, for their first pennant in 28 years. Lou finished the season hitting .355, second only to Ted Williams, and had 18 homers and 106 runs batted in, all career highs. He was easily named the Most Valuable Player in the league.

The Indians went on to beat the Boston Braves in six games in the 1948 World Series. Veeck happily admitted his mistake. He tore up Lou's $50,000 a year contract and gave him a new one for $75,000.

Lou was an innovator of sorts. Back in 1946, he had belted five extra-base hits in one game, the first time that had been done since 1889. But nevertheless the Red Sox won the game, 11–10, on three home runs by Ted Williams. When Williams came to the plate in the second game that day, Lou positioned himself on the right side of the infield, putting three infielders

between first and second. The so-called Boudreau Shift was not always successful, but it offered a new brand of defense that became more widely used in the 1960s.

By 1949 Lou was the senior manager in the league, with the exception of Connie Mack, and he was only 32 years old. He batted .284 that year as the Indians fell to third, and .269 in 1950 with Cleveland finishing fourth. Veeck had departed by now, and the new general manager, Hank Greenberg, released Lou on November 22, 1950. Al Lopez was hired as manager and the fans were predictably outraged.

Five days later, the Red Sox signed Boudreau as a utility infielder. Playing for Steve O'Neill in 1951, Lou hit .267 in 82 games. In 1952 he was named manager of the Red Sox, played four games without a hit, and concluded his playing career with a .295 batting average. The Red Sox finished sixth that year and placed fourth in both 1953 and 1954.

Lou became the first manager of the Kansas City Athletics in 1955. He remained there for three lackluster seasons, with the A's finishing sixth, eighth, and seventh. While still a big name in Cleveland, Boudreau was no longer considered a miracle man. Thus, there was no great outrage when he was released by the Athletics after the 1957 season.

Lou's only other attempt at managing occurred in 1960, when he moved down from the Chicago Cubs broadcast booth to change jobs with Charlie Grimm on May 5. Lou was 54–83 with the seventh-place Cubs. At the end of the season he returned to the broadcast booth, where he carved out a lengthy new career.

Lou was elected to the Hall of Fame in 1970. Cleveland Mayor Carl Stokes then renamed a street near Municipal Stadium, Boudreau Boulevard—a testimony to the lasting popularity of the boy manager in the city of Cleveland.

LOUIS BOUDREAU, JR.

Cleveland 1939–1950
Boston (A.L.) 1951–1952

G	AB	R	H	2B	3B	HR	RBI	Avg.
1646	6030	861	1779	385	66	68	789	.295

(Top picture, opposite page) University of Illinois basketball star Lou Boudreau, facing camera, plays in a game against St. John's University at Madison Square Garden in 1937. Boudreau planned to become a basketball coach until a Cleveland scout came calling that year. (Below) A baseball classic: In the 1948 World Series opener against the Braves, Boudreau appears to tag out Phil Masi who dives back to second base. But umpire Bill Stewart, at right, signals safe. (Above) Manager Boudreau, at right, watches his pitching ace, Bob Feller. Feller was in a slump, but Boudreau told reporters, "We'll sink or swim with Feller," and the championship was his vindication.

Roger Bresnahan (1879-1944)

Roger Bresnahan was a versatile, fiery athlete who was best known as Christy Mathewson's catcher and for his pioneering the use of shin guards and other catching equipment.

Roger Philip Bresnahan was born on June 11, 1879. Throughout his playing career, Bresnahan had everyone believing that he was born in Tralee, Ireland, and he came to be known as "The Duke of Tralee." However, it was discovered years after his retirement that he had been born in Toledo, Ohio. Both his parents came from County Kerry in Ireland, and his mother was of the O'Donahue clan. Bresnahan lived in Toledo all his life.

At the age of 18, Bresnahan signed with the Washington Senators of the National League as a pitcher. He had played many positions in amateur leagues and on the sandlots, but he considered pitching his finest talent.

Roger made his debut on August 27, 1897, hurling a six-hit, 3–0 victory over St. Louis. He showed excellent control, walking only one batter. Washington placed seventh in the 12-team league that year, and Bresnahan was at once a most pleasant surprise. He started five games in all and posted a 4–0 record, walking only 10 men in 41 innings.

But when the season ended, the Senators and Roger failed to agree on what an 18-year-old pitcher with a perfect record should be earning. Bresnahan secured his release and went home. In 1898 he pitched for the local minor league club in Toledo (part of the Inter-State League) and split four decisions. The following year Roger pitched three games for Minneapolis in the Western League. He also tried his hand at catching, first moving behind the plate in a game in which he had been removed as pitcher.

The 1900 season was yet another bizarre one for Roger. He played with the Cubs late in the year after spending most of the summer as a semipro in Toledo. Roger appeared in one game with the Cubs, caught, and went hitless in two times at bat. During four seasons of professional baseball, Roger had now appeared in only 15 games, usually late in September after his semipro schedule had been completed.

But with the turn of the century came the birth of the American League, and room for many young players with major league ambitions suddenly appeared. Bresnahan was among those who left the Cubs, and he signed with the Baltimore Orioles, managed by John McGraw.

Roger Bresnahan was the best protected catcher of his era—the early 1900s. He pioneered the use of shin guards, despite the jeers of fans and players, and improved the catcher's mask. (Opposite page) The fully padded Bresnahan in action. (Above) He crouches below the wide stance of batter Honus Wagner. (Below) The runner, Wagner again, slides into home, but too late, and Bresnahan nails him.

Before long Roger was recognized as one of the better catchers in the league. His principal batterymate was Joe McGinnity, who pitched 382 innings that year. Roger appeared in 86 games and batted .263. McGraw, although a third baseman by trade, knew enough about catching to pass on many of the finer points to Roger. From that season on, the 5'8" 180-pounder made catching his primary position.

The Orioles finished last in 1902, but Roger lifted his average to .274 and hit 4 home runs in 66 games. He also spent some time at third base and in the outfield.

The Baltimore franchise was to shift to New York the following year, but McGraw, McGinnity, and Bresnahan would not accompany the team. McGraw had already received an offer to return to the National League as manager of the Giants. He took his biggest stars, McGinnity and Bresnahan, along with John Cronin and Frank Bowerman, and put them in Giant uniforms on July 6, 1902.

Roger returned to the National League with a reputation for outstanding defense and excellent speed. He stole 211 bases in his career, with a season's high of 34 in 1903, his first full year with the Giants. That was a fine all-around year for "The Duke." Roger batted .350, with 142 hits in 111 games, and spent considerable time in center field. As a leadoff hitter, he pounded 30 doubles, 8 triples, and 4 home runs. Roger remained in the leadoff spot even when catcher became his sole position in 1905.

The 1905 season was an important one in Roger's career. He batted .302 and handled the pitching of McGinnity and Christy Mathewson, as the Giants played in their first World Series under McGraw. In the Series, Roger caught Christy's record-setting three-shutout performance against the Athletics. He batted .313 in the five games and took home a full winner's share after refusing to join his teammates in agreeing to split the Series money evenly with the Philadelphia players.

Borrowing the idea from cricket players, Roger in 1907 donned shin guards behind the plate for the first time. Other catchers had worn shin protection under their heavy woolen socks, but Roger was the first to openly wear the guards. Fans and other players jeered. Pittsburgh manager Fred Clarke was among the most vocal critics of the innovation, calling them unsafe to sliding base runners. But the National League approved their use, and they have been worn ever since.

Roger also wore a crude form of batting helmet that year. Early in the season he had been beaned by Andy Coakley and missed 30 days. Upon returning, Roger

placed a leather protector over his cap, but the idea was unpopular and even Roger gave it up. Bresnahan is also credited with bringing about improvements in the catcher's mask. He was undoubtedly the best-protected catcher in baseball at that time.

By 1908 McGraw was determined to help Roger acquire a managing job, for his better playing days were behind him and he clearly possessed the characteristics of a good manager. McGraw's personal fondness for Roger led to a meeting late in 1908 between the St. Louis Cardinal management and Bresnahan in a St. Louis hotel room. Roger agreed to move to the Cardinals as manager and catcher for a salary of $10,000 a year, and McGraw received Bugs Raymond, John Murray, and George Schlei in return.

Roger's managerial career did not have an easy start in St. Louis. The 30-year-old skipper was constantly at battle with umpires and was suspended several times. His club finished seventh, but owner Stanley Robison never lost faith in Roger. Nor did Robison attempt to interfere.

Roger continued to fight with the umpires in 1910. During one game, he stationed all of his players out of position to protest a decision that went against the Cardinals. Roger divided the catcher's duty with Ed Phelps but recognized that he was slowing down. The team again placed seventh in 1910.

In 1911 the Cardinals advanced to fifth place, but it was not a pleasant year. A train wreck on July 11 badly unnerved the team, destroying the momentum they had begun to build. No one was injured. Robison died earlier in the year and the team was inherited by his niece, Mrs. Schuyler Britton ("Lady Bee"), baseball's first female executive.

At first, Lady Bee was a great fan of Roger's. She presented him with a new five-year contract at $10,000 a season, plus a separate arrangement calling for 10 percent of the club's net earnings. But when she came to know The Duke better, she regretted her quick judgment. Roger always seemed to use crude, vulgar language in Mrs. Britton's presence, and this so insulted her sensibilities that she fired Roger after a sixth-place finish in 1912. An out-of-court settlement brought him an additional $20,000, less than he was actually entitled to by the terms of his contract.

The whole season was a frustrating one for Roger. The President of the Philadelphia Phillies, Horace Fogel, accused Roger of intentionally benching his best players against the Giants to help his old teammates win the pennant. Bresnahan demanded that his name be cleared by the National Commission, and the three-man board banished Fogel from baseball.

Following his release by the Cardinals, Roger signed as a player with the Cubs. Bresnahan spent three seasons in Chicago as a part-time catcher, and in 1915 he was named manager. It was an uneventful season: Chicago finished fourth with a 73–80 record, and Roger closed out his playing career with a lifetime .279 average. Only seven times in his career had he played more than 100 games in a season. Nevertheless, he was a team leader and probably the best catcher of his era.

Fired after only one season as Cubs' manager, Bresnahan returned to Toledo, where he bought the American Association franchise and managed the team through the 1923 season. In off-seasons, he served as a hotel detective in his hometown.

Roger returned to McGraw as a coach from 1925 to 1928. His only other association with the major leagues came in 1930 and 1931 when he coached for Bucky Harris in Detroit.

Roger died in Toledo on December 4, 1944, at the age of 65. One year later, he was inducted into the Hall of Fame.

ROGER PHILIP BRESNAHAN

Washington (N.L.) 1897
Chicago (N.L.) 1900, 1913–1915
Baltimore (A.L.) 1901–1902
New York (N.L.) 1902–1908
St. Louis (N.L.) 1909–1912

G	AB	R	H	2B	3B	HR	RBI	Avg.
1410	4480	684	1251	222	72	26	531	.279

Probably the best catcher of his time, Bresnahan went on to become a manager but had less success in that role.

Dan Brouthers (1858-1932)

Dan Brouthers was the most powerful hitter of his day. A strapping 6'2" 200-pounder with a bushy mustache, Dan captured five batting titles.

Dennis Brouthers—the Irish family pronounced its name to rhyme with "smoothers"—was born on May 8, 1858, in Sylvan Lake, New York, near the town of Wappingers Falls on the banks of the Hudson River. It was on the sandlots in this upstate New York town that Dan learned to play baseball.

Dan began playing semipro ball in 1876, the year the National League was formed. He joined the Wappingers Falls Actives, serving as a lefthanded pitcher with a good fastball and a tricky curve, an unusual pitch at the time. His strong shoulders made him a powerful hitter and he was soon converted into a first baseman, filling the role of cleanup hitter in lineups for many years. Although Dan at first was considered somewhat awkward, he became an adept fielder and a stylish base runner.

After three seasons of semipro ball in the Hudson Valley, Dan signed with the Troy Haymakers of the National League in 1879. He pitched three games for Troy that season, lost two of them, and became a full-time first baseman. The Troy club finished in last place in the four-year-old league. In total, the team managed only four home runs during the entire season, and Dan blasted all of them.

In 1880 Brouthers played briefly with Troy's National League team, and also with independent teams in Baltimore and Rochester, before joining the Buffalo N.L. club in 1881. There he teamed with center fielder Hardie Richardson, left fielder Deacon White, and catcher Jack Rowe to give Buffalo the so-called Big Four of the National League, a devastating attack which helped the club finish a strong third in 1881. The players were beloved by Buffalo fans, and none more so than big Dan, who in 1882 won his first batting title with a .368 average. His eight home runs the previous year, good enough to lead the league, had made him the most feared hitter in the Buffalo lineup.

Dan repeated as batting champion in 1883 with an average of .371, leading the league in hits (156) and triples (17). He continued to enhance his reputation with a .325 average in 1884.

The Buffalo team, however, was in serious financial difficulty by 1885. In an effort to salvage the franchise, the team sold Brouthers, Richardson, Rowe, and White to the Detroit club of the National League in mid-September for approximately $7500, a sensational sum at the time. This desperation move on the part of the Buffalo team promised to change the course of the entire pennant race. Because the

transaction was made strictly for economic reasons, National League President Nick Young attempted to void the deal, ordering the four players to return to Buffalo. When the players refused, they were permitted to join Detroit but ordered not to participate in games against pennant contenders. The confusion surrounding the decision caused them to miss all remaining games during the final three weeks of the season. The Buffalo franchise folded at the close of the season anyway.

Brouthers gained his great national recognition during his Detroit years, hitting some of the longest home runs on record at that time. It was the era of the so-called dead ball, and a home run of any measure was a rarity. One day in Washington Dan belted a home run which for years was used as the standard to which long-distance homers were compared. In 1886 he hit a wooden structure beyond the outfield fence in Boston known as "Sullivan's Tower," knocking off a number of fans. It was a famous incident of the day.

Detroit won the pennant in 1887, Brouthers' second year with the club. It was a most eventful season for Dan; he batted .419 with 239 hits, hit safely in 107 of 122 games, but lost the batting title to Cap Anson by a mere two points. It should be noted, however, that in the 1887 season walks counted as hits.

During that same season, Dan joined John Montgomery Ward and Ned Hanlon in presenting a series of players' grievances to the National League. They asked to discuss the reserve clause and to have the full salary figure written into a player's contract each season. It was one of the first attempts at player unity in the area of labor negotiations. Nothing came of the attempt at the time, but a few years later it was looked upon as the beginning of a major player revolt.

Dan had achieved a measure of fame by being the first man to win consecutive batting titles, in 1882–1883, and he was considered to be the first great lefthanded hitter. But it was not until his Detroit days that he became a sensation wherever he played. The sight of Dan coming to bat, with the outfielders moving back to the fences, caused fans throughout the National League to roar their approval.

A year after their 1887 pennant, the Detroit club finished fifth and disbanded at the end of the season. The players were promptly awarded to other clubs in the league, with Brouthers going to Boston. There, he signed a $4700 contract and won

Dan Brouthers's laced, prison-striped shirt and high boots (circa 1880s) may look dated, but the dapper six-footer's knickers are trim even by modern standards.

his third batting title, registering a .373 mark for the second-place Bostonians. But on November 4, 1889, serving as what today would be called "player representative," Dan spoke for the Boston players in announcing the formation of the "Players League." The new league was born out of the Brotherhood of Professional Baseball Players, headed by the Giants' Monte Ward. King Kelly jumped to the new Boston team as manager. Hardie Richardson, Dan's old teammate, also signed up to rejoin Brouthers on another pennant winner. Dan hit .345 in the Players League's only season.

In 1891 Brouthers signed with Boston of the American Association, making it three different Boston teams in three seasons. Dan again found himself on a pennant winner, and again he won a batting championship, this time with an average of .349.

The following year, Brouthers returned to the National League, hooking up with Brooklyn (managed by Ward), and tied Cupid Childs for the batting championship with a .335 average. Dan also led the league in hits (197), doubles (33), and triples (20).

As if he had not traveled enough, Brouthers really started to move around when his Brooklyn days ended after one more year. In January 1894 Dan and Willie Keeler were traded to the Baltimore Orioles. Brouthers became the most feared hitter in Baltimore's legendary lineup, which also included John McGraw, Hughey Jennings, Joe Kelley, and Wilbert Robinson. Baltimore won the 1894 pennant and Dan compiled a batting average of .345. Curiously, this was only two points better than the team average for the year. Brouthers and McGraw formed a strong friendship which lasted until Dan's death.

Brouthers was sold to Louisville for $700 in May of 1895. The following year he went to Philadelphia, closing out his major league career with a .349 lifetime batting average. Altogether, Dan played on nine National League teams during his career—still a major league record.

But Dan was not quite through with baseball. He went to the Eastern League, played for Springfield, Toronto, and Rochester. He still displayed a booming bat, even at the age of 39, when he hit .415 in 126 games for Springfield in 1897 to win another batting title.

Leaving professional ball after the 1899 season, Brouthers came out of retirement three years later to play briefly with New London of the Connecticut League and then played for the Poughkeepsie entry of the Hudson River League for three seasons. In 1904, at the age of 46, he won the batting championship of the league with a .385 average.

As a favor to McGraw, Dan closed out the 1904 campaign by appearing in two home games for the New York Giants as a gate attraction. In 1906 he bought the Newburgh team in the Hudson River League and served as owner-manager until the middle of the season.

McGraw hired Dan as a scout in 1907, and then served as his employer for over 20 years at the Polo Grounds in New York, where Dan worked as a night watchman and press box attendant.

Dan died on August 2, 1932, in East Orange, New Jersey, at the home of a son. He was 74. In 1945 Brouthers was named to the Hall of Fame.

DENNIS BROUTHERS

Troy (N.L.) 1879–1880
Buffalo (N.L.) 1882–1885
Detroit (N.L.) 1886–1888
Boston (N.L.) 1889
Boston (P.L.) 1890
Boston (A.A.) 1891
Brooklyn (N.L.) 1892–1893
Baltimore (N.L.) 1894–1895
Louisville (N.L.) 1895
Philadelphia (N.L.) 1896
New York (N.L.) 1904

G	AB	R	H	2B	3B	HR	RBI	Avg.
1658	6725	1507	2349	446	212	103	1056	.349

Moredecai Brown (1876-1948)

Mordecai "Three Finger" Brown turned a serious injury into an advantage and became one of the best pitchers in the first decade of the twentieth century.

Mordecai Peter Centennial Brown was born in Nyesville, Indiana, on October 19, 1876. The year was the one-hundredth anniversary of the United States, hence the name "Centennial." It was also the first year of the National League.

Nyesville was a mining town, and Mordecai worked in the mines as a teenager. But at the age of seven, while visiting his uncle David Beasley's farm, Mordecai had stuck his right hand under a corn chopper, and half of the index finger was chopped off. The thumb and middle finger were also badly injured. Mordecai returned to the farm a few weeks later with his hand in a splint. Playfully chasing a hog around the field, he fell and further mangled the hand.

The damaged hand worked to Brown's advantage when he became a pitcher. It gave his pitches an unusual hop, causing his natural sinker ball to behave like a knuckleball and giving his curve ball extra zip. Mordecai never had a powerful fastball, but his breaking pitches frustrated hitters for years.

Brown was not self-conscious about his injury. For years his uncle displayed the chopping machine to curious tourists, and eventually Brown claimed the machine himself and set it up for display in his garage.

In 1898 Brown was a semipro third baseman for Coxville, a team composed entirely of miners from the community. One day the Coxville pitcher fell and injured his arm, and Brown was pressed into service. He responded with a 9–3 victory over Brazil, Indiana. Brazil then offered Brown more money to play for them, and he jumped at the opportunity.

In 1901 the switch-hitting righthander signed his first professional contract, receiving $60 a month to pitch for Terre Haute in the Three-I League. Mordecai was a sensation there, winning 23 games to lead the league and earning the nickname "Three Finger." The following season he compiled a record of 27–15 for Omaha in the Western League, completing every game he started. After these two auspicious seasons, the St. Louis Cardinals purchased Mordecai for the 1903 campaign.

The Cardinals finished in last place in 1903, and although Brown was 9–13 for a club that won only 43 games, it was felt that his physical handicap would always prevent him from achieving stardom. Thus, at the end of the season the Cards traded Brown and catcher Jack O'Neill to the Chicago Cubs for pitcher Jack Taylor.

Miner Brown achieved instant notoriety in Chicago. On the team that featured the famous Joe Tinker-Johnny Evers-Frank Chance infield, Mordecai was 15–10 in his first year. The Cubs placed second in 1904 and third in 1905, when Brown posted an 18–12 record.

On June 13, 1905, Brown locked into a great pitching duel with Christy Mathewson of the Giants. Mathewson had a no-hitter through eight innings, and Brown a one-hitter. Mathewson stopped the Cubs in the ninth; Brown then lost the game, 1–0.

Brown did manage to wreak revenge on Mathewson, however. No pitcher ever matched Mordecai's success against the Giants' ace. Between July 12, 1905, and October 8, 1908, Brown beat Mathewson nine consecutive times. Their matchups became tremendous gate attractions, whether in New York or in Chicago. For his career, Brown defeated Matty 13 times in 24 decisions.

In 1906 Frank Chance was both first baseman and manager of the Cubs. Chicago won a record 116 games and lost only 36, finishing 20 games ahead of the second-place Giants. Brown was the leader of the pitching staff with a 26–6 record, including 9 shutouts and what would have been computed to be a 1.04 ERA had such statistics been kept at the time. Included was the first of five one-hitters thrown by Brown, a post-1900 National League record later tied by Grover Cleveland Alexander and Jim Maloney.

The Cubs faced the "Hitless Wonders," the Chicago White Sox, in the 1906 streetcar Series. True to form, the American League entry batted only .198 in the Series. But the Cubs compiled only a .196 average, and the White Sox won the Series in six games. Brown lost the opener, 2–1, at West Side Park, blanked the Sox, 1–0, in the fourth game at Comiskey Park, but got bombed in the final game, 8–3, when he allowed seven runs in only one and two-thirds innings.

Brown posted a 20–6 record in 1907 as the Cubs won another flag, but Chance bypassed him as a starter in the first four World Series games against Detroit that fall. Instead, Chance preferred the trio of Orval Overall (twice), Jack Pfiester, and Ed Reulbach. Brown pleaded with Chance to pitch the fifth game, hoping to atone for the previous year's disappointments. Finally, at game time, Chance handed the ball to Brown, who went out and beat the Tigers,

2–0, to clinch the Cubs' first World Championship.

The 1908 season was probably the most dramatic one in the league's 32-year history. The Giants had virtually won the pennant when Fred Merkle, their young first baseman, neglected to run to second on a game-winning hit and was ruled out. The game against the Cubs was declared a tie, and it was ruled that should the season end in a tie, the game would be replayed. Sure enough, New York and Chicago finished tied for first.

The replay of the tied game was scheduled for the Polo Grounds. Pfiester was selected as starting pitcher for the Cubs since Brown had been in 6 of the last 13 games en route to a 29–9 season. One of the largest, most unruly crowds in baseball history jammed the park for baseball's first "playoff." Brown, by his own recall, claimed to have received many death threats from the "Black Hand." Mathewson started for the Giants, but when Pfiester allowed a run in the first inning and had two men on, Chance wasted no time in calling Brown in from the bullpen.

Battling his way through the fans who lined the field, ignoring their taunts and threats, the Miner took the mound after only a few warmups, struck out Art Devlin to end the inning, and went on to win the game, 4–2, as the Cubs rallied for four runs in the third. The players received police protection the next morning as they headed for Detroit and the World Series.

Brown had had a tremendous year. He handled 108 chances without an error on the mound, serving virtually as a fifth infielder with the Tinker-Evers-Chance and Harry Steinfeldt unit. He became the first pitcher to hurl four consecutive shutouts, accomplishing the feat between June 13 and July 4. And in the World Series, Brown beat the Tigers in relief in the first game and shut them out in the fourth game.

The Cubs dropped to second place in 1909 even though Mordecai posted a league-leading 27 victories. But in 1910, when Brown was 25–14, the team won another pennant. In the five-game World Series loss to the Philadelphia Athletics, Mordecai posted a 1–2 record.

Brown led the league with 53 appearances in 1911, compiling a 21–11 record for the last of his six successive 20-victory seasons. In 1912, with his salary raised to $7000, he suffered a knee injury and pitched in only 15 games with a 5–6 record. Brown supplemented his income that year by tutoring Fowler McCormick, grandson of John D. Rockefeller, in the art of pitching. McCormick pitched for Princeton University.

The Cubs' attempt to return Brown to the minor leagues following the 1912 season created a furor in baseball circles, and he subsequently was traded to Cincinnati for pitcher Grover Lowdermilk. Although he was only 11–12 for the Redlegs, it was a better fate than the possibility of spending the year at Louisville.

In 1914 Brown jumped to the Federal League, serving as player-manager of the St. Louis club. He was relieved as manager in July, remained as a pitcher until August, and then was sent to the Brooklyn Feds. He had a combined 14–11 record that season. In 1915 Mordecai pitched for the pennant-winning Chicago Feds, posting a 17–8 mark. When the league folded, he returned to the Cubs under the general peace agreement signed with the major leagues.

Brown's return to the Cubs lacked the excitement of his first stay with the team. Whereas he had been a pitching star on four championship Chicago teams, he was now just another arm on a poor pitching staff. The team finished fifth, and Brown had a 2–3 record in 12 games. In his final major league appearance, on Labor Day of 1916, he was beaten, 10–8, by Mathewson, who was making his only appearance for Cincinnati after being traded by the Giants.

When Brown was sent to the minors following the 1916 season, there was none of the furor which accompanied the attempt four years earlier. This time, it was merely an accepted move for an aging star.

Brown pitched for Columbus of the American Association in 1917 and 1918, posting 10–12 and 3–2 records, respectively. He then moved to Terre Haute, where his career had begun, and served as pitcher and manager in 1919. He recorded a 16–6 mark that season at the age of 42; then, in September, Brown managed Indianapolis of the American Association. He returned again in 1920 to Terre Haute, where he compiled a 4–6 record during limited appearances on the mound.

After his professional career, Mordecai managed a semipro team in Lawrenceville, Illinois, which represented the Indian Refining Company. He opened a gas station in Terre Haute and ran it until 1946. Brown resided in the Indiana town with his wife, Sallie, until his death on February 14, 1948. One year later, he was inducted into the Hall of Fame.

MORDECAI PETER CENTENNIAL BROWN

St. Louis (N.L.) 1903
Chicago (N.L.) 1904–1912, 1916
Cincinnati 1913
St. Louis (F.L.) 1914
Brooklyn (F.L.) 1914
Chicago (F.L.) 1915

G	IP	W	L	Pct	H	R	ER	SO	BB	ERA
411	2697	208	111	.652	2284	863	inc.	1166	548	inc.

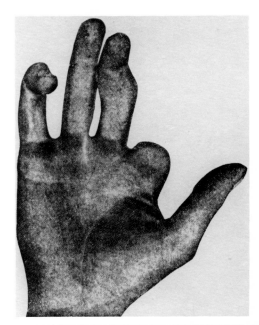

Morgan Bulkeley (1837-1922)

Morgan Gardner Bulkeley was not, in truth, a very significant figure in the history of baseball. But he was a man of great stature in government and business, and by serving as the first president of the National League, he brought dignity and respect to the organized development of the game.

Bulkeley was born on December 26, 1837, in East Haddam, Connecticut, the son of Eliphalet Adams Bulkeley and the former Lydia S. Morgan. He was descended from the Reverend Peter Bulkeley, the first settler of Concord, Massachusetts. Eliphalet Bulkeley had been an attorney, a member of the state legislature, and, in 1850, the founder of the Aetna Life Insurance Company.

The Bulkeleys moved from East Haddam to Hartford in 1846. Morgan attended public schools in Hartford but left at the age of 14 to serve as office sweeper at Aetna for one dollar a week. His father wanted Morgan to go to Yale, where he had graduated, but Morgan did not receive his degree until 1889, when he was 51.

In 1852 Morgan left Hartford to work at his uncle's dry goods store, H. P. Morgan & Co., in Brooklyn. Young Bulkeley learned the merchandising business and within seven years had raised himself from an errand boy to a partner in the firm. He also developed an interest in politics, first instilled in him by his father, one of the founders of the Connecticut Republican Party.

Morgan enlisted in the New York National Guard in 1861 and served as a private during the Civil War. He fought in the Virginia campaigns under General George McClellan. After the war Morgan returned to Brooklyn and his uncle's business.

When his father died in 1872, Morgan returned to Hartford. Thomas Enders had succeeded the senior Bulkeley as president of Aetna, but Morgan was named to the board of directors. He also organized the United States Bank in Hartford and became the principal backer of the local professional baseball team—a member of the National Association, baseball's first major league.

The National Association originated in 1871, but each new season saw a loss in profits and a lessening of public trust. Bedlam reigned and the league seemed near collapse. In the winter of 1875–1876, Chicago's William A. Hulbert and his star pitcher, Albert G. Spalding, drafted the constitution for a new league, the National League. The draft was presented to other club owners at a meeting in the Grand Central Hotel in New York City on February 2, 1876.

Represented at the meeting were teams from Chicago, St. Louis, Hartford, Boston,

Louisville, New York, Philadelphia, and Cincinnati. Bulkeley, a rising 38-year-old executive, represented the Hartford team. He asserted that baseball was merely a pastime for him, and thus he did not devote his full energies to the game.

Hulbert had the wisdom to see the value of Bulkeley's association with the league. As a highly regarded citizen, Bulkeley would bring greater respectability to the game. It was also necessary, Hulbert thought, to select an Easterner as the league's top representative.

Hulbert nominated Bulkeley for president of the new league. Officially, a drawing was held, with the first name drawn to become president and the second to become vice-president. Bulkeley's name appeared first, and with that simple act he became the first National League president.

Bulkeley accepted the honor but informed those present that he would probably serve no more than one year. This was accepted by the league owners, and the league got off to a good start. Chicago won the pennant in 1876, while Bulkeley's Hartford Dark Blues, managed by Bob Ferguson, finished third. Tommy Bond was the top pitcher on the club; the inventor of the curve ball, Candy Cummings, was also on the Hartford pitching staff.

As expected, Bulkeley resigned after one year. He was not even present at the league meeting in December 1876, which was called to expel two teams—the Mutuals and the Athletics—for failing to fulfill their schedules. Hulbert, the actual founder of the league, became the second president and served for six years. Bulkeley remained president of the Hartford club in 1877, but the franchise soon shifted to Brooklyn, ending Bulkeley's affiliation with baseball. He remained an avid sports fan, particularly of horse racing, and served as a member of the National Trotting Association for 30 years.

While baseball prospered, so too did Bulkeley's career. He was elected alderman in Hartford in 1876. In 1879 he resigned from his bank to become president of Aetna Life following the retirement of Thomas Enders.

Bulkeley remained president of Aetna for the remainder of his life. During those years, Aetna grew into the largest general insurance company in the nation. Yearly income grew from $6 million to $80 million. In 1907 Bulkeley added the Aetna Casualty and Surety Company to handle the growing businesses of accident, health, liability, and automobile insurance.

In 1885 Bulkeley married Fannie Briggs Houghton. They had two sons and a daughter.

In 1880 Bulkeley was elected to his first of four terms as mayor of Hartford. He earned the reputation of a humanitarian when he sheltered the children of a man who had killed his wife. Each election gave Bulkeley a larger plurality, and in 1888 he was nominated by the Republican Party for the governorship of Connecticut.

Bulkeley's first campaign for the position was successful. Although he was actually defeated by Luzon Morris in the popular election, the legislature awarded the victory to Bulkeley, and he became the state's thirty-sixth governor.

Bulkeley did not run for reelection in 1890, but in a strange turn of events he continued as governor for two additional years. Neither candidate in 1890 secured the constitutional majority needed for election. The state legislature was unable to declare a winner, one house being Democratic and the other Republican. Bulkeley, citing a clause in the state constitution which stated that a governor shall remain in office until his successor is duly elected, retained the governorship.

The controversy became a matter of national interest, particularly when Governor Hill of New York refused to recognize Bulkeley and would not transact business with the state of Connecticut.

The state controller, a Democrat, had the superintendent of the state capital building install a new lock on the governor's office in an attempt to keep Bulkeley out. Bulkeley, arriving with his personal bodyguards, called for a crow-bar and personally pried open the door. Thereafter, he was known as the "Crow-Bar Governor."

Eventually, the Supreme Court of Connecticut upheld his right to remain in office, and Bulkeley used some $300,000 of Aetna funds to finance state programs. The state paid Aetna back with interest.

When his term as governor ended in 1893, Bulkeley returned to Aetna. In 1896 he was a delegate to the Republican National Convention that nominated William McKinley for president. Bulkeley himself received 39 votes for the vice-presidential nomination.

In 1904 Bulkeley was elected to the United States Senate. There he earned a reputation as a Republican opponent of President Theodore Roosevelt, particularly over Roosevelt's dishonorable discharge of an entire battalion of Black soldiers. Some of the men had allegedly been disorderly in Brownsville, Texas, and when none of them would testify against the guilty, the entire battalion was discharged. Bulkeley fought the President long and hard on the issue.

In his second year as senator, Bulkeley announced on the floor of the chamber that it was the intention of Aetna and other Connecticut insurance companies to fully cover all damage caused by the San Francisco earthquake.

Bulkeley was defeated in his bid for a second senatorial term in 1910, and although he remained active in the campaigns of others, his personal political career had past. However, he remained active as the head of Aetna until his death on November 6, 1922 at the age of 84.

Baseball enshrined the first American League president, Ban Johnson, in the Hall of Fame in 1937. The committee felt it appropriate to place Bulkeley, the first National League president, in the Hall, too. The honor perpetuated a name that might otherwise have been lost in the annals of baseball.

Bulkeley, shown here in his Aetna Life office, got involved in baseball as a financier. His bank backed Hartford's professional team, a member of the National Association, the first major league.

53

Jesse Burkett (1868-1953)

Jesse Burkett batted over .400 three times in his major league career, a feat later duplicated only by Ty Cobb and Rogers Hornsby.

The exact date of Jesse Cail Burkett's birth is disputed, and Jesse himself never knew it for certain. It is given in various sources as December 4, 1868, or February 12, 1870; most sources list the former date. The place was Wheeling, West Virginia.

Jesse spent much of his youth swimming and fishing in the Ohio River. At the age of 12, he dove into the river, while scores of adults looked on, in an unsuccessful attempt to rescue a drowning girl. The event brought tears to Jesse's eyes even when he recalled it in his eighties.

Burkett began his professional baseball career in 1888 as a pitcher for Scranton in the Central League. He won over 20 games that season and advanced in 1889 to Worcester of the Atlantic Association, earning $125 a month and posting a 39–6 record. Used occasionally at second base, Burkett also batted .280. He bought a small home in Worcester and settled there for the remainder of his life.

Indianapolis owned the rights to Burkett in 1889, but when the club folded the following year Jesse was among the players transferred to the New York Giants. He began the 1890 season as a member of the Giant pitching staff, but his record was a poor 3–10 (some sources list it as 1–11). Despite a .309 batting average as an outfielder, Burkett was sold to Cleveland in 1891.

The Cleveland Spiders—so named because all their players seemed to be long-limbed—farmed Jesse to Lincoln of the Western Association, where he gave up pitching and devoted his attention to becoming a good-hitting outfielder. The results were immediate: he averaged .349 in 93 games and earned a promotion to the Spiders toward the end of the 1891 season. Jesse batted .271 and began to show the exceptional bunting ability that would earn him many base hits each season.

Burkett stood only 5'8" and weighed 155 pounds. The lefthanded hitter was noted for his line drives; only once did he hit as many as 10 home runs in a season. He also developed the ability to foul off third strikes with bunts while waiting for a better pitch.

Jesse's first full season with Cleveland was 1892, and he batted .278 for the second-place, rough-and-tumble Spiders of Patsy Tebeau. In the playoff with Boston—the first- and second-place teams met in a postseason series—Cleveland lost in six games (one tie). Cy Young was the Spiders' pitching star.

Early in his career with the Spiders, Jesse earned the nickname "Crab." It was based on his somewhat testy disposition

Jesse Burkett boasted he could average .300 just by bunting, and perhaps he could have. His exceptional bunting, combined with his line drives, took him over .400 in three seasons, the last in 1899. (Opposite page) Burkett strikes the classic outfield catching poses of his era.

and on his frequent exchanges of insults with bleacher fans. For some reason, Jesse was particularly sensitive to his physical resemblance with former Spider Jack Glasscock, and when fans teased him about being Jack's son, he would go into a rage. Although Jesse did not smoke, drink, or chew tobacco, his fiery behavior on the field often caused trouble.

There was an incident in 1896 when Burkett was thrown out of both games of a double header; it required six Louisville policemen to escort him from the park. The following day, Burkett, Tebeau, Jimmy McAleer, and Ed McKean were each fined $200 in police court for precipitating a riot. In 1903 Jesse was fined $50 for punching Washington manager Tom Loftus in the nose after an exchange of vile language during a game.

Off the field, Jesse was a different man, noted for his passion for vanilla ice cream and his patience with young fans.

Burkett had his first big season at bat in 1893, hitting .373 in 124 games. In 1894 Jesse compiled a batting average of .357, and in 1895 he reached the .400 plateau for the first time, hitting a sensational .423 to lead the National League. Jesse also led the league with 235 hits, while scoring 149 runs and stealing 47 bases.

Cleveland won the 1895 Temple Cup competition against Baltimore in a series marked by stone throwing at visiting players in both cities.

In 1896 Jesse batted .410, with 240 hits, 159 runs scored, 585 at bats, and 133 games played—all league-leading figures. Again Cleveland compiled the second-best record in the league, but they lost the Temple Cup to the Orioles in four straight games.

Crediting his success at the plate to "the ol' confeedience," as he pronounced it, Jesse boasted that he could hit .300 just by bunting. In 1897 he batted .383, and in 1898 he finished with .345, leading the league with 215 hits. At that point the Spiders folded, and owner Frank Robison transferred his better players to his St. Louis team. Burkett and Young were the most prominent of those transferred.

In his first year at St. Louis, Jesse batted over .400 for the third time. His average was .402, but he was bested in his attempt for a third batting crown by Philadelphia's Ed Delahanty, who hit .408. In the five years from 1895 to 1899, Jesse averaged .392 with 1117 hits.

Burkett stayed with St. Louis for three

years, winning his third batting championship in 1901 with a .382 average and 228 hits.

In 1902 the young American League moved its Milwaukee franchise to St. Louis and hired Jimmy McAleer, Burkett's old teammate, as manager. McAleer persuaded seven players, including Jesse, to jump from the Cardinals to the Browns. Jesse became the first regular left fielder on the new club. He batted .306, a somewhat disappointing showing considering his past performances.

Burkett's age began to affect his playing abilities. He batted .296 in 1903, and .273 in 1904. Jesse still bunted frequently, and he was highly sensitive to any mention of his diminished speed or advancing age.

In January 1905, Jesse was traded to the Boston Red Sox for outfielder George Stone. Happy to be playing near his home, he batted only .257 in 149 games and was released when the season ended. His lifetime average was a hefty .342, and he fell only 128 hits short of 3000.

Having saved his money carefully, Jesse then invested it in the Worcester team of the New England League. While serving as owner, manager, and outfielder, Jesse led the league with a .344 average in 1906. He ran the club through the 1913 season and always allotted himself playing time despite his age. His Worcester club won four successive pennants from 1906 to 1909. In 1911 Jesse hit .342 for 243 times at bat.

In 1916 he managed the Lawrence entry of the Eastern League for the first half of the season, then shifted to the helm at Hartford for six weeks, and eventually finished the season managing Lowell. Burkett played his final 24 professional games that year and had 8 hits in 38 times at bat. In 1917 he became coach of the Holy Cross College baseball team, helping to develop such future big leaguers as Joe Dugan, Jigger Statz, and Rosy Ryan in his four years at the school. Jesse also scouted for the New York Giants during that period, and in 1921 he was made a coach under John McGraw.

Although not officially listed as a coach in 1922, Burkett was employed by McGraw as a "keeper" for a wild young pitcher named Phil Douglas. But the eccentric Douglas escaped him during the season and Burkett gave up the job.

Jesse returned to the managerial position at Worcester for 1923 and 1924, and he continued to scout for the Giants into the 1940s. He also served briefly as manager for Lewiston of the New England League in 1928 and 1929 (the team shifted to the Northeastern League in the latter season),

and for Lowell of the New England League in 1933.

Residing in Worcester and frequently hosting old baseball friends who would visit Boston, Jesse was one of the few remaining people active in the game from the nineteenth century. In his later years he was troubled with hardening of the arteries, which confined him to bed for several years.

When he was elected to the Hall of Fame in 1946, Jesse commented, "It took them a long time, and I thought they weren't going to pick me because everybody had forgotten me."

Jesse died in Worcester on May 27, 1953.

JESSE CAIL BURKETT

New York (N.L.) 1890
Cleveland (N.L.) 1891–1898
St. Louis (N.L.) 1899–1901
St. Louis (A.L.) 1902–1904
Boston (A.L.) 1905

G	AB	R	H	2B	3B	HR	RBI	Avg.
2063	8389	1708	2872	314	185	70	952	.342

Roy Campanella (b.1921)

One of baseball's great power-hitting catchers, Roy Campanella—along with Jackie Robinson, Duke Snider, Gil Hodges, Pee Wee Reese, and Carl Furillo—was a member of the feared "Boys of Summer" that propelled the Brooklyn Dodgers to five pennants between 1949 and 1956. During his remarkable 10-year career, cut short by a tragic automobile accident in 1958, he won three Most Valuable Player awards.

"Campy" was born on November 19, 1921, in Philadelphia, Pennsylvania. He was reared in the Nicetown section of North Philadelphia by his black mother and Italian father. A happy and ambitious boy, Roy contributed to the family income by selling newspapers, cutting lawns, shining shoes, and helping his brother with a milk delivery route. His greatest delight was watching the Philadelphia Athletics play at Shibe Park. As a youngster, he played sandlot ball with a team called the Nicetown Colored Athletic Club. Eventually, Roy joined the local American Legion Team, Loudenslager Post No. 366.

Although Roy's roly-poly physique was ideal for a catcher, who must present a compact target to the pitcher and be able to block the plate with authority, that was not the only factor in his decision to become one. In trying out for the Simon Gratz High School team, he found that no one had signed up for catcher and so chose that position to ensure making the team.

In 1937, when Roy was only 15, he joined a semiprofessional Negro team known as the Bacharach Giants for weekend games in Pennsylvania, New York, New Jersey, and Connecticut. The $25 weekend fee went straight to Mrs. Campanella, along with a promise that Roy would attend services at the Baptist Church on Sunday morning.

While the team was in New York, Roy was approached by the manager of the Baltimore Elite Giants, one of the better teams in the Negro National League. He rode to Norristown, Pennsylvania, for a tryout with the Elite Giants and signed a contract.

Roy immediately became the team's regular catcher, and although no records were kept, he caught over 200 games a year for a top salary of $150 a month. He spent his winters adding more playing time in Puerto Rico, Mexico, Cuba, and Venezuela.

In 1939 Roy married for the second time (his first marriage, although brief, had produced two children). His new wife, Ruthe, traveled around the country with him as the Elite Giants finished third in 1939.

Deferred from military service as the father of two children, Campanella in the middle of the 1942 season jumped to the Mexican League, where he earned $1000 a month. Baltimore lured him back in 1944 with a $3000-per-month contract.

Following completion of the 1945 schedule, Roy was invited to play a postseason series against major league players. During that series Roy received word that Brooklyn Dodger president Branch Rickey wanted to speak to him. They talked in general terms about the possibility of a black player entering the majors. The conversation was purely general, and it ended with Rickey merely asking Campy not to sign with any major league club without first talking to him. Rickey was laying the groundwork for the entrance of black players into organized ball, and on October 23, 1945, newspapers reported that Jackie Robinson had signed with the Dodgers.

During the winter of 1945–1946, Rickey again contacted Campanella, this time in Caracas, Venezuela, where Roy was playing winter ball. Branch offered him $185 a month to play for Nashua in the New England League. The money was far below his Negro League salary, but Roy decided to take the offer. At the age of 24, with nine years of professional experience already behind him, Roy became a pioneer in organized baseball.

At Nashua in 1946, Roy played for manager Walter Alston and roomed with pitcher Don Newcombe, two men who would be part of the great Dodger successes in the 1950s. Roy batted .290 with 13 homers and 96 RBIs in 1946 and was named Most Valuable Player in the league. He even managed the club on occasions when Alston was absent or had been ejected.

In 1947 Roy was advanced to Montreal in the Triple-A International League, the club Jackie Robinson had broken in with the year before. Again he had a fine season, batting .273 with 13 homers and 75 RBIs. Roy trained with Brooklyn in 1948 and came north with the team, but he appeared in just three games before being sent to St. Paul in May. Rickey told Campanella he wanted him to break the color line in the American Association.

But after 35 games and a .325 showing with 13 more homers and 39 RBIs, manager Leo Durocher insisted on having Campy back. Roy returned as a 26-year-old rookie

Karate? A new dance step? Actually it is catcher Roy Campanella tagging out Billy Martin in the 1953 World Series between the Yankees and the Dodgers. Campanella won his second MVP award that year, hitting .312 and slugging 41 home runs to break a record for catchers.

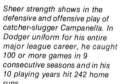

Sheer strength shows in the defensive and offensive play of catcher-slugger Campanella. In Dodger uniform for his entire major league career, he caught 100 or more games in 9 consecutive seasons and in his 10 playing years hit 242 home runs.

to take over regular catching duties for Brooklyn. He played 83 games that season and batted .258 with nine homers.

An easy-going man, Campanella did not think in racial terms. In this respect he was very different from the intense Jackie Robinson. The two were never close, though both contributed mightily to the great Dodger team that was then taking shape.

In 1949 the Dodgers won the National League pennant, with Roy batting .287 and hitting 22 homers. It was the first of nine consecutive seasons in which he caught 100 or more games.

The Dodgers narrowly lost pennants in both 1950 and 1951, but Roy's prestige in the league mounted. In 1951, he won the first of his three Most Valuable Player awards, batting .325 with 33 homers and 108 runs batted in. Number 39 was a big man among the faithful Brooklyn fans.

In 1952 and 1953, the Dodgers won

back-to-back pennants. Roy earned his second MVP award in the latter season, belting 41 home runs, a record for catchers. (Johnny Bench surpassed the figure later, but he played some games in the outfield.) Campy led the National League with 142 runs batted in (playing 144 games) and batted .312.

The Dodgers failed to win the pennant in 1954, but the next year they captured their first World Championship. Roy won his third MVP award that year, batting .318 with 32 homers and 107 RBIs, and then added two homers in the World Series against the Yankees. Never much of a Series hitter, Roy batted only .237 in 32 World Series games.

Roy batted a measly .219 in 1956, but came back in 1957 to hit .242 and lead the league in fielding percentage for the fourth

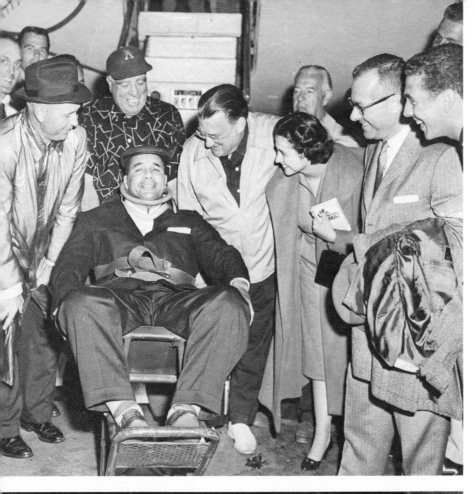

time. By then he had established a successful liquor store in Harlem, had a fine home on Long Island, and was earning nearly $50,000 a year.

At the close of the 1957 season, owner Walter O'Malley announced his decision to move the Dodgers to Los Angeles. The move to the West Coast was one of the things on Campanella's mind at 3:34 A.M. on January 28, 1958. Driving home to Long Island from his store in Harlem, Roy skidded on a slick spot on an S curve and slammed into a telephone pole. He was pinned inside his overturned car for a half-hour before his twisted body could be pried loose. His fifth and sixth cervical vertebrae were fractured and dislocated. He was paralyzed from the chest down.

The recovery was not an easy one for Roy. His wife left him after a time and died shortly thereafter, leaving him with four children. Destined to spend the remainder of his days in a wheelchair, barely able to feed himself, the great athlete despaired. But slowly his spirit revived, and he adjusted to a new life. O'Malley paid him his full salary and made him a spring training coach. In 1959 the Yankees and Dodgers played an exhibition game in his honor at the Los Angeles Coliseum. A crowd of 93,-103 people attended—an all-time record for baseball. Roy conducted television and radio interview programs from his wheelchair, remarried, and settled in Westchester County, New York. His liquor store remained his major source of income. He worked in the promotion department of the New York Mets in 1978, and then rejoined the Dodgers organization as a member of the community relations department for the 1979 season, moving at last to the West Coast.

In 1959 Roy published his autobiography, *It's Good to be Alive.* It was made into a television movie in 1974. By then repeated illnesses and hospital stays had reduced his once powerful frame. But he remained a beloved and revered figure to baseball fans, and an inspiration to the handicapped everywhere.

In 1969 Roy was inducted into the Hall of Fame. "There's a bit of little boy in every good ballplayer," he told the audience. That was the essence of Roy's career—baseball was a game, not a cause.

ROY CAMPANELLA

Brooklyn 1948–1957

G	AB	R	H	2B	3B	HR	RBI	Avg.
1215	4205	627	1116	178	18	242	856	.276

Campanella's fans, not least among them the players themselves, remain true. (Above) A throng greets him as he descends from a plane. (Below) He is still a star at the 1975 Old Timer's Game in Shea Stadium, where he's met by Willie Mays.

Max Carey (1890-1976)

Max Carey led the National League in stolen bases 10 times during a 20-season career, primarily with the Pittsburgh Pirates. His records for career steals, games played, and putouts by an outfielder stood for more than 40 years after his retirement.

Maximilian Carnarius was born on January 11, 1890, in Terre Haute, Indiana, of German ancestry. His family was religious and Max entered Concordia College in Fort Wayne to study for the Lutheran ministry. In addition to his theological studies, he pitched and played shortstop for the Concordia baseball team.

In the summer of 1909, Max and a friend went to see the South Bend team of the Central League play. The South Bend shortstop, Ray "Speed" Kelley, had recently been sold to Washington, and his replacement, Joe Claffey, did not distinguish himself on the diamond. Max told his friend, "I can play better than that guy," and he almost went into the clubhouse to see manager Aggie Grant about the situation.

Thinking better of it, Max hunted out Grant at the downtown hotel and offered his services, producing a medal he had won as a track sprinter at Concordia. Grant was impressed and offered Max a tryout the following day. The tryout went well, and Max was given a contract.

With a year of college remaining, Maximilian Carnarius changed his name to Max Carey to protect his amateur status and his scholastic eligibility. Max played in 48 games as a shortstop for South Bend, hit .158, and committed 24 errors. Despite the weak showing, he was invited to rejoin the club after school let out the following summer.

In the fall of 1909, Max returned to his theological studies at Concordia College and received his degree the following spring. Reporting to South Bend at the start of the 1910 season, Max found a new manager, Eddie Wheeler, and a fine new shortstop, Alex McCarthy. Wheeler positioned Carey in left field, and he remained an outfielder throughout his career.

The 1910 season was a considerably better one for Max. He played in 96 games, batted .293, and stole 36 bases. At the end of the Central League season, he and McCarthy were purchased by the Pittsburgh Pirates. That ended Carey's plans to enter the ministry. Max made his major league debut on October 3 against the Cardinals, and the following day he played again. In the two games Carey smacked three hits in six at bats.

Honus Wagner, the star of the Pirates, urged the young speedster to keep his legs in shape during the winter. Max took the

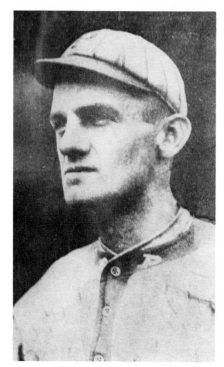

Max Carey was one of the biggest base thiefs in baseball. In his entire career, from 1910 to 1929, he stole 738, a National League record until 1974. A scientific basestealer, Carey studied pitchers and learned their pickoff moves. (Opposite page) Carey batting. He averaged over .300 seven times in his career.

advice and spent each winter of his career running to maintain a fine slender build. He stood 5'11½" and weighed 170 pounds. Although he was a natural righthanded hitter, Max taught himself to switch-hit.

Early in the 1911 season, an injury sent manager Fred Clarke to the bench and Carey replaced him in left field. When Clarke returned to action a few weeks later, Carey was assigned to center field and installed as the Pirates' leadoff man. In his first full major league season, Max batted .258 and stole 27 bases. He was not known for his power but was a good spray hitter who drew numerous walks. Twice in his career Carey led the National League in bases on balls.

But stolen bases were Max's forte. He did not have the reckless baserunning style of a Ty Cobb, and no one ever accused him of a spikes-high slide to get into the base. Rather, Carey was a scientific base stealer who studied the pitchers and learned their pickoff moves. As the National League's most prominent base runner since Billy Hamilton in the nineteenth century, Max kept the art of base stealing alive after it had fallen out of fashion.

Players called Max "Scoops" after a nineteenth century first baseman named George "Scoops" Carey, but the name did not catch on. The name "George" did, however, and "Max George Carey" became his contract signature.

In 1912 Max played 150 games and batted .302, one of six seasons in which he topped the .300 mark. He also led the league's outfielders with 369 putouts that year, the first of a record nine seasons in which he headed that department. By the time his career had ended, Max collected 6363 putouts, a record that stood until Willie Mays surpassed it. But Carey's 339 assists—70 higher than Roberto Clemente's total—including four league-leading seasons, remains a record.

In 1913 Max led the league in both times at bat (620) and runs scored (99). He also earned his first stolen-base crown, pilfering 61 bases. Nine additional stolen-base crowns would be garnered by Max.

The Pirates, meanwhile, were playing first-division ball under Fred Clarke, with Wagner remaining the team leader. But in 1914 the team dropped to seventh and remained in the second division for four

years. Max led the league in stolen bases in 1915 (36), 1916 (63), and 1917 (46). In 1918 the club rallied and finished fourth, as Max captured his fourth straight theft crown with 58.

Illness kept Max on the sidelines for a large part of the 1919 season. Playing in only 66 games, he batted .307 and stole only 18 bases. Still the Pirates led the league with 196 stolen bases.

Max returned to full-time duty in 1920, hit .289, and achieved a league-leading figure of 52 stolen bases. In 1921 Frankie Frisch stole 49 bases to beat Max, who had 37, but Carey batted .309 as the Pirates made a great run for the pennant, finishing second.

Then in 1922 Max enjoyed a season on the bases unmatched for excellence. While batting .329 with 140 runs scored and 207 hits, he stole 51 bases in 53 attempts, a .962 percentage. On July 7 that year, Carey enjoyed one of the finest days a hitter every experienced, reaching base nine times in an 18-inning, 9–8 loss to the Giants. Max collected six hits in six at bats, drew three walks, stretched a single into a double, recorded seven putouts, and stole three bases including home.

While never particularly noted for his hitting, Max set a National League career record for the most times with five or more hits in a game (nine). And on June 22, 1925, he had two singles in an inning twice in one game for a record.

Max led the league again in steals in 1923 (51), 1924 (49), and 1925 (46). Late in 1924—one of the four consecutive seasons in which he scored 100 or more runs—Max scored 20 runs in a 15-game stretch. In 1923 he tied teammate Pie Traynor for the National League lead in triples

with 19, as the Pirates hit 111 for the season.

The Pirates finally captured the pennant in 1925. It was Max's fifteenth full season with the club and, in addition to winning his tenth stolen-base title, he recorded a career-high batting average of .343 for manager Bill McKechnie. In the World Series against Washington, Max batted .458 with 11 hits in the 7 games, including 4 doubles and 3 stolen bases.

He played the final two Series games with broken ribs, and in the finale, hitting against Walter Johnson, Max had four hits, scored three runs, drove in two, and stole a base. The Pirates won the game, 9–7, and took the World Championship. Max received a raise to $16,000 a year the following season.

Club morale should have been at a peak in 1926, but unfortunately for the Pirates it was not. Fred Clarke, Max's first Pirate manager, was named a vice-president and assigned to direct the club along with McKechnie in the dugout. His presence was resented by some players, particularly Max, when teammate Carson Bigbee reported that Clarke had suggested to McKechnie that he bench Max.

Carey, the team captain, called a meeting of the players to vote for either Clarke or McKechnie as manager. The unusual action resulted in an 18–6 vote for Clarke, a suspension without pay for Carey, and his release to Brooklyn on waivers in July.

Bothered by sinus trouble, Max batted only .231 that year, then .266 in 1927, .247 in 1928, and .304 in 19 games in 1929 before drawing his release. He never enjoyed the popularity in Brooklyn that he had become accustomed to in Pittsburgh.

Max returned to the Pirates in 1930 as a coach, but he quit after the season and sat out a year. In 1932 he was hired to replace Wilbert Robinson as Brooklyn manager. With his arrival, the name of the team was changed from the Robins to the Dodgers. Max hired Casey Stengel as a coach, bought Hack Wilson from the Cubs, and battled with the front office over decision making. The Dodgers placed third in 1932 and sixth in 1933. Although Max had signed a 1934 contract, he was fired shortly before spring training began and

replaced by Stengel. Casey made sure Max was properly recompensed before agreeing to manage the club.

Max settled in Miami Beach with his wife, Aurelia, and their two sons. In 1940 he returned briefly to baseball as manager of the Miami team in the Florida East Coast League. He subsequently organized the All-American Girls Professional Baseball League, and during World War II he served as a race-track official. In 1955 Max managed Cordele of the Georgia-Florida League for the last half of the season, and the following year he managed Louisville of the American Association during the latter part of the season.

Carey's 738 career stolen bases stood as the National League record until Lou Brock surpassed it in 1974. In 1961, the same year that Billy Hamilton was elected, Carey joined his predecessor in base-running heroics in the Hall of Fame. Max Carey died in Miami Beach, Florida, on May 30, 1976 at the age of 86.

MAX GEORGE CAREY

Pittsburgh 1910–1926
Brooklyn 1926–1929

G	AB	R	H	2B	3B	HR	RBI	Avg.
2469	9363	1545	2665	419	159	69	797	.285

Carey in the outfield: His 6363 career total putouts were tops in the major leagues until Willie Mays chalked up more, but his 339 assists still stand as a record. He led the National League in putouts for nine seasons and in assists for four.

Alexander Cartwright (1820-1892)

The first man to formulate the rules of baseball, clearly distinguishing it from any type of British game, was Alexander Joy Cartwright. By drafting these rules and by establishing the first amateur team, Cartwright can today be cited as the man who virtually invented baseball. But not until the 1930s did he receive his just due.

Cartwright was descended from a long line of British sea captains. The first Cartwrights settled in Nantucket around 1660. Alexander Joy Cartwright, Sr., settled in New York in 1816, where he married Esther Rebecca Burlock; they produced seven children, three boys and four girls. The first child was named Alexander Joy Cartwright, Jr., and his birthdate was April 17, 1820.

Coming as he did from a prosperous family, young Alick led a happy life in the open fields of New York. He and his friends played a variety of ball games, but since considerable anti-British sentiment still remained, their parents sought to divert the children's interests from the British games of cricket, rounders, and town ball.

Cartwright also had a great interest in fire fighting, and in 1835 he nearly died of pneumonia after watching a raging, all-night blaze in the city. He never lost interest in fire departments and served at various times as a volunteer fire fighter. One of his brothers, Benjamin, became one of New York City's first fire commissioners.

In 1836 Alexander Cartwright, Sr., lost his fortune and become an insurance inspector, but the family retained its place in New York society.

In 1842 young Alick married Eliza Ann Gerritse Van Wie of Albany and accepted a position as a teller at the Union Bank in New York. A dashing figure at 6'2" and 210 pounds, Alick was considered quite handsome.

In 1842 Cartwright also joined the Knickerbocker Engine Company as a volunteer fireman, but the company disbanded in 1843. In July 1845, fire destroyed the Union Bank, and Alick and his brother Alfred opened a book and stationery shop on Wall Street.

The new location brought Alick together with a group of rising young businessmen in New York's financial district. Being something of an organizer, he began to plan sporting events for his large circle of friends. They first started to play ball in the Murray Hill section of Manhattan in 1845, and by September their rules were starting to make their game distinct from all previous games. Cartwright suggested that the group organize itself with written rules and a name, and on September 23, 1845, the Knickerbocker Base Ball Club emerged.

Cartwright and the Knickerbockers insti-

tuted a formal constitution for the team. They also decided to play in the more open expanses of Hoboken, New Jersey, a short ferry ride across the Hudson River from New York City.

The site selected was Elysian Fields, now located at Hudson and 12th Streets in Hoboken. A famous lithograph by Currier and Ives depicts one of the first baseball games played on Elysian Fields.

While the rules of baseball have changed significantly from those first established by Cartwright, his rules distinguished the game from town ball, in which runners were declared out when hit by a thrown ball. Twenty rules were adopted on that September day, and they were put in writing by two members of the team, known as the Committee on By-Laws.

The twenty rules follow:

1. Members must strictly observe the time agreed upon for exercise, and be punctual in their attendance.

2. When assembled for practice, the President, or in his absence the Vice-President, shall appoint an Umpire, who shall keep the game in a book provided for that purpose, and note all violations of the By-Laws and Rules during the time of exercise.

3. The presiding officer shall designate two members as Captains, who shall retire and make the match to be played, observing at the same time the players put opposite each other should be as nearly equal as possible; the choice of sides to be then tossed for, and the first in hand to be decided in a like manner.

4. The bases shall be from "home" to second base, forty-two paces; from first to third base, forty-two paces, equidistant. [42 paces equaled 90 feet.]

5. No stump match shall be played on a regular day of exercise.

6. If there should not be a sufficient number of members of the Club present at the time agreed upon to commence exercise, gentlemen not members may be chosen in to make up the match, which shall not be broken up to take in members that may afterwards appear; but in all cases, members shall have the preference, when present, at the making of a match.

7. If members appear after the game is commenced they may be chosen in if mutually agreed upon.

8. The game to consist of twenty-one counts, or aces; but at the conclusion an equal number of hands must be played.

9. The ball must be pitched, and not thrown, for the bat.

10. A ball knocked out of the field, or outside the range of the first or third base, is foul.

(Above) The Knickerbockers, the first formally constituted baseball club. Alexander Cartwright is at top center, and to his right is probably his brother Alfred. For all their superior organization, the Knickerbockers lost their first game against another team, the New York Nine, played June 19, 1846, in Hoboken's Elysian fields.

(At right) Cartwright's latticed bungalow in Honolulu. He arrived in Hawaii in 1849 on what was to have been an around-the-world adventure. Instead he stayed there the rest of his life.

11. Three balls being struck at and missed and the last one caught is a hand out; if not caught is considered fair, and the striker bound to run.

12. A ball being struck or tipped and caught either flying or on the first bound is a hand out.

13. A player running the bases shall be out, if the ball is in the hands of an adversary on the base, or the runner is touched with it before he makes his base; it being understood, however that in no instance is a ball to be thrown at him.

14. A player running who shall prevent an adversary from catching or getting the ball before making his base, is a hand out.

15. Three hands out, all out.

16. Players must take their strike in regular turn.

17. All disputes and differences relative to the game, to be determined by the Umpire, from which there is no appeal.

18. No ace or base can be made on a foul strike.

19. A runner cannot be put out in making one base, when a balk is made by the pitcher.

20. But one base allowed when a ball bounds out of the field when struck.

The Knickerbockers had 28 players in that first game, and Cartwright was the pitcher for one of the sides. The club played at least 14 recorded games in Hoboken that fall, and it purchased a specially designed scorebook for its records. Cartwright's side appears to have lost more often than it won.

On April 10, 1846, the Knickerbockers officially opened a well-structured new season, scheduling games every Tuesday and Friday afternoon. On June 19 that year, in what many consider the first game against another team, Cartwright served as umpire and saw the Knickerbockers lose to the New York Nine, 23–1.

The Knickerbockers wore the first baseball uniforms, outfitting themselves in blue pantaloons, white flannel shirts, straw hats, and patent leather belts. Despite their name, they never wore knickers, which was the fashion of the day. The team never turned professional, as most amateur teams eventually did in the New York area, and it continued to play on Elysian Fields into the early 1870s before disbanding.

Cartwright remained with the club for only four years. By his own method of scorekeeping, he played 121 games, scored 448 runs, and was retired 354 times.

An adventuresome man eager to try something new, Cartwright suddenly left New York on March 1, 1849, and never returned. Having read of the California gold rush, he set out for the West Coast, more interested in the adventure than in fortune seeking. He traveled by conestoga wagon from Newark, New Jersey, along with a small party. Whenever the group stopped, Alick would organize a baseball game for both the travelers and any local residents. He thus introduced baseball to such cities as Pittsburgh, Columbus, Springfield, Indianapolis, St. Louis, Jefferson City, Independence, Kansas City, Topeka, Casper, Lodi, Oakland, and finally San Francisco, where he arrived early in July of 1849.

Cartwright remained in San Francisco for but a few days. He fell ill with dysentery and was advised to go to Hawaii for a recovery. His intention then was to continue on to China and eventually return to New York. But the strapping young man, descended from generations of sea captains, became so seasick on the voyage to Hawaii that he vowed never to set foot on a boat again. He sent for his wife and three children, who arrived early in 1852, and spent the remainder of his life in Hawaii.

Cartwright became a prominent figure in the Islands, befriending King Kamehameha and serving as a diplomat for five Hawaiian rulers. He established his own firm as a whaling agent and commission merchant. Cartwright also ran a general merchandise business, hotel, bowling alley, and billiard hall. He organized the Honolulu fire department and even served as fire chief from 1850 to 1859. His businesses made him quite wealthy, and he found time to introduce the sport of baseball to the Hawaiian Islands.

Cartwright died on July 12, 1892, at the age of 72. His death went virtually unnoticed in the United States, and he was long forgotten as having had anything to do with the invention of baseball.

In the early 1900s, the National League appointed the Mills Commission to investigate the origin of baseball. The commission came to support the theory that Abner Doubleday invented the game in Cooperstown, New York. As baseball was preparing to celebrate its centennial with festivities in Cooperstown, Cartwright's grandson, Bruce Cartwright, Jr., wrote to baseball officials and was able to produce his grandfather's extensive diaries. These documents not only charted Cartwright's early baseball experience but also provided a vivid account of traveling westward during the gold rush era. After a review of his diaries, Cartwright was given due recognition and inducted into the Hall of Fame in 1938. A year later Babe Ruth visited his grave in Hawaii, paying tribute to the man who laid out the first baseball diamond.

Firefighting was another of Cartwright's loves. Here, in his later years, he wears the uniform of the Honolulu Fire Department he organized in 1850. In Hawaii, he became a wealthy businessman, befriended royalty, and introduced baseball.

Henry Chadwick (1824-1908)

The only professional sportswriter enshrined in the Hall of Fame is Henry Chadwick, who was inducted in 1938. Chadwick was a prominent figure in baseball from its inception as a professional sport until his death. For his contributions to the framing of the rules of the game and the method of scoring, as well as for his prolific writing as baseball journalist and historian, Chadwick has been called the "Father of Baseball."

Henry Chadwick was born on October 6, 1824, in Jessamine Cottage, St. Thomas Exeter, England. His father, Sir James, was the editor of the *Western Times* of Exeter. Henry's brother, 24 years his senior, was Sir Edwin Chadwick, an outstanding civil servant who achieved notoriety in 1842 with his publication of *The Sanitary Condition of the Labouring Population.*

With the exception of Edwin, the Chadwicks emigrated to the United States in 1837, settling in Brooklyn, New York. Henry remained a resident of Brooklyn for the remainder of his life. He received a careful education and at 19 became a contributor to the Long Island *Star.*

As a boy, Chadwick played cricket and rounders. He viewed his first baseball game at 23 when the young journalist traveled with his bride to Hoboken, New Jersey, to see the famed Knickerbocker Base Ball Club in action at Elysian Fields.

Chadwick's imagination was at once captured by this new sport, but he still covered cricket matches when he joined the young New York *Times* in 1856. Two years later, as a member of the staff of the New York *Clipper,* he devoted himself exclusively to baseball. Soon recognized as the nation's first important sportswriter, Chadwick remained with the *Clipper* for 31 years.

During that span, Chadwick's work appeared in a number of newspapers and publications. With the *Clipper's* blessings, he compiled the first printed rule book on baseball, which was published in 1859. The book standardized the loosely interpreted rules which tended to vary from town to town. After covering the Civil War for the New York *Tribune,* Chadwick joined the sports department of the New York *Herald* in 1864, and then joined the New York *Sun,* meanwhile retaining his affiliation with the *Clipper.*

His writing grew more prolific, as did his reputation. Chadwick became editor of the first weekly devoted entirely to baseball, *Ball Players Chronicle,* which published from June 1867 through July 1869. He edited a weekly fans' newspaper, *The Metropolitan,* which was a journal of events at New York's Polo Grounds from 1882 to 1884.

For more than 45 years, Chadwick contributed to the Brooklyn *Eagle,* serving as

Henry Chadwick, baseball's primary early historian, is the only professional sportswriter in the Hall of Fame. He compiled the first printed rule book on baseball in 1859.

chief baseball writer and, for a time, as sports editor. He also wrote for *Outing Magazine, Sporting Life,* and *The Sporting News,* baseball's "bible."

Although his style was considered to be at times "high-brow," no doubt owing to his proper English upbringing, his books and pamphlets were well read, and sold successfully. Chadwick never owned a typewriter, penning all of his material in a handsome longhand.

Chadwick was the first to compile such reference and "how-to" books as *Beadle's Dime Base Ball Guide* (1860), *Haney's Base Ball Book of Reference* (1866–1870), and *DeWitt's Base Ball Guide* (1869–1880). The Beadle book sold more than 50,000 copies a year, and the DeWitt Guide was a forerunner of the *Official Baseball Guide,* which Chadwick edited for Spalding Publishing Company from 1881 to 1908. The Official Guide, today published annually by Spink Publications, is the running history of the game. It was Chadwick's recognition of the need for an accurate historical record which launched the book to its highly regarded place in sports.

In 1872 Chadwick published the first listing of all professional baseball players, including their heights, weights, birthplaces, birthdates, and home towns, a form still commonly seen in modern rosters. In 1877 and 1878, he edited *Our Boys Base Ball Guide,* a guide to the game's slang which could be used by British sportswriters when Albert Spalding led an American tour to England. The book contained such terms as "passed ball," "double play," "pop up," "grounder," "assist," and "fungo."

Prompting from Spalding propelled Chadwick to turn out many instructional booklets, including *The Art of Batting, The Art of Base Running,* and *The Art of Fielding.* He also authored how-to booklets on cricket, handball, and one of his great hobbies, chess.

While baseball and chess were consuming interests with Henry, he managed to be married for 60 years and to rear two daughters. Music was yet another area of interest to Chadwick. Having worked briefly in his younger days as a piano teacher, he maintained his ability by composing and daily practice.

To those who followed Chadwick's career, it was difficult to envision the man as anything but a baseball buff. Surely, no sportswriter has ever approached in sheer quantity his numerous volumes of work. Although his books were successful, he continued in the field of journalism, contributing to the New York *World,* the New York *Evening Telegram,* the *Tribune,* and a sports paper known as the *Mercury.* His statistical reports were syndicated in many other eastern dailies.

Chadwick assumed the position of editor for the *Spalding Guide* in 1881 when Lewis Meacham died. At times Chadwick would use the pages of the *Guide* to express his personal opinion about the manner in which he thought the game should be played. Occasionally, his refined background probably inhibited his understanding of the players. Since the athletes lacked Chadwick's education and high standards, it would appear ludicrous for him to impose these qualities upon the players. He expected players to behave like proper English cricketeers, often lecturing them in print on the evils of drinking, on frequenting undesirable places, and on earning an unnecessarily high salary. The fans were also subject for his pen, particularly their rowdyism.

Chadwick's great battle was with gamblers. Although he accepted small-scale wagering between players, he feared the onset of mutual betting at baseball games. Largely through his condemnations of "pool-setting," the newly formed National League took a hard line against any manner of betting in 1876.

Harry Wright, another Englishman and a friend of Chadwick's, took exception to his repeated warnings on gambling, publicly scolding Henry by stating, "he uses words he doesn't understand." Clearly, Chadwick's writing was meant for the reading public and not for the athletes themselves.

"Father Chadwick," as he was called by the late 1880s, refuted his nickname, claiming that the "game never had a father. All I or anyone else has done is develop a field exercise long before we took serious note of it." Henry believed the game to have evolved from rounders, and he opposed the findings of the Mills Commission, which was organized in 1905 to determine the origin of the game. The commission presented the General Abner Doubleday theory, which has since been generally dismissed as unfounded. It was one of the few areas in which Spalding and Chadwick disagreed.

Chadwick invented the scoring system for keeping a play-by-play and refined the box score for newspaper use. He was appointed vice-president of the Baseball Reporters Association of America in 1887, the first organized group of sportswriters.

In 1867 Chadwick accompanied a professional team from Washington on an extended western tour. He pitched briefly, one of the few times that he participated in the game as an adult, but served principally as official scorekeeper. The only loss incurred by the team was to Forest City, which in 1871 became one of the teams forming the first professional league, the National Association. Chadwick served as chairman of the rules committee for the Association, following a 12-year stint as rules chairman for the amateur National Baseball Association.

Chadwick was an opponent of the Brotherhood rebellion of 1890. A foe of home run hitters, he acknowledged that only an "intelligent minority" appreciated scientific hitting. At various times, Chadwick would predict either doom or immortality for baseball, depending on his mood and recent events. But as the game grew and the demand for accurate information increased, he was regarded as the baseball authority.

When the National League sought to offer Chadwick a $600 pension during a time of need, New York Giants' president Andrew Freedman accused Henry of biting the hand which fed him. In protest, Chadwick boycotted all Giant games, and Spalding eventually led a drive to oust Freedman.

In 1894 the National League bestowed lifetime honorary membership on Chadwick. When he was present at a game, umpires often conferred with him over interpretation of rules. Chadwick fought hard for honest baseball and saw it grow into the national pastime.

When Chadwick turned 80 in 1904, President Theodore Roosevelt saluted him as the "Father of Baseball." Henry remained the editor of *Baseball Guide* through 1908. That April, he attended opening day at the Polo Grounds despite a fever, and developed pneumonia. He died in Brooklyn on April 20, 1908. Flags in all parks were lowered to half-staff. His longtime friend, Al Spalding, paid for an elaborate baseball monument at the Chadwick gravesite in Greenwood Cemetery, Brooklyn.

(Far left) One of Chadwick's baseball manuals. He wrote how-to books and reference books and invented the play-by-play scoring system. (Left) Chadwick's gravestone was a memorial from Al Spalding, for whose firm Chadwick edited the Official Baseball Guide.

Frank Chance (1877-1924)

In the first decade of the twentieth century, the Chicago Cubs captured four pennants. Their first baseman, cleanup hitter, and manager was the anchor of the Tinker-to-Evers-to-Chance double-play combination, burly Frank Chance.

Frank Leroy Chance was born on September 9, 1877, in Fresno, California, where his father was a bank executive. At Washington College in Irvington, which he entered in 1893 to study dentistry, Frank served as catcher for the baseball team.

Frank played semipro baseball and came to the attention of a former Cincinnati Red Stocking player, Cal McVey. After watching Chance play for several years, McVey wrote to Chicago manager Cap Anson, "Chance is the most promising player I have ever seen." The Cubs summoned Chance, and his dental aspirations were soon forgotten.

When Chance reported to Chicago, Anson was no longer manager, having been replaced by Tommy Burns. The spring-training camp was located in West Baden, Indiana, in 1898, and Chance was not particularly impressive. But physically he was massive, standing 6'0" and weighing 190 pounds. The players immediately began to call Chance "Husk."

Frank made his major league debut on April 29, 1898, going into the game in the late innings to catch Clark Griffith. He was discouraged at once by his performance, and after the game he told Burns of his intention to quit. Sportswriter Harold "Speed" Johnson talked Chance out of it, and Frank hung on as a catcher.

Chance was not a very competent catcher, constantly banging his fingers, breaking them on foul balls, and serving only as backup man to Tim Donahue. But he enjoyed his role, and took to the position more and more.

In 1902 Frank Selee took over as Cubs' manager. Late in July, Selee announced that Chance would be stationed at first base. Chance had batted .288, .289, .305, and .289 in his first four years and seemed to be a strong righthanded hitter. Frank's reaction was to again threaten to quit—he had grown to love catching.

At first base, Chance joined with shortstop Joe Tinker and second baseman Johnny Evers to form the famous double-play combination that Franklin P. Adams would immortalize in 1910 in his newspaper column with the poem:

These are the saddest of possible words—
   Tinker to Evers to Chance
Trio of Bear Cubs and fleeter than birds—
   Tinker to Evers to Chance
Thoughtlessly pricking our gonfalon bubble,
Making a Giant hit into a double,
Words that are weighty with nothing but
   trouble—
   Tinker to Evers to Chance

Frank's fortunes improved quickly once he moved to first base. In 1903, his first full season as a regular, he batted .327 and led the league with 67 stolen bases. In 1904, when Selee's health began to fail, Chance was appointed field captain of the team. He batted .310 that year and stole 42 bases. Fans did not measure the skill of a player by the amount of home runs blasted in those days. Undoubtedly, a man of Frank's size, would today be expected to hit more home runs (Chance had only 20 for his career), but in those days he served ably as cleanup batter in the Cub lineup.

Ill with tuberculosis, Frank Selee left the team in 1905. Chance was appointed his successor in July, and the team rallied to a 40–23 finish to capture third place. Frank's personal contribution was a .316 batting average.

In 1906 Chance assembled a great team. The poetic infield was completed by the acquisition of third baseman Harry Steinfeldt from Cincinnati. Pitchers Ed Ruelbach, Mordecai Brown, and Jack Pfiester won 64 games among them, and the Cubs registered a record 116 victories to finish 20 games ahead of the second-place Giants. Chance led the league with 57 stolen bases and 103 runs scored while batting .319, fifth in the league. Newspaper reporter Charlie Dryden hailed him as "The Peerless Leader."

The Cubs lost the 1906 World Series to the White Sox in six games, but the club returned to Series competition in 1907 after winning the pennant with 107 victories, finishing 17 games ahead of Pittsburgh. Frank hit .293 for the year and led the league's first basemen in fielding percentage. In the fall classic, the Cubs swept the World Series, winning four in a row over the Tigers after battling to a tie in the opening game.

The Cubs captured their third straight pennant in 1908, capping the season with another World Championship, again at the expense of Detroit. Chance hit .272 in the regular season and .421 in the World Series, but it was as a manager that he was now famed, particularly after the Cubs defeated the Giants on the last day of the season to win the pennant.

That game was a consequence of the famous "Merkle boner" incident. Several weeks before, the Giants' Fred Merkle had neglected to touch second base on an apparent game-ending hit, and the resultant tie, called by umpire Hank O'Day, necessitated a makeup game on the day after the regular season ended. Chance started Jack Pfiester, but lifted him in the

Chance, batting, throwing, and catching for the Chicago Cubs. He joined the club as a catcher, but against his wishes was moved in 1902 to first base, where his exploits became legendary. Later, he became manager, led his team to two World Championships and, in 7½ years, had a won-loss average of .665.

Frank Chance (left) signs a contract to manage New York's American League team for the 1913 season, the year the Highlanders moved to the Polo Grounds and became the Yankees. Club president Frank Farrell is at right.

first inning for Three Finger Brown. The Peerless Leader personally contributed three hits, including a key double, as the Cubs won the game, 4–2, and the pennant.

Frank had a habit of getting hit by pitches. The problem became serious after the 1908 season when headaches began to trouble him. Chance wore some added protection in his cap starting in 1909, but he still had difficulty backing away from high inside pitches. As a result, he never played as many as 100 games a season again.

In 1909 the Cubs won 104 games but finished second to Pittsburgh. However, they returned in 1910 to win their fourth pennant in five years with another 104 wins. In the World Series, won by Philadelphia in five games, Chance batted .353 to give him a career Series mark of .310.

The Cubs placed second in 1911. Rumors began circulating in 1912 that Heinie Zimmerman was undermining Chance in hopes of obtaining the managing position. Chance challenged Zimmerman to a fight to settle the issue, and apparently won it. Chicago finished third in 1912, but on September 28, owner Charles Murphy announced that Chance would not return as manager. Indignant fans protested loudly. Frank's record in seven and one-half years as Cub manager was 753–379, a .665 percentage. When released, Frank revealed that his salary had been a mere $5500 a year, compared with Fred Clarke's $15,000 in Pittsburgh and John McGraw's $18,000 in New York. (Chance did have a 10 percent stock holding in the team.)

Cincinnati was the first to claim Frank on waivers, but when the opportunity to manage the Yankees arose, the Reds graciously stepped aside. The Yanks then bought Chance for $1700, and New Yorkers held a parade to welcome him.

Chance was the first Yankee manager. With their move into the Polo Grounds in 1913, the New York Highlanders were renamed as the "Yankees." Unfortunately, Chance's stay in New York was not a pleasant one. The club finished seventh in 1913. Chance was through in mid-September of 1914 and returned home to California. He was paid $3300 for the remaining year of his contract.

Frank was not affiliated with baseball in 1915, but in 1916 he purchased the Los Angeles Angels of the Pacific Coast League, managing the club for two years before selling it at a profit.

Deaf in one ear as a result of repeated beanings, Frank remained at home in California until the Boston Red Sox convinced him to take on the managerial duties in 1923. Boston had been a lowly second-division team after they traded Babe Ruth to the Yankees, and Chance saw little hope for improvement. "This bunch will unquestionably finish last," he told reporters in spring training. They did, and out went Chance. It was a difficult season, for Frank was not popular with the players and had special difficulty in getting along with pitcher Lefty O'Doul.

In the fall of 1923, shortly after he had been released by the Red Sox, the Chicago White Sox sought the popularity of Frank's name in Chicago and hired him to manage. But his health was failing, and a bad case of asthma forced him to decline the job. As a replacement, the White Sox hired Johnny Evers.

Chance returned to California, where he died on February 15, 1924. Tinker, Evers, and Chance were together inducted into the Hall of Fame in 1946.

FRANK LEROY CHANCE

Chicago (N.L.) 1898–1912
New York (A.L.) 1913–1914

G	AB	R	H	2B	3B	HR	RBI	Avg.
1232	4279	796	1273	195	80	20	596	.297

Oscar Charleston (1896-1954)

Oscar Charleston was one of the first great stars of the Negro Leagues, and a man who devoted almost his entire life to the game of baseball.

Oscar McKinley Charleston was born on October 12, 1896, in Indianapolis, Indiana. It was said that he was named after President William McKinley, although McKinley was not elected until a month after Oscar's birth. Oscar's father, Tom Charleston, was a construction worker who had moved to the Midwest from South Carolina. His mother, the former Mary Thomas, came from Tennessee, where her father, a carpenter, helped to construct Fisk University in Nashville. Oscar was the seventh of 11 children, 8 of them boys.

Baseball and Oscar seemed to form a comfortable relationship as soon as he was old enough to meet his friends in the neighborhood yards. He attended Public Schools 23 and 17 in Indianapolis, and he held a paper route, delivering the *Morning Star* to over 100 customers each day. He always carried a baseball with him, tossing it as he delivered his papers.

Although his build was on the stocky side, even when he was a boy, he had good speed and showed a great interest in the game. The local professional team, the Indianapolis ABCs, hired him as batboy, and he enjoyed working out with the club. But he had a restlessness about him that took him to new locations throughout his life. At the age of 15, following the lead of an older brother, he enlisted in the Army and was made a member of the black 24th Infantry, stationed in the Phillipine Islands. There, his athletic ability really began to grow.

In the Phillipines he had a chance to run track, and he turned in impressive times in the 220-yard dash (23 seconds) and the 120-yard high hurdles (15.1 seconds). He also played service ball, and by 1914 he was the only black player in the Manila League. This was a feat he was unable to duplicate during his adult life because of the unwritten color code that kept black players out of organized baseball until 1946.

Late in 1914, Oscar was transferred to Hawaii, and his commanding officer, on a trip to Army Command School in Leavenworth, Kansas, paved the way for Oscar to enter professional ball. When his discharge came a few months later, Oscar joined the local Indianapolis ABCs, where he began to emerge as one of the finest players in the Negro Leagues.

The Indianapolis club, owned and operated by C. I. Taylor and Tom Bowser, was a fine one, and Oscar was able to maneuver himself into the center field job where his defensive prowess could not be denied.

Charleston stood about 5'11" and weighed 185 pounds at the time, but later he developed a weight problem and ballooned up to nearly 230. He was a lefthanded batter and thrower and, in those early years, a complete player. He could not only run fast, but with good instinct, and he was a frequent stolen base threat. He hit for average and he hit for power, although statistics from the Negro Leagues are so sketchy that it is difficult to say anything other than that league experts claimed he normally hit close to .370 with 30 home runs. He was often compared to Tris Speaker, for he too played a short center field, had great rear pursuit of a ball, and had a fine throwing arm.

While playing for the ABCs, Oscar married a local girl, Helen Grubbs, but the marriage soon ended in divorce.

Changing teams was common in the Negro Leagues. The contracts were not as rigid as in organized ball, and the lure of more money was always a strong inducement to jump. In 1919, Oscar joined the Chicago American Giants, run by Rube Foster, for whom he played left field. By now he was well established in the league, and a recognized .300 hitter. Teammates knew him fondly as "Charlie."

It was around this time that Oscar began playing winter ball in Cuba, making baseball a year-round job. He was a great star in Cuba year after year, and although at times he spent a few weeks in Mexico or the Dominican Republic, he always made Cuba his principal winter base.

Although the records are vague, it is believed that he returned briefly to Indianapolis in late 1920 after two years in Chicago, but no records indicate for certain that he played again with the ABCs. He cared deeply for his family and always sent money home to his mother. In any case, he joined the St. Louis Giants in 1921, a team run by Charlie Mills. At the end of the season he had his first chance to play against major league competition, as the Giants faced the St. Louis Cardinals in a five-game, postseason series. The Cardinals won three of the games, but Oscar left a mighty impression by hitting four home runs in one game, two of them off Cardinal star Jess Haines.

In 1922 Oscar played briefly for the St. Louis Stars, and then returned home again to play for the ABCs, earning $325 a month, or $125 more than anyone else on the club.

He spent the next two years back with Indianapolis and then accepted an offer to play and manage for the Harrisburg Giants in Pennsylvania. Colonel Strothers, owner of the club, handed him the dual job, and Oscar was his own best player. Rap Dixon was probably the next best player on the club.

It was in Harrisburg that Oscar married the daughter of a Methodist bishop, Jane Blaylock. Although never especially religious himself, he was at one point coaxed by Jane to visit her father's Sunday School class to meet the children. When teammates heard that "Charlie's teaching Sunday School," they could not believe it. His reputation was one of a gruff, rugged man, never one to shy away from a fight, and always one to battle umpires and opponents. He had a quick temper, and was often impatient with players less gifted than himself. Most acknowledged, however, that he was basically a gentle person.

Oscar and Jane were together often, even on road trips, as Oscar owned a car and took her along. The couple finally separated after about 20 years of marriage. They had no children.

Reaching for still a better offer, Oscar moved to the Philadelphia Hilldale club for the 1928 and 1929 seasons. In 1929 he was reported to hit .396 with 99 hits in 250 at bats, 37 of the hits being for extra bases. He was also credited with 22 stolen bases. On the bases, his reputation tended more toward Ty Cobb, for he slid hard with spikes high.

He was not a fast liver, and not a night person. He was usually asleep by 11 P.M., and was known as an early riser who took long walks before breakfast.

At Hilldale he became close friends with Judy Johnson and Biz Mackey. After his two seasons at Hilldale he joined the Homestead Grays for the 1930 and 1931 seasons, happy to be earning a steady paycheck during the Depression, no matter how poor were the travel and hotel conditions of the Negro Leagues.

In 1932, Oscar became playing-manager of one of the finest baseball teams ever assembled, the Pittsburgh Crawfords. Operated by Gus Greenlee, the team was a virtual all-star squad of the Negro Leagues, featuring, in addition to Charleston, Satchel Paige, Josh Gibson, Judy Johnson, and Cool Papa Bell. Few major league clubs ever had as many future Hall of Famers. Oscar was by now approaching his twentieth year of play and was something of a father figure. He was also one of the most popular players in the game—and he helped himself by leading the Crawfords to a 99-36 record in that first year, while batting a .363 in 135 games with 19 triples and 13 home runs.

Oscar managed Pittsburgh until 1938, and while the club was never quite as strong as in that first year, it was the "class" of the league. Charleston, now getting heavy, moved himself to first base, and continued to bat .300 even as he reached his fortieth birthday. He was never considered a great manager, for everyone knew how good the Crawfords were, but he did command the respect of his players and he had good baseball knowledge.

In 1939 he played briefly for the Toledo Crawfords, a team which replaced his old ABCs in the Negro American League. He then moved east to play and manage the Philadelphia Stars, Eddie Gottlieb's club. His tenure with the Stars did not bring any great success in the standings, but he was a popular figure to have running the club. And he still took his turns at bat.

Oscar remained with the Stars until 1945, when he signed to play for Branch Rickey's Brooklyn Brown Dodgers in Ebbets Field. Rickey was preparing to sign Jackie Robinson at the end of the season, but unfortunately for Oscar the breaking of the color line was coming too late for him.

The Brown Dodgers lasted only one year, and Oscar returned to the Stars in 1946, as the Negro Leagues began to fail with the entrance of black players into organized ball. Oscar took a fling at managing the Indianapolis Clowns, baseball's answer to the Harlem Globetrotters, and he took a team of all-stars on a tour of Canada, rooming with Satchel Paige to make certain that Paige was around to pitch the games. By 1949 Charleston had retired as a player and settled down in Philadelphia, taking a job in the baggage department at the Pennsylvania Railroad Station. He worked there for several years, but a bad back injury finally halted him.

Oscar died in Philadelphia on October 5, 1954, a week before his fifty-eighth birthday. Funeral services were held there, and in Indianapolis, where he was buried.

In 1976 he became the seventh player from the Negro Leagues to be elected to the Hall of Fame.

OSCAR McKINLEY CHARLESTON

Negro Leagues 1915–1946
(no records available)

(Above) Manager Charleston, left, talks to some of the top talent in a team made up of stars, the Pittsburgh Crawfords, in 1932. Right from Charleston are Rap Dixon, Josh Gibson, Judy Johnson, and Jud Wilson. (Below) Charleston, center, and two of his players on the Indianapolis Clowns, which combined skill and antics in the style of basketball's Globetrotters.

Jack Chesbro (1874-1931)

Jack Chesbro's best season was topped off by a pennant-losing wild pitch, but he survived the memory of that disappointing day to earn a reputation as a great pitcher.

John Dwight Chesbro was born on June 5, 1874, in North Adams, Massachusetts. The first team that Jack was ever associated with was the Houghtonville Nine, one of the many western Massachusetts sandlot teams for which he would play.

In 1894 Jack and several friends answered an advertisement for employment at the state mental hospital in Middletown, New York. The boys did some work with the patients but spent the majority of their time playing for the hospital team. The team coach was Pat McGreehy, who educated Jack in the finer points of pitching.

While working at the asylum, Chesbro acquired the nickname "Happy Jack," a reflection of his genial personality. The nickname reemerged several years later when he was pitching in the big leagues.

The 1895 season was Jack's first as a professional. He signed a contract with the Albany club of the New York State League. On May 20, the Albany team collapsed, and Jack was transferred to Johnstown of the same league. But on July 6, the entire league folded. Although his record was an unimpressive 7–10, Jack managed to finish the year with Springfield in the Eastern League, winning all of his three decisions.

In 1896 Jack signed with Roanoke of the Virginia League. He had compiled a 7–11 record when his club folded on August 20. Jobless, he traveled to Cooperstown, New York, where he pitched semipro ball. This occurred several years before Cooperstown gained notoriety as the "Birthplace of Baseball," and by pitching there Jack later claimed the distinction of being the only Hall of Famer who actually pitched in the town where the Hall of Fame was established.

With the opening of the 1897 season, Chesbro landed a job with the Richmond club of the Atlantic League. The broad-shouldered righthander, who stood 5'9" and weighed a chunky 180 pounds, posted a 16–18 record in his first season at Richmond. He was strictly a fastball and curveball pitcher during his minor league days, although he later learned to throw the spitball with great success.

In 1898 Jack worked in 40 games for Richmond and had a 23–15 record. The Baltimore Orioles had an opportunity to purchase Chesbro at that time, but they passed him up. In 1899 Jack returned to Richmond.

Had the Atlantic League been more proficient at compiling averages and distributing them to major league teams, Jack might not have spent so much time at

Richmond that year. Not until mid-season did anyone recognize that he had a 17–4 record, all complete games. In July, the Pittsburgh Pirates bought Chesbro for $1500 and put him on the mound against the Giants in the Polo Grounds. The result was a 4–1 loss.

Pittsburgh was managed at the time by Patsy Donovan, and the club's top pitchers were Sam Leever and Jess Tannehill. Jack's contribution was a 6–10 record in 19 appearances.

In 1900, Jack's first full season in the major leagues, Fred Clarke assumed the managerial reins and the Pirates jumped from seventh to second place. The addition of Honus Wagner to the lineup was a great asset, but Jack assisted with a 14–12 record for 32 appearances.

In 1901 the Pirates won their first National League pennant, compiling a 90–49 record. Jack registered his first 20-victory season, posting a 21–9 record for the top winning percentage in the league. He also tied for the league lead with six shutouts. There was no World Series.

The Pirates finished first again in 1902 with a sensational 103–36 record. Chesbro led the league with 28 victories (including a 12-game winning streak), hurled 8 shutouts, and lost only six times. That was the season Jack began to throw the spitball.

Seizing an opportunity to earn more money, Chesbro in 1903 jumped to the New York Highlanders, who were in their maiden American League season. The club, later to be known as the Yankees, had been moved from Baltimore, and a strong team was being assembled to compete with the Giants. Clark Griffith came from Chicago to manage the club. Hilltop Park in upper Manhattan was selected as the Highlander's home field.

Jess Tannehill also jumped the Pirates to join New York, but to Pirate owner Barney Dreyfuss's delight, neither Chesbro nor Tannehill enjoyed great years. Tannehill was only 15–15, and Chesbro, while winning 21 games, lost 15 and had only 1 shutout. The Highlanders finished fourth, while Pittsburgh won yet another pennant and participated in the first World Series.

But the nature of the game was different for Jack Chesbro in 1904: he enjoyed the finest season of any pitcher in the twentieth century. Jack completed each of his first 30 starts (he had a record 51 starts in all), hurled 48 complete games, made 4 relief appearances, led the league with 454 innings pitched, struck out 240 batters (a Highlander-Yankee record), and was not

Three pictures show the style of spitball hurler Chesbro, who holds the Highlander-Yankee title for the most strikeouts in a season—240, accomplished in 1904. That year he set an American League record of 41 victories, but cost his team the pennant on a wild pitch. Chesbro never made excuses for it, but later his widow attempted to have the play blamed on the catcher.

As these photos show, Fred Clarke threw right and batted left. He did both brilliantly, batting .315 over his career and once throwing out four base runners in one game, a feat accomplished only eight times in major league history. Clarke played full time for 15 years even while managing.

The symbol of success: for Fred Clarke, a new Studebaker.

In 1901, Clarke's second year as manager, the Pirates captured the National League pennant by seven and one-half games over second-place Philadelphia. Clarke helped his own cause with a .316 batting average and 22 stolen bases. A daring base runner who started many fights on the field by using his elbows to jar the ball loose from fielders, Clarke stole 527 bases in his career. He led the league in 1898 with 66.

In 1902 the Pirates won 103 games to capture another pennant. The margin of victory over second-place Brooklyn was 27½ games, easily the largest margin ever recorded in the major leagues.

The 1903 Pirates made it three consecutive pennants, topping the Giants by six and one-half games. They then faced the Red Sox in the first modern World Series. Clarke hit .351 in the regular season but batted only .265 in the Series, which the Red Sox won in eight games.

Clarke continued to perform well in left field while directing the team. In 1911 he recorded 10 putouts in one game, and in 1910 he threw out four base runners in a single game, a feat accomplished only eight times in major league history. Clarke's game may have been helped by flip-up sunglasses, which he introduced to baseball.

Unlike many player-managers who appeared in the lineup only occasionally, Fred played full-time for 15 seasons as manager. In 1904 a leg injury limited him to 70 games, the only year between 1885 and 1911 in which he played in fewer than 100 games. The leg injury contributed to the Pirates' fall to fourth place that year. In 1905 the club rose to second, then finished third in 1906, second again in 1907, and third in 1908. Finally, in 1909, they won their fourth pennant under Clarke, compiling a 110–42 record to beat the Cubs by six and one-half games. Wagner was the only player on the team to bat over .300, leading the league with .339. The 36-year-old Clarke hit .287 and won his second consecutive putout title in the outfield. Clarke hit only .211 in the World Series, won by Pittsburgh over Detroit in seven games.

Clarke remained a regular for two more seasons, but in 1910 he secured Max Carey from South Bend (Central League) to groom as his successor. At the end of the 1911 season, Clarke virtually closed his playing career; he appeared in only 12 games over the next 4 years. Second place in 1912 was the closest he came to another pennant. After the Pirates finished fifth in 1915, Clarke was replaced as manager by Jim Callahan. On September 23, 1915, Pirate fans staged a gala "Fred Clarke Day" in Forbes Field, presenting Fred with a book signed by thousands of admirers. In return, Clarke played four innings, collecting his final hit in two at bats to finish his career with a .315 average.

Clarke then retired to his ranch in Kansas, but he returned to Pittsburgh as a coach in June 1925. In 1926 Barney Dreyfuss appointed him vice-president and assistant manager of the team. As vice-president he outranked manager Bill McKechnie, but on the bench he certainly did not. When Clarke criticized players during games while sitting in the dugout, rebellion and dissension followed.

Max Carey, now captain of the team, and players Carson Bigbee and Babe Adams called a meeting with McKechnie to bring the matter to a head. McKechnie did not attend the meeting, but the team voted 18–6 in favor of Clarke's authority. News of the meeting reached the press, and Dreyfuss received word while vacationing in Europe.

Carey was suspended and then waived to Brooklyn; Bigbee and Adams were released. At the end of the year, Clarke sold his stock in the club and left town; McKechnie was released.

Clarke prospered on his "Little Pirate Ranch" in Winfield, Kansas. In 1937 he served as chairman of the National Baseball Congress semipro tournament in Wichita. He was also president of the National Association of Leagues for the Sandlot Clubs.

In 1945 Clarke was elected to the Hall of Fame. He died in Winfield on August 14, 1960, shortly before what would have been his eighty-eighth birthday.

FRED CLIFFORD CLARKE

Louisville 1894–1899
Pittsburgh 1900–1915

G	AB	R	H	2B	3B	HR	RBI	Avg.
2204	8584	1620	2703	358	219	65	1015	.315

John Clarkson (1861-1909)

In the 1880s, when the distance from the mound to home plate was 50 feet, John Clarkson was considered one of the best pitchers in baseball.

John Gibson Clarkson was born on July 1, 1861, in Cambridge, Massachusetts. His father was a well-to-do jewelry manufacturer from whom he inherited his handsome features. John had two Harvard-educated brothers, Walter and Arthur, both of whom also took a fling at professional baseball. Walter, 17 years younger than John, pitched for the New York Highlanders (1904–1907) and Cleveland Naps (1907–1908) with a combined 20–18 record. Arthur, nicknamed "Dad," was five years younger than John, and he posted a 39–39 record while pitching for New York, Boston, St. Louis, and Baltimore in the National League from 1891 to 1896.

John broke into professional baseball as a major leaguer, signing his first professional contract with Worcester in 1882. A member of the National League at the time, Worcester had the worst record of the eight clubs in the league, finishing with an 18–66 mark. In the second season of the 50-foot pitching distance (it had previously been 45 feet), John was signed since club owners thought that a local boy might boost the poor attendance figures. Had the team not been local, and had it not been so poorly staffed, John doubtless would have taken his normal course through the minor leagues.

However, Clarkson found himself in the minors when Worcester disbanded at the end of the 1882 season. John, as a free agent, was lost in the shuffle of players trying to sign on with other clubs. Quiet and meek in his younger years, John did not approach other clubs for employment. Instead, he was scouted and signed by Saginaw of the Northwestern League, where he spent one and a half years. In that half-season of 1884, John pitched 10 shutouts and had a strikeout-walk differential of 399 to 45. While pitching in Grand Rapids, Michigan, he was observed by Cap Anson, manager of the Chicago White Stockings. Anson's No. 2 pitcher, Fred Goldsmith, was beginning to fade, and Anson was looking for a replacement. He found his object in Clarkson, signed him to a contract, and merely paid the price of a railroad ticket from Saginaw to Chicago.

John pitched in 14 games for the White Stockings at the close of the 1884 season. He won 10, lost only 3, and had 12 complete games. Larry Corcoran, the club's premier pitcher, pitched 517 innings that season, compiled a 35–23 record, and gave Clarkson an idea of the mound work to be expected.

If John Clarkson looks more like a banker (above) or a dancer (opposite page), blame it on the photography of the 1880s, for indeed he was a top-notch baseball pitcher, master of the "drop curve" and change-up, and winner of 327 games over his major league career.

Corcoran was gone early in the 1885 season. Anson made Clarkson his No. 1 pitcher, using Jim McCormick as the alternate. Clarkson thereupon compiled one of the greatest pitching records of all time. He racked up 53 wins against 16 losses, pitched 622 innings, started 70 of the White Stockings' 112 games, and completed 68 of them. He registered 10 shutouts, 318 strikeouts, and only 99 walks. On July 27, he pitched a 4–0 no-hitter against Providence. He recorded a 12-game winning streak during the season, leading the league in victories, shutouts, innings pitched, strikeouts, and complete games.

The White Stockings won the 1885 pennant, edging the Giants by two games. The third-place Phillies finished 31 games out of first although each team played only a 112-game schedule.

A World Series was attempted between Chicago and St. Louis (American Association champions), but no winner emerged, as each club won three, lost three, and tied one. The second game was declared a tie, after Charles Comiskey pulled his Chicago team off the field in a protest.

In 1886 Clarkson again led Chicago to a National League pennant. He did not match his superlative record of the 1885 season, but he nonetheless did register a 35–17 record, completing 51 games in 53 starts. For the season, the White Stockings edged Detroit by two and one-half games.

Another World Series was scheduled between the Browns and the White Stockings following the season, and it was agreed that the winner would receive the entire gate assets. The games were considered to be the best of the early "World Series," with the fans wildly enthusiastic and the games exciting. Clarkson shut out St. Louis, 6–0, in the opener, won the third game, 11–4, lost the fourth, 8–5, and had a 3–0 lead in the sixth and deciding game when he permitted St. Louis to tie the score. In the tenth inning, a wild pitch permitted the Browns' Curt Davis to slide home—"the $15,000 slide" as it was called—and St. Louis won the championship.

Davis's slide became more famous than Clarkson's pitch, and Clarkson never suffered the memory of his unfortunate delivery. Instead, he returned in 1887 to post a 38–21 record, leading the league in victories and completing 55 of 58 starts.

John was not the easiest man to manage, as Anson later pointed out. He developed a terrible temper and had an extremely sensitive disposition. Adverse criticism would cause John to sulk and he might not win another game for weeks. He was one who constantly needed praise and encouragement to deliver his best.

During the off-season before the 1888 campaign, John was sold to Boston for the enormous sum of $10,000. His batterymate, the colorful Mike "King" Kelly, had been sold by Chicago to Boston the year before for the same price. Armed with its new "$20,000 battery," Boston suddenly had an established team.

The Chicago players were bitter over the sale. The money represented more than two and one-half years of Clarkson's salary, but the transaction netted John nothing. In effect, the incident was an early example of player discontent.

Chicago placed higher than Boston in 1888, finishing second to Boston's fourth, but Clarkson was 33–20 and completed all of his 53 starts. He was at the peak of his form now. In style of pitching, John relied primarily on his "drop curve" and change-up.

Clarkson also derived a measure of success on the mound by wearing a shiny belt buckle that reflected the sun into the batter's eyes. However, the deception was soon acknowledged to be contrary to the game's rules, and Clarkson was forced to abandon it. He was also noted for his acute memory, which retained the strengths and weaknesses of opposing batsmen.

Although generally on the serious side, John once demonstrated his belief that a game should be called for darkness by throwing a lemon to his catcher. The umpire, Jack Kerin, called the pitch a strike and, when shown the lemon, ended the game.

In addition to his prowess on the baseball field, John was a fine billiards player. His strong hand was able to spin a billiard ball completely around the table with one twist of his fingers, a feat which won him many bets.

In 1889 John compiled a 49–19 record, but Boston lost the pennant to New York by one game when Pittsburgh defeated Clarkson on the final day of the season. He really worked overtime that season, hurling 629 innings and 69 complete games, including two complete-game victories on September 12. Down the pennant stretch, John was called on to pitch on eight consecutive days. He also set National League fielding records for pitchers that season which still stand, handling 206 chances and recording 168 assists.

John remained loyal to the National League in 1890, rejecting an offer from the Players' League, and posted a 26–18 record for Boston. It was later reported that league officials had given John

$10,000 to remain with Boston. As a result of this contention, John and 14 other players were branded traitors to the players' cause, and his popularity among players fell.

Boston won pennants in both 1891 and 1892, with Clarkson and Kid Nichols the big men. John was 34–18 in 1891, a year in which no World Series was held.

In 1892 Clarkson had recorded an 8–6 mark in 16 games for Boston when arm trouble curtailed his playing time. This alone might have led to his release, but concurrently Boston attempted to cut the salary of John and other players to reduce its operating expenses. When Clarkson refused, Boston released him, conveniently citing arm trouble as the cause.

John immediately accepted an offer from Cleveland. He pitched in 29 games for the Spiders, winning 17 of 27 decisions. The league had a split season that year, with Boston winning the first half and Cleveland the second. Thus, John contributed to two championship clubs in the same season.

Cleveland placed third in 1893, but John was a fading veteran and Cy Young the rising star on the staff. Clarkson was 16–18 that year, and in 1894 he compiled an 8–8 record to wrap up his career. Ned Hanlon, running the Baltimore Orioles, offered John a sizable sum of money to sign with his pennant-bound club, but Clarkson decided to retire. Hanlon instead signed John's brother, Arthur.

John moved to Bay City, Michigan, and opened a cigar store, which he ran until 1906. He then suffered a mental breakdown, was declared insane, and spent most of the remainder of his life in a mental hospital. He was visiting relatives in Cambridge when he died of pneumonia on February 4, 1909.

John's 327 career victories made him one of only 14 pitchers in baseball history to record 300 triumphs. In 1963 his achievements were rewarded by selection to the Hall of Fame.

JOHN GIBSON CLARKSON

Worcester (N.L.) 1882
Chicago (N.L.) 1884–1887
Boston (N.L.) 1888–1892
Cleveland (N.L.) 1892–1894

G	IP	W	L	Pct.	H	R	ER	SO	BB	ERA
517	4514	327	176	.650	4384	inc.	inc.	2013	1192	inc.

Roberto Clemente (1934-1972)

Roberto Clemente captured four National League batting titles and collected 3000 hits during his 18-year career with the Pittsburgh Pirates. He became the first Hispanic player elected to the Hall of Fame.

Roberto Walker Clemente was born on August 18, 1934, in Carolina, Puerto Rico, near San Juan. He was the youngest of seven children, six of them boys. His father was the foreman of a sugar plantation, manager of a grocery and meat market, and owner of some trucks. Young Roberto developed his physical strength by helping to unload the trucks.

The temperate climate in Puerto Rico enabled Roberto to play baseball the entire year, and it quickly became his dominant passion. He played softball on the playgrounds and hardball in municipal leagues. He also squeezed a rubber ball for hours, helping to develop one of the strongest throwing arms in baseball. Roberto's hero was Monte Irvin, then a Negro League star who played winter ball in Puerto Rico each year.

In high school Roberto starred in baseball and track. His teacher and playground coach, Roberto Marin, tipped off a scout for the Santurce professional team, Pedro Zorrilla, about his student's talents. After observing young Clemente several times, Zorrilla offered Roberto a $5000 bonus, a $60-per-month contract, and a new baseball glove. While still in high school, Clemente began to play for Santurce.

Roberto played three winters for Santurce between 1952 and 1955, attracting the attention of big league scouts in America. Latin players had just begun to enter major league baseball after having been generally barred along with blacks for many years. Minnie Minoso was already in the major leagues at this time, and Mexico's Bobby Avila had won the 1954 American League batting championship.

Clemente batted .356 for Santurce during the winter of 1952–1953. The following winter, Dodger scout Al Campanis came to town and organized a clinic for 100 boys. Clemente participated, showed the ability to do everything well, and Campanis offered him a $10,000 bonus.

Nine other clubs also awaited Roberto's high school graduation in order to extend offers, including one of $30,000 from the Milwaukee Braves. But Roberto gave his word to Campanis and stuck to the agreement.

Although he was only 19, Clemente was assigned to the Dodgers' top minor league team, the Montreal Royals of the International League. But baseball regulations interfered with his first season as a player. A rule in effect at the time stated that any player receiving a bonus of more than

$4000 had to be placed on the major league roster after one minor league season. If not, another club could draft the player for a mere $4000.

The Dodger club in the mid-1950s was loaded with talent. They knew it would be difficult to make room on their roster for Clemente, so they attempted to "hide" their find at Montreal by using him sparingly, hoping to discourage other clubs from drafting him. He was sent to bat only 148 times in 1954, and hit .257 with 2 homers and 12 RBIs. The Dodgers were satisfied that a player with such an undistinguished record would not be drafted.

However, the Pittsburgh Pirates claimed Clemente on November 22, 1954. Clyde Sukeforth had watched Roberto in batting practice at Montreal and had recognized his great potential. The Pirates made him their No. 1 selection, and the Dodgers lost Roberto for $4000.

Clemente joined the last-place Pirates in 1955 and found a place in the regular line-up, batting .255 with 5 home runs in 124 games. It was not a sensational debut, but Clemente had moved into a major league lineup at the age of 20 while still going through the adjustments of learning English.

At one point during his rookie season, Roberto switched to a lighter bat, and the change in swing caused a back injury that plagued him for several years. The backache was one of many injuries that befell Clemente during his career. Few were serious, and many teammates and opponents began to label him a hypochondriac, a charge that remained with Roberto throughout his career.

In 1956 the Pirates advanced a notch to seventh place and Clemente hit .311. It was the first of 13 seasons in which he would surpass the .300 mark, including a span of eight consecutive years between 1960 and 1967. In the following three seasons (1957–1959), the Pirates began to assemble a quality major league team, although Roberto batted under .300 each time.

In 1958 Clemente put on a great show with his powerful arm, recording 22 assists and winning his first of five assist titles among outfielders. That he should capture the title as late as 1966 and 1967 was a remarkable achievement, for by then most runners respected his arm and few dared

The classic duel between batter and pitcher unfolds. (Left) Clemente at bat waits for the pitch from Jim Palmer of the Baltimore Orioles in the first inning of the sixth game of the 1971 World Series. (Above) The climax: Clemente connects for a triple. The Pittsburgh Pirates went on to win the Series.

As Vera Clemente hugs her hero husband, the scoreboard above spells out the story of that day, September 30, 1972. The story should have gone on to more such celebrations for Clemente. In fact, the milestone hit was his last.

to go from first to third on singles to right field.

In 1960 the Pirates were headed for a World Championship. Playing with Clemente under manager Danny Murtaugh were such stars as Bill Mazeroski, Dick Groat, Bill Virdon, Dick Stuart, Smokey Burgess, Don Hoak, Bob Skinner, Bob Friend, Vern Law, and Roy Face. It was an exciting club, and Pittsburgh fans went wild over their champions, who defeated the Yankees in a thrilling seven-game Series when Mazeroski hit a last-of-the-ninth home run in the final contest.

For the season, Clemente batted .314 with 16 homers; in the World Series, he batted .310. Groat won the Most Valuable Player award and Clemente felt bypassed because of his Puerto Rican background.

Roberto often expressed his emotions about being overlooked by writers and fans. He resented the lavish attention paid to such American-born stars as Willie Mays and Hank Aaron, believing himself to be equally deserving. Clemente and Mays were brilliant outfielders, and both caught fly balls in the unique "basket" style— waist high with glove up. Neither copied the other, for both arrived in the majors with this particular style.

In 1961 Clemente won his first of four batting titles. He batted .351 with 201 hits, his first of four seasons of 200 hits or better. Physically he was in excellent shape, and even his back had ceased to bother him. A six-month winter hitch in the Marines in 1957 had worked the pain out, and at 5'11" and 185 pounds he was trim and handsome.

Clemente captured his second batting title in 1964, the year he married Vera Zabala. They later had three sons. He batted .339 in 1964, and won his third title in 1965 with a .329 mark. In 1966 Roberto relinquished the batting title to teammate Matty Alou, but he hit 29 homers and drove in 119 runs, earning the league's MVP award despite the Pirates' third-place finish.

Roberto won his fourth and final batting championship in 1967, hitting .357 with 23 home runs. In 1968 Clemente batted .291 and failed to make the All-Star team for the only year between 1960 and 1971. But in 1969 he returned to hit .345. The following year, Roberto led the Pirates to the Eastern Division title with a .352 batting average. As Clemente reached his late thirties, his hitting seemed to improve each season.

The Pirates lost the Championship Series to the Reds in 1970, but in 1971 they captured both the National League flag and the World Championship. Roberto batted .341 in the regular season and then put on a sensational exhibition in the 1971 World Series, batting .414 with 12 hits, 2 of them homers, and some tremendous fielding plays. He was named the top player of the Series. In accepting postseason awards, he took the opportunity to speak out on behalf of the Puerto Rican people.

Bothered by injuries in 1972, Roberto batted .312. The Pirates again finished first in their division, but lost in the playoff to the Reds. On September 30, Clemente collected his three thousandth and final hit— he was only the eleventh man to reach that total.

Following the 1972 Championship Series, Roberto returned to his suburban home near San Juan. He had played and managed in the Puerto Rican winter leagues in previous years, but this winter he devoted his time to work for a sports city for San Juan youngsters.

In the final week of December, an earthquake destroyed the city of Managua, Nicaragua. Clemente helped to organize relief missions to the city. On New Year's Eve, he boarded a small DC-7 with four others to fly emergency supplies to the decimated city. Shortly after taking off, the plane exploded and crashed into the ocean. Clemente's body was never found.

The event shocked not only the baseball world but also the island of Puerto Rico, where Clemente had become a national hero. Three days of official mourning were declared, during which people lined the beaches as divers searched for his remains. Radio stations canceled regular programming. A special election was held to vote Clemente into the Hall of Fame at once, bypassing the regulation of a five-year waiting period. In tribute to Clemente's accomplishments as a humanitarian and a player, the Pirates of 1973 wore patches on their sleeves with Roberto's uniform number, 21, circled in black. Each spring for the next several years, the Pirates played a series of exhibitions in San Juan, so that Clemente's dream of a "sports city" would be realized, in his name.

ROBERTO WALKER CLEMENTE

Pittsburgh 1955–1972

G	AB	R	H	2B	3B	HR	RBI	Avg.
2433	9454	1416	3000	440	166	240	1305	.317

Ty Cobb (1886-1961)

Ty Cobb is considered by many baseball experts to have been the greatest player in the game's history. Those who dispute the claim usually select Babe Ruth as the foremost star. Although these two men share this high esteem, they were totally different. Ruth was an amiable, pleasure-loving extrovert; Cobb, a harsh, driving, and lonely perfectionist.

The complex life of Tyrus Raymond Cobb began on December 18, 1886, in Narrows, Georgia. He was particularly devoted to his father, Professor W. H. Cobb, the local schoolmaster and a Georgia state senator. The senior Cobb hoped his son would study at West Point or go to law school, but when Ty decided to enter professional baseball Professor Cobb supported his decision wholeheartedly.

Ty signed his first professional contract in 1904 at the age of 17. But when he batted only .237 in 37 games for the Augusta entry in the Sally League, the team released him.

Leaving professional baseball, Ty joined a semipro outfit in Anniston, Alabama. He batted .370 in 22 games, which prompted Augusta to give him a second chance the following year. But in 1905 an event outside the baseball circle had a deep impact on Ty's life. The elder Cobb, seeking to catch his wife in an unfaithful act, climbed through the bedroom window of the Cobb home and was shot and killed by the startled Mrs. Cobb, who mistook him for an intruder. Whether that event remained the cruel and bitter spike in Cobb's introverted nature can only be left to speculation. Those who knew Ty thought it was the principal cause of his rage. Whatever the reasons, Cobb's personality certainly made him one of the most disliked players in baseball history.

From the time he first put on a Detroit Tiger uniform on August 30, 1905, Cobb was unpopular with his teammates. He ate his meals alone and kept to himself. Whereas he was determined to be the best player on the team, his relentless drive, reckless slides with spikes high on the basepaths, and meager .240 batting average as a rookie only nurtured his teammates' resentment. Some players passed years without speaking to Cobb.

In 1906 Ty signed a $1500-per-year contract, played in 97 games, and batted .320. It was the first of 23 consecutive seasons in which the master of hitting would bat .320 or better. He won 12 batting titles, 9 of them consecutively, and compiled the highest lifetime average in the game, .367. In fact, Cobb's lifetime average has remained higher than any individual season's average of any player, aside from Ted Williams (twice) and Stan Musial (once), since 1942!

Three times Cobb bettered the .400 mark. He set lifetime records for games played (3,033), times at bat (11,429), stolen bases (892), and total hits (4,191). In regard to career hits, Cobb is the only player to pass the 4000 mark. Although he played in the so-called dead-ball era and hit only 118 home runs, he ranks high in extra-base hits and total bases.

In 1906, Cobb's first full year in the major leagues, Detroit finished in sixth place under manager Bill Armour. Ty was the club's leading hitter. When Hughey Jennings became manager in 1907, Cobb won his first of nine consecutive batting championships, hitting .350 and leading the league with 212 hits and 116 runs batted in. The Tigers won the pennant but lost the World Series in five games (one tie) to the Cubs, with Cobb managing a scanty 4 hits in 20 at bats.

With an outfield composed of Ty Cobb, Sam Crawford, and Davy Jones, the Detroit Tigers became one of the great baseball teams of the early twentieth century. Detroit captured another pennant in 1908, edging Cleveland by a mere half-game. Cobb batted .324 and led the league in hits, doubles, triples, and runs batted in. He batted .368 in the Series loss to Chicago.

The Tigers captured their third consecutive pennant in 1909 as Cobb batted .377. The World Series featured a classic matchup between Ty and the Pirates' Honus Wagner. Cobb was quoted as saying, "I'll show that kraut," and threatened to spike Wagner on the basepaths. Wagner, the favorite in the Series, hit .333; the brash Cobb batted only .231 as Pittsburgh won in seven games. There was no rematch—it was Cobb's last World Series.

Personal duels between Cobb and opponents were not uncommon. In 1909 there was the celebrated spiking of Philadelphia's Home Run Baker, and for years fans debated whether it had been intentional. Cobb once engaged in a terrible brawl with the New York Giants' Buck Herzog during an exhibition game, continuing the fight later in the club's hotel and badly beating up the smaller man. Ty was often accused of racial bigotry, and he once was sued by a hotel chambermaid whom he beat up when she resented his calling her "nigger."

Cobb fought with many others in the game, including umpire Billy Evans and teammate Germany Schmidt. He also fought with his two wives, both of whom divorced him, and he was never close to

Ty Cobb (bottom row, extreme left) with the
Royston Rompers, his first organized team.
Cobb's father, a schoolmaster and Georgia state
senator, dreamed of seeing his son go to West
Point or law school, but finally endorsed the
young man's decision to play pro ball.

his children. Cobb's autobiography, written in the closing years of his life, was a bitter recall of personal vendettas. Numerous people regretted that such a talented player should be so obstinate and bitter, but most individuals merely avoided Cobb and classified him as trouble.

Detroit failed to win the pennant in 1910, but Ty hit .385 for his fourth batting crown. In 1911 he scaled the .400 mark for the first time, batting .420 with 248 hits and winning his only Most Valuable Player Award.

In 1912 he engaged in a bitter holdout with Detroit owner Frank Navin, teaming with three other players in a unified demand for higher salaries. While the three others yielded before opening day, Ty did not sign until May 1 (although he did play on opening day), at which time he settled for $11,332.55. Eventually, Cobb's salary soared to $50,000. By investing his money wisely, notably in a new soft drink called Coca-Cola, Ty became a wealthy man.

If the long holdout of 1912 affected Cobb's play, the only evidence was that his .420 batting average in 1911 slipped to .410. In 1915 Cobb not only achieved his ninth consecutive batting title, but he stole bases at a record clip. His theft mark was 96 that season, a record which stood until Maury Wills of the Los Angeles Dodgers stole 104 bases in 1962.

In 1916 Cobb batted .371, but Cleveland's Tris Speaker captured the crown with an average of .386. Cobb recovered the title the following season with an average of .383. He also topped the league in 1918 and 1919 with marks of .382 and .384, respectively.

By 1920 the Tigers were a seventh-place club under manager Jennings, and Cobb's average had dropped to .334. To everyone's surprise, the club appointed Cobb manager in 1921. The move, which coincided with the coming of Babe Ruth to the Yankees, failed to revive the Tigers' fortunes.

The team finished in sixth place in 1921; Cobb hit .389 and lost the batting title to teammate Harry Heilmann by five points. The Tigers finished third in 1922, with Cobb hitting .401 in the year in which George Sisler batted .420.

Detroit placed a distant second in 1923 (Cobb hit .340), third in 1924 (.338), fourth in 1925 (.378), and sixth in 1926 (.339). On November 2, 1926, the baseball world was stunned when the Tigers released Cobb as both player and manager. Surely, fans reasoned, Cobb retained his batting skills, and the mystery of his dismissal puzzled their minds.

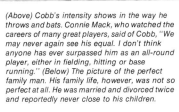
(Above) Cobb's intensity shows in the way he throws and bats. Connie Mack, who watched the careers of many great players, said of Cobb, ''We may never again see his equal. I don't think anyone has ever surpassed him as an all-round player, either in fielding, hitting or base running.'' (Below) The picture of the perfect family man. His family life, however, was not so perfect at all. He was married and divorced twice and reportedly never close to his children.

87

Dirt flying, Ty Cobb slides safely into third. Jimmy Austin is the third baseman. Base runner par excellence, Cobb stole a record 892 bases in his career, but his style did not contribute to his popularity with other players. All too often, he slid with high-flying spikes aimed carefully at the baseman. An unfriendly loner, Cobb was not a favorite with teammates either.

When Tris Speaker, player-manager of Cleveland met a similar fate a few weeks later, reporters unearthed the real story.

The American League president, Ban Johnson, had come into possession of two letters, one written by Cobb and the other by pitcher Joe Wood, which appeared to support a claim that a 1919 game between Detroit and Cleveland had been "fixed" by Cobb and Speaker for betting purposes, with the Tigers winning as planned. Baseball was shaken by the involvement of two such prominent figures in a scandal, and Commissioner Kenesaw Mountain Landis was not eager to pursue its resolution. Subsequently, Landis cleared both players of the charges, and Ban Johnson, who had committed himself to the decision that "neither would ever play in the American League again," resigned a short time later.

Both Speaker and Cobb were restored to their respective rosters, but both were once again released. Speaker then signed with Washington, and Cobb contracted with Connie Mack in Philadelphia. In his first season as an Athletic, 1927, Cobb batted .357. The following year, at age 41, he hit .323 and terminated his career.

Thereafter, Cobb lived a lonely existence, wealthy but friendless, never mellow or regretful. He had played diligently and arduously in single-minded pursuit of perfection, and no player ever came closer to it on the baseball diamond.

In his later years Cobb helped to establish scholarships and funded a medical center in his father's name in Royston, Georgia. Acts such as these helped ease his long-standing reputation for frugality.

In 1936 Ty Cobb received the most votes in the first Hall of Fame election. He died in Atlanta on July 17, 1961.

TYRUS RAYMOND COBB

Detroit 1905–1926
Philadelphia (A.L.) 1927–1928

G	AB	R	H	2B	3B	HR	RBI	Avg.
3033	11429	2244	4191	724	297	118	1954	.367

(Above) Detroit fans honor their superstar on Ty Cobb Day. (Left) After playing for Detroit for 21 years, Cobb signs with Philadelphia.

Mickey Cochrane (1903-1962)

Mickey Cochrane is considered by many in the baseball world to have been the finest catcher in the game's history. If there was one ability that set him apart from other catchers, it was his speed, which he displayed over a 13-season career with Philadelphia and Detroit in the American League.

Gordon Stanley Cochrane was born on April 6, 1903, at Bridgewater, Massachusetts, not far from Boston. Only his mother called him Gordon; "Mickey" seemed to better fit the son of John Cochrane, a Boston Irishman. The senior Cochrane was a caretaker for a wealthy New England family.

Mickey not only dreamed of playing in the big leagues, but he also hoped to manage a major league club. Upon graduating from high school, Mickey enrolled at Boston University where he participated in baseball, track, football, basketball, and boxing. He was a halfback and place kicker on the school's football team. A 52-yard field goal was perhaps the greatest feat of his football days.

Mickey worked his way through college as a saxophonist in a jazz band, a dishwasher, and a semipro ball player who assumed the name "Frank King" to protect his amateur status.

It was under the name Frank King that Mickey signed his first professional contract—with Dover of the Eastern Shore League in 1923. Although he had already received his degree from the university, he retained the alias to protect himself from failure at Dover; if he did not succeed, he reasoned, he could always try somewhere else under his real name.

But Mickey played well at Dover, volunteering to catch when that position became vacant. With the exception of one game in the outfield in 1932, Mickey was solely a catcher.

At Dover, Mickey batted .322 in 65 games and impressed Tom Turner, owner of the Portland team in the Pacific Coast League. But the Dover price tag was too steep for a minor league team. Connie Mack, also alerted to Cochrane's worth, agreed to take over the operation of Portland from Turner. Mack then negotiated the sale of Mickey to Philadelphia for $50,000. This was in addition to the $150,000 Connie invested in Portland simply to sign Cochrane.

Assigned to Portland in 1924, Mickey appeared in 99 games and batted .333. The following season, at age 22, he joined the Athletics and immediately replaced Cy Perkins as the team's regular catcher. He appeared in 134 games and batted .331 with 6 home runs and 55 runs batted in. It was the first of 11 consecutive seasons in

Mickey Cochrane dreamed bigger than most little boys; even as a child he knew he wanted to be a major league manager. He fulfilled that dream after proving himself invaluable as a catcher in situations like those on the following page. (Above right) He tries to tag a baserunning former teammate, Jimmy Dykes. As a runner (lower picture) Cochrane slides in to avoid opposing catcher "Muddy" Ruel.

which Mickey caught more than 100 games; in 5 of these seasons he caught 130 or more games—evidence of remarkable stamina in the most physically grueling position on the diamond.

Jimmie Foxx joined the Athletics as a catcher in 1926, but there was no way even the powerful Foxx could displace Cochrane from his position. Instead, Foxx was converted into a first baseman to get his bat into the lineup. Mickey than remained behind the plate for the A's for nine years.

In 1926 Mickey batted .273, one of only three seasons in which he failed to top .300 during his first 11 years in the majors. In 1927 he hit .338 and drove in 80 runs, and in 1928, when Philadelphia finished in second place (only three games behind the Yankees), Mickey captured the league's Most Valuable Player award. Although his batting average was only .293, his leadership qualities were outstanding, and he received the bulk of credit for the Athletics' fine showing that year.

The following year, 1929, saw the Athletics achieve the first of three consecutive pennants. Mickey's teammates included Jimmie Foxx, Lefty Grove, Al Simmons, Jimmy Dykes, and Bing Miller. Mickey batted .331 that year, batted in 95 runs, and caught 135 games. In the World Series, won by the A's in five games over the Cubs, Mickey registered a .400 mark.

Cochrane, a durable lefthanded hitter who stood 5'10½" and weighed 180 pounds, returned in 1930 to bat .357, a career high. He scored 110 runs, drove in 85, and belted 42 doubles. Lefty Grove won 28 games and again Philadelphia captured the pennant. Cochrane not only offered field leadership, but he also helped tame the hair-trigger temper of Grove. In the World Series, Mickey hit two home runs against the Cardinals, and the Athletics retained the World Championship.

In 1931 the A's achieved their third consecutive pennant. Grove won 31 games and Simmons hit .390. Cochrane batted .349, smacked 17 home runs, and drove in 89 runs. In the World Series, however, the Cardinals turned back the Athletics. Pepper Martin ran wild on the bases, stealing five, and batted .500. The A's catcher bore considerable blame for Martin's running, but keen observers recognized that Pepper was running off the Philadelphia pitchers, not Cochrane.

The Athletics never won another pennant for Connie Mack, and he soon began to sell the better players to save the team from financial collapse. Cochrane remained with the A's through 1933, reaching career highs in homers (23) and RBIs (112) in 1932 and hitting .322 the following year.

Replacing his catcher would not be an easy task, but in December 1933, Mack

accepted $100,000 from the Detroit Tigers for Mickey. Detroit threw in a catcher named John Pasek, but Pasek never made the Athletics.

Detroit was looking for more than the league's best catcher. (Of course, many claimed that distinction for the Yankees' Bill Dickey.) Actually, the team was searching for a manager to replace Bucky Harris, who had gone to Boston. Owner Frank Navin toyed with the idea of hiring Babe Ruth to manage the Tigers, but at the urging of Walter Briggs, a major stockholder in Detroit, Navin grabbed Cochrane.

Fulfilling his boyhood dream of managing a major league club, Mickey immediately worked wonders with the fifth-place Tigers of 1933. He remodeled the team into the first-place Tigers of 1934, adding himself and Goose Goslin to a lineup that already included Hank Greenberg and Charlie Gehringer. Mickey batted .320 for Detroit (matching his eventual lifetime batting average) and led the Tigers to 101 victories, beating the second-place Yankees by seven games. But in the World Series the "Gashouse Gang" Cardinals, led by Dizzy and Paul Dean, defeated Detroit in seven games. Mickey batted only .214.

Cochrane's Tigers won another pennant in 1935, again edging the Yankees, but this time the club captured the World Championship with a six-game Series victory over the Cubs. Mickey hit .292 for the Series.

The 1935 pennant-winning season proved to be "Black Mike's" last big year as a player. He batted .319 in 115 games. When the Tigers slipped badly in 1936, letting the Yankees finish well ahead of them, the pressures of both playing and managing became burdensome to Mickey. He suffered a nervous breakdown and was hospitalized. Playing in only 44 games that season, Mickey batted .270.

Returning as manager in 1937, Mickey would have been wise to have retired as a player. He started strongly at the plate and owned a .306 batting average after 27 games. But on May 25, a 3–1 pitch from the Yankees' Bump Hadley hit Mickey on the right temple. He was unconscious for ten days, and his life was considered in danger.

Mickey rallied, however, and even wanted to return as an active player. But Briggs,

now the owner of the club, would not hear of it, and thus the beaning ended Cochrane's playing career at the age of 34.

Mickey managed the team to another second-place finish in 1937, but the club had only a 47–50 record the following year when Briggs replaced him with Del Baker on August 6. Detroit fans gave the deposed Cochrane a rousing farewell as he left town two days later.

Leaving the manager's job also meant severing his tie with the Tigers as a vice-president and member of the board. Cochrane left baseball at that point; he invested in a Wyoming dude ranch, and for a short time he represented a trucking firm.

During World War II, Cochrane directed the athletic program at the Great Lakes Naval Training Station. The war claimed the life of his only son, Gordon, Jr.

Mickey was elected to the Hall of Fame in 1947. He returned to baseball uniform in 1950 to serve as a coach under Connie Mack. He then became general manager of the Athletics late in May that year before being eased out at the close of the season. Mickey also scouted for the Yankees in 1955 and for the Tigers in 1960. The following year he was named a vice-president of the Detroit club, serving in that position until his general nervous state, coupled with a respiratory ailment, claimed his life on June 28, 1962, in Lake Forest, Illinois.

GORDON STANLEY COCHRANE

Philadelphia (A.L.) 1925–1933
Detroit 1934–1937

G	AB	R	H	2B	3B	HR	RBI	Avg.
1482	5169	1041	1652	333	64	119	832	.320

Many experts call Cochrane the greatest catcher of all time.

Eddie Collins (1887-1951)

The longest major league career of the twentieth century belonged to Eddie Collins, second base star for the Philadelphia Athletics and Chicago White Sox for 25 years. Only Jim McGuire, a journeyman catcher with a dozen different teams, spanned more seasons (1884–1912).

Edward Trowbridge Collins was born on May 2, 1887, in Millerton, New York, and reared in Tarrytown, New York. Small in stature as a youth, he eventually grew to 5'9" and weighed 175 pounds.

At the age of 16, Eddie enrolled at Columbia College, serving as quarterback on the football team. To help earn tuition money, he played semipro baseball in the summer. Following his junior year, an Athletics scout recommended Collins to Connie Mack, the A's owner and manager.

In his first meeting with Connie Mack, Collins was addressed as "Sullivan" to hide his identity from a Boston sportswriter present at the time. Mack thought the writer might recognize Collins s name from Columbia-Yale football games, and had he signed Eddie under his real name, it would have threatened his college eligibility. Recalling the somewhat shady incident years later, Connie merely called it the accepted practice of the time.

Disguised by his pseudonym, Eddie joined the Athletics in 1906 for their final western trip, playing six games and batting .235. However, upon returning to Columbia for his senior year, he found his eligibility stripped—not for playing with the Athletics, but for having participated in semipro ball in New England. Eddie was instead appointed coach of the Columbia baseball team, a rare honor for an undergraduate.

After graduating from Columbia, Eddie returned to the Athletics in 1907, and under his real name appeared in 14 games and batted .250. He also played four games for Newark in the Eastern League—the only minor league games he ever played.

In 1908 Collins played 102 games for the A's and batted .273. He had originally joined the club as a third baseman, played shortstop occasionally in 1907, but now was positioned at second base. By the time his career ended, Collins had played in more games and handled more chances than any second baseman in baseball history.

By 1909 Collins was ready to move into the regular lineup. He bested Danny Murphy in the competition for the second-base job, batting .346 with 198 hits in 153 games. It was the first of 8 consecutive seasons—and 18 seasons in all—in which Eddie would hit .300 or better. Although Ty Cobb dominated the batting charts at the time, and Eddie never captured a batting

championship, Collins became one of the few players to reach the mark of 3000 career hits, compiling a lifetime batting average of .333.

While not a power hitter (47 home runs was his career total), Collins was dazzling on the basepaths. He stole 67 bases in 1909, and then led the league with 81 the following season. He won three additional base-stealing titles and finished with 743 career thefts, third only to Lou Brock and Ty Cobb. Collins shares the all-time World Series stolen base title of 14 with Brock.

Philadelphia won the 1910 pennant by 14½ games over the New York Highlanders. Eddie batted .322 and stole 81 bases. In Philadelphia's World Series victory over the Cubs, the 23-year-old Collins batted .429 with a record nine hits in the five games. Four of the hits were doubles.

The Athletics repeated as league champions in 1911, with Eddie batting .365, but they slipped to third place in 1912 despite a .348 showing from Collins. That season he led the league with 137 runs scored (his first of three consecutive runs scored titles) and electrified the baseball world by twice stealing 6 bases in games 11 days apart.

In 1911 Connie Mack installed Stuffy McInnis at first base. Home Run Baker was at third and Jack Barry played shortstop. With Collins at second, the group became known as the "$100,000 infield." The Athletics won pennants in 1913 and 1914, making it four in five years for Philadelphia, and Collins captured the Most Valuable Player award in 1914 with a .344 average, 181 hits, and 122 runs scored.

Following the season, Collins was sold to the Chicago White Sox. Two circumstances led to the startling deal. The first was Connie Mack's desire to sell his big stars and rebuild the club; the second was Collins's threatened move to the newly born Federal League, whose Chicago team had made Eddie a substantial offer.

Thus, on December 8, 1914, Collins was purchased by the Chicago White Sox for $50,000. Ban Johnson, the American League president, helped to negotiate the transaction since it was deemed necessary to have a player of Collins's stature on the White Sox in order to successfully compete with the Feds.

Collins, of course, sought a substantial salary, for he held the power of jumping to

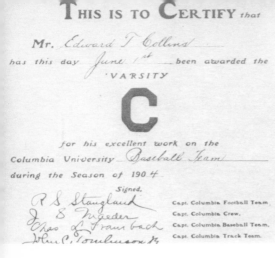

the new league. Negotiating from strength, Eddie achieved a $15,000-per-year contract for five years. The salary was undoubtedly the highest paid by the White Sox to that point, and it was considerably higher than that of any of the Sox players.

Eddie, nicknamed "Cocky" for his aggressive style of play, still hit and ran the bases as if unaffected by the transaction. He batted .332 in his debut season with the White Sox , and registered a .308 mark the following year. Although his batting average fell to .289 in 1917, the White Sox captured the pennant and Eddie hit .409 in the World Series, a classic best remembered for the Giants' Heinie Zimmerman chasing Collins across the plate with the winning run in the final game. For years Zimmerman was famous for his "bonehead play," but as Collins pointed out, there was no one at the plate to receive a throw.

After playing 97 games in 1918, Eddie enlisted in the Marines, but World War I ended before he was sent overseas. Returning to a baseball uniform in 1919, Eddie helped Chicago capture the pennant. But the Sox lost the World Series to Cincinnati. It was a bitter blow to Collins when eight of his teammates were charged a year later with conspiring to fix the Series. Although all eight were acquitted in court, Baseball Commissioner Kenesaw Mountain Landis banished them from baseball. As a consequence of the fix, the 1919 White Sox became known as the Black Sox.

Eddie maintained his own high standard of play into the early 1920s, reaching a career-high batting average of .360 in 1923. After the team finished last in 1924, Eddie was named player-manager for the 1925 season. Under Collins the White Sox finished fifth for two successive years, during which he compiled .346 and .344 batting averages. On November 11, 1926, the White Sox released Collins as both player and manager. One month later, Connie Mack again signed him to play for Philadelphia.

Eddie batted .338 in 95 games for the Athletics in 1927. He then served principally as a pinch-hitter the following season, batting .303 in 36 games. He coached the young Philadelphia infielders in 1929 and 1930, batting a total of nine times in the two years. After the 1930 season, Collins remained strictly a coach. The Athletics won pennants in 1929, 1930, and 1931, and Collins received a full share of the Series money each year.

In 1929, after Miller Huggins had died, the Yankees offered their managing job to Collins, but Connie Mack assured Eddie that he should stay with the Athletics to be groomed as Mack's successor. Little did either know that Connie would remain manager through 1950.

In February 1933, Eddie accepted an offer from Tom Yawkey, new owner of the Boston Red Sox (and a fellow alumnus of Tarrytown High School), to go to Boston as vice-president, treasurer, and business manager. The Red Sox had finished last in 9 of the previous 11 seasons, and therefore the job posed a real challenge to Collins. He accepted the position and moved his family to Boston. His son, Eddie Jr., later played briefly for the Athletics in 1939, 1941, and 1942, batting .241.

Collins earned respect as a fine baseball administrator, and he helped buy Ted Williams from San Diego while on a rare scouting trip. Gradually, Boston returned to respectability, winning a pennant in 1946.

Bothered by heart trouble while running the Red Sox, Eddie remained at his job until he died on March 25, 1951, at the age of 63. Collins had been inducted into the Hall of Fame in 1939, the fourth year in which elections were held.

EDWARD TROWBRIDGE COLLINS

Chicago (A.L.) 1915–1926
Philadelphia (A.L.) 1906–1914, 1922–1930

G	AB	R	H	2B	3B	HR	RBI	Avg.
2826	9949	1818	3311	437	186	47	1307	.333

Eddie Collins in action: (Right) Running the bases, for which he was almost as famous as Ty Cobb, and (at left) pulling in a high one at second base. (Upper left) The certificate for his Columbia C in baseball, but in college he was probably better known as the quarterback on the football team. While still a junior, he signed with Connie Mack, Philadelphia Athletics' longtime owner and manager, under a false name to protect his amateur status for college play. Although he was not identified during the few games he played with the A's that year, Collins's eligibility was stripped anyway for playing semipro ball in other summers. Unable to play, Collins became coach of Columbia's baseball team.

Jimmy Collins (1870-1943)

As the outstanding third baseman at the turn of the century, Jimmy Collins gave third base play its present form.

James Joseph Collins was born on January 16, 1870, in Niagara Falls, New York. With the roar of the mighty falls in the background, Jimmy learned to play ball in the early days of the National League. He attended St. Joseph's College in Buffalo, but in 1893, before receiving a degree, he accepted a contract with the Buffalo team of the Eastern League. Signed as a shortstop, Jimmy appeared in 76 games and batted .286, but he committed 65 errors and was not considered a promising prospect.

The following year Collins set his credentials aright, hitting .352 with a league-leading 198 hits and, more importantly, reducing his errors to 21 while leading the Eastern League outfielders with 34 assists. Suddenly, Jimmy was in demand.

The Providence manager, Billy Murray, had seen Collins in action, and he urged Frank Selee of the Boston National League team to purchase him. Selee did in 1895, and Jimmy reached the major leagues. On May 17 of that season, Boston loaned Collins to the Louisville Colonels of the National League, for the latter team was in need of an extra outfielder. The practice was common at the time.

Jimmy made his mark at Louisville during a series with the powerful Baltimore Orioles. On May 31, the Louisville third baseman, Walter Preston, made four errors in one game while trying to field bunts by the pesky Orioles. In desperation, the Louisville manager asked Collins to finish out the game at third. Oriole shortstop Hughey Jennings teased Collins with the promise that he would not bunt in Jimmy's direction, but Collins challenged him to try it. Collins turned in a brilliant performance, stopping the Oriole attack of Jennings, John McGraw, Willie Keeler, and Joe Kelley. The Orioles were pennant-bound, the Colonels doomed to finish last in the 12-club league, but Collins earned a reputation that day as a third baseman with exceptional fielding range. On June 13, he was permanently shifted to third base.

When it came to playing third base, Jimmy Collins was in a class by himself. He was the first man to charge bunts and play them barehanded, flipping the ball in one motion to first base. He also could range toward the line or to his left, and he did not stay within a short distance of the bag as was the custom in those days.

Jimmy's exceptional fielding skills resulted in 601 chances accepted in 1899

and 252 putouts in 1900, both of which remain among the longest-standing fielding records.

Collins returned to Boston in 1896. An ankle injury limited his playing time to 83 games, but he nonetheless batted .300 in his first full season at third base.

At Boston, Collins was a member of the finest nineteenth-century infield. Fred Tenney played at first, Bobby Lowe at second, and Herman Long at shortstop. The quartet worked many unusual pickoff plays, and they developed new ways of covering bases for each other.

Boston won the 1897 National League pennant, but lost to Baltimore in the Temple Cup series, four games to one. That season Collins achieved a career-high batting average of .346. The Temple Cup series, played between the American Association and National League champions, was a forerunner of the modern World Series.

Boston repeated its title in 1898, with Jimmy leading the league with 14 home runs and batting .337. The home run total represented one of the highest pre-1900 figures in baseball.

Jimmy remained at third base for the Boston Beaneaters in 1899 and 1900, batting .275 and .299. Then, in a move that rocked Boston, the popular Collins accepted an offer from Charlie Somers, new owner of the Boston team in the American League, and jumped the Beaneaters. The new American League team was at first called the Invaders, later the Somersets, by 1903 the Puritans, and eventually the Red Sox.

Collins was hired by the new franchise as both third baseman and manager. Chick Stahl, Buck Freeman, and Parson Lewis soon followed Collins across town to join the American League. Cy Young and Lou Criger, an outstanding battery, came over from St. Louis, and Collins soon had a respectable club. In 1901 Boston finished second to Clark Griffith's Chicago White Sox, with Collins batting .329 in 138 games. In 1902 Collins batted .325 as Boston finished third. In 1903 he led the team to the pennant with a 91–47 record, contributing a .296 average himself.

The year 1903 saw the first modern World Series, in which the Boston team faced Fred Clarke's Pittsburgh club. Boston surprised the experts by beating Pittsburgh, five games to three, each player earning a winners' share of $1182. Collins saw the postseason matchup as a possible permanent contest because "it gives the players a chance to pick up a little extra money!"

Boston captured another pennant in 1904, with Collins participating in a record 156 games at third base. But the New York Giants manager, John McGraw, refused to

Collins at third for the Red Sox, which he joined as player-manager in 1901 for the sensational salary of $4000, twice what he had been earning with the Boston Beaneaters of the National League.

recognize the American League as a major league and therefore prohibited his team from playing in a postseason series. Hence there was no World Series in 1904.

Collins batted .276 in 1905 as his team fell to fourth place. In 1906 the club was heading for a last-place finish when Jimmy was released as manager late in the season. It was a disappointing year for Collins. A knee injury limited his playing time to 37 games, the team collapsed, and the pressure of managing began to hurt his playing abilities.

Collins began the 1907 season at third base as usual. He roomed with his old teammate and now the new manager, Chick Stahl. Collins was shocked one day during spring training to return to their room and find Stahl dead through suicide.

Despite a good start at the bat, Jimmy was traded on June 7 to Connie Mack's Philadelphia Athletics for an infielder named Jack Knight. Boston fans, in whose eyes Collins ranked second only to heavyweight boxing champion John L. Sullivan in popularity, gave Jimmy a rousing sendoff. Collins finished the season in Philadelphia with a .279 average.

Jimmy ended his major league career with the Athletics in 1908, batting .217. In 14 major league seasons, he had collected 1999 hits and compiled a .294 batting average.

Turning to the minor leagues in 1909, Collins managed Minneapolis of the American Association. In 1910 and 1911, he directed the Providence club of the Eastern League. He played third base on a regular basis in 1909 and 1910, but he was clearly past his prime.

After the 1911 season, Jimmy returned to Buffalo with his wife and two daughters. He invested his savings in real estate, living well until the Depression depleted his capital. He was then employed by the Buffalo City Parks Department.

Collins' interest in baseball never left him. For the remaining 22 years of his life, Jimmy served as president of the Buffalo

Municipal League. Eventually, he faded somewhat from the public consciousness, especially when a latter day infielder named Eddie Collins (no relation) erased memories of the previous great Collins.

At one time, Jimmy believed that hitting as a skill had been neglected by baseball rule makers. But he lived to see hitting surpass pitching as the game's emphasis and the dead-ball era give way to the age of the home run.

Jimmy died of pneumonia in Buffalo on March 6, 1943, at the age of 73. In 1945 he was elected to the Hall of Fame.

As late as 1961, baseball historians polled by *The Sporting News* rated Collins the greatest all-time third baseman. With the passage of years, Pie Traynor, or perhaps Brooks Robinson, has generally supplanted Collins in the minds of the experts. But every skill that Traynor or Robinson mastered at third base was conceived by the infielder from Niagara Falls.

JAMES JOSEPH COLLINS

Boston (N.L.) 1895–1900
Louisville (N.L.) 1895
Boston (A.L.) 1901–1907
Philadelphia (A.L.) 1907–1908

G	AB	R	H	2B	3B	HR	RBI	Avg.
1718	6792	1057	1999	333	117	62	985	.294

Earle Combs (1899-1976)

Earle Combs was the center fielder and leadoff hitter for the famed "Murderers Row" teams that the New York Yankees fielded in the late 1920s. He was known as "the table setter" for Babe Ruth and Lou Gehrig since he was often on base when the two power hitters came to bat.

Earle Bryan Combs was born to a large Scotch-German family on May 14, 1899, in Pebworth, Kentucky. He was one of seven children in the immediate family, but the Combs clan extended to hundreds of members, and they held frequent reunions and parties. The Combs family even published its own newspaper.

The elder Combs ran a farm and hoped to see Earle become a teacher. Earle accepted this aspiration and, after completing local schools, enrolled in Eastern Kentucky State Teachers' College. Today the school (now called Eastern Kentucky University) has a building known as Earle Combs Hall, which is used by athletes as a dormitory.

At Eastern Kentucky, Earle played the outfield and found his speed an asset in covering ground. During the summer, the game of baseball was frequently played around the Combs farm. Earle's father made baseballs and also organized the games.

After graduating in 1921 with his certification and degree, Earle accepted the position of elementary school teacher for $37 a month. Each day, he would hitchhike eight miles to the little red schoolhouse in the area. Soon thereafter, he gave up teaching and acquired a $40-per-month job with the High Splint Coal Company in Pleasant Grove. Officially hired as a carpenter, he was in fact hired to manage and play for the company's baseball team.

Earle entered professional baseball in 1922, shortly before his twenty-third birthday. He signed with the Louisville Colonels of the American Association, managed by Joe McCarthy. McCarthy worked with Earle and instilled confidence in his game.

Combs was a gifted athlete with a perfect batting eye and beautiful form at the plate. He neither smoke nor drank, and stood 6'0" and weighed 185 pounds. He batted left and threw right, lacking only a good throwing arm to be a complete player. But Earle compensated for this disadvantage by hustling to get to the ball and quickly releasing his throw.

Earle batted .344 for Louisville in 1922. The following season, he played in 166 games and banged out a league-leading 241 hits to produce a .380 average. Included were 127 runs scored, 145 runs batted in, and 14 home runs—the only season he would reach double digits in homers. It required little effort by McCarthy to peddle Earle's name to major league clubs since they all appeared interested.

Earle Combs was the first link in the Combs-DiMaggio-Mantle center field lineage during the long Yankee dynasty. Although his teammates Ruth and Gehrig usually got more publicity, Combs was very often on base when the famed sluggers got up to bat. Many said it was Combs who made the lineup work effectively. (Opposite page) Combs demonstrates the classic form at bat for which he was noted. His career average was a solid .325, and he led the league in triples three times.

In New York, the Yankee owner, Colonel Jacob Ruppert, was spending a considerable amount of money to build a winning team. And with the opening of Yankee Stadium in 1923, Ruppert was extremely eager to field an all-star cast. Lou Gehrig had joined Babe Ruth in the lineup, and Ruppert laid out $50,000 to purchase Combs from Louisville.

Earle made the club easily in spring training, and when Whitey Witt started slowly at the bat, Combs replaced him in center field. He was quickly a sensation, batting an even .400 in his first 24 games. But in June Earle fractured an ankle in a slide and was out for the remainder of the season, with the exception of one pinch-hitting appearance in September.

The 1925 season, therefore, was actually Earle's first full year in the majors, and he became one of the few rookies in history to collect more than 200 hits. Earle played 150 games, batted .342 with 203 hits, but the Yanks finished in seventh place.

Batting leadoff, the line-drive hitting Combs managed to find the gaps in the outfield at Yankee Stadium, collecting a great many triples as a result of the distant power alleys. Three times (1927, 1928, 1930) Earle belted more than 20 triples in a season, leading the league on each occasion.

In 1926 the Yankees returned to the top of the league for their fourth pennant under manager Miller Huggins. Earle batted .299, scored 113 runs, and then hit .357 in the World Series, which was won by the Cardinals. Earle had 10 hits in the seven-game Series.

The following season, 1927, is considered the Yankees' finest, and perhaps the greatest team in baseball history was then assembled. Combs was flanked by Babe Ruth and Bob Meusel in the outfield. While the Babe was hitting 60 home runs and the team was winning 110 games, Earle was leading the league with 231 hits, an all-time Yankee record. He batted .356, scored 137 runs, drove in 64, and collected 36

doubles, 23 triples, and 6 home runs as a leadoff batter. Earle led the league's outfielders with 411 putouts. He also enjoyed another fine World Series, batting .313 and scoring the winning run in the deciding game against Pittsburgh.

In 1928 Earle hit .310 for the pennant-winning Yankees, collecting 21 triples and again leading the league in putouts with 424. A broken finger forced him to the bench for the 1928 World Series, but Huggins sent him up in the final game as a pinch-hitter. With his finger in a splint, Earle delivered a sacrifice fly.

The Yankees did not capture another pennant until 1932, but Combs continued to distinguish himself as one of the outstanding center fielders in baseball. He batted .345 in 1929, but the late-season death of Huggins left Combs deeply saddened.

In 1930, under manager Bob Shawkey, Earle hit .344. And in 1931, Joe McCarthy, his old manager at Louisville, replaced Shawkey as Yankee helmsman. Combs was delighted with the reunion, and he batted .318 in the leadoff spot.

The Yankees captured the league championship in 1932 and met the Cubs in the World Series. During the regular season, Earle had batted .321 with 190 hits. In his fourth and final World Series, he recorded a .375 average with six hits in four games. In the fourth and final game, Earle scored four runs as the Yankees topped the Cubs, 13–6.

"Hark! to the Tombs / Here comes Earle Combs" was the rhyme of the day, but it was not easy to obtain publicity on a club whose roster included Ruth and Gehrig. Still, many players and sports buffs appreciated Earle's abilities. In fact, many thought that he was the player who made the Yankee lineup work effectively.

Earle and his wife, the former Ruth McCollum, whom he married in October 1922, would spend winters raising livestock on a farm in Lexington, Kentucky. The very image of the gentleman farmer, Earle became known as "The Colonel" as his hair turned prematurely gray.

In 1933 Earle played 122 games and batted .298, only the second time he failed to reach the .300 mark. But his brilliant efforts came to an abrupt halt in 1934. Earle was off to his usual fine start, batting .319 after 63 games, with the Yankees in first place. Pursuing a long drive hit to left-center field in St. Louis on July 24, Combs

crashed at full speed into the concrete wall and fell unconscious. Rushed to the hospital, he lay in a coma for hours. The diagnosis was a fractured skull and torn muscles of the right shoulder. Doctors thought that he would probably never play again.

But Dr. Robert Hyland of St. Louis operated on Earle, actually restoring his playing ability. Combs amazed everyone by returning in 1935 to play in 89 games and bat .282—the lowest mark of his career, but still an admirable one for a player so badly injured.

But with the season's end, Earle decided to retire. The Yankees had purchased Joe DiMaggio from San Francisco to replace him, and Earle thought it was an opportune time to end his career.

Combs moved onto the coaching lines for the Yankees, staying through the 1944 season, and collected seven more World Series checks. In 1947 he coached for the St. Louis Browns. He then coached for the Red Sox from 1948 through 1952, and his final job in uniform came as a coach with the 1954 Philadelphia Phillies.

Back home, Earle was a member of the State Banking Commission and the Chairman of the State Board of Regents. He was the pride of Lexington, Kentucky, and a popular guest at old timers' gatherings.

Ill health finally forced Earle to cancel public appearances in 1973, but he remained the first link in the great Yankee centerfield lineage of Combs-DiMaggio-Mantle, all Hall of Famers. Earle's selection occurred in 1970. He died in Richmond, Kentucky on July 21, 1976 at the age of 77.

EARLE BRYAN COMBS

New York (A.L.) 1924–1935

G	AB	R	H	2B	3B	HR	RBI	Avg.
1455	5748	1186	1866	309	154	58	629	.325

His days of sliding safely into base for the Yanks (top picture) were long over, but Earle Combs was still signing autographs for young admirers in his seventies (left).

Charles Comiskey (1859-1931)

Charles Albert Comiskey was the only baseball player ever to rise to the sole ownership of a major league baseball team. He was founder, owner, and president of the Chicago White Sox from 1900 to his death in 1931.

Comiskey was born on August 15, 1859, in Chicago, the third child in a family of eight. His father, John, had emigrated from Ireland in 1848 and had become a Democratic leader and an alderman from Chicago's seventh ward.

Young Charlie became a plumber's apprentice, but his principal interest was baseball. There were many open fields outside of downtown Chicago, and he took advantage of every opportunity to participate in baseball games.

In 1876 Comiskey was scheduled to deliver a truck load of bricks for the dedication of a new office building at which his father was to preside. En route, he stopped to join a game and never made the delivery. His father arrived, saw Charlie engrossed in pitching, and took the truck himself. Charlie never again devoted his time to anything but baseball.

Comiskey played for an independent team in Elgin in 1877, but he really began his career in 1878 by joining the Dubuque Rabbits. The club was headed by Ted Sullivan, a well-known organizer of minor league teams in the Midwest. Sullivan acquired a job for Comiskey as a representative of the Western News Company while he continued to play semipro ball for Dubuque. Primarily a first baseman, Charlie played almost every position on the small teams of that period.

Comiskey earned $50 per month with Dubuque. He was a teammate of the great pitcher, Hoss Radbourn, in 1879 when Dubuque played in the Northwest League. Comiskey also met his future wife, Nan Kelly, in Dubuque; they were married in 1882.

In 1882 Comiskey was purchased by the St. Louis Browns of the American Association, then a major league. Owner Chris Von der Ahe signed Charlie to a pact amounting to $125 per month and installed him at first base. As a first baseman, Comiskey introduced the style of play which continues today. He placed himself several yards away from the base, a location that gave him considerable range but required the pitcher to cover the base on ground balls hit to the right of the first baseman. Comiskey became noted for this innovation.

Von der Ahe named Comiskey manager, captain, and first baseman late in the 1883 season. The Browns finished fourth the following year, and Comiskey batted .241. The well-built righthanded-hitting player,

who stood 6'0" and weighed 180 pounds, was earning the respect of everyone in the Association.

Comiskey's stature was heightened in 1885 when he led the Browns to their first of four consecutive pennants. His club met Cap Anson's Chicago Colts in a "world series," in which each club won three games and tied one. Comiskey removed his team from the field as a protest during the tie game, and the series was never played to a conclusion.

In 1886 the Browns captured another pennant. In the series, Comiskey's club beat the Chicago Cubs, four games to two.

The Browns achieved a third pennant in 1887, as Comiskey batted .368. A tedious 15-game playoff was held after the season, with Detroit winning 10 games and St. Louis 5. In 1888 Comiskey became the first manager since Harry Wright to win four consecutive pennants, although he again lost the postseason series to Jim Mutrie's Giants, six games to four.

During his St. Louis days, Comiskey was called "The Noblest Roman of the National Baseball Field." The title was later shortened and modified to "The Old Roman," Comiskey's lasting baseball nickname.

After finishing second in 1889, Comiskey jumped at the opportunity to manage a club in his home town. He acquired the Chicago franchise in the rebel Players' League in 1890 but had a disappointing year, finishing fourth and failing to draw many people. Jimmy Ryan was his best player; Comiskey himself played, batting only .248. The league folded after one year, and Comiskey returned to manage the Browns to a second-place finish in 1891 while batting .265.

In 1892 the National League absorbed the American Association, and Comiskey received the job of managing the Cincinnati Reds. His three years in Cincinnati were uneventful, the Reds finishing fifth, seventh, and tenth (out of 12 teams), but he formed an important friendship with the sports editor of the Cincinnati *Commercial Gazette,* Ban Johnson.

After the 1894 season, Comiskey's urgings helped to establish Johnson as president of the new Western League. In 1895

OFFICIAL SCORE CARD

WORLDS CHAMPIONSHIP SERIES

ST. LOUIS BROWNS

COMISKEY

CHAMPIONS OF THE ASSOCIATION

the Sioux City franchise was transferred to St. Paul, and Comiskey became player-manager and owner. It was Charlie's final season as a player, and he participated in 17 games, hitting .343.

Comiskey operated the St. Paul club until 1899, at which point Johnson and "Commy" decided to seek major league status for their league. No matter was as important to them both as installing a franchise in Chicago, and, after considerable prompting, the National League agreed in 1899 to permit another club in Chicago. But the team would not be recognized as having major league status, and the Cubs would have a right to draft its players. Furthermore, they could not play north of 35th Street, so as not to infringe on the Cubs' territory.

This was a start for the American League, and the St. Paul franchise was moved to Chicago in 1900, with Comiskey as sole owner and president. Following the 1900 season, Comiskey induced Clark Griffith of the Cubs to jump to his team as pitcher and manager. The act signaled open warfare between the two leagues as Griffith pitched the White Sox to the first American League pennant while the Cubs finished fifth in the National League.

Griffith was an enormous asset to Comiskey, but Charlie agreed to release Griffith in 1903 to manage the New York franchise "for the good of the league." The next Chicago pennant came in 1906 with the "Hitless Wonders," managed by Fielder Jones. The team compiled a collective batting average of only .230, but Chicago edged Griffith's Highlanders by three games and then beat the Cubs in six games in the World Series.

In 1910 Comiskey borrowed enough money to build Comiskey Park, the first perfectly symmetrical stadium in the country. Improvements and additions were made over the years, and today the park remains the oldest major league park in the country and is still highly functional. The park was selected as the site of the first All-Star game, played in 1933.

Following the 1913 season, Comiskey and John McGraw led their teams on a combined world tour, playing in Tokyo, Hong Kong, Manila, Brisbane, Sydney, Melbourne, Ceylon, Cairo, Naples, Nice, and London (before King George V). The two men buried an old difference dating back to 1901 when Comiskey had blocked McGraw's efforts to disguise a black player, Charlie Grant, as an American Indian and get him into organized baseball.

In 1917 the White Sox won the World Championship under Pants Rowland. During World War I, Comiskey donated 10 percent of his gross receipts to the American Red Cross, but his generosity was confusing to his players, who were low-salaried and generally discontented.

In 1915, White Sox owner and president Comiskey (at right) chats with new manager Clarence Rowland. (Opposite page) A scorecard from the 1885 "World Series" between the Browns, managed by Comiskey, and Cap Anson's Chicago Cubs. During one game, with the score tied, Comiskey led his team off the field in a protest. The two teams split the other six games—and neither emerged world champion.

It was such discontent that led eight members of the 1919 pennant-winning White Sox to conspire to fix the World Series against Cincinnati. Rumors were rampant during the Series, in which the heavily favored White Sox were defeated, and Comiskey pressed for an investigation. He held up the World Series checks of Ed Cicotte, Claude Williams, Chick Gandil, Swede Risberg, Joe Jackson, Happy Felsch, Buck Weaver, and Fred McMullin, and argued with his former friend, Ban Johnson, over the depth of the investigation. Finally, a year later, the story broke wide open, the issue went to court, and Commissioner Landis banned the eight players from further participation in professional baseball.

It was a crushing blow to Comiskey. His club was in ruins, the game itself was shaken, and his open expression of no confidence in Ban Johnson had permanently destroyed his best friendship. The two had first quarreled over the assignment of pitcher Jack Quinn to the Yankees in 1918, but the Series fix was the final blow.

Comiskey fell into bad health and generally withdraw from active participation in the running of the club. He retained Kid Gleason, who assumed the reins in 1919, as manager through 1923, then replaced him with Frank Chance. Subsequently, Johnny Evers, Eddie Collins, Ray Schalk, Lena Blackburne, and Donie Bush piloted Comiskey's team. The club never raised itself from the second division, and in fact the White Sox did not win another pennant until 1959, the first year the Comiskey family was not affiliated with its operation.

There were those in the baseball world who said that the 1919 "Black Sox" scandal had killed Comiskey, but "The Old Roman" led a quiet existence until he died on October 26, 1931, at his estate in Eagle River, Wisconsin. He was elected to the Hall of Fame in 1939.

CHARLES ALBERT COMISKEY

St. Louis (A.A.) 1882–1889, 1891
Chicago (P.L.) 1890
Cincinnati (N.L.) 1892–1894

G	AB	R	H	2B	3B	HR	RBI	Avg.
1383	5813	984	1564	206	68	29	inc.	.269

Jocko Conlan (b. 1899)

By the time Jocko Conlan reached the major leagues, umpires were treated with considerably more dignity than they had been accustomed to in the early days of baseball. Seldom were pop bottles flung from the bleachers, and no more dark, secret passages out of town were necessary to escape angry fans. The refinement of the game and the fans tended to keep umpires out of the spotlight as they went about their business in quiet, efficient ways. Nevertheless, Jocko Conlan emerged as a colorful and outstanding umpire, only the fourth selected for the Hall of Fame, and the first from baseball's modern era.

John Bertrand Conlan was born on December 6, 1899, in Chicago. Because he was an aspiring baseball player, Conlan listed his birthdate as 1902. He did not correct the "error" until his autobiography was published following his retirement.

Conlan was one of nine children born to a Chicago policeman. His father died when he was three, and the burden of rearing the family fell on John's mother.

Johnny, who did not receive his nickname until he reached professional baseball, grew up in the shadows of Comiskey Park. He recalled playing sandlot ball as early as his seventh birthday. While attending All Saints Parochial School, Conlan played in the same school league as future Giants' star Freddy Lindstrom. Johnny was a pitcher and first baseman in those days, and he also filled in as a temporary batboy for the White Sox during the 1912 and 1913 seasons. He would show up at morning workouts, take care of the bats, and shag fly balls in the outfield for the big leaguers.

One day in Comiskey Park, Johnny found himself the last boy on the field. Spotting a glove on the ground, he quickly picked it up and tucked it under his shirt. Upon his arrival home, he discovered the glove belonged to Chicago coach Kid Gleason. After treasuring the mitt for a few weeks, Conlan sold it for $2. Approximately 14 years later, while in Miami for spring training, Jocko confessed his childhood crime to Gleason. Gleason received it good naturedly, and said he hoped he had started Johnny on a good career.

Johnny's professional career began in 1920 when he was signed by the Tulsa club as an outfielder. Without ever playing for Tulsa, he was quickly traded to Wichita of the Western League. The 5'7½" 160-pound lefthanded-hitting Conlan proceeded to bat .247 in 117 games. But when the season was winding down to its final few weeks, Johnny's older brother, a former pitcher in the Midwest and Eastern Leagues, came to visit. Feeling somewhat homesick, Conlan left the team one week

Jocko Conlan fulfilled a boyhood dream of playing with the Chicago White Sox and then discovered his real calling—as an umpire. A jolly Irishman who loved to sing, he put up with no nonsense on the field and was not hesitant about ejecting troublemakers. (Opposite page, above) Jocko Conlan as a young outfielder. (Below) Conlan monitors the play at base after switching from player's flannels to umpire's somber dark suit.

early and returned home. The result was a suspension for the entire 1921 season. Unhappy over the penalty, Johnny defied orders not to play with an "outlaw" circuit composed of other contract jumpers. As a result, after 10 games of the 1922 season with Wichita, he was again suspended for the full season.

Johnny strongly believed that his punishments were excessively cruel. He traveled to the minor league meetings that winter to have the suspension rescinded, and his plea was accepted. In 1923 Conlan participated in 167 games for Wichita, batting .311 with 204 hits and 18 home runs. He led Western League outfielders with 465 putouts.

After the season, Conlan was sold to Rochester of the International League, where he played for manager George Stallings. It was at Rochester that a sportswriter pinned Conlan with the nickname "Jocko," not for being a bench-jockey as was commonly believed, but probably as an imitation of a Jocko Conlon, a Boston Braves infielder in 1923. Players often borrow monickers of other players to nickname new arrivals with similar last names.

Jocko had an outstanding season at Rochester in 1924, batting .321 with a league-leading 214 hits in 165 games. He supplemented his $2500 salary by becoming a licensed New York State fight referee, his first experience as an official. But umpiring was still a distant occupation.

In 1925 Conlan held out briefly and finally signed for $5200, a healthy minor league salary. Jocko hit .309 that year, and then batted .286 in 1926, after a major league transaction collapsed. Conlan had been ticketed to go to Cincinnati in exchange for Tom Sheehan, Elmer Smith, Chet Fowler, and $17,500 when he hurt his knee sliding home. The injury negated the deal, and Conlan instead was sold to Newark in 1927. There he spent the following three seasons, hitting .300 or better each year.

In 1926 Jocko married Ruth Anderson; they later had a son and a daughter. The son, John, eventually became an Arizona state senator.

In 1920 Conlan was purchased by Toledo, where he played for manager Casey Stengel. The two went on to become close friends. But after one season with Toledo, Conlan was dealt to Montreal (International League), where he played for two years.

By then, Jocko had compiled 12 minor league seasons.

Released by Montreal early in 1933, Jocko decided to retire from organized baseball and become a playground instructor in Chicago. However, on July 1, 1934, with injuries having depleted their outfield, the Chicago White Sox, his boyhood dream team, offered Jocko a chance. The team was managed by Jimmie Dykes, and although it included such players as Zeke Bonura, Luke Appling, Mule Haas, Al Simmons, George Earnshaw, and Ted Lyons, it was a last-place club. Jocko participated in 63 games and batted .249.

In 1935 the club improved its standing to fifth, and Conlan contributed a .286 average in 65 games as a reserve outfielder.

One day late in July of 1935, the White Sox were playing a Sunday twin-bill in an extremely hot St. Louis ballpark. Umpire Red Ormsby was overcome by heat at the close of the first game. Since only a two-man crew had been assigned, this left Harry Geisel without a partner to umpire the second game. Conlan, sidelined at the time with a sprained thumb, volunteered to work the bases. Dykes laughed at the suggestion, but Browns' manager Rogers Hornsby approved of the notion. Dykes therefore agreed, and Conlan worked that game in his White Sox uniform. He handled the task well and was involved in only one minor argument—when he called his teammate, Luke Appling, out on a slide.

With Ormsby still too weak to work, Conlan filled in as umpire again the following day, and the league paid him $50 for his efforts.

At the conclusion of the year, the White Sox general manager, Harry Grabiner, asked Conlan if he would consider umpiring as a career. At the major league level, the profession offered a pension, a feature which players did not at the time receive. Grabiner arranged for Conlan to meet with the American League president, Will Harridge, and Harridge offered Jocko $300 per month to umpire in the New York-Penn League.

Conlan had hoped to start in the majors, but the league ruled it out after experiencing difficulty in a similar incident with Fred Marberry a few years earlier.

Jocko thus went to the New York-Penn League, spent two years sharpening his skills, and even turned down a minor league managing job in 1937 when given a chance to pilot Birmingham. From 1938 to 1940, he umpired in the American Association.

In 1940 Jocko was scouted by American League umpire Tom Connolly, but he was ruled out as "too small." That same year National League president Ford Frick offered Jocko a job upon the recommendation of senior umpire Bill Klem.

Klem broke Jocko in during spring training in Havana in 1941. The only issue of difference between the two concerned the use of the inside chest protector favored by Klem. Jocko conformed to the National League standard by wearing it. But after receiving two broken collarbones, a broken elbow in the 1950 World Series, and a foul tip into his larynx, he abandoned it in favor of the pillow-type chest protector worn in the American League. Jocko was also the only umpire who made all signals with his left hand. In later years he was distinctive for wearing a bow tie during games.

Jocko made his presence in the National League known in 1941 when he ejected 26 men from games. Whereas Connolly prided himself on seldom ejecting anyone, Klem told Conlan never to passively accept abuse from anyone. A quick mind and fast reflexes made Conlan a highly respected umpire throughout the league, and although he and Leo Durocher were constantly at odds, the two respected each other.

A jolly Irishman who enjoyed singing, Jocko was all business on the field. He frequently received the call to work the big games. He had the honor to umpire in all four National League playoffs—1946, 1951, 1959, and 1962. Conlan was also named to umpire in six World Series (1943, 1945, 1950, 1954, 1957, and 1961) and six All-Star games (1943, 1947, 1950, 1953, 1958, and 1962).

Conlan developed a spur in his heel in 1963, and other ailments began to impede his mobility the following season. He retired after the 1964 campaign, receiving standing ovations throughout the league when his final appearance in each city was announced. Jocko served for a few weeks as a substitute umpire in 1965, giving him 25 years in total as a National League umpire.

Jocko and his family settled in Scottsdale, Arizona, following his umpiring career, and in 1967 his autobiography, *Jocko,* was published. Conlan was inducted into the Hall of Fame in 1974.

Tom Connolly (1870-1961)

British-born Tom Connolly never played baseball but became the outstanding umpire in the formative years of the American League.

Thomas Henry Connolly was born in Manchester, England, on December 31, 1870. At the age of 13, Tom and his family emigrated to America, settling in Natick, Massachusetts. All the other boys in town played baseball so Tom purchased a rule book and taught himself the game. He became the most learned fellow in the area concerning the rules of the game, but he never had the desire to play. At the age of 15, he was asked to manage the local YMCA team. But Tom declined the offer, preferring to umpire. And that he did, working the YMCA games in addition to school and sandlot contests throughout Natick and the surrounding communities.

When he was a young man of 23, Tom was spotted by National League umpire Tim Hurst, who found Tom's approach to the game and his sharp knowledge of the rules appealing. Hurst recommended Connolly to Tim Murnane, a well-known Boston baseball writer and the president of the New England League. Murnane accepted the recommendation and gave Connolly his first professional job in 1894. Tom remained in the New England League for four seasons.

In 1898 Tom was promoted to the National League, a difficult assignment in that era. The players were rough, the conditions poor, and the league office tended to support the powerful club owners rather than the umpires. It was an arduous life. Tom remained in the National League for the entire 1898 and 1899 seasons, but midway through the 1900 campaign, he became disillusioned when the league failed to support him after a dispute with a player. Quiet but stern, the 5'7" 135-pounder left the league and returned home to Natick to ponder his future.

At this time, Ban Johnson was forming the new American League, preparing to claim major league status in 1901. Connie Mack, who would become the founder of the Philadelphia franchise, had never seen Connolly umpire but had heard positive comments concerning his ability. Mack recommended him to Johnson as a possible umpire for the new league. Johnson contacted Connolly at his home in Natick, hiring him for the 1901 season.

Tom had the distinction of umpiring the first American League game. It was played in Chicago on April 24, 1901, and was won by the home team, 8–2, over Cleveland. All three other games scheduled that opening day were rained out, and therefore it was no matter of dispute to determine which was the first game.

The American League offered umpires more protection and support for their decisions than did the National League. Connolly himself was once reprimanded by Ban Johnson for "not acting with sufficient dispatch" when Washington manager Tom Loftus berated St. Louis's Jesse Burkett. Burkett proceeded to punch Loftus in the nose, and Connolly received the warning to act tougher. This he did, tossing 10 players out of games in his maiden season.

Conditions for umpires remained crude in these early days of the league. Connolly once had to row out of Boston in the middle of the night after threats from fans. In August of his first season, Baltimore's Joe McGinnity was fined and suspended for 12 days for spitting in Connolly's face. Ban Johnson always supported the decisions of his umpires, calling them "the boss of the game, and a representative of the league."

Not only did Connolly umpire the first American League game, but he also opened ball parks in Boston (Fenway Park), Philadelphia (Shibe Park), and New York (twice—first Hilltop Park, home of the Highlanders, and in 1923, Yankee Stadium).

The unobtrusive Connolly was also selected to umpire the first modern World Series, played in 1903 between Pittsburgh and Boston. Tom shared the assignment with the National League's Hank O'Day. It was his first experience working with another umpire, for until 1909 umpires almost always worked alone. They usually positioned themselves behind the catcher but had the responsibility for calls on all the bases and on fair and foul balls. In 1909 the rules were finally amended to allow two umpires on the field for each game.

Tom umpired a total of eight World Series, serving in 1908, 1910, 1911, 1913, 1916, 1920, and 1924, in addition to the 1903 series.

Although Tom ejected players frequently early in his career, including a famous dismissal of Chicago's Frank Chance in the 1910 World Series, he later earned a reputation for never ejecting men. He prided himself on keeping players in the game and advised other umpires to resort to ejection only as a final measure.

The last occasion on which Tom ejected a player occurred in 1922. The player was Babe Ruth, and it turned out to be Ruth's last ejection in baseball as well. Ruth had started to run toward the stands in the Polo Grounds in chase of a fan when Connolly put his small frame in front of Ruth and stopped him from the mad charge.

Umpire Connolly had a reputation for
handling difficult players without ejecting
them. The last player he ever tossed out of
a game was an angry Babe Ruth, who was
about to take on a taunting fan in a game in
1922.

Ruth hollered and fought, but Connolly
kept him from the attack, admonishing
Ruth with "You ought to be ashamed of
yourself." Apparently, the plea was effective; Ruth ended his tantrum and walked
slowly to the clubhouse in center field.
Connolly received applause from the
crowd.

It required an act of courage for Connolly to call Detroit's Ty Cobb out after an
apparent game-tying triple in the ninth
inning sent the home-team fans into a flurry of excitement. Connolly calmly
announced that the triple was void—Cobb
had stepped over the plate in swinging at
the pitch. Cobb, himself a battler, recognized Connolly's breaking point and
admitted that he never argued with Tom
when the back of the ump's neck grew red.

Connolly's authority on the field was all
the more impressive when one considers
his slight frame. Not until later years did
his weight finally reach 170 pounds.

Connolly became the senior umpire on
the American League staff, and, as such,
the counterpart of the legendary Bill Klem
in the National League. In June 1931, at the
age of 60, Tom finally stepped down as an
active umpire, accepting the position as
chief of staff of American League umpires.
His office was located in Chicago, and he
worked directly for league president Will
Harridge. He often would travel around the
country, quietly attending major league
games to observe his umpires at work. In
later years, Cal Hubbard served as Connolly's assistant in this capacity.

Connolly finally announced his retirement from the American League on January 14, 1954, at the age of 83. He was still
bright and alert, and had served for many
years as a member of the Rules Committee. In 1953 Connolly and Bill Klem
became the first umpires selected for
inclusion in the Hall of Fame. That year he
was also given a lifetime gold pass to baseball games, something generally presented only to players with a minimum of
20 years major league service.

Tom Connolly died at his long-time
home in Natick, Massachusetts, on April
28, 1961, at the age of 90.

Roger Connor (1857-1931)

Indirectly, it took Hank Aaron to get Roger Connor the recognition he deserved. For when Aaron broke Babe Ruth's lifetime home run record in 1974, baseball fans wondered whose record the Babe had broken. The answer was Roger Connor's.

Roger Connor was born on July 1, 1857, in Waterbury, Connecticut, his lifelong home. His parents were Irish immigrants from County Kerry who settled in the Washington Hills section of the town. Roger was one of eight children in a rather athletic family. A younger brother, Joe, was also a professional ballplayer, and another brother, Dan, was the head groundskeeper in the Waterbury ballpark. It was an uncle who fostered the children's interest in baseball, and Roger began playing ball when he was eight.

His first experience with the organized sport came with the town team, the Monitors of Waterbury, in 1876. Roger was a lefthanded-throwing third baseman then, and his size was a great factor in making him a star on the club. Although he was only 18 years old, he was already a six-footer and was quite well developed.

Roger played for the town team for two years, but in 1878 he ventured away from home to join the New Bedford club in a more competitive league. After a few weeks he was lured into joining the town team in Holyoke, Massachusetts, where his reputation as a powerful hitter began to form.

Holyoke was Roger's club for the 1878 and 1879 seasons, and he seemed to save his best performances for the club's archrival, Springfield. Many a time Roger belted long home runs into the Connecticut River during games between the two clubs. The Springfield manager was Bob Ferguson, who in 1880 was given the job of managing Troy of the National League. Ferguson quickly signed both Connor and his star teammate, pitcher Mickey Welch, and hauled them off to the upstate New York town. It was major league baseball, 1880 style, the fifth year of play for the National League.

Roger was still a third baseman, despite the fact that he was lefthanded all the way. In that first year of top-grade baseball, he batted .332 with three home runs in 83 games. It was his first of 12 seasons over the .300 mark, during a major league career which spanned 18 years.

A dislocated shoulder early in 1881 forced Roger to switch to first base upon his return to the Troy lineup. He found the position to his liking, and although he was never known as a great fielder, he became quite adept at scooping balls out of the dirt. He twice managed to lead the league's first basemen in fielding percentage.

Despite such prominent players as Buck Ewing, Tim Keefe, and Mickey Welch, Troy was only fifth in 1881 and dropped to seventh in 1882. Roger hit .288 and .327 for

Roger Connor, home-run king of another era. His 131 lifetime homers was a record until Babe Ruth revolutionized the game. (Opposite page) Connor dressed for baseball in the fashion of the late 1800s and (below) the weathervane that was a landmark for years on his Waterbury, Connecticut home.

those two years, but demonstrated his great strength in 1882 by leading the National League with 17 triples. He went on to lead the league in triples five times, topping double figures on 12 occasions, with a high of 26 in 1894. His 227 career triples are topped only by Sam Crawford, Ty Cobb, Honus Wagner, and Jake Beckley.

But power was not so valued in the nineteenth century; players tended to admire a good hit-and-run man more than a home-run hitter. This did not deter Roger, however, who enjoyed using his strength and his power. The fans appreciated them, too, and Roger turned into a highly popular star—not only for his power, but because when called upon he could execute the necessary bunt plays.

The Troy franchise was shifted to New York in 1883, and Roger enjoyed a .362 season. He was nearly 6'2" and weighed 190 pounds, but he later would broaden out to 220 pounds and would really stand out on a baseball field. Jim Mutrie, who took over the management of the New York club in 1885, is credited with nicknaming his team the "Giants"—after his pride in his players' physical appearance. Roger was probably the man he most had in mind, and the nickname may have been born out of Connor's size.

Roger was also a graceful runner. He would slide feet first and then bounce up in an instant upon reaching the base. The soft-spoken Connor stole 252 bases during his career.

Roger's first really big year was 1885, the year Mutrie took over. Connor led the league with a .371 average, 169 hits and 15 triples, as the Giants finished second to Cap Anson's Chicago club. It was Connor's only batting championship.

After a .355 showing with seven home runs in 1886, Roger really began hitting the long ball in 1887. That year he belted 17 home runs for his first of three home run titles and his first of six seasons in double figures.

Connor played for his first pennant winner in 1888, as the Giants bested Chicago by eight and one-half games. Although Roger's average fell from .383 to .291 (walks had counted as hits in 1887), he led the league in both triples (17) and home runs (14). On May 9, 1888, he feasted on Indianapolis pitching by hitting three home runs in one game, only the sixth time that had been done in the National League.

"Dear old Roger," as New York fans liked to call him, starred again for the 1889 Giants, who once more were National League champs. On July 10 of that year,

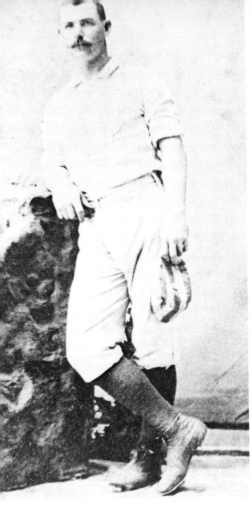

playing in the Polo Grounds at 110th Street and Fifth Avenue in Manhattan, Roger hit one of the longest home runs ever seen. He connected with one of his well-loved low pitches and sailed the ball out onto 112th Street. A group of Wall Street brokers, watching from the stands, were so impressed that they passed the hat and collected $500, with which one of them bought an inscribed gold watch for Connor as a souvenir of the occasion.

Gifts were not unusual for Roger once a season ended, for this hero of Waterbury was honored annually with a banquet in his hometown. He was a dashing figure, with a broad, handlebar mustache, and a strong, confident walk.

The 1890 season was one of turmoil for the National League, as most star players left their clubs and joined the Players League, an outgrowth of the Brotherhood of Professional Base Ball Players. Connor, along with Ewing, Keefe, and Monte Ward, had organized the Giants' chapter in 1885, and out of this the new league was formed to "promote high standards of professional conduct and to encourage and benefit the players." Roger was a stubborn advocate of the new league, and even a visit to his Waterbury home by the Giants' owner John B. Day failed to get him to return to the fold. From this resistance he became known as "The Oak," and with Buck Ewing as manager, Roger and the New York team finished third, with Connor hitting .372. But the league disbanded after the one season, and Roger was back with the Giants in 1891, hitting seven home runs and batting .293.

In 1892 the Giants dealt Roger to Philadelphia, but after one year they reclaimed him and kept him until midseason of 1894 when they traded him to the St. Louis Browns of Chris von der Ahe. As the first man in history with 100 career home runs, Roger was well received in St. Louis. He enjoyed one of his best days when, on June 1, 1895, against his old teammates, the Giants, he went 6 for 6 with two doubles and a triple as the Browns pasted a 23–8 defeat on pitcher Jouett Meeker, who pitched a complete game.

Following the 1895 season, Roger's wife gave him a beautiful weather vane, fashioned out of two baseball bats, and placed atop their Waterbury home. Although one of the bats was broken off in a storm, the weather vane became a landmark in Waterbury and was preserved long after

the Connors died and the house was sold.

In 1897, after 13 consecutive years of more than 100 games a season, Roger began to slow down. This was to be his final year in the National League. He hit his 131st and last home run that season, a record which stood until Babe Ruth hit his twenty-ninth home run in 1921, 24 years later.

Roger finished the 1897 season at Fall River in the New England League. He then bought the Waterbury team of the Connecticut League, put his wife to work as box office attendant, and had his adopted daughter sell tickets. Roger was owner, manager, and first baseman of the team, and although he now wore glasses he was a standout at bat, hitting .319 in 1898, and then leading the league with a .392 average in 1899. He still wore the lucky shamrock on his uniform that had been his symbol since he had begun playing.

Bill Klem, later a Hall of Famer, began his umpiring career in the Connecticut League, and he recalled Roger, after having a play called against him, once saying, "Young man, let me congratulate you for umpiring a fine ballgame today." The sentiment touched Klem, and he always saw to it that baseball remembered Roger.

Connor operated the Springfield team in 1902, still playing first base at the age of 45, but he called it a career after that season. His brother Joe was the manager of the team, and Roger hit .259. (Joe Connor was a catcher for the Boston Nationals, and for the Cleveland, Milwaukee, and New York clubs in the American League between 1900 and 1905, although never as a regular.)

Upon retirement, Roger was appointed school inspector for the city of Waterbury, and by horse and wagon he went from school to school to supervise maintenance operations. He remained quite a hero in his hometown.

In 1920, due to poor health, he was forced to retire, and he lived a simple life until he died on January 4, 1931, in Waterbury. It is doubtful that Babe Ruth ever heard of him.

Connor was generally forgotten until Hank Aaron's pursuit of Ruth's home-run record. He was finally chosen for the Hall of Fame in 1976.

ROGER CONNOR

Troy (N.L.) 1880–1882
New York (N.L.) 1883–1889, 1891, 1893–1894
New York (P.L.) 1890
Philadelphia (N.L.) 1892
St. Louis (N.L.) 1894–1897

G	AB	R	H	2B	3B	HR	RBI	Avg.
1987	7807	1607	2535	429	227	131	1078	.325

Stan Coveleskie (b. 1889)

There were five boys born to the Kowalewskie family of Shamokin, Pennsylvania, a coal-mining town near Scranton. All five played baseball. The oldest, a pitcher named Jacob, was killed during the Spanish-American War before he had an opportunity to play professional baseball. Frank, another pitcher, played with the Union League in 1907, an "outlaw" league that was not recognized by organized baseball. John, a third baseman and outfielder, played in the minor leagues and failed to pass a spring trial with the Philadelphia Athletics.

Harry, who changed his surname to Coveleskie, was the first brother to achieve success. He rose from the coal mines to reach the major leagues with the Philadelphia Phillies at the age of 21, earning the reputation of "The Giant Killer" when he beat New York three times in a five-game series late in 1908. The "Merkle boner" incident had created in effect a pennant tie between the Cubs and the Giants. But it was Harry Coveleskie's pitching, as much as Fred Merkle's baserunning, which cost the Giants the 1908 pennant. Harry later pitched for Cincinnati and Detroit. His career spanned nine years, during which he compiled an 81–57 record.

Stanislaus Kowalewski, or Stan Coveleskie, was the youngest in the family. Whereas Harry threw lefthanded, Stan was a righthander. And whereas Harry had fleeting success, winning 66 of 103 decisions from 1914 to 1916, Stan had a 14-year career in which he reached the 20-victory circle five times.

Stan was born on July 13, 1889. At the age of 12, he joined the older men in the mines, working as many as 72 hours a week for a salary of $3.75, or approximately a nickel per hour. The work day lasted from before sunrise until after sunset, six days a week. Remarking on the fact that he only saw the sun on Sundays, Coveleskie claimed "I'd have been great in night baseball."

Although many sources spell Stan's last name "Coveleski," Stan claimed they were all in error, including his Hall of Fame plaque. He signed his name with an "ie."

There was no time for young Stan to play organized baseball, but he amused himself in the evenings by throwing stones at tin cans set up by his home. Night after night he would fire the stones at the cans, perfecting his control. In 1908 he was asked to join a team in Shamokin, partly due to his reputation of accurately knocking down tin cans but also, of course, because his brother had reached the major leagues.

Stan posted a 6–2 record for Shamokin in the Atlantic League in 1908. In 1909 he played for the Lancaster, Pennsylvania team in the Tri-State League. Strictly a control pitcher who threw the standard fastball, slowball, and curve, Stan led the

Stan Coveleskie had no time for sandlot baseball as a boy, so he taught himself to pitch by throwing stones at tin cans each evening. As a Cleveland star (opposite page), his style looks easy, but his trademark was control. He threw consistently into the strike zone and finished games quickly.

league in 1909 with 23 victories, losing only 11 times. In 1910 he achieved a 15–8 mark, and in 1911 he posted a 15–19 record, although he walked only 65 men in 272 innings.

Eager to leave Lancaster, Stan managed to be transferred to Atlantic City, a club in the same league, in 1912. There he posted a 20–13 mark, and earned a call from Connie Mack, manager of the Philadelphia Athletics.

Coveleskie made his debut with Mack in September, relieving on two successive days and then pitching a three-hit shutout the following day. He concluded his month in the major leagues with a 2–1 record for five games. The 178-pound righthander showed good control, but he nonetheless found himself locked out of any future with the Athletics, who had a four-man pitching rotation of Chief Bender, Jack Coombs, Eddie Plank, and another newcomer, Herb Pennock. Mack knew there was no slot for Stan, and he sent Coveleskie to Spokane in the Northwest League for more seasoning in 1913.

Stan was 17–20 for Spokane that season, and in 1914 he won 20 and lost 15 while leading the league with 214 strikeouts. But Mack then lost Coveleskie's contract in a misunderstanding with Spokane, and Stan found himself attached to the Portland club of the Pacific Coast League in 1915. It would be his eighth minor league season.

The 1915 season proved to be a turning point for Covey. In addition to his three regular pitches, he developed a spitball, a legal pitch at the time, which he managed to throw with great control. By a turn of his wrist, he could make the ball break either up or down. It virtually added two pitches to his assortment, and after recording a 17–17 mark with a league-leading 64 appearances, Coveleskie was promoted to the major leagues in 1916, joining the Cleveland Indians of manager Lee Fohl.

Stan enjoyed a fine rookie season, winning 15, losing 12, and walking only 58 batters in 232 innings. Control was always the key to Stan's success, and he preferred to let the opposition hit the first pitch rather than attempt to strike them out. Frequently he would retire the side on three or four pitches, and in one game he threw only strikes for the first seven innings. Coveleskie was also one of the fastest workers in the game.

In 1917 the Indians jumped from sixth place to third. Stan hurled a league-leading nine shutouts, posting a 19-14 record with a 1.81 earned-run average, third best in

the league. The Indians continued to climb in 1918, reaching second place. Stan achieved his first 20-victory season compiling a 22–13 record and a 1.82 earned-run average. That year Harry Coveleskie terminated his major league career with the Detroit Tigers. Harry and Stan always refused to pitch against each other, despite urgings from their respective owners.

Known as "The Silent Pole" to the Cleveland fans, Stan was indeed quiet, but he enjoyed a hearty laugh. He once threw teammate Joe Sewell into a lake during spring training and rowed away, telling Sewell it was the only way for him to learn how to swim. Sewell nearly drowned.

Coveleskie was 23–12 in 1919, the year Tris Speaker replaced Fohl as manager, and again the club finished second. But 1920 turned out to be a banner year for the Indians. They won the pennant by two games over Chicago, with Stan posting a 24–14 record and leading the league in strikeouts. The Indians faced Brooklyn in the World Series.

Stan emerged as the hero of the Series, won by the Indians, five games to two. He set back Brooklyn in the first game, 3–1, the fourth game, 5–1, and the deciding seventh game, 3–0. Each victory was a five-hitter. As the first pitcher since Christy Mathewson (in 1905) to win three Series games, Coveleskie threw only 72, 78, and 82 pitches in the three games. Matty had pitched three shutouts, whereas Coveleskie had allowed two runs. But the results were equivalent, and Stan registered a brilliant 0.67 ERA for the Series.

After 1920, the spitball was outlawed except for those who had previously been throwing it. Thus Stan and 16 other pitchers were permitted to continue employing the pitch. The tobacco-chewing Coveleskie recorded a 23–13 mark in 1921, his fourth consecutive 20-win season, but the Yankees captured their first pennant that year, beating the Indians by four and one-half games.

Stan compiled a 17–14 record in 1922, but in 1923 he dropped to a 13–14 mark,

When Stan Coveleskie was 12, he joined the older men in his family in this coal mine. Working from sunup to sundown, he earned $3.75 a week. "That is why I started chewing tobacco," he said, "to keep the dust from drying out my mouth." From such a severe boyhood, all five Coveleskie boys, of which Stan was the youngest, went on to play baseball. Stan followed his brother Harry into the majors.

although he led the league with a 2.76 ERA. But in 1924 his earned-run average jumped to 4.05, he posted a 15–16 record, and, as far as manager Tris Speaker was concerned, Coveleskie was finished.

On December 12, 1924, Stan was traded to the Washington Senators for pitcher Byron Speece and outfielder Carr Smith in what amounted to a waiver transaction. Various critics gave Stan little chance of even making the team in 1925, for the Senators were just coming off a pennant-winning season under manager Bucky Harris.

But Coveleskie proved the skeptics wrong, leading the league with a 20–5 record and a 2.84 ERA. His won-lost percentage was even better than that of teammate Walter Johnson, who was 20–7. Stan was working strictly on control and the spitball at this point, and his strikeout total was under 60 for the third successive year.

Stan hurled a complete game in the second contest of the 1925 World Series against Pittsburgh, but lost, 3–2. He also started the fifth game but lasted only six and one-third innings, losing, 6–3. The Pirates went on to capture the Series in seven games. Nevertheless Stan's combined ERA for five Series games was a low 1.74.

Stan remained with Washington for another year and a half, going 14–11 in

1926, and 2–1 in 1927 before drawing his release on June 12. He then returned to Shamokin until the following year when the New York Yankees signed him. Stan started eight games for the 1928 World Champion Yankees and posted a 5–1 record, despite a 5.74 earned-run average. He was not with the team for the World Series, however, having drawn his release before September 1.

In 1929 Stan received an offer to play semipro ball in South Bend, Indiana. He and his wife, whom he had married in 1922, decided to settle there. Stan operated a filling station, but gave it up after a few years. He then settled into a quiet, simple life of fishing, getting by on a limited income, partly through a "fix-it" operation in his garage. Coveleskie was elected to the Hall of Fame in 1969 and despite a 1972 heart attack, continued to enjoy a daily routine of fishing.

STANLEY COVELESKIE

Philadelphia (A.L.) 1912
Cleveland 1916–1924
Washington 1925–1927
New York (A.L.) 1928

G	IP	W	L	Pct.	H	R	ER	SO	BB	ERA
450	3092	214	141	.603	3055	1237	982	981	802	2.88

Sam Crawford (1880-1968)

Although he played in the shadow of Ty Cobb during his career with the Detroit Tigers, Sam Crawford was considered in his time to be the hardest hitter in baseball. He holds the distinction of being the only player to have led both major leagues in home runs.

Samuel Earl Crawford was born on April 18, 1880, in Wahoo, Nebraska. When Sam entered professional baseball, he was given the nickname "Wahoo Sam." He grew so fond of it that throughout his adult life he signed all letters and autographs as "Wahoo Sam Crawford," and he requested that the name be used on his Hall of Fame plaque.

The elder Crawford owned the Wahoo General Store, but Sam became an apprentice barber, working in the local shop as a sweeper and occasionally cutting the hair of a wandering tramp for practice. It was difficult work for Sam, who much preferred playing ball.

Sam was an accomplished lefthanded pitcher and an outfielder for the Wahoo town team of the late 1890s. When Sam was 18 years old, the team borrowed a horse-drawn wagon with which they were able to tour Nebraska, playing teams in other communities and passing the hat to meet expenses.

While playing for the Wahoo club in the town of West Point, Nebraska, Sam was offered money to remain and play solely for West Point. He accepted the offer and the team captured the state championship. Shortly thereafter, Sam was noticed by John McIlvaine, a player with the Chatham club in the Canadian League. McIlvaine arranged for Sam to be signed to a $65-a-month contract with his club, and in May 1899, Sam formally ended his career as a barber and became a professional baseball player.

A strong six-footer with large hands and feet, Sam possessed great power and was primarily a line-drive hitter. He played in 43 games for Chatham and registered a .370 batting average, but the league folded in July and Sam landed with Columbus, Ohio, of the Western League. Columbus transferred to Grand Rapids a few weeks later, and Sam, unaffected by the transition, hit .333 in 60 games. Toward the end of the season, Crawford was purchased by Cincinnati.

Sam's 87 hits with Grand Rapids in 1899 were a significant statistic. After the Western League evolved into the American League and claimed major league status in 1901, the National Commission, the three-man ruling body of baseball, decreed that any Western League players who joined an American or National League club should have their Western League statistics

counted as major league totals. League statisticians, however, came to overlook the ruling with the passing of years. Sam's career total of hits, therefore, stood at 2964 rather than 3051, which would have made him one of the select few to reach 3000 career hits.

Sam joined the Redlegs on September 10, 1899, barely one year after he had been touring Nebraska in a wagon for the Wahoo team. He broke into the big leagues with five hits in eight at bats during an unusual double header, in which Cincinnati played Cleveland in the first game and Louisville in the nightcap. The performance earned Sam a regular position in the Cincinnati outfield.

The 1899 season was a lengthy one, and Sam managed to play in 31 games with a .307 average, two doubles, and eight triples. The high triples total became characteristic of Sam's career, for with his wide-open stance and strong swing he became the leading three-base hitter in baseball history, belting 312, 15 better than Cobb. In doing so, Sam led both leagues in triples, captured a total of six triples titles (three of them consecutively, 1913–1915), and tied Joe Jackson's American League record for triples with 26 in 1914.

Sam was not a particularly speedy runner, but he had good sense on the bases and stole as many as 41 bases in one season (1912). He also stretched many doubles into triples by knowing when not to hesitate as he rounded second base.

In 1900 Sam hit .270 for the Redlegs, a seventh-place club. But in 1901 he batted .335 and led the National League with 16 home runs. The entire league had only 224 homers for the season.

Various baseball historians believe that Crawford was held back more than any other player in the dead-ball era. They contend that Crawford might have challenged Babe Ruth for home run titles had the two played simultaneously.

After a .333 season in 1902, Sam, who was earning $150 a month, was attracted by a better contract offer from the young American League. He signed contracts with both Cincinnati and Detroit in 1903, and when a peace agreement was finally arranged, he was awarded to Detroit. Several years later, Crawford helped form one of the great outfields in American League history, first with Cobb and Davy Jones,

Crawford in the field and at the plate: Usually playing left field, he was part of one of the greatest outfields in American League history, Crawford-Cobb-Jones and later Crawford-Cobb-Veach. At bat, he hit a record 312 triples in his career. Experts say he would have slugged home runs in Babe Ruth style had it not been for the dead ball of the time.

and later with Cobb and Bobby Veach. Crawford generally had the distinction of batting fourth in the lineup, and he usually played left field. When Cobb came into the major leagues in 1905, he was the center fielder. Sam also had the distinction of pinch-hitting for Cobb on April 24, 1906, lining a single.

In his first American League season, Sam played under manager Ed Barrow and batted .332 with a league-leading 25 triples. He hit over .300 11 times in his major league career with a high of .378 in 1911, but he never captured a batting title.

The club's leading hitter in 1903, Crawford fell to .247 the following season as Detroit finished seventh. Barrow was then replaced as manager by Bobby Lowe. In 1905 Sam rebounded to hit .297 with 10 triples, his lowest triples total between 1900 and 1916.

In Cobb's first full season with the Tigers, 1906, the team finished sixth under manager Bill Armour. Sam batted .295 that year, and he followed it with a .323 performance. The 1907 season marked the first of three consecutive pennant winners in Detroit under new manager Hughey Jennings. Unfortunately, the Tigers lost all three World Series, the first two to Chicago and the 1909 series to Pittsburgh. Thus neither Cobb nor Crawford, two of the game's greatest players, ever were affiliated with a World Championship club.

Similar to the remainder of his team, Sam's World Series performances were not noteworthy. He batted .238 in the 1907 Series, repeated the mark in 1908, and then hit .250 in 1909 for a combined .243. He rapped three doubles and a home run (off the Pirates' Babe Adams) in the 1909 Series.

In 1908 Sam belted seven homers to capture the American League title, thus making him the only man ever to lead both leagues. He batted .311 that year and .314 in 1909, leading the league with 35 doubles in the latter season.

The Tigers never achieved another pennant during Sam's era, but he nonetheless continued to excel on the diamond. He was a favorite of the Tiger fans and the most popular player on the team. Cobb, of course, was extremely unpopular. The relationship between the two was strained, and they supposedly did not speak to each other for several years. Sam believed the silence to have began when he grounded into four double plays in one game with Cobb on first.

In addition to three consecutive triples titles, with totals of 23, 26, and 19, between 1913 and 1915, Sam shared the home-run crown in 1914 with Home Run Baker. Both men belted eight.

Crawford batted .299 in 1915 and .286 in

1916, his final season as a regular at the age of 36. In 1917, while limited to 61 games and 104 at bats, Sam hit a mere .173. It gave Crawford a lifetime batting average of .309.

Sam received an offer to play with Los Angeles in the Pacific Coast League the following year, and he moved with his wife, Mary, to the West Coast and spent four seasons with the Angels. In 1918 Crawford hit .292, but in 1919 he belted 41 doubles, 18 triples, and 14 homers for a .360 average in the expanded Pacific Coast League schedule. In 1920 he led the league with 21 triples and batted .332. And in 1921, at the age of 41, Crawford played 175 games and collected 199 hits for a .318 average.

After the 1921 season, Sam retired as a player and moved to Burbank, California, where he tended his garden. His only return to baseball was a four-year umpiring stint in the Pacific Coast League from 1935 to 1938, but he gave it up, calling umpiring a thankless and lonely profession.

An articulate and well-read man, Sam was once considered to be a player who would make a good addition to the three-man National Commission, the ruling body of baseball prior to the establishment of the office of Commissioner. But the idea of adding a player to the Commission was never realized.

The Crawfords had moved to the town of Pearblossom near the Mojave Desert when Sam received word in 1957 that he had been named to the Hall of Fame. He led a quiet existence in his later years; even his neighbors were unaware that Crawford had been a baseball player, let alone one of the greatest in the game's history.

Sam died on June 15, 1968, in Hollywood, California, at the age of 88.

SAMUEL EARL CRAWFORD

Cincinnati 1899–1902
Detroit 1903–1917

G	AB	R	H	2B	3B	HR	RBI	Avg.
2505	9579	1392	2964	455	312	95	1525	.309

Joe Cronin (b. 1906)

In a professional baseball career of more than 50 years, Joe Cronin was a minor league player, a major league player, a manager, a general manager, and a league president.

The son of Irish immigrants, Joseph Edward Cronin was born in San Francisco on October 12, 1906, only a few months after the great San Francisco earthquake had left the Cronin family and thousands of others penniless. Joe attended Mission High School, but after a fire leveled the school he transferred to Sacred Heart. At the age of 14, in an era when tennis was considered a "society" pastime, he captured the junior tennis championship of San Francisco. In high school Cronin played soccer and basketball. Tall and thin, he stood 6 feet but weighed barely 160 pounds.

While his brothers contributed to the family income by working as manual laborers, Joe became a junior clerk at the Hibernia Bank. After graduating from Sacred Heart, he turned down a baseball-basketball scholarship offer from St. Mary's College so that he could continue to assist his family. He worked as a playground instructor and played semipro ball in Napa, a small town across the bay, earning $15 per game as a shortstop.

In 1925 Pittsburgh Pirate scout Joe Devine offered Cronin a professional contract. After signing, he was assigned to the Johnstown, Pennsylvania club in the Mid-Atlantic League, a considerable distance from home but not far from Pittsburgh. At Johnstown, Joe appeared in 99 games and batted .313 with 18 doubles, 11 triples, and 3 home runs. His lean body never produced much power—only 6 times in his career did he hit 10 or more home runs—but he was clearly adept at handling the bat.

The following year Joe advanced to Pittsburgh, only to find himself sitting on the bench and watching Glenn Wright play shortstop. Wright was a good ballplayer who batted .294 during an 11-year career, and young Cronin was not about to replace him. Neither could he count on playing third base, occupied by a future Hall of Famer, Pie Traynor. Joe played in only 38 games for the Pirates, collecting 22 hits for an average of .265, before being farmed out to New Haven in the Eastern League for more playing time. At New Haven he batted .320 in 66 games.

Returning to the Pirates in 1927, Cronin again spent most of the season on the bench. Led by such stars as Paul and Lloyd Waner, Kiki Cuyler, and Pie Traynor, the Pirates captured the National League pennant. Shortstop Glenn Wright batted .281 but committed a league-leading 45 errors. Cronin appeared in only a dozen

games, recording 5 hits in 22 at bats and driving in 3 runs. He did not play in the four-game World Series against the Yankees, but he did receive a full loser's share of the Series money—$3,985.47.

Obviously committed to Wright at shortstop, the Pirates in 1928 sold Cronin to Kansas City of the American Association. Joe's National League career was behind him—50 games and a .257 batting average. At Kansas City, rusty from inactivity in the previous year, the 21-year-old infielder fumbled balls at both short and third and batted a mere .245. Cronin was scheduled to be demoted to Wichita when he was spotted by Joe Engel, a scout for the Washington Senators. The Senators purchased Joe for $7500, a reasonably high price for an unproven minor leaguer.

During the remainder of the 1928 season, Cronin batted .242 in 63 games for the Senators. Washington owner Clark Griffith was not impressed, but his secretary and niece, Mildred Robertson, was. Seven years later she and Cronin married.

During the off-season, Joe chopped trees and ran, in order to add weight to his frame. His fielding became almost graceful and his batting improved. In his first full season with the Senators, 1929, Joe batted .283. In 1930 he exploded with a .346 average, including 203 hits, 14 homers, and 126 RBIs. Although the Senators finished eight games behind pennant-winning Philadelphia, Cronin was selected the American League's Most Valuable Player.

In 1931 Cronin's average dropped to .306—close to his lifetime mark of .302—but he repeated his RBI total of 126. He also led the league in games played for the second successive year. In 1932 Cronin batted .318 and led the league with 18 triples.

Clark Griffith was now disenchanted with his manager, the former great pitcher, Walter Johnson. Nine years before, he had selected his 27-year-old second baseman, Bucky Harris, as player-manager, and the Senators captured the pennant. In the hope of repeating that success, Griffith offered the 26-year-old Cronin the same challenge for 1933. After consulting Johnson, Cronin accepted.

It was a fine year for the Washington club. Cronin's Senators won 99 games, eight more than the Yankees, and captured what would be their last pennant. Cronin batted .309 and led the league with 45 doubles; he also led the league's shortstops in fielding. Nevertheless, the Giants captured the World Series.

Player-manager Cronin of the Washington Senators cannot stop Chicago catcher Johnny Pasek from sliding safely between his legs in a 1934 game. The year was a disaster for the Senators, as they fell to seventh place from their previous pennant position.

The following year, 1934, was a disaster. The Senators plummeted to seventh place with a 66–86 record as injuries plagued the team. Cronin himself was hurt, and his batting average fell below the .300 mark for the first time in five years. The highlight of the season was the All-Star game. Cronin, playing shortstop, managed an American League team that included such stars as Babe Ruth, Lou Gehrig, Jimmie Foxx, Al Simmons, Charlie Gehringer, Bill Dickey, and Heinie Manush. Joe is remembered as one of five future Hall of Famers who were struck out in succession that day by Carl Hubbell.

In October 1934, Boston Red Sox owner Tom Yawkey offered Griffith an incredible $250,000, plus shortstop Lyn Lary, for Cronin. Griffith consulted with Joe, received for him a firm contract offer of $50,000 a year for five years as player-manager, and, with Joe's permission, made the trade.

Cronin managed the Red Sox from 1935 through 1947. Until 1945 he remained an active player. Under Cronin, the Red Sox finished second four times and did not win a pennant until 1946. As a regular with the Red Sox, Cronin batted over .300 four times. In 1938 he hit .325 and led the league with 51 doubles. In 1943 he hit five pinch-hit home runs (the previous record for a *career* had been five), a feat that established Cronin as one of the great clutch hitters. The shortage of players during World War II kept Cronin active at least as a pinch-hitter until April 19, 1945, when he fractured his right leg. Joe never played again.

The Red Sox captured their only pennant under Cronin in 1946 when they won 104 games. The St. Louis Cardinals, however, captured the World Series crown. In Cronin's final year as manager, 1947, the Red Sox finished in third place.

From manager of the Red Sox, Cronin in 1948 moved up to become vice president, treasurer, and general manager of the club. He held the position for 11 years—a long tenure in baseball—until he was named president of the American League in January 1959. Only one other person

had ever risen from player to league president: John Tener.

During Cronin's two terms as president, the American League expanded, first to 10 teams, then to 12, necessitating divisional play and a playoff system. Two controversial decisions marked his tenure. In 1970 he fired umpires Al Salerno and Bill Valentine for "incompetence" after they were discovered to be organizing an umpire's union. In December 1973, he vetoed the Yankees' contract with manager Dick Williams, whose release by the Oakland A's was in some doubt, while at the same time approving the Tigers' signing of former Yankee boss Ralph Houk. Both decisions aroused intense criticism.

In January 1974, at the end of his second term as president, Cronin became chairman of the American League, the presidency going to Lee MacPhail. Cronin had twice been mentioned as a candidate for the position of commissioner, but the post was not offered to him.

Cronin was elected to the Hall of Fame in 1956.

JOSEPH EDWARD CRONIN

Pittsburgh 1926–1927
Washington 1928–1934
Boston (A.L.) 1935–1945

G	AB	R	H	2B	3B	HR	RBI	Avg.
2124	7577	1233	2285	515	117	171	1423	.302

Cronin bats for the Boston Red Sox, which he managed from 1935 to 1947 before moving into the general-manager slot. As a regular for the Red Sox, he batted over .300 four times. Later, he slugged five pinch-hit home runs in one season—the previous lifetime record having been five.

Candy Cummings (1848-1924)

Candy Cummings is credited with being the inventor of the curveball. While Candy did not throw the ideal curveball, his innovation has become an essential part of every pitcher's repertoire.

William Arthur Cummings was born of Scotch descent on October 17, 1848, in Ware, Massachusetts. His parents moved the family to Brooklyn, New York, when Arthur (as he was then called) was two years old.

The idea of a curve ball first came to Cummings as a teenager. Idly hurling half a clam shell across the beach in Brooklyn with some friends, he observed the irregular course of its flight and decided to attempt a similar throw with a baseball. Using a nickel baseball, he began to work on his curve. With a flick of the wrist and a late release from his fingers, he finally achieved the curved trajectory. His friends, although witnesses to the feat, scoffed at the idea, refusing to believe their own eyes. It was years before the curve was accepted as more than a mere optical illusion.

Arthur played baseball at boarding school in Fulton, New York, and with a boys' team that played its games in Carroll Park, Brooklyn. While a player with an amateur team known as the Star Juniors, he was credited with winning 37 of 39 games, pitching every game for the team despite a rather frail physical appearance. Even as an adult, Arthur stood only 5'9" and never weighed more than 120 pounds.

His performance with the Star Juniors was so impressive that Joseph Legett, operator of Brooklyn's Excelsior Club, obtained permission from Arthur's parents to sign him. The Excelsiors were New York City's best amateur team, and the invitation to join was a great honor.

Arthur pitched for the Excelsiors in 1866 and 1867. His first game was a 24–12 victory, a typical score of the day, over the Eureka team of Newark, New Jersey. The Excelsiors drew large crowds, including a visit by President Andrew Johnson. Cummings came to be known as "Candy," a term of admiration for anything considered meritorious. "The candy" was a popular expression for "the best."

In 1867 Cummings and the Excelsiors traveled to Boston to play some of the local teams—including Lowell, Tri-Mountain, and Harvard College. Against Harvard, in a game played on Soldier's Field in Cambridge, Candy first used the curveball extensively. The players were stunned by the odd behavior of the pitch, and at the end of the game Candy was asked to demonstrate the pitch to players and fans. Rules at the time required a pitcher to keep both feet on the ground while delivering the ball, making it difficult to muster much

speed on the pitch. But Cummings had advanced far beyond any pitcher who attempted to throw the curve, and he was the only one who could clearly explain it.

Other pitchers who threw the early curveball included Alphonse Martin, Bobby Mathews, Fred Goldsmith, and Joseph Mann. Candy's claim to its invention was often disputed, but in the 1890s the National League established a commission that ruled Cummings should receive full credit.

In 1868 Candy joined the Stars of Brooklyn and spent four years with the "championship team of the United States and Canada," as they billed themselves. It was a fine club, and with Cummings pitching the majority of the games, the Stars defeated the Mutuals of New York, 24–12, in a "battle of champions." The Mutuals were one of the few local teams considered above amateur level; some of their players openly admitted receiving money for playing. But when Cummings again beat the Mutuals in 1871, this time by a 14–3 score, the abilities of this so-called professional team were called into question. To allow only three runs in those days was a rare feat, and Cummings was widely acclaimed for the performance.

The Mutuals persuaded Candy (with money) to join their club in 1872, at last establishing Cummings as a full-fledged professional. It was during that season that Candy believed his curveball was perfected.

The Mutuals were a member of the National Association, the first major league, and Cummings pitched all their games in 1872, winning 34 and losing 19. Contracts were not widely respected in those days, and Candy had in fact signed with three different teams before settling on the Mutuals.

In 1873 he pitched for the Lord Baltimores, winning 29 and losing 14, while demonstrating good ability at bat despite his small stature. He transferred to the Philadelphia Athletics in 1874, winning 28 and losing 26, before joining the Hartford Dark Blues, another National Association club.

Candy was a well-known star at this point, and at 27 he was considered a veteran. After Tommy Bond joined Hartford, Candy no longer did all the pitching. But Candy pitched enough to post a 34–11 record in 1875, followed by a 16–8 mark in 1876, the first year of the National League. On September 9 of that season, he became the first pitcher to hurl two complete-game victories on the same day, twice pinning defeats on Cincinnati.

Hartford finished third in the 13-club National Association in 1875. Their standing remained stationary in 1876 as Chicago captured the first National League pennant. Bond now pitched more frequently than Cummings, and many pitchers were learning to throw and master the curve.

In 1877, at a baseball convention in Pittsburgh, the first minor league was formed. It was called the International Association, a forerunner of the American Association and the International League. Candy was elected the Association's first president. It was a loosely structured league composed of 13 teams, each of which was required to pay a $10 entry fee and to put forth an additional $15 if it wished to compete for the league championship. The league, and Candy's presidency, lasted two years.

Cummings pitched briefly for the Lynn, Massachusetts team in the International Association (Candy was player-president!), winning only one of eight decisions. He secured his release in July and signed with the Cincinnati Reds of the National League, while still retaining the presidency of the International Association. But Cummings was less than sensational. Many pitchers were throwing harder curves, and Candy was unable to achieve success.

The fans, the management, and especially the press were unusually cruel to Candy. One paper wrote, "This thing of examining scores of the games in which the Cincinnati Reds play, and seeing from 18 to 25 hits each game piled up against Cummings' record, is getting sickening. His presence on the team is demoralizing. Unless the evil is remedied, the club on its return will not attract 100 people to the games. No change could be for the worse."

Whether Candy resigned or was released from the Redlegs is uncertain. Nevertheless, he did not return with the team to Cincinnati, causing the same newspaper to write, "Whether he left voluntarily or was urged to do so by the directors was not stated. No one who has pride in the game will mourn this loss to the club."

Candy pitched briefly for Forest City of Cleveland in 1878, after which he returned to Ware, Massachusetts, his birthplace. His health was poor and his baseball career was finished at the age of 30. In 1884 Cummings moved to Athol, Massachusetts, where he played for the local amateur team. In 1896 he was prominent at ceremonies honoring Harry Wright, delighting the crowd with a display of slow curveballs. He moved to Fitchburg in 1901, but returned to Brooklyn after a few months. In 1902 Candy returned to Athol, where he established a successful paint and wallpaper business that lasted for thirty years.

Candy gave up his painting business in 1920 and moved to Toledo, Ohio, where he spent the last four years of his life in poor health. He died in Toledo on May 17, 1924. In 1939 Candy was inducted into the Hall of Fame.

WILLIAM ARTHUR CUMMINGS

Mutuals (N.A.) 1872
Baltimore (N.A.) 1873
Philadelphia (N.A.) 1874
Hartford (N.A.) 1875
Hartford (N.L.) 1876
Cincinnati (N.L.) 1877

G	IP	W	L	Pct.	H	R	ER	SO	BB	ERA
245	inc.	146	92	.613	inc.	inc.	inc.	inc.	inc.	inc.

(Left) An old sketch of Candy Cummings, throwing his brand new curveball. With a flick of the wrist and a late release of his fingers, he made the ball take a route it never had taken before. He had gotten the idea while throwing clamshells on the beach as a teenager.

Kiki Cuyler (1899-1950)

Kiki Cuyler might have been one of the greatest Pittsburgh Pirate players had not an argument with management ended his stay with the club after only four seasons. Ten times in his career, Kiki batted over .300. He played on four pennant-winning teams.

Hazen Shirley Cuyler was born of Irish-German parents on August 30, 1899, in Harrisville, Michigan. As a boy, friends called him by half of his surname, "Cuy." He remained "Cuy" to all who came to know him until 1923, at which time sportswriter Blinky Horn of Nashville, hearing infielders yelling "Cuy! Cuy!" on fly balls, simply tabbed Cuyler as "Kiki." Thereafter, that was to be his name.

Cuyler was both a pitcher and an outfielder in high school. After spending three months at the U.S. Military Academy at West Point, Cuyler acquired a job as an auto-top builder for Buick in Flint, Michigan. Like many promising young players of the day, his primary assignment was with the company's baseball team, of which he was the star player.

In the depression of 1920, Buick closed its Flint plant and disbanded its baseball team. Before the 1920 season was completed, Cuyler caught on with Bay City, a team in the Michigan-Ontario League, as a pitcher-outfielder. Early in his stay there, he was badly spiked while sliding into second base. When he returned to action a week later, it was strictly as an outfielder. Kiki never pitched again.

A righthanded hitter exclusively, Cuyler stood 5'11" and weighed 185 pounds. He neither smoked nor drank. His hobbies included hunting, golf, and photography, and he was an excellent dancer. Many thought that he approached the ideal of the "All-American boy." He matured early and married Bertha Kelly at the age of 18; they later had two sons.

Cuyler enjoyed a fine season with Bay City in 1921, batting .317 in 116 games. At the end of the season, Pittsburgh purchased Kiki. He played in one game for the Pirates, going hitless in three at bats. In 1922 he was farmed out to Charleston of the South Atlantic League, batted .309, and again finished the season in Pittsburgh. This time, he participated in only one game, serving as a pinch-runner.

In 1923 Cuyler again played in the minor leagues, this time with Nashville of the Southern Association. Kiki had a brilliant year, hitting .340 with 65 extra-base hits and 68 stolen bases. He received the league's Most Valuable Player award, an automobile. Again, Kiki finished the season in Pittsburgh, playing 11 games and batting .250. But in 1924 he remained with the Pirates and replaced Carson Bigbee as the club's regular left fielder.

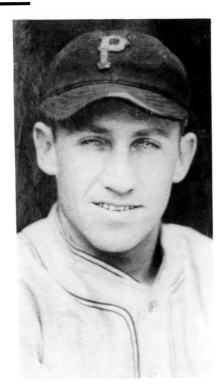

It was but a brief time before Pirate fans were hailing Kiki as the "new Ty Cobb." There was little he failed to accomplish in his rookie season. He batted .354, the fourth highest average in the league, drove in 85 runs, hit 16 triples, and stole 32 bases.

Max Carey, the most feared base stealer in the National League, was a teammate at the time. He gave Kiki numerous pointers, and when Max retired, Cuyler assumed his slot as the league's champion base stealer. Kiki captured four theft titles (1926, 1928–1930); in 1925, he swiped 41 bases in 54 attempts.

The 1925 season, only his second in the majors, was perhaps Cuyler's finest. He batted .357, collected 220 hits, scored 144 runs (a Pirate record and a league-leading figure), compiled 366 total bases (also a Pirate record), belted 43 doubles, 26 triples, 17 homers, and drove in 102 runs. In reward for his efforts, which included a record-tying 10-consecutive hits, he finished second to Rogers Hornsby in Most Valuable Player voting. The Pirates captured the 1925 National League pennant, thanks in great measure to Kiki's performance.

Appropriately, Cuyler was the hero of the 1925 World Series. The Washington Senators were seeking their second consecutive World Championship, and the Series went down to the seventh game. A great catch by Cuyler kept the deciding game close, but in the eighth inning, Washington led, 7–6, with Walter Johnson pitching. In the last of the eighth, the Pirates tied the score, 7–7, and an error by Roger Peckinpaugh put the winning runs in scoring position. Kiki stepped up to the plate, made the sign of the cross, and banged a two-run double off Johnson to put Pittsburgh ahead, 9–7. The Pirates held on to win, and 5000 Pirate fans greeted Cuyler outside of Forbes Field and carried him to his home on their shoulders.

Riding the crest of his popularity, Kiki recorded another fine season in 1926, batting .321 and leading the league again in runs scored with 113. But his honeymoon with Pittsburgh was about to end suddenly.

Kiki was hitting .300 as the 1927 season unfolded, but he was not hitting the ball with the authority he had previously shown. Manager Donie Bush positioned him in center field, but Cuyler insisted on playing right. Bush placed him second in the batting order, whereas Cuyler, with little confidence in his hit-and-run abilities, preferred batting third. In June, an ankle

Cuyler kept in shape winters by playing for the Flint, Michigan, Pontiac Tool Shop basketball team. Before breaking into professional ball, Cuyler had a job with the Flint Buick plant, where his main assignment had been with the company's baseball team. (Opposite page) An older Cuyler plays for the Brooklyn Dodgers in 1938, his last year in the major leagues.

injury sidelined him. On August 6, Kiki failed to slide into second base; he was fined $50 and removed from the game. Bill Terry of the Giants, witnessing the play, defended Cuyler's act, but Bush would accept no explanation. Pirate president Barney Dreyfuss backed his manager, and Cuyler was benched.

Even when Clyde Barnhart was injured and an opening appeared in the outfield, Cuyler remained on the bench while rookie Adam Comorosky got the call. Cuyler barely played the remainder of the 1927 season, which terminated in another Pittsburgh pennant. In the World Series, Kiki did not appear in a single game. The fans, watching the Pirates being defeated in four straight games by the Yankees, shouted "We want Cuyler" throughout the Series, but to no avail. Cuyler's career as a Pirate had ended.

After the season, Cuyler composed a lengthy explanation of his actions for a Pittsburgh newspaper. He spoke of the future which the Pirates could have had with an outfield composed of Cuyler and the Waner brothers. But on November 28, Kiki was traded to the Cubs for Sparky Adams and Pete Scott.

After hitting only .285 in his first season with the Cubs, Kiki bounded back in 1929 to bat .360 with 102 RBIs. He helped Joe McCarthy's Cubs beat out Bush's Pirates for the pennant, a fact that no doubt delighted Kiki. And in the World Series, Cuyler hit Athletic pitching for a .300 average.

The Cubs placed second in 1930 and third in 1931, but Cuyler hit .355 and .330 for the two seasons. His lifetime batting average at that point was .335, and he was as popular in Chicago as he had been in Pittsburgh. In 1932, although Cuyler's average dropped to .291, the Cubs won the pennant. Kiki was thus playing for his fourth pennant winner. He hit .278 in the four-game Series, collecting two singles, a double, a triple, and a homer, finishing his World Series play with a .281 average.

In 1933 Kiki reinjured a foot he had fractured the previous spring and played in only 70 games, batting .317. The injury substantially diminished his base stealing ability, but he remained a consistent hitter and retained his strong throwing arm. In 1934, the year in which he was selected

to the National League All-Star team, he batted .338 for the Cubs. But in July 1935, Cuyler was released by the Cubs and signed two days later by Cincinnati. He finished the season with a disappointing .258 average.

Cuyler's old abilities reemerged in 1936 as he batted .326 in 144 games. But in 1937 his average plummeted to .271, and at the end of the season Cuyler was given his unconditional release by the Reds.

The Brooklyn Dodgers, in the habit of acquiring aging stars in those days, signed Cuyler in February 1938. He made a good enough showing in spring training to go north with Burleigh Grimes's club, thus beginning his fifteenth full season in the major leagues. Employed strictly as a reserve outfielder, Kiki batted .273 and thus closed out his major league career with a .321 lifetime average.

Cuyler was in demand as a minor league manager, but never received an offer for a big league job. He managed Chattanooga in 1939, 1940, and part of 1941, finishing first, fourth, and fourth, respectively. On August 6, 1941, he was appointed coach under manager Jimmy Wilson of the Cubs, and he remained in that capacity through the 1943 season.

In 1944 Cuyler returned to the Southern Association, where he had been Most Valuable Player in 1923, and assumed the managerial helm of the Atlanta Crackers. The team placed second in 1944 and captured pennants in both 1945 and 1946. In 1947 his club finished fifth, and in 1948 sixth. Cuyler's career record as a manager was 633–523, a .548 percentage.

Cuyler spent the 1949 season as a coach with the Boston Red Sox under his old skipper, Joe McCarthy. The team lost the pennant by one game to the Yankees. Before the 1950 season began, Cuyler experienced serious heart trouble. He died en route to a hospital in Ann Arbor, Michigan, on February 11, 1950. He was only 50 years old.

Kiki Cuyler was elected to the Hall of Fame in 1968.

HAZEN SHIRLEY CUYLER

Pittsburgh 1921–1927
Chicago (N.L.) 1928–1935
Cincinnati 1935–1937
Brooklyn 1938

G	AB	R	H	2B	3B	HR	RBI	Avg.
1879	7161	1305	2299	394	157	127	1065	.321

Dizzy Dean (1911-1974)

One of the most colorful men to play professional baseball, the star of the St. Louis Cardinals' "Gas House Gang," Dizzy Dean condensed a brilliant pitching career into a few short years. Between 1932 and 1936, he won 120 games. In 1934 he became the last National League pitcher to achieve 30 victories in one year.

Dizzy was born Jay Hanna Dean on January 16, 1911, in Lucas, Arkansas. Years later, out of respect for a neighbor's son who had died, he changed his name to Jerome Herman Dean. Jay's mother died when he was three. His father was an itinerant farm worker who traveled the Southwest in search of work. Jay and his brothers worked the cotton fields at an early age, and his formal education ended with the fourth grade. At the age of 16, Jay enlisted in the Army. It was during Dean's Army years that he received the nickname "Dizzy," which has since become as famous a baseball nickname as "Babe" or "Yogi."

After three years service in the Army, Dizzy traveled to San Antonio, Texas, to work for a public service company and to pitch for the company baseball team. He had learned to pitch in the Army, and he sharpened his skills with the company team. In 1930 Don Curtis, a Cardinal scout, spotted Dizzy pitching and signed him to a professional contract.

Assigned to St. Joseph in the Western League, Dizzy won 17 games, lost eight, and worked 217 innings before the end of August. He was promoted to Houston (Texas League), posted a quick 8–2 record, and made the Cardinal team by the end of the season. Diz made his only start for manager Gabby Street that September, pitching a complete-game, three-hit, 3–1 victory over Pittsburgh.

Dean continued to make a good impression on the mound during spring training in 1931, but he was a cocky kid who did not hesitate to report late to practice. The Cardinals, having captured the 1930 pennant without Diz, decided they could repeat in 1931 the same way. And they were right. The Cardinals won the 1931 pennant by 13 games while Dizzy was winning 26 games at Houston with a 1.57 earned-run average and 303 strikeouts. All were league-leading figures.

It was obvious that a place had to be found on the Cardinal roster for Dean in 1932, but to his misfortune the 1932 Cardinals finished in a tie for sixth place. Dean emerged as the staff's top pitcher with an 18–15 record. He posted league-leading totals in innings pitched (286) and strikeouts (191).

Frankie Frisch replaced Street as manager in 1933 and the Cardinals finished

fifth, with Diz winning 20 and leading the league in games pitched (48) and strikeouts (199). He lost 18 games but it was his strikeouts that had the crowds talking. On July 30, in the first game of a doubleheader against the Cubs, Dean struck out 17 batters to set a major league record. (The record stood until Bob Feller fanned 18 in 1938. Feller in turn has been surpassed by Steve Carlton, Tom Seaver, and Nolan Ryan, each of whom struck out 19 batters.)

Baseball in 1934 offered the nation a needed escape from Depression woes, and the Cardinal "Gas House Gang" had a crew of stars. Besides Dean and Frisch, there were Rip Collins, Leo Durocher, Ducky Medwick, and Pepper Martin. Dizzy was also joined on the club by his brother, Paul Dean, younger by two years. Naturally, Paul was quickly nicknamed "Daffy," but the coinnage was not appropriate. Paul was considerably more level-headed and less inclined to practical jokes and bragging than was Diz.

In his first year with the Cardinals, Paul Dean accomplished one feat that always eluded Dizzy—pitching a no-hitter. He performed the feat in the second game of a September 21 double header against Brooklyn after Dizzy had registered a three-hitter in the opener. Dizzy's postgame comment was: "If I'd known Paul was going to do that, I'd have pitched one, too!"

In 1934 Dizzy posted a sensational 30–7 record, an .811 winning percentage, to lead the Cardinals to the pennant. (Not until 1968, when Denny McLain reached the mark for Detroit, did another pitcher win 30 games.) He topped the league with 195 strikeouts and was selected as Most Valuable Player.

Prior to the 1934 World Series, Dizzy told the world: "Me an' Paul will win two games each." His boast was accurate; Diz won games one and seven, and Paul games three and six, in downing the Tigers.

Dizzy was earning $25,000 a season at this point, the highest salary ever paid to a pitcher to that time. But Paul was receiving a typical Depression baseball salary—$3000—and Dizzy staged a brief strike during the 1934 season on his brother's behalf. Occasional sitdown strikes were not unusual for Dizzy, nor was his practice of missing exhibition games or placing an occasional bet on another sporting event. Many years later he was called in for questioning in a major Detroit gambling investigation, but he was never personally involved in trouble with the law.

(At left) Dean warms up for his company baseball team in San Antonio, Texas, where a Cardinal scout spotted him in 1930. This is believed to be the first picture of Dean in a baseball uniform. (Below) The brothers Dean, Paul, left, and Dizzy. In the 1934 World Series, each pitched two victories.

Dizzy's baseball wagering was on a small, friendly level. One day he bet a dollar that he could strike out Vince DiMaggio four times in one game. Dean struck him out the first three times up, but on the fourth, the eldest DiMaggio brother lifted a foul pop behind the plate. As catcher Bruce Ogrodowski prepared to catch the ball, Dean raced in from the mound screaming, "Drop it, drop it!" The stunned rookie catcher let it fall, and Dean returned to the mound and struck out Vince for the fourth time.

There were hundreds of similar Dean legends, but the DiMaggio story is generally believed to hold more weight than most.

In 1935 Paul Dean won 19 games for the second successive year, and brother Diz contributed 28 victories, again leading the league with 182 strikeouts. Unfortunately, the Cubs staged a late spurt to beat the Cardinals out of the pennant.

The brothers' partnership came to a close in 1936 when Paul experienced arm trouble. He never again won more than four games in a single season. Dizzy, however, led the National League in games (51) and innings (315) and posted a 24–13 record. He was the starting and winning pitcher in the 1936 All-Star game, hurling three shutout innings.

When he was named to the 1937 All-Star team, Dizzy was inclined to pass it up and go fishing, but his wife Pat urged him to play, telling him that he owed it to baseball. Dizzy started the game and had two outs in the third inning when Lou Gehrig homered. That brought up the Indians' Earl Averill, who lined a shot that struck Dizzy's foot. Dean retrieved the ball and threw Averill out, but his big toe had been broken.

It was not the broken toe that ended Dizzy's great career. Rather, it was his own insistence, against almost everyone's advice, on pitching with the toe in a splint. The injury forced Dean to alter his delivery to favor the ailing foot and to stride unnaturally. Sure enough, while he was pitching soon after the All-Star game, Dean felt a pop in his right arm. That was the end of his fastball.

Dizzy finished the 1937 season with a 13–10 record. Three days before the start of the 1938 season, he was traded to the Cubs for three players and $185,000. Despite his lame arm, he pitched 13 games

for Chicago that year, posting a 7–1 record, a 1.80 ERA, and walking only 8 batters in 75 innings. In the 1938 World Series, he pitched two games for the Cubs, allowing six runs in eight innings. Dean was only 27 years old, but he would never again be a big winner.

In 1939 Dizzy compiled a 6–4 record in 96 innings, and in 1940 he posted a 3–3 mark in just 54 innings. He should have been approaching his peak, but instead he was nearing his end. Dizzy went to Tulsa to finish out the 1940 season, recording an 8–8 mark. Returning to the Cubs in 1941, he pitched only one inning, was released, and then signed as a coach on May 14. Two months later, he accepted a job broadcasting Cardinals and Browns games on a St. Louis radio station. With his quick wit and misuse of grammar ("the runner slud into second") Dizzy became a well-known and popular announcer. He reached national fame on television in the 1950s, doing network telecasts of the Game of the Week and many commercials. His weight, which had been around 200 pounds as a player, soared to almost 300 as a broadcaster, and he was easily recognizable both by voice and appearance.

On the final day of the 1947 season, Dizzy pitched four shutout innings for the Browns as part of a promotional stunt. His major league record for just eight full seasons and parts of four others was 150–83, a .644 won-lost percentage.

Retiring from a full-time broadcasting job in the late 1960s, Dizzy and his wife lived comfortably in Wiggins, Mississippi. Dean was elected to the Hall of Fame in 1953.

On July 17, 1974, he suffered a heart attack in Reno, Nevada, and died at the age of 63.

JAY HANNA DEAN

St. Louis (N.L.) 1930, 1932–1937
Chicago (N.L.) 1938–1941
St. Louis (A.L.) 1947

G	IP	W	L	Pct.	H	R	ER	SO	BB	ERA
317	1966	150	83	.644	1921	776	663	1155	458	3.04

(Above) Dean, announcing for a St. Louis radio station, where with his boisterous good humor he continued to delight baseball fans long after his playing days were over. Later, a generation of fans, who never saw him play, loved Dean as a television personality. (Opposite page) The famous form of the great Dizzy Dean is demonstrated as he neared the end of his career.

Ed Delahanty (1867-1903)

One of the finest hitters of the nineteenth century, Big Ed Delahanty holds the distinction of being the only player to win batting championships in both the American and National Leagues. His death, which occurred while he was still an active player, ended a career in which Ed compiled a .346 lifetime batting average—a figure surpassed only by Ty Cobb, Rogers Hornsby, and Joe Jackson.

Edward James Delahanty was born on October 31, 1867, in Cleveland, Ohio, of French-Irish ancestry. The family name had originally been "de la Hante." Ed was one of seven boys and two girls. Four of Ed's brothers reached the big leagues, giving the Delahanty Family the distinction of being the only family to produce five major leaguers.

Bill Delahanty was drafted by Brooklyn, but he never reached the big leagues due to an injury. Tom Delahanty played 19 games for Philadelphia, Cleveland, Pittsburgh, and Louisville between 1894 and 1897, batting .239. Joe Delahanty played 269 games for the St. Louis Cardinals between 1907 and 1909, batting .238. Jim Delahanty had a 13-year career (1901–1913) with 8 clubs, batted .283 lifetime, and led the Detroit Tigers with a .346 average in the 1909 World Series. Frank Delahanty played for four clubs between 1905 and 1915, totaling 287 games and batting .226.

Ed was the oldest brother and the most successful on the field. A sandlot star in Cleveland, he left home in 1887 to play ball for Mansfield of the Ohio State League, telling his parents that he could earn $3000 a year playing baseball. They did not believe him, but he eventually went on to earn that and more.

At Mansfield, playing second and first, the righthanded-hitting Delahanty batted .355 in 73 games. He joined the Wheeling team of the Tri-State League in 1888 and was easily the best hitter there. Harry Wright, manager of the Philadelphia Phillies of the National League, paid Wheeling $1900 for Ed's contract. At the age of 20, Delahanty was a big leaguer.

Ed did not have a fast start in Philadelphia. After having batted .408 at Wheeling, he hit only .228 in 74 games for the Phillies while playing mostly second base. But in 1889 Ed began to find his form and batted .293. He developed a style of "bad ball" hitting, frequently standing on his toes and reaching out for near-wild pitches, punching hits all over the field. At 5'10" and 170 pounds, Delahanty was unusually strong for his era and was promptly labeled "Big Ed." Fans and players usually referred to him simply as "Del."

Ed joined the Players' Brotherhood League in 1890, banding with many of the more established stars in the rebel cause. He played for Cleveland, batted .296, and became a full-time outfielder. He also recorded one of his biggest days at bat when, on June 2, he went 6-for-6 against Chicago's Mark Baldwin. Included in the six hits were three singles, two doubles, and a triple. Four years later, on June 16, 1894, Delahanty again achieved a 6-for-6 performance, this time against a pair of Cincinnati pitchers. He thus became one of only five players in baseball history to record a pair of 6-for-6 days.

The Players' League folded after one season, and Ed rejoined the Phillies, still seeking the form which would make him one of the most feared batsmen of his day. But Delahanty batted a meager .250 in 1891, and it was not until 1892 that he finally reached the .300 mark, hitting .313 with a league-leading 33 doubles.

Ed was surrounded by great teammates during the 1892 season. Roger Connor, Sam Thompson, Billy Hamilton, Gus Weyking, and Tim Keefe also wore Philadelphia uniforms.

Firmly settled in the outfield, Ed had his first great season at bat in 1893 when he recorded a .371 batting average and led the National League with 19 home runs, a sensational total for the dead-ball era. Only five players up to that point had ever hit more homers in a single season.

In 1894 Ed posted his first of two .400 seasons. He was also one of only eight men in baseball history to twice reach the .400 mark. But the .400 average was not sufficient to lead the league. In fact, Ed placed only fourth that year, trailing Hugh Duffy, Tuck Turner, and Sam Thompson. Turner and Thompson were teammates of Ed's, and Philadelphia recorded a team batting average of .349 for the season.

Fans loved to come out and watch Ed's long-ball hitting. Once he broke a somewhat weakened baseball in two when he made contact with it. In 1892 the St. Louis third baseman, George Pinckney, anticipating a bunt, was felled by a Delahanty line drive that broke his ankle.

Ed hit .399 in 1895, leading the league with 47 doubles and, according to some, topping the league in pints of beer consumed. In 1896 he batted .394 and led the league with 13 homers and 42 doubles. On July 13, 1896, Big Ed Delahanty became the second player in baseball history to blast four home runs in a single game. All the homers occurred with Chicago's Adonis Terry pitching, and Ed's performance drove the fans wild with excitement. With the fences distant, all were inside-the-park homers. In the first inning, Ed belted a homer to left. In the third, he lined a single over short. In the fifth he homered to right, and in the seventh he homered to center. When Delahanty stepped to the plate in the ninth, the fans were screaming, and the center fielder had moved back to a distance of almost 500 feet, bringing a smile to Ed's face. He proceeded to rip the pitch deep to right-center for his fourth homer.

The following year Big Ed batted .377 and recorded 10 consecutive hits over a two-game period on July 13 and 14. After slipping to an average of .335 in 1898, Delahanty returned in 1899 to lead the league with a .408 batting average, including league-leading figures in hits (234) and doubles (56).

Ed and teammate Napoleon Lajoie held out the following season, each seeking more than the $2400 maximum salary allowed by league rule. Eventually, Delahanty received $3000 and Lajoie $2600, although Lajoie was told he received the same amount as Ed. Delahanty was now a 12-year veteran, and he had finally fulfilled his boast to his parents that he would earn $3000 in baseball. Big Ed batted .319 in 1900 and .357 in 1901, continuing at the $3000 salary figure. The American League had entered the scene the previous year, and Ed jumped to the Washington Senators for the 1902 season at a salary of $4000.

Ed immediately found a home in the American League, batting .376 to capture the batting title. At the close of the season,

the Giants' John McGraw made Ed a substantial offer to return to the National League as a New Yorker. McGraw even advanced Ed $4500.

New York was where the money was, and Ed was thrilled all winter awaiting 1903. But as the season approached, the two leagues settled their differences and agreed to respect the reserve clause and each other's players. Delahanty was ordered to return to Washington and to refund McGraw's $4500. Most of it had already been lost at the race tracks.

Delahanty was furious. He swore that he would never play for Washington again; he went so far as to seek a job in the outlaw California State League. Eventually, but still protesting, Big Ed joined the Senators for the 1903 season.

Although he was hitting close to .340, Delahanty was deeply in debt trying to repay McGraw. He also had marital difficulties and drank excessively. Late in June, his manager, Tom Loftus, suspended him.

Disheartened, Ed accompanied the team to Detroit, but from there he took the Michigan Central Railroad toward New York in order to visit his wife. He departed on the 4:25 P.M. train and headed for the dining car, where he consumed five drinks and brooded over his troubles. Eventually, he became rowdy and boisterous. The train's

conductor tried reasoning with Ed, but to no avail. At Fort Erie, Ontario, on the Canadian side of the International Bridge over the Niagara River, a group of trainmen threw Ed off. Weeping and enraged, Ed began to chase the train across the bridge. In his drunken state, he had trouble negotiating the railroad ties. At the center of the bridge, a railman with a lantern warned him to get back, the drawbridge was opening. But Ed fought with the man, and when the scuffle had ended, Delahanty had slipped through the ties and fallen into the dark Niagara River. He was swept over Niagara Falls. The date was July 2, 1903.

There was no sign of Ed for a week. His teammates were certain that he would appear, as did his wife. Eventually, Ed's body was found mangled against a wharf 20 miles south of the bridge. He was identified by his dental records.

Big Ed Delahanty was named to the Hall of Fame in 1945.

EDWARD JAMES DELAHANTY

Philadelphia (N.L.) 1888–1889, 1891–1901
Cleveland (P.L.) 1890
Washington (A.L.) 1902–1903

G	AB	R	H	2B	3B	HR	RBI	Avg.
1825	7493	1596	2593	508	182	98	1464	.346

Delahanty in the field. Associates described his fielding ability as graceful and powerful, but the fans came to see him hit. Twice he went 6 for 6, once he blasted 4 home runs in one game, and once he even broke a baseball in half when he connected.

Bill Dickey (b.1907)

Throughout the 1930s, Bill Dickey and Mickey Cochrane vied for honors as the best catcher in the American League. Dickey had the advantage of being a member of the New York Yankees, playing on eight pennant-winning clubs.

William Malcolm Dickey was born on June 6, 1907, in Bastrop, Louisiana, one of seven children. His father, a railroad worker, moved the family to Kensett, Arkansas, in 1914, and Bill remained an Arkansas denizen thereafter.

Bill had an older brother, Gus, who played semipro ball, and a younger brother, George, who caught 170 games for the Red Sox and the White Sox between 1935 and 1947. Bill attended high school in Searcy, Arkansas, where he played the infield and pitched for the school team in addition to the Kensett town team. He enrolled in Little Rock College and joined the baseball team as a pitcher and catcher. At 6'1½" and 185 pounds, Dickey had an unusual build for a catcher, being somewhat tall and lanky, but he possessed great agility, a strong throwing arm, and keen baseball sense.

While substituting for a college teammate on a town team in Hot Springs, Bill was spotted by Lena Blackburne, manager of the Little Rock team in the Southern Association. Blackburne, who would later manage the White Sox (1928–1929), signed Dickey several days later, and Bill caught his first three professional games at the close of the 1925 season. He collected 3 hits in 10 times at bat.

In 1926 Dickey was optioned to the Muskogee, Oklahoma team in the Western Association, batting .283 in 61 games. Recalled by Little Rock, Bill compiled a .391 average in 21 games, but he was again optioned for the 1927 season, this time to the Jackson, Mississippi team in the Cotton States League. At Jackson he batted .297 in 101 games, leading the league's receivers in both putouts and assists.

Still not considered to be of major league caliber, Bill returned to Little Rock in 1928. Although he was hitting .300 after 60 games, most clubs assumed he was strictly bound to the Chicago White Sox, who had an informal working agreement with Little Rock. However, the Yankees were never a team to take such suppositions for facts. Therefore, they sent scout Johnny Nee to observe Dickey, and when the report was favorable, they purchased him. Bill played three games at Buffalo, and then finished the 1928 season with the Yankees, participating in 10 games.

Bill joined one of baseball's legendary teams. The Yankees of that era were the "Murderers' Row" club, strong at every

position except catcher. The infield featured Lou Gehrig, Tony Lazzeri, Mark Koenig, and Joe Dugan; the outfield was composed of Babe Ruth, Earle Combs, and Bob Meusel; and the pitching staff included George Pipgras, Waite Hoyt, Bob Shawkey, Herb Pennock, and Wilcy Moore. Dickey completed the lineup, beginning a chain of outstanding Yankee catchers that later included Yogi Berra, Elston Howard, and Thurman Munson. And the Yankees were always considered a strong club because of an able field leader behind the plate.

In his rookie season, Bill played 130 games, batting .324 with 10 home runs. It was the first of 13 consecutive seasons in which he would appear behind the bat in more than 100 games, a record for catchers. He never played another position in the majors.

Bill hit .339 in 1930, the year in which Shawkey replaced the deceased Miller Huggins as Yankee manager. In 1931 Joe McCarthy assumed the managerial duties. McCarthy established the "Yankee image" of businesslike efficiency on the playing field and a highly professional demeanor off the field. Gehrig and the soft-spoken Dickey, close friends and two of the club's biggest run producers on the field, were the two who most exemplified "class" off the field. Joe DiMaggio, a few years younger, soon joined them.

Bill's first pennant experience came in his fourth year with the club, when he batted .310 for the season and then .438 in the World Series sweep of the Cubs. But for Bill, the year was marked by a 30-day suspension for breaking the jaw of Washington's Carl Reynolds in a one-punch battle at home plate. Although the Yankees fell from first in 1933 and 1934, Bill's contribution was noteworthy as he batted .318 and .322. But along with the remainder of the club, Dickey slumped in 1935, batting under .300 for the only time in his first 11 major league seasons (.279).

The Yankees bounced back in 1936 to capture the pennant. Dickey enjoyed a .362 season, the third highest mark in the American League. He hit 22 home runs and drove in 107 runs, the first of four consecutive seasons in which he had more than 100 runs batted in. In the World Series, Bill hit a disappointing .120 as the Yankees defeated the Giants in six games.

Dickey also had a superlative year in 1937 with a .332 batting average, 29 home runs, and 133 runs batted in. In 1938 Bill played 132 games, batting .313 (his career average) with 27 home runs and 115 runs batted in. Again it was a pennant-winning season for the Yankees, and Bill batted .400 in the World Series victory over Chicago.

Dickey enjoyed his last big season in

It's all over for runner Danny Litwhiler of the St. Louis Cardinals as he heads straight into the outstretched arms of Bill Dickey, who has the ball in his right hand. Umpire Ed Rommel watches the play. Litwhiler had tried to score from first on a double in the second inning of the first game of the 1943 World Series.

Yankee catcher Bill Dickey in action. Dickey's entire major league career was with the Yanks, and he did his share toward boosting the "Murderer's Row" team into nine World Series during his tenure.

1939, batting .302 with 24 homers and 105 RBIs. Again, the Yankees captured the pennant and the World Series.

By 1940 the even-tempered, lefthanded-hitting Dickey began to experience the effects of his considerable playing time. His batting average dropped to .247 that year, and in 1941 he caught 100 games for the final time, batting .284. The Yankees won pennants in 1941, 1942, and 1943, using Bill as a part-time catcher the latter two seasons with good results (.295 and .351). In 1943, at the age of 36, Dickey smacked a big two-run homer in the sixth inning of the fifth game of the World Series to give the Yankees a 2–0 victory over the Cardinals and the World Championship. After the Series, Bill enlisted in the navy, spending 1944 and 1945 in the Pacific theater.

Rejoining the Yankees in 1946, Bill found himself the backup catcher to Aaron Robinson. On May 24, McCarthy resigned as manager and Dickey was hurriedly appointed his replacement. Bill received the job because of his seniority and the general respect he enjoyed among the players, but he did not particularly enjoy his duties. Although he achieved a 57-48 record as manager, Dickey was not disappointed when Johnny Neun replaced him on September 12 to finish out the schedule. The Yankees finished third.

With his playing career now behind him, Bill returned home to manage the Little Rock team in 1947. At season's end the team had posted a 51–103 record, and Dickey never attempted to manage thereafter. He did play his final eight professional games that season, batting .333.

Retiring from baseball in 1948, Bill became employed at Stephens, Inc., a Little Rock investment firm. His brother, George, ran the company, and the two did quite well over the years in the selling of securities. Bill remained active in the company until 1972.

Dickey reappeared in a Yankee uniform in 1949, when Casey Stengel, in his first year as manager, brought Bill to New York to work with Yogi Berra behind the plate. Dickey remained on the coaching staff for Stengel through 1957. As a member of the Yankees, Bill earned eight additional World Series shares.

Bill scouted for the Yankees in 1958 and 1959, and then returned as a coach for part of the 1960 season.

Dickey was elected to the Hall of Fame in 1954. In 1972 the Yankees retired uniform No. 8, which Dickey and later Berra had worn, in a ceremony at Yankee Stadium.

WILLIAM MALCOLM DICKEY

New York (A.L.) 1928–1946

G	AB	R	H	2B	3B	HR	RBI	Avg.
1789	6300	930	1969	343	72	202	1209	.313

Joe DiMaggio (b. 1914)

Yankee center fielder Joe DiMaggio was the most graceful and admired player of his day. His popularity grew to heroic proportions long after his playing career ended.

Joe was born of Italian immigrant parents on November 25, 1914, in Martinez, California. The San Francisco area remained his home during and after his baseball career. On his birth certificate, the name read Giuseppe Paolo DeMaggio, Jr., but it became Joseph Paul DiMaggio upon his entrance into school.

The DiMaggio family consisted of five boys and four girls. Two of Joe's brothers, Dominic and Vince, also played in the major leagues. Dominic became a star with the Boston Red Sox between 1940 and 1953. Vince had an unspectacular 10-season career with 5 National League clubs between 1937 and 1946.

During Joe's infancy, the DiMaggios moved to a small home near Fisherman's Wharf in San Francisco. The DiMaggio brothers spent many of their free hours playing ball together. Joe attended Galileo High School, but he left after one year to work in a cannery. In addition, Joe also earned a slight salary playing semipro ball as a shortstop and first baseman.

At the age of 17, the San Francisco Missions of the Pacific Coast League offered DiMaggio a contract. But Vince was already playing for the rival San Francisco Seals, and Joe decided to join his brother. Joe made his professional debut at the close of the 1932 season, playing three games and batting .222.

DiMaggio returned to the Seals in 1933 at a salary of $250 per month. Tall (6'2") and thin, Joe had been awkward at shortstop; now he was repositioned to the outfield. His performance in the 1933 season was one of the finest ever recorded in the Pacific Coast League. Joe hit safely in 61 consecutive games, an all-time record for professional baseball. He batted .340, drove in a league-leading 169 runs, and banged out 259 hits while playing 187 games in the expanded PCL schedule. San Francisco toasted the new hero of the Bay Area.

In 1934 Joe batted .341 in 101 games, but he suffered a knee injury that diminished the interest of major league teams. Both Boston and Pittsburgh backed off; the New York Yankees, encouraged by their western scouts, Bill Essick and Joe Devine, became the only bidders. Recognizing that the injured knee made him a questionable prospect, the Yankees purchased Joe on November 22, 1934, for $25,000 and five minor league players. He was immediately optioned to San Francisco for the 1935 season so that he could continue to receive medical treatment for his knee.

Joe batted a sparkling .398 in 1935, with

34 home runs and 154 runs batted in. Invited to the Yankee spring training in 1936, Joe drove from San Francisco to St. Petersburg with fellow Bay residents Tony Lazzeri and Frank Crosetti, eager to show the major leaguers his skills.

Sportswriters placed considerable pressure on Joe, billing him as a new Babe Ruth since Ruth had left the Yankees just a year and a half earlier. But Joe's big-league career started disappointingly when his instep was accidentally burned during heat treatment for a twisted ankle. As a result, he did not make his debut until May 3, 1936, at which time nearly 25,000 Italian residents of New York turned out at Yankee Stadium waving Italian flags.

Joe opened his career in right field, but one month later, after Ben Chapman was traded to Washington, he moved to center. His rookie year brought a .323 average, 29 home runs and 125 runs batted in. He led the league with 15 triples, displaying speed, power, a strong throwing arm, and the ability to hit in the clutch. In addition, the quiet youngster came to exemplify what was called "Yankee class," joining Lou Gehrig and Bill Dickey as those most representative of the kind of style that manager Joe McCarthy wanted to display.

In the 1936 World Series—the first of 10 in which he would play—Joe made one of his many memorable catches in center field. In the second game against the Giants, won by the Yanks, 18–4, Joe caught the final out in deep center field at the Polo Grounds, and he then raced up the clubhouse stairs without breaking stride. The surest-handed fielder in the game, Joe made a similar catch in 1939 behind the flagpole in Yankee Stadium, hauling in a tremendous drive by Detroit's Hank Greenberg.

Joe's roommate was pitcher Lefty Gomez, an outspoken, happy-living sort, who was a perfect complement to the shy, uncertain DiMaggio. The two remained close friends, and Lefty could always be counted on to bring a smile to Joe's face.

In 1937 Joe led the league with 46 home runs while batting .346 and driving in 167 runs. It was a career high in homers for Joe, who as a righthanded hitter was always bothered by the depth of left field at Yankee Stadium. Despite that obstacle, his 361 career home runs placed him fifth on the major's all-time list at the time of his retirement.

Joe held out during the first two weeks of the regular season in 1938, finally settling for $25,000. He frequently found himself having to argue for a higher salary, but in 1949, he became the American League's first $100,000 player.

Joe batted .324 in 1938. The following year he hit .381, winning his first batting championship and the league's Most Valuable Player award. He had a fine opportunity to reach the .400 plateau that year, but eye trouble in the final three weeks dropped him from a high of .412 in early September.

Following the 1939 season, Joe married Dorothy Arnold. A son, Joe, Jr., was born two years later. The marriage failed after Joe's return from World War II, but he remained devoted to the child.

In 1940 Joe captured his second successive batting championship with a .352 average, but for the first time since he had joined the Yankees the team failed to win the pennant. The 1941 season proved the most memorable of Joe's career. He batted safely in 56 consecutive games, an all-time major league record. His streak, during which he hit .406, ran from May 15 to July 17. Cleveland pitchers Al Smith and Jim Bagby stopped the streak with the help of two great plays at third base by Ken Keltner. Joe quickly ran up another quick streak of 17 games. He won his second

MVP award that year, despite a .406 season by Boston's Ted Williams.

After batting .305 in 1942, Joe was drafted into the army. During his three years in the service, he played ball at home and in the Pacific. But those years away from professional baseball at the peak of his career definitely depleted his lifetime statistics.

Joe returned to the Yankees in 1946, batting .290. In 1947 he earned his third MVP award, hitting .315 in a pennant-winning season.

A hero throughout the country at the time, DiMaggio was immortalized in a song, "Joltin' Joe DiMaggio," recorded by the Les Brown Orchestra. "The Yankee Clipper," as he had come to be known, had another great season in 1948, winning the home run title (39) and RBI crown (155), and batting .320. But during the season a bone spur developed in his right heel, causing intense pain and eventually

(Above) Teammates applaud Joe DiMaggio, whose hit against the Senators had just made it 42 consecutive games in which he hit safely, shattering a record. DiMaggio's hitting streak eventually totalled 56 games between May 15 and July 17, 1941. (At left) Staff Sgt. DiMaggio disembarks from a Navy transport in Hawaii during World War II. (Opposite page) The toast of San Francisco, 19-year-old Joe slugs one for the San Francisco Seals in 1934. Although bothered by a knee injury, DiMaggio was purchased that year by the Yankees for $25,000 and five major league players.

driving Joe into retirement.

DiMaggio missed the first two months of the 1949 season as a result of the heel ailment, returning to the lineup in Boston in mid-June. In his first games for manager Casey Stengel, Joe had what he later called his most satisfying series. He belted four home runs in three games, earning the cheers of the Fenway Park fans.

At the end of the season, the Yankees staged a "Joe DiMaggio Day" in Yankee Stadium. Despite a bad virus, he helped the team beat Boston that day to gain another pennant.

The painful heel continued to affect Joe in 1950, but he managed to bat .301 and belt 32 homers. In 1951, with Mickey Mantle having arrived as his likely successor, Joe batted only .263 with 12 home runs. Announcing his retirement at the age of 37, he turned down a fourth consecutive $100,000 contract for 1952. "When baseball is no longer fun," he said, "it's no longer a game." The Yankees retired his uniform, No. 5.

Joe hosted the Yankees' pregame television shows in 1952. He had developed poise and charm, and had become increasingly handsome with the passing of the years. In later years, he was frequently called on to make television commercials.

In 1954 Joe married Marilyn Monroe, the voluptuous Hollywood actress. Although the marriage lasted only nine months, the two remained very close until Marilyn's suicide in 1962. Her death affected Joe deeply, and he became a decidedly introverted person in his middle age.

In 1968 the Oakland A's owner, Charles O. Finley, persuaded Joe to serve as batting coach and vice-president of the club. Joe spent two years with the A's and received some credit for aiding in the development of Reggie Jackson. Joe retained an interest in a family restaurant in San Francisco, and he devoted his free time to golf and public relations.

Elected to the Hall of Fame in 1955, Joe always remained the featured attraction of old timers' gatherings. In 1969 he was named the "Greatest Living Player" in a centennial poll of sportswriters. In 1979 he was named to the Baltimore Orioles' board of directors after his friend, Edward Bennett Williams, purchased the franchise.

JOSEPH PAUL DiMAGGIO

New York (A.L.) 1936–1951

G	AB	R	H	2B	3B	HR	RBI	Avg.
1736	6821	1390	2214	389	131	361	1537	.325

DiMaggio watches the ball soar over the fence. His tremendous follow-through shows in this picture of the great Yankee, who was renowned not only as a hitter but also as the surest-handed outfielder in the game.

Hugh Duffy (1866-1954)

Hugh Duffy who spent 68 years in professional baseball, accomplished the feat of hitting .438 in 1894, the highest average ever recorded in baseball under current rules.

Duffy was born of Irish parents on November 26, 1866, in River Point, Rhode Island. As a youngster, he worked in a blue-dye shop, where the labor involved in lifting heavy masses of wet cloth out of machines developed great strength in his wrists. In his teens, Duffy journeyed to Jewett City, Connecticut, to work in a mill, augmenting his salary by playing semipro baseball on weekends for $30 per month. On Sundays, he would wear a baseball uniform under his church clothing, and head for the baseball field after attending morning worship. In 1885 Duffy increased his earnings to $50 per month with a team in Winstead, Connecticut.

Hugh signed his first professional contract with Hartford of the Eastern League in 1886. He appeared in seven games and compiled a .278 batting average. Although a pitcher and shortstop during his amateur and semipro days, he now played right field.

Duffy transferred to Springfield in 1887, and he was batting .350 after 17 games when he was scouted by Salem manager George Fessenden. Fessenden bought Duffy's contract from Springfield for $25, believing that he had picked up a great bargain. But when Salem owner George Vickery found out about the purchase, he was enraged. Telling Duffy that the price was ludicrous, Vickery gave him a contract for $5 a week plus board. The contract included the provision that if Duffy failed to have a good week, the $5 would be withheld.

Playing under this stringent provision, Duffy, in his first game at Salem (New England League), committed five errors and struck out three times. Vickery immediately fired the 20-year-old Duffy, and then also sold the club that same night. The new owners gave Hugh another chance, but he wound up the year at Lowell in the same league. His batting average for Salem and Lowell was .428, with 16 home runs in 78 games.

Duffy was earning a mere $100 per month at Lowell when Tim Murnane offered him $1200 to play for Cap Anson in Chicago. A better offer soon came from Mike Kelly in Boston, forcing Murnane to increase his bid to $2000, with $500 in advance. Duffy accepted the contract and reported to Anson in Chicago, only to find that the legendary "Cap" was disappointed by his new player. "We've got a bat boy—what are you doing here?" he asked Duffy. "I'm your new outfielder," Hugh replied, but Anson remained unaffected.

He considered Duffy (who stood 5'7" and weighed 168 pounds) too small and light for major league baseball. Duffy sat on the bench for the next two months.

In July, right fielder Billy Sunday, later the famous evangelist, was sold to Pittsburgh, and Duffy finally received his chance. He responded with a .282 batting average, including seven home runs, four of which were struck before Duffy collected his first double or triple.

Anson drilled Duffy constantly and repositioned him in center field, where Hugh established a reputation as one of the better defensive players in the game. At bat, Duffy developed a style of lifting his front leg before hitting the ball. He became a good place hitter who could unload the long ball as frequently as any player despite his small stature.

When asked about his hitting technique in later years, Duffy could only reply, "It comes natural. You just walk up there and hit!"

As a full-time player with Chicago in 1889, Hugh led the National League in games played (136) and times at bat (584) while hitting .312.

The Players League was formed in 1890, and Hugh was one of many players to jump from the National League. It was a rather short jump: Duffy merely went crosstown to play right field for Charles Comiskey's team, where he batted .328. Duffy established the unique distinction of compiling a lifetime .300-plus batting average in four different major leagues.

When the Players League collapsed after one season of operation, Hugh signed in 1891 with Boston of the American Association, a major league. He was named captain of the "Reds" and batted .341, second in the league to teammate Dan Brouthers. The Reds won 93, lost only 42, and were the Association champions that season.

The American Association folded after the 1891 season, consolidating with the National League to form a 12-team circuit. Duffy shifted to the Boston Beaneaters, where he would spend the next nine seasons.

As center fielder and captain of the Beaneaters in 1892, Duffy joined right fielder Tommy McCarthy, another 5'7" New Englander, to form Boston's "Heavenly Twins." Great friends on and off the field, Duffy and McCarthy excelled in the execution of the hit-and-run play. Duffy was also an excellent base runner. In fact, he stole 597 bases during his career, with a high of 83 in 1891.

Boston captured the 1892 postseason

Hugh Duffy played on two Chicago teams and managed one during his baseball career that spanned 68 years and took him to teams in both the American and National Leagues as well as the ill-fated Players League. Until a year before his death at 87, he travelled south every spring with the Red Sox.

playoff with Cleveland, five games to none, with one tie; Duffy led all batters with 12 hits. In 1893 he played on his third successive pennant winner, while leading the National League with a .378 batting average and 149 runs scored.

In 1894 the rules were changed to move the pitcher's mound from 50 feet to home plate to its present distance of 60 feet, 6 inches. The alteration in rules naturally hurt pitchers, who had to readjust the speed and distance of their deliveries. As a result, 1894 was a hitter's year; the league batting average was .309. But the player who enjoyed the greatest success in the National League was Duffy. Compiling a 26-game hitting streak along the way, Hugh batted .438, leading the league with 236 hits, 50 doubles, and 18 home runs. The average, unmatched since, was bested only by an 1887 figure (James O'Neill of the American Association hit .492). Duffy's figure actually remains the higher, for in the 1887 season walks were counted as hits.

Toward the tail end of the 1894 season, Duffy knew only that he was leading the league in hitting. He played the final game of the schedule rather than take his teammates' advice to ride the bench in order to protect the title. Duffy collected five more hits that day.

"They only published averages once a month in those days," he later recalled, "and I didn't know whether I'd hit .428 or .438, but I knew I'd won the title."

His teammates gave him a watch charm with five diamonds, and fans throughout New England showered him with gifts. Hugh had become a very significant figure in Boston sports. Despite his superlative year, Duffy's salary for 1895 rose only $12.50 a month to the National League maximum of $2400 a season.

Hugh remained with Boston through the 1900 season, adding four more years of .300 or better averages but failing to capture another batting title. He played for two more pennant winners, the 1897 and 1898 teams.

Duffy was then one of the pioneers who formed the American League in 1901. Hugh and his brother-in-law met in Philadelphia to convince Ban Johnson that Boston would be an opportune location for an American League franchise. Duffy even played a major part in selecting the Huntington Avenue site for the Boston ball park. Eventually, Duffy was given the managing job for the Milwaukee franchise. He became a popular figure in the city and the German residents came to call him "Duffmeier."

Hugh remained in Milwaukee even when the city returned to Western League competition in 1902–1903 after the American

League club had shifted to St. Louis. In 1904 Duffy acquired the job as Connie Mack's Philadelphia rival, managing the Phillies for three seasons. His team finished in eighth place the first year and fourth the following two seasons. He played his final National League games those years, winding up with a .330 career batting average.

Duffy had saved his money wisely and owned considerable real estate. But his passion for baseball tied him to the game for the remainder of his life. He was the owner and manager of Providence in the Eastern League from 1907 to 1909, playing 37 games in his final season at the age of 41.

Hugh managed the Chicago White Sox to sixth- and fourth-place finishes in 1910 and 1911, then returned to manage in Milwaukee of the American Association in 1912. Subsequently, he purchased the Portland team of the New England League and managed it for four years starting in 1913. In 1917, 1918, and 1919, Duffy served as a scout for the Boston Braves, while also serving as a college baseball coach, first at Boston College and later at Harvard. In 1920 he managed Toronto of the International League.

A man who seldom drank and whose greatest profanity was "by jingoes," Duffy always found a place in baseball. The Red Sox hired him as manager for 1921 and 1922, shortly after they had broken up a fine club by selling Babe Ruth and other stars to the New York Yankees. The Red Sox finished fifth and eighth under Hugh's tenure. Two years after being fired as manager, Duffy returned to the Red Sox as a scout. He served the organization as director of its tryout camp and baseball school, and as a general goodwill ambassador. Until 1953, he traveled south with the team each spring, putting on a uniform every day.

Duffy was inducted into the Hall of Fame in 1945. He died on October 19, 1954, in Allston, Massachusetts, at the age of 87. His 68 years in professional baseball is a figure surpassed only by Connie Mack.

HUGH DUFFY

Chicago (N.L.) 1888–1889
Chicago (P.L.) 1890
Boston (A.A.) 1891
Boston (N.L.) 1892–1900
Milwaukee (A.L.) 1901
Philadelphia (N.L.) 1904–1906

G	AB	R	H	2B	3B	HR	RBI	Avg.
1722	6999	1545	2307	310	117	103	1299	.330

Billy Evans (1884-1956)

Billy Evans was active in professional baseball for more than 45 years as an umpire, author, and club executive.

William George Evans was born on February 10, 1884, in Chicago. The Evans family moved to Duquesne, Pennsylvania, and then to Youngstown, Ohio, while Billy was still a child. Although the family was not wealthy, considerable attention was given to ensure the proper education of the children. Billy's father, the superintendent of the Ohio Steel Works, enrolled his son in Rayen Prep. Young Billy's grades were sufficient for him to gain acceptance to Cornell University as a law student. At Cornell, Billy participated in football, track, boxing, and baseball, playing for coach Hughey Jennings, the famed Baltimore Oriole infielder.

After two years at Cornell, Billy was forced to leave school when his father died. A friend of his father's gave him a job as a reporter and jack-of-all-trades for the Youngstown *Vindicator.* It was not long before Billy became sports editor of the paper at a salary of $18 per week.

One of Billy's regular assignments was to cover the Youngstown games in the Ohio Protective Association, a semipro circuit. Reporting to the park one day in 1903, he discovered that no umpire had attended. Youngstown manager Marty Hogan and visiting Homestead manager Charley McCloskey approached Evans and requested his services. Billy was not enthused, but when he was offered $15 for the day, he accepted the job. Several times during the next two years, he umpired games, supplementing his income from the newspaper.

In 1905 Billy broke into organized baseball, joining the umpiring staff of the Ohio-Pennsylvania League. Late in the season, working a Niles-Youngstown game with two out in the ninth, a walk would enable Niles to tie the score while an out would give the game to Youngstown. The pitcher broke off a sharp curveball, and Evans courageously called it strike three, precipitating a riot on the field that required police protection for poor Billy.

One individual in the stands that day agreed with the call and thought that he had seen an excellent umpiring job under difficult circumstances. The man was Jimmy McAleer, manager of the St. Louis Browns, who happened to be on a scouting assignment that very day. McAleer soon recommended Evans to American League president Ban Johnson.

Johnson arranged for a meeting with young Evans, and the two were duly impressed with each other. Evans always held Johnson in great esteem, as did most umpires, for he always supported the umps against club owners. Johnson gave Evans a contract for the 1906 season at a salary of $1800. At the age of 22, Evans

became the youngest umpire to reach the major leagues, and the only umpire ever to jump from Class C in the minors directly to the major leagues.

Billy immediately set a new tone for umpires. He was a fastidious dresser, both on and off the field, and a man who avoided fights through his imperturbable manner. When a batter would shout that Evans had missed the pitch by a foot, Billy would point out that the batter had missed the last pitch by a foot and a half. When a pitcher sarcastically asked Evans, "How many pitches are you allowed to miss a game?", Billy calmly replied, "About twelve."

Only once was Billy involved in a fight. The incident involved the fiery Ty Cobb challenging Evans to meet him under the stands to settle a dispute. Billy accepted. Although few witnesses were present, the bout was said to have been fast and brutal, with Cobb winning easily. Neither side reported the incident to the league office.

In Billy's second season as an umpire, a near riot followed a St. Louis-Detroit game, and Billy was struck by a pop bottle thrown from the stands. He suffered a fracture of the skull and was near death for several days in a hospital. The family of the 18-year-old boy who had thrown the bottle remained by Evans's bedside until the crisis passed. Eventually, despite urgings from Ban Johnson, Billy did not press charges, instead permitting the boy to be released in his mother's custody.

In 1910 Billy started a newspaper column. He was the only active baseball figure who wrote a regular column, and eventually it became syndicated to more than 100 newspapers throughout the country. The column proved so successful that in 1920 the Scripps-Howard newspapers talked Evans into leaving his syndicate to become sports editor of Newspaper Enterprise Association. Billy remained in that position from 1920 to 1927, writing 3000 words each day for his "Billy Evans Says" column while remaining an umpire. Occasionally Evans would have a ghost writer do the writing, but usually the words were his own.

Evans frequently wrote for *The Sporting News,* helping to compile their *Knotty Problems of Baseball* book, and wrote what was considered to be the authority on his profession, *Umpiring From the Inside.*

On the field, Billy was credited with instituting the practice of having four umpires on the field during the World Series. It followed a dispute in his first World Series, 1909, when Evans and his partner, Bill Klem, had to ask the bleacher fans in Pittsburgh where a ball had landed. Billy also worked the World Series of 1912, 1915, 1917, 1919, and 1923; the later Series was the first to be played in Yankee Stadium. The 1919 Series between the Chicago "Black Sox" and the Cincinnati Redlegs was marked by charges of a fix. But at no time did gamblers approach Evans, a man noted for his integrity.

A group headed by Alva Bradley bought the Cleveland Indians in November 1927, and offered Evans the new position of general manager. He accepted, terminating his umpiring career after 22 seasons.

Billy remained the Cleveland general manager for eight years. The team finished seventh his first year, and then third three times and fourth four times. During spring training in 1933, when none of the three Cleveland newspapers could afford to send a writer to New Orleans, Billy wrote three stories each day on their behalf.

When the Indians attempted to reduce Billy's salary following the 1935 season, he resigned on November 18. Three months later, the Boston Red Sox hired Evans as farm director. Owner Tom Yawkey and general manager Eddie Collins wanted to establish a strong minor league system, and they believed Evans to be the man for the task. Billy's largest contribution to Boston was his insistence on the purchase of the Louisville franchise in the American Association as a means of obtaining shortstop Pee Wee Reese. The deal was completed in September 1938, but the Red Sox sold Reese to Brooklyn. That action eventually led to Evans's resignation in the fall of 1940.

Billy retired from baseball briefly in 1941 to become general manager of the Cleveland Rams in the National Football League. The job lasted one season, and Evans returned to baseball on December 3, 1942, as president of the Southern Association. Billy observed the rival Texas League fold during the manpower shortage of World War II, but he fought to make his league

financially successful. Evans managed to increase attendance from around 700,000 prior to his arrival to a high of more than two million a year between 1944 and 1946. His determination to speed up the games was said to have been a major factor in making the sport more popular.

While working under a five-year contract in the Southern Association, Billy updated the league's constitution and compiled one of the best record books of any minor league.

On December 14, 1946, Billy returned to the major leagues, accepting a five-year contract with the Detroit Tigers as vice-president and general manager. Twice his clubs finished second to the Yankees, but he failed to produce a pennant winner. A month before his contract expired in 1951, Billy was replaced by long-time Detroit hero Charlie Gehringer. Evans then retired from baseball at the age of 67.

Billy died at his home in Miami on January 23, 1956, at the age of 71. In 1973 he became the third umpire elected to the Hall of Fame, joining Bill Klem and Tom Connolly in the membership.

Umpire Billy Evans watches John "Shane" Evans slide safely as Joe Dugan waits for the relay that came too late. All calls were not so easy. After Evans and his partner Bill Klem had to ask the fans where a ball had landed during the 1909 World Series, Evans insisted that baseball adopt the practice of having four umpires on the field during Series games.

Johnny Evers (1881-1947)

Johnny Evers, middle man of the famous Chicago Cubs Tinker-to-Evers-to-Chance double-play combination, was a scrappy second baseman who played for 5 pennant winners in 16 major league seasons.

John Joseph Evers was born on July 21, 1881, in Troy, New York. Troy was a major league city at the time, with the local National League club boasting such players as Roger Connor, Tim Keefe, Mickey Welch, and Buck Ewing. But the city lost its franchise after the 1882 season and was replaced by the New York club. Evers thus never had ample opportunity to appreciate major league baseball in his hometown.

He would have appreciated it, too, for Johnny was a keen student of the game. Unlike most players, who knew little of baseball's history, Evers made a careful study of the game. When Johnny was a player, he would go to bed at night with a copy of the rule book and the latest issue of *The Sporting News,* looking for whatever edge he could gain. Weighing barely 100 pounds, Johnny needed every advantage.

Evers signed his first contract with the local Troy Cheer-Ups of the New York State League in 1902, receiving $60 per month from club owner Lou Bacon. Late in the season, Chicago Cub manager Frank Selee dispatched a scout to Troy to watch pitcher Alex Hardy, a promising young prospect. The scout was in Troy for only a few days when he received a telegram from Selee: "Lowe broke leg. Bring back infielder too."

Bobby Lowe, the veteran Cub second baseman, had indeed put himself out of action for the remainder of the season. Evers at the time was hitting .285 for Troy, but he had committed 65 errors playing at second and short. Nevertheless, both he and Hardy were purchased from Bacon for $250.

The pair joined the Cubs in Philadelphia on Labor Day. Johnny was given the only available uniform, which was much too large for his 5'9", 105-pound frame. Cub teammates laughed at Evers. At 21, he looked perhaps seven years younger. Evers played both ends of a double header at shortstop that day, but he did not distinguish himself. The players, thinking the little fellow would be killed playing in the majors, would not even allow him to ride the team bus. Johnny had to climb on top of the bus after the game to return to the hotel.

Evers played three games at short and then was moved to second base. On Labor Day, the names Joe Tinker, Johnny Evers, and Frank Chance appeared in a lineup together for the first time.

Tinker, Evers, and Chance were not the greatest double-play combination in baseball history, nor perhaps even in their era. But in 1910, Franklin P. Adams, finishing up a column in the New York *Evening Mail,* wrote "Baseball's Sad Lexicon."

> These are the saddest of possible words—
> Tinker to Evers to Chance
> Trio of Bear Cubs and fleeter than birds—
> Tinker to Evers to Chance
> Thoughtlessly pricking our gonfalon bubble,
> Making a Giant hit into a double,
> Words that are weighty with nothing but trouble—
> Tinker to Evers to Chance.

The poem immortalized the trio in the annals of baseball.

Johnny finished out the 1902 season hitting .225 in 25 games with the Cubs. In 1903, after signing a $100-per-month contract, the hard-nosed Irishman surprised even his teammates by batting .293 and hitting 27 doubles. Evers showed himself to be a pesky hitter, capable of hitting to all fields, but without power. Players labeled him "The Trojan" after his birthplace.

Evers was also known as "The Crab," both for his manner of moving about the infield and for his testy disposition, particularly toward umpires. As a small man, Johnny was constantly battling to get ahead. In 1909 he staged what seemed to be his millionth argument with umpire Bill Klem. Evers challenged Klem to appear at the National League office the following day to settle the dispute. Klem agreed, but Evers wagered Klem $5 that he would not show up. Bill did not appear although Johnny did, and for weeks, every time the two were on the same field, Evers would demand his money. He would scratch a large "5" with his bat in front of the batter's box, and hold up five fingers in Klem's direction whenever he caught his eye. Klem finally paid the debt on a train when he could no longer tolerate such insistence.

Johnny was such an abrasive heckler that even teammate Frank Chance admitted that he would prefer to have Evers playing the outfield. Also, Joe Tinker refused to speak to Johnny for years over a 1905 incident involving the failure of Evers to share a taxi to an exhibition game. Evers's baserunning style, with spikes high and belligerent demeanor, reminded many of Detroit's Ty Cobb.

Chicago captured the 1906 and 1907 pennants, with Evers hitting .255 and .250, and stealing 49 and 46 bases, in those years. In 1908 he batted .300 and had 36 stolen bases, becoming both an offensive and defensive star in the game.

(Above, from left to right above) It's Tinker to Evers to Chance, the Chicago Cubs' infield threesome immortalized in "Baseball's Sad Lexicon," a poem written by columnist Franklin P. Adams. (Below) Evers tags out a Cincinnati runner at second.

Johnny helped the Cubs notch their third consecutive pennant in 1908 simply by knowing the rule book better than anyone. On September 4, at Pittsburgh, the Pirates had beaten the Cubs in ten innings, 1–0, but on the game-winning hit the Pirate runner on first base failed to touch second. Umpire Hank O'Day ignored Ever's protests but promised that he would not allow the same incident to occur. "It's one rule that nobody enforces," said O'Day, "but remind me next time and I'll call it an out."

The next occasion came shortly thereafter. In an historic game at the Polo Grounds in September, Fred Merkle, the runner on first, failed to touch second while the apparent game-winning run was being scored. As bedlam broke loose, with the Giants seemingly having assured themselves of the pennant, Evers frantically called for the ball and jumped up and down on second base, screaming for O'Day (coincidentally, the umpire again) to call the runner out. O'Day did, and the incident, "Merkle's boner," became legendary. Whether Evers had the actual ball or a new one was debated for years, but the controversial out forced a replay of the game on the day after the regular season ended. The Cubs won the game to break the pennant deadlock with the Giants.

In the 1908 World Series, Johnny hit .350 for the second successive year, as the Cubs beat the Tigers in five games. The Cubs captured the World Championship again in 1910, but a broken leg forced Johnny to miss the Series. Illness in 1911 limited Evers to only 44 games, but he returned in 1912 to hit an amazing .341 with only 18 strikeouts in 478 at bats. The average ranked fourth in the league; manager Frank Chance's Cubs finished in third place.

Chance was fired after the season, and Evers was named manager. His weight had reached 140 pounds now, but his average fell to .285, and once again the Cubs finished third. John had signed a four-season, $10,000-per-year contract in 1913, but when the Federal League was formed in 1914, he sought more money. Charles Weeghman of the Chicago Federal League team offered John $30,000 in cash and a five-year, $75,000 contract to jump. Evers gave the Cubs an opportunity to match the offer, but owner Charles Murphy considered it a resignation and released him.

The National League, fighting to maintain as many stars as possible, would not honor the release papers. Instead, league president John Tener helped negotiate a trade of Evers from the Cubs to the Braves for infielder Bill Sweeney. Evers received a

$25,000 bonus from the transaction and remained a National Leaguer.

Johnny's arrival in Boston was magnificent. It coincided with the emergence of Rabbit Maranville as a star shortstop, and the two helped pace the Miracle Braves—in last place on July 4—to the 1914 National League pennant. Johnny batted .279, sparkled in the field, and received the Chalmers Award—a new car—as the Most Valuable Player in the National League for the 1914 season. In the World Series sweep of the Athletics, Johnny hit .438 to give him a lifetime Series average of .316.

Johnny remained in Boston until July 1917. His playing time dropped to under 100 games a year beginning in 1915, but the Braves certainly received their money's worth from him. Released by the Braves on July 12, 1917, Evers signed with the Philadelphia Phillies, with whom he finished the season and his playing career. (He later played one game each for the White Sox and Braves while coaching with them.) His career average was .270.

During the following two years, Johnny managed a shoe store in Chicago and a sporting goods store in Troy. He returned to baseball in 1920 as a coach with John McGraw of the Giants. In 1921 he again managed the Cubs, compiling a 42–56 record before being fired in midseason. In 1922 and 1923, he was a coach under Kid Gleason with the White Sox. Johnny then became manager of the team in 1924 after illness forced Frank Chance to relinquish the reins. The club finished last. Evers did not return again to baseball until 1929 when he was named assistant manager of the Braves. He served in that capacity for four years and then scouted for the Braves in 1933 and 1934. Evers managed the Albany club of the International League in 1935, and he served as vice-president and general manager of the Albany team in the Eastern League in 1939.

In addition to his sporting goods business in Troy, John was superintendent of city-owned Bleeker Stadium in Albany. He and his wife lived near the park.

In 1942 Evers suffered a paralytic stroke but recovered sufficiently to attend his Hall of Fame induction in 1946. That year Tinker, Evers, and Chance were elected together. On March 28, 1947, another stroke killed him at the age of 65.

JOHN JOSEPH EVERS

Chicago (N.L.) 1902–1913
Boston (N.L.) 1914–1917, 1929
Philadelphia (N.L.) 1917
Chicago (A.L.) 1922

G	AB	R	H	2B	3B	HR	RBI	Avg.
1776	6136	919	1659	216	70	12	538	.270

(At right) Evers demonstrates the batting style he developed to become an offensive as well as defensive star. (Below) He poses with officials on Evers Day in Chicago in 1913, the year Evers took on managing duties for the Cubs.

Buck Ewing (1859-1906)

Considered by Connie Mack to be the greatest catcher of all time, Buck Ewing starred for the New York Giants in the nineteenth century and helped to revolutionize the art of catching.

He was born William Ewing in Hoaglands, Ohio, on October 27, 1859. Hoaglands was a small town just outside Cincinnati, and Ewing was one of the first sandlot players to emerge into professional stardom from the Cincinnati area. He spent many hours studying the game when the Cincinnati Red Stockings, the nation's first professional team, were making a name for themselves.

Boyhood friends nicknamed Ewing "Buck," a name which stayed with him throughout his life. After he reached stardom, the former marble-playing star of Cincinnati was referred to as William Buckingham Ewing by a sportswriter, and some journalists accepted that as his real name. But "Buckingham" was totally fictitious.

Working as a teamster for $10 a week in 1878, Buck added to his income by playing semipro ball with the Mohawk Browns. He spent two seasons with the Browns and one year with the Cincinnati Buckeyes before joining Rochester of the National Association in 1880, where he participated in 13 games and batted .148. Buck completed that season with the Troy Haymakers of the National League, becoming a full-time player for the team in 1881 at a yearly salary of $1000. He caught for pitchers Tim Keefe and Mickey Welch and filled in at shortstop, third base, and the outfield. Rosters were smaller in those days, and it was not unusual for a man to play many positions. During his career, Buck played all nine, even posting a 3–3 record in nine games as a pitcher in the majors.

Buck batted .243 in 1881 and .274 in 1882, the final year of Troy's existence as a major league team. At the end of the season, many of the Troy stars, including Ewing, were transferred to the New York Giants. Joining Buck on this new team were Keefe, Welch, Roger Connor, and John Montgomery Ward.

Ewing was an immediate sensation with the New York fans. The 5'10", 188-pound, righthanded-hitting Ewing belted 10 home runs to lead the league, hit .306, and was given substantial credit for handling pitchers Keefe and Welch.

Mickey Welch could never praise Ewing sufficiently. He considered Buck the greatest player of all time, a real "thinking man's player." Welch credited Ewing with originating the pregame clubhouse meeting, and he recalled Buck's careful study of opponents in search of any psychological advantage.

Buck was a master behind the plate. He was one of the first catchers to switch from an unpadded glove to the "pillow style" similar to that in use today. He received considerable ribbing about the change, as players usually do when they introduce the novel, but he silenced his critics by becoming the best defensive catcher of his day. Buck was the first catcher to make the throw to second base from a crouch position, saving precious seconds when attempting to throw out base stealers. He always behaved politely to umpires, reasoning that a little politeness now might result in a favorable call later.

As a base stealer, Buck was second only to Monte Ward on the Giants. He always recorded a high percentage of success despite only average speed; his success was primarily due to his knowledge of pitchers and the ability to get a good jump. There was a famous base-stealing incident one day with the Giants when Ewing swiped both second and third, and then shouted for all to hear, "Now I'm stealing home!" Sure enough, with a dazzling run and a hard slide, he scored. The scene was reproduced as a lithograph and sold well throughout New York City as one of baseball's first novelty items.

Buck was not without superstition, adding to the appeal of this gentle, good-natured man. He considered it good luck to have the team's mascot spit on his lumber before he batted, and young fans of the era imitated his example, much to the disgust of their parents.

In 1884 Buck led the league with 18 triples, again demonstrating his outstanding baserunning abilities. He batted .278 that year and played every position.

The following year, Ewing, influenced by Monte Ward, was one of nine members of the Giants to sign a document forming a chapter of the Brotherhood of Professional Baseball Players. This early attempt at unionizing players was Buck's first involvement in the "politics" of the game.

The 1885 season saw Buck hit .304, which he followed by a .309 showing in 1886. In 1887 he batted .365 in a season cut short by a broken finger.

In 1888 the Giants won their first pennant, with Buck serving as leadoff hitter. He batted .346 in the 10-game postseason series against the champions of the American Association, Charles Comiskey's St. Louis team. Buck became the hero of the deciding game when he belted a home run and a bases-loaded double.

Prior to the start of the 1888 season, Monte Ward resigned as team captain over a salary dispute, and Ewing was chosen as his successor. A team captain in those days was actually closer to the role of manager as we know today, with the "manager" of the club more concerned

Buck Ewing was noted as a "thinking man's player," but he could arouse fans with his razzle-dazzle, too. Once, after stealing second and third, he shouted, "Now I'm stealing home." He made it.

with gate receipts and transactions with the players.

The Giants repeated as pennant winners in 1889. Buck batted .327 for the season and earned $5000; in the playoff victory over Brooklyn, he batted .250.

In 1890 Ward led a players' revolt that resulted in the formation of the Players League, also known as the Brotherhood League. Ewing was among the many players who jumped the National League, seeking more money and less ownership control of their lives.

Ward went to Brooklyn, and Ewing moved across the street to the other Polo Grounds to manage and catch for the New York team of the Players League. As the most popular member of the Giants, he brought along many fans with him—but also a host of attorneys representing the interests of the Giants. The Giants sued on the strength of the reserve clause to retain the rights to Ewing, but the court ruled in Ewing's favor, noting the absence of "mutuality" in the standard professional baseball contract.

John B. Day, the Giants' owner, offered Buck $10,000 to leave the Brotherhood and return to the Giants. A document was prepared announcing that Ewing would return to the National League in 1891 because the Players League was proving financially unsuccessful. When other players refused to support the statement, Ewing decided against signing. But nonetheless many players believed that Buck had betrayed the players' cause.

Meanwhile, Buck managed the New York team to a third place finish in 1890, batting .350 and handling, among other pitchers, his brother, John. When the league folded after one season, Buck in 1891 rejoined the Giants; John remained with his brother for another season.

Buck injured his throwing arm in 1892 but retained his value at the plate by hitting .320. Following the season, he was traded to Cleveland for shortstop George Davis.

He spent the following two years in the Cleveland outfield, batting .371 and .255.

When Cleveland released him in 1894, Buck signed a contract to manage and play first base for Cincinnati. There he succeeded Charles Comiskey as Red Stockings manager. Only in that first season did he play regularly, batting .317. His team finished eighth in the 12-team league.

In 1896 the club finished third, and Buck limited his own playing time to 67 games, compiling a .282 batting average. He made his final appearance at the plate in 1897, when the Red Stockings finished fourth.

Buck remained with Cincinnati for two additional seasons, the team finishing third and sixth. Among Buck's innovations were morning bunting sessions, which were not well received by the players but helpful in Red Stockings victories.

Ewing retired from baseball in 1900 a wealthy man, thanks to land investments in the western United States. He was out of touch with the baseball world and living in Cincinnati with his wife and two children when diabetes and paralysis claimed his life on October 20, 1906, at the age of 47.

In 1939 he was elected to the Hall of Fame.

WILLIAM EWING

Troy (N.L.) 1880–1882
New York (N.L.) 1883–1889, 1891–1892
New York (P.L.) 1890
Cleveland (N.L.) 1893–1894
Cincinnati (N.L.) 1895–1897

G	AB	R	H	2B	3B	HR	RBI	Avg.
1281	5348	1118	1663	237	179	66	inc.	.311

Red Faber (1888-1976)

Red Faber, the last American League pitcher permitted to throw the spitball, compiled 254 career victories for the Chicago White Sox between 1914 and 1933.

Urban Charles Faber was born on September 6, 1888, in Cascade, Iowa, of Luxemburgian descent. His father operated Faber's Hotel in Cascade, and Red worked there for many winters between baseball seasons.

Red, so named for the color of his hair, was sent to boarding school for two years in Wisconsin, and then was moved to St. Joseph's College in Dubuque for another two years. During this period, he learned to pitch, becoming a successful amateur player.

When the St. Joseph team played a game against the Dubuque club of the Three-I League, Faber so impressed those professionals that they offered him $100 per month to join their club. The salary amounted to more money than Faber had ever made, and it was a rather good minor league income for the time. Therefore, Red left school and joined the Dubuque team in 1909.

It was at Dubuque that a teammate taught Red the art of throwing a spitball. Many pitchers tried it during the days of its legality, but few mastered it as well as did Faber. He would moisten the tips of the index and middle fingers on his right hand with tobacco juice, and release the ball with a snap of the wrist. The ball had no spin and its sharp downward trajectory made it extremely difficult to hit.

Red appeared in 15 games in 1909 and posted a 7–6 record. After the season, the Pittsburgh Pirates purchased him from Dubuque, but without giving him a trial they returned him to Dubuque for the 1910 season.

That was a big year for Red. Although his record was only 18–19, he worked 334 innings, struck out 200 batters, and on August 18 hurled a perfect game, defeating Davenport, 3–0. It was only the third perfect game in the history of professional baseball. Red allowed only one ball to be hit out of the infield during his performance.

This feat, of course, drew considerable attention to the 21-year-old righthander, but the Pirates had the rights to him and again he was brought up to the majors after the minor league season. But once again the Pirates failed to use him, and in 1911 Red was sold outright to Minneapolis of the American Association.

After only six innings at Minneapolis, Faber was shipped to Pueblo of the Western League, where he compiled a 12–8 mark. He spent 1912 and 1913 at Des Moines of the Western League. Those

were fine years, for he was 21–14 in 1912, and 20–17 with a league-leading 265 strikeouts in 1913.

The owner of the Des Moines club, former White Sox infielder Frank Isbell, tipped off Chicago's Charles Comiskey about Faber. Shortly thereafter, the White Sox bought his contract for $35,000.

At the end of the 1913 season, Comiskey and John McGraw organized a world tour for the White Sox and Giants. Faber, although still a minor leaguer, accompanied the Sox westward with the Giants until the entire party arrived in Seattle, the point of departure. At that juncture, New York's Christy Mathewson changed his mind about going, and McGraw was short one pitcher. Comiskey offered to lend him Faber for the trip, and McGraw was pleased to accept.

Thus without ever having appeared in a major league game, Red was headed around the world, pitching for the Giants against his own team. He had a wonderful trip, beating the White Sox in Hong Kong, Cairo, Brisbane, and Melbourne before losing an eleven-inning game in London. McGraw was so impressed that he offered Comiskey $50,000 for Faber, but the offer was turned down.

Jim Callahan was the Chicago manager in Red's rookie season. Red pitched that year to such old timers as Napoleon Lajoie and Home Run Baker. By the time he threw his final pitch in 1933, Luke Appling was a teammate.

Red recorded a 10–9 mark in his rookie season, making a modest impression on the sixth-place club. It was not an unusual spot for the White Sox to finish, and through much of Red's career he was saddled with mediocre clubs. Nevertheless, he managed to finish his career 42 wins above .500.

Faber had a spectacular sophomore campaign, posting a 24–14 record, second in the league in victories only to Walter Johnson. He appeared in 50 games, which tied Harry Coveleskie for the league lead, and posted a 2.55 earned run average. His efforts helped Chicago to a third place finish under new manager Pants Rowland. Red pitched 300 innings for the first of four times in his career, and the 20-victory season was also the first of four times in that elite circle.

Faber was not essentially a strikeout artist; he fanned 182 in 1915, but he topped the 100 figure on only three other occasions and generally allowed the hitters to pound his spitball into the ground for outs. Red always took special pride in a game in which he threw only 67 pitches, with only

Right-hander Faber hurls the ball. A 20-game winner four times, Faber's greatest achievement was winning three games in the 1917 World Series against the New York Giants to lead the White Sox to victory.

three pitches in each of three innings.

In 1917, Faber's fourth with the team, the White Sox captured the American League pennant. Red pitched far better than his 16–13 record would indicate. He allowed 92 runs that season, only 53 of which were earned, and his 1.92 ERA placed him fourth in the league.

The 1917 World Series was Red's finest hour. He beat the Giants three times during the Series, won by Chicago, four games to two. Red started and won the second game, 7–2; lost the fourth game, 5–0; and won the fifth game, 8–5, in relief. Two days later Red posted a 4–2, complete-game victory to give Chicago the World Championship.

Although winning three games in one Series was a widely heralded feat, Red practically became better remembered for his poor baserunning. In one game, he singled, went to second on a ground out, and then set out to steal third. When the dust of his slide had cleared, he found to his dismay teammate Buck Weaver already occupying the base; Red was tagged out.

Faber was a switch-hitter, but held little authority with the bat. His lifetime batting average was .134 with three home runs.

After winning four of five decisions during the first two months of the 1918 season, Red enlisted in the navy and wound up playing service ball. He returned to the White Sox in 1919, underweight and bothered by an ankle injury. The injury kept him out of action during the 1919 World Series and untouched by its scandal. The suspension of the eight players accused of throwing the Series virtually ended the pennant-contending years of the White Sox. The club did not capture another flag until 1959, but Faber continued to be a durable and effective pitcher.

Red married in 1920 and settled in Chicago. His first wife died in 1942, and five years later he married Fran Knudtzon, who bore him his only child, Urban II. Popular with players and fans, humble, and basically an Iowa farmboy throughout his life, Red was not only remembered as an "honest" member of the 1919 White Sox, but also as a gentleman.

Although the White Sox were divorced from the pennant race, Red compiled a 23–13 record in 1920, and posted a 25–15 mark in 1921 with a league-leading 2.47 earned-run average. In 1922 Faber again led the league in ERA with 2.80, also led with 353 innings pitched, and had a 21–17 record, completing 31 of the 38 starts.

Red's biggest seasons were behind him at that point. He recorded a 14–11 mark in 1923. The following year an arm injury limited his appearances to 21 games and a 9–11 record. He appeared to make a comeback in 1926 when he posted a 15–8 record for the fifth-place club, but a sore arm in 1927 diminished his record to 4–7.

"Fabe" stood 6'1" and weighed 195 pounds, but it was his spitball and not his fastball that made him effective. The spitball was declared illegal in 1920, except for a select few whose trade depended on the pitch. Faber, who lasted in the majors until 1933, thus was throwing the last legal spitballs in the American League. Only Burleigh Grimes of the National League outlasted Faber.

Red won 13 games in both 1928 and 1929, and he even recorded 10 victories in 1931 at the age of 42. He always considered Al Simmons of Philadelphia to be his most difficult batter, but he managed to pitch to almost every other player with great success.

Working mostly in relief, Faber posted a 2–11 record in 1932, and a 3–4 mark in 1933, hurling his final game in an exhibition series against the Cubs at the end of the season—and shutting them out. Faber was then 45 years old, but he believed that it was merely a bad knee which slowed him down.

Red retired from baseball and opened a bowling alley in Greys Lake, Illinois, which he operated until 1946. That year, Ted Lyons was named manager of the White Sox, and he called upon Red to assume the duties of pitching coach. The job lasted through the 1948 season, at which time both Lyons and Faber were released. Red then returned to work for the Cook County Highway Department as a surveyor. He retired from that job in 1965. Red died in Chicago on September 25, 1976 at the age of 88.

In 1964 Red Faber was selected for induction into the Hall of Fame.

The Faber method of winning was not on strikeouts, but rather on the least possible number of pitches. Generally, batters would hit his spitball into the ground for fast outs.

URBAN CHARLES FABER

Chicago (A.L.) 1914–1933

G	IP	W	L	Pct.	H	R	ER	SO	BB	ERA
669	4087	254	212	.545	4104	1813	1430	1471	1213	3.15

Bob Feller (b. 1918)

Bob Feller learned to pitch on an Iowa farm, reached the major leagues at the age of 17, and went on to become the American League's strikeout champion seven times.

Robert William Andrew Feller was born on November 3, 1918, on his family's farm in Van Meter, Iowa. As a youngster he played catch with his dad, developing a strong throwing arm by the time he was six. Young Robert built great strength through farming chores and practiced throwing a baseball against the sides of barns.

Bob played for his father's town team in a field carved out of the family's 360-acre farm; he also graduated to semipro ball for a salary of $30 per game. It was while playing semipro ball that Bob was scouted by Cleveland's Cy Slapnicka at the urging of a teammate.

Baseball rules prohibited a major league club from signing a boy still in high school. Therefore, Slapnicka signed the 16-year-old Feller and filed the contract as a minor league arrangement with Fargo-Moorhead of the Northern League. The following year, 1936, the contract was transferred to New Orleans, another Cleveland farm team, and Bob was placed on the "voluntary retired list" to further keep him hidden.

Meanwhile, Feller continued to pitch semipro ball. When he starred for Des Moines in a national tournament, he came to the attention of other clubs. The Detroit Tigers, after offering Bob a $9000 bonus and a trip to the World Series for the Fellers, discovered him to be Cleveland property. An investigation was called.

Commissioner Landis, an opponent of a rule that made it legal for a minor league team to sign a player that could not be contracted by a major league team, decided in favor of the Indians but made the club pay Des Moines $7500 to balance the claim. Des Moines (the Western League team, not the semipro team) accepted the payment. Thus was halted a potential bidding war for Feller that might have resulted in as much as a $100,000 bonus for young Bob.

Without ever having pitched a professional game, Bob took the mound in Cleveland's League Park in July 1936 to hurl an exhibition game against the St. Louis Cardinals. All were anxious to see what this widely heralded 17-year old could do, and Bob put on quite a performance with eight strikeouts in three innings. Home plate umpire Red Ormsby called Bob the fastest pitcher he had ever seen—including Walter Johnson. Feller certainly threw at top velocity; at one point in his career his fastball was clocked at 98.6 miles per hour.

Bob made a few relief appearances before he received his first start in mid-August, facing the St. Louis Browns. The result was a 4–1 victory with 15 strikeouts. In September he tied Dizzy Dean's single game strikeout record by fanning 17 Philadelphia Athletics. Bob finished his rookie season with a 5–3 record, 76 strikeouts in 62 innings, and a 3.34 earned-run average. After the season, he returned to Iowa to finish high school.

Returning to the Indians in 1937, Bob was brought along slowly by manager Steve O'Neill. He had arm trouble that year, was limited to 149 innings, and posted a 9–7 record. He struck out 150 batters.

In 1938 Ossie Vitt became the Cleveland manager, and Bob had his first full season of pitching. On April 30, Feller hurled his first of a record twelve one-hitters, allowing only a bunt single in the sixth inning. No pitcher has ever approached that number of one-hitters, and Bob eventually added three no-hitters, tying the major league record. (Sandy Koufax and Nolan Ryan later pitched four each.)

Bob captured 17 of 28 decisions in 1938, struck out 240 men for his first strikeout title, but walked 208 batters, an American League record. It was necessary for Bob to have a strong arm because he always threw a considerable number of pitches in a game, walking nearly as many batters as he struck out. Upon retiring from baseball, Feller had walked more batters than any other pitcher—1764, a total later surpassed by Early Wynn. Bob's 2581 strikeouts, however, placed him an impressive third behind Walter Johnson and Cy Young at the time of his retirement. Warren Spahn, Bob Gibson, and Mickey Lolich have since exceeded Bob's total.

Feller recorded his first 20-victory season in 1939, leading the American League with a 24–9 mark, 297 innings, and 246 strikeouts. Not yet 21, Bob had already achieved 55 victories in the major leagues.

In 1940 Feller won a career high of 27 games, losing only 11, and registered a league-leading 2.62 ERA. He struck out 261 and walked only 118, his best ratio to date. On April 16 that year, he pitched the only opening day no-hitter in major league history, stopping the Chicago White Sox cold. Cleveland lost the 1940 pennant to Detroit by one game, and a silent rebellion bred between manager Vitt and his players. Only Feller voiced his opinions publicly, as he would frequently do as the years went by. Bob said, "Oscar makes us nervous . . . I wouldn't want to play for him next year."

Vitt was gone in 1941 and Roger Peckinpaugh assumed the managerial reins, but

the club nevertheless fell beneath the .500 mark and finished fourth. Bob turned in another stellar performance, winning 25 games to lead the league again. He also led in games (44), innings (343), hits allowed (284), strikeouts (260), and walks (194).

Bob entered the navy in 1942, serving as a gun-crew chief on the U.S.S. *Alabama* during World War II. The war took almost four years out of Feller's playing career, certainly berefting him of a 300-victory career. During his stint in service Bob developed a slider, an excellent third pitch that made him, many believed, an even better pitcher when he returned to the game in 1946.

Discharged from the navy late in the summer of 1945, Bob pitched nine games at the end of the season. The following year would reveal if his four-year absence had depleted his skills. The results satisfied everyone—Feller won 26 games in 1946, pitched 371 innings, had a 2.18 ERA, and set the major league record of 348 strikeouts in a single season (later broken by Sandy Koufax and Nolan Ryan). Included was an April 30 no-hitter in Yankee Stadium.

Following the 1946 season, Bob became the first player to incorporate himself, establishing Ro-Fel, Inc. The label "incorporated" gave Feller tax advantages that enabled him to make a fortune from his many endorsements, personal appearances, and pitching clinics. His wife, the former Virginia Winther, was secretary of the corporation, and his father-in-law was vice-president. Bob was earning $80,000 a year at this point, the highest salary ever paid a pitcher, and his investments increased his yearly earnings to nearly $150,000. In effect, Feller became the first baseball player to reap substantial gains from the use of his name in a business sense.

Bob organized a team of major leaguers in the fall of 1946 to tour the country with a Negro League all-star team headed by Satchel Paige. The two formed a mutual admiration society, and Bob became highly regarded by the black community for advocating Paige's election to the Hall of

(Above) Robert William Andrew Feller, age 10, in his first baseball uniform, and (at right) a few years later as a high school basketball player. (Below) Feller is fourth from left, front row, in this picture of the Oak View team of Iowa.

150

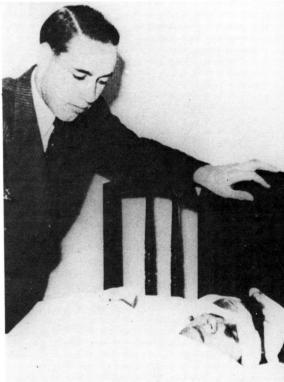

(At left) The Feller windup. (Above) The denouement of a freak accident: Feller visits his mother in a Chicago hospital after she was struck by a foul tip from her son's delivery in Comiskey Park in 1939. (Below) Father Bill Feller comes to the city to see his son in a 1938 game.

151

Fame years later. But much of that regard was lost during a heated debate in 1969 between Feller and Jackie Robinson over the place of blacks in baseball front offices.

Feller posted a 20–11 record in 1947, but it was not until 1948, his eighth full season, that the Indians captured a pennant. Player-manager Lou Boudreau sparked the team to the title that season. Feller won 19 games, third highest on the Indian pitching staff behind Bob Lemon and Gene Bearden. In the opening game of the World Series against the Braves, Bob and Johnny Sain locked into a scoreless pitching duel. In the eighth inning, the Braves' Phil Masi was ruled safe in a close pickoff play at second base; then Tommy Holmes singled in Masi with the game's only run. It was, according to Feller, his toughest defeat.

Bob also started the fifth game before 86,268 fans in Cleveland, but he permitted seven runs and eight hits in six and one-third innings to suffer his second defeat.

After dropping to 15 wins in 1949 and 16 in 1950, Bob recorded his final 20-victory season in 1951 when he posted a 22–8 mark for the highest winning percentage in the league. On July 1 that year, he stopped the Tigers, 2–1, for his third no-hitter. It was Feller's last big season, and the final time he struck out more than 100 batters.

As a spot starter in 1954, Bob posted a 13–3 record for a team that won a league record of 111 games. But Feller was not used in the World Series; Wynn, Lemon, Mike Garcia, and Art Houtteman had passed him in the starting rotation.

Bob worked in 25 games in 1955 with a 4–4 record, and in 1956 he recorded an 0–4 mark. After the 1956 season, the eight-time All-Star retired. His uniform, No. 19, was never worn again by a Cleveland player.

Feller served as a scout for the Indians in 1958, but that was his only job in baseball following his retirement. His business interests supported him, and he owned his own plane and cabin cruiser. Bob was considered a wealthy man, but in 1969 he revealed serious financial trouble which surprised those who knew the shrewd right-hander. Feller's marriage ended in divorce in 1971, and he married Anne Thorpe in 1974.

Bob was elected to the Hall of Fame in 1962, his first year of eligibility, being listed on 93 percent of the ballots cast. But high percentages were typical of Robert Feller, who compiled a 266–162 lifetime record for a .621 winning percentage.

ROBERT WILLIAM ANDREW FELLER

Cleveland 1936–1956

G	IP	W	L	Pct.	H	R	ER	SO	BB	ERA
570	3828	266	162	.621	3271	1557	1384	2581	1764	3.25

Feller winds up to deliver a final strike to Detroit's Hank Greenberg during the 1945 season. Feller pitched only nine games that year, following his return from the Navy in late summer. But he came out of the Navy with a new pitch, a slider, that made him better than ever.

Elmer Flick (1876-1971)

Elmer Flick was accomplished enough as a player to be sought in a trade for Ty Cobb, but his team, the Cleveland Indians, vetoed the transaction. A lifetime .315 hitter, Flick starred for the Phillies and the Indians during his 13-year career.

Elmer Harrison Flick was born on January 11, 1876, in Bedford, Ohio. He signed his first professional contract at the age of 20 with the Youngstown team of the Inter-State League. Either Flick was too outstanding for the league or the sport just came too easy for him, for in 31 games Elmer batted .438 with 34 runs scored. He had his troubles in the field but appeared to be a naturally gifted hitter.

The outfield was always Elmer's position, and he owned a good arm with good range. For the majority of his career, Elmer was positioned in right field. Standing 5'8½" and weighing 165 pounds, Flick threw righthanded and batted lefthanded.

In 1897 Youngstown transferred Elmer's contract to Dayton, also of the Inter-State League. Yet, he remained superior to most of the Inter-State League pitching; he compiled a .386 average in his first full season of professional ball. In 126 games, he scored 135 runs and collected 183 hits. Elmer also recorded 25 assists in the outfield, a high total.

With two fine years under his belt, Elmer was purchased by the Philadelphia Phillies for the 1898 season. It was not the ideal club for a promising young outfielder to join: the Phillies had a sensational outfield trio in Ed Delahanty, Dick Cooley, and Big Sam Thompson. But Thompson was vulnerable, for a bad back had begun to reduce his effectiveness.

The Phillies trained in the spring of 1898 at Cape May, New Jersey. Elmer appeared with his homemade bat, which had been turned on a lathe by the young outfielder. It was merely one of the reasons Elmer was noticed that spring. The other was his hitting, which had seasoned veterans observing him.

Thompson opened the season in rightfield, but a back injury sidelined him after only a few games. That was all the opportunity Flick required. He stepped in against Boston on April 26, banged two singles off Fred Klobedanz, and started on the trail toward a brilliant career.

The 1898 Phillies were slightly better than a .500 club, but Delahanty, Thompson, and Napoleon Lajoie were all members of the team, giving the Phillies four future Hall of Famers. Flick celebrated his rookie season with a .318 batting average, which included 8 home runs, and 29 stolen bases.

With a year's major league experience, Elmer batted .344 in 1899, placing him

among the league's top 10 hitters. He also stole 31 bases and scored 101 runs. The Phillies hit a collective .301 that year and finished a respectable third in the 12-team league.

In 1900 Elmer belted 11 home runs, falling short by one to the league's champion, Herman Long. Scanty attention was paid to home runs in those days. Of greater interest was Elmer's .378 batting average, which was second only to Honus Wagner's .381. Elmer collected 207 hits that year, scored 106 runs, and stole 37 bases.

The 1901 season proved to be another fine campaign for Flick; he batted .336 and scored 111 runs. But it also became his final season of National League play. For his four seasons with the Phillies, Flick compiled a .345 batting average.

In 1902 Flick followed the lead of some more established stars and jumped to the newly formed American League. Lajoie had preceded him a year earlier in moving crosstown to play for Connie Mack's Philadelphia Athletics. Mack dispatched the baseball editor of the Philadelphia *Inquirer,* Frank Hough, to serve as his agent in recruiting players. With the promise of better playing conditions and a higher salary, Hough lured Flick to the American League.

Elmer played only 11 games for the Athletics in 1902. The Phillies went to court to prevent Lajoie from participating in the new league. The subsequent court decision forbade Lajoie or any other former Phillies from playing for any team other than the Phillies while in the state of Pennsylvania. Obviously, Connie Mack could not retain players who could play only road games. Rather than allow the players to return to the National League, he dealt all of those affected to other American League clubs. On May 16, Flick was sold to the Indians. A few weeks later, Lajoie also joined Cleveland.

While many of the National League stars who moved to the new league enjoyed fine seasons, Elmer batted under .300 for the first time in 1902, hitting .295. Cleveland, under manager Bill Armour, finished fifth. In 1903 Flick played in all of the Indians' 142 games, leading the league in games played. Cleveland moved up to third place, and Flick's average rose to .299. Then in 1904, Elmer batted .303 and tied for the league leadership with 42 stolen bases.

The 1905 American League season was marked by its peculiarity. Nine pitchers won 20 or more games, and the entire league batted only .241. Only Willie Keeler at .302 and Flick at .306 managed to top the .300 mark; in fact, Flick captured the batting championship with the lowest league-leading average until 1968, at which time Boston's Carl Yastrzemski gained the title with a .301 performance.

Flick became famous for this record, which was an unfair reflection of the man.

After all, Elmer had once batted .378 only to lose the title by three points. His .306 batting title became his most memorable achievement—it was Elmer's only batting championship.

Lajoie had become the Indians' manager in 1905, but Elmer's performance failed to bring Cleveland home higher than fifth. In 1906 Elmer raised his average to .311, but league hitters arose from their slumber as six players topped his mark. One of the six was a rookie outfielder on the Tigers named Ty Cobb, who was creating trouble for Detroit manager Bill Armour, Flick's former boss.

Armour departed after the 1906 season, and Hughey Jennings assumed the Tiger reins. Jennings immediately sized up Cobb as nothing but a nuisance. As far as Jennings was concerned, Flick, a fine gentleman, was as good a player as Ty. Their base-stealing abilities at the time were comparable, and their hitting was relatively equivalent after Cobb's first full season.

During spring training of 1907, Jennings offered Cobb in exchange for Flick. Cleveland owner Charlie Somers pondered the offer, then turned it down. He valued Flick highly and knew of the trouble Cobb might create.

As a counteroffer, Somers offered Bunk Congalton, a three-year man who had batted .320 in 1906. Fortunately for the Tigers, the deal fell through. Cobb remained a Tiger until 1926, earning recognition as the best player in the game. Congalton was peddled to Boston, where he proved the .320 season of 1906 to be a fluke.

But the Indians were still proud of Flick in 1907. He batted .302 and swatted 18 triples, leading the American League in that department for the third consecutive season. Only Sam Crawford, the all-time triples leader, and Zoilo Versalles, a 1960s Minnesota Twin, ever led the league for three consecutive years in triples.

But by opening day of 1908, Cleveland realized that the spurned Cobb trade was a grevious error. A mysterious stomach ailment felled Elmer that year in New Orleans. Some blamed it on the drinking water, but Flick was the only player affected. Many considered it to be ulcers, but no doctor ever properly diagnosed the case.

Elmer played only nine games in 1908, collecting seven hits. In 1909 he played in 66 games and batted .255. And in 1910, Elmer appeared in 24 games and hit .265. Flick's mysterious illness thus ended his career prematurely.

Nevertheless, Elmer had compiled a .315 career average. He played for Toledo in 1911 and hit .326 in 84 games. Elmer then batted .262 for the Mud Hens in 1912 before retiring from baseball at age 36.

Flick, his wife, Rosella, and their five daughters, moved to Warrensville Heights, Ohio. A popular old timer, Flick attended many baseball functions. Illness and a broken hip prevented Elmer from attending his Hall of Fame induction in 1963, but he arrived one year later, bent and walking with a cane. Tears filled the 88-year-old man's eyes as he viewed his plaque for the first time. It was one of the most moving scenes ever observed in Cooperstown.

Elmer died on January 9, 1971, two days before what would have been his ninety-fifth birthday.

ELMER HARRISON FLICK

Philadelphia (N.L.) 1898–1901
Philadelphia (A.L.) 1902
Cleveland (A.L.) 1902–1910

G	AB	R	H	2B	3B	HR	RBI	Avg.
1480	5597	948	1764	266	170	46	756	.315

Elmer Flick appears to be doing a Highland Fling in the outfield. Flick's fame was for his hitting, and his base stealing.

Whitey Ford (b. 1928)

Whitey Ford pitched on 11 pennant-winning Yankee teams, was victorious in more World Series games than any pitcher in history, and compiled the highest winning percentage of any hurler with more than 200 career victories.

Edward Charles Ford was born on October 21, 1928, on East 66th Street in Manhattan, the son of James and Edith Ford. Most of his youth was spent in the Astoria section of Queens. He graduated from the Manhattan High School of Aviation with a perfect attendance record and thoughts of becoming an airplane mechanic.

Eddie played high school ball and saw duty as a pitcher-first baseman for the "Thirty-Fourth Avenue Boys," an amateur team in the Queens-Nassau League. When the team was invited to play in the Hearst Sandlot Classic, an annual New York City event, Eddie was spotted by the chief Yankee scout, Paul Krichell. Krichell brought Ford to an April tryout session in Yankee Stadium, urged him to pitch during the summer, and then signed him in October for a $7000 bonus, outbidding the Red Sox and the Dodgers.

The 18-year-old Ford brought his natural curveball to Butler of the Middle Atlantic League for the 1947 season. By midseason that year, with Ford on the road to a 13–4 record, the Dodgers realized they had dropped out of the bidding prematurely.

In 1948 the 5'10", 180-pound lefthander moved up to Norfolk in the Piedmont League, where he posted a 16–8 record with a 2.58 earned-run average. In 1949 he recorded a 16–5 mark at Binghamton in the Eastern League, and wondered why Casey Stengel did not elevate him up to the Yankee roster. Ford led the league with a 1.61 ERA that season.

Ford opened the 1950 season at Kansas City, the Yankees' top club in the American Association. After winning six of nine decisions, he finally received the call from Stengel.

The fair-haired, 21-year-old Ford, now nicknamed "Whitey" by former Yankee lefthander Lefty Gomez, was hit hard in his first two appearances, but he then reeled off nine consecutive victories to finish his rookie campaign with a 9–1 record. Always noted for his calmness under pressure in his later years, Whitey first demonstrated this talent in 1950 when Stengel started him in September in a crucial game against Detroit. The Tigers held a half-game lead over New York, but Whitey stopped them, 8–1, to send the Yankees into first place and on their way to a pennant.

In the World Series sweep of Philadelphia, Whitey pitched the deciding fourth game. He would have notched a shutout victory had not Gene Woodling misplayed

an outfield fly. But Ford won the game, 5–2, for his first of a record 10 Series victories.

On April 14, 1951, Whitey married Joan Foran and moved to a home on Long Island. The Fords had three children; the middle one, Eddie, was drafted number one by the Boston Red Sox in 1974.

The army drafted Whitey just when he was enjoying the finest moments of his life, and Ford spent two full seasons at Fort Monmouth, New Jersey, in the Signal Corps. At one point, he escaped serious injury after a fall of 15 feet from a telephone pole. For the remainder of his hitch, Ford worked in a radar truck.

Admittedly heavy and out of shape upon returning to the Yankees for the 1953 season, Whitey had to work himself back into a competitive spirit. Never lazy, but never an advocate of running as necessary exercise for a pitcher, he required only a few weeks to regain his form. Shortly thereafter, his great curveball and "sneaky" fastball were keeping batters off stride, and Whitey went on to post an 18–6 season in another pennant-winning year for the Yankees.

Stengel always used Ford carefully. Never part of a rigid, four-day rotation, Whitey would pitch whenever Stengel thought it was best for him to work. As a result, the most games he ever started during the Stengel era was 33 in 1955.

But the work pattern agreed with Ford. He posted a 16–8 mark in 1954, a year in which the Yankees finished second, and then recorded an 18–7 mark in 1955, tying for the league lead in victories. In September of that year, he equaled a major league record by pitching two consecutive one-hitters. And he led the league with 18 complete games, earning selection as the league's "Pitcher of the Year" by The Sporting News.

In the 1955 World Series against the Dodgers, Whitey compiled a 2–0 record with a 2.12 ERA. With the departure of Allie Reynolds, Vic Raschi, and Ed Lopat, Ford became the top pitcher on the Yankee staff.

In 1956 Ford captured his first of two ERA titles, posting a 2.47 mark to complement a 19–6 record, the top winning percentage in the league. His control was vastly improved, and he was recognized as one of the craftiest workers in the game. Various players, coaches, and managers accused Ford of doctoring baseballs, or having his catcher, Yogi Berra or Elston Howard, perform the act, but Whitey only smiled when the suggestion was made, preferring to keep the hitters guessing.

Teenager Eddie Ford (second from left, front row) and his teammates of the Thirty-fourth Avenue Boys. It was when this team played in the Hearst Sandlot classic that a Yankee scout spotted the young pitcher and signed him for a $7000 bonus in 1946.

Whitey's closest friend on the team was Mickey Mantle, the country boy from Oklahoma who looked to Ford for the city sophistication necessary for survival in New York. The two were involved in a famous brawl in New York's Copacabana night club early in 1957 while celebrating Billy Martin's birthday. The five Yankees present that night were each fined $1000, but generally Whitey's behavior was respectable, and he enjoyed tremendous popularity with teammates, fans, and the media.

Whitey did have shoulder problems, however, and these limited his 1957 season to 24 games and an 11–5 record. Ford recovered in time for the World Series, during which he posted a 1–1 record against Milwaukee.

In 1958 Whitey led the league with a 2.01 ERA, helped by 7 shutouts; he won 14 decisions, lost 7, and returned to the top of his game. In 1959, however, the Yankees dropped to third place, and for the first time in Ford's career, his losses reached double figures. Whitey compiled a 16–10 record, and in only one other season would he lose in double figures.

The 1960 season was a disappointing one for Ford. Still used irregularly, Whitey posted a disappointing 12–9 record for Stengel's final Yankee team, and he was bypassed for the opening game of the World Series. Stengel later conceded that perhaps Ford should have started, as the Yanks lost in seven games to the Pirates. Ford's Series performance that year was flawless. He hurled two complete game shutouts, winning 12–0 and 10–0. Ralph Houk, who succeeded Stengel as Yankee manager, immediately remarked that Whitey would be his No. 1 pitcher, would work every fourth day, and would be, as Elston Howard described him, "The Chairman of the Board."

Working in the regular rotation in 1961, Ford enjoyed his finest season. He compiled a 25–4 record, his first 20-victory season, which included a streak of 14 consecutive wins. He struck out 209 in a league-leading 283 innings, and he captured the Cy Young Award as the major leagues' top pitcher.

In the 1961 World Series, Ford won two more games and broke the long-standing record of 29⅔ consecutive scoreless World Series innings set by Babe Ruth when he was a pitcher with the Red Sox. Whitey extended his streak to 33⅔ in the 1962 World Series. The same year that Ford broke Ruth's pitching record, teammate Roger Maris surpassed Ruth's season home run record of 60.

Ford recorded a 17–8 mark in 1962, and won his tenth Series game that fall against the Giants. Whitey enjoyed a 24–7 season in 1963, again leading the league in victories, winning percentage, and innings pitched. But Sandy Koufax outpitched him in the opening game of the 1963 World Series, and Whitey lost again to the Dodger star in the fourth and deciding game.

The Yankees' final pennant of their dynasty, and Ford's last superlative season, came in 1964. Whitey posted a 17–6 record with a 2.13 ERA, surpassing Red

Ruffing as the Yankees all-time biggest winner. He was hit hard in the 1964 Series, however, losing his eighth and final series decision. Thus the books closed on a host of World Series records which included most games pitched (22), opening games started (8), innings (146), strikeouts (94), walks (34), victories (10), and losses (8).

Ford had doubled as pitching coach under manager Berra in 1964, and he was earning $80,000 as the highest paid pitcher in the league. But in 1965, Whitey gladly relinquished the coaching chores when Johnny Keane became Yankee manager.

Ford compiled a 16–13 record in 1965 with a 3.25 ERA. In 1966 his left shoulder began to trouble him again, and a circulation blockage was discovered. He was perspiring on only one side and was unable to pitch more than a few innings each time out. Whitey had posted a 2–5 mark in August when he underwent an operation which finished him for the season.

Ford returned in 1967 to post a 1.64 ERA in seven appearances, but his inability to pitch complete games bothered him, and he announced his retirement on May 30. The Yankees hired him immediately as a scout and minor league pitching coach, and in 1968 Whitey was made first base coach of the club.

But Ford left the Yankees at that point to pursue his many business interests, which included a syndicate that purchased the Boston Celtics, work as a customer's man in a brokerage house, and investment in a large Long Island country club. Whitey remained close to the Yankees by serving as a television commentator during home games and as a special spring training pitching instructor.

In 1974, the year in which Ford returned to the Yankees as a full-time pitching coach, he and Mantle were elected to the Hall of Fame. In May 1975, a circulatory problem caused Whitey to black out after pitching batting practice, and he was forced to bring a halt to his coaching career. He returned as a spring training instructor and special assignment scout for 1976, and was appointed Commissioner of the National Professional Softball League in 1977.

EDWARD CHARLES FORD

New York (A.L.) 1950–1967

G	IP	W	L	Pct.	H	R	ER	SO	BB	ERA
498	3171	236	106	.690	2766	1107	976	1956	1086	2.74

Whitey Ford hurls against the Cincinnati Reds in the 1961 World Series opener in Yankee Stadium. Ford won the game in a two-hit shutout.

Jimmie Foxx (1907-1967)

One of baseball's most powerful hitters, Jimmie Foxx belted 30 or more home runs and drove in over 100 runs for 12 consecutive seasons as a member of the Philadelphia Athletics and the Boston Red Sox. Until the late 1960s, the muscular "Double-X" placed second only to Babe Ruth in career home runs, with 534 over his 20-year span.

Foxx was born on October 22, 1907, at Sudlersville, Maryland, the son of an Irish farmer. Inspired by his grandfather's tales of the Civil War, young Jimmie ran away at the age of 10 to enlist as a drummer boy in World War I. But the army did not accept dream-filled drummer boys of that age, and Jimmie returned to the farm, performed his chores, and dedicated himself to athletics. His first ambition was to run track, but as Jimmie grew, speed became one of the lesser attributes of his powerful physique, and he turned to baseball.

While playing for Sudlersville High School and local sandlot teams, Foxx was invited to try out with Easton of the Eastern Shore League, a team managed by Frank "Home Run" Baker, the great Philadelphia and New York infielder (1908–1922). In May 1924, though only 16, Jimmie left home to sign his first professional contract. Short of catchers, Baker persuaded Jimmie to try out behind the plate. He caught 76 games for Easton that year and batted .296 with 10 home runs.

The solid season aroused the interest of two major league clubs—the Philadelphia Athletics and New York Yankees. Both sought to purchase Foxx from Easton, but Baker's loyalty to Connie Mack decided the issue. Baker had always respected Mack and hoped to return a favor to him one day. Selling Mack Foxx seemed a large enough favor, and the deal was consummated.

Foxx finished the 1924 season with Philadelphia sitting at Connie Mack's side, a 16-year-old muscleman unable to move Mickey Cochrane from behind home plate. It was not until the following May that Foxx played in a game, and he lined a pinch-hit single off Vean Gregg to launch his major league career. But Jimmie played infrequently for the A's in 1925, and after batting only nine times (with six hits), he was optioned to Providence in the International League, where he caught 41 games and batted .327.

Foxx spent the entire 1926 season on the Philadelphia roster, but he appeared in only 26 games and batted .323. Twelve of Foxx's games that year were behind the plate, three were in the outfield, and the remainder were pinch-hitting appearances. His roommate was Mickey Cochrane, the man standing between Foxx and

regular play, but at the age of 18 Jimmie was content to enjoy the big leagues and play when he could.

His playing time increased in 1927 to 61 games, and he hit the first three home runs of his career. Shifted to first base and catching only five games, Foxx hit .323 in 130 at bats. Philadelphia finished in second place, 19 games behind the legendary Yankee team of that season.

By 1928 it was clear that a place in the lineup would have to be found for Foxx's valuable bat. He was hitting well even with infrequent chances, and his run-producing potential was evident. Mack inserted Jimmie into the lineup by playing him at first base in 30 games, behind the plate in 20 games, and at third base in 61 games. The constant movement of position did not hurt Foxx at bat; he contributed to a fine Philadelphia season with a .328 average and 13 homers in 118 games. The A's finished only three games behind the Yankees.

In 1929 Foxx displaced Joe Hauser at first base and began his record streak of 12 consecutive seasons of 30 homers or better. He belted 33 that year in 149 games, driving in 117 runs and batting .354, which tied him for the fourth best average in the league. Foxx and Al Simmons combined for 67 homers and 275 runs batted in as they led the A's to the first of three successive pennants, aided by Hall-of-Fame teammates Mickey Cochrane and Lefty Grove.

Philadelphia captured the 1929 World Series in five games, with Foxx batting .350 and slamming two homers. The winning share amounted to $5620, a large sum considering that Jimmie's annual salary at the time was only $5000. Foxx, in fact, was never well paid in comparison to other stars of his period partly because of the financial difficulties of the Philadelphia franchise. His top salary, late in his career with Boston, was $32,000.

In 1930 the Athletics won another pennant. Jimmie contributed a .335 average with 37 homers and 156 runs batted in, finishing third in the league behind Lou Gehrig and teammate Simmons. He batted .333 in the World Series, which Philadelphia captured from St. Louis in six games. In that Series, Foxx hit what he considered to be his biggest homer—a ninth-inning blast off Burleigh Grimes with one man on to give the A's a 2–0 victory and set the stage for the clincher two days later.

That Series home run may have been his most famous, but it certainly was not his longest. Foxx had the strength to hit 600-foot homers, but in those days distances

were not measured. He is one of few men to have reached the upper deck in left field at Yankee Stadium and to have cleared the outfield stands at Chicago's Comiskey Park.

Connie Mack captured his last of three consecutive pennants in 1931. Not until 1972, when the team was based in Oakland, did the Athletics gain another flag. Foxx hit 30 homers and drove in 120 runs, but his average slipped to .291, one of only three seasons in which he slipped below the .300 mark as a regular. In the seven-game World Series loss to the Cardinals, the big first baseman hit .348 to give him an 18-game Series average of .344.

The pennants were behind Philadelphia by 1932, but Foxx's big years remained ahead. His finest season was probably 1932 when he fell only two short of Babe Ruth's home-run mark of 60. Foxx would have reached the figure had not two homers been "rained out" when games were stopped before the fifth inning. Detroit's Hank Greenberg equaled Foxx's 58 in 1938. Only Roger Maris, with 61 home runs in 1961, surpassed both Foxx and Ruth.

Along with the 58 homers, Foxx drove in a league-leading 169 runs and batted .364, missing the batting title and Triple Crown by only three points. The performance of 1932, in which Foxx played in every game, earned him his first of three Most Valuable Player Awards.

Foxx repeated his homer and RBI titles in 1933, with 48 and 163, respectively, and he also added the batting title (.356) to earn the Triple Crown and Most Valuable Player award. He was also adept enough at first base to lead the league in assists. In that 1933 season, Jimmie hit four consecutive home runs over two games to tie a major league record. But the undervaluation of Foxx's talents continued; he actually received a pay cut from $16,333 to $16,000 as the reward for his two finest years. Money was tight in Philadelphia and would become even tighter.

In 1934 Foxx relinquished all three hitting titles, but he still belted 44 homers, drove in 130 runs, and averaged .334. In the standings and at the box office, the Athletics were on a more drastic downward course. In 1934 the team slipped to fifth place with a 68–82 record. In 1935 they crumbled to last, winning only 58 games. Foxx tied Greenberg in the latter season for the home-run lead with 36 and batted .346 with 115 RBIs. But the franchise was in trouble, and Foxx remained the only star Connie Mack had not sold. By the end of 1935, Mack was compelled to make that move. On December 10, Connie traded Foxx and pitcher John Marcum to Boston for two unheralded players (Gordon Rhodes and George Savino), and $150,000, the latter being the important part of the transaction for Philadelphia.

At Boston, Foxx took advantage of the short left-field wall and put his righthanded power to work. In his first season with the Red Sox, Jimmie belted 41 homers and hit .338. After dropping to 36 homers in 1937, he really unleashed the power in 1938, hitting 50 homers, driving in 175 runs, and batting .349. The latter two figures led the league, but that was the year Greenberg hit 58 homers, depriving Foxx of another Triple Crown, but not of his third MVP award.

Foxx won his fourth and final home run title in 1939, hitting 35 for Boston; he then belted 36 homers in 1940 and 19 in 1941, his final season as a regular.

Jimmie was 34 years old in 1942. He had enjoyed his share of Scotch and had seen his better days. He was batting .270 for the Red Sox when he was released on waivers to the Chicago Cubs on June 1, completing his American League career with a .331 league mark. The Cubs tried to platoon Foxx with Phil Cavarretta at first base, but Jimmie had lost his skills and batted only .205. He wisely retired after the 1942 season, but with World War II depriving the major leagues of their top attractions, the Cubs lured Foxx out of retirement in 1944. Foxx managed to collect only 1 hit in 20 times at bat, and the Cubs appointed Jimmie manager of their Portsmouth team in the Piedmont League on August 25.

As though he had not convinced everyone that he could still play if he wished, Foxx signed with the Philadelphia Phillies in 1945. He actually played 89 games for the Phils, batted .268 with seven homers, and pitched in nine games, becoming a moderately successful pitcher in his last year, posting a 1.57 ERA for 23 innings, winning one decision and losing one. Foxx then finally decided to retire as a player. He managed St. Petersburg of the Florida International League in 1947, appearing as a pinch-hitter in six games, and managed Bridgeport of the Colonial League for part of 1949. His last connection with baseball came as a coach with Minneapolis of the American Association in 1958.

In 1951 Jimmie Foxx was named to baseball's Hall of Fame—six years after his last major league game. Had Jimmie played one more season, he would have qualified for baseball's pension plan, which went into effect in 1946. Foxx was one player it would have benefitted. Never wise with money and always quick to pick up a check, Jimmie had made several unwise investments resulting in financial hardship for the majority of his postbaseball years.

In his last years, Foxx resided near Cleveland, where he suffered a heart attack in 1963. On July 21, 1967, while visiting his brother in Miami, he choked on a piece of meat and died.

JAMES EMORY FOXX

Philadelphia (A.L.) 1925–1935
Boston (A.L.) 1936–1942
Chicago (N.L.) 1942, 1944
Philadelphia (N.L.) 1945

G	AB	R	H	2B	3B	HR	RBI	Avg.
2317	8134	1751	2646	458	125	534	1921	.325

During the 1931 World Series, Philadelphia's Foxx prepares to throw the ball after putting out St. Louis Cardinal Jim Bottomley at first. Foxx's team lost the Series that year to the Cards.

Ford Frick (1894-1978)

As National League president and later Commissioner of Baseball, Ford C. Frick quietly presided for 32 years over some of the greatest changes in baseball.

Ford Christopher Frick was born on December 19, 1894, in Wawaka, Indiana, the only boy among five children. His father had been employed as a railroad worker, but at the time of Ford's birth he devoted the majority of his time to farming.

Much of Ford's childhood was spent in Bloomfield, Indiana, a town of 250 residents. He played baseball with other youngsters, and his interest in the game grew.

After completing high school in 1910, Frick enrolled at Fort Wayne International Business College. In 1911 he took a job as a stenographer and typist for a company that manufactured engines for windmills. Ford soon began to report sporting events for newspapers in Terre Haute and Indianapolis to help pay his way through DePauw University in Greencastle, Indiana, from which he graduated in 1915 with an A.B. degree. He lettered in baseball at DePauw, playing first base for the college team.

For reasons of health, Frick moved to Colorado after graduation and became a teacher of business English in Walsenburg. In September 1916, he married Eleanor Cowing; the couple had one child, Frederick.

Taking an assistant professorship at Colorado College in Colorado Springs, Frick moonlighted as a reporter for the Colorado Springs Gazette. During World War I, he did rehabilitation work at the Veterans Bureau in Denver. Following the war, Ford returned to Colorado Springs, where he became a partner in an advertising agency. He also resumed his journalism career with the Colorado Springs Telegraph, beginning a sports column.

As fortune would have it, a retired printer working at a Colorado sanitarium was impressed by Frick's writing and sent a batch of clippings to Arthur Brisbane, an associate of famed publisher William Randolph Hearst. Brisbane, based in New York, made a point of seeing Frick when he passed through Colorado on a trip west. After their meeting, Brisbane offered Ford a job. Frick accepted and then traveled to New York.

In 1922 Ford was assigned to the sports staff of the New York American; his task was to cover the Giant and Yankee baseball games in the Polo Grounds. Later, Frick tended to specialize in the Yankees and became a close friend of Babe Ruth, serving as a ghost writer for the Babe from 1924 to 1932. He reportedly earned as much as $10,000 working with Ruth on newspaper and magazine articles.

In 1923 Brisbane switched to the New York Evening Journal and took Frick with him.

Frick remained on the staff of the Journal until 1934, earning a reputation as one of the outstanding baseball writers in the country. In addition, he was one of the few writers who ventured into sports broadcasting, a field generally viewed as show-business oriented. His background as a factual, hard-working newsman set him apart from many of his radio colleagues.

Frick handled news and sports, and he was also an announcer on the Andre Kostelanetz program at one point. In 1929 Ford commenced work for radio station WOR in New York, doing a daily news broadcast each day at noon and a sports report at 7 P.M. Frick remained with WOR for six years, and in midseason of 1931 he was at the microphone for the first baseball broadcast in New York City—the Brooklyn Dodgers had finally lifted the broadcast blackout. Four announcers covered the game; Frick was joined by Graham McNamee, Ted Husing, and Sid Loberfeld, each representing rival stations. Frick also handled the final, decisive series of the 1931 season between Brooklyn and St. Louis.

In 1933 Frick narrated re-creations of all Giant road games over WOR, using Western Union play-by-play. For his skills, Ford earned the high regard of Giants' manager John McGraw. McGraw's opinion was important for it led to Frick's first baseball administrative post. In February 1934, Frick departed from journalism and broadcasting to succeed Cullen Cain as head of the National League Service Bureau, which was a forerunner of a public relations department.

In October of that year, John A. Heydler retired as National League president. The league did not have far to look for a successor. Although only 40 years old, Frick was chosen to be the eleventh National League president in November 1934.

One of Frick's earliest accomplishments, and one of his proudest, concerned the construction of the Baseball Hall of Fame. Stephen Clark, a Cooperstown, New York, philanthropist and historian, had set out to establish a baseball museum in the town considered to be the birthplace of baseball. In 1935 Clark personally set up a museum, after collecting rare baseball treasures from around the country. At about the same time, Frick visited New York University's Hall of Fame for Great Americans, and he was intrigued by the idea of immortalizing baseball pioneers and players. Ford sold the idea to baseball executives (although Commissioner Landis was not a strong supporter of the plan), suggesting that the Baseball Writers' Association of America handle the voting. The first election was held in 1936, and by 1939, in a celebration of the game's centennial, the National Baseball Hall of Fame and Museum was dedicated. The annual day of induction has since become a significant event of the baseball year.

Three clubs were in financial trouble when Frick became league president— Brooklyn, Philadelphia, and Boston. Ford helped to arrange their sale to more financially stable hands.

Bill Veeck, who would battle Frick often throughout the years, claimed to have sought the purchase of the Phillies in 1944 in order to stock the team with Satchel Paige and other Negro League stars. But the Phillies were awarded to lumber dealer William Cox, who soon thereafter departed from the baseball scene.

Frick supported Branch Rickey in 1947 when the Dodger owner finally integrated baseball by bringing Jackie Robinson to Brooklyn. When the St. Louis Cardinals threatened to strike if Robinson took the field against them, Frick took a firm stand. "Tell them this is America and baseball is America's game," Frick told Cardinal owner Sam Breadon. "If they go on strike, they will be barred from baseball."

Frick's action prevented a strike, and black players began to move into organized baseball in greater numbers. Indeed, the National League was quicker to sign blacks than the American League, which helped end the supremacy of the Yankee-dominated American League.

Frick presided over the National League for 17 years, during which time every club except the Pirates won a pennant. In July 1951, the contract of Baseball Commissioner Happy Chandler expired. There was a heated battle for succession, the principal candidates being Warren Giles, General Douglas MacArthur, Ohio Governor Frank Lausche, Dr. Milton Eisenhower, and Frick. On the sixteenth ballot, Ford was elected to a seven-year term. He was reelected in 1958 for an additional seven years.

Frick's era as Commissioner was eventful, but he maintained a low profile and often allowed the league presidents to handle troublesome matters. He made 17 appearances before congressional anti-trust committees to defend the reserve clause, for which he was frequently criticized as an "owners' commissioner." But such criticism was to be expected since it was the owners who had elected Frick.

Franchise shifting commenced in 1953 when the Boston Braves moved to Milwaukee. Shortly thereafter, the St. Louis Browns shifted to Baltimore and the Philadelphia Athletics to Kansas City. The greatest furor arose when the Dodgers and Giants abandoned New York for the West Coast in 1958.

A third league, the Continental, was proposed in 1960, but it never came into existence. Instead, the two existing leagues expanded, the American League adding Minneapolis-St. Paul and Los Angeles in 1961, and the National League following a year later with Houston and the New York Mets.

During Frick's domain, television reve-

nue became a chief source of income for baseball. In 1954 Ford helped to prepare a $13-million package with the National Broadcasting Company for a Game of the Week telecast, including continued NBC coverage of the World Series and All-Star Game.

One of Frick's most controversial decisions occurred in 1961 while Roger Maris was threatening to shatter Babe Ruth's 34-year-old record of 60 homers in one season. Ruth had accomplished his feat in a 154-game schedule, but Maris was playing in a 162-game season. Late in the season, Frick ruled that unless Maris matched Ruth's mark in 154 games, both records would be listed in the books. Although no asterisk was ever used in publication, the verdict came to be known as the "Asterisk Decision."

In 1965 baseball adopted the free-agent draft, giving each club an equal opportunity to sign players.

Frick's second term came to a close in December 1965, at which time he retired to his home in Bronxville, New York, from where he had commuted daily to his New York City office. His interests included Indian lore and stamp collecting.

In 1970 Ford Frick was named to the Hall of Fame, an appropriate honor for the man who had conceived the idea. In 1973 Frick's book, *Games, Asterisks and People*, was published as a tribute to the game to which he had devoted so many years.

Frick suffered several strokes in his later years and died on April 8, 1978, in Bronxville, New York, at age 83.

Commissioner Frick presents miniature World Series flags and diamond rings to victorious Dodgers in 1960: from left, Charlie Neal, Gil Hodges, Wally Moon, and Walter Alston, manager.

Frankie Frisch (1898-1973)

Frankie Frisch was a member of more pennant-winning teams than any player in National League history. This feat was more than mere coincidence—the legendary "Fordham Flash" was a valuable contributor to each of the eight championship teams for which he played.

Frank Francis Frisch was born on September 9, 1898, in New York City, the son of a wealthy linen manufacturer. He grew up in the borough of the Bronx. While his father did not discourage Frank's interest in athletics, he would have preferred to have him enter the family business or devote closer attention to chemistry.

Frankie enrolled at Fordham Prep and went on to attend Fordham University. Entering college in 1915, he played baseball, football, and basketball, served as captain of all three teams, and earned second-team All-America selection in 1918 as a football halfback. He also participated in track.

Frisch left Fordham after two years and worked in a New York brokerage firm. When World War I broke out, he enrolled in the Student Army Training Corps at Fordham. At the close of the war, Frankie returned to his regular studies and graduated Fordham in 1919.

Art Devlin, Fordham baseball coach and a former New York Giant, urged Giant manager John McGraw to scout Frisch. McGraw sent scout George Gibson to observe the youngster, and when the report was favorable, young Frank was offered a contract.

Frisch, however, would not play in the minor leagues. Frankie had the opportunity to enter business with his father, and he preferred that career to anything except playing in the major leagues. McGraw bought the argument and signed Frisch to a major league contract. On June 17, 1919, Frankie was sent up to the plate to pinch-hit against Grover Cleveland Alexander in the Polo Grounds. Frisch reached base on an error, and his major league career was underway.

McGraw recognized Frisch's speed but knew he lacked the range to play shortstop, his college position. McGraw converted him into a second baseman and third baseman; eventually Frisch won his fame at second. Frankie never enjoyed a reputation for good hands, but he possessed quick reflexes and had great pursuit of a ball. Four times he led the National League in fielding; in 1927 he achieved a major league record by handling 1037 chances at second base.

As a batter, Frisch could hit from either side of the plate. Only Mickey Mantle, who hit with considerably more power, and Pete

Rose rival Frisch's claim as the finest all-time switch-hitter. Frank was a natural left-handed hitter, but McGraw persisted in having him swing both ways. When Frisch batted righthanded, he held the bat in an odd, crosshanded style until McGraw took him in tow.

Larry Doyle, a .289 hitter, was the Giants' second baseman in 1919. But Doyle was 33 years old, and Frisch was cast as his likely successor. This was made more evident by the strong bond of friendship that developed between McGraw and Frisch. Frankie's aggressive, scrappy style of play appealed to McGraw, who generally looked with disdain upon college-educated players.

Frankie, a 5'10", 185-pound hustler, played 54 games in 1919 but batted only .226. He spent considerable time adjacent to McGraw on the Giant bench, and he learned much about the game from the Giants' skipper.

Playing third base in 1920, Frank hit .280 in 110 games and drove in 77 runs. The Giants finished second to the Dodgers that season, but the club was about to embark on a string of four successive pennants.

The first league title came in 1921, with Frisch still stationed primarily at third, but this time batting .341 with 211 hits and 100 RBIs. Included were 31 doubles, 17 triples, and 8 home runs. Frankie also stole 49 bases, a career high and his first of three stolen-base titles. (He again led the league with 48 in 1927 and 28 in 1931.)

In Frisch's first World Series, against the Yankees, he batted .300. It was his lowest average during his four World Series years with the Giants.

Frank batted .327 for the 1922 season and .471 in the World Series, collecting 8 hits in 17 times at bat. It was during this season that Frisch moved to second base on a full-time basis.

The Giants captured the pennant again in 1923, with Frisch leading the league with 223 hits and batting a career high of .348. Although he never won a batting title, Frisch batted .300 or better 13 times, missing only once between 1921 and 1934. In the 1923 World Series, Frankie batted .400—his second .400 Series average in succession.

In 1924 the Giants achieved their fourth pennant in four years. Frisch batted .328 and tied for the runs scored title with 121.

The Giants fell to second place in 1925 and fifth in 1926. Frisch batted .331 and .314 for those years. In 1926, while serving as team captain, Frisch fell out of favor with McGraw. The Giants' manager had been taking out his frustrations on his captain, and it finally took its wear on Frisch in St. Louis. Frisch jumped the club and did not return until the team reached home several days later. Although he publicly resolved the incident with McGraw, the relationship was never the same. Frankie's last big act for the Giants was a September home run that defeated Cincinnati and gave the Cardinals the 1926 pennant.

Not only did Frisch help the Cardinals to the pennant, but on December 20 he was traded to the team. The transaction sent Frisch and pitcher Jimmy Ring to St. Louis for Rogers Hornsby, the darling of the Cardinal fans.

St. Louis rooters were outraged by the trade, and Frisch himself would have preferred to remain in his hometown. But Frankie captured the affections of the Cardinal fans with his play, and ultimately the Cardinals clearly got the better of the deal.

Frisch had a great debut season in St. Louis, missing the Most Valuable Player award by one vote. He batted .337 with 208 hits as the Cards finished second. Hornsby batted .361 for New York but the Giants finished third, and Rogers was traded again after the season. Frisch would stay with St. Louis for the remainder of his playing career.

The 1928 Cardinals returned to the World Series. Frisch, who hit .300 during the season, managed to bat only .231 in the Series. He never achieved the same October magic in St. Louis that he had displayed in New York. His career World Series average wound up at .294 with 58 hits in 50 games.

In 1929 the Cardinals captured the pennant again, with Frankie batting .334. Then came a .346 season for Frisch in 1930 and still another flag for the Cardinals. Frisch drove in 114 runs that year despite the limited power that produced only 105 career home runs. Although he was never a long-ball hitter. Frankie batted No. 3 in the Cardinal lineup and was a noted clutch hitter.

Frisch also held the distinction of belting the first two home runs in All-Star game history for the National League, smacking one each in the 1933 and 1934 contests.

Frankie was awarded the 1931 Most Valuable Player trophy in the first year of voting by the Baseball Writers' Association. Batting .311 during the season, Frisch again proved to be the sparkplug of another Cardinal pennant.

Frankie's first sign of slowing down occurred in 1932. He was hitting under .300 and appeared to lack the old sparkle. Some accused Frisch of not trying his hardest. Angered by manager Gabby Street's reluctance to speak out in his behalf, Frisch personally revealed that badly charley-horsed legs had slowed him down considerably. "If I was managing," said Frisch, "I'd certainly tell the press about a player's injury!" It was his first mention of managing, and the baseball world now began to look at him as a possible successor to Street.

That's Frank Frisch holding the football (above) in the photo of the Fordham Prep gridiron squad. Frisch went on to Fordham College in 1915 and became captain of the football, baseball, and basketball teams. (Below) He is about to take a shot at the basket.

Frisch slides safely twice. (At left) third baseman Jimmy Johnson receives the ball a moment too late. (Below) It is Fred Schliebner reaching for a ball that does not come in time. Umpire at right is Bob Hart.

With the team at a 46–45 mark on July 24, 1933, Street was dismissed and Frisch was appointed player-manager. At 34 he was young but full of experience, and it seemed to be a wise choice. Frankie batted .303 that year and the Cardinals posted a 36–26 record under his management.

By 1934 the Cards had assembled the legendary "Gashouse Gang" of colorful, capable players. The cast included the Dean brothers, Rip Collins, Joe Medwick, Pepper Martin, and Leo Durocher, with Frisch the manager and leader. The team chalked up 95 victories and another pennant. The World Series was the eighth for Frisch the player and his first as manager. In the deciding game, Frankie belted a bases-loaded double to ignite a seven-run inning that brought the World Championship to St. Louis.

Limiting his playing time after the 1934 campaign, Frisch was active through 1937, calling it quits as a player at the age of 40. As manager, he led the Cardinals to a second-place finish in 1935, a tie for second in 1936, and fourth in 1937. The 1938 Cardinals dropped to sixth, and Frisch was fired on September 10.

In 1939 Frankie became a radio announcer for the Boston Braves, and then managed the Pittsburgh Pirates from 1940 through 1946. His teams fared poorly, but Frisch provided an element of interest through his frequent arguments with umpires. He did not hesitate to open an umbrella during a game to demonstrate his belief that it should be called because of rain.

After his Pirate stint, Frisch returned to the radio booth to serve as the Giants' announcer in 1947. He returned to uniform in 1948 as a Giant coach under Leo Durocher. By virtue of his 1947 election to the Hall of Fame, Frankie was now recognized as one of the greats in the game. He became an oft-quoted man who believed that modern baseball could not compare with his era for quality of play.

The Chicago Cubs named Frisch manager in June 1949. He was employed by the Cubs until July 21, 1951, failing to improve the Chicago team.

Out of baseball, Frankie tended his garden in his suburban home in New Rochelle, New York; he then moved with his wife, Ada, to a five-acre farm in Quonochontaug, Rhode Island. His wife died in 1971, and Frisch remarried a year later. On February 8, 1973, Frisch was badly injured in an automobile accident and never recovered. He died on March 12, 1973, in Wilmington, Delaware.

FRANK FRANCIS FRISCH

New York (N.L.) 1919–1926
St. Louis (N.L.) 1927–1937

G	AB	R	H	2B	3B	HR	RBI	Avg.
2311	9112	1532	2880	466	138	105	1242	.316

Pud Galvin (1856-1902)

Pud Galvin pitched more innings than any hurler apart from Cy Young, and he was one of only 14 pitchers to record 300 or more lifetime victories. In a career bridging the eras of underhand and overhand pitching, Galvin never worked from the modern pitching distance of 60 feet, 6 inches, and never wore a glove larger than his hand.

James Francis Galvin was born in the Kerry Patch section of St. Louis, Missouri, on Christmas Day, 1856. James took an early liking to baseball and rapidly became one of the best amateur players in the St. Louis area, playing with men considerably older than himself. He and his catcher and close friend, Tim Sullivan, formed one of the best batteries among town teams in Missouri.

St. Louis adopted its first professional club in 1875 when the top amateur team, the Red Stockings, or Reds, decided to play for a salary. Shortly thereafter, a second professional team, the St. Louis Browns, was formed in the city. The Reds grabbed Galvin before the Browns had the opportunity to do so, and records indicate that Jim compiled a 4–2 record in nine games for the Reds, the fourth-place team in the National Association's final season of operation.

"Pud" (so named because he made pudding out of the hitters) played independent ball with a different St. Louis Red Stockings team in 1876. He pitched a pair of no-hitters that year, including one against a very strong team, the Cass Club of Detroit.

When the Reds disbanded following the 1876 season, Pud joined the Allegheny club of Pittsburgh, where he and his wife settled and resided for many years. This was Pittsburgh's first professional team, and it was a member of the International Association, baseball's first minor league. Galvin pitched 19 games during the season and recorded four shutouts. One of his victories was a 1–0 win over Boston's ace, Tommy Bond, who posted a 40–17 record that season. Galvin's home run won the game.

Pud was a good hitter as well as a brilliant pitcher. During his career, he played 51 games in the outfield and two at shortstop on days that he did not pitch. But his height was only 5'8" and his weight nearly 200 pounds—making it difficult for him to offer much range at any position other than pitcher. Weight was a continuous problem for "The Little Steam Engine," as sportswriters called him. His round, handlebar-mustached face was easily recognizable on any baseball field.

Galvin was also known as "Gentle Jeems." As the name suggests, he was a modest, unassuming man. He seldom drank and his only vice appeared to be spending money. Part of his problem in

saving money was his large family—Pud had 11 children and was a devoted father. He once laughingly claimed that he could start his own baseball team and call it the "Galvanized Nine!"

Jim had excellent control and set a National League record for fewest walks in a career of 4000 or more innings pitched. His strong arm enabled him to take the mound almost every other day, and Pud recorded the most complete games in National League history. He never developed a curveball and his fastball was his primary pitch. Galvin was especially adept at holding runners on base, for his delivery, as Cap Anson argued for years, approximated a balk.

Galvin joined the Buffalo Bisons of the International Association in 1878 and remained with the club in 1879 when it became a member of the National League. The team captured the 1878 minor league flag and made the Bisons the only pennant-winning club for which Galvin played.

In 1879, his first season in the National League, Jim posted a 37–27 record for the third-place Bisons, who won 46 games in all. The following season, he pitched his first of two National League no-hitters, beating Worcester, 1–0, on August 20. Galvin's other no-hitter occurred on August 4, 1884, against Detroit; the Bisons won the game, 18–0. Two days earlier, Jim recorded a one-hitter. Three days after the no-hitter, he pitched a three-hit shutout, and the very next day he pitched 12 innings only to lose, 1–0. It was one of the most remarkable performances of any pitcher during such a short span.

Pud posted a 20–37 mark in 1880 for a team with a 24–58 record. When Galvin threatened to jump to an independent team in San Francisco if he did not receive $900 promised him in back pay, Buffalo finally came up with the money. Pud augmented his income by working as a steamfitter in Pittsburgh during winter months.

Jim remained in Buffalo into the 1885 season. In both 1883 and 1884, he won 46 games. In the latter season, he shut out each of his seven opponents at least once, leading the league with a dozen whitewashings. The Bisons were managed by Jim O'Rourke in 1884, and the club finished a respectable third. Pud's most memorable victory that season was a 2–0 decision over Old Hoss Radbourne which snapped a 20-game winning streak for Providence.

Late in 1885, Pud was transferred to Allegheny of the American Association. The sale price from Buffalo was a hefty $2500, of which Galvin received $700 in cash. He also received a $1000 raise, putting him near the $3000 class. Pud posted

Galvin was that rarity, a good hitter as well as pitcher. As a minor league pitcher, he once shut out the opponent 1–0, chalking up that one run himself with a homer.

a 3–7 record for Allegheny to close out the 1885 season. In 1886 his record stood at 29–21 before the Allegheny club withdrew from the Association in order to join the National League for the 1887 season. This move marked the beginning of the Pittsburgh Pirates.

Galvin became the star pitcher for Pittsburgh in 1887 and had the distinction of winning the first two games for the new National League club. He beat John Clarkson of Chicago, 6–2, and Lady Baldwin of Detroit, 8–3, to spark the Pirates to a fine start. But despite a 28–21 season from Jim, the club finished in sixth place.

Pittsburgh remained sixth in 1888 with Jim registering a 23–25 record. In 1889 Ned Hanlon replaced Horace Phillips as manager in midseason, and the team advanced to fifth. Galvin compiled a 23–16 record.

Now 33 years old and one of the "elder statesmen" of the game, Jim would have preferred to see a peaceful settlement to the Brotherhood rebellion in 1890, which led to the formation of the Players' League. Galvin had hoped the dispute would merely lead to higher National League salaries, and he was discouraged when most of the National League stars jumped to the new circuit. But Pud followed suit and went with Hanlon's Pittsburgh team, contributing a 12–13 record to the sixth-place club. Two other pitchers on the staff notched better records than Galvin.

When the Players' League folded after one season, Pud happily returned to the Pittsburgh club in the National League. But there he found his salary cut in half and two other pitchers—Mark Baldwin and Silver King—hired to handle the bulk of the work. The team finished last; Baldwin posted a 22–28 record and King 14–29. Galvin, shunted aside, registered a 14–13 mark.

A finger injury in 1892 finished Galvin's career with Pittsburgh. Released after 12 games, he signed with St. Louis, where he had begun to play as a boy. Pud was popular in his birthplace but ineffective on the mound, posting a disappointing 5–6 record for the Cardinals.

Galvin might have continued his playing career had he fully recovered from a leg injury suffered in a collision with Cap Anson in 1885. Pud's weight was now well over 200 pounds (he ultimately soared to 300 pounds after his retirement).

Galvin attempted to umpire in the National League, but he retired from the profession after two seasons. He returned to Buffalo, where he was a highly regarded man, and pitched two games for the Eastern League team in 1894. During Pud's glory days in Buffalo, he had become friendly with Mayor Grover Cleveland, and when Al Spalding and Cap Anson visited Cleveland in the White House years later, the President inquired about the health of his "old friend Pud Galvin."

Following his retirement, Pud opened the largest saloon in Pittsburgh, employing nine bartenders. But the business failed, and it seemed typical of Galvin's fate that each of the nine employees went on to open his own establishment. Pud was wiped out.

Galvin took a construction job and moved into a rooming house in the "Little Canada" section of Pittsburgh's North Side. When Pud died on March 7, 1902, the event went virtually unnoticed. A major flood nearby occupied the newspaper columns. Pud died so destitute that friends had to hold a benefit to pay for his funeral. Only six of the 11 children outlived their father.

Sixty-three years after his death, and 29 years after the first election, Pud was inducted into the Hall of Fame as one of the winningest pitchers in baseball history.

JAMES FRANCIS GALVIN

St. Louis (N.A.) 1875
Buffalo (N.L.) 1879–1885
Allegheny (A.A.) 1885–1886
Pittsburgh (N.L.) 1887–1889, 1891–1892
Pittsburgh (P.L.) 1890
St. Louis (N.L.) 1892

G	IP	W	L	Pct.	H	R	ER	SO	BB	ERA
685	5959	361	309	.539	6334	inc.	inc.	1786	744	inc.

Lou Gehrig (1903-1941)

The most durable player ever known to major league baseball was Yankee first baseman Henry Louis Gehrig, a quiet, powerful man who spent the majority of his career in the shadow of Babe Ruth.

Gehrig was born on June 19, 1903, at 309 East 94th Street, in New York City. His German parents had immigrated to New York in 1900, and Lou was the only one of their four children to survive infancy. His father was a janitor, his mother a domestic, and the family struggled to get by. Lou, as Gehrig was generally known, was a devoted son who remained close to his parents throughout his life.

At the High School of Commerce in Manhattan, Lou excelled in sports, but his father disdained "such nonsense." After graduation in 1921, Lou signed a professional baseball contract with Hartford in the Eastern League. He played in a dozen games there under the surname of "Lewis" and batted .261.

In 1922 Gehrig enrolled at Columbia University, aided by his mother's work as a fraternity house domestic. Lou pledged a fraternity—Phi Delta Theta—which today keeps his name in the college memory by presenting an annual award to the major league player best exemplifying Gehrig's high character.

Lou played on the Columbia baseball team, but the school, and indeed the entire Ivy League, was caused considerable embarrassment when Gehrig's participation at Hartford the previous year under an assumed name was discovered. Once a man received payment for sports, as Lou did in the Eastern League, he was declared ineligible for collegiate athletics.

After one year at Columbia, and upon the conclusion of the baseball season which he was forced to sit out, Lou was offered a contract by New York Yankee scout Paul Krichell. Against the wishes of his father, he decided to accept and received a $1500 bonus from the Yankees.

Lou joined the Yankees in June 1923 (the year Yankee Stadium opened), and made seven brief appearances. But Wally Pipp was playing an outstanding first base, and the Yankees decided that Lou would profit from more experience in the Eastern League. Thus, Lou was shipped to Hartford in the beginning of August. He returned to the Yanks after Hartford had completed its schedule. At Hartford Gehrig had batted .304 in 59 games. The young ballplayer stood 6'1" tall, and his 212 pounds were solid muscle. Despite his youth, Lou felt ready to take his place in the Yankee line-up.

Gehrig opened the 1924 season with Hartford, where he batted .369. Called up

by the Yankees on August 31, Lou collected 6 hits in 12 at bats for a .500 average. He never played minor league ball again.

Lou opened the 1925 season on the Yankee bench, with Pipp remaining the starting first baseman. On June 1, Gehrig had a pinch-hitting assignment. The following day, Pipp went to manager Miller Huggins complaining of a headache. Huggins suggested that Pipp take the day off (which he did, going to the race track), and Miller gave Gehrig the starting role at first base. Lou never left the Yankee lineup for 14 seasons, establishing a record of 2130 consecutive games played.

Lou's durability, in addition to his magnificent build and great strength, caused him to be nicknamed "The Iron Horse." He came to symbolize the "class" on which the Yankees prided themselves. Always polite, respectful, and well dressed, he was clearly the inspiration of the team and, appropriately, was the team's appointed captain.

This went well with his teammates, and their respect for Lou was authentic. But in the eyes of the press and the public, Gehrig would never surpass Babe Ruth's popularity.

Ruth, wearing uniform No. 3, and Gehrig, No. 4, batted back-to-back in the Yankee lineup from 1925 until 1935 when Ruth left the Yankees. Gehrig never possessed the great flair and crowd-pleasing ability of Ruth, and by his own admission, the fans would still be talking about The Babe while Lou was at bat.

The figures, of course, also favored Ruth. Gehrig was able to capture only one home run title outright during the years they were teammates, smacking 49 in 1934. In 1931 Lou tied Ruth with 46, but only a fluke prevented Gehrig from capturing the title with 47. Gehrig, running with his head down, passed a runner and was credited only with a triple. That gave him 46 homers, not 47, and he was forced to share the home run title with Babe.

After batting .295 in his rookie season, Gehrig never slipped under .300 until 1938. In 1926 he batted .313, led the league with 20 triples, and drove in more than 100 runs for the first of 13 consecutive years. Gehrig's career total of 1991 RBIs is third only to Ruth and Hank Aaron in baseball history. His RBI totals, aided by Ruth frequently being on base ahead of him, reached peaks of 174 (1930), 175 (1927), and 184 (1931), the latter being an American League record.

In 1927 Gehrig captured his first Most Valuable Player award (he also won in 1936) by hitting 47 home runs and batting

Gehrig has a brief triumph as a Columbia University athlete: (right and below) in baseball uniform and playing on the quadrangle; (far right) on the gridiron. Gehrig's college playing days ended quickly when it was discovered he had played pro ball in 1921.

.373. Ruth belted 60 homers that year as the heart of the 1927 Yankee batting order came to be known as "Murderer's Row." Gehrig's honor was a tribute to the leadership he displayed on the Yankees.

In World Series play, Gehrig was at his finest. He played on eight Yankee pennant winners (1926–1928, 1932, 1936–1939) and hit a combined .361 with 10 homers and 35 runs batted in. In 1928, against the Cardinals, Lou batted .545 with four homers and nine RBIs in just four games; and in 1932, against the Cubs, Gehrig hit .529 with three homers and eight RBIs in four games.

Gehrig's finest day on the field came on June 3, 1932, at Philadelphia when he smacked four consecutive home runs in a single game, the first man in the twentieth century to accomplish the feat. The first three homers were hit off George Earnshaw, and the fourth against Leroy Mahaffey. On three other occasions (1927, 1929, and 1930), the lefthanded-hitting Gehrig belted three in one game. Gehrig had a career total of 493 home runs, which placed him second only to Babe Ruth at the time of his retirement.

For all of his exploits, Gehrig's salary was always dwarfed by Ruth's. The Babe earned $80,000 per year at his peak, while Gehrig, not a good bargainer, made a high of $39,000.

When Ruth left the Yankees in 1935, Gehrig stood alone at last. But the following year, a much-heralded rookie, Joe DiMaggio, joined the team. Before long he had replaced Gehrig as the talk of the baseball world.

In 1934 Lou won baseball's Triple Crown, reaching a career high of 49 home runs, driving in 165 runs and winning his only batting title with a .363 mark. Two years later, Lou matched the 49 figure to gain his final home-run title.

Gehrig married Eleanor Twitchell, a wealthy Chicago debutante, on September 29, 1933. Until that time, he had lived with his parents, for whom he had bought a home in 1928 in New Rochelle, New York.

In 1938 Gehrig's batting average slipped to .295, with 29 homers and 114 RBIs—fine credentials, but quite a bit below his previous showings. He failed to drive in a single run in the 1938 World Series, and there arose a question of his health the following spring. His weight was falling, and the once great hulk of a man was not filling out his uniform as well.

Lou opened the season as usual at first base, but on May 2, 1939, after having collected only four hits in the first eight games, he sent word to manager Joe McCarthy that he wanted to talk to him.

"I think I'm hurting the team," Lou told his manager. "Maybe it would be better if I took a rest for a while."

Gehrig, the "Iron Horse," in motion in 1938, still smashing out long ones, although that year the illness that was to claim his life began to take its toll.

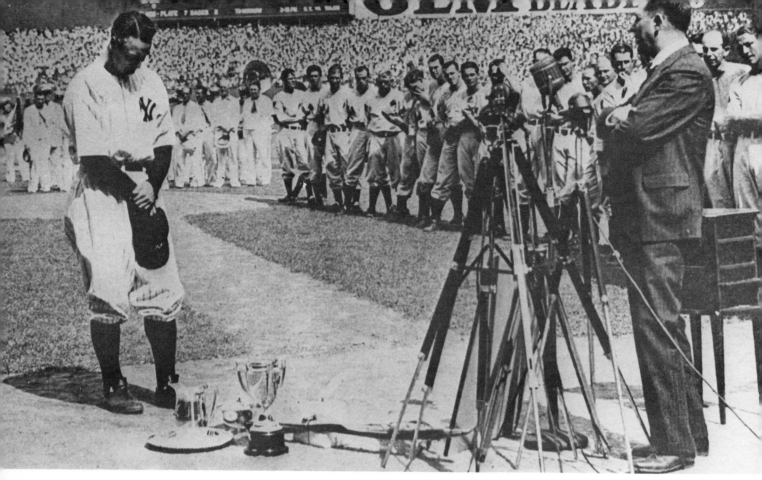

Lou Gehrig Day, July 4, 1939, after doctors had given him only two years to live. Faced with that bleak prospect, Gehrig, at left, told teammates and fans, "I consider myself the luckiest man on the face of the earth."

When the lineups were posted on the scoreboard in Briggs Stadium, Detroit, the fans knew Gehrig's streak was over. As captain of the club, he took the lineup to home plate before the game—a lineup with the name Babe Dahlgren written in at first base. The fans stood and gave Gehrig a tremendous ovation, and Lou returned to the dugout in tears. After 2130 games—14 full seasons—Gehrig, the six-time All Star, rode the bench.

Early in June, Lou entered the Mayo Clinic for tests, which showed that he had amyotrophic lateral sclerosis—a hardening of the spinal cord, producing symptoms similar to polio. The rare disease, known today as "Gehrig's Disease," was fatal, and he was cautiously given just two years to live.

Hurriedly, the Yankees arranged a day in Lou's honor. It was held on July 4, 1939, in Yankee Stadium before 61,808 fans. The 1927 and 1939 Yankees stood by as a tearful Lou, recalling all that baseball had meant to him, said, "Today, I consider myself the luckiest man on the face of the earth." Babe Ruth, never a close friend, but always identified with Lou, gave him a great hug in an emotional scene. Suddenly, and perhaps for the first time in his

career, Lou was fully appreciated by the baseball fans. But it was too late. He never played another game, serving merely as inspiration for the remainder of that year in the Yankee dugout.

The Baseball Writers' Association voted Lou into the Hall of Fame that summer, and the Yankees retired his uniform—the first man ever to be so honored.

Mayor Fiorello LaGuardia appointed Lou to the New York City Parole Commission following the 1939 season, and Lou worked diligently with youth groups until a month before his death on June 2, 1941, 17 days before what would have been his thirty-eighth birthday.

In 1941 the Yankees dedicated a monument to Lou in Yankee Stadium, and the following year Gary Cooper portrayed Gehrig in a memorable movie, "Pride of the Yankees."

HENRY LOUIS GEHRIG

New York (A.L.) 1923–1939

G	AB	R	H	2B	3B	HR	RBI	Avg.
2164	8001	1888	2721	535	162	493	1991	.340

Charlie Gehringer (b. 1903)

Charlie Gehringer could perform almost any feat on a baseball field, but he did it so effortlessly, and with so little flair or color, that he came to be called "The Mechanical Man." The nickname obscured his true brilliance, for Charlie was one of the greatest second basemen in the history of the American League.

Charles Leonard Gehringer was born on May 11, 1903, in Fowlerville, Michigan, a small farming community approximately 60 miles north of Detroit. When Charlie and his brother, Al, were not helping out with the chickens, cows, and pigs on the family farm, they laid out a baseball field near their property and practiced each day after school. Eventually, Charlie starred for his high school and town teams, and he then went on to play football and baseball for the University of Michigan.

After completing one year of college, Charlie decided upon a career in professional baseball. The year was 1924, and Bobby Veach had just terminated a 12-year career in the Detroit outfield, having been sold to Boston in January. Still loyal to the Tigers, however, Veach arranged for Gehringer to try out at Navin Field in Detroit under the eye of Tiger manager Ty Cobb. Veach had been impressed by the youth after a friend had recommended him, and Bobby now passed his impression along to Cobb.

Gehringer, at this time a third baseman, accepted a small minor league contract and reported to London in the Michigan-Ontario League. Immediately, he was ordered to learn second base, for Fred Haney and Bobby Jones were already keeping the Tigers well-manned at third.

Gehringer adjusted to his new position with ease and batted .292 in 112 games. At the close of the 1924 season, Charlie reported to the Tigers and played five games, collecting six hits for a .545 batting average. In 1925 Gehringer was optioned to Toronto, where he hit .325 with 25 home runs and 108 runs batted in. Again he joined the Tigers at the end of the campaign, but this time it was to stay. Charlie played the final eight games that season, replacing the Tigers' regular second baseman, Frank O'Rourke. In 1926 O'Rourke was demoted to utility infielder, and Charlie played his first of 16 consecutive seasons as the Tigers' second baseman.

The 5'11" lefthanded-hitting Gehringer attributed substantial credit to Ty Cobb for molding him into a major-league hitting star. Charlie batted .277 as a rookie, but only once thereafter (until 1941) did he fall below the .300 mark—the year was 1932, and his batting average .298.

Although the Tigers at one point considered moving Gehringer to shortstop, he remained a second baseman for his entire career. Playing 2205 games at second for

Detroit, Charlie led the league in games played four times and played in more than 150 contests in nine different seasons. His only movements from second were a brief, six-game stint at third base in 1926, and a stay of nine games at first base in 1931. He played second with unmatched grace, eventually setting an American League record by leading the league in assists seven times.

In 1927 George Moriarty replaced Cobb as Tiger manager. Gehringer hit .317 that year, scored 110 runs, and helped Detroit rise from sixth to fourth in the standings.

Noted for his quiet demeanor, Gehringer, it was said, was a fellow who said hello on opening day and goodbye when the season ended. With his sad, expressionless face, Gehringer lent himself to "The Mechanical Man" image.

Charlie lifted his average to .320 in 1928, but he enjoyed his first particularly outstanding season in 1929, leading the league in games played, runs scored, hits, doubles, triples, and stolen bases, while also leading American League second basemen in putouts and fielding percentage. His .339 batting average dispelled all doubts about his capabilities at the plate, and his 215 hits marked the first of seven seasons in which he would surpass the 200 mark. Five of the seasons (1933–1937) were consecutive. The 28 stolen bases in 1929, a low total to lead the league, was a career high for Charlie, who never attempted to steal many bases.

Bucky Harris was appointed Tiger manager in 1929, but the Tigers remained a sub-.500 club. In 1930, despite a .330 season from Gehringer, Detroit again finished fifth.

Charlie injured his throwing arm in 1931 and was limited to 101 games. It was the only serious injury of his career, but he still managed to hit .311 for the season. Without Gehringer in the lineup regularly, however, the Tigers fell to seventh place.

Charlie came back in 1932 to play 152 games, driving in 107 runs and batting .298. For an infielder other than a first baseman to drive in more than 100 runs, as Gehringer did seven times, was a rare accomplishment.

The Tigers continued to flounder in 1933, and late in the season coach Del Baker replaced Harris as manager. Charlie hit .325 that year with 105 RBIs. He became the second baseman in the major's first All-Star contest, held on July 6 in Chicago. Although he went 0–3, Charlie's combined average for six All-Star games (20 at bats) was a sparkling .500, an All-Star game record.

In 1934 Mickey Cochrane assumed the

managerial reins and led the Tigers to the pennant. Gehringer, now a nine-year veteran at the age of 31, hit .356 with 11 homers and 127 RBIs. The batting average placed him second only to Lou Gehrig in the American League, and his RBI total was the fifth highest. Although the Tigers lost the World Series in seven games to St. Louis, Charlie batted .379 with 11 hits.

The Tigers repeated as league champions in 1935, with Gehringer batting .330, belting 19 homers, and driving in 108 runs. The Tigers then captured the Series, besting the Cubs with Gehringer batting .375.

Detroit finished second to the Yankees in 1936. Charlie collected 227 hits for a .354 average. Included were 60 doubles, seven short of the major league record and a total that has not been reached since. Only five times in baseball history has the figure been surpassed, and the mark helped to place Gehringer as the fifth leading doubles (574) hitter at the time of his retirement.

In 1937 Charlie registered a career-high batting average of .371 to capture the championship. His mark was 20 points higher than the runnerup, Lou Gehrig. Gehringer also captured the league's Most Valuable Player award, despite the fact that the Yankees won the pennant.

Gehringer belted 20 home runs, a career high, in 1938 and batted .306. He followed this performance with a .325 mark in 1939.

In 1940 the Tigers enjoyed another pennant-winning season. Although Charlie batted .313 during the season, he hit only .214 in the World Series, bringing his career Series average to .321.

In 1941 Gehringer batted a disappointing .220, but he led the league's second basemen in fielding percentage for the ninth time. Recognizing that his skills had begun to fade, Charlie prepared to retire. But the onset of World War II drained the Tiger dugout of players, and Charlie agreed to remain on the roster as a pinch-hitter and reserve infielder.

Serving as coach and pinch-hitter in 1942, Charlie went to the plate 45 times, collecting 12 hits for a .267 average. The part-time service marked the end of his playing career. After the 1942 season, Charlie entered the Navy as a lieutenant and served in its Fitness Program through the war years.

Following his discharge, Gehringer returned to Detroit and went into business with Ray Forsyth, a local automobile dealer. The two men became successful at selling interior inventions to automobile manufacturers in Detroit. While his top baseball salary had been a creditable $35,000, his postbaseball career became a more profitable one.

In 1949, the year of his election to the Hall of Fame, Charlie married Josephine Stillen. He had previously lived with his mother in a suburban home near Detroit throughout his Tiger career, but she had died in 1946.

Charlie was coaxed back into baseball in August 1951 by Tiger owner Walter O. Briggs. Up until then Gehringer had spent his time tending to business and playing golf. Briggs wanted Gehringer to serve as general manager, and Charlie held the position for two years, finally hiring Muddy Ruel to replace him following the 1953 season. Gehringer admitted to a lack of preparation for the assignment, and he was astute enough to recognize his own shortcomings in the position.

Gehringer remained a vice-president of the Tigers until 1959 when he retired from baseball. As reserved in retirement as he was when a player, Charlie remained one of the most polished professionals ever to have played second base.

CHARLES LEONARD GEHRINGER

Detroit 1924–1942

G	AB	R	H	2B	3B	HR	RBI	Avg.
2323	8858	1773	2839	574	146	184	1427	.321

(At left) Gehringer in 1934 when his team, the Detroit Tigers, won the American League pennant. Gehringer (center above) returns to the Tigers as general manager in 1951. With him are, from left, Gerry Priddy, Aaron Robinson, Red Rolfe, and Dizzy Trout.

Josh Gibson (1911-1947)

Josh Gibson was considered the finest slugger ever to play in the Negro Leagues. Numerous baseball experts believe that if Gibson had been given the opportunity to play in the major leagues, he might have rivaled Babe Ruth for the prestige of being the game's premier power hitter. But Josh died in 1947, before Jackie Robinson broke the color line with the Brooklyn Dodgers.

Joshua Gibson was born on December 21, 1911, in Buena Vista, Georgia. His parents, Mark and Nancy Gibson, extracted a meager existence from their small farm. Josh was the first of three children. His younger brother, Jerry, later played one season (1943) in the Negro Leagues with Cincinnati.

In 1923 Mark Gibson traveled north to visit relatives in Pittsburgh and to try to establish a better means of support for his family. He found employment as a laborer for Carnegie-Illinois Steel, and he sent for his family early in 1924. Josh later called the move to Pittsburgh's North Side "the greatest gift Dad ever gave me."

Josh had completed the fifth grade in Georgia, and he continued his elementary school education in Pittsburgh. After completing ninth grade at the Allegheny Pre-Vocational School, he dropped out to work as an apprentice in an air-brake factory. By now, sports was his overwhelming interest. He became not only an accomplished playground baseball player, but an outstanding swimmer, winning several medals in Pittsburgh's summer recreation programs.

Before long Josh had established a reputation as the best young ballplayer in town. Gibson was always the first selected in choose-up games, and he could always be relied upon to strap on rollerskates and travel as far as six miles to Bellevue to participate in sandlot games.

Josh wore his first baseball uniform at the age of 16, catching for the Gimbels Athletic Club, an all-black amateur team in Pittsburgh. While he occasionally played the outfield during his baseball career, he was principally a catcher, his barrel-chested frame lending itself to that position. Gibson stood 6'1", weighed 215 pounds, and had broad shoulders and thick arms. With his friendly disposition and a pleasant face, Josh tended to reflect his boylike innocence.

Gibson was not a first-rate defensive player, and he often had trouble with foul pops. But Josh was a rugged competitor who worked hard at improving his game.

Gibson was a fan of the Pittsburgh Pirates in the days of Paul and Lloyd Waner and Pie Traynor, but all Josh could hope for was an opportunity to play with the Homestead Grays, the local team in the Negro American League. In 1929 and 1930,

Josh caught on with the Crawford Colored Giants, a semipro club. He helped organize the team's schedule. Crawford would play other semipro clubs under a free admission policy, passing a hat among the crowd to raise money. Rarely did Josh receive more than a few dollars for each game.

On July 25, 1930, the defending champion Kansas City Monarchs came to Pittsburgh for a series with the Grays. The Monarchs, featuring Satchel Paige, carried a portable lighting system with them, and the July 25 game would be the first night game ever played in Forbes Field.

Joe Williams, a hard-throwing pitcher, was to work for the Grays that evening, but early in the game the Homestead catcher walked off the field rather than handle Williams' fastballs under the poor lighting. Judy Johnson, the Homestead manager, had seen Gibson catch semipro games and knew that the 18-year-old strongboy was an excellent prospect. Fortunately for Johnson and Gibson, Josh was in the stands that night. Johnson signaled him to the field, and a crowd of 30,000 waited while Gibson suited up. Josh did not collect any hits that game, but he did find a place for himself with the Homestead Grays.

Recognizing the need to polish up his catching skills, Josh caught batting practice and then the regular games. He never seemed to play as much baseball as he desired. Later on in his career it was not uncommon for Josh to play 200 games a year with his Negro League teams, and then play winter ball in Mexico or the Carribean. An old roommate remembered Josh spotting a sandlot game from his hotel window and racing down the stairs to join the action. And this was after a double header in which Gibson had caught both games.

Josh had simple pleasures and lived a clean life at that point. While other players would go drinking at night and searching for women, Josh would frequent ice cream parlors. Josh married in 1930, but his wife died in childbirth a year later when Josh, Jr., and a twin sister were born. The children were reared by Josh's sister while Gibson played ball.

Record keeping was, at best, haphazard in the Negro Leagues, especially since many of the games were exhibitions. Only Sunday games counted in league standings to prevent the better teams from spurting too far ahead. Thus, no one knows for certain how many home runs Gibson hit, but estimates reach as high as 84 in a single season. Undoubtedly, Josh

(At right) Gibson catches for the Pittsburgh Crawfords, a team that boasted many of the all-time great black players before the color line was broken in the majors. (Opposite page) Gibson rounds third for the Homestead Grays in a 1944 game against the Baltimore Elite Giants in Washington's Griffith Stadium, where Negro League ball outdrew the Senators. The series of pictures below shows the Gibson follow-through.

Playing to packed stands in Chicago's Comiskey Park, Josh Gibson makes it safely home during the 1944 Negro All-Star game. That Gibson was a slugger of at least Babe Ruth's ilk was recognized by all who followed baseball.

was one of the strongest hitters in the sport, and he accomplished many of his great feats in major league parks.

Gibson is reported to have been the only man ever to hit a fair ball out of Yankee Stadium, belting one high over the upper deck in left field. The ball landed in the far reaches of the visitors' bullpen on the way down. Since it had cleared the roof before its descent, it was considered out of the park.

Josh repeatedly hit tape-measure home runs in Washington's Griffith Stadium, where Negro League baseball outdrew the Washington Senators. Clark Griffith, seeing the great crowds that turned out to watch Gibson, considered signing him and breaking the color line in the 1930s. But nothing came of the idea. Walter Johnson had told Griffith that Gibson was worth one-quarter of a million dollars.

While stars like Joe DiMaggio and Ted Williams soared toward six-figure contracts, Gibson seldom received a salary of more than $10,000 per year for a full 12 months of baseball. In his peak earning years in the early 1940s, Josh collected about $1000 per month, far above the league's average but well below Satchel Paige, who was far more of a showman than the quiet Gibson.

After reportedly belting 75 home runs for Homestead in 1931, Gibson and several other Negro League stars jumped to the Pittsburgh Crawfords, who were owned by Gus Greenlee. Paige was also a member of the team and, with Gibson, formed one of the greatest baseball batteries. Cool Papa Bell, Judy Johnson, Oscar Charleston, Ted Page, Leroy Matlock, and Jimmie Crutchfield were other fine players on the team. Gibson spent five years with the Crawfords, earning his greatest fame with them. His habit of hitching up his sleeve while waiting for the pitch, lifting his leg slightly, and then swinging with all his might were well known even to white audiences.

After the 1934 season, a group of Negro League stars faced a group of major league stars in a series of nine exhibition games. Only Dizzy Dean could defeat Paige, and Gibson hit well against all the major league pitchers.

When the Crawfords disbanded following the 1936 season, Paige went to Kansas City and Gibson decided to return to Homestead. Greenlee, the Crawford owner, maintained that he still owned Gibson, and eventually a trade was worked out in which Gibson and Judy Johnson went to Homestead for two journeymen players, Pepper Bassett and Henry Spearman.

Gibson played ball in the Dominican Republic before spring training ended in 1937, but by July he was back leading the Grays to their first pennant. Josh remained with Homestead until 1940, at which time he jumped to Mexico for two years, taking advantage of the high altitude and thin air to hit tremendous home runs.

Josh received a salary of $6000 playing for Veracruz, but when Homestead filed a $10,000 suit against Gibson and laid claim to his home in Pittsburgh, he returned to the Grays and the suit was dropped.

Gibson's skills began to slip during the war years. He had taken to drinking, and while it never caused him to miss a game, he was occasionally suspended for "failing to observe training rules." In fact, a suspension caused Josh to miss the 1945 Negro League All-Star game, the only one in which he failed to play.

Plagued by recurrent headaches and apparent cartilage damage to his knees, Josh's abilities started to fade. When talk arose of black players entering organized baseball, he listened with interest and brooded silently when others were offered jobs in 1946 and no overtures came his way. Josh was considered a bad risk by major league clubs in view of his age and failing health.

On January 20, 1947, Gibson became ill at his mother's home in Pittsburgh. Josh told her that he thought he was having a stroke and as she sought to cheer him by bringing in his trophies, he fell asleep and died. Cause of death was listed as a cerebral hemorrhage.

Josh never saw Jackie Robinson play in the majors. More regrettable was that millions never saw Josh in major league competition. Josh, Jr., played in the Mid-Atlantic League in 1948, but that was as close as the Gibson family came to reaching the major leagues.

In 1972 a special committee established to place Negro League stars in the Hall of Fame selected Josh Gibson, who at last found himself a teammate of baseball's immortals.

JOSHUA GIBSON

Negro Leagues 1930–1946

No records available.

Lefty Gomez (b.1908)

One of the finest pitchers in the history of the New York Yankees, Lefty Gomez was a four-time 20-game winner who compiled a perfect record in World Series play. He was also one of the greatest wits to play professional baseball.

Vernon Gomez was born on November 26, 1908, in Rodeo, California. Although he was of Spanish-Irish descent, Gomez never learned the Spanish language.

The nickname "Lefty" was tagged to Gomez while he starred on the mound for Richmond High School in California. He weighed a scanty 146 pounds at the time, but the 6'2" southpaw could really fire the baseball.

Nick Williams, manager of the San Francisco Seals of the Pacific Coast League, signed the 19-year-old Gomez to a contract in 1928. Lefty was optioned to Salt Lake in the Utah-Idaho League, where he led the circuit in appearances (39) and strikeouts (172). His record was a mediocre 12–14, but he showed sufficient poise to be promoted to the Seals in 1929.

In the Coast League, Lefty posted an 18–11 record and topped the league with a 3.44 earned-run average. He pitched 267 innings and struck out 159 batters. Despite his frail appearance, he received the recommendation of Yankee West Coast scout, Bill Essick, and was purchased by the club for $35,000.

Joining the 1930 Yankees, Lefty found himself a member of the great Murderers' Row team headed by Babe Ruth and Lou Gehrig. Although only 21, Lefty's quick wit immediately made him popular with the established stars, and he developed an especially good rapport with Ruth.

In subsequent years Babe would bet Gomez $500 each season that he would not collect 10 hits during the year. Lefty always liked to kid about his hitting. He took exception to the omission of his name from the list of great hitters struck out by Carl Hubbell in the 1934 All-Star Game. Hubbell struck out Ruth, Gehrig, Jimmie Foxx, Al Simmons, and Joe Cronin in succession. After Bill Dickey singled to end the string, Hubbell also fanned Gomez, but Lefty's name was never included with the "other great hitters."

Lefty found himself in deep water in the majors in 1930. After 15 appearances, Gomez had posted a 2–5 record with a 5.55 ERA. He was then farmed out to St. Paul of the American Association to work on his control, fielding, and the ability to hold runners on. He improved the latter technique by speeding his release of the ball from the stretch position. His exceptionally high kick had previously given runners the opportunity to take big leads.

Lefty also improved his fielding and perfected a slow curveball, which in time would become his best pitch. He posted an 8–4 record with St. Paul and was recalled for the 1931 season, Joe McCarthy's first as Yankee manager.

Lefty's first full year in the majors was a great success. He recorded a 21–9 mark, with a 2.63 ERA and 150 strikeouts. It was the beginning of a great Yankee career for Lefty, who had only one losing season thereafter.

In 1932 Gomez posted a 24–7 record, and the Yankees returned to the World Series after a three-year absence. Lefty started the second game of the Series against the Cubs, defeating another thin hurler, Lon Warneke, 5–2. He called the victory his greatest thrill in baseball. It was the first of six consecutive World Series victories recorded by Gomez; he never suffered a defeat. That mark remains the finest pitching record ever posted in Series competition.

Already famed for his sense of humor, Lefty signed a 12-week contract after the Series to perform a vaudeville routine in his Yankee uniform at Madison Square Garden. But the act failed and was canceled after three weeks. Of greater interest to Gomez at this point was his romance with Broadway actress June O'Dea, whom he married on February 26, 1933.

Lefty had his finest season in 1934, but the Yankees failed to win the pennant. Gomez had increased his weight to 175 pounds, and he was really humming the ball past the hitters. Lefty compiled a 26–5 record that year, leading the league in victories, percentage (.839), innings (282), strikeouts (158), ERA (2.33), and complete games (25). All that prevented Lefty from winning 30 games was a freak accident in Washington—his spikes caught on the pitching mound and he wrenched his arm.

Arm difficulties continued to plague Gomez during the following two seasons, in which he posted 12–15 and 13–7 records, both far from his established form. Nevertheless, he retained that fine slow curve, his ability to fool hitters, and his technique of keeping them off stride. In 1936 he captured two more World Series games for the Yankees. Gomez also made the Series memorable by pausing on the mound to watch an airplane fly overhead.

Lefty bounced back in 1937 to post a league-leading 21 victories against only 11 losses, and to again top league pitchers in strikeouts (194) and ERA (2.33). In the World Series against the Giants, he recorded two complete game victories and allowed only three runs in 18 innings.

Lefty Gomez's exceptionally high kick makes a dramatic picture. Gomez had to learn to compensate for the kick with a fast release of the ball, since in his early playing days the kick gave base runners time to take big leads.

In 1938 Lefty permitted only three home runs during his 239 innings pitched. However, "El Goofy" was in danger of his first World Series setback that fall when, trailing the Cubs in the second game, 3–2, he left for a pinch-hitter. But the Yankees rallied on the strength of a Frank Crosetti home run to give Gomez his sixth and final World Series victory. Johnny Murphy saved the game for Gomez in relief, a common occurrence at that stage of Lefty's career. Gomez never failed to give Murphy credit when recalling his own success.

Lefty's final World Series appearance came in 1939, following a 12–8 regular season. He started the third game against Cincinnati but retired after one inning because of a sore arm.

Gomez experienced serious arm trouble in 1940 as the Yankees fell to third place, and the high-kicking southpaw pitched only 27 innings, splitting six decisions and posting a 6.67 ERA. The Yankees attempted to trade him to the Dodgers after the season, but like most clubs Brooklyn considered Gomez to be finished and thus passed him by.

Unable to deal him, the Yankees retained Gomez on the roster in 1941. Lefty proved to be a surprise, leading the league with a .750 winning percentage on the strength of a 15–5 record. Lefty was unusually wild that season, but he always seemed crafty enough to come out the victor. On August 1, he set a major league record by walking 11 batters en route to a shutout over St. Louis, 9–0.

Selected for seven All-Star games, Lefty became the winning pitcher in three (1933, 1935, and 1937) and the losing pitcher in one (1938).

Arm trouble finally caught firm hold of Lefty in 1942. Although only 33 years old, he pitched but 80 innings and posted a 6–4 record. He did not appear at all in the World Series against the Cardinals.

On January 25, 1943, Lefty was sold to the Boston Braves. The Yankees and Gomez parted on the best of terms, and he always considered himself a Yankee regardless of the uniform he wore.

Braves' manager Casey Stengel took Gomez north with the team after spring training, but Lefty did not appear in a single game and was released on May 19. Five days later, the Washington Senators signed him. But after pitching and losing one game, Gomez called it quits.

The Yankees hired Lefty to manage their Binghamton farm team (Eastern League) in June 1946. He pitched two games in his two seasons at Binghamton.

The clever Gomez, his manner now that of a professional comic, turned to radio work and banquet speaking, earning plaudits wherever he appeared. He was a close friend of Joe DiMaggio, and was the one man who could be relied upon to bring a smile to Joe's usually serious face.

Lefty became a representative of Wilson Sporting Goods, serving the company as a goodwill ambassador. He also served baseball in a similar capacity wherever he spoke. Gomez and his son were involved in a land-investment company which did well, but another son was killed in a motorcycle accident in 1973.

In 1972 Lefty was elected to the Hall of Fame, joining teammates Babe Ruth, Lou Gehrig, Joe DiMaggio, Bill Dickey, Red Ruffing, Earle Combs, and Manager Joe McCarthy in Cooperstown.

VERNON GOMEZ

New York (A.L.) 1930–1942
Washington 1943

G	IP	W	L	Pct.	H	R	ER	SO	BB	ERA
368	2503	189	102	.649	2290	1091	929	1468	1095	3.34

Goose Goslin (1900-1971)

Goose Goslin was a member of five pennant-winning teams in the American League, and also participated in every World Series game ever played by the Washington Senators.

Leon Allen Goslin was born on a small farm in Salem, New Jersey, on October 16, 1900. He acquired his love for baseball early in life, and consequently would often bicycle 10 miles or more to participate in sandlot games. Farm chores built up Goslin's strength, and a day seldom passed in which the burly youth did not sharpen his skills as a pitcher.

Leon quit school at the age of 14 when his father became ill and in need of assistance to run the farm. Eventually, the farm was sold and the family moved to downtown Salem.

Goslin earned some money playing semipro ball in southern New Jersey, but, as he described it, "I'd have paid them to let me play."

While pitching semipro ball, Goslin was discovered by International League umpire Bill McGowan. McGowan told young Goslin that he could get him a job in Rochester, but Bill soon learned that the Rochester club had a full complement of pitchers. Considering himself obligated to the youngster, McGowan arranged for him to sign with the Columbia, South Carolina, team in the Sally League.

Goslin never forgot McGowan's efforts, and he later urged Clark Griffith, influential owner of the Senators, to help bring McGowan into the American League. Bill then went on to become the league's senior umpire, serving for 20 years (1925–1944).

Goslin's father wanted his boy to be a farmer, but young Goslin was so full of the enthusiasm for baseball that nothing could restrain him from joining the Columbia team in 1920. While Goslin's early pitching record was a respectable 6–5 mark, with a 2.44 earned-run average, manager Zinn Beck was not impressed. Constantly ducking hard foul liners near his third-base coaching box, Beck decided to end Goslin's pitching days by converting him into an outfielder. As a hitter that first year, Goslin batted .317 in 90 games. The origin of the nickname "Goose" has never been pinned down. It either derived from his bulbous nose or his method of chasing fly balls—circling beneath them and waving his arms. In either case, the name did not originate until Goslin played professional ball. Once it was tagged on him, it applied for the remainder of his life, and Goslin always called himself "Goose."

Goslin had a sensational season at Columbia in 1921. He led the Sally League with a .390 batting average, 214 hits, 124 runs scored, and 131 runs batted in. He

also belted 16 home runs, 13 triples, and 38 doubles. Manager Beck, a friend of Clark Griffith, tipped off the Washington Senators owner to Goslin, and Griffith sent scout Joe Engel to observe him. When he received no word from Engel after several weeks, Griffith forgot about Goose.

Late in the 1921 season, Griffith was dining with his friend Jack Dunn, owner of the Baltimore Orioles minor league club. In the course of conversation, Dunn revealed his intent to purchase Goslin for $5500. Griffith promptly bought Goslin the next morning for $6000.

Joining Washington late in the 1921 campaign, Goslin appeared in 14 games and batted .260. In 1922 he went to spring training hopeful of earning a starting position. But he wandered away from the training camp one day and worked out with a local track team, repeatedly tossing the 12-pound shotput. His throwing arm became sore and never regained its strength. With his arm gone, Goose had lost his only defensive skill, for he was not particularly graceful, quick, or adept at playing the outfield.

That same year he suffered a fracture of the wrist, but by the close of the 1922 season, Goose had participated in 101 games and batted .324. It was the first of 11 seasons in which Goslin would hit .300 or better, leading to a lifetime average of .316.

In 1923 Goslin hit an even .300 and tied for the league lead with 18 triples. Then in 1924, the Senators, under manager Bucky Harris, captured their first pennant, edging the Yankees by two games. Goslin led the team with a .344 average, and he also led the league with 129 runs batted in, his only RBI crown despite 11 seasons of 100 or more RBIs. But Goslin was competing against strong company in those days, notably the Yankee duo of Babe Ruth and Lou Gehrig.

Always a great clutch player, Goslin batted .344 in the 1924 World Series, collecting 11 hits, including 3 home runs. Washington bested the Giants in seven games.

In 1925 the Senators again won the pennant, with Goslin hitting .334, collecting 201 hits, and leading the league with 20 triples. Although the Pirates bested the Senators in seven games in the World Series, Goslin batted .308 in the Series with another three homers.

Goose's first batting championship came in dramatic style on the final day of the 1928 season. He and St. Louis' Heinie Manush were locked head to head for the championship, and both sought it badly.

As luck would have it, the two were opposing left fielders on the final day of the schedule in St. Louis. Manush collected two hits in three times at bats for a .378 mark; Goslin was but a fraction ahead. An out on his last at bat would cost him the title, a walk or a hit would win it. Goose was inclined not to take his turn at bat, but teammates warned him of the possible criticism if he did not. Goslin went up to the plate and the count quickly reached 0–2. On the following pitch, he poked "a lucky hit" to right field to win the championship with a .379 average.

A year and a half later, Goose was traded to St. Louis for Alvin Crowder and Manush, the deal being completed on June 14, 1930. Goslin hit .308 that year, then .328 and .299 in the following two campaigns with the Browns.

On December 14, 1932, Goslin was dealt back to Washington in a six-player trade. He helped the Senators win their last pennant in 1933, hitting .297 in the regular season and .250 in the World Series.

A great fastball hitter who swung so hard that he often landed on the seat of his pants, Goslin was a popular player with a flair for colorful play.

At times a great power hitter, Goose enjoyed a home run output of 37 in 1930, a season in which he also drove in 138 runs. Three times the lefthanded hitter belted three homers in a single game (in 1925, 1930, and 1932). But Goslin also held the unique record of grounding into four double plays in one game (1934).

The depression-riddled Senators could no longer afford to pay Goslin in 1934, and he therefore was traded to the Tigers for outfielder Jonathan Stone on December 14, 1933. Griffith undoubtedly believed that Goose's better playing days were past.

To Griffith's surprise, Goslin helped turn the Tigers around for new manager Mickey Cochrane. He came through in 1934 to bat .305 with 13 home runs and 100 runs batted in, earning great fame with the bleacher fans in Detroit, who greeted him with cheers of "Yeah Goose!"

During the 1934 World Series, won by the Cardinals in seven games, Goslin became involved in a heated argument with umpire Bill Klem, calling him "Catfish," a sure way to provoke Klem's anger. Goslin apologized to Klem the following day on a crowded elevator, but the distraught Klem called Goslin virtually every name he could conjure up. When passengers reported the incident, Commissioner Landis fined Klem $200. Goslin received no penalty, a rare case of the player besting an umpire.

The 1935 World Series was Goslin's finest hour. After batting .292 in the regular season, Goose averaged .273 in the Series, but he won the sixth and final game with a ninth-inning single off the Cubs' Larry French. Cochrane had opened the inning

with a base hit, advanced to second on a ground out by Charlie Gehringer, and then Goslin won the World Championship with his line single to right.

Detroit fans went wild over The Goose, and he needed transportation to his hotel in a police cruiser to protect him from adoring crowds. The excitement of that moment seemed to propel Goslin through the following season; he hit .315 with 24 homers and 125 RBIs for the Tigers at the age of 35.

Goslin had a poor year in 1937, hitting only .238 in limited duty. In May 1938, the Tigers released him. Griffith then telephoned from Washington to see if his old hero would give the Senators a third try. Goslin agreed and so traveled to the nation's capital to finish his career. It was not a grand finale. Goslin batted only .158 in 38 games, and he never even completed his final at bat, wrenching his back on a swing and giving way to a pinch-hitter for the only time in his career.

Goslin became player-manager for Trenton of the Inter-State League in 1939–1940, and strictly a manager in 1941, his last baseball job. In December 1940, he married Marian Wallace, who died in 1959.

Retired from baseball, Goose returned to his 66-acre plot in Bayside, New Jersey, where he operated a fishing resort. He enjoyed a relaxing life, frequently playing golf and vacationing in Florida. He became disappointed at being repeatedly passed over by Hall of Fame voters, especially when Manush was elected in 1965.

Finally, in 1968, Goslin was elected. He was quite moved by the honor. One year later, Goose retired from his business; he then lived alone for the remainder of his life in a small home.

A heavy smoker, Goslin developed cancer, and in July 1970, he had his larynx removed. On May 15, 1971, he died in a hospital in Bridgeton, New Jersey, just three days after Manush had passed away.

LEON ALLEN GOSLIN

Washington 1921–1930, 1933, 1938
St. Louis (A.L.) 1930–1932
Detroit 1934–1937

G	AB	R	H	2B	3B	HR	RBI	Avg.
2287	8654	1483	2735	500	173	248	1609	.316

(Above) Goose Goslin at bat. Goslin's swing was so hard that it sometimes landed him on the seat of his pants. (Below) Goslin slides in under Rube Lutzke, who has to jump to catch a ball that arrives too late.

Hank Greenberg (b.1911)

Apart from Jimmie Foxx, Hank Greenberg hit more home runs from the right side of home plate in one season than any player in baseball history. In 1938 he belted 58 home runs, just two short of Babe Ruth's record, and a total which tied Foxx's output in 1932. Such awesome power was not surprising from this New York strongboy who went on to star for the Detroit Tigers.

Henry Benjamin Greenberg was born on New Year's Day, 1911, in the Greenwich Village section of New York City. His parents were Rumanian immigrants, and his father earned a good living in New York's garment center. By the time Hank was seven years old, the Greenberg family—three boys and a girl—was able to move to the Crotona Park section of the Bronx. There, Hank lived in a fashionable, 16-room house not far from the site of Yankee Stadium.

Greenberg sharpened his developing baseball skills in Atlantic Highlands, New Jersey, where his parents had a summer home. He was a schoolboy star at James Monroe High School in the Bronx, playing for coach Irwin Dickstein. Basketball was his better sport, however, because of his height (6'3½"). But Hank's first love was baseball, and he habitually worked long hours to overcome his somewhat awkward style on the field.

Paul Krichell of the Yankees was the first scout to take notice of Hank's talents, and he offered him a $7500 bonus to sign with the local American League club. The Washington Senators bid $12,000, and the Detroit Tigers followed with an offer of $9000. None of the bids particularly impressed David Greenberg, who wanted his son to attend college.

John McGraw of the Giants had an opportunity to observe Greenberg, and he did so with the knowledge that a local Jewish player on his team would be a tremendous gate attraction. But McGraw thought Hank too clumsy for the game and passed him over.

Meanwhile, Hank reasoned that his limitations would keep him at first base, and with Lou Gehrig a fixture there for the Yankees, he ruled out any future with that club.

The Tigers then returned to talk David Greenberg into agreeing to a contract which would permit Hank to go to college first. His permission was received and Hank enrolled at New York University while the property of the Tigers.

In the spring of 1930, Hank, overwhelmed by his desire to play ball, left N.Y.U. and was assigned to Hartford of the Eastern League, where he batted .214 in 17 games. The Tigers then dropped him to Raleigh of the Piedmont League, and Hank responded with a .314 average, 19 home runs, and 93 runs batted in in 122 games. At the end of the season the Tigers called Hank up, and he grounded out as a pinch-hitter in his only appearance.

Farmed to Evansville of the Three-I League in 1931, Hank hit .318 with 15 homers. He was becoming a better first baseman, building up his tall body to 215 pounds and getting the most out of his powerful arms. With Beaumont of the Texas League in 1932, Hank batted .290 and led the league with 123 runs scored and 39 homers. He also drove in 131 runs.

In 1933 Detroit manager Bucky Harris installed Hank as the club's regular first baseman. Although the Tigers finished fifth that season, Hank batted .301 and tied teammate Charlie Gehringer for the club lead with 12 home runs. It was the first of eight consecutive seasons in which Greenberg hit .300 or better, but Hank became far better known for his power-hitting achievements.

Mickey Cochrane became the Tiger manager in 1934, and he led the team to its first pennant since 1909. Hank's contribution was a .339 average, 26 home runs, and 139 runs batted in, the latter being the third highest total in the league. Although he batted .321 with seven RBIs in the 1934 World Series, Hank also struck out nine times. Dizzy and Paul Dean captured that Series for the Cardinals.

In his third year in the majors, 1935, Hank won the American League's Most Valuable Player award. He batted .328 with 36 homers and 170 runs batted in as the Tigers again won the pennant. Hank tied Jimmie Foxx for the league lead in home runs, and his RBI total was 51 higher than runner-up Lou Gehrig of New York. These were the first of four home run and RBI titles which Hank would win. Although Detroit captured the World Series, Greenberg set the ignominious record of committing three errors at first base. He was batting only .167 when forced out of action after the second game with a broken wrist.

The wrist mended over the winter, and Hank jumped off to a fast start in 1936, batting .348 through the first 12 games. But then Washington outfielder Jake Powell ran into Hank at first base and refractured the wrist. The injury kept Greenberg sidelined for the remainder of the season, and it left open to speculation his home run potential upon his return.

But Greenberg came back in grand style in 1937, belting 40 homers and driving in 183 runs, just one short of Gehrig's American League record. Hank also batted .337 and collected 200 hits.

In 1938 Hank exploded for 58 home runs, equaling the record for righthanded batters set earlier by Foxx. Ruth's record of 60 was only 11 years old at that point,

In 1938, the cameras were following Greenberg's every swing as he moved up toward Babe Ruth's 60–home-run mark. These shots were taken in Yankee Stadium, when the Detroit slugger had 45 homers to his credit. He ended the season with 58, 2 short of the Babe, tying Jimmie Foxx's second place total, and setting a record for right-handed home runs. (Opposite page) Greenberg leaps to catch a high fly.

and Hank's home run chase did not cause the sensation that Roger Maris's did in 1961. Hank had belted 58 homers with five games remaining, but in the crucial final weekend against Cleveland, he was stopped in his bid for the record. Eleven times that year Hank swatted two homers in a single game, a record for a season.

When Hank slipped to 33 homers and 112 RBIs in 1939, the Tigers attempted to cut $10,000 from his $40,000 salary. But when they further informed him of plans to move him to the outfield in 1940, he demanded and received a $10,000 raise, making him the highest paid player in the league.

The shift to the outfield was necessary to make room at first base for Rudy York on the Tigers. York was slower and less graceful than Greenberg, and it was impossible to place him anywhere else. Hank approached his new position with ardent dedication, and the handsome bachelor came through with a .340 season and titles in both home runs (41) and RBIs (150). The tremendous performance earned him his second MVP award, and it helped the Tigers capture another pennant. Hank batted .357 in the World Series against Cincinnati, but the Tigers lost in seven games.

Now 30 years old, Hank opened the 1941 season with Detroit after his draft board had deferred him because of flat feet. But responding to public criticism, the board reexamined Greenberg in May. After appearing in 19 games that spring, he was drafted into the Army as a private. Hank received a discharge on December 5, but he reenlisted when Pearl Harbor was attacked two days later. This time Greenberg reached the rank of captain in the Army Air Corps. He served a year in China and took part in the first bombings of Japan in June 1944.

Hank returned home on July 1, l945, to rejoin the Tigers, and 47,729 fans turned out to welcome him to Briggs Stadium. He homered in his first game and went on to bat .311 with 13 homers and 60 RBIs for 78 games, proving that his skills were undiminished after nearly four full seasons out of the game.

On the final day of the 1945 season, Hank blasted a grand-slam home run in the ninth inning at St. Louis to win the pennant for the Tigers. It was one of baseball's most dramatic home runs.

Rudy York was traded to Boston in 1946, and Hank returned to first base with a contract calling for $55,000. His credit at Gimbels' Department Store in New York was also good, for he had married Bernard Gimbel's daughter, Caral. Greenberg made the year a fine one by leading the league in home runs with 44 and in RBIs with 127. The Tigers finished second to Boston that season.

Hank's average slipped to .277 in 1946, and the Tigers began to feel the 35-year-old slugger might be slowing down despite the home run and RBI crowns. Nevertheless, Hank was totally surprised when he heard on his car radio, on January 18, 1947, that he had been sold to Pittsburgh after the entire American League had waived on him.

Financially successful through wise stock investments, Hank considered retirement. However, the Pirates offered him a magnificent contract that he promptly accepted. For many years it was believed that he received $100,000, but the Pirates payroll records refute this claim.

Hank roomed with young Ralph Kiner at Pittsburgh that year, and although the club finished last, the two sluggers, one fading and the other coming on, gave the fans plenty to cheer about. Left field in Forbes Field was shortened and nicknamed "Greenberg Gardens," and Hank bowed out with 25 homers and a .249 average. His advice helped Kiner to a 51-homer season.

Retiring as a player after the 1947 season, Hank joined an old admirer, Bill Veeck, at Cleveland the following season as a vice-president and farm director. The Indians captured the 1948 pennant, and two years later, after Veeck left the Indians, Greenberg became the club's general manager. He was also general manager when the Indians won the 1954 pennant with a league record of 111 victories.

In 1956 Hank Greenberg was elected to the Hall of Fame. Three years later he rejoined Veeck, this time with the Chicago White Sox, and served as vice-president from 1959 (a pennant-winning year) through 1963, after which he left baseball to devote more time to his Wall Street interests and the tennis courts. His marriage to Caral Gimbel ended in divorce (he remarried in 1965), but one of his children from the marriage, Steve Greenberg, became a baseball star at Yale University and was subsequently drafted by the Washington Senators in 1970.

HENRY BENJAMIN GREENBERG

Detroit 1930, 1933–1946
Pittsburgh 1947

G	AB	R	H	2B	3B	HR	RBI	Avg.
1394	5193	1051	1628	379	71	331	1276	.313

Clark Griffith (1869-1955)

Clark Griffith earned the nickname "The Old Fox" as a pitcher for Cap Anson's Chicago Colts in 1895. He retained the name throughout his long career, most of which was spent as the owner of the Washington Senators.

Clark Calvin Griffith was born on November 20, 1869, in a log cabin in Clear Creek, Missouri. His parents had traveled to Missouri by covered wagon two years earlier. Clark was the fifth of six children born into this simple Welsh family.

When Clark was only two years old, his father was accidentally killed by a rifle shot while hunting. That left his mother, a stoic, pioneer woman, to rear the family. At the age of 10, Clark contributed to the family income by trapping animals for their fur. He was also selected as mascot for the local baseball team.

Clark developed malaria in 1883, and the family moved to Bloomington, Illinois, for reasons of his health. There he recovered from the disease and became a fine pitcher for his school team. In 1887 Griffith earned $10 for pitching the local Hoopeston team to victory over Danville in a semi-pro game. His performance brought him a contract offer from the Bloomington Central Interstate League team for $50 a month. After winning 10 of 14 decisions, Clark was sold to Milwaukee of the Western Association for $700. His salary was increased to $225 a month, and he concluded the 1888 season with a 12–10 record for Milwaukee.

Physically, Clark was not a big man. He stood only 5'8", and although listed at 175 pounds, he never appeared quite that heavy. No skill came easily to Clark in an age when size was considered important to success in athletics. As a pitcher, Griffith used every possible trick to get hitters out, scuffing up baseballs beyond recognition and using all sorts of substances to make them especially difficult to hit. Later, players wondered why Griffith became such a strong advocate of the abolition of the spitball in 1920.

At Milwaukee, Clark did quite well. Playing for manager James A. Hart, he posted an 18–13 mark in 1889 and a 27–7 record in 1890. In 1891 Clark reached the major leagues, hurling for St. Louis of the American Association. When he was not on the mound, he was assigned to the gate to collect tickets; clubs operated on small budgets in those days. In midseason of 1891, he was sold to the Boston franchise of the Association. Although Griffith finished the year with a 17–7 record, with Boston winning the pennant, he developed a sore arm and was unable to pitch in the final weeks of the season. Boston cut him loose during the winter.

In an effort to work out his arm trouble, Clark signed with Tacoma, a team in the Pacific Northwest League. He compiled a 13–7 record there in 1892, and the following year he acquired a job with Oakland in the Coast League. Clark pitched in 48 games at Oakland and won 30. But when he had trouble collecting his salary from the financially troubled franchise, he left the team and took a job singing in a honky-tonk music hall.

Griffith's break came late in the 1893 season. Hart, his Milwaukee manager, now owned the Chicago team, and he wired Griffith to ask him to join his pitching staff. With arm trouble behind him, Clark became the biggest winner on Cap Anson's club in 1894, posting a 21–11 record. In 1895, his second year with Chicago, he acquired the nickname "The Old Fox." For seven seasons Griffith was a National League pitching star, winning more than 20 games in all but his final season. During that period, he developed a particular dislike for John McGraw, and the two often battled on the playing fields.

Griffith's outstanding pitching performance was a 1–0 win over Rube Waddell of Pittsburgh on June 19, 1900. Clark went the 14-inning distance and allowed only five hits.

In 1901 Griffith became one of the first stars to jump to the new American League. Charles Comiskey of the Chicago team had urged him to do so, adding the offer of managing the White Sox. While continuing to star on the mound for Chicago (he was 24–7 in 1901), Griffith also led the White Sox to the first American League pennant, edging Boston by four games. There was no World Series that year.

In the interests of the American League, Comiskey released Griffith, allowing him to become manager of the New York Highlanders in 1903. Forerunners of the Yankees, the team had just been shifted from Baltimore, and it was important for the league to establish a strong franchise in New York to compete with McGraw's Giants.

Griffith by now was fading as a pitcher, but he posted a 14–10 record in New York's first season; the team finished fourth. In 1904 the club lost the pennant on the final day of the season on a wild pitch by 41-game winner Jack Chesbro. But the strong showing firmly established the New York American League team as a solid franchise.

Griffith remained with the Highlanders until 1908. He won his two hundred and fortieth and final game as a pitcher in 1906 (even though he made appearances as late

(Above) Griffith warms up with the Highlanders, which he managed from 1903 to 1907. (Below) He watches the Senators' spring training in 1913.

as 1914 with Washington). Clark was not getting along with the New York owners, Frank Farrell and Bill Devery, objecting to their advice on how to manage. In midseason of 1908, Clark quit to take a scouting job with the Cincinnati Reds.

But Griffith, an American Leaguer at heart, had his mind set on the managing job in Washington. But in 1909 the managership remained with Joe Cantillon, and Griffith became manager of the Reds. He ran the club for three years, finishing fourth, fifth, and sixth, respectively. In 1911 Clark became the first to scout Cuban players, signing Rafael Almeida and Armando Marsans for Cincinnati. In later years, Griffith nearly broke baseball's color line by signing Josh Gibson after having watched the Negro League star fill the Washington stadium with crowds larger than the Senators drew. But Griffith never took the big step, and Branch Rickey finally made the breakthrough in 1946.

After the 1911 season, Griffith had the opportunity to purchase a 10 percent interest in the Washington Senators, of which he now became manager. Clark mortgaged his Craig, Montana, ranch to raise the money ($27,000), and at the age of 42 he became a limited partner of the team and its $7500-per-year manager.

One of Griffith's first acts in 1912 was to invite President William Howard Taft to throw out the first ball of the season, a ritual which became a Washington tradition. The Senators' second-place finishes in 1912 and 1913 were Griffith's best showings as manager.

During the Federal League uprising in 1914, Clark met personally with his star pitcher, Walter Johnson, and kept him from jumping to the new league. It took financial assistance from Comiskey to keep Johnson in Washington.

In 1919 Griffith and Philadelphia grain dealer William Richardson purchased 80 percent of the Senators, and Griffith was installed as president in 1920. That was also his last season as team manager.

Griffith took a chance in 1924 and appointed 28-year-old Bucky Harris as player-manager. The Senators bested the Yankees for the pennant and the Giants for the World Championship that year. In fact, 1924 proved to be the only World Championship season in Senator history.

The team also won pennants in 1925 and 1933, losing the World Series each time. With the exception of those three seasons, the Senators were primarily a second-division team operating on a small budget. Fans enjoyed the saying, "Washington is first in war, first in peace, and last in the American League."

Griffith was not above hiring comical players to boost attendance, employing men such as Al Schacht, Nick Altrock, and Germany Schaefer. Despite his poor teams, Griffith did have some quality players, such as Sam Rice, Goose Goslin, Heinie Manush, Joe Cronin, Johnson, Harris, and Harmon Killebrew (his last great signing).

During World War I, Griffith organized the Griffith Bat and Ball Fund, which sent 3000 baseball equipment kits to the armed forces overseas.

An early opponent of night baseball, Griffith wound up scheduling more night games than anyone during World War II. The impetus was President Roosevelt calling upon Clark to provide war workers with the opportunity to see games.

Griffith and his wife, the former Ann Robertson, had no children of their own, but they adopted seven children of Ann's brother. One daughter married manager Joe Cronin, and another married pitching coach Joe Haynes. One son, Sherry Robertson, played for the Senators. Another, Calvin, succeeded Clark Griffith as president, and, with brothers William and James, transferred the franchise to Minneapolis-St. Paul as the Twins in 1961.

In December 1949, the Richardson estate sold its 40 percent share of the club to John J. Jachym and Hugh Grant, but the new owners voted to retain Griffith as president. When Connie Mack retired in 1950, the 80-year-old Griffith became the dean of the American League.

Griffith was elected to the Hall of Fame in 1946. President Harry S. Truman attended ceremonies in his honor at Griffith Stadium in 1948. Clark Griffith died on October 27, 1955, in Washington, shortly before what would have been his eighty-sixth birthday.

CLARK CALVIN GRIFFITH

St. Louis (A.A.) 1891
Boston (A.A.) 1891
Chicago (N.L.) 1893–1900
Chicago (A.L.) 1901–1902
New York (A.L.) 1903–1907
Cincinnati 1909
Washington 1912–1914

G	IP	W	L	Pct.	H	R	ER	SO	BB	ERA
416	3370	240	140	.632	3372	inc.	inc.	962	800	inc.

Burleigh Grimes (b. 1893)

Burleigh Grimes pitched for seven major league clubs and won 270 games, but he is best remembered as the last pitcher legally permitted to throw the spitball. He hurled his last spitter in 1934, concluding a 19-year career in the major leagues.

Burleigh Arland Grimes was born on August 18, 1893, in the north country of Emerald, Wisconsin, where lumbering was the chief industry. Burleigh was appropriately named, for at full maturity "burly" was an accurate way to describe this rough-and-tumble warrior who stood 5'10" and weighed 195 pounds.

His father, a lumberman, was the manager of a local semipro baseball team, but he died shortly after whetting Burleigh's appetite for the game. In order to help his mother, Burleigh went to work in a lumber camp as soon as he was old enough, contributing one dollar a day to the family purse. One day, young Grimes was nearly killed when one of the four horses he was driving tripped over a tree stump, toppling seven tiers of 16-foot logs on top of him. When the lumberjacks pulled him out from beneath the debris, they were amazed to find him alive.

At the age of 18, Burleigh signed his first professional contract with Eau Claire of the Minnesota-Wisconsin League. But if a professional contract signifies payment for being a team member, perhaps Burleigh did not actually qualify; the league folded on July 1, and Grimes never received a salary.

Burleigh then returned to the lumber camp, but he tried baseball again in 1913, pitching for Ottumwa of the Central Association. He won six of eight decisions, striking out 67 batters and walking only 22 in 70 innings. Sold to Chattanooga soon thereafter, Grimes posted a 6–7 record for the club, but he was still learning the pitcher's trade. In 1914 Burleigh moved quickly from Chattanooga to Birmingham (both in the Southern League), and then on to Richmond of the Virginia League. During this period, Grimes learned to throw the spitball, not a very sanitary pitch but, properly thrown, a highly effective one.

Burleigh threw the spitter differently than most pitchers, who held it loosely and let it fly. His grip was a tight one, and he used slippery elm to moisten the ball. On a good day, his ball would break between seven and eight inches. But like most successful spitball pitchers, much of his skill depended upon deception—the batter never actually knew if Grimes was throwing the pitch. Usually, he was not. Many years later, the Philadelphia Phillies discovered that Burleigh's cap moved when he actually spit on the ball. Grimes solved the problem by wearing a larger hat.

At Richmond in 1914, Burleigh came into his own. He posted a 23–13 record in

296 innings, striking out 190 batters. That was the first of three successive minor league seasons of note. Returning to Birmingham in 1915, Grimes compiled a 17–13 record, and he followed that campaign with a 20–11 season in 1916.

On the basis of his three-year mark of 60–39, the Pittsburgh Pirates purchased Grimes in August 1916. Had Burleigh begun with a flourish, he might have had a long career with the Pirates. But his record in 1916 was an insignificant 2–3. Then in 1917, Grimes suffered through a 3–16 season with the Pirates. His earned-run average was a creditable 3.53, but he could not shake a bad losing streak and allowed it to get the better of him.

One day the Pirates were traveling to Cincinnati, and Burleigh was in the throes of an 11-game losing streak. When manager Hugo Bedzek told writers on the train that he was removing Grimes from the pitching rotation, Burleigh and Bedzek exchanged angry words. Soon they were slugging it out and rolling all over the train in battle. Apparently, Bedzek admired Grimes's spunk, for he started him the following day—Grimes lost. Eventually, Burleigh's losing streak ended at 13.

On January 8, 1918, Grimes was traded to Brooklyn with Charlie Ward and Al Mamaux for George Cutshaw, Casey Stengel, and $20,000. Suddenly, everything seemed to right itself for Burleigh. He posted a 19–9 record, a 2.13 earned-run average, and a league-leading 40 mound appearances that year. Burleigh had become, at the age of 25, one of the best pitchers in the National League.

After spending time in the service during the winter, Burleigh returned to the Dodgers in 1919 to post a 10–11 record under manager Wilbert Robinson. Injuries throughout the season diminished his effectiveness, but Robinson developed a great respect for Grimes. At times, their tempers obscured their mutual respect. They also might not speak for weeks, but generally, they got along well.

The 1920 season ended with a pennant for Brooklyn. Burleigh contributed his share with a 23–11 record, producing the top winning percentage in the league. His spitball was really hopping that year, and everyone was paying close attention to it, for prior to the 1920 season the joint rules committee of the major leagues decided to outlaw the application of any foreign substance to the baseball. They made exceptions for 17 active major league pitchers whose livelihoods depended on the specialty pitch. Grimes was one of the pitchers

permitted to use the spitter until he retired, and he earned the distinction of being the last legal spitball pitcher.

"Old Stubblebeard" (he never shaved on a day he was scheduled to pitch) started the second game of the World Series in 1920 against Cleveland. Burleigh pitched a seven-hit shutout, winning 3–0. But in the fifth game, he failed to field a bunt and then gave up the first grand-slam home run in World Series history (to Elmer Smith), as Brooklyn lost, 8–1. Grimes also lost the seventh and final game, 3–0, as Stan Coveleskie shut out the Dodgers.

Burleigh remained in Brooklyn through the 1926 season, winning more than 20 games on three other occasions. He posted a 22–13 record in 1921, 21–18 in 1923, and 22–13 in 1924. He led the league in strikeouts in 1921 with 136, and in innings pitched in both 1923 and 1924. But he also holds the ignominious distinction of leading the majors in earned runs allowed three times (1922, 1924, and 1925). As a fielder, he established a record by leading the league's pitchers in chances accepted seven times.

In 1927 the Dodgers traded Grimes to the Giants in a complicated, three-team transaction. For manager John McGraw, Grimes notched a 13-game winning streak and produced a 19–8 record, but he was traded to Pittsburgh the following winter for Vic Aldridge. It was one of McGraw's worst deals; Aldridge compiled a 4–7 record that year, his last in the majors, whereas Grimes worked in 48 games for the Pirates, posted a 25–14 record, and led the league in innings pitched and victories. The Pirates were delighted to have him back, and the club especially enjoyed his 5–0 record against McGraw's Giants that season.

Grimes compiled a 17–7 record in 1929, and then on April 9, 1930, he was traded to the Boston Braves for Percy Jones and cash. Two months later, he was peddled to the St. Louis Cardinals for Bill Sherdel and Fred Frankhouse. Burleigh finished the 1930 season with a 16–11 record, finding himself a member of the pennant-winning Cardinals. Grimes lost the opening game of the 1930 World Series, 5–2, to Philadelphia's Lefty Grove, and George Earnshaw bested him, 2–0, in the fifth game for Burleigh's fourth successive Series defeat.

Grimes regained his October form the following year when, after a 17–9 season, he posted two victories in the Series, beating Grove, 5–2, with the assistance of his own two-run single, and besting Earnshaw, 4–2, in the final game, with Bill Hallahan getting the last out. It was a courageous finish for Burleigh, who played with packed ice around his abdomen during the final seven weeks of the season, refusing to yield to an inflamed appendix.

But in December 1931, Burleigh was traded to the Cubs for Hack Wilson and Art Teachout. After a 6–11 season, he found himself in his third consecutive World Series. However, he was hit hard in two brief appearances and failed to distinguish himself against the Yankees.

After opening the 1933 season with the Cubs, Grimes was waived to the Cardinals in August, sent to the Yankees early in the 1934 season, and finally concluded the 1934 season with Pittsburgh. With the Pirates for the third time in his career, he won his two hundred and seventieth and last major league game. The Pirates released him in September 1934.

In 1935 the big righthander embarked on a managing career with Bloomington of the Three-I League. In 1936 he came in seventh with the Louisville Colonels of the American Association, but Brooklyn hired him to replace Casey Stengel as manager in 1937; the club finished sixth. In 1938 Grimes actually predicted that his club would finish last, and despite a seventh-place finish, Larry MacPhail fired him at the end of the season.

Burleigh managed Montreal of the International League in 1939. He was at the helm of Grand Rapids of the Michigan State League in 1940 until a fight with an umpire in July caused him to receive a full year's suspension.

Grimes managed Toronto in the International League from 1942 to 1944, Rochester in the same league in 1945 and 1946, and Toronto again for part of 1947. Burleigh's 1943 club was the only pennant winner.

Grimes scouted for the Yankees from 1947 to 1952, managed Toronto again in 1952–1953, coached for the Kansas City Athletics in 1955, scouted for the club in 1956–1957, and then scouted for the Baltimore Orioles from 1960 to 1971.

Burleigh Grimes was elected to the Hall of Fame in 1964. A lifelong Wisconsin resident, Burleigh married Inez Marguerite Martin in 1940. After her death, he married Zerita Brickell, widow of former major leaguer Fred Brickell, whose son Fritz had a brief big league career.

BURLEIGH ARLAND GRIMES

Pittsburgh 1916–1917, 1928–1929, 1934
Brooklyn 1918–1926
New York (N.L.) 1927
Boston (N.L.) 1930
St. Louis (N.L.) 1930–1931, 1933–1934
Chicago (N.L.) 1932–1933
New York (A.L.) 1934

G	IP	W	L	Pct.	H	R	ER	SO	BB	ERA
615	4178	270	212	.560	4406	2048	1636	1512	1295	3.52

(Above) Grimes at 1928 spring training for the Pirates. (Below) As a Dodger, Grimes lets lose his famous temper.

Lefty Grove (1900-1975)

In baseball's centennial poll of the greatest living players, conducted in 1969, Lefty Grove was named the greatest living left-handed pitcher for his brilliant performances on the mound with the Philadelphia Athletics and Boston Red Sox.

Robert Moses Grove, who was usually called either "Lefty" or "Mose" as a player, was born on March 6, 1900, in Lonaconing, Maryland. With his three brothers, Lefty went to work in the coal mines at 50 cents per day to increase the family income. His formal education ended with the eighth grade.

Lefty worked briefly as an apprentice glass blower and a railroad worker. At the age of 17, he had his first encounter with organized sandlot baseball. Three years later he signed to pitch for Martinsburg in the Blue Ridge League.

After six games at Martinsburg, where he compiled a 3–3 mark, Lefty was sold to Jack Dunn, owner of the International League's Baltimore Orioles, for $2000. Although a minor league team, the Orioles paid well, and Lefty earned as much as $7500 per year in Baltimore. He would have preferred to be in the major leagues, but he was comfortable in Baltimore and was a fine gate attraction. Those reasons combined to keep Grove in the minors for four and one-half years, during which he compiled a 109–36 record for the Orioles. His best season was 1924, when he posted a 27–6 record and led the league in strikeouts for the fourth consecutive year, having reached as many as 330 whiffs in 1923. Unfortunately, Lefty's control was not particularly sharp, and he led the league in walks in three of the four years as well.

At last, Connie Mack worked out the purchase of Grove from his friend Dunn. The Athletics agreed to give Baltimore $100,000 in 10 installments, plus an additional $600, to make the purchase price higher than that paid for Babe Ruth.

Considering the substantial price, the publicity that accompanied it, Grove's minor league records, and the fact that he was already 25 years old, Lefty's rookie season was somewhat disappointing. Philadelphia finished second to Washington in 1925, but Grove compiled only a 10–12 record with a 4.75 ERA. Fast and wild, he led the league with 116 strikeouts, but he also walked 131 batters, high for the league.

In 1926 Lefty evened his record to 13–13, increased his strikeouts to 194, and dropped his walks to 101. He also led the American League with a 2.51 earned run average, the first of his nine ERA titles.

At the age of 27, Lefty won 20 games for the first time, going 20–12 with a team that ran a distant second to the famed 1927 Yankees. Now the ace of Connie Mack's

staff, Grove tied George Pipgras in 1928 for the league lead in victories with 24, and he won his fourth strikeout title in four major league seasons. Again the Yankees captured the pennant, but their margin had been trimmed to just three games by the A's.

In 1929 the Athletics won their first of three consecutive pennants, with Grove leading the way from the mound each year. Lefty posted a 20–6 record in 1929 and led the league in winning percentage, earned run average, and strikeouts.

In the A's 1929 World Series victory over Chicago, Lefty hurled six and one-third innings of shutout relief ball when Connie Mack attempted to fool the Cubs by using Howard Ehmke instead of Grove in the opener. Although always noted as a starter, Lefty was a good relief pitcher. He compiled a record of 33 victories and 55 saves, with an earned run average of 2.84, in relief.

In 1930, five of Lefty's 28 victories were achieved in relief, and he saved an additional nine games. Lefty recorded a 28–5 mark, again leading the league in winning percentage, ERA, and strikeouts (with a career high of 209). His 2.54 ERA can best be appreciated when it is realized that American League clubs had a combined .288 batting average in 1930, with three clubs topping .300 and 37 regulars batting better than .300. Runner-up Wes Ferrell finished with an ERA of 3.31.

The Athletics again captured the pennant in 1930, taking the World Series with St. Louis in six games for a second successive World Championship. Grove won the first game, beating Burleigh Grimes, 5–2; lost the fourth game to Jesse Haines, 3–1; and won the fifth game with two flawless relief innings when Jimmie Foxx hit a two-run homer in the ninth to break a scoreless tie.

As great a season as 1930 had been, it was all a prelude to 1931, in which Lefty received the first American League Most Valuable Player award voted by the Baseball Writers' Association. Lefty captured 31 of 35 decisions that season, including a streak of 16 consecutive victories between June 8 and August 19. The four games lost that year were by the narrow margins of 2–1, 7–5, 1–0, and 4–3. Lefty registered his seventh consecutive strikeout title and led the league with a 2.06 ERA, 57 points better than the runnerup, Lefty Gomez of the Yankees. Grove's control was no longer a problem: he walked only 62 men in 289 innings.

Grove's 31 victories in 1931 marked the last time an American Leaguer would win 30 or more games until Denny McLain of Detroit accomplished the feat in 1968.

Lefty Grove hurling the ball for Boston, where he was traded when Athletics longtime manager Connie Mack decided to sell all his stars and rebuild his team from scratch in 1934. Mack always called Grove his finest pitcher ever.

Grove accepts the first American League Most Valuable Player award, voted by the Baseball Writers Association in 1931. He won 31 out of 35 games that season and led the league with a 2.06 ERA.

The Athletics achieved their third consecutive pennant in 1931, but the Cardinals captured the World Series in seven games. Lefty won the opener, 6–2, lost the third game, 5–2, and won the sixth game, 8–1, on a five-hitter. The Series proved to be his last.

Lefty continued to enjoy success, recording a 25–10 season in 1932 with another ERA title, and tying for the league's victory lead in 1933 with a 24–8 mark. But Philadelphia was slipping in the standings, attendance was falling, and it was time for Connie Mack to sell his stars and rebuild. Mack had done it earlier in the century, and he was ready to do it again. Grove, along with Max Bishop and George Walberg, was sent to the Red Sox for Hal Warstler, Bob Kline, and $125,000.

Preceding Grove to Boston was his reputation as a bad loser. Lefty had a terrible temper, and he had never hesitated to holler at a teammate, break down a door, or talk back to Connie Mack. Bucky Harris, the Boston manager, prepared himself for the lanky 6'3" lefthander.

In his first year in Boston, 1934, Lefty was bothered by arm trouble. The Red Sox could not help but feel cheated when Grove showed an 8–8 record and a 6.52 ERA for 22 games. Critics were ready to write him off, believing that no lefthander could ever enjoy success in Fenway Park with its short left field fence, but Lefty bounced back in 1935. Although lacking his former speed, Grove had become craftier. With his great curveball, Lefty compiled a 20–12 record. He led the league in ERA, had six shutouts, and reached the 20-victory circle for the last time in his career. Boston, however, played only around .500 ball under new manager Joe Cronin that year.

Lefty won 17 games in each of the next two seasons. In 1938 he posted a 14–4 record, followed by a 15–4 mark in 1939. Both years he led the league in ERA, making it nine ERA titles in all. While no longer winning 20 games, striking out 100, or pitching 200 innings, Grove nevertheless showed himself to be one of the most knowledgeable players in the game.

Fourteen victories short of 300 after 1939, Lefty won seven games in 1940 and seven the following season. It had been a struggle to reach the 300 club, but only 11 pitchers before him had accomplished the feat, and Lefty had not won his first major league game until he was 25 years old. One hundred and eight of his 300 victories were recorded between 1930 and 1933.

Despite his lack of education, Lefty was prudent in handling his finances, investing in government bonds. Financially secure and aware that he was no longer the athlete he once was, Grove retired on December 7, 1941. The announcement went generally unnoticed, however, for the Japanese attacked Pearl Harbor on that day.

Lefty, his wife, Ethel, and two children, lived in Lonaconing, Maryland, after his playing days. Ethel died in 1959. In retirement, Lefty devoted considerable time and money to youth leagues in both Philadelphia and his hometown in Maryland. He remained close to Connie Mack, who always rated Grove his greatest pitcher.

Lefty Grove was inducted into the Hall of Fame in 1947. He died on May 22, 1975 of a heart attack in Norwalk, Ohio.

ROBERT MOSES GROVE

Philadelphia (A.L.) 1925–1933
Boston (A.L.) 1934–1941

G	IP	W	L	Pct.	H	R	ER	SO	BB	ERA
616	3940	300	141	.680	3849	1594	1339	2266	1187	3.06

Chick Hafey (1903-1973)

Had Chick Hafey not been plagued by poor health throughout his career, he might have become the game's greatest right-hand hitter. That was the opinion of both Branch Rickey, who employed him, and John McGraw, who opposed him. Despite his ill health and poor vision, Hafey compiled a lifetime .317 batting average in the National League.

Charles James Hafey was born on February 12, 1903, in Berkeley, California. For many years Hafey lied about his age, claiming to be one year older. When he broke into organized ball at the age of 20, he thought scouts would be more impressed if they thought he was 21. The extra year stayed with Hafey throughout his career.

Chick had an older brother, Albert, who pitched in the Pacific Coast League with Portland in 1913. In later years he also had three nephews who played professional baseball: Bud Hafey, an outfielder with four major league clubs (1935–1939); Tom Hafey, an infielder with the Giants (1939) and the Browns (1944); and Will Hafey, a minor league pitcher.

Chick was an athletic star at Berkeley High School, serving the baseball team as a pitcher and the football team as a halfback. After graduation he could have gone to the University of California, but instead he traveled to Bradenton, Florida, in the spring of 1923 to try out for the St. Louis Cardinals.

Branch Rickey, managing the Cardinals, watched the workouts carefully, looking for prospects among hundreds of boys. Hafey was not particularly impressive as a pitcher, but he looked good in the batting cage. Although Chick did not appear physically strong (he stood 6'1" and had a top weight of 185), he drove hard line drives down the third-base line. He also showed good speed going to first and a strong and accurate arm in warmups. Suitably impressed, Rickey signed Chick and told him, "From now on, you're an outfielder."

The shy, soft-spoken Hafey was placed on the roster of the Fort Smith club in the Western Association. Rickey had just begun to organize his farm system, and Hafey became one of its first significant products. Chick played 144 games at Fort Smith and batted .284 with 72 extra-base hits. It was a fine showing for his first year away from the pitching mound.

In 1924 Chick opened the season with Houston of the Texas League, where he batted .360 with 68 extra-base hits. Although the Cardinals owned 59 percent of the club, the Houston president had the right to sell his players, and he notified Rickey that another major league club was offering $35,000 for Hafey's contract. Without hesitation, Branch wrote a check for

$35,000 and sent it to Houston. (Since 59 percent wound up back in St. Louis, the price that the Cardinals paid was actually $20,650.) Chick played 24 games for St. Louis at the end of the 1924 season, hitting .253.

Chick opened the 1925 season with Syracuse of the International League, but when Rickey moved to the Cardinals' front office and Rogers Hornsby became manager, Hafey was recalled and moved into the lineup as the left fielder. Chick played in 93 games that season, virtually his rookie year, and batted .302 with 57 runs batted in. It marked the start of an outstanding career.

In 1926 Chick batted only .271 and was frequently hit by pitches. Although his playing time was limited to 78 games, he helped contribute to the Cardinals' first pennant. Chick played in all seven games of the World Series against the Yankees, but he batted only .185, which, unfortunately, proved typical of his World Series performances.

Although Hafey complained of vision problems in 1927, he batted .329. A teammate, Specs Toporcer, was wearing glasses on the field, a rarity at the time, but Chick would not yield to the suggestion that he have his eyes checked, especially after batting .329.

Hafey frequently found himself embroiled in salary disputes with Rickey, but before the 1928 season he signed a three-year contract calling for annual salaries of $7000, $8000, and $9000, respectively. If the security diminished his competitiveness, no one noticed. He repeatedly belted hard line drives down the third-base line, causing people to call him the National League's answer to Jimmie Foxx.

In 1928 Chick batted .337 with 27 home runs and 111 runs batted in, but he managed only three singles in the World Series. The Yankees swept the Series in four games, and there was little that any Cardinal did.

Chick batted .338 in 1929, with 29 home runs and 125 runs batted in. That was the season in which he finally agreed to wear glasses. In 1930 he compiled a .336 batting average with 26 homers and 107 RBIs. Chick batted .273 against the Athletics in the World Series that year, including five doubles. He experienced no trouble with Lefty Grove's pitching, going to right field on the Philadelphia southpaw rather than down the left field line.

For the three years covered by his contract, Chick had batted .337 with 82 home runs, 343 runs batted in, 310 runs scored,

Chick Hafey hitting and fielding for the Cincinnati Reds. The Reds paid him $15,000 in 1932, more than he had ever made as a St. Louis star.

132 doubles, 27 triples, and 500 hits. The Cardinals had captured two pennants, and Hafey was considered one of the best hitters in the league.

For the 1931 season, Hafey requested a $15,000 contract. But Rickey, citing the Depression, called the salary outrageous. After a long and highly publicized holdout, Hafey signed 10 days before the start of the season for $12,500. At that point, Rickey informed Chick that he would not be paid until the front office considered him physically fit to play ball. Since he had missed most of spring training, it enabled the club to deduct $2100 from his salary.

Hafey was furious with Rickey and the Cardinals, but he did not allow his anger to affect his play. He was locked in an exciting, three-way race for the league's batting championship, competing with the Giants' Bill Terry and his own roommate and best friend, Jim Bottomley.

At the end of the year, Hafey had batted .3489, Terry .3486, and Bottomley .3482. Chick thus captured the closest batting race in history; the Cardinals also won the 1931 pennant by 13 games. Chick gave considerable credit for his performance to the Cardinals' team physician, Dr. Robert F. Hyland, who finally convinced Hafey to wear glasses. Chick may have stood out on the field with his specs on, but he certainly stood out among the batting leaders as well.

In the spring of 1932, Hafey and his wife, Bernice, reluctantly drove to Florida to negotiate a contract. Hafey proposed a salary of $17,500, which included the $2100 deducted the previous year. Rickey offered $13,000, a $500 raise.

Hafey became enraged at Rickey's terms, hopped into his car, and drove home with his wife to their ranch in Walnut Creek, California. He remained there until he received word on April 11 that he had been traded to Cincinnati for Harvey Hendrick, Benny Frey, and perhaps as much as $50,000 in cash.

Rickey remained unperturbed, for he had Joe Medwick ready to replace Hafey. Chick happily joined the Reds, who were, unfortunately, a last-place club, but they paid him $15,000.

Battling the flu and sinus trouble the entire year, Chick hit .344 in 83 games to lead the club. In 1933 he participated in the first All-Star game, collecting one hit in four trips, and he batted .303 during the regular season. But Hafey's health was not good, and his sinus problem continued to plague him. Although he had 568 at bats in 1933, Chick belted only seven home runs, far below his performances in the 1928–1930 period. In 1929 he had tied the National League record of 10 successive hits, but he no longer hit the ball with that kind of authority.

The 1934 season was his last campaign as a regular player. He played in 140 games and belted 18 homers while batting .293. It was a personally satisfying year, but the Reds finished last while the Cardinals captured the pennant.

Chick began the 1935 season with a shoulder injury, but he returned to the lineup late in April. On May 24, he participated in the first night game in major league history, after Larry MacPhail had installed lights at Crosley Field. The dampness of the evening greatly troubled Chick's sinus condition, and, seeing night baseball as an example of the future, he became sullen.

Early in June, Hafey wrote a note to his roommate which announced his retirement. Since the Reds had recently acquired both Babe Herman and Kiki Cuyler, they were not very disturbed over the matter. Chick then returned home peacefully to hunt, fish, and tend to his ranch.

Hafey sat out the remainder of the 1935 season and all of the 1936 campaign. In 1937 he decided to attempt a comeback and played in 89 games for the Reds, hitting .261 with nine home runs. At that point, he called it a career.

Chick returned home to his ranch again, followed the progress of baseball as it moved to the West Coast, and was somewhat overshadowed by the more colorful members of the Cardinals' championship teams.

In 1971 Chick Hafey was inducted into the Hall of Fame. He died on July 2, 1973, in Calistoga, California, at the age of 70.

CHARLES JAMES HAFEY

St. Louis (N.L.) 1924–1931
Cincinnati 1932–1935, 1937

G	AB	R	H	2B	3B	HR	RBI	Avg.
1283	4625	777	1466	346	67	164	833	.317

Jesse Haines (1893-1978)

The St. Louis Cardinals spent a small fortune to obtain pitcher Jesse Haines in 1919, but their gamble proved successful. Jesse compiled 210 victories for the Cards during his 18-year career.

Jesse Joseph Haines was born in Clayton, Ohio, on July 22, 1893, of English-German ancestry. His father was a part-time carpenter who also worked for the road department and served as an auctioneer. His mother reared a family of four boys after the death of an infant daughter.

Jesse's first experience with baseball occurred during his school years in Clayton. He became a good pitcher with his school team, possessing a strong arm and great strikeout ability. But this style of pitching did not prove to be his forte as a professional.

Jesse played semipro ball in Clayton and attended a country school until he was 16 years old. In the fall of 1913, he signed his first professional contract, joining the Dayton club of the Central League. He worked the final game of the season for Dayton, defeating Evansville.

In 1914 Jesse pitched in 33 games for Saginaw of the South Michigan League, compiling a 17–14 record with 159 strikeouts in 258 innings while walking only 52. He had started the season with Fort Wayne of the Central League, and then was transferred to Saginaw. Jesse was strictly a fastball-curveball pitcher in those days, and he was considered to have exceptional control.

In the middle of the 1915 season Jesse found himself with the Detroit Tigers on a trial basis. But the Tigers found no opportunity to work him into a game, nor did they manage to do so when he was again on their roster in 1916. The only pitching Jesse did in those years was in the minor leagues. He played for Saginaw again in 1915, and had a 10–5 record when the league folded on July 1. In 1916 he journeyed to Springfield of the Central League, posting a 23–12 record with a 1.68 earned-run average in 310 innings.

Returning to Springfield in 1917, Jesse compiled a 19–10 mark with a 1.83 ERA. In 1918 he captured 12 of his first 16 decisions with Topeka-Hutchinson of the Western League. Finally, he was purchased by the Cincinnati Reds.

The 1918 Reds were managed by Christy Mathewson, but the former Giant star failed to see any potential in Haines. Battling John McGraw for a second-place finish, Mathewson used Haines in only one game late in July. In his five-inning appearance, Jesse allowed only one run, one walk, and five hits. But that was the extent of his Cincinnati career, for the Reds returned the 6'0", 180-pound righthander to Hutchinson, which in turn sold him to Tulsa in 1919.

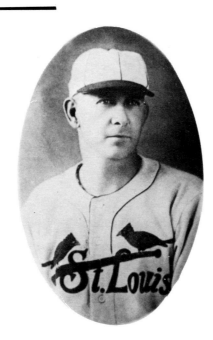

Now almost 26 years old and in his seventh minor league season, Jesse was despondent. He compiled a 5–9 record at Tulsa before moving up to Kansas City of the American Association, where he concluded the 1919 season by posting a 21–5 mark and a 2.11 earned-run average. With only 52 walks and 66 strikeouts in 213 innings, Jesse had discovered the best pitching method for him: let the batters hit the ball. He saved his arm for critical situations and concentrated on keeping the ball down. Throughout his career Jesse always allowed many hits, but he permitted very few walks, had a relatively small number of strikeouts, and he usually finished on top. One would not dispute his style, for he had now become a pitcher, not a thrower.

The Cardinals in 1920 were operating with scanty funds, but Branch Rickey liked what he saw of Haines. Rickey thus was willing to reach into the American Association and spend some money. He managed to convince the club's directors of Jesse's value, and the Cards borrowed $10,000 from a bank to purchase Haines.

Jesse was the last player the Cardinals would buy for more than a quarter of a century, and $10,000 was a substantial investment at that time. But Jess was to spend 18 years pitching in a Cardinal uniform, tying Pittsburgh's Babe Adams for the National League record for most years pitching with one club.

As a rookie in 1920, Jesse led the National League with 47 appearances, 37 of which were starts and 19 of which were complete games. Although his earned-run average was 2.99, he compiled only a 13–20 record, becoming one of the few rookies ever to pitch enough to lose 20 games. Jesse struck out 120 men that year, the only occasion in his major league career in which he reached three figures in that department.

Jesse's outstanding game in the 1920 season was a 17-inning loss to the Cubs' Grover Cleveland Alexander. Haines hurled 10 consecutive hitless innings before eventually succumbing to defeat, 3–2. The paths of Haines and Alexander would cross again in a memorable game six years later.

Jesse was a poised, unemotional man on the mound, and his serious face reflected his calm nature. But he was a tough competitor, and in 1921 he helped lift the Cardinals from fifth to third place. His 18–12 record made him the leading winner on the St. Louis staff.

In 1922 Jesse posted an 11–9 mark, but in 1923 he achieved his first of three 20-victory seasons with a 20–13 record and a

3.11 earned run average (fifth in the league). He struck out 73 and walked 75, a typical Haines season.

Jesse suffered through a horrible 8–19 season in 1924, but he had the distinction of pitching the only no-hitter in the league when he stopped the Braves, 5–0, on July 7. It was the first no-hitter thrown by a Cardinal since George Bradley in 1876 (which was the first no-hitter in the National League).

Haines rebounded somewhat in 1925 with a 13–14 record, and in 1926, under manager Rogers Hornsby, Jesse helped the Cardinals to their first National League pennant with a 13–4 season. Used sparingly by Hornsby, Haines started 21 games but had one of his better records.

The 1926 World Series produced Jesse's greatest fame. He relieved Bill Sherdel in the first game at Yankee Stadium, a game won by the Yankees, 2–1. Jesse returned to start the third game and shut out New York, 4–0, with a five-hitter. All the hits were harmless singles. In that game, Jesse belted a home run. Not for another 16 years would the Yankees be shut out in a World Series game.

The series homer was something of a fluke, for Jesse was not a good hitter. He batted only .186 for his career, with three regular-season home runs.

Haines started the seventh game of the 1926 Series, one of the most famous October games ever played. The Series was tied 3–3, and Jesse had his fine knuckleball hopping that day. It was thrown right off the knuckles, not from the fingertips as many other "knuckleball" pitchers handled it.

Jesse worked hard in the seventh game, but after he walked Lou Gehrig with two out in the seventh inning, filling the bases, Hornsby visited the mound. Spotting a bad blister on Jesse's knuckle, Hornsby called in Grover Cleveland Alexander from the bullpen. Haines, listening on the clubhouse radio, heard Ol' Pete strike out Tony Lazzeri and go on to save the game and the World Championship for the Cardinals.

Jesse chalked up his largest victory total in 1927, when he compiled a 24–10 record, but the Pirates won the pennant. He returned in 1928, at the age of 35, to produce a 20–8 record for the pennant-winning Cards. The Yankees swept the World Series this time, and Jesse was tagged with the loss in the third game.

Haines posted a 13–10 record in 1929, and a 13–8 mark in 1930, another pennant season in St. Louis. In the 1930 World Series, the 37-year-old knuckleballer beat Philadelphia, 3–1, with a four-hitter in the fourth game.

Jesse recorded a 12–3 mark in 1931, but arm trouble began to slow him down, and he was not available for Series duty.

Haines had a 3–5 record in 1932, 9–6 in 1933, and 4–4 in 1934, as the Cardinals' famed Gashouse Gang won another flag. Haines, by now known as "Pop" to the rowdy young Cardinals, pitched primarily in relief and made his final World Series appearance.

Jesse was still pitching in relief for the Cardinals as late as 1937, when at age 44 he completed his eighteenth season. His two hundredth victory came late in 1935, and he concluded his career with 210 wins. In 1938 the Brooklyn Dodgers hired Haines as a coach. It was Jesse's last baseball job.

Haines had married in 1915 and settled in Phillipsburg, Ohio, where he operated a garage during the off-seasons. After his retirement from baseball, he maintained the garage and also served seven terms as auditor in Montgomery County, Ohio, from 1938 to 1965.

Jesse Haines was elected to the Hall of Fame in 1970. He died on August 5, 1978, at the age of 85.

JESSE JOSEPH HAINES

Cincinnati 1918
St. Louis (N.L.) 1920–1937

G	IP	W	L	Pct.	H	R	ER	SO	BB	ERA
555	3207	210	158	.571	3460	1556	1298	981	871	3.64

Jesse Haines, pitcher and family man. The shot with his wife and baby daughter was taken on a visit to relatives in Dayton, Ohio, after the Cardinals' World Series triumph over the Yankees in 1926.

Billy Hamilton (1866-1940)

In an era when stolen bases occurred more frequently than home runs, no player stole more bases than Billy Hamilton.

Of Scotch descent, William Robert Hamilton was born on February 16, 1866, in Newark, New Jersey. He never grew to be more than 5'6" and weighed a chunky 165. He had heavy, stumpy legs, but they did not hinder his speed nor his ability to cover considerable ground from his center field position.

Billy attended local schools and played on the sandlots of New Jersey and Clinton, Massachusetts. He signed his first professional contract at the age of 22, joining the Worcester club of the New England League, for which he played 61 games, scored 76 runs, stole 70 bases, and batted .352 in 1888.

Such figures as these were typical of Billy Hamilton's career. In fact, he managed to score 1690 runs in 1578 major league games, an incredible average of better than one per game. Only Harry Stovey, who scored 1492 runs in 1486 games (mostly in the American Association between 1883 and 1889), is credited with a comparable record. No twentieth-century player has approached the feat.

Hamilton finished the 1888 season with Kansas City of the American Association, which was a major league. The club finished in last place, winning only 43 of 132 games. Billy did not contribute much with his .250 average in 35 games, but he did steal 23 bases.

In 1889 the Kansas City team advanced to seventh place, and Billy had his first complete major league season, batting .301 in 137 games and leading the Association with 117 stolen bases. Although an impressive total, the stolen base figure was not the highest recorded in the American Association. In 1887 a Scotch-born outfielder named Hugh Nicol had swiped 138 bases.

It is important to consider that between 1886 and 1897 a runner was credited with a stolen base if he advanced an extra base on a hit. For example, if a man singled and the runner went from first to third, the runner was credited with a stolen base. Thus there is no way of comparing the totals of Hamilton and Nicol against today's figures. One can only compare contemporaries, and among them Hamilton was the best.

Another factor that helped to inflate Hamilton's stolen-base totals was the distance between the catcher and home plate. Catchers then stood much farther back, often catching pitches on a bounce. Also, the art of holding a runner on base had not yet been perfected by pitchers.

The lefthanded-hitting Hamilton was signed by Harry Wright for Philadelphia's

National League team in 1890. The Phillies were a third-place club, but Hamilton immediately led the league with 102 stolen bases. He also batted .325, the second highest average in the league, and scored 131 runs in 123 games.

Billy captured the 1891 batting championship with a .338 average, and he also led the league in runs scored (142) and hits (179). His crowning achievement that year, however, was his incredible 115 stolen bases, a record destined to withstand challenges by such players as Ty Cobb and Maury Wills. Not until 1974 did St. Louis's Lou Brock break the record. Noted for his head-first slides, Hamilton became known as "Sliding Billy," and he was a great favorite of the fans.

In the 1891 season, Hamilton was flanked in the Philadelphia outfield by Ed Delahanty and Sam Thompson, both future Hall of Famers, like himself. Although Philadelphia never finished first during Hamilton's years with the club, its outfield was one of the best in baseball history. In 1894 the trio had a combined batting average of .401.

After hitting .330 in 1892 and .395 in an 1893 season shortened for him when he contracted typhoid fever early in August, Billy had another sensational season in 1894. In addition to stealing 99 bases to lead the league, Hamilton set an all-time record of 196 runs scored. This sensational total included a streak of 24 consecutive run-scoring games between July 6 and August 2. Once on base, Billy had a constant green light and the freedom to ignore coaches' signals. In one game he was credited with seven stolen bases, tying the 1881 record set by George Gore—a mark not equaled since.

Playing against the rough and ragged Cleveland Spiders that year, little Billy was grabbed by the shirt as he rounded third by Cleveland third baseman Chippy McGarr. McGarr tossed Hamilton into the grandstand wall in frustration, but fortunately no injury was incurred.

For the 1894 season, Billy compiled a .399 batting average, with Delahanty hitting .400 and Thompson .404. But Philadelphia could finish no better than fourth.

Billy captured his final stolen base title in 1895, swiping 95 bases for the Phillies in addition to hitting .393. His 166 runs scored gave him his third runs title, and he topped the 200-hit mark for the second successive year.

In 1896 Billy was involved in a heavily publicized trade. He was sent to the Boston Beaneaters in exchange for their team captain, Bill Nash. Boston wanted Hamilton to replace the fading Tommy McCarthy

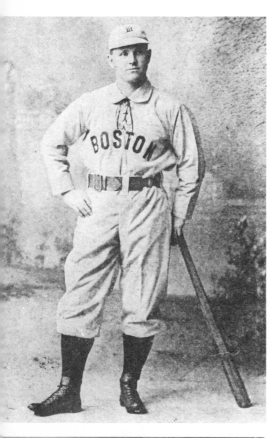

in center field, and the club desired Billy's base-stealing talents in the leadoff slot of the lineup. Hamilton's on-base average was always very high. In fact, he led the National League in walks five times during his career (1891, 1894–1897). His career high of 126 walks in 1894, combined with 223 hits, meant that he reached base at least 349 times in 131 games played.

With Boston in 1896, Billy set a club record of 93 stolen bases, while leading the team with a .363 average. In 1897 he participated in the thrilling pennant race between Boston and the Baltimore Orioles, a race so close and attracting such crowds that players were limited to two passes for each game. It was a marvelous year for baseball attendance.

In a dramatic September series in Baltimore, Boston pulled away and wound up winning the pennant by two games. Hamilton led the league with 153 runs scored (his fifth and last title) and batted .344. The Beaneaters compiled a team average of .319.

Boston captured the opening game of the 1897 Temple Cup series, but Baltimore then swept four straight. When it was later revealed that the teams had secretly decided to split the money evenly, William Chase Temple withdrew his cup. Thus the playoffs between first- and second-place teams came to an end. Hamilton contributed little to the final Temple Cup series, and his error on a routine fly ball in the fourth game caused his manager to bench him in the fifth and deciding contest.

Boston again finished in first place in 1898, but a knee injury limited Billy to 109 games. Still, he hit .367 and stole 59 bases. A leg injury in 1899 further limited Hamilton's playing time, for he saw action in only 81 games, batted .306, and stole only 19 bases. In 1900 he batted .332 and scored more than 100 runs for the eleventh time in his career.

Billy rejected a contract offer from the Boston team in the American League in 1901, and he batted .292 for the Boston Nationals in his final major league season.

Billy terminated his career with a record 937 stolen bases. He also set the National League mark with 797 thefts. Both figures are included in record books, although the modern marks of Ty Cobb and Lou Brock are generally accepted.

After his major league days, Billy began a long career as a minor league manager, playing for his teams through 1910. He managed Haverhill of the New England League from 1902 to 1904, Harrisburg of the outlaw Tri-State League from 1905 to 1908, and Lynn of the New England League in 1909 and 1910. Hamilton captured three minor league batting championships during that period, hitting .412 for Haverhill in 1904 (also leading the league with 113 runs, 168 hits, and 74 stolen bases), .333 with Haverhill in 1907, and .332 with Lynn in 1909.

Billy scouted for the Red Sox in 1911 and 1912, and then went to Fall River of the New England League as a nonplaying manager in 1913. In 1914 he managed Springfield of the Eastern League. His final job in professional baseball came in 1916 when he was manager and part owner of the Worcester team (Eastern League) in his home town.

Unlike many players of his era, Billy had invested his earnings wisely and owned a considerable amount of property. It enabled him and his wife, Rebecca, to live comfortably at their home in Worcester until he died on December 16, 1940.

Billy Hamilton was selected for membership in the Hall of Fame in 1961.

WILLIAM ROBERT HAMILTON

Kansas City (A.A.) 1888–1889
Philadelphia (N.L.) 1890–1895
Boston (N.L.) 1896–1901

G	AB	R	H	2B	3B	HR	RBI	Avg.
1578	6262	1690	2157	225	94	37	736	.344

(Above) Billy Hamilton as a Boston batting star. In his five years with the Beaneaters, Hamilton averaged .363, .344, .367, .306, and .292. (Below) Hamilton when he was with his first major league team, Kansas City of the American Association.

Will Harridge (1881-1971)

When the American League hired Will Harridge as a secretary in 1911, he had never seen a game of baseball, let alone played in one. But Will went on to achieve a long and distinguished career as a baseball executive even though he lacked the color and personality that might have made him better known.

William Harridge was one of six children born to British parents in the Hyde Park section of Chicago on October 16, 1881. His parents had come from England five years earlier, and Will (he was never known as Bill) made the Chicago area his home throughout his life.

As a teenager, Will acquired a job as an office boy with the Wabash Railroad. After graduating from high school, he enrolled in a Chicago business college in order to learn stenography. His new-found skills soon earned him a more trusted spot at the Wabash. One of his jobs was to handle the massive paperwork connected with arranging travel for the baseball clubs riding the Wabash. This experience brought him to the attention of Ban Johnson, president of the American League. In December 1911, Johnson hired Harridge as his personal secretary.

Johnson was at once impressed with Harridge's abilities as a secretary, particularly his stenography. Will, in fact, took shorthand notes throughout his career with the league, generally giving them to his own secretary for transcription.

Harridge had earned only $90 per month with the Wabash Railroad, but Johnson raised his salary to $200 per month and retained him as private secretary throughout his administration, which lasted until 1927.

Late in his career as league president, Johnson came into a heated debate with Commissioner Landis and eventually with the American League club owners. In 1927, after battling Johnson over an alleged betting scandal involving Ty Cobb and Tris Speaker (the two were found innocent), league owners voted to give Johnson a leave of absence. This left Harridge in a precarious position.

When Johnson returned two months later to try to regain control, he found Harridge at his desk. Ban was somewhat angered by the presence of his former secretary, sensing a transfer of loyalty, and Will was forced to move into his own office down the hall. He finally returned when Johnson submitted his resignation on October 17, 1927. At that point, the league elected Ernest S. Barnard, former president of the Cleveland Indians, as the league's second president. Harridge was then elected league secretary for a three-year term.

Both Barnard and Harridge were reelected in 1930, but on March 27, 1931,

Barnard died, only 16 hours before Ban Johnson himself also died. That left the presidency open, and Harridge was one of the candidates considered for the office. Since Harridge was not an aggressive man, some owners had misgivings about his qualifications. Will himself offered to stay on as acting president for one year to give the club owners a chance to evaluate his performance.

But White Sox owner Charles Comiskey would not hear of such a compromise. The post needed filling, and Harridge was his man. Largely through Comiskey's efforts, Harridge was nominated at a special meeting in Cleveland on May 27, 1931, by Phil Ball of the Browns. "I nominate Will Harridge for president and treasurer," Ball said, "and I hope he's not elected, for if he is, we are going to lose a damn good secretary."

Will was elected to a three-year term, and then reelected in 1934. In 1938, 1947, and 1956, he was reelected for 10-year terms, never signing a written contract, but serving honorably for nearly 28 years.

Harridge's toughness was tested early in his presidency. In the spring of 1932, Chicago manager Lew Fonseca and three players were charged with attacking umpire George Moriarty during a game in Cleveland. Harridge weighed the circumstances and fined the four White Sox $1350.

Not one to carry a grudge, and always one to recognize talent, Will hired Fonseca four years later as the chief of his newly created promotion department and later placed him in charge of a new film division. When Harridge assumed office, only he and a secretary occupied the offices at 310 South Michigan Avenue in Chicago. Harridge expanded the staff to include a publicity department and a supervisor of umpires.

Only a few weeks after the Fonseca incident, Will ran up against the strongest owner in the league, New York's Jacob Ruppert. Ruppert's star catcher, Bill Dickey, had punched Washington outfielder Carl Reynolds in the jaw, causing a fracture. Although Dickey was a man of high character and without a previous incident upon his record, Harridge suspended the Yankee receiver for 30 days and fined him $1000. The outraged Ruppert did not speak to Harridge for a year, but in 1935 became a vice-president of the league and a strong Harridge supporter.

In 1933 Arch Ward of the Chicago *Tribune* came to Will with an idea for an All-Star game as a charity affair. Harridge was doubtful that the league owners would accept it, and he thought a newspaper in each city would soon want to sponsor such a game. But Will liked the idea and gave it his backing. With his support, the first All-Star game was played in 1933, and it has been an annual affair since.

The job of league president was seldom an exciting one, unless a fine or suspension put the office in the newspapers. Generally, schedule making was the principal duty of the office. The American League was a highly stable unit of eight teams from the time Harridge joined the league until late in 1953 when the St. Louis Browns shifted to Baltimore. One year later, the Philadelphia Athletics moved to Kansas City.

As early as 1941, Harridge conferred with men interested in moving the St. Louis Browns to Los Angeles. But when World War II intervened, the matter was tabled and not reopened during Harridge's presidency. During the war, Will was a leader in the struggle to keep baseball going despite the absence of many stars.

Will and National League president Warren Giles imposed a mandatory $50 fine on pitchers who intentionally threw at hitters, leaving the judgment to the umpires. As further protection for batters, Will made it mandatory in 1958 for hitters to wear helmets. Until that time, only Phil Rizzuto of the Yankees had regularly worn one, having borrowed the idea from Branch Rickey.

Will championed the cause of free admissions to games for servicemen and opposed premature expansion of the league. But he did envision the day when each league would be composed of 12 teams, and he did predict that there would eventually be 3 major leagues.

Harridge seldom took the liberty of a vacation, and his hobbies were few. He played bridge and took delight in gardening at his home in Wilmette. He enjoyed long rides in the country and occasionally played golf. In June 1911, he had married Maude Hunter, and their only son, William L.H. Harridge, became a noted Chicago surgeon. It was on the advice of his son that Will decided to retire in 1958. With eight years remaining on his $50,000-per-year contract, Will decided to pass the job on to a younger man, Joe Cronin.

One of Harridge's last acts involved the heavily publicized fining of Ted Williams for spitting toward the fans during a 1958 game in Kansas City. It showed Will's determination to treat stars and journeymen equally.

Maude Harridge died on November 6, 1956. Thereafter Will lived a quiet life in Wilmette. After retiring as league president, Will held the title of Chairman of the Board of the American League until his death.

In 1967, at the age of 86, he accidentally struck an 83-year-old pedestrian while driving in Chicago, killing the man. Harridge, however, was immediately cleared of any wrongdoing.

Will's son died in March 1971, a tragedy he found difficult to accept. One month later, on April 9, Will passed away at a nursing home in Evanston, Illinois, at the age of 89.

In 1972, Will Harridge was selected for membership in the Hall of Fame.

Harridge (at right) meets with National League president Ford Frick, left, and Baseball Commissioner Judge Kenesaw Mountain Landis in Chicago in 1943 to discuss wartime travel difficulties for the major league teams.

Bucky Harris (1896-1977)

Bucky Harris managed the Washington Senators to their first and only world championship when he was 27 years old. Although he continued in baseball until the age of 75, that achievement remained his most memorable.

Stanley Raymond Harris was born on Ball Street in Port Jervis, New York, on November 8, 1896. His mother was of Swiss parentage, and his father, Thomas, was a Welsh coal miner who had emigrated to America. Thomas was a decent semipro ballplayer in the United States, and the one-time batterymate of Hughey Jennings. Stanley, who acquired the nickname "Bucky" from neighborhood friends at an early age, had an older brother, Merle, who taught him to play baseball and basketball.

Bucky's parents were divorced shortly after the family moved to Pittston, Pennsylvania, and Bucky quit school at the age of 13 to work as a breaker boy in the coal mines. Eventually, he graduated to the weighmaster's office in a responsible position that paid $4.30 a week.

Jennings, who lived in nearby Scranton, had seen Harris play shortstop on local mine teams and wired an invitation to the little infielder to try out with Detroit in Waxahachie, Texas, during spring training in 1916. Unfortunately, Jennings was ill when Harris arrived for the tryout. Coach Jimmy Burke gave Harris a quick workout at the strange position of third base, found him rather ordinary, and dismissed him as just another benchwarmer. Although Bucky was with the Tigers when the season opened, he failed to play in any games and was soon sent home to Pittston.

After a few months, however, Jennings offered Harris a job as third baseman for the Muskegon club in the Central League. Bucky signed a $125-per-month contract, played five games, and was released. Rather than return home, Harris sat in the stands and watched his replacement play poorly. The fans began hollering for Bucky's return. Rehired, he played in a total of 55 games and batted .166. Again, he was released.

Jennings found Harris another job in 1917, this time with Norfolk of the Virginia League. But the advent of American involvement in World War I caused the league to fold, and Harris transferred to the Reading team in the New York State League. With Reading, Bucky settled down to play second base, hit .250, and seemed to find himself. His very signing was an accident, however, for George Wiltse, the Reading manager, had thought he was signing Bucky's older brother.

The New York State League folded after the 1917 season, but Wiltse brought Harris to Buffalo of the International League the

following year and played him as the regular second baseman at a salary of $175 per month. In midseason Bucky jumped the club and signed with the Baltimore Drydocks, an independent team that featured Joe Judge and Dave Bancroft in the infield. Harris played well there, and he returned to Buffalo in 1919 to hit .282 in 120 games. The 5'9½", 156-pound, righthanded-hitting Harris was now ready for the majors.

Harris had an unsuccessful tryout with the New York Giants in midseason of 1919. But fortune was in Bucky's favor later in the year when Washington Senator owner Clark Griffith saw him play in a double header against Reading. Playing with a broken finger, Harris impressed Griffith enough to command a $5000 purchase price. Harris still had an opportunity to play for the Giants, and the Athletics also showed an interest, but Wiltse left the choice to Bucky. Sensing a greater opportunity to excel in Washington, Harris went there. He broke in late in August and, with Walter Johnson on the mound for Washington, hit a two-run single in his first appearance at the plate. But he misjudged a popup in the thirteenth inning and Johnson lost the game, 5–4. It was a tough debut for the rookie, but Johnson's understanding attitude made Harris feel welcome.

Bucky surprised many people in 1920 when he hit .300 and proved adept at handling the double play. By 1922, veteran Roger Peckinpaugh had joined the club as shortstop, and he was making an even better infielder out of Bucky. No one ever claimed that Harris was a master hitter or a great fielder, but he was a dependable performer who served the club well.

The youngest regular on the team as the 1924 season approached, Bucky was in disfavor with Griffith, who discovered that Harris had played semipro basketball contrary to team orders during the off-season. But Donie Bush had been fired as Washington manager, and the job needed filling. Harris was playing golf in Florida when Griffith called to offer him the job. Harris wired back, "I'll take that job and win Washington's first American League pennant." Bucky tipped the Western Union clerk $20 to send the same wire four times in the following four hours.

Harris had not even been certain of a regular job for 1924, as Griffith had been trying to obtain Eddie Collins from Chicago that winter. But suddenly "The Boy Manager" took the helm. No one expected much from Washington, and not one writer accompanied the team on its first trip. But Bucky began to win with Judge, Peckinpaugh, Sam Rice, Goose Goslin, Muddy Ruel, and Johnson. By season's end, Harris and the Senators were the toast of baseball, beating out the Yankees for the pennant by two games.

The ball is already in Harris's glove as Frankie Frisch tries to regain second. This thrilling play in the last game of the 1924 World Series contributed to the Senators' victory under "the boy manager"—Bucky Harris.

Bucky then outfoxed John McGraw of the Giants, and the Senators captured the World Series in seven games. Harris started righthander Curly Ogden in the deciding game, allowed him to face two batters, and then switched to George Mogridge, a lefthander, to counter the presence of young Bill Terry in the Giants' lineup. It was McGraw's last Series.

Harris set records that October for most chances, double plays, and putouts by a second baseman in a World Series. Bucky collected 11 hits and batted .333; he also belted two home runs, a rarity for a player who hit only nine in his career. Bucky repeated his pennant success with the 1925 club, but the Senators lost the World Series in seven games to Pittsburgh.

In 1926 Bucky married Elizabeth Sutherland, daughter of former Senator Howard Sutherland of West Virginia. They honeymooned in Paris, and the Harrises were the talk of Washington social circles.

By 1928, Harris had slowed down on the field, a fact Griffith attributed to continued basketball playing. After the season, Griffith traded Bucky to Detroit for Jack Warner, an infielder. The Tigers at once named Bucky manager. Under his direction, Detroit finished in the second division five consecutive times. In 1931 Harris concluded his playing career with a lifetime .274 batting average.

Griffith retained a certain fondness for Harris. In 1935, after Harris had managed the Red Sox to a fourth-place finish the previous year, Griffith rehired Bucky to run the Senators, succeeding Joe Cronin, whom Griffith had sold to Boston. All of Bucky's contracts were for one year, and his club was lackluster and financially poor. Although his ability to discipline was at times criticized, Harris was considered a good manager and popular with players. He managed Washington from 1935 to 1942, finishing in the first division only in 1936 with a fourth-place showing.

Two days after the 1942 season ended, Griffith fired Harris again: Bucky was then hired by William Cox, new owner of the Philadelphia Phillies. When Harris publicly called Cox a "jerk," his lone National League season was hastily concluded, and he left with the team in sixth place on July 28.

In 1944 and 1945, Bucky managed and served as general manager for the Buffalo Bisons in the International League, and then in 1946 he filled only the executive position. Harris had an opportunity to become general manager of Detroit late in 1946, but he elected to take Larry MacPhail's offer to join the New York Yankees "in an executive capacity." The job turned out to be Yankee manager, and

Bucky promptly won the 1947 World Championship, managing such greats as Joe DiMaggio, Phil Rizzuto, and rookie Yogi Berra. In 1948 the Yankees lost the pennant by only two and one-half games, but with MacPhail gone, the new management dismissed Harris and hired Casey Stengel.

Bucky spent the 1949 season managing San Diego of the Pacific Coast League. In 1950 he returned to Washington to begin his third term as Senator manager. Harris remained with Washington for five years, finishing in the second division each time. Everyone knew the Senators simply lacked the money to buy star players.

Bucky managed the Tigers for a second time during the 1955 and 1956 seasons, finishing fifth both times. That concluded a managerial career which spanned 29 major league seasons, a mark surpassed only by Connie Mack and John McGraw. And although 20 of those seasons were spent with second-division clubs, Harris was regarded as one of baseball's most knowledgeable managers.

The Red Sox hired Bucky in October 1956 as an assistant to Joe Cronin, the club's general manager. Harris had been Joe's manager in his rookie season with the Senators, playing second while Joe played short. With Cronin's advancement to American League president in 1959, Harris was named to succeed him. Unfortunately, the assignment was shortlived. On September 27, 1960, after the Sox had finished in seventh place, and with the impending retirement of Ted Williams, Harris was fired. The White Sox hired him as a scout, despite his increasing poor health.

Harris returned to the expansion Washington Senators in 1963 (his fourth term in Washington, equaling President Roosevelt's record, as one writer quipped) to handle "special assignments." Bucky did some major league scouting, but with the passage of ownership to Robert Short, his duties became limited due to his failing health. When the Senators moved to Texas after the 1971 season, Bucky's baseball career ended.

Ill with Parkinson's disease and confined to a nursing home in Bethesda, Maryland, the 78-year-old Harris was named to the Hall of Fame in 1975. He died on his 81st birthday, November 8, 1977.

STANLEY RAYMOND HARRIS

Washington 1919–1928
Detroit 1929, 1931

G	AB	R	H	2B	3B	HR	RBI	Avg.
1264	4736	722	1297	223	64	9	506	.274

Gabby Hartnett (1900-1972)

During his long career as a catcher (1922–1940) and player-manager (1938–1940) with the Chicago Cubs, Gabby Hartnett was considered the finest backstop in the National League.

Charles Leo Hartnett was born on December 20, 1900, in Woonsocket, Rhode Island, but was reared in Millville, Massachusetts. His father was a streetcar conductor and bus driver, and Charles Leo was the first of 14 children. The nickname "Gabby" was bestowed upon him by a Chicago sportswriter during his rookie year in the major leagues. Although it was widely accepted, his teammates always called him "Leo."

In the spring of 1921, while he was working in a steel and wire mill in Worcester and playing semipro ball, Hartnett was offered a contract by Jack Mack, manager of the Worcester team in the Eastern League. Gabby immediately became Worcester's regular catcher, playing in 100 games and batting .264. During the year, Jesse Burkett, a former star and then scout for the New York Giants, observed Hartnett's performance for John McGraw. Burkett reported that Hartnett's hands were too small and that he would never become an accomplished major league catcher. At the end of the season, Hartnett was sold to the Chicago Cubs for $2500.

Gabby made his major league debut with Chicago in the 1922 season opener, catching Grover Cleveland Alexander. However, Gabby played infrequently during his first year—Bob O'Farrell was the regular catcher—and batted only .194 in 31 games. But Alexander took a particular liking for the 21-year-old rookie and asked that Hartnett be his catcher whenever he pitched.

O'Farrell remained the regular catcher in 1923, but Gabby saw more action, catching 39 games and playing first base in 31 games. He batted .268 and hit his first eight major league home runs. The following year Hartnett replaced O'Farrell as the Cubs' regular catcher, appearing in 111 games and batting .299 with 16 home runs and 67 runs batted in. It was the first of 12 seasons—8 of them (1930–1937) consecutive—in which Hartnett caught in 100 or more games, a National League record.

The Cubs finished last in 1925, winning only 68 games, but Gabby batted .289 with 24 home runs and topped all National League catchers in putouts and assists. He was improving steadily. In 1928 Gabby reached the .300 plateau for the first time in his career, batting .302 in 120 games.

The 1929 season was a great one for the Cubs but hardly for Hartnett. Joe McCarthy was manager, Rogers Hornsby played second base, and the lineup included Charlie Grimm, Kiki Cuyler, Hack Wilson,

and Riggs Stephenson. In the second spring training game on Catalina Island, something snapped in Hartnett's arm when he made a throw to second base. Gabby caught only one game that year and was limited to 22 at bats for the entire season. With Zack Taylor behind the plate, the Cubs won the pennant by 10½ games.

If anyone had to prove his ability in 1930, it was Hartnett. The 6'1", 218-pound slugger reclaimed his first-string job by appearing in a career high of 141 games, batting .339 with 37 home runs and 122 RBIs—both also career highs. His 172 hits and 84 runs scored that year likewise were career highs. He led all National League catchers in fielding, a feat he accomplished six times during his career.

The 1930 Cubs slipped to second place, and Joe McCarthy was replaced as manager by Hornsby. The Cubs did not capture another pennant until 1932, when Hornsby was replaced as manager by Cub first baseman Charlie Grimm. Hartnett contributed a .271 season to the pennant drive and finally had a chance to catch in a World Series.

The American League champions that year were the Yankees, managed by McCarthy. This was the Series in which Babe Ruth is alleged to have pointed his finger to the center field bleachers before hitting a home run there off Cub pitcher Charlie Root. Hartnett, the catcher, claimed it never happened that way. Ruth, he recalled, merely gestured and said, "It only takes one to hit." The Yankees swept the Series in four games.

For the first All-Star game in 1933, Hartnett was named starting catcher for the National League. He also caught the next four All-Star contests, including the memorable 1934 contest in which Carl Hubbell struck out Babe Ruth, Lou Gehrig, Jimmie Foxx, Al Simmons, and Joe Cronin in succession. "Just throw them what you throw me," Hartnett advised the great Giant pitcher at a first-inning mound conference.

Under Grimm, the Cubs captured the 1935 pennant, and Hartnett batted .344. It was the first of three consecutive seasons in which Gabby batted over .300, culminating in 1937 when he batted .354. In the 1935 World Series, the Cubs faced Mickey Cochrane's Detroit Tigers. Cochrane was generally considered to be the best catcher in the American League (others might have named Bill Dickey), and Hartnett the best in the National League. The Tigers won the Series in six games, and both Cochrane and Hartnett batted .292.

The Cubs finished second in each of the following two seasons. In 1938, with the Cubs in third place with a 45–36 record, six and one-half games behind the league-leading Pittsburgh Pirates, Cub owner Phil

(At right) Hartnett is almost hidden in complete catchers' gear. (Below) Hartnett, at left, receives a scroll signed by 2500 fans on September 7, 1939, the day he caught his 1727th big league game and broke a catcher's endurance record. Presenting the scroll at right is Ray Schlak, who had set the previous record 10 years earlier.

Wrigley fired Grimm and named Hartnett player-manager. The Chicago fans and press were skeptical. Hartnett was a good-natured Irishman; could Gabby discipline his teammates? Hartnett met the challenge with a seriousness that surprised most outsiders. He proved to be a smart manager who sometimes took the less obvious path to achieve a victory.

The climax of the season came on September 28, 1938, in a head-to-head clash with the Pirates, who held a half-game lead over the Cubs in the pennant race. The score was tied, 5–5, as darkness spread over Wrigley Field after the eighth inning. With no lights in the park, the umpires huddled and decided to play one more inning before calling the game.

The Pirates went down in order in the top of the ninth, and Mace Brown, the Pittsburgh reliever, retired the first two Cubs in the last of the ninth. Up to the plate stepped the skipper, 37-year-old Gabby Hartnett, as 34,465 fans prayed for a miracle. The count went to two strikes and then Hartnett swung at a curve ball and rocketed it over the ivy-covered walls of Wrigley Field into the left-field seats. Of his 236 home runs, this was his most memorable. Chicago fans went wild; the win put the Cubs in first place, and they clinched the pennant two days later.

The 1938 World Series, however, was another four-game sweep for the Yankees. Gabby himself collected only one hit in the Series. During the Hartnett years, the Cubs lost all four of the World Series in which they played.

Gabby managed the Cubs to a fourth-place finish in 1939, batting .278 himself. In 1940 the Cubs slipped to fifth place, and Gabby hit only .266 in 37 games. On November 13, 1940, the Cubs released Hartnett as both player and manager. Gabby signed with the New York Giants as a player-coach, and in 1941, at the age of 40, he played in 64 games and batted .300. It was a good point at which to bow out as an active player.

For the next several years Gabby managed in the minor leagues—at Indianapolis (1942), Jersey City (1943–1944), and Buffalo (1946). No major league job beckoned, and his baseball career appeared to be ended. Gabby then became an avid golfer and bowler, opening a bowling alley and sporting goods store in Lincolnwood, Illinois. In 1965 Gabby returned to baseball as a coach with the Kansas City Athletics. Luke Appling also coached that season, giving the A's a pair of Hall of Famers on the coaching lines. Gabby held the job for one year and then became a scout and public relations man for the A's.

Elected to the Hall of Fame in 1955, Gabby Hartnett thereafter became a frequent guest at old timers' baseball gatherings. He died at his home in Park Ridge, Illinois, on December 20, 1972, his seventy-second birthday.

CHARLES LEO HARTNETT

Chicago (N.L.) 1922–1940
New York (N.L.) 1941

G	AB	R	H	2B	3B	HR	RBI	Avg.
1990	6432	867	1912	396	64	236	1179	.297

Harry Heilmann (1894-1951)

Harry Heilmann was a line-drive hitter who won four batting championships in the American League. With nine more well-timed hits, he would have become the only player to hit .400 four times.

Harry Edwin Heilmann was born in San Francisco on August 3, 1894, of German-Irish parentage. He attended St. Mary's High School in Oakland and had registered at Sacred Heart College, a Christian Brothers' school, in 1913 when Jimmy Richardson, a scout for the Portland team in the Pacific Coast League, induced him to play professional baseball. Harry's father could not believe that anyone would receive a salary for playing ball, and Harry himself had doubts when his bonus for signing turned out to be a spaghetti dinner.

Two brothers named McCredie owned a pair of professional teams in Portland—the Pacific Coast League club and the Class B team in the Northwest League. Harry was optioned to the lower classification on May 15, and he batted .305 with 11 home runs while playing both first base and the outfield.

The Detroit Tigers, at the suggestion of former White Sox manager Fielder Jones, drafted Harry on September 12, 1913, for $1500. Harry did not play at all with Detroit in 1913, but in 1914 he appeared in 67 games for the Tigers and hit .225. Slow afoot and without a defensive position he could play well, Heilmann was nicknamed "Harry the Horse" by his teammates. In the first inning of a game on May 22, he committed three errors in the outfield to set a major league record. Heilmann was clearly unprepared for the big leagues, and in 1915, manager Hughey Jennings farmed him to San Francisco of the Pacific Coast League, where he played first base and batted .364 in 98 games.

Harry never excelled on defense, but he spent the majority of his career in the outfield, with stints at first base and a brief trial at second. He was strictly a hitter, and a great one. His home run totals were never extraordinary, but sharp line drives were his specialty. The righthanded-hitting, 6'1" 200-pounder was as fearsome a power hitter as the Tigers had before Hank Greenberg appeared.

Heilmann returned to Detroit in 1916 and batted .282 in 136 games. He followed that performance with season averages of .281 and .276 in 1917 and 1918. In 1919 Harry finally surpassed the .300 mark, batting .320 but leading the league with 31 errors at first base. In 1920 he hit .309 and committed a league-leading 19 errors.

Ty Cobb became manager of the Tigers in 1921. Although few players were friendly with Cobb, Heilmann was an exception. Not only did the two remain close friends for life, but Cobb turned Harry's career around in that first season. Cobb instructed Heil-

mann to move his feet close together, with his bat held right down on the end and resting on his shoulder. Cobb's batting tips and patience paid off; Harry captured the 1921 batting championship with a .394 mark, leading the league with 237 hits and ranking fifth with 19 home runs.

The 1921 batting crown marked the first of four titles for Heilmann. Oddly, they came in alternate years—1921, 1923, 1925, and 1927. Asked about the coincidence, Harry would laugh and explain that it always occurred in the last year of a two-year contract, and that he was putting on a salary drive.

His averages in those four championship years were .394, .403, .393, and .398. If Heilmann had made four additional hits in 1921, four more in 1925, and one more in 1927, he would have compiled four .400 years. Unfortunately, Harry seldom beat out an infield hit, costing him many points each year.

In 1925 Tris Speaker held a lead of approximately 15 points over Heilmann as September approached, but a leg injury placed Speaker on the bench for most of the month. Heilmann started to swing a hot bat and the lead began to shrink. Finally, in a double header on the final day of the season, Harry collected six hits in nine at bats to beat Speaker, .393 to .389.

In 1927, while Babe Ruth was winning the home run crown and Lou Gehrig the RBI title, Heilmann was locked in a close batting race with Al Simmons. Al finished at .392 in an East Coast game on the final day, and Heilmann knew he could ride the bench during the second game of his double header and capture the title. But nevertheless Harry played, collected seven hits in nine trips to the plate, and finished with a .398 average.

Although capable of the long ball, his hits usually bounded off the fences. Eight times Harry hit 40 or more doubles in a season. Despite his lack of speed, which limited him to an average of 6.6 stolen bases per year, he reached double figures in triples nine times. His best home run season was 1922 when he belted 21—10 of them in Philadelphia. That accomplishment remains a single-season record for home runs in a visited ballpark. But the 1922 season was also the only year between 1921 and 1929 that Harry failed to drive in 100 or more runs.

The years in which Harry, or "Slug" as he was called, did not capture batting titles were by no means failures. He batted .356 in 1922, fourth best in the league; .346 in 1924, fifth in the league; and .367 in 1926, fourth in the league. And although his

The Harry Heilmann batting style. Heilmann became a four-time batting champion in the 1920s and averaged .342 for his career, thanks to the tutelage of Ty Cobb, who helped Heilmann correct his early batting faults.

fielding was still not strong, his powerful arm cut down 31 baserunners in 1924 to lead the league's outfielders in assists.

Bothered by a drinking problem, Harry would at times become involved in improbable situations off the field. On one occasion, he drove his Austin into a building, down the steps, and directly up to the bar in a speakeasy. The car had been given to him at a big "Harry Heilmann Day" at Navin Field on August 9, 1926.

Heilmann, who had served briefly as a quartermaster on submarines in the Pacific during World War I, was a personable, generous, and outgoing man. He was a close friend of Ruth and Cobb, two very different personalities. Harry's only regret was that he never played for a pennant winner.

After batting .328 in 1928 and .344 in 1929, Harry, to everyone's surprise, was waived out of the American League on October 29, 1929. The Cincinnati Redlegs immediately claimed him. Harry joined a seventh-place Cincinnati club in 1930 and batted .333 in 142 games. Bob Meusel, purchased from the Yankees, and Curt Walker shared the Cincinnati outfield with him.

During the 1930 season, Harry was nearly sold to the Brooklyn Dodgers for $60,000. Since his salary was $20,000, and it had cost the Reds $40,000 to buy him from Detroit, the deal promised to net the Redlegs $20,000. But Cincinnati manager Dan Howley turned the deal down, and when Heilmann spoke to Reds' owner Sidney Weil to convince him to make the transaction, Weil supported his manager. Harry had wanted the trade because of the chance to play with a pennant winner, but the Dodgers folded down the stretch and finished fourth anyway.

Heilmann missed the entire 1931 season with arthritis. Attempting a comeback in 1932, he played in only 15 games and batted .258. Harry finished the season as a coach for the Reds, and he then returned to his home in Detroit with his wife and son.

At first Heilmann tried to reestablish his insurance business, which had been wiped out in the 1929 stock-market crash. This and several other business ventures failed. The Tigers hired Harry in 1933 to be their radio announcer. It turned out to be a highly popular move; Harry was well received by Detroit fans, and he held the job for the remainder of his life.

In 1951 Heilmann became ill during spring training, spending several weeks in a Detroit hospital. He returned to the broadcast booth on April 28, remained with the club through June 24, and then returned to the hospital with lung cancer.

Cobb came to visit him and whispered that Harry had been elected to the Hall of Fame. But the announcement was premature since the election was not actually held until 1952, seven months later. On July 9, 1951, the eve of the All-Star game in Detroit which he had been selected to announce on network radio, Harry died.

HARRY EDWIN HEILMANN

Detroit 1914, 1916–1929
Cincinnati 1930, 1932

G	AB	R	H	2B	3B	HR	RBI	Avg.
2146	7787	1291	1660	542	151	183	1549	.342

Billy Herman (b. 1909)

One of the National League's most consistently dependable infielders during the 1930s and early 1940s, Billy Herman participated in ten All-Star games and played for four pennant winners during his career with the Chicago Cubs and Brooklyn Dodgers.

William Jennings Herman was born on July 7, 1909, in New Albany, Indiana. Some sources listed his full name as William Jennings Bryan Herman, but although he was named after the famed attorney and presidential candidate, "Bryan" was never a legal part of his name. His father, a machinist, and his mother reared ten children, of whom Billy was the ninth born.

Billy's earliest experiences with baseball were not typical of future major league stars. He was not the best player in his neighborhood and never the first selected for sandlot teams. At New Albany High School, Billy failed to crack the regular lineup, serving only as a utility infielder. Although not particularly outstanding at basketball either, it was considered his better sport.

His skills in baseball improved following his high school graduation. Farm chores had helped to add strength to his body, enabling Billy to catch on with various semipro clubs, particularly in nearby Louisville, Kentucky. There, he acquired a job in a veneer factory and played for the factory team. Billy also participated in a church league, and when he pitched his club to a championship, he was rewarded with a trip to Pittsburgh to see the first two games of the 1927 World Series.

Also in 1927, the 18-year-old Herman married Hazel Steproe. They had one child, Billy III. The marriage ended in divorce in 1960.

With his semipro success a matter of record, Billy signed a handsome $250-per-month contract (a figure explained by his local appeal) for the 1928 season with the Louisville Colonels of the American Association. But Louisville farmed him to Vicksburg of the Cotton States League, for which the 155-pound righthanded hitter played three infield positions and batted .332. Billy spent the final week of the season with Louisville.

Billy did not have the strength to hit the long ball and he therefore developed a style of hitting to all fields. Even when his weight increased to 195 in later years, he never changed his batting style, enabling him to produce steady .300 seasons.

Louisville farmed Billy to Dayton of the Central League in 1929. He continued to hit the ball well, batting .329 in 138 games. Now established at second base, Herman led the league in total chances. He again completed the season with Louisville, hitting .323 in 24 games.

Billy spent the entire 1930 season with the Colonels and batted .305 with 86 runs batted in. Many considered him ready for the major leagues, but with the opening of the 1931 season he returned to Louisville for his fourth minor league season. Again, Billy belted the ball sharply, batting .350 through early September when the Chicago Cubs bought his contract.

The 1931 season was the last one in which Rogers Hornsby would play regularly, and as manager of the team, The Rajah was eager to find a replacement at second. Herman appeared to be a likely candidate.

A fine hit-and-run man noted for good bat control, Billy also proved at once to be a fielder of durability and great range. Between 1931 and 1941, he never played a single game at any position other than second base. He led National League second basemen in putouts a record seven times, and also topped the league in assists on three occasions. Five times during the 1930s, Billy handled more than 900 chances in a season.

Playing daily during September 1931, Billy broke into the big leagues by hitting .327 for the Cubs. Having made a strong impression, Billy was handed the regular job for 1932.

In the 1932 campaign, Billy tied for the National League lead in games played with 154, batting .314 with 102 runs and 206 hits, only one of which was a home run. It was a fine rookie showing.

The Cubs fired Hornsby on August 2. Charlie Grimm, his replacement, then led the club to the National League pennant. Herman hit .222 in the four-game World Series loss to the Yankees, a Series best remembered for the "called shot" home run by Babe Ruth.

The Cubs finished third in 1933, but Herman and shortstop Billy Jurges were recognized as the finest keystone duo in the league, with the possible exception of Frankie Frisch and Leo Durocher of St. Louis. Billy hit under .300 for the first time in his professional career in 1933 (.279), and shouldered part of the blame for the Cubs' fall. But in the field, Billy led the league in putouts. On June 28, he recorded 16 putouts in a double header, including 11 in the first game. Both totals established records.

Herman made his first of 10 All-Star game appearances in the 1934 contest. He always appeared to play his best during these midsummer games, and in 10 games between 1934 and 1943, he collected 13 hits in 30 at bats for a .433 average.

During the regular 1934 season, Billy batted .303 but the Cubs remained in third place. In 1935 the Cubs returned to the World Series; Billy hit a career high of .341 during the regular season, fifth best in the league. He topped the National League in hits with 227, and in doubles with 57, the latter figure establishing an all-time Cub record. One year later, he equaled the mark for a two-year total of 114.

Billy batted .333 in the 1935 World Series and connected for a rare home run off Tiger pitcher Tommy Bridges in the sixth and deciding game, won by Detroit, 4–3. Herman drove in all three Cub runs in the contest.

Billy hit .334 and .335 in the following two seasons as the Cubs placed second both times. But in 1938, despite a drop in average to .277 by Billy, the Cubs captured the pennant and met the Yankees in the World Series. New York handled the opposition easily, however, sweeping four consecutive games. Billy collected only three singles and batted .188.

With his salary a handsome $21,000 and his popularity high, Herman became one of the best known athletes in Chicago and a fixture at second base for the Cubs.

Charlie Grimm had been replaced as manager by Gabby Hartnett in 1938, and Hartnett yielded to Jimmie Wilson in 1941. Wilson seemed threatened by the presence of Herman on the club since Billy was a close friend of owner William Wrigley, had a leadership flair about him, and was one of the few Cubs enjoying a good season. Thus, many blamed Wilson's fear of losing his job for the trade of May 6, 1941, which sent Herman to the Brooklyn Dodgers for John Hudson, Charley Gilbert, and a reported $65,000.

"I just bought a pennant," said Dodger boss Larry MacPhail, whose team had not captured the flag since 1920. Brooklyn fans went wild over the arrival of their long-time foe. Billy immediately replaced Pete Coscarart at second, teaming with Dolph Camilli, Pee Wee Reese, and Cookie Lavagetto to give the Dodgers a fine infield. Brooklyn, led by Durocher, did indeed win the pennant, only to lose the World Series to the Yankees. Billy batted .125 to end his career Series play with an average of .242.

Herman hit a mediocre .256 for the Dodgers in 1942, but he bounced back in 1943 to bat .330, second in the league to Stan Musial. Billy also drove in a career high of 100 runs (third in the league) despite a season's total of only two home runs.

Billy spent the 1944 and 1945 baseball seasons in the Navy, serving in Honolulu. He then returned in 1946 to bat .298 in a season divided between Brooklyn and the Boston Braves, to whom he was traded on June 15 for Stew Hofferth. On September 30, 1946, Herman was again traded, this time to Pittsburgh in a six-player trade. Billy was immediately named player-manager of the Pirates. The team finished in a tie for the cellar in 1947, but record crowds turned out to watch the home run heroics of Hank Greenberg and Ralph Kiner. Billy played in 15 games and batted .213 for a career average of .304. The day before the close of the regular season, Herman was fired.

Billy managed Minneapolis of the American Association in 1948, and he then returned home in 1949 to New Albany

where he had a partial interest in a paint factory. Charlie Dressen convinced Herman to play for Oakland of the Pacific Coast League in 1950, and Billy batted .307 to close out his playing career. In 1951 Herman managed Richmond of the Piedmont League, and from 1952 to 1957 he coached with Brooklyn and collected four more World Series checks. He moved to Milwaukee in 1958, coaching for its pennant-winning club that season and remaining with the club through 1959.

From 1960 to 1964, Billy coached for the Boston Red Sox. He became manager of the club in 1965, lasting two seasons before Dick Williams succeeded him and led the Sox from ninth place to the pennant in 1967.

Billy coached for the California Angels in 1967. He then joined the Oakland A's as a scout from 1968 to 1974. In 1968 Billy also managed their Gulf Coast League farm club at Bradenton.

An excellent golfer and bridge player, Billy moved to Palm Beach, Florida, in 1956. He remarried in 1961, and in 1975 he was elected to the Hall of Fame. In 1976 Billy Herman joined the San Diego Padres as minor league hitting coach and special assignment scout. He retired after the 1979 season.

WILLIAM JENNINGS HERMAN

Chicago (N.L.) 1931–1941
Brooklyn 1941–1946
Boston (N.L.) 1946
Pittsburgh 1947

G	AB	R	H	2B	3B	HR	RBI	Avg.
1922	7707	1163	2345	486	82	47	839	.304

Herman stretches to pull in the ball. Renowned for his fielding feats, he led the National League second basemen in putouts a record seven times and topped the league in assists in three years. He and shortstop Bill Jurges combined to form one of the best keystone duos in the league.

Harry Hooper (1887-1974)

The Boston Red Sox captured four World Championships between 1912 and 1918, and their great outfield of Duffy Lewis, Tris Speaker, and Harry Hooper contributed substantially to their success. Although only a .281 lifetime hitter, Hooper was such a fine player that he eventually joined Speaker in the Hall of Fame.

Harry Bartholomew Hooper was born on August 24, 1887, on the Elephant Head Homestead in Bell Station, Santa Clara County, California. He was a competent baseball player as a youngster, and although a natural righthanded hitter, he taught himself to bat from the left side to obtain a better jump toward first base. But Harry's ambition was engineering, not baseball. He graduated from St. Mary's College in 1907 with a degree in civil engineering. During his senior year, he joined the Oakland team in the outlaw California State League to help finance his education. By no means did he consider professional baseball as a career.

The 5'10" outfielder had an agreement with Oakland owner Bob McMinnamen that he would receive his release upon graduation in June 1907, at which time he would be free to pursue his engineering career. But one day Charlie Graham, manager of the Sacramento club, expressed an interest in the 19-year-old Hooper. McMinnamen arranged for Hooper to say nothing of his planned "retirement," and he agreed to give Hooper half the sale price if a deal could be arranged with Sacramento. Hooper made it clear that he planned to go into engineering, but this did not trouble Graham, who promised to obtain a job for Harry as a surveyor in addition to playing ball.

At last the transaction was accomplished. Hooper was sold to Sacramento for the embarrassing sum of $25, of which he received $12.50. When he reported to Sacramento, Graham kept his promise by acquiring him a job as a surveyor for the Western Pacific Railroad. Hooper earned $85 per month playing ball in addition to $75 per month from the railroad. He considered baseball a sideline, but Graham took a different view.

Harry hit .301 in 1907 and .344 in 1908. Late in the 1908 season, Boston Red Sox owner John Taylor came to town to scout players. Taylor's wife originally came from California, and he used the opportunity of visiting relatives to find new players for his "Speed Boys" in Boston. Hooper was just such a man.

Since the California State League was not within organized baseball, Taylor had to negotiate directly with Hooper. Harry still wanted to be an engineer, but Graham urged him to travel to Boston and try baseball for a few years. Taylor further enhanced the contract offer of $2800 per

year by explaining that the Red Sox would soon be building Fenway Park and might need Hooper's assistance in its design.

Hooper took the offer and never again practiced engineering. Although Harry had no role in the construction of Fenway Park, he never regretted choosing baseball.

Harry went to spring training with Boston in 1909 and found himself generally ignored in favor of the veterans. Early in the season, however, injuries enabled him to break into the lineup. Immediately, Harry started to hit. For the following 12 seasons, he remained a fixture in the Boston lineup.

Harry excelled as a leadoff batter with his good speed. Defensively, he had a strong, accurate arm and great range, and he developed a style of sliding to make great catches. Speaker, Boston's center fielder, played very shallow, and Hooper was therefore responsible for a considerable territory in deep right-center field. Harry soon became one of the most graceful fielders in the game.

Hooper batted .282 in his rookie season, and he then hit .267 and stole 40 bases in 1910. He had a fine .311 season in 1911, one of the only two seasons over the .300 mark with Boston. During this period, manager Patsy Donovan added new talent to the team. In 1912, under manager Jake Stahl, and in their first season in Fenway Park, the Red Sox won 105 games to run away with the pennant.

Boston faced John McGraw's Giants in the 1912 World Series, and the Red Sox won it in eight games. In the sixth inning of the final game, Hooper fell into the stands while robbing Larry Doyle of a home run. Despite long and loud protests by the Giants that the catch was illegal, it was allowed and the Red Sox won the game in 10 innings, 3–2. Hooper batted .290 for the Series.

Harry batted with a wide-open stance, took a very short stride, and swung with an upper-cut at the ball. Although not noted as a power hitter, he recorded double figures in triples nine times. Harry was an intelligent player who earned the position as Red Sox captain when Ed Barrow became manager in 1918.

The Red Sox did not capture the pennant in either 1913 or 1914, but in 1915, under manager Bill Carrigan, the club won the pennant despite a disappointing .235 season by Hooper. In the 1915 World Series against Philadelphia, Harry performed more last-minute heroics. In the fifth and final game of the Series, played in Shibe Park, Philadelphia, Harry hit two home runs to equal his season's total. Both home runs bounced into the temporary stands built around the outfield; both would be called ground-rule doubles under today's rules. The latter of the two blasts occurred in the top of the ninth inning and gave the Red Sox a 5–4 victory and another World Championship.

The Red Sox captured another pennant in 1916. Harry batted .333 in the five-game World Series victory over Brooklyn.

A fourth pennant came Boston's way in 1918, and the Red Sox squared off against the Cubs in the World Series. Discovering that for the first time Series money would be shared with the second, third, and fourth-place teams in addition to the pennant winners, Red Sox and Cub players staged a sit-down strike prior to the fifth game as 25,000 fans sat and waited in Fenway Park. The players had already agreed to donate 10 percent of their earnings to the Red Cross to help with the war effort, and they now were suddenly confronted with the prospect of receiving the smallest shares in Series history.

Hooper, captain and spokesman for the Red Sox, presented the players' point of view. The National Commission, composed of the two league presidents and the president of the Cincinnati club, listened but would not alter their position. Hooper stated that the players wanted a guaranteed winners' share of $1500. Ban Johnson, American League president, answered by talking of the "glory of baseball."

Although disgusted, the teams decided to play for the enjoyment of the fans, provided that no punitive action was taken against the clubs. The Red Sox won the Series. The winners' share was $1102, and the losers received $671—both were the smallest figures in Series history. Despite the promise of no penalties, the players never received the diamond lapel pins selected as World Championship awards.

As team captain, Hooper was the man who convinced Ed Barrow to install Babe Ruth in the outfield to make full use of his bat. The move, of course, became a historic one, but Ruth and many other Red Sox players were soon traded or sold to the Yankees by the financially hard-pressed Boston owner, Harry Frazee. Having batted .312 in 1920, Hooper held out in 1921 for $15,000, knowing he would never receive the sum. Harry was delighted to leave the deteriorating Red Sox when Frazee traded him to the White Sox during spring training for Shano Collins and Nemo Liebold. Charles Comiskey gave him a three-year blank contract on which Hooper wrote in a salary of $13,250 per year.

Despite a broken hand, Hooper played in 108 games for the White Sox in 1921, hitting a career high of .327. In 1922 Harry batted .304 with 11 homers and 80 runs batted in, and he then hit .288 in 1923 and .328 in 1924.

After hitting .265 in 1925, Hooper was offered a 1926 contract calling for $7000.

Hurt by Comiskey's action, he wrote a letter recalling his fairness in filling in a modest figure on the blank contract in 1921. In reply, Hooper received his unconditional release in the mail.

Harry sat out the entire 1926 season. Returning to baseball in 1927, he played the outfield for the San Francisco Missions in the Pacific Coast League, batted .284, and announced his retirement.

At home in Santa Cruz, California, with his wife, Esther, Harry briefly tried real estate. He then enjoyed a two-year coaching position at Princeton University (1931–1932). During the Depression, he took a temporary job as postmaster in Capitola, California, but remained on the job for 25 years.

In 1971, at the age of 84, Harry Hooper was elected to the Hall of Fame. He died on December 18, 1974, at Santa Cruz, California.

HARRY BARTHOLOMEW HOOPER

Boston (A.L.) 1909–1920
Chicago (A.L.) 1921–1925

G	AB	R	H	2B	3B	HR	RBI	Avg.
2308	8784	1429	2466	389	160	75	813	.281

Boston Red Sox captain Hooper leaves the bench to get in on the action. Hooper led the team in a sitdown strike during the 1918 World Series to protest a decision to share Series money with the second, third, and fourth place teams. (At right) Hooper is about to head for first base.

Rogers Hornsby (1896-1963)

Brash and outspoken Rogers Hornsby, the man with the highest lifetime and single-season batting averages in National League history, was also one of the most traveled men in the game. During his 23-year major league career, "The Rajah" played on five different teams, and then managed five different teams.

Rogers Hornsby was born on April 27, 1896, in Winters, Texas, and was given his mother's maiden name. In his early baseball days he was frequently called "Roger," but by the time his career had ended there was no one associated with the game who did not know the correct first name.

Rogers began his professional career as he turned 18, signing as a shortstop with Hugo, Oklahoma, of the Texas-Oklahoma League in 1914. Later that season he joined the Denison, Texas, team in the same league. His mother, a great baseball fan, encouraged Rogers to make a career in the game.

Hornsby batted only .232 in 1914, playing 113 games with 91 hits and just 3 homers. In 1915 he played with Denison and produced a .277 mark in 119 games. Late in the season, the 140-pound, right-handed hitter was purchased for $500 by the St. Louis Cardinals, managed by Miller Huggins. Art Butler was the regular shortstop at that time, and Hornsby appeared in only 18 games that year, hitting .246. The Cardinals finished in sixth place.

In his first four full seasons with the Cardinals (1916–1919), Hornsby played primarily third base or shortstop. He batted .313, .327, .281, and .318 those years, leading the National League in triples in 1917. He also earned a reputation as an outspoken young man who did not hesitate to criticize a teammate or a manager, and who was brash enough to let the world know that he was the finest hitter in the league.

In 1920 Hornsby moved to second base, switching positions with Milt Stock. During the next two decades he would gain the reputation as one of the greatest second basemen in baseball history. Hornsby hit .370 that year (besting runner-up Ross Youngs of the Giants by 19 points), leading the league in hits (218), doubles (44), and runs batted in (94). Much of his improvement at the plate could be attributed to added weight. Huggins had coaxed him up to 160 pounds, and Branch Rickey, his manager from 1919 to 1925, pushed Rogers to build up his weight to 200 pounds—none of it fat. The added strength increased Hornsby's home run output from 5 in 1918 to a record high of 42 just four years later.

The years 1921–1925 witnessed the greatest half-decade of hitting ever known in baseball. Winning the batting title each season, Rogers compiled marks of .397, .401, .384, .424, and .403. Although it was no longer as common to hit .400 as it had

been before the turn of the century, Hornsby passed the .400 mark three times in the five seasons; his five-year batting average was .402 with 1,078 hits. Three times in that span he led the league in hits (235 in 1921, 250 in 1922, and 227 in 1924). He also won three doubles championships during that span (44 in 1921, 46 in 1922, and 43 in 1924), a triples title (18 in 1921), three runs-scored titles (131 in 1921, 141 in 1922, and 121 in 1924), and three RBI titles (126 in 1921, 152 in 1922, and 143 in 1925). Rogers also captured two home run championships with 42 in 1922 and 39 in 1925; the former mark stood as the major league record for second basemen until broken in 1973 by Atlanta's Dave Johnson. The .424 average compiled in 1924 remains the highest batting average recorded in the major leagues in the twentieth century. In 1925 Hornsby won his first of two Most Valuable Player awards.

The five-year performance was breathtaking. Not even Ty Cobb, winner of many batting titles in the American League, approached such heights. Hornsby was now considered by many the greatest hitter in the game, and his brash confidence led the Cardinals to name him player-manager on June 1, 1925. The team had won only 13 of 38 under Rickey, and with Hornsby at the helm, leading the way with his own bat, the Cardinals won 64 and lost 51 to finish in fourth place. Hornsby had completed 10 seasons with the Cardinals at this point without ever having played on a pennant winner.

That was to change, however, in 1926. Hornsby's average tumbled to .317 with only 11 homers, but the Cardinals captured their first pennant. The prime contributors to the pennant effort were future Hall of Famers Jim Bottomley, Chick Hafey, Jesse Haines, and Grover Cleveland Alexander. In the World Series, Hornsby brought in the great 39-year-old Alexander to strike out the Yankees' Tony Lazzeri in the seventh game, enabling the Cards to win the world championship.

The Series victory should have been the peak of Hornsby's career. But Rogers had a dispute with Cardinal owner Sam Breadon over an exhibition game late in the 1926 season. Consequently, Hornsby was offered only a one-year contract for $50,000 as player-manager in 1927 rather than the three-year contract he expected. A parting of the ways was imminent.

On December 20, 1926, one of the most famous trades of baseball's first half-century was completed: Hornsby to the New York Giants for their great second baseman Frankie Frisch and pitcher Jimmy Ring. Free of managerial responsibilities (John McGraw was running the show in New York), Rogers hit .361 and led the league in games played and runs scored.

A great issue of the day was the obligatory unloading of Hornsby's stock in the Cardinals; Rogers had owned 1000 shares, which he had bought at $45 per share. The shares were now valued at $120 each, and to pay Hornsby, the eight National League club owners contributed $5000 apiece to settle the matter.

Hornsby got along no better with Giant owner Charles Stoneham than he had with Breadon. Rogers spent only one year in New York. On January 10, 1928, he was dealt to the Boston Braves for outfielder Jimmy Welsh and catcher Shanty Hogan.

Jack Slattery was the Braves' manager, but Hornsby was far too strong a personality to be just another player on the club. On May 23, 1928, with the team's record a miserable 11–20, Hornsby was named player-manager. But Rogers had little success as manager, with the team winning only 39 while losing 83 and finishing in seventh place. He did, however, win his seventh batting title with a .387 average.

With the Braves badly in debt, Judge Emil Fuchs, their owner, was forced to trade Hornsby at the end of the 1928 season to the Chicago Cubs for five players and $200,000. Even Hornsby advised Fuchs to make the transaction for the financial well-being of the club.

With Chicago in 1929, under manager Joe McCarthy, Hornsby led the league in games played, a proud feat at age 33, and batted .380 with 39 homers and 149 runs batted in. He also captured his second Most Valuable Player award. The Cubs won the pennant, and Hornsby played in his second and last World Series, which the Cubs lost to Philadelphia in five games.

On September 23, 1930, Joe McCarthy was fired as Cub manager. Hornsby was named to replace him and the club won the last four games of the season to finish in second place. In 1931 Hornsby led the Cubs to a third-place finish. He played in 100 games for the last time in his career, batting .331 with 16 home runs and 90 runs batted in. In 1932 Rogers limited himself to only 19 games. On August 2, 1932, with the team at 53–44, Hornsby was fired. Charlie Grimm assumed the managerial reins and led the team to the pennant. The players cut Hornsby completely out of their World Series money.

It was a disappointing year for Hornsby

(At left) Hornsby ready to connect. His career batting average was .358, second only to Ty Cobb's in major league records, and tops in National League history. (Above) He watches the action from the St. Louis dugout.

on another front as well. Commissioner Landis called him in to discuss his betting on horses. Hornsby always seemed to have financial difficulties; he gambled heavily and lost a reported $100,000 in the 1929 stock-market crash. His married life reflected a similar instability, for he was divorced twice.

In 1933 his old friend, Branch Rickey, bailed Rogers out by signing him to return to the Cardinals. Hornsby batted .325 as second baseman and pinch-hitter in the early part of the season. In June he was named manager of the cross-town rival, the St. Louis Browns. Rogers managed the American League team from July 27, 1933 to July 20, 1937, when Jim Bottomley replaced him. Under Hornsby, the Browns finished eighth, sixth, seventh, seventh, and eighth, respectively. Rogers played occasionally in emergencies, batting .299 in 67 games over those five seasons. That brought his career batting average to .358, second only to Ty Cobb.

Thereafter followed a long "exile" to the minor leagues. Hornsby coached for Baltimore of the International League in 1938, and then was named manager of Chattanooga of the Southern Association in July 1938. He managed Baltimore in 1939, Oklahoma City of the Texas League from June 1940 to June 1941, Fort Worth of the Texas League in 1942 and 1943, Beaumont of the Texas League in 1950, and Seattle of the Pacific Coast League in 1951. After 15 years in the minors, Hornsby returned to the major leagues in 1952 to again manage the Browns. But on June 9 he was dismissed. The Cincinnati Reds brought him back to the National League on August 1 to handle the managerial duties. His stay in Cincinnati lasted just over one year; he was fired on September 17, 1953.

Out of baseball for four years, Hornsby was hired as Chicago Cub coach for 1958 and 1959, New York Met scout in 1961, and Met coach in their first season, 1962.

A man who always prided himself on his eyesight and would never even attend a movie, Hornsby underwent an operation for cataracts late in 1962. While in the Chicago hospital, he had a heart attack and died on January 5, 1963.

Rogers Hornsby was elected to the Hall of Fame in 1942.

ROGERS HORNSBY

St. Louis (N.L.) 1915–1926, 1933
New York (N.L.) 1927
Boston (N.L.) 1928
Chicago (N.L.) 1929–1932
St. Louis (A.L.) 1933–1937

G	AB	R	H	2B	3B	HR	RBI	Avg.
2259	8173	1579	2930	541	168	301	1579	.358

Waite Hoyt (b.1899)

Waite Hoyt was brought up on the sandlots of New York City, and he went on to play for all three New York teams before his 21-year career ended. His greatest fame came as leader of the mound staff for the great Yankee teams of the 1920s.

Waite Charles Hoyt was born on September 9, 1899, in Brooklyn, New York. His ancestry was English-German-French. His father made a living as a singer, and the touch of show business always remained in Waite.

Baseball in Brooklyn at the turn of the century was a daily game for youngsters. When Waite was not attending P.S. 92, he would be on the sandlots learning to pitch. At Erasmus Hall High School he became the focus of the city's baseball league by compiling a 31–2 record and pitching three no-hitters.

Early in 1916, while still only 16 years old, Waite ventured to Ebbets Field in hope of a tryout. Despite his great record at nearby Erasmus Hall, the Brooklyn club showed little interest.

Waite had been observed by Red Dooin, a scout for John McGraw's New York Giants, and Red invited young Hoyt to the Polo Grounds for a better look. Shortly thereafter, Waite's father signed a Giants contract for his son (who was still a minor), and Waite was assigned to the Mt. Carmel team of the Pennsylvania State League. When the league folded, he was transferred to Hartford of the Eastern League, and then to Lynn of the same league, posting a combined 4–5 record.

Waite continued to move about in 1917. Opening the year at Memphis of the Southern Association, Waite had a 3–9 record, and then a 7–17 mark in 28 games at Montreal of the International League, where he compiled a 2.51 earned run average.

Dissatisfied with the shuffling from town to town, Waite longed to find a permanent home in the majors. In 1918 he had a 5–10 record for Nashville of the Southern Association when at last he received a call to report to the Polo Grounds in June. The 18-year-old righthander, already a broad-shouldered 5'11½" and 183 pounds, was handed the ball only once by McGraw. Waite pitched one inning and retired three consecutive batters, striking out two. To his dismay, he was optioned to Newark of the International League a few days later.

Waite recorded a 2–3 mark with a 2.09 ERA for Newark. Before the 1918 season ended, the Giants notified him that he was being moved to New Orleans. It then appeared obvious to Waite that the Giants would never recognize his skills. He packed his bags and acquired a job with an independent team in Baltimore known as the Dry Docks. With the start of World

War I, Hoyt spent the winter in Officer's Candidate School at Middlebury College in Vermont.

Waite's break came in the midsummer of 1919 when the Boston Red Sox bought his contract from New Orleans. Hoyt joined Babe Ruth, Sam Jones, Herb Pennock, and Allen Russell on Ed Barrow's pitching staff. His record for the remainder of the season was 4–6, but on September 24 he distinguished himself by retiring 30 consecutive Yankee batters in a 13-inning, 2–1 loss. No batter reached base between the second and eleventh innings, but Waite's performance was overshadowed by Babe Ruth's twenty-eighth home run, which established a new single-season record.

In 1920 Ruth moved to the Yankees, and Hoyt compiled a 6–6 record for Boston. But the Yankees had not forgotten his 1919 outing against them, and Barrow, now with the Yankees, effected an eight-player trade on December 15 that brought Hoyt and catcher Wally Schang to the Yankees.

"Schoolboy" Hoyt, as he was known, became an immediate sensation with the Yankees. When the Yankees won their first pennant in 1921, Hoyt recorded a 19–13 mark. In the World Series Waite delighted himself no end by pitching 27 innings against McGraw's Giants without allowing an earned run. He pitched a two-hitter in the second game, winning, 3–0; scored a 3–1 win in the fifth game, with the Giant run being unearned; and was handed the ball by manager Miller Huggins to pitch the eighth and deciding game. The Giants scored a run in the first inning on an error by shortstop Roger Peckinpaugh, and Art Nehf stopped the Yankees the remainder of the game for a 1–0 win. But Hoyt had certainly distinguished himself.

After his World Series heroics, Waite became quite a personality. His playboy life, despite prohibition, rivaled that of Babe Ruth, and the two became close off-the-field friends—even though at one point they passed two years without a word. On the mound, Waite maintained a casual gait which some interpreted as arrogance, but it helped to build his reputation as a star.

In 1922 Hoyt again won 19 games, but he lost his only Series decision as the Giants again won the World Championship. In 1923, in the club's first year in Yankee Stadium, Hoyt posted a 17–9 record, and the Yanks finally beat the Giants in the Series for their first world championship. Waite did not record a decision in the 1923 World Series.

The Yanks did not capture the pennant in either 1924 or 1925. For the two years Hoyt compiled a combined 29–27 record. In 1925 he was fined $200 for throwing the ball into the stands when manager Miller Huggins brought in a relief pitcher to replace him.

The Hoyt delivery. Hoyt's manner on the mound was so relaxed that more critical observers called it arrogant—but that did no harm to the superstar status he achieved shortly after his twenty-second birthday, when he pitched 27 innings without allowing an earned run.

In 1926 Waite posted a 16–12 record. In the World Series against St. Louis, Hoyt scored a victory but lost the deciding game when Grover Cleveland Alexander relieved Jesse Haines for the Cardinals and struck out Tony Lazzeri with the bases loaded.

By 1927, Waite was earning a handsome $16,000, plus a $2500 bonus for notching 20 victories. The 1927 Yankees may have been the best team ever assembled, and Hoyt was their standout pitcher, leading the league with a 22–7 record. He scored his fourth World Series victory against the Pirates that fall.

In 1928 Hoyt's salary was increased to $20,000 including his bonus. Besides compiling a 23–7 record during the regular season and notching two victories in the World Series, Waite made news by spending his free time studying for a mortician's license. His father-in-law was a funeral director in Brooklyn and Waite considered the possibility of joining the business. He became known as "The Merry Mortician," but when his marriage broke up, so too did his interest in the funeral business.

After the 1928 season, Waite went on the vaudeville stage as a singer. The versatile and well-spoken Hoyt also amused himself by learning to paint with oils.

In 1929 Hoyt's record fell to 10–9. Then in 1930, with former teammate Bob Shawkey now installed as manager, Hoyt's Yankee days ended. He and Shawkey argued over pitching plans, and on May 30 Hoyt was traded with Mark Koenig to the Detroit Tigers in one of Ed Barrow's poorer deals. The Yankees received Owen Carroll, George Wuestling, and Harry Rice, none of whom contributed significantly.

Waite remained in Detroit for little more than one year. He posted an 11–10 record in 1930 but had contributed nothing in 1931 when he was waived to the Philadelphia Athletics in June. The deal meant that Hoyt had now played for John McGraw, Miller Huggins, and Connie Mack, an education in itself.

For the Athletics in 1931, Hoyt compiled a 10–5 record, giving him a combined 13–13 season record, and found himself on another pennant winner. Waite appeared in one Series game that fall, lasted six innings and received the loss, which gave him a 6–4 World Series record. At the time, Hoyt had earned more Series victories than any pitcher in baseball.

Connie Mack released Waite in January 1932, and his hometown team, the Brooklyn Dodgers, signed him. But his stay in Brooklyn was brief. He was released by the Dodgers in June. Signed immediately by the Giants, shortly after McGraw had resigned in favor of Bill Terry, Waite finished the year with a 6–10 record. Obviously, he was no longer a pitcher of superlative ability.

In November 1932, Hoyt was released to Pittsburgh. One day in Pittsburgh he marched over to the Chicago Cubs' dugout, after receiving considerable bench-jockeying, and announced, "If you guys don't shut up, I'll put on my old Yankee uniform and scare you to death!" The reference was to the 1932 World Series, swept by the Yanks over the Cubs.

Hoyt remained in Pittsburgh until midway in the 1937 season. In 1935 he was present to see Babe Ruth swat three home runs against his club for the Babe's final big day with the Boston Braves.

Released by the Pirates in June 1937, Waite joined the Dodgers and finished his career with Brooklyn in 1938, losing all three of his decisions before drawing his final release in May. He had won 237 games in his career.

Hoyt then became one of the first athletes to work in broadcasting, first with the Dodgers for two years and then with Cincinnati, where he spent 24 seasons as Reds' announcer. He retired in 1966 but made a one-year comeback in 1972, a pennant-winning season for the Reds.

Waite Hoyt was named to the Hall of Fame in 1969.

WAITE CHARLES HOYT

New York (N.L.) 1918, 1932
Boston (A.L.) 1919–1920
New York (A.L.) 1921–1930
Detroit 1930–1931
Philadelphia (A.L.) 1931
Brooklyn 1932, 1937–1938
Pittsburgh 1933–1937

G	IP	W	L	Pct.	H	R	ER	SO	BB	ERA
675	3762	237	182	.566	4037	1780	1500	1202	1003	3.59

Cal Hubbard (1900-1977)

Cal Hubbard is the only man with the distinction of belonging to both the baseball and the football Halls of Fame. His football recognition came as a player; his baseball recognition came as an umpire.

Robert Cal Hubbard was born on October 31, 1900. He was one of the five children of Robert and Sally Ford Hubbard, farmers in Keytesville, Missouri. Cal was always known by his middle name in order to avoid confusion with his father.

Even as a youth he was generally selected as an umpire at neighborhood baseball games. Big for his age, he was a fine football player, but his bulk made him somewhat awkward in baseball and his friends would invite him to umpire. His imposing size, both then and later, helped to earn him respect as an official. He grew to be 6'3" and weighed 255 pounds, but he was so physically imposing that college football scouts frequently listed him as 6'6".

Cal was raised on the family farm, but education was stressed and he was sent off to a school in Glasgow, Missouri, where the quality of education was considered higher. He was back at Keytesville High School for graduation, and then enrolled in a business college in nearby Chillicothe, Missouri. But his boyhood idol, Bo McMillan, was the football coach at Centenary College in Louisiana, and when McMillan offered Hubbard a chance to play football there, no further encouragement was needed. McMillan had been a star quarterback for Centre College and had gained national recognition when he had led his club to a victory over Harvard.

At Centenary, Cal also participated in baseball and track, but he was considered poor on the diamond and played only because of the small enrollment at the school. But on the gridiron he was soon earning rave notices. Installed as a tackle, it quickly became clear that Hubbard was the finest player in the conference. Had the school been larger, he probably would have been considered for All-American, or at least All-South honors.

In 1923, his second year at Centenary, Cal was switched to end, and led his team to a 10–1 record. As he continued to develop, he joined the boxing and wrestling teams.

Then, in 1924, McMillan became the coach at Geneva College in Beaver Falls, Pennsylvania, and he took Hubbard with him. Supporting himself by working in the local steel mill, Cal spent two seasons at Geneva and developed a reputation as a hard-hitting blocker with mobility, agility, and the ability to pursue his man. In 1926 he earned All-American honors as a right end, and soon professional clubs were seeking his services. McMillan sat down with him and studied the offers, then urged him to sign with the New York Giants. Thus

it was that Hubbard went to New York for the 1927 season, acting, with Steve Owen, as tackle on a fine Giant team. Cal even caught some passes that year as the Giants used him as an eligible receiver on screen-pass plays.

In 1928 Cal was back with the Giants, but he was not happy with the big city. He was still a Missouri farm boy at heart, and when the Giants played the Packers in Green Bay, Wisconsin, Cal decided that that town was much more to his taste. He discussed the situation with Giants business manager John March, and March worked out a trade in which, for the 1929 season, Cal went to the Packers for halfback Al Bloodgood.

It turned out to be a great trade for Green Bay, and Hubbard was soon earning recognition as one of the stars of the National Football League. His movements were brilliant for a man of his size, and he could run the 100 in 11 seconds. George Halas, coach of the Bears, called him "the best lineman I ever saw." In November of 1929, playing in the Polo Grounds against his old Giant teammates, Cal became perhaps the game's first linebacker. Coach Curly Lambeau slipped him behind the defensive front line, and Cal roamed all over the field that day, leading the Pack to a 20–6 upset of New York.

Meanwhile, Hubbard began spending his summers as a baseball umpire. It all began in the summer of 1928 when he wrote to William G. Bramham, president of the Piedmont and Southeastern leagues, to apply for a job—and got it. The times were not easy for an umpire, and Hubbard toiled between the two leagues for the 1928 and 1929 seasons, learning the fine points of the game as he went. He came to be considered one of the leading experts in baseball, and before long he could quote directly from the rule book. But there were times, as in 1929 after a game in Macon, when he had to sneak out of town by rail following an uproar at the ballpark.

His football career, meanwhile, was only approaching its peak. The Packers were undefeated in 1929, and also won the NFL title in 1930 and 1931. All-Pro teams were selected for the first time in 1931, and Hubbard was an easy selection. The honor was repeated in both 1932 and 1933.

But in the summertime it was always back to umpiring. In 1930 he split the year between the Piedmont League and the South Atlantic League. In 1931 he worked the Piedmont again, and also entered the Triple-A International League, a big step toward the majors. In 1932 he worked in the Western League but settled into the International League for the summers of 1933, 1934, and 1935.

(Above) The 1927 New York Football Giants, with Hubbard seventh from left, top row. A country boy at heart, Hubbard was not too happy in the Big Apple and talked the Giants into trading him to Green Bay for the 1929 season. It was a great move for Hubbard, as the Packers were undefeated that year and NFL champs in 1930 and 1931 too. In the meantime, Hubbard was spending summers as a minor-league baseball umpire, building up his reputation for his second career. (At left) Hubbard takes the classic lineman's pose.

Umpiring was now taking Hubbard away from summer football practices, and as he reached his middle thirties, he realized that his future was in baseball. He did not play football at all in 1934, but served instead as line coach at Texas A&M. The Packers had him on the inactive list in 1935, and on October 29, 1936, his old team, the Giants, signed him. He played a game against Detroit but was soon sold to Pittsburgh, and then announced his retirement as a player.

The 1936 season was not only Cal's last as an NFL player but it was his first as an American League umpire, for American League President Will Harridge had purchased him from the International League at the start of the season. He was, of course, well known to sports fans, but as a rookie umpire he worked steadily with his partner Dick Nallin, adjusting to his new responsibilities. Cal's size let him retain an outwardly cool personality on the field, and he was seldom involved in arguments. Yet White Sox catcher Mike Tresh once recalled, "Cal told me that if I didn't shut up he'd hit me so hard on top of my head it would take a derrick to get me back to ground level!"

Umpire Hubbard gets an earful from two other future Hall of Famers, Lou Gehrig (No. 4) and Bill Dickey of the Yankees. Hubbard generally kept a cool head in such disputes and earned the nickname "His Majesty" by his regal behavior on field.

By 1938, Cal was good enough to be assigned to work the World Series, played between the Yankees and the Cubs. Cal later worked the World Series of 1942, 1946, and 1949. He received three All-Star game assignments: 1939, 1944, and 1949.

His final tie to football came during the winters of 1941 and 1942 when he served as head coach at his alma mater, Geneva College. He had received an A.B. degree in 1927.

By the post-World War II years Cal was considered one of the finest umpires in baseball, and younger fans were hard pressed to remember any of his football heroics.

In off seasons, Cal liked to tend to his 300-acre cattle farm in Milan, Missouri, where he settled with his wife and two sons. (He remarried in 1966 after the death of his first wife.) Although Cal was an opera lover, his main hobby was bird and goose hunting. It was on a hunting trip, following the 1951 season, that tragedy ended his umpiring career. He was struck in the right eye by a shotgun pellet, his vision was damaged, and he was forced to give up umpiring.

Will Harridge, one of Hubbard's great admirers, at once appointed him "Supervisor of Umpires" for the American League, with his responsibilities including the hiring and firing of his former colleagues. He was thus frequently on the road, touring the parks to watch his charges in action.

Cal remained in that post until he retired in 1969. Not one to seek the headlines, he remained in the background during the controversial 1968 firings of American League umpires Al Salerno and Bill Valentine, but it was his bad reports on the pair that had led league president Joe Cronin to dismiss them.

Cal also spoke out against the spitball ban, calling the existing rule "unenforceable."

Although known to some as "His Majesty," because of his regal manner on the field, Cal was humble enough to admit that seldom did he call a "perfect game."

In 1963, Cal was among the first group of men chosen for the Professional Football Hall of Fame in Canton, Ohio. That same year he was also named to the National Football Foundation Hall of Fame for college players.

In 1976 he was selected for the Baseball Hall of Fame, making him the only man to be so honored in two sports.

On October 17, 1977, Hubbard died of cancer in St. Petersburg, Florida.

Carl Hubbell (b.1903)

Carl Hubbell took one pitch—the screwball—perfected it to a fine art, and used it to record 15 winning seasons in his 16-year playing career with the New York Giants.

Carl Owen Hubbell was born on June 22, 1903, in Carthage, Missouri, and reared on a pecan farm in Oklahoma. As a boy he worked on the farm and as a cotton chopper. After graduating from high school, he worked for an oil company. But in August 1923, with impressive credentials as a schoolboy and sandlot pitcher, Carl signed a professional contract with the Cushing team in the Oklahoma State League. He started the following year with Cushing as well, but the club folded early in the season and Carl moved on to the Ardmore team in the Western Association, where he pitched 12 innings and won his only decision. Hubbell closed out the 1924 season with Oklahoma City in the Western League, appearing in two games and splitting two decisions.

Carl returned to Oklahoma City in 1925 for his first full professional season in one city. He pitched in 45 games, won 17 and lost 13, but walked 108 batters against only 103 strikeouts. Clearly, he needed polish.

By this time, Carl had begun to throw the screwball, a "reverse curve" that broke *in* to a lefthanded hitter. Hubbell, being lefthanded, understood that most hitters looked for a curve that would break *away* from a lefty.

Following the 1925 season, Jack Holland, owner of the Oklahoma City team, sold the 22-year-old Hubbell to the Detroit Tigers for a reported $20,000. Carl reported to the Tigers for spring training, only to be warned by manager Ty Cobb not to employ the screwball. The screwball—or "butterfly pitch," as it was then known—was thrown in a most unnatural way, and the Tigers feared that it would ruin their pitcher's valuable arm.

Hubbell did not pitch a single inning in spring training, and Detroit farmed him to Toronto in the International League. With orders not to throw the screwball, Carl recorded only an unimpressive 7–7 mark with a 3.77 earned-run average.

Carl returned to spring training with the Tigers in 1927, and again he was forbidden to throw the screwball. With his best pitch prohibited, Carl's confidence and control collapsed. Again Hubbell failed to make the club, and he was assigned to Fort Worth of the Texas League. After pitching in two games with the club, he was sent to Decatur in the Three-I League. But even his 14–7 record with a 2.53 earned run average failed to restore his confidence. With five minor league seasons under his belt, Hubbell seriously questioned his future in baseball.

Carl made it through spring training in 1928, but the Tigers released him outright to Beaumont of the Texas League when the season opened. Beaumont manager Claude Robertson saw nothing wrong with the screwball and told Carl to use the pitch. It had been two years since Carl had thrown a screwball in a game, and to regain its effectiveness was an arduous process. But Carl mastered the pitch and finished the season with a 12–9 record, 116 strikeouts, and only 45 walks.

The New York Giant scout in Texas at the time was Dick Kinsella. A delegate to the 1928 Democratic National Convention in Houston, Kinsella became bored with politics and went to see a Texas League game. There he saw Hubbell lose a 1–0 decision in 11 innings. Impressed, Kinsella called John McGraw, the Giants' manager. On Kinsella's recommendation, the Giants purchased Hubbell from Beaumont for $30,000, and Carl immediately joined the Giants.

Carl's first Giant start came against Pittsburgh, and he was rocked for seven runs in the second inning. But McGraw sought out Hubbell the next day, told him he was impressed by what he saw, and restored the confidence of the shocked pitcher.

Carl settled down after his disappointing debut to capture 10 of his 16 decisions as a Giant rookie. With an ERA of 2.83 in 14 starts and 6 relief appearances, Hubbell had established himself as a major leaguer.

In 1929 Carl became the Giants' leading winner with an 18–11 record, and the team finished in third place. With his control steadily improving, Carl posted records of 17–12 (1930), 14–12 (1931), and 18–11 (1932). He soon received the nickname "King Carl."

John McGraw resigned as Giant manager on June 2, 1932, and first baseman Bill Terry took over as player-manager. The 1933 Giants pitching staff featured Hubbell, Hal Schumacher, Freddy Fitzsimmons, and Roy Parmelee. Terry and Mel Ott, Hubbell's roommate, provided the hitting power as the Giants captured their first pennant since 1924, besting second-place Pittsburgh by five games. Hubbell compiled a 23–12 record, a sensational 1.66 earned-run average, 10 shutouts, and a league-leading 309 innings pitched. He was voted the league's Most Valuable Player, never an easy award for a pitcher, who often works only twice a week.

In the 1933 World Series against Washington, Carl won the first and fourth games as the Giants easily defeated Joe Cronin's Senators in five games.

Although Carl had pitched an 11–0 no-hitter against Pittsburgh on May 8, 1929, he always considered a 1933 game against St. Louis to be the best performance of his career. On July 2 of that year, Carl matched arms with the Cardinals' Tex Carlton. Hubbell pitched an 18-inning shutout, allowing only six hits, striking out 12, and not permitting a single base on balls. The Giants won the game in the eighteenth when Hubbell beat out a double-play grounder to keep the inning alive; second baseman Hughie Critz then delivered the game-winning single off relief pitcher Jesse Haines.

If the 18-inning victory was Hubbell's finest regular season game, certainly his most memorable outing occurred the following season. Carl received the starting assignment for the second All-Star game, played in the Polo Grounds on July 10, 1934. The American League starting lineup consisted of:

Charlie Gehringer, 2b
Heinie Manush, lf
Babe Ruth, rf
Lou Gehrig, 1b
Jimmie Foxx, 3b
Al Simmons, cf
Joe Cronin, ss
Bill Dickey, c
Lefty Gomez, p.

Every one of those American League players is today in the Hall of Fame. Gehringer opened the game with a single and Manush walked. Hubbell's catcher, the Cubs' Gabby Hartnett, walked to the mound and told Carl, "Throw the screwball—it always gets me out!" Carl then went to work on Babe Ruth, 39 years old but still fearsome. Hubbell retired Ruth on a called strike three, and Gehrig fanned on four pitches. He then struck out Foxx to the roar of the crowd.

The tall and thin Hubbell, 6'1" and 175 pounds, strode to the mound in the second inning and faced Simmons, then Cronin. He fanned both, making it five consecutive strikeouts—five of the best hitters ever to bat in succession in one game. It was a remarkable accomplishment, and although the American League rallied to win the game, 9–7 (Hubbell departed after the maximum of three innings with a 4–0 lead), his performance remains the most memorable achievement in the history of the All-Star game.

During the regular season in 1934, Carl posted a 21–12 record and led the league with a 2.30 ERA. It was the second of five consecutive years in which he won 20 or more games. His masterful performances earned him the nickname "The Meal Ticket," a title which manager Bill

Terry did not particularly enjoy. But Carl was as important to the Giants then as Christy Mathewson had once been.

In 1935 Carl compiled a 23–12 mark. In 1936 the Giants returned to the World Series behind Carl's 26–6 record, which included 16 consecutive victories at the end of the season. The Yankees captured the World Series that fall, with Hubbell winning the first game but losing the fourth in a six-game setback. As in 1933, Carl was voted the Most Valuable Player in the National League.

Carl began the 1937 season with eight consecutive wins, giving him 24 consecutive victories over a two-year span. He finished the year with a 22–8 mark and a league-leading 159 strikeouts. The whiff crown in 1937 was his only strikeout title, but Carl maintained a ratio of strikeouts to walks of nearly three to one.

The Giants again captured the pennant in 1937, but once more the club lost to the Yankees in the World Series. Carl split another two decisions in the Series, giving him a lifetime Series record of 4–2 with a 1.79 earned-run average.

The screwball, as Ty Cobb had warned many years before, took its toll on Hubbell's arm. Carl had experienced arm trouble sporadically throughout his career. Its most serious effects occurred in 1938 when Hubbell made only 22 starts and fell to a 13–10 record. Never again did Carl approach the 20-victory circle. In each of the following four years he won 11 games, including an 11–12 record in 1940, his only losing season.

Finally, in 1943, Carl ended his career at the age of 40. His 253 lifetime victories represented the record for National League southpaws until Warren Spahn broke it years later. Only Mathewson placed ahead of Hubbell on the all-time Giant pitching charts.

A man of keen baseball sense, Carl was named director of the Giants' farm system on December 2, 1943. His title was later changed to director of player development. Carl retained the position to the end of the Giants' New York era in 1957 and onward with the team to San Francisco. He still held the vital position after such modern Giant stars as Willie Mays, Willie McCovey, Juan Marichal, and Orlando Cepeda had completed their Giant careers. In 1977 Hubbell began his 50th season on the Giant payroll, still as lean and trim as the day he joined the club. Illness that year finally sent him to Arizona and retirement, but he continued to serve the Giants as an honorary scout.

Carl Hubbell was elected to the Hall of Fame in 1947.

CARL OWEN HUBBELL

New York (N.L.) 1928–1943

G	IP	W	L	Pct.	H	R	ER	SO	BB	ERA
535	3591	253	154	.622	3461	1380	1188	1677	725	2.98

(Opposite page and at left) From high kick through release, the windup and delivery of Carl Hubbell's screwball, a reverse curve that broke into a left-handed batter. Although Cobb warned Hubbell that it was an unnatural pitch and would ruin his arm, Hubbell threw it for many fame-filled seasons. (Above) He sits in the Giant dugout with manager Bill Terry, left.

Miller Huggins (1880-1929)

Miller Huggins, for 12 years a fine infielder in the National League, piloted the New York Yankees to six pennants during the 1920s.

Miller James Huggins was born on March 27, 1880, in Cincinnati, Ohio. He was brought up on the sandlots of Cincinnati's fourth ward, a rough neighborhood, especially for one so small in size. Huggins never grew to be more than 5'4", and upon reaching the major leagues, he weighed a scanty 125 pounds.

His father, a devout Methodist, was an English-born grocer. Because the senior Huggins would never have permitted Miller to play ball on Sundays, Miller broke into professional ball under the name "Proctor" out of respect for his father.

The name also helped to preserve Miller's amateur status, as he entered the University of Cincinnati at his father's wishes to study law. A faculty member, future President William Howard Taft, took a liking to the young Huggins and advised him either to concentrate on law or baseball, but not to attempt both. Huggins received his law degree but never practiced. In fact, he never held a single position outside of baseball.

Miller began his minor league career in 1899 with Mansfield of the Inter-State League, playing shortstop and third base. He experimented with and adopted switch-hitting, a rare talent in those days. But Hug had to compensate for his short stature in various ways.

In 1900 Miller left professional baseball briefly to take a job as a semipro second baseman for Julius and Max Fleischmann, owners of a resort hotel in New York's Catskill Mountains. Huggins was a great favorite of the Fleischmanns, and they kept in close touch in later years.

Hug returned to organized ball in 1901, joining St. Paul of the Western League. He played 129 games and batted .322. When St. Paul moved to the American Association in 1902, Hug stayed with the club and hit .328. In 1903, while still with the Saints, Huggins topped the .300 mark again, batting .308.

During the winter months Hug worked out with weights to build his strength. Gradually, he developed greater power in his arms.

The Cincinnati Reds, long in search of a second baseman, quietly purchased Miller in the winter of 1903–1904. In spring training, manager Joe Kelley told reporters, "I've got a second baseman who'll make you all forget Bid McPhee—Miller Huggins."

Not everyone was as impressed as Kelley. McPhee had a great reputation in Cincinnati, and Huggins was not as physically imposing. After sitting on the bench on

opening day, Huggins earned a place in the lineup in the second game of the season. He collected a single, two walks, and a stolen base, and then survived a hard collision at second with the Cubs' John Evers. Huggins batted leadoff during his rookie season and hit a respectable .263. At second base, he covered considerable ground and was soon called "Little Mr. Everywhere."

The Reds were never a pennant contender while Huggins played with the team, but Miller developed a fine reputation on the bases and in the field. He batted as high as .292 (1906), which came as a great surprise in later years to Babe Ruth, who thought his manager had never reached the .240 mark.

After the 1909 season, during which Huggins had played only 49 games for manager Clark Griffith, Miller was dealt to the Cardinals with Rebel Oakes and Frank Corridon for Fred Beebe and Alan Storke. Cardinal manager Roger Bresnahan had personally sprung the deal in an effort to acquire the peppery Huggins. In his first year as a Cardinal, Hug batted .265. On June 1, 1910, he received four walks and sacrificed twice, setting a record with six unofficial times at bat in one game. Hug scored 101 runs that season, and he increased the figure to 106 in 1911, tying for second in the league.

During the winter of 1912–1913, Bresnahan was fired and Huggins was named to succeed him. Miller was the personal choice of Mrs. Helene Britton, "Lady Bee," the new owner of the team. Bresnahan's vulgar language in her presence had made her determined to replace him with the more gentlemanly Huggins.

Miller, known as "The Rabbit" during his Cardinal days, assumed the managerial reins of a poor St. Louis team that promptly finished last. But his contract was renewed for 1914, and he lifted the team to third place, the highest Cardinal finish since the National League's first season (1876).

Huggins held strict control in St. Louis. He advised the club on trades and hired his friend, Charley O'Leary, as coach. Hug continued to play second base for the Cards through 1915. In 1914 he stole 32 bases but set a record by being thrown out 36 times.

In 1916 rookie third baseman Rogers Hornsby joined the club. Hug remained stationed at second base, but he promised friends that "I'll quit when the fans tell me I'm no longer filling the bill." One day late in 1915, Miller committed two errors on routine ground balls, the fans booed, and he sat himself down. Hug appeared in 18

(Top) Huggins at bat, where his performance was respectable, although not spectacular. (Below) The smiles of Huggins, now Yankee manager, and Yank owner Jacob Ruppert reflect the fortunes of the great team.

games in 1916, but he then turned the position over to Hornsby.

The Cardinals finished last in 1916 and third in 1917. Those were disappointing years for Hug. After the 1916 season, Lady Bee announced her intention to sell the team. She offered Huggins the opportunity to buy the Cards, but while Miller was in Cincinnati raising the money from the Fleischmanns, she sold the club to barrister James C. Jones. Jones acquired Branch Rickey from the Browns to manage the team, and Huggins' job was gone.

The Yankees were seeking a manager for 1918. Wild Bill Donovan had been fired, and the Yankee owners, Colonels Ruppert and Huston, battled over his successor. Ban Johnson, American League president, praised Huggins to Ruppert and had J. G. Taylor Spink, publisher of *The Sporting News,* serve as messenger to Huggins. Miller met with Ruppert during the 1917 World Series, was offered double his previous salary, and accepted the job.

Huston, away in France during the War, wanted Wilbert Robinson and was infuriated by Ruppert's selection. It caused a major conflict between the two which ended only when Huston sold out to Ruppert following the 1922 World Series.

Huggins, "The Mite Manager," was placed under considerable pressure, but the Yankees finished fourth in 1918 and third in 1919. Then, at Huggins' suggestion, the Yankees purchased Babe Ruth from Boston and changed the course of baseball history. After finishing in third place in 1920, the Yankees captured pennants in 1921, 1922, and 1923, launching a baseball dynasty that produced 29 pennants in 44 years.

Miller respected Babe Ruth's talents, but Ruth was his chief antagonist on the team. An undisciplined man to begin with, Ruth could not withstand orders from the 5'4", 145-pound manager. Babe broke all training rules, berated his manager to anyone who would listen, and frequently embarrassed Huggins in front of the other players. On more than one occasion, Babe held Miller over the side of a moving railroad car just for laughs.

By 1925, Huggins' patience had passed its limit. Babe did not hit a home run until June 11, was badly out of shape, and the club was mired in seventh place. Late in August, prior to a game in St. Louis, Huggins pulled Ruth off the field and informed him that he was being fined $5000 and suspended indefinitely.

The fine was the largest ever imposed on a baseball player. Ruth hurled every conceivable insult at Huggins, and The Babe sought to appeal the fine before Commissioner Landis. But Landis was not in town, and Ruth pleaded his case before Ruppert and general manager Ed Barrow.

The two backed Huggins completely, and Ruth finally apologized, paid his fine, and returned to the field after one week. Huggins seldom had trouble with Babe thereafter, and out of respect for Miller the money was not returned to Babe until after Huggins had died.

In 1927 Huggins managed perhaps the greatest team in baseball history. It was known as "Murderers' Row," and included Ruth, Lou Gehrig, Tony Lazzeri, Mark Koenig, Joe Dugan, Earle Combs, and Bob Meusel, plus pitchers Herb Pennock, Wilcy Moore, Waite Hoyt, Urban Shocker, and Dutch Reuther. Only 25 men played for the Yankees that year, and the club captured 110 games during the season and four consecutive victories in the World Series.

Huggins, a rich man through wise stock investments, helped advise his players on the market. Many became financially successful as a result of his counsel.

In 1928 Huggins won his sixth Yankee pennant and third World Championship. But by 1929, after three successive pennants, the team appeared lackluster, and Connie Mack's Athletics captured the flag. Huggins worried more than usual, and he appeared ill at times. A bachelor, Miller was being cared for by his sister, but his weight was dropping and his appetite was decreasing. One day late in September, he told coach Art Fletcher, "Take the reins, Art. I'll be back tomorrow."

But Huggins never returned. He had been suffering from neuritis, and a carbuncle below his left eye had poisoned his entire system, resulting in erysipelas. He died in New York on September 25, 1929.

Players cried when they heard the news of Miller's death. Ruth, sobbing openly, said, "He was a great guy, was Hug."

Yankee Stadium's first center field monument was dedicated to Huggins, and it was later flanked by monuments to Ruth and Gehrig. In 1964 Miller Huggins joined many of his illustrious players in the Hall of Fame.

MILLER JAMES HUGGINS

Cincinnati 1904–1909
St. Louis (N.L.) 1910–1916

G	AB	R	H	2B	3B	HR	RBI	Avg.
1573	5558	948	1474	146	50	9	318	.265

Monte Irvin (b. 1919)

Of the players selected for the Hall of Fame by the Committee on the Negro Leagues, Monte Irvin accomplished the most in the major leagues, helping the New York Giants to two pennants.

Monford Irvin was born on February 25, 1919, in Columbia, Alabama, the seventh of ten children born to Cupid Irvin, a farmer, and his wife, the former Mary Eliza Henderson. The family moved to Orange, New Jersey in 1927. At Orange High School, he earned 16 varsity letters and became one of the finest schoolboy athletes in New Jersey's history. Irvin was all-state in four sports—baseball, football, basketball, and track, where he competed in the javelin and shot-put events.

Among the many scholarships offered to Monte in his senior year was one from the University of Michigan, where he might have played football in the same backfield as Tom Harmon and Forrest Evasheski. But the Irvin family could not afford the transportation to Michigan, and Monte therefore accepted a scholarship from Lincoln University, a predominantly black institution in Pennsylvania.

Under the assumed name "Jimmy Nelson," Monte joined the Newark Eagles of the Negro National League in 1937. An all-around athlete, Irvin had speed, power, a great throwing arm, and tremendous desire. He made the all-star team in 1939, and the following season he batted .368. After spending the summer of 1942 playing ball in Mexico, Irvin entered the U.S. Army, serving with the Army Engineers in Europe during World War II.

Before he entered the service, Monte had been quietly scouted by Branch Rickey of the Dodgers, who even then had ideas of integrating baseball. But while he was overseas, Monte's name became lost in the shuffle. By his own admission, too, it took him time to return to form once he rejoined the Eagles in 1946. By then, Rickey had signed Jackie Robinson, despite the feeling of those in the Negro Leagues that Irvin would have been a better choice at the time.

Somehow, other players received the call into organized ball before Monte. Irvin led the Negro National League in hitting in 1946 with a .389 average, but Don Newcombe, Roy Campanella, Dan Bankhead, Larry Doby, Hank Thompson, and Willard Brown were all signed to major league contracts previous to Irvin's entry.

When the Eagles disbanded following the 1948 season, Monte was claimed by Brooklyn. However, the Eagles' owner, Mrs. Effie Manley, contended that she owned the rights to Monte's contract and threatened to go to court to retain him. Baseball Commissioner Happy Chandler, not wishing to do legal battle with the Negro Leagues, ruled in Mrs. Manley's favor, and the Dodgers retracted their claim.

The 6'2" 195-pounder was playing ball for Almendares in the Cuban Winter

League in 1949 when Alex Pompez, a scout for the New York Giants, offered him a contract. Monte was assigned to Jersey City of the International League for the 1949 season. He had finally entered organized baseball at the age of 30.

Monte started quickly at Jersey City, and he was hitting .373 with 9 home runs and 52 runs batted in after 63 games when he and Hank Thompson were called up by the Giants. But Monte failed to find a place in the regular lineup that season. He appeared in only 36 games, batted .224, and was one of the first players cut in spring training in 1950.

Returning to Jersey City, Monte regained his confidence and batting stroke. In 18 games there, over a three-week period, Irvin collected 26 hits in 51 times at bat for a sensational .510 average, including 10 home runs and 33 runs batted in.

Hurriedly, he was called back by the Giants. On his second day with the team, Monte belted a grand-slam home run. By June he had become a regular in the lineup. When left fielder Whitey Lockman suffered an appendicitis attack, Irvin was placed in left, where he displayed one of the finest throwing arms in the league. Upon Lockman's return several weeks later, Monte was moved to first base, where he was less than graceful, but still a regular. Irvin finished the 1950 season with a .299 average and 15 home runs.

In 1951 Monte opened the season at first, but in May he traded positions with Lockman and returned to his more natural left field slot. The Giants started poorly, but Irvin was swinging a good bat. He also helped rookie Willie Mays to adjust to the major leagues and became Willie's most trusted friend. The two remained close throughout Willie's illustrious career.

Trailing the Brooklyn Dodgers by 13½ games in mid-August of 1951, the Giants caught fire and put on one of the greatest pennant drives in National League history, with Irvin leading the way. Monte seemed to collect key hits daily down the stretch, batting nearly .400 in the season's final six weeks. As the regular season came to a close, the Giants tied the Dodgers for first place. The dramatic three-game playoff ended in the ninth inning of the final game when Bobby Thomson homered into the left field stands at the Polo Grounds. For the season, Monte batted .312 with 24 home runs and a league-leading 121 runs batted in.

The Yankees captured the 1951 World Series, but Monte was the Series star with 11 hits in 24 times at bat for a .458 average. In the opening game, he stole home.

The Most Valuable Player award for the 1951 season went to Roy Campanella, with Stan Musial second and Irvin third. It was the high point of Monte's career, and his salary for 1952 was increased to $25,000.

On April 2, 1952, as spring training was drawing to a close, Monte broke his right ankle sliding into third base during an exhibition game against Cleveland in Denver, Colorado. The break was serious, and Irvin did not return to the lineup until August 1. But it was not the same Monte Irvin. Although he batted .310 in 46 games, his speed had vanished. Suddenly, Monte played like a tired 33-year-old, not like the ever-youthful Irvin. With Mays in the service and Irvin missing most of the year, the Giants finished second in 1952, four and one-half games behind the Dodgers.

Monte batted .329 in 1953, but on August 9 he reinjured his ankle sliding home against St. Louis. The injury seemed to deplete his batting skills as well as his speed.

The 1954 Giants captured the pennant. Monte contributed some key hits along the way, but his average for the season was only .262. He batted only .222 in the Series sweep of the Indians.

After playing 51 games for the Giants in 1955, during which he hit a mediocre .253, Monte was sent to Minneapolis of the American Association. There he batted .352 in 75 games, prompting the Chicago Cubs to draft him for the 1956 season when he was left unprotected by the Giants. For the last-place Cubs in 1956, Monte hit .271 in 111 games. That marked the end of his major league playing career.

Monte and his wife, Dee, lived in suburban New Jersey. Personable and well liked, Irvin worked for a major brewery in New York, kept himself in prime physical condition, and made numerous speaking appearances. In 1967 and 1968, he scouted for the New York Mets, and then in August 1968 he was hired as a public rela-tions representative in Commissioner Bowie Kuhn's office.

Monte was made a member of the committee to select Hall of Famers from the Negro Leagues. In 1973 the committee, with Monte not participating, selected Irvin both for his performances in the Negro Leagues and for his fine National League career.

MONFORD IRVIN

Negro, Cuban, and Mexican Leagues 1937–1948
New York (N.L.) 1949–1955
Chicago (N.L.) 1956

The following figures apply only to Monte Irvin's National League career. No records exist from the Negro, Cuban, and Mexican Leagues.

G	AB	R	H	2B	3B	HR	RBI	Avg.
764	2499	366	731	97	31	99	443	.293

Major league totals only

(At left) Irvin flanked by hospital nurses after he broke an ankle sliding into third base during an exhibition game in 1952. The accident threatened his career, but he bounced back to hit .329 in 1953. (Above) Irvin greets his fans on Monte Irvin Day in 1951.

Hughey Jennings (1870-1928)

Hughey Jennings was a star infielder with the Baltimore Orioles and a successful manager of the Detroit Tigers during a career that spanned 35 seasons.

Hugh Ambrose Jennings was born on April 2, 1870, in the coal-mining town of Pittston, Pennsylvania. Of Scotch-Irish parents, he was one of four children. Hughey received no formal education until his baseball career commenced, and he went on to attain a law degree from Cornell.

Freckle-faced and red-headed, Hughey was an active youngster, but not a particularly tall one for his age. He finally grew to 5'9" and weighed 165 pounds, but in his teens he attempted to get by as a 90-pound catcher with a bad arm. In hopes of building up strength in his arm, Hughey actually baked it in a brickyard kiln.

In 1890 Jennings was catching for a semipro team in Leighton, Pennsylvania, when the Allentown team of the Eastern Interstate League signed him. He batted .320 in 13 games while playing shortstop primarily, and he was then signed by Louisville of the American Association (a major league) for the 1891 season.

Jennings continued to show a good bat that year, hitting .300 in 81 games, but the league had low-quality pitching and his hitting was not fairly tested.

When Louisville moved into the National League in 1892, Jennings received that test and nearly failed it. He batted only .232 for a team that finished ninth out of 12 clubs. His basic problem was keeping his foot from stepping into the bucket, a common failing of hitters.

In mid-June of 1893, Jennings was traded to the Baltimore Orioles along with Harry Taylor for Tim O'Rourke and cash. It was a major transaction for the Orioles, who were on their way to winning pennants for manager Ned Hanlon in 1894, 1895, and 1896, and a Temple Cup playoff in 1897. The club was one of the most colorful ever assembled. In addition to Jennings, the team included John McGraw, Willie Keeler, Joe Kelley, and Wilbert Robinson, all future Hall of Fame members. Jennings struck up a lifelong friendship with McGraw, who helped him to overcome his hitting problem by pitching to him while his back was against a wall.

The results were gratifying—Jennings batted .332 in 1894, .386 in 1895, .398 in 1896, and .353 in 1897. He also became adept at being hit by pitches, living by the credo "Hit or get hit." In 1896 Hughey was struck by pitches 49 times, a major league record that stood until Montreal's Ron Hunt was hit 50 times in 1971. Jennings claimed to have been hurt on only one of the 49 occasions. He also stole as many as 73 bases in a single season (1896), compiling a career total of 373.

Jennings proved to be a natural leader, and in 1894, his first full season with the

Orioles, he was appointed captain of the team. This was a high honor for a 24-year-old. In the late 1890s, Hughey was almost returned to Louisville in a straight deal for Honus Wagner, but the trade fell through when Jennings personally wired the Louisville owner: "Don't consent to deal. Am in no condition. Will play no more this season. Bad arm." Hughey did indeed have a bad arm, which forced him to switch from shortstop to first base.

In the summer of 1899, Jennings, Keeler, Kelley, and Hanlon moved from the Baltimore Orioles to the Brooklyn Superbas (the teams were under the same ownership). As a result of that move, the Superbas won the National League pennant in both 1899 and 1900. Playing at first base, Jennings hit .270 in 1900.

At this time Jennings became an officer in the Players' Protective Association. The Association was shortlived, but it led to the birth of the American League.

During winters Jennings studied law at St. Bonaventure University and later at Cornell. At Cornell, he also coached the baseball team. One night, he dove into the unlit Cornell swimming pool. The pool, however, had been drained, and Jennings fractured his skull. Eventually, he received a law degree from Cornell, was admitted to the Pennsylvania bar, and built up a successful practice in Scranton.

In 1901 and 1902, Jennings was first baseman and captain of the Philadelphia Phillies; the team finished second and seventh, respectively. He returned briefly to Brooklyn in 1903, played a mere six games, and was appointed manager of the Baltimore Orioles (members of the Eastern League at the time). Jennings acquired valuable managing experience during his four seasons there. He also played shortstop and second base, hitting as high as .328 in 1903.

Several teams became interested in Jennings as a major league managerial candidate, and the Detroit Tigers acquired him from Baltimore for $1500 in 1907 and handed him the job. Jennings brought home pennants in each of his first three seasons with the Tigers, although failing each time to capture the World Series. Not until Ralph Houk of the 1961–1963 Yankees performed the feat would another manager win pennants in his first three seasons in the American League.

The greatest asset to Jennings, of course, was the presence of Ty Cobb on his club. Jennings made no bones about his dislike for the temperamental superstar, but he realized early that, if left alone, Cobb would greatly benefit the club. Hughey almost traded Cobb that first year,

(Above) A tiger made of flowers is presented to Jennings in 1907, his first year as Detroit manager and the first of three consecutive years he led the team to a pennant. The sequence at left shows the war dance Jennings performed each day, punctuated with whoops of "Ee-yah." Intended to encourage his player, the shouting unnerved players and fans alike.

but when no offers of value came, he retained him.

As Tiger manager, Jennings would direct the club each day from the third-base coaching box. He became famous for a war-like cry of "Ee-yah," which he would shout at his team in encouragement. Where the cry originated, no one was certain. Some believed it to evolve from "That's the way" to "Way-uh" to "Ee-yah." Jennings offered the theory that he had acquired it from a Hawaiian-born pitcher, John Williams, as an island expression for "watch out." Hughey also had the habit of plucking the grass from the third-base area and chewing it during the game.

Jennings' yell replaced the obnoxious whistle that he had used during his first season as manager. American League president Ban Johnson had ordered Jennings to put the whistle away or face a 10-day suspension. Lawyer Jennings challenged Johnson's decree, won his point, but retired the whistle.

Jennings remained the Detroit manager through 1920 when the club finished seventh. Although he was still highly regarded as a field leader, the Tigers had not won a pennant in 11 seasons. The club owners then decided to make Ty Cobb player-manager. Cleveland had just won the 1920 pennant by using Tris Speaker in a similar manner.

John McGraw snapped up Jennings immediately, making him his third base coach and "assistant manager." It was a newly created post, and Jennings handled it well, helping the Giants to pennants in his first four seasons as coach.

In 1925, when McGraw fell ill, Jennings managed the team for the majority of the season. The Giants finished second, eight and one-half games behind Pittsburgh.

The responsibility of handling a team that had just captured four consecutive pennants eventually took its toll on Jennings. He suffered a nervous breakdown after the 1925 season and was sent to a sanitarium in Asheville, North Carolina. Hughey never returned to baseball.

Jennings, who had been involved in a serious automobile accident in 1911 which resulted in another fracture of his skull, suffered an accident in 1927 that caused him to walk with a cane thereafter. In January 1928, he suffered an attack of spinal meningitis. He died on February 1, at Scranton, Pennsylvania, leaving a wife and daughter.

Hughey Jennings was elected to the Hall of Fame in 1945.

HUGH AMBROSE JENNINGS

Louisville (A.A.) 1891
Louisville (N.L.) 1892–1893
Baltimore (N.L.) 1893–1899
Brooklyn 1899–1900, 1903
Philadelphia (N.L.) 1901–1902
Detroit 1907–1909, 1912, 1918

G	AB	R	H	2B	3B	HR	RBI	Avg.
1264	4840	989	1520	227	88	19	840	.314

Ban Johnson (1864-1931)

Founder of the American League, Ban Johnson served as its president from 1900 to 1927

Byron Bancroft Johnson was born in Norwalk, Ohio, on January 5, 1864. He was descended from a long line of ministers and educators, his father being of both professions. The Johnsons moved to Avondale, Ohio, where Ban learned to play ball during his youth.

Ban entered Oberlin College, but disliking the religious emphasis there, he transferred to Marietta College. Joining Marietta's baseball team, he developed a reputation as a good catcher, handling fast pitching without the use of a glove, chest protector, or mask. Johnson was a husky, chesty fellow who resembled future President Theodore Roosevelt both in appearance and style.

Ban graduated from Marietta in 1887 and took a job as a sportswriter for the Cincinnati *Commercial-Gazette*. While in Cincinnati, he formed a close friendship with Reds manager Charles Comiskey, and the two spent long hours talking about baseball's future. The National League had been formed in 1876, but Johnson even then believed that a third league (the American Association operated through 1891) could compete successfully for players and customers.

In 1893 a minor league known as the Western League, founded in 1879, folded. Johnson, eager to get a foothold in a minor league operation, sought to revive it.

While on a scouting mission for Cincinnati owner John T. Brush after the 1893 season, Comiskey met some former Western League participants who agreed to reorganize. Comiskey sold them on the idea of Johnson as league president. On November 20, 1893, representatives of franchises from Sioux City, Toledo, Indianapolis, Detroit, Kansas City, Milwaukee, Minneapolis, and Grand Rapids met in Detroit, elected Johnson president, and revived the league. Brush, who also operated the Indianapolis club as a Cincinnati farm team, attended the meeting only briefly, but he was considered an opponent of Johnson's because of Ban's criticism of the owner in a newspaper article. Johnson took a cautious one-year leave of absence from the *Commercial-Gazette,* but the revived Western League flourished and Johnson never returned to journalism.

At the end of the 1894 season, Brush fired Comiskey as the Cincinnati manager. Comiskey took over the Western League's Sioux City franchise and transferred it to St. Paul. Johnson persuaded Connie Mack to purchase the Milwaukee franchise; Mack later moved it to Philadelphia. Other

franchise shifts in the Western League included Detroit to Columbus, then Toledo to Detroit, Grand Rapids to St. Joseph (and back again), and Columbus to Buffalo.

In 1899 the National League reduced its membership from 12 clubs to 8 by cutting Washington, Cleveland, Baltimore, and Louisville. Johnson immediately added Cleveland to his league, replacing Grand Rapids. He also had Comiskey move his St. Paul franchise to Chicago. On October 11, 1899, at a league meeting in Chicago, the name of the Western League was changed to American League.

The American League operated in 1900 as a minor league, and Johnson ran it in an efficient and dignified manner. No liquor was sold in its parks, no profanity was allowed on the field, and Johnson's umpires had total authority. Women were encouraged to attend the games in the newly painted or remodeled parks. Johnson even attempted to end organized rooting, although he never quite accomplished this feat.

After the 1900 season, Johnson announced that he was raising his collection of teams to major league status, with or without the consent of the National League. He enticed players to his league by waiving the $2400 salary limit that prevailed in the National League. Johnson had eight good franchises—Chicago, Boston, Detroit, Philadelphia, Baltimore, Washington, Cleveland, and Milwaukee. His managers included Clark Griffith, Jimmy Collins, George Stallings, Connie Mack, John McGraw, and Hugh Duffy.

The National League refused to recognize the American League as an equal, despite the fact that 111 of the 182 players in the new league in 1901 were former National League players.

Johnson was elected league president for a 10-year term, establishing his offices in the Fisher Building in Chicago. He was reelected in 1911 for 20 additional years, which was increased by five in 1925, giving Ban a term that would have expired in 1935.

The league continued to attract such National League stars as Napoleon Lajoie, Cy Young, Ed Delahanty, Wilbert Robinson, and Willie Keeler. McGraw, hampered by the obligation to respect umpires, found the league unsuitable to his style of play, and he returned to manage the Giants in the National League. After the 1902 season, the Baltimore franchise was shifted to New York, where the team became the Highlanders and later the Yankees.

Chicago won the league's first pennant, and Philadelphia captured the flag in 1902. By 1903, with players jumping back and forth between leagues, the National League agreed to recognize the American

League, and Johnson helped to draft the National Agreement of Professional Baseball, which brought the raiding to an end.

The ruling body of baseball became the National Commission, consisting of Johnson, the National League president, and Garry Herrmann, president of the Reds. Johnson was the dominant personality, and he was unquestionably the most influential executive in baseball.

The first World Series was held in 1903. Boston's upset of Pittsburgh gave the American League parity at once with the National League.

Not as far as John McGraw was concerned, however. When the Giants captured the 1904 National League pennant, McGraw refused to allow his team to meet the American League champions, the Red Sox, in a Series. But in 1905 McGraw relented and the two-league matchup has been a fixture ever since.

The American League not only grew, but it prospered and soon surpassed the National League in the fame of its players. Thanks to a decision by the National Commission, George Sisler was awarded to the St. Louis Browns in 1915 rather than to the Pittsburgh Pirates, who had signed him as a minor. Babe Ruth and Ty Cobb, perhaps the game's greatest players, were both American Leaguers. During Johnson's

reign, the American League won 14 of 24 World Series.

One of the first breaks in Johnson's power occurred when the 1919 "Black Sox" scandal rocked baseball and threatened its hold on the American public. Eight members of the Chicago White Sox were accused of conspiring to throw the Series. Johnson pressed ahead with a full investigation, ending his friendship with White Sox owner Comiskey, who refused to believe that his players were guilty.

Other club owners also objected to Johnson's investigation. To restore baseball's reputation for integrity, the owners decided to replace the three-man National Commission with an independent baseball commissioner. For this position they selected Judge Kenesaw Mountain Landis, who had no previous connection with the game. This was clearly a circumvention of Johnson's powers, and Johnson forever after disputed the authority of Landis.

With Landis ruling the game, Johnson was crushed. His health declined and his spirits left him. The American League was entering its finest era, but Johnson knew he no longer had control of its operation.

In 1927 another seamy affair rocked the game. Dutch Leonard, a retired pitcher, produced a letter from Ty Cobb to Joe Wood that apparently involved both Cobb and Tris Speaker in the fixing of a late-season game in 1919. Johnson came down hard on the two great stars, seeking to terminate their careers. When Leonard refused to confront the accused face to face, the case no longer seemed plausible. Judge Landis reinstated the two players and let the matter drop.

Johnson was enraged, but the club owners, with the exception of Phil Ball of St. Louis, supported Landis. The owners decided to strip Johnson of his powers while permitting him to retain his title. But Johnson hastily scribbled his resignation on a piece of paper and flung it at the Yankees' Jacob Ruppert in July 1927. The resignation took effect at the close of the 1927 season.

Johnson was entitled to $320,000 in unpaid salary for the remaining years on his contract, but he refused the money for work he would not be able to do. He then retired with his wife to Spencer, Indiana. Johnson died of diabetes on March 28, 1931, at St. John's Hospital in St. Louis, Missouri.

Ban Johnson was elected to the Hall of Fame in 1937.

An attempt to form a third major league ends in an agreement in Cincinnati in early 1916, disbanding the young Federal League. Ban Johnson, American League president, sits far right. Other principals in the decision were, standing left to right, Weeghman, Sinclair, Bruce, and Gwinner, and, seated, Gilmore, Tener, and National Commission Chairman Herrmann.

Judy Johnson (b.1899)

In the days before black players were permitted to participate in organized baseball, it was fashionable to brand the better players with nicknames reflecting their relative abilities. The nicknames managed to make at least a few of the black players recognizable to the general sporting world. Josh Gibson, for example, was called the black Babe Ruth. Buck Leonard, a first baseman, was the black Lou Gehrig. And the best third baseman of the Negro Leagues happened to play most of his games in the same town (Pittsburgh) as Pie Traynor. Thus Judy Johnson became known as the black Pie Traynor.

William Julius Johnson was born in Snow Hill, Maryland, on October 26, 1899, the second of three children. Known as Billy as a boy, he found himself a teammate of a veteran player named Judy Gans in the early 1920s. Since Johnson resembled Gans, and as his middle name was Julius, teammates began calling the youngster Judy as well. The name stuck.

Judy's father, originally a seaman, moved the family to Wilmington, Delaware, in 1906 and took a job with a trolley company. His ambition for Billy was to have the boy become a prize fighter, and to prepare him for this career, he bought two sets of boxing gloves—one for Billy, and one for his sister, Mary Emma. Mary Emma, at 12, was four years older than Billy, and quite a tomboy. In addition, their father established rules that prohibited Billy from striking his sister in either the face, chest, or stomach. The results were usually destructive to Billy, and he soon grew tired of boxing.

Billy played football and baseball for integrated town teams in Wilmington. Since Howard High School offered no sports program, those street games were the extent of his experience. After one year of high school, Judy quit and took a job as a stevedore at Deep Water Point, New Jersey. With the end of World War I, Judy returned to Wilmington. Shortly thereafter, he began to play weekend baseball for the Chester Giants in Pennsylvania. The games earned him $5 plus transportation, and he soon was able to increase his playing time by adding Thursday games to his schedule.

By 1918, after impressing the rival Bacharach Giants during games in Atlantic City, Billy signed a contract with the club to begin his professional career. But still he earned just $5 per game.

In 1919 and 1920, Judy played for the Madison Stars of Philadelphia. Most of the semipro teams he encountered by this time were strictly black, as he was now advanced enough in professional baseball

to be bound by the prohibition of participation with any white leagues.

In 1921 the Madison Stars sold Johnson to Hilldale, a Philadelphia-based club, for $100. He earned $150 a month as their third baseman.

Judy had a strong arm and good range at third. He managed to buy a new glove each season, even in an era when equipment was hard to come by. He also played a good part of his career with two pairs of baseball shoes—one for good fields and one for bad fields, of which there were many.

Judy stood 5'11" and weighed 150 pounds during his playing days. Right-handed all the way, Johnson was not much of a power hitter, seldom hitting more than two or three home runs each year. But he was a good line-drive hitter with an excellent batting eye, and his averages were usually in the mid-.300s. Statistics were a matter to which the Negro Leagues paid little attention, and for the most part no accurate records exist. But from time to time, newspapers would report a batting average or two just to keep the league in line with the white leagues.

Late in 1923, Judy married Anita Irons, an attractive girl who used to attend the Hilldale games and root for him. The two were still married when Johnson was elected to the Hall of Fame 51 years later.

By 1924, Johnson had established a reputation as the Negro Leagues' best third baseman, and he was a key member of the Hilldale club which participated in the first Negro World Series. Judy led all hitters in that series with a .341 batting average. The following season, although suffering a broken arm while playing shortstop, Judy managed to hit what is believed to be his career high of .392.

Baseball was Judy's life virtually 12 months a year. In the early 1920s, he spent winters playing for hotel teams in Florida, wearing the name of the establishment on his uniform shirt as a means of advertising the place, or in the Cuban Winter League, where he generally played second base and shortstop, seldom playing his regular third-base position.

And, of course, there were always the barn-storming tours against white all-star teams. In these games the black stars achieved most of their national fame. Johnson held his own against such opponents as Rogers Hornsby, Jimmie Foxx, Muddy Ruel, Heinie Manush, and even Babe Ruth.

Johnson even maintained a friendship with Pie Traynor, to whom he was often compared. Connie Mack paid Johnson tribute in the late 1920s when he said, "If Judy were only white, he could name his own price."

Johnson remained with Hilldale in 1929,

(Top left) Johnson during his days in the Philadelphia-based Hillsdale club, which participated in the first Negro World Series. Johnson was the Series' leading hitter, with a .341 batting average. (Top right) He mans third base. (Below) The Murderers' Row of the Pittsburgh Crawfords, the most famous Negro League team ever: from left to right, Oscar Charleston, Josh Gibson, Ted Paige, and Judy Johnson.

and in 1930 he joined the Homestead Grays as a player-manager. The team, based in Pittsburgh, paid him $500 per month, his top baseball salary. In 1930 Johnson served as Josh Gibson's first manager, for the powerful young catcher began his career that season. Like most veterans of the Negro Leagues, Johnson, without reservation, cited Gibson as the finest hitter he ever saw.

Although not an especially fast base runner, Judy had good running sense, and in general had good baseball instincts in all aspects of the game. He was therefore looked to for advice and guidance by many young players.

After one year with Homestead, Johnson returned to the Darby Daisies (formerly Hilldale) in 1931 as player-manager. And then in 1932, he went to the Pittsburgh Crawfords, the most famous team in the Negro National League, where he joined future Hall of Famers Gibson, Satchel Paige, and Cool Papa Bell. Johnson was named captain of the club, and the Crawfords won the pennant in 1935 and the second-half race in 1936.

These were difficult days for the Negro Leagues. Traveling conditions were poor, with as many as nine men being stuffed into a single automobile for rides of hundreds of miles. Many restaurants, particularly in the South, would refuse to serve the players and not offer them rest room facilities. Lodging was always uncertain. But these were the Depression years in the United States, and the players were happy to be holding jobs.

Johnson remained with the Crawfords through 1937. Oscar Charleston was the manager of this strong club, and sportswriters frequently compared the lineup to the "Murderers' Row" of the Yankees. The four men who formed the heart of the potent Pittsburg lineup were Rap Dixon, Josh Gibson, Jud Wilson, and Johnson, the frailest of them all but perhaps the most durable. With the exception of a broken arm, Judy seldom was injured and seldom missed a game.

Upon his retirement as an active player, Judy returned to Wilmington and took a job as a supervisor on the shipping platform of Continental Can Company. In 1940 he and his younger brother, John, opened a general store in Wilmington. When the store closed several years later, Judy returned to Continental Can and remained there until his return to baseball in 1954.

By that time, Jackie Robinson had broken the color line, and black players were emerging as a force in the game. Johnson had always regretted his inability to play in the white leagues, but like every other black player he had merely accepted it as part of the system.

The Philadelphia Athletics hired Judy as a coach and scout in February 1954, assigning him to help the two young black players on their roster, Bob Trice and Vic Power. Judy's job was to find the pair housing in spring training and guide their entry into the major leagues. Johnson at one point watched young Hank Aaron in a semipro game and urged the Athletics to invest the $3500 bonus required to sign Hank. But the club passed on the idea.

After two years with the Athletics, Johnson became a scout for the Milwaukee Braves, where he was credited with the discovery and signing of Billy Bruton. Judy's daughter, Loretta, also discovered Bruton, and the two were married shortly thereafter.

When John Quinn, general manager of the Braves, transferred to the Philadelphia Phillies in 1959, Johnson accompanied him as a scout and was helpful in the signing of Richie Allen in 1960. Judy retired from the Phillies in 1973, spending most of his time in the vegetable garden at his Marshalltown, Delaware, home.

Judy was a member of the Committee on Negro Baseball Leagues, whose responsibility it was to select Negro League stars for inclusion in the Hall of Fame. Withdrawing from the voting in 1975, Judy Johnson became the sixth player selected by the committee.

WILLIAM JULIUS JOHNSON

Independent team and Negro Leagues 1921–1937

No records available.

Judy Johnson and his wife, Anita, outside a ball park named in his honor on November 9, 1975, the year he was elected to the Hall of Fame.

Walter Johnson (1887-1946)

The man considered to have been the hardest-throwing pitcher in the history of baseball is Walter Johnson, the 21-year veteran of the Washington Senators who posted brilliant records with a perennially poor team.

Walter Perry Johnson was born on November 6, 1887, in Humboldt, Kansas. He was the son of Swedish farmers who had moved to Kansas by wagon train from Pennsylvania. In 1901 the family moved to Olinda, California, hoping to strike it rich in the oil fields. No oil came the Johnsons' way, but they earned a living by providing mule teams for the oilmen.

By the age of 14, Walter had a strong, athletic build, and he was a catcher on the local Oil Field Juniors baseball team. With his strong arm, Walter would have been the best pitcher on the team, but there was no one on the club capable of catching him.

While playing semipro ball in the Northwest in 1907, Johnson, then 19, attracted the attention of a traveling liquor salesman. The salesman sent telegrams and letters to Washington manager Joe Cantillon, whose team had lost 95 games the previous year. Cantillon then sent his injured catcher, Cliff Blankenship, to Idaho, where Johnson was pitching while working for the Idaho Telephone Company, digging post holes. Blankenship saw Johnson fire his fastball for 12 innings in a 1–0 loss, liked what he saw, and received authorization to offer the 6'1" righthander a $100 bonus and a contract for $350 per month.

It was a long trip from Idaho to Washington, D.C., and Walter's father made sure that travel expenses were included before Walter signed the contract. With no minor league experience, Walter was on his way.

Johnson joined the Washington Senators in August 1907. It was still a terrible team headed for a last-place finish with a 49–102 record. Johnson made his major league debut against the pennant-bound Detroit Tigers, whose lineup included Ty Cobb and Sam Crawford. Walter was locked in a 1–1 duel until the eighth inning when Cobb beat him with some daring baserunning. But Johnson had made a fine impression on the Tigers, and soon earned the nickname "The Big Train." The name was bestowed by sportswriter Grantland Rice, and it referred to the speed of Johnson's fastball. Rice compared the blazer to the fastest mode of transportation at the time, and the nickname stuck.

Another name that applied to Johnson among his teammates was "Barney," derived from race car driver Barney Oldfield. It had nothing to do with the speed of Johnson's pitches, but rather with the speed at which Walter drove an automobile. It was the only vice of an ordinarily

shy, humble man who did not smoke, drink, or swear.

Johnson compiled a 5–9 record in 14 appearances in his rookie season of 1907, striking out 70 men and walking only 16 in 111 innings. Speed and control were to remain Johnson's trademarks throughout his career; he never developed more than just a fair curveball, relying strictly on the fastball even as he neared 40.

Although the Washington Senators were not a good team in 1907, Johnson was in the major leagues and eager to make a long career. In 1908 he was the No. 2 starting pitcher on the team, behind 29-year-old Long Tom Hughes. Hughes won 18 games in 1908, and Johnson added 14 victories; the pair accounted for 32 of the 67 victories posted by Washington.

Johnson pitched six shutouts that season, including a record-setting three consecutive blanks against New York on September 4, 5, and 7. (Sunday ball being prohibited by law in New York, there was no game on September 6.) He pitched a six-hitter on Friday, winning 3–0; a four-hitter on Saturday, winning, 6–0; and a two-hitter in the first game of a Monday double header, winning, 4–0. The great showing, coming near the end of the season, made Johnson the No. 1 man in Washington's plans for the following year, but it did little to increase his salary of $2700 per year.

From opening day, when a heavy cold prevented him from pitching, 1909 was a disappointing year for Johnson. He won only 13 games and lost 25. The Senators managed only 42 victories that year and slipped to last place again.

But the 1910 season was different, right from opening day. The team had a new manager, Jimmy McAleer. Johnson received the opening-day assignment, and President William Howard Taft threw out the first ball. The ceremony marked the first time the Chief Executive performed this task, and Johnson became associated with it by being the opening day pitcher for Washington 14 times (with nine victories and seven shutouts). Johnson collected the autographed "first" baseballs of Presidents Taft, Wilson, Harding, Coolidge, and Hoover. The entire collection was given to the Baseball Museum by his son after Walter died.

The 1910 season, although producing another seventh-place finish for Washington, was a big one for Johnson, who won 25 games, lost only 17, pitched eight shutouts, and struck out 313 batters. It was the first of 12 strikeout titles for Walter, who holds the career record of 3508 strikeouts.

Twice Johnson topped the 300-whiff mark for one season, and on five other occasions he surpassed 200.

The 1910 season marked the first of 10 consecutive seasons in which Johnson won 20 or more games. In that decade the Senators averaged only 76 victories per year, and Johnson averaged 26. Walter also pitched a career high of 374 innings in 1910, leading the American League. (He led the League in innings pitched in four other seasons, 1913–1916.)

Johnson duplicated his 25 victories in 1911, then jumped to 32 wins in 1912, a year in which he appeared in 50 games and struck out 303 batters. But all of these great feats were just a tuneup for his finest season, 1913.

The Senators were now a respectable club, having finished second in 1912 with Clark Griffith as their new manager. Johnson could not be stopped in 1913, and the Senators came within six and one-half games of Connie Mack's pennant-winning Athletics. Johnson notched winning streaks of 14, 11, and 10 games during the season. He pitched 12 shutouts and five one-hitters. Between April 10 and May 14, Walter pitched 56 consecutive shutout innings. He led the league in innings pitched (346), strikeouts (243), winning percentage (.837), and victories (36 against only 7 losses). It was the first year in which earned-run averages were computed by the league, and Johnson set a record with 1.14, a mark unsurpassed by any major leaguer until St. Louis's Bob Gibson posted a 1.12 ERA in 1968. Johnson's 1913 season was one of the greatest ever put together by a major league pitcher, and Walter received his first Most Valuable Player award.

The following season Johnson won 28 games, notching 10 shutouts, 225 strikeouts, and a 1.72 earned-run average. He was now earning $12,000 from the Senators, and he believed his worth to be more. That was when the new Federal League came calling.

The Federal League offered Johnson a $16,000 contract plus a $10,000 bonus to jump and play for Chicago. The Chicago team, the best in the new league, was managed by Joe Tinker, the old Cub infield star. It was certainly an offer worth considering, and Clark Griffith was not ready to match it since Johnson had "slipped" to 28 victories.

Finally, Griffith agreed to match the $16,000 salary, but not the $10,000 bonus. To obtain the money, Clark virtually blackmailed the White Sox owner, Charles Comiskey, reminding him that Johnson's move to Chicago would undoubtedly take fans away from the Sox. Comiskey gave Griffith the money, Griffith gave it to Johnson, and

(Top left) Future major-league pitching sensation Walter Johnson in uniform for Waiser, Idaho. (At right) He pitches for Washington in 1915. (Below) He passes on some tips of the trade to his young sons, from left to right, Walter Jr., Eddie, and Bob.

Johnson turned it over to his brother to bail him out of a business debt. Walter was set in Washington.

The Big Train continued to pile up victories, heading for a career total of 416 that was bettered only by Cy Young. Walter won 20 or more games every year through 1919. In 1920 a sore arm reduced him to 21 appearances and an 8–10 record. Despite his poor overall showing, Walter pitched the only no-hitter of his career in 1920, beating Boston, 1–0, on July 1. An error by second baseman Bucky Harris prevented it from being a perfect game.

The 1–0 score was typical of Johnson's career. He was involved in 1–0 decisions 64 times, winning 38. Johnson recovered from the sore arm, but scored only 17, 15, and 17 victories between 1921 and 1923. Many thought the end was approaching for the 36-year-old righthander.

But Johnson's fastball was as good as ever, and finally, in 1924, Walter was on a pennant winner. With Harris making his debut as manager, and such capable teammates as Joe Judge and Goose Goslin, the Senators posted 92 victories to edge the Yankees by two games. Johnson compiled a 23–7 record and led the league in victories, strikeouts, winning percentage, shutouts, and earned run average. He also captured his second Most Valuable Player award.

Johnson won one game and lost two in the World Series as the Senators beat the Giants for their only World Championship. Walter's victory came in relief in the deciding game.

The Senators repeated their pennant-winning feat in 1925, with Johnson compiling a 20–7 record, but the club lost the World Series to Pittsburgh in seven games. Johnson won two of three decisions in that Series.

Definitely on the decline now, Johnson posted a 15–16 record in 1926. During spring training in 1927, a line drive off the bat of teammate Joe Judge broke his leg. Johnson came back to win 5 of 11 decisions that year, but it was his last hurrah. A bad case of the flu cut 35 pounds off his 200-pound frame the following spring. Griffith then sent Walter to Newark in the International League as manager. At Newark, Johnson put himself into one game and walked the only man he faced. It was his only minor league appearance.

The following year, 1929, Johnson was named manager of the Senators. In his four years at the helm, Washington finished fifth, second, third, and third again. Following the 1932 season, he was replaced by Joe Cronin. In June 1933,

Johnson was appointed manager of the Cleveland Indians; the club finished fourth in 1933, third in 1934, and was in fifth place when Walter was fired in August, 1935. His reputation for patience, so well established when he was the only player of accomplishment on hapless Washington clubs, was severely tested as a manager. Walter was not considered a successful one.

Johnson married in 1913, but his wife died in 1930 at the age of 36, leaving him with five children. That might have been part of his difficulty in his years as manager.

In 1936 Johnson joined Ty Cobb, Honus Wagner, Babe Ruth, and Christy Mathewson in the first group of players elected to baseball's Hall of Fame.

Walter owned a farm in Maryland, near a high school in Bethesda named in his honor. There he spent most of his time after his retirement. He dabbled in politics but lost a 1940 congressional election. He served for one season as a radio announcer for the Senators. Mostly, he raised cattle and hunted foxes.

A brain tumor paralyzed Johnson in April, 1946, and he died in Washington on December 10 that year, at the age of 59.

WALTER PERRY JOHNSON

Washington 1907–1927

G	IP	W	L	Pct.	H	R	ER	SO	W	ERA
802	5924	416	279	.599	4920	1902	inc.	3508	1353	inc.

(Above) Walter Johnson pitching for the Senators in the 1924 World Series against the Giants. It was Johnson's only Series and the Senators' only championship. (At left) He announces a Senator game on radio during a one-year broadcasting fling.

Tim Keefe (1857-1933)

Tim Keefe was one of six nineteenth century pitchers to win more than 300 games. He accomplished the feat in only 14 major league seasons. In six consecutive campaigns, Tim scored 32 or more victories.

Timothy John Keefe was born on New Year's Day, 1857, in Cambridge, Massachusetts. His father, Patrick, a native of Ireland, was a builder of factories. Pat Keefe was working on the construction of a factory in the South when the Civil War broke out. The Confederates expected him to join their cause, but Pat would not put on a grey uniform to fight against his Union brothers, Frank and John Keefe, and he was imprisoned for three years. During his imprisonment, Pat was required to work on the manufacture of bullets. Both of his brothers were killed in the war.

Tim was nine years old when his father returned home. Baseball was only a game as far as Pat Keefe was concerned, and he wanted Tim to learn mathematics and go to college.

But at the age of 18, Tim took a job as an "amateur" player for the Franklin Juniors of Cambridge. Most amateur teams were composed of men employed in some nominal job; they were actually hired by a company to play for their organization's team.

In rapid succession, Tim donned the uniforms of the Cambridge Tremonts, the Boston Mutuals, the Lewiston Androscoggings, Our Boys of Boston, New Bedford, Westboro, and Clinton. While still an amateur, he was recognized as the best hurler in New England. Pitching was done underhand in those days, with the pitcher standing 45 feet from the batter.

In 1879 Tim broke into professional baseball with the Utica team of the National Association, a minor league. Before the season was completed, he was pitching for New Bedford. In 1880 he hurled for Albany of the National Association, and was so accomplished that the nearby Troy team of the National League purchased his contract. Although Troy was a much smaller city than Albany, the Troy club was well financed.

At Troy, Keefe first teamed with Smiling Mickey Welch. Between the pair all the club's pitching was handled. Troy finished fourth in 1880, with Welch winning 34 games, while Keefe, whose debut on August 6 was a 4–2 win over Cincinnati, posted a 6–6 record.

In 1881 Welch and Keefe virtually matched each other as Troy finished fifth. Tim compiled a 19–27 record that year, but he completed each of his 46 starts for 413 innings of work.

Tim still posted a losing record in 1882 when Troy finished seventh. He notched a 17–26 mark while leading the club in innings pitched.

After the 1882 season, the Troy club was dropped by the National League. John B. Day, taking over the new league franchise in New York, obtained most of the Troy players, including Mickey Welch, for the Giants. Tim, however, went to the New York Metropolitans, managed by Day's partner, Jim Mutrie.

Keefe's first year in New York was a successful one. He compiled a 41–27 record and led the league with 360 strikeouts, 68 appearances, and 619 innings pitched— incredible totals by today's standards. On July 4, he won both ends of a double header, allowing only three hits in the two games.

In 1884 overhand pitching was legalized, but Tim continued to throw underhand for fear that the unnatural motion of overhand pitching would lead to arm injuries. He had good speed and a fine curveball, but his big pitch was a changeup or, as it was called in those days, a slowball. Tim was one of the first to find success with this pitch, for which he is considered a pioneer of off-speed deliveries.

The spotlight often fell on Tim in 1884, as the Mets won the American Association pennant. Between June 23 and August 10, Tim won 19 consecutive games. Nine of the victories came on the road, as he beat every club in the league.

One of the nineteen successive victories occurred on July 16 in a game that he left after two innings, leading 9–0. Under today's rules, Keefe would not have received the victory. That is one of the reasons why Rube Marquard's 19 consecutive victories in 1912 is a more widely recognized record.

Tim had the distinction on October 23 that year of pitching in the first "World Series" game ever played. The Mets faced Providence in a postseason playoff, with Providence representing the National League. In the historic game, played before 2500 fans, Old Hoss Radbourn beat Keefe and the Mets, 6–0. Tim also lost the second game, and Providence captured the series in three games.

After the 1884 season, Day and Mutrie transferred the two best players on the Mets—Keefe and Dude Esterbrook—to the New York Giants, provoking a storm of protest. Admission to Giants games was 50 cents, and to Met games only a quarter. By moving these two popular players to the higher-priced club, Day and Mutrie were simply making a good business deal.

Keefe was not with the Giants for very long when John Montgomery Ward, a teammate, formed the Brotherhood of Professional Base Ball Players. Ward was elected president and Keefe secretary. While most players spent their evening hours on the town, Tim remained in his hotel room to teach himself shorthand. His first opportunity to put it to practice was with the Brotherhood, and he took an active part in recruiting members.

Tim was gentlemanly, serious, and well-regarded. He stood 5'10½", weighed 185 pounds, and threw righthanded. Although he possessed a handsome, bushy mustache that the fans seemed to like, Tim always tried to avoid public attentions.

With the Giants, Keefe again shared the pitching assignments with Mickey Welch. In his first season with the club, he posted a 32–13 record. Seven of his victories were shutouts, and he struck out 228 batters. The Giants finished only two games behind Cap Anson's champion Chicago Colts.

Tim won 42 games in 1886, leading the league in appearances (64), innings pitched (535), and complete games (62). Keefe and Welch worked 1034 innings that season.

Thirty-five more victories came Tim's way in 1887, but the Giants finished only fourth and seemed to be slipping. However, they rebounded in 1888 to win the National League pennant. Tim's 35–11 record proved to be the top victory total and best winning percentage in the league, and he also led the circuit in strikeouts (335) and shutouts (8). Had earned-run averages been computed then, Tim would have captured the crown with his 1.74 mark.

The 1888 campaign marked the eighth consecutive year of 30 or more victories for "Sir Timothy," and he starred in the postseason series against St. Louis, pitching four complete-game victories in which he allowed 5 earned runs and 18 hits in 35 innings. Three of the four wins were against the Browns' star, "Silver" King. The Giants beat St. Louis in six games.

The Giants were a dapper-looking team in those days. Their tight-fitting black uniforms were designed by Tim himself. He negotiated the sale of the garments and made some money on the deal.

In 1889 the Giants captured the pennant again. Tim was 28–13 in the regular season but 0–1 in the World Series, won by New York, six games to three, over Brooklyn.

After the 1889 season, the Brotherhood revolted. Tim, a leader of the cause, jumped to Buck Ewing's New York team in the new Player's League. Tim ranked only fourth on the new pitching staff, however, with a 17–11 record, as the club finished third. When the league folded after one year, Keefe returned to the Giants for the 1891 season. But in August he drew his unconditional release after seeing limited action and compiling a 2–5 record.

Signed by the Philadelphia Phillies, Tim posted a 3–6 mark for the club during the remainder of the 1891 season. He had a good year for the Phillies in 1892, compiling a 19–16 record in 312 innings of work at the age of 35. But the 1893 season was his last. Tim appeared in 22 games and had a 10–7 record.

Tim remained in the game for two additional seasons as a National League umpire, but in 1896 he left baseball and opened a real estate business in Cambridge. A heart attack felled him on April 23, 1933, at the age of 76.

In 1964 Tim Keefe was named to the Hall of Fame.

TIMOTHY JOHN KEEFE

Troy (N.L.) 1880–1882
New York (A.A.) 1883–1884
New York (N.L.) 1885–1889, 1891
New York (P.L.) 1890
Philadelphia (N.L.) 1891–1893

G	IP	W	L	Pct.	H	R	ER	SO	BB	ERA
599	5050	344	225	.605	4452	inc.	inc.	2542	1225	inc.

The Keefe pitching style back in the days of underhand pitching. Keefe's pitching advice was: learn control first and worry about speed and curves later.

Willie Keeler (1872-1923)

In an era of rough and tumble baseball players, a small, gentlemanly Irishman named Willie Keeler made his mark as one of the finest hitters in the game.

William Henry Keeler was born on March 13, 1872, in Brooklyn, New York, before it became a borough of New York City. His father was the oldest horse-car trolley driver on the DeKalb Avenue Line.

Willie was a small child, and at full maturity he stood only 5'4½" and weighed 140 pounds. But Willie developed great athletic ability playing on the sandlots in Flatbush, Flushing, Arlington, and Plainfield, New Jersey.

Keeler was a member of a semipro team known as the Acmes when he received his chance to break into professional ball. In upstate New York, the Eastern League had a team in Binghamton. When the club's third baseman, John Rainey, broke a leg, a replacement was urgently needed.

The Binghamton manager, Frank Leonard, asked a well-traveled player, Gus Moran, if he had any suggestions. Moran, having seen Keeler play for the Acmes, recommended him. Two scouts were sent to watch Willie play a game against the Cuban Giants. They liked what they saw and signed him.

Willie had been a pitcher and an infielder during his semipro days. He was only a fair pitcher, working from the 50-foot distance. Although it was unusual to have an infielder other than a first baseman who threw lefthanded, Willie played short in his first game for Binghamton, and pitched his second. He gave up 18 hits in a losing cause and never took the mound again.

Keeler eventually was installed at third base and began to shine there. He played 93 games for Binghamton, enough to qualify for the Eastern League's batting title, which he won with a .373 average. He collected 153 hits, but his 48 errors indicated that perhaps the infield was not his station.

Late in the 1892 season, Keeler was purchased by the New York Giants. He played in 13 games for New York and batted .306. Again he played third base, where he committed seven errors.

After playing seven games for New York, Keeler was sold to Brooklyn in July 1893. The Giant manager, John Montgomery Ward, later regretted the sale, confessing that he failed to recognize what a fine player "Wee Willie" would turn out to be. After playing some 20 games for Brooklyn, Keeler was farmed to Binghamton in late August.

In January 1894, Brooklyn traded Willie and Dan Brouthers to the Baltimore Orioles for third baseman Billy Shindle and outfielder George Treadway. Shindle, in a

Willie Keeler was asked the secret of his batting success. "Hit 'em where they ain't," he replied, coining one of baseball's immortal lines. (Opposite page, top) He shows the high grip on the bat with which he could bunt or find a hole in the infield. (Below) The man known as "Bushel Basket" pulls down a high ball.

13-year career, batted .269, while Treadway was a .284 hitter for four seasons. Both Keeler and Brouthers wound up in the Hall of Fame.

Willie became an instant hit in Baltimore. Joining Ned Hanlon's fine club, he teamed with Hughey Jennings, John McGraw, Joe Kelley, Wilbert Robinson, and Brouthers to establish one of the finest teams in baseball history. All six were later elected to the Hall of Fame, and for four consecutive seasons the Orioles participated in the Temple Cup "World Series." They lost to New York in the 1894 competition and to Cleveland in 1895, but then the Orioles beat Cleveland in four consecutive games in 1896 and stopped Boston in five games in 1897. Throughout, Keeler was an important part of the attack.

Keeler used one of the lightest bats ever employed in baseball. It measured only 30 inches in length and weighed a mere 29 ounces. He handled it with great dexterity and became one of the outstanding bunters in the game. Before the rule was instituted that a batter was declared out if he bunted foul after two strikes, Willie would foul off dozens of pitches with bunts until he got just what he wanted.

Long flies were not part of Keeler's offensive game. In fact, he hit only 32 home runs in his career.

Keeler mastered the "Baltimore chop," pounding high bouncers over infielders' heads as they charged potential bunts. He and McGraw, alternating between the first and second spots in the batting order, were the first to perfect the hit-and-run play. Willie always seemed able to aim the ball at vacated holes in the infield. And should the hit-and-run fail, it was a good bet that Keeler would steal second. He swiped 519 bases in his career, with a high of 73 in 1896.

Willie's bat control extended to a remarkable strikeout showing. Although official statistics were not compiled on strikeouts, some sources claim that he went through the entire 1898 season (564 at bats) without a strikeout.

Hanlon shifted Keeler to right field, where Wee Willie displayed a surprisingly good throwing arm and became noted for brilliant catches. Older writers recall seeing him battle the barbed wire atop outfield fences to catch long fly balls.

While his teammates were colorful, exciting, and reckless, Willie was shy, quiet, and polite. His small size—he appeared no bigger than the bat boy—made him a fan favorite. Everyone loved the underdog.

A sportswriter, reportedly Abe Yager of the Brooklyn *Eagle,* once asked Willie his hitting secret. "Keep your eye clear and hit

'em where they ain't,'' he replied, and the expression "hit 'em where they ain't" took its place among baseball's famous quotes.

In 1894 Willie batted .368 with 218 hits. For eight consecutive seasons, he collected more than 200 hits a year; no player has ever matched that record. Willie had 221 hits in 1895 and batted .395. In 1896 he collected 214 hits and recorded a .392 average.

But 1897 was Keeler's finest year. He hit safely in the first 44 games of the Orioles' schedule, from April 22 to June 18. It was the major's longest consecutive-games hitting streak until Joe DiMaggio broke the mark with his 56-game streak in 1941. By the end of the year, Willie had collected 243 hits, a record that stood until 1920 (broken by George Sisler), and had batted .432, the second highest average in baseball history (Hugh Duffy hit .438 in 1894). Keeler not only won the batting title, but he repeated a year later with a .379 average on 214 hits, which included 202 singles, an all-time major league record.

At the end of the 1898 season, the Baltimore team was broken up. Ned Hanlon was dispatched to Brooklyn to manage the Superbas, and with him went Keeler, Jennings, and Kelley. The transfers made the 1899 Brooklyn team the best club in the National League and Willie celebrated his return home with a .377 average, fourth in the league.

Brooklyn repeated as champions in 1900, with Willie hitting .366 and leading the league with 208 hits. When the American League was formed in 1901 and began raiding star players, Keeler remained loyal to the Nationals despite his paltry $2400 salary, the league maximum. It was enough money for Willie, a bachelor.

Keeler once told a writer, "I'm thinking of all those suckers, the owners, paying me for playing ball. Why, I'd pay my way to get into their parks if that was the only way I had to get in a ball game!"

After two more years with Brooklyn, Willie finally yielded to a tempting financial offer. The New York Highlanders, formerly the Baltimore franchise, began play in 1903. Owners Frank Farrell and Bill Devery offered Willie $10,000 to play for the club. Since he would not have to move, Willie found the offer irresistible and became baseball's first $10,000 player.

Keeler was, after Napoleon Lajoie, the biggest name in the American League. Since the Highlanders later became the Yankees, Keeler was therefore the first in the great line of Yankee stars. Willie batted .318 in 1903, and in 1904, with the club losing the pennant on the last day of the season, he hit .343. It was Keeler's last great season. In the following two campaigns he batted .302 and .304, closing out a streak of 15 consecutive seasons over the .300 mark in the major leagues.

When the end came, it came fast. In 1907, at the age of 35, Willie suddenly dropped to a .234 batting average. In 1908 he hit .263, and in 1909, .264.

Early in the 1908 season, Highlander manager Clark Griffith became disgusted and quit over a dispute with management. Frank Farrell decided that he would like Keeler to take over the club, but Willie, getting wind of the impending offer, disappeared, and Farrell, unable to contact him, appointed Kid Elberfeld as manager. The shy Keeler simply lacked the confidence to manage a team of men physically larger than himself.

Old friend John McGraw gave Willie a job as a pinch-hitter in 1910 with the Giants, and Keeler collected 3 singles in 10 times at bat.

In 1911 Willie returned to the Eastern League, hitting .277 for Toronto before calling it a career. His lifetime .345 batting average is one of the highest recorded in baseball history. Just as Babe Ruth was known as the best home run hitter during baseball's home run era. Keeler was proclaimed the best at hitting singles during the so-called dead-ball era.

In 1914 Willie coached for the Brooklyn team in the Federal League, and in 1915 he was a scout for the Boston Braves.

Keeler made 376 Pulaski Street in Brooklyn his lifelong address, and he died at his home on New Year's Day, 1923.

Willie Keeler was elected to the Hall of Fame in 1939.

WILLIAM HENRY KEELER

New York (N.L.) 1892–1893, 1910
Brooklyn (N.L.) 1893, 1899–1902
Baltimore (N.L.) 1894–1898
New York (A.L.) 1903–1909

G	AB	R	H	2B	3B	HR	RBI	Avg.
2124	8564	1720	2955	234	155	32	810	.345

Joe Kelley (1871-1943)

Joe Kelley was one of the great stars of the legendary Baltimore Orioles of the 1890s. Unlike some of his illustrious teammates, he did not achieve great success later in his career as a manager. As a result, his name is not widely remembered today.

Joseph James Kelley was born on December 9, 1871, in Cambridge, Massachusetts, and learned to play ball in the public parks around Boston.

Kelley's first ambition was to pitch for the Boston team in the National League, and at the age of 19 he came close to realizing that dream. Joe signed his first professional contract with the Lowell club of the New England League, posting a 10–3 record in 14 mound appearances. He also batted .331 and stole 21 bases in 57 games as an outfielder.

Midway through the 1891 season, Boston purchased him. Why the transaction was made was a mystery to Kelley, although he was naturally pleased. Boston already had an outstanding pitching staff, headed by future Hall of Famers John Clarkson and Kid Nichols. Kelley appeared in 12 games as an outfielder with Boston that season and hit .244.

For the 1892 season, the handsome Irishman journeyed to Omaha to play in the Western League, where he worked on improving his outfield play. Kelley batted .330 in 49 games and was sold to Pittsburgh in June.

At Pittsburgh, Joe played in 56 games. In September he was traded to Baltimore for the Orioles' deposed manager, George Van Haltren. Joe played the final 10 games of the campaign with the Orioles and batted .246 for the season.

Kelley's first season as an Oriole regular was 1893 when he came under the direction of the brilliant manager, Ned Hanlon. Ned was beginning to assemble one of the best baseball clubs of the nineteenth century, and Kelley was destined to become a key part of it.

Hanlon had Kelley arrive at the park as early as eight o'clock in the morning to work on his bunting and baserunning. The hard work led to Kelley's development as a complete player. He became a great left fielder, famed for long running catches and hard, accurate throws to the infield. Joe perfected a fine batting eye and became adept at beating out bunts and stealing bases. In 1893 he hit .312, the first of 12 consecutive years in which he batted .300 or better.

Kelley, who stood 5'11" and weighed 190 pounds, was a man of great magnetism on the field. He had the spirit of a field leader and was a great exciter of the fans. They were particularly amused by his curious habit of keeping a pocket mirror under his cap and admiring himself between pitches while standing in left field.

Another Kelley trick and a specialty of the Oriole outfield was the practice of hiding extra baseballs in the high grass in case a ball was hit between them. One day in 1894 Kelley chased down the real ball while center fielder Steve Brodie threw in the planted one. That marked the end of this stunt for the Orioles.

In addition to Kelley in left field and Brodie in center, Willie Keeler played right field, giving the Orioles a sensational outfield. Other players on the team included Kid Gleason, John McGraw, Hughey Jennings, and Wilbert Robinson. All went on to managerial success, leaving the name Joe Kelley hidden in the background. Joe's fling as a manager did not measure up to their record of success, but as a player, he was one of the "Big Four" along with McGraw, Jennings, and Keeler.

Kelley had a fabulous 1894 season. He batted .391 with 199 hits and 45 stolen bases in 129 games. His season was highlighted by a record-setting 9-for-9 performance in a double header on September 3. In the first game Kelley collected three singles and a triple, and in the second game four doubles and a single. The feat still stands in baseball record books.

In 1894 Pittsburgh stockbroker William Chase Temple donated an expensive cup to be awarded to the winner of a postseason series between the first- and second-place teams in the National League. The Temple Cup was won that year by the second-place Giants in four successive games over the first-place Orioles.

Seeking revenge in 1895, the Orioles were again beaten for the Temple Cup, this time going down four games to one. But in 1896 Baltimore captured the Cup with a four-game sweep of Cleveland, and in 1897 they retained the Cup by downing Boston in five games. The four consecutive pennants made the Orioles the most highly regarded team of the 1890s.

During that period, Kelley played an important role in the team's success. He followed his 1894 performance with season averages of .371, .370, and .390; he also stole 90 bases in 1896.

In off-seasons, Joe was the superintendent of a draying business in Baltimore. He married Margaret Mahon, daughter of John J. Mahon, the owner of the Orioles and a leading political figure in Maryland.

The 1898 Orioles dropped to second place in the standings and were mired in serious financial trouble. Mahon sold his interest in the club, and Kelley and Ned Hanlon were transferred to the Brooklyn Superbas of the National League in February

1899. Keeler and Jennings also made the move to Brooklyn. Under Hanlon's management, Brooklyn won the 1899 pennant as team captain Kelley hit 330.

Brooklyn captured the pennant again in 1900, with Kelley hitting .318. Joe had now been a member of a first-place club in six of seven seasons.

The Superbas finished third in 1901, and the following January Joe jumped to the new American League, returning to the city of his greatest triumphs, Baltimore. But there he was part of a last-place club which the following winter would be shifted to New York to become the Highlanders (later the Yankees). Kelley remained with the club for only a short time. When teammate McGraw left the club to manage the Giants, Kelley briefly managed Baltimore and then returned to the National League with the Cincinnati Redlegs.

After only two weeks with Cincinnati, Kelley was named manager, succeeding Bid McPhee and Frank Bancroft, both of whom had done little with the club. Kelley brought a 33–26 showing out of the team to bring the Reds home fourth. As player, he batted .327 in 37 games.

Kelley's best performance as Cincinnati manager was an 88–65 third-place finish in 1904, but the following season the Reds finished fifth. Nothing during those years gave him as much satisfaction as beating his old teammate, John McGraw, but the Giants won 32 of the 42 games played between New York and Cincinnati during the 1904 and 1905 seasons.

Joe's final season as Cincinnati manager was 1905, but he remained on the team as a player in 1906 when his old mentor, Ned Hanlon, replaced him as manager. In 1907 Kelley went to Toronto of the Eastern League as manager, and he batted .322 while playing first base.

In 1908 Joe finally returned to Boston as manager of the National League club. There he made the mistake of urging a trade for New York Giant catcher Frank Bowerman. Bowerman spent the year undermining Kelley's authority. He finally threatened to quit if Boston owner George Dovey did not fire Kelley and appoint him manager.

Dovey and Kelley had not been getting along well to begin with, and the owner did indeed ask Kelley to resign late in the season. By having Bowerman as a player-manager for 1909, Dovey could also save the $5000 salary being paid to Kelley.

After some hesitation, Kelley quit. The breaking point occurred at a September 24 Old Timers' gathering in Boston, which brought together such stars as Al Spalding, George Wright, and Jim O'Rourke. Kelley made a speech that night regretting the caliber of players of those days in comparison to the great nineteenth century stars. Shortly thereafter, he resigned.

Kelley lost his final two games as Boston manager to the Giants, thereby setting up the playoff situation between New York and Chicago necessitated by the Fred Merkle "boner" incident of 1908.

Kelley returned to Toronto and managed the club from 1909 through 1914, playing his final games in 1910. Joe was one of four New York Yankee scouts in 1915 and 1916, and his last job in baseball was as a coach with Brooklyn in 1926.

Kelley lived in Baltimore with his wife and two sons. There he died on August 14, 1943, the last surviving member of the old Baltimore Orioles.

In 1971, long after he had been forgotten by baseball fans, Joe Kelley was named to the Hall of Fame.

JOSEPH JAMES KELLEY

Boston (N.L.) 1891, 1908
Pittsburgh 1892
Baltimore (N.L.) 1892–1898
Brooklyn 1899–1901
Baltimore (A.L.) 1902
Cincinnati 1902–1906

G	AB	R	H	2B	3B	HR	RBI	Avg.
1827	6982	1424	2245	353	189	66	1194	.321

(At left) A pose of Kelley scooping up a ball at first base, but actually his slot was left field. (Above) Kelley flanked by teammates: from left, Germany Schaeffer, Wild Bill Donavan, Kelley, and Duke Farrell.

George Kelly (b.1895)

George "Highpockets" Kelly was the first baseman for four New York Giant championship teams in the 1920s, and he was one of the National League's hardest hitters during that period.

George Lange Kelly was born on September 10, 1895, in San Francisco. His father, James, was a Civil War veteran and a captain on the San Francisco police force for more than 30 years. The elder Kelly was a strong disciplinarian who instilled belief in law and order in the Kelly children—seven boys and two girls. George was the seventh child.

George's mother was the former Mary Lange, sister of Bill "Little Eva" Lange, an outstanding outfielder with Chicago from 1893 to 1899. During the latter year, Bill's wife made him give up the game.

There was a sandlot next to the Kelly home on Spruce and Jackson Streets, and George learned to play baseball there after school. His Uncle Bill taught him the fine points of the game after his retirement and return to San Francisco. It made a tremendous impression on the neighborhood kids when they discovered that George had such a famous uncle.

George attended Polytechnic High School for three years, but he quit after his junior year to play semipro ball at Golden Gate Park. Kelly was 16 years old and thought himself ready to help earn some money for the large family. But although the league was considered semipro, the only money George ever collected was on 25-cent bets made by the players before the games started.

Al Earle organized a 30-team West Coast semipro league in which George participated, receiving only expense money for road games. Conditions were poor, there were no locker rooms, and the players usually changed in the back of a local pool room. There was no grandstand at Golden Gate Park, and only a wire fence kept fans off the field. The fields bordered each other, and one team's right fielder might be playing in another game's left field.

Kelly received his first professional contract offer in 1914. Uncle Bill recommended George to Mike Lynch, manager of the Spokane club in the Northwestern League. Lynch was a former teammate of Bill Lange, and he valued Bill's suggestion. But before George ever played a single game, he was transferred to Victoria of the same league when Charlie Brooks, the Victoria first baseman, broke a leg. Kelly's contract called for a salary of $150 per month.

George batted .250 that year in 141 games, dividing his time between the outfield and first base. He was hitting close to .300 in 1915 when New York Giant scout Dick Kinsella came to Victoria to observe George. As fate would have it, Kinsella became ill and never saw George play, but he wired home a favorable report to John

McGraw anyway. McGraw purchased George for $1500 on August 19.

Standing 6'4" and weighing 190 pounds, the long-legged Kelly was immediately nicknamed "Highpockets" by New York sportswriters. Hal Chase was the Giants' first baseman, but McGraw was searching for a successor. Kelly, unaccustomed to the hot New York summer and far removed from the Northwestern League, could not get untracked. He batted only .158 to close out the 1915 season, and in 1916 he played 49 games and batted .158 again. The fans booed George, but McGraw stuck with him, insisting that one day he would make good.

But George started the 1917 season no better. Therefore, when McGraw needed room on his roster for a pitcher, he reluctantly sold George to Pittsburgh on a conditional basis. The understanding was that Kelly would be returned if he did not make the club.

Again, Kelly failed. He played only eight games for the Pirates, collected two hits in 39 at bats, and was returned to the Giants. McGraw promptly optioned him to Rochester of the International League, and George batted .300 in 32 games.

Kelly put in a year's military service in 1918, seeing duty at San Antonio Field. He then returned to Rochester in 1919 to hit .356 in 103 games, second in the league. McGraw brought him back in August, and George hit .290 in 32 games. He had finally found his major league stroke.

Chase was gone in 1920, and Kelly was handed the first-base job. He played 155 games, batted .266, and tied for the National League lead in runs batted in with 94.

In 1921 George notched his first of six consecutive .300 seasons, batting .308 and leading the National League with 23 home runs—an impressive total for anyone but Babe Ruth at that time. George also drove in 122 runs, finishing only four behind defending co-champion Rogers Hornsby.

The Giants won their first of four consecutive pennants that year and met the Yankees in the World Series. Although Kelly batted only .233, he had a memorable Series, setting records for chances accepted (93) and assists (7) by a first baseman as well as records for strikeouts (10) and times at bat in one inning (2). He was somewhat of a hero in the eighth and deciding game, won by the Giants, 1–0, when his ground ball was misplayed, leading to the Giants' only run. And in the ninth inning, with Aaron Ward on first base and one out, Home Run Baker hit a hard grounder toward the hole between the second and first basemen. Johnny Rawlings made a great play and fired to Kelly to retire Baker. Ward tried to advance to third, but Kelly rifled a perfect strike to

(Above) First baseman Kelly picks up a grounder. (Below) Kelly hits a hard one. He is the only man to hit home runs in three consecutive innings in one game.

Frankie Frisch at third, and the Giants completed a double play and captured the world championship.

McGraw admired Kelly's strong arm and always used it to advantage. He sent him ranging into the outfield as a cutoff man, and George was able to nail many advancing runners. George led the league's first basemen in assists in 1920, 1921, and 1922.

George hit .328 in 1922, and then batted .278 in the World Series win over the Yankees. In 1923 he batted .307 and became the only man to hit home runs in three consecutive innings in a game, accomplishing the feat during a 5-for-5 day (15 total bases) on September 17. On June 14 of the following season, George again belted three homers in one game, driving in all the runs in an 8–6 Giant victory. That year, Kelly also belted home runs in six consecutive games, collecting seven in the process, a National League record later tied by Walker Cooper and Willie Mays, and a major league record finally broken by American Leaguer Frank Howard.

In the field, George had great range and was even able to put in some playing time at second base. He set league records at first for putouts and chances in 1920; he also had 19 putouts in one game during the 1923 World Series. In the 1924 World Series against Washington, George hit his only Series homer, connecting off Walter Johnson in the opening game. For the season, Kelly led the league in RBIs with 136 while hitting .324 with 21 homers.

In 1923 George's younger brother, Ren, had a taste of the majors, pitching one game for the Athletics. George himself had hurled five shutout innings back in 1917 in a meaningless final game of the season. He was a most versatile athlete, and McGraw claimed, "He had more important hits than any player I ever had."

When Bill Terry arrived in 1924, George was shifted to the outfield to get Terry into the lineup. It was not a pleasant year for George, as he, Frankie Frisch, and Ross Youngs were implicated in a betting scandal involving shortstop Jimmy O'Connell and coach Cozy Donlan. Commissioner Landis and the assistant district attorney of New York, George Brothers, investigated the case and cleared Kelly, Frisch, and Youngs, but it was an embarrassing situation.

George batted .309 in 1925 and .303 in 1926. But with Terry at first and Kelly's value high, McGraw traded George to Cincinnati in January 1927 for Edd Roush, recognized as the league's best centerfielder. Neither player was pleased with the deal, but the unusual exchange of two future Hall of Famers was a tribute to both.

"Kell," as the players called him, earned $18,500 in 1927 and batted .270 for the Reds. He hit .296 in 1928 and .293 in 1929, setting a Cincinnati record in the latter season with 45 doubles, a mark later broken by Frank Robinson.

In July 1930, although hitting .287 after 51 games, George was released to Minneapolis at the age of 34. He might have been doomed to the minors had not Charlie Grimm been injured at Chicago. The Cubs purchased George after his .361 showing at Minneapolis, and he batted .331 in 39 games for them.

But Kelly was back at Minneapolis in 1931, hitting .320 with 20 homers in 155 games. The big righthanded hitter, a line-drive hitter by nature, could still belt the long ball. In 1932, when Del Bissonette of Brooklyn was injured, Kelly was purchased by the Dodgers and closed out his major league career by hitting .243 with his last four home runs. He concluded the season with Jersey City of the International League, hitting .294.

In 1933 George played 21 games for Oakland of the Pacific Coast League and hit .232. But he was happy to be there; he had purchased a home in Millbrae, California, in 1929, two years after his marriage to Mary Helen O'Connor. With their three children, the Kellys remained Millbrae residents thereafter.

George was a coach for Cincinnati in 1935, 1936, and 1937, and he then moved on to Boston to join Casey Stengel as a coach with the Braves. He spent six years with Boston, leaving after the 1943 season to work as a machinist in a San Francisco engineering firm.

In 1946 Kelly scouted for the Reds, and he returned to the club as a coach in 1947 and 1948. The following year he scouted for Oakland. From 1950 to 1953, Kelly coached at Oakland for managers Charlie Dressen, Augie Galan, and Mel Ott. In 1954 he assumed the only managerial position of his career and brought Wenatchee to a last-place finish in the Western International League, a successor to the league where he had begun his career some 40 years earlier.

After leaving Wenatchee, George worked as a dispatcher of ground transportation at the San Francisco International Airport until his retirement at age 65 in 1960.

In 1973, still in fine health and with an erect posture, the 77-year old Kelly was named to the Hall of Fame.

GEORGE LANGE KELLY

New York (N.L.) 1915–1926
Pittsburgh 1917
Cincinnati 1927–1930
Chicago (N.L.) 1930
Brooklyn 1932

G	AB	R	H	2B	3B	HR	RBI	Avg.
1622	5993	819	1778	337	76	148	1019	.297

King Kelly (1857-1894)

Baseball's first "matinee idol" was Mike "King" Kelly, the handsome, carefree, swaggering star of the National League's early days.

Michael Joseph Kelly was born on December 31,1857, in Lansingburgh (now known as Troy), New York. His father, an Irish immigrant, served in the Union army in the Civil War. After the war, the elder Kelly reenlisted and moved the family to Washington, D.C. Mike had his first experience with baseball on the Washington sandlots.

When ill health forced the senior Kelly to resign from the army, he moved his family to Paterson, New Jersey. There, young Mike established his own team and, as soon as he was old enough, grew a mustache like that of his hero, Joe Start of the New York Mutuals.

When Mike was 18 years old, he decided to try a career as a silk weaver, but he found the 12-hour days in the mills not to his liking. Although baseball was hardly a profession at the time, Kelly played some semipro ball in Port Jervis and Paterson for $3 per week. In 1877 he and a friend, Eddie "The Only" Nolan, gave Paterson a team with two future major leaguers. Later that year he joined Columbus for his final fling at semipro ball.

In 1878 Mike joined the Cincinnati Buckeyes as a right fielder. He collected only one hit in his first 21 times at bat, but he then caught fire and finished the season with a .281 batting average. The following year, playing third base and catching, he batted .348. After the season, he barnstormed on the West Coast, where Chicago's Cap Anson took notice of him. Anson offered Mike a job with the White Stockings in 1880, and after a week of negotiating over a $100 salary difference, Kelly accepted.

Mike earned the nickname "King" from the Chicago fans. Players called him "Kel," and in later years the names merged into "King Kel." In Chicago he developed a new sliding technique, the original hook slide, that made him famous. When he got on base, fans would yell, "Slide, Kelly, slide!" A song by that name became popular in the 1890s:

> Slide, Kelly, slide!
> Your running's a disgrace!
> Slide, Kelly, slide!
> Stay there, hold your base!
> If someone doesn't steal you,
> And your batting doesn't fail you,
> They'll take you to Australia!
> Slide, Kelly, slide!

Although not especially fast, Mike was in a class of his own on the basepaths, stealing as many as 84 bases in 1887.

Kelly also experimented with head-first slides and trick plays that took advantage of loopholes in baseball rules. For example, he would knock the ball out of fielders'

hands or drop his catcher's mask on the plate to trip runners. And if the game's lone umpire was not alert, Mike would skip a base entirely and run directly from second to home. One day, while Mike was on the bench, a foul pop was lofted near the dugout. Mike immediately hollered, "Kelly now catching for Flint," and made the putout. Although the plays often led to heated arguments, Kelly became an extremely popular player with both fans and players.

In addition to his sliding innovations, Mike is sometimes credited with the invention of the hit-and-run play. He was also one of the first catchers to use finger signals to pitchers while recognizing the need for his fielders to know what pitch was coming. As an outfielder, he was among the first to play close behind the infield to back up plays.

Although his pay was slight, Mike lived in high style. He drank heavily, insisting that ale and wine were good for him. He spent a fortune on clothes, dressing in pointed patent-leather shoes and a high silk hat, and gambled considerable sums of money at race tracks. Reporting late one season and ordered to get in shape by visiting the Turkish baths, Mike was discovered instead at the race track while his teammates were playing ball. As Cap Anson, his Chicago manager, said, "Mike's only enemy is himself."

Nevertheless, in seven seasons with Chicago, Mike helped the club to five pennants—1880, 1881, 1882, 1885, and 1886. In 1882 his slide, which forced the ball out of George Wright's glove, led to two runs and a pennant-clinching victory by Chicago over Providence. In 1886 Kelly led the National League with a .388 batting average and 155 runs scored.

When Chicago owner Al Spalding could not meet his salary demands for the 1887 season, Kelly was sold to the Boston Beaneaters for a record $10,000. The sale was the talk of baseball for months. Boston agreed to pay Kelly the maximum salary of $2000, plus an additional $3000 for the use of his picture in team advertising.

Spalding had to explain to disappointed Chicago fans that Kelly's drinking was a bad influence on the younger players, and that his mere five-hit performance in the 1886 playoffs indicated that his skills were slipping.

Mike became Boston's new hero. The "$10,000 Beauty" played all positions. In his first season, with walks counted as hits, he batted .394 and stole 84 bases. Fans presented him with a house and an expensive carriage drawn by two white horses, in which he would proudly ride to the park

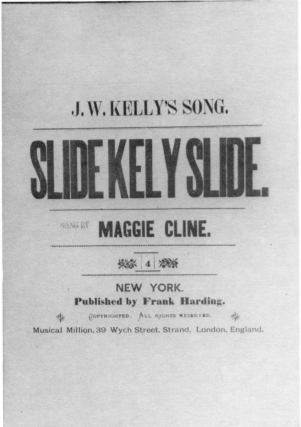

Immortalized in oils and in song, King Kelly was in a league of his own on the base paths, stealing as many as 84 bases in 1887. The painting above, "Slide Kelly Slide," showing his headlong plunge into second, was done by Frank O. Small in the 1880s. The song of the same name was popular in the 1890s, although, as the picture at left shows, the publisher spelled Kelly's name wrong.

each day. At the peak of his fame, fans would sometimes stop the carriage, unhitch the horses, and lead him to the park themselves. Kelly was one of the first players to be asked for autographs. In 1888, employing a ghost writer, Mike published one of the first baseball books, *Play Ball: Stories of the Ball Field.*

Mike had an off-season job as a starter at a race track. He also performed some vaudeville sketches, reciting "Casey at the Bat" on the stage. Once when the Beaneaters were introduced to President Grover Cleveland, Kelly squeezed the President's hand until the President winced. His teammates, thinking it humorous, followed in turn.

Mike batted .318 in 1888, then .293 in 1889. When the Players' League was formed by the Brotherhood in 1890, Mike was one of those who left the National League, despite a $4000 salary with the Beaneaters. He was then given the managerial reins of the Boston franchise in the rebel league. On behalf of the National League, Spalding, his old boss, secretly offered Mike $10,000 and a blank, three-year contract not to jump. Mike thought it over and then turned Spalding down, saying he "couldn't go back on the boys."

Loaded with such talent as Dan Brouthers, Harry Stovey, Hoss Radbourne, and Hardie Richardson, Kelly's team captured the Players' League's only pennant. Kelly's personal contribution was a .324 batting average. But the league folded after one season, and Mike went to the American Association, serving as player-manager for the Cincinnati franchise of Chris Von der Ahe. The team was in serious financial trouble, and in August Von der Ahe sold the club to Milwaukee interests and gave Kelly the option to join any other team in the Association. Mike chose Boston and was welcomed back by 10,000 adoring fans. After only four games with Boston's American Association team, Mike jumped to the Beaneaters and inspired the club to an 18-game winning streak and the National League pennant.

In 1892 Boston again won the pennant, but by this time Mike was hitting only .201 and nearing the end of his career. Eager to have a strong New York franchise in the league in 1893, Boston sent Mike to New York, where he caught 16 games and hit .315 to close out his major league career with a .313 batting average.

With his big-league career behind him, Mike opened a saloon in New York City in partnership with umpire "Honest John" Kelly (no relation). In 1894 he took a job as manager and catcher for Allentown in the Pennsylvania State League.

There was still a call for Mike on the Boston stage, and so in November he took a boat from New York to Boston to appear at the Palace Theater. On the boat Kelly caught a bad cold that developed into typhoid-pneumonia. Mike died at Boston Emergency Hospital on November 8, 1894, at the age of 36. He left his wife penniless; he had even given his best suit of clothes to a tramp on the ill-fated boat ride. The steamship company provided a suit for Mike's funeral.

Five thousand Bostonians turned out at the Elks Hall to view Mike's body as he lay in state. Baseball's first hero was elected to the Hall of Fame in 1945.

MICHAEL JOSEPH KELLY

Cincinnati (N.L.) 1878–1879
Chicago (N.L.) 1880–1886
Boston (N.L.) 1887–1889, 1891–1892
Boston (P.L.) 1890
Cincinnati (A.A.) 1891
Boston (A.A.) 1891
New York (N.L.) 1893

G	AB	R	H	2B	3B	HR	RBI	Avg.
1434	5922	1359	1853	351	109	65	795	.313

Boston's $10,000 beauty, King Kelly. In 1887, that was an unheard of sum for a baseball player, but the Boston Beaneaters paid it gladly to get Kelly from Chicago. For his part, Kelly got the maximum $2000 salary, plus an additional $3000 for the use of his picture in advertising.

Ralph Kiner (b.1922)

No baseball player in history, including Babe Ruth and Hank Aaron, ever matched the record established by powerful Ralph Kiner. Ralph either led or tied for the league lead in home runs in each of his first seven seasons in the major leagues. Ruth, who belted home runs in an era when few others did, never recorded a streak of more than six consecutive seasons.

Ralph McPherran Kiner was born in Santa Rita, New Mexico, on October 27, 1922. His father, a baker, died when Ralph was only four years old. His mother moved with the boy to Alhambra, California, and supported the family of two by working as a registered nurse.

Physically large for his age and athletic by nature, Ralph attended Fremont Grammar School and received his introduction to baseball through playground softball. By the time he was 13 years old, Ralph was good enough to play semipro ball in the Alhambra area, and he impressed onlookers with mighty home runs.

At Alhambra High School, Ralph was the team's pitcher and leading home run hitter, averaging almost a homer per game. On days that he did not pitch, he played either short, second, or third, considerable ground for a large fellow.

Continuing in the semipro leagues, Ralph joined a team called the Yankee Juniors. It was supported by the New York Yankees and run by their west coast scout, Bill Essick. Each player wore hand-me-down Yankee uniforms, and Kiner had the thrill of wearing George Selkirk's old No. 3.

At the time Ralph was old enough to be seriously scouted, the Yankees showed considerable interest and offered him a standard Class D contract. But the Yankees were loaded with talented outfielders, the position into which Ralph had settled. He could envision only a five- to six-year minor league apprenticeship with little hope of making the Yankees.

The Giants, Redlegs, and Browns also made good offers, but all stipulated Class D beginnings. A fine offer came from the local Pacific Coast League club, the Hollywood Stars, who offered Ralph one-half of whatever they could sell him for to a major league team. It was an interesting and unusual bid.

Kiner selected the Pittsburgh Pirates after many sessions with their scout, Hollis Thurston. The Pirates were not a strong club and thus did not offer the heavy competition to reach the majors. Pittsburgh management had considered the club's most recent campaign, the 1940 season, a good one since the Pirates had managed to play just slightly over .500 ball under Frankie Frisch. But Pittsburgh did not have a strong farm system and so was able to offer Ralph a Class A pact. For a bonus, Ralph received $3000, with the promise of

an additional $5000 when he reached the major leagues.

In the meantime, Kiner attempted to continue his education. He attended Pasadena Junior College during the winters of 1940, 1941, and 1942, and spent six weeks at the University of Southern California before realizing that baseball had to occupy the majority of his time.

The 165-pound youngster, a righthanded hitter, reported to Albany of the Eastern League in 1941 and promptly tied for the league lead by playing in 141 games. But his 11 home runs did not indicate that there would be a substantial power production in his future. Back at Albany again in 1942, Ralph increased his home run output to 14, good enough to lead the league. Again he topped the league in games played while batting .257.

In 1943 he was promoted to the Toronto Maple Leafs of the International League. He played 43 games, hit only two home runs, and was batting .236 when he was inducted into the Navy Air Corps. Ralph trained as a flier in Corpus Cristi, Texas, and served in Hawaii. The naval training added strength to his arms and back, and he left the service in 1946 at 6'2" and 195 pounds.

Reporting to spring training with the Pirates at San Bernardino, California, Kiner donned uniform No. 4 and became the talk of the camp when he belted two home runs against the White Sox during an exhibition game in Pasadena. Frisch decided to open the season with Kiner in the lineup.

Ralph was immediately popular on the lackluster team. The Pirates finished seventh, losing 91 games, and Frisch failed to complete the year as manager. But Kiner belted 23 home runs to lead the league for the first of seven consecutive seasons. It was a low total for a league leader (Johnny Mize was runnerup with 22), but Kiner had become the first rookie since Harry Lumley in 1906 to lead the National League, and his total established a Pittsburgh record for one season.

The American League home run champion that season was Detroit veteran Hank Greenberg, who had hit 44. Thus it was with a flurry of excitement that the Pirates purchased the 36-year-old Greenberg for the 1947 season. Forbes Field offered a short left field for the mighty Greenberg, and the area became popularly known as "Greenberg Gardens." Hank belted 25 home runs in his only season with the Pirates, but his real contribution came through his helpfulness to Kiner, his roommate and close friend.

Although 11 years apart in age, the two got along quite well, and they remained friends long after their careers ended. Hank gave Ralph many valuable batting tips, and Kiner increased his batting average to .313 while driving in 127 runs and challenging Babe Ruth's home run record by belting 51 four-baggers. Only a slump of two homers in the final 14 games prevented Kiner from being a more serious challenger, and Ralph settled for a tie for the league lead with Mize. Kiner established a record that season by belting eight home runs in four consecutive games. In addition to this fact, he twice smacked three homers in a single game. Although the Pirates finished in a tie for last place, the club drew a record 1,283,531 fans, thanks largely to the presence of Hank and Ralph.

Immediately recognized as bright and well spoken, Ralph was named player representative by his teammates. He was also named National League player representative at the time the major league pension plan was instituted.

With Greenberg retired in 1948, his "Gardens" were renamed "Kiner's Korner," and Ralph offered proof that it was unnecessary to play for a New York club to receive considerable national attention.

"Ozark Ike," as his teammates called him, benefited from his southern California residence and received much publicity over a single date with Elizabeth Taylor. For a while, he seriously dated actress Janet Leigh.

Striking up a friendship and business relationship with Pirate announcer Bob Prince, Ralph was involved in a series of endorsements and promotional tie-ins, few of which earned him much money. But at least it kept his name in the papers, and Prince got Ralph established as a radio and TV personality, producing and at times co-hosting interview shows for Ralph. Kiner became one of the first baseball players to have his own television program.

In 1948 the Pirates managed to finish fourth, and Ralph again tied Mize for the homer crown with 40. Homers were the only offensive department in which Stan Musial failed to lead the league.

Soon Kiner's salary passed Musial's, making him the top salaried man in the league. By 1951 Ralph was earning $90,000, which caused teammate Fritz Ostermueller to observe, "Home run hitters drive Cadillacs—single hitters drive Fords." Kiner never said that himself, but the remark was frequently attributed to him.

Kiner's home run hitting capabilities became more prolific with each passing season. In 1949 he belted 54, two short of Hack Wilson's league record. Four of the blasts came with the bases loaded, and his career total of 12 grand slams tied Rogers Hornsby's league mark. Sixteen of Kiner's

1949 homers came in September. His total of 101 homers in 1949 and 1950 set a two-year National League record. In five All-Star games, Ralph hit three homers. When he won his fifth straight homer crown in 1950 (with 47), he was named National League Player of the Year by *The Sporting News*.

Following a .309 season with 42 homers in 1951, Ralph married Nancy Chaffee, the fourth-ranked women's tennis player in the country. They had three children but were divorced in 1969 when Ralph married the former Barbara Batchelder and adopted her two daughters.

Kiner captured his seventh home run title in 1952, sharing the lead with Chicago's Hank Sauer with 37. And then on June 4, 1953, in a deal which shocked Pittsburgh fans, Kiner became a teammate of Sauer's when he was dealt to the Cubs with three other players (including Joe Garagiola) for six Cubs and an estimated $100,000.

Eddie Mathews led the league in homers with 47 that year, stopping Ralph's streak (Kiner placed fifth in the league with 35). In 1954 Kiner dropped to 22 homers, and he then was traded to Cleveland for the 1955 season. Bothered by a slipped disc which caused considerable back pain, Ralph knew the end was near. After hitting only 18 homers in 1955, he retired at the age of 33.

Kiner took a job as general manager of the San Diego Padres of the Pacific Coast League from 1955 to 1960, and then in 1961 was hired as a radio announcer by the Chicago White Sox. One year later, he was signed by the New York Mets to join their newly formed television and radio team and to host pregame and postgame television shows. The trio of Kiner, Lindsey Nelson, and Bob Murphy, became the longest-running three-man broadcasting team in baseball history.

Maintaining homes in St. Petersburg, Florida, and Rye, New York, Kiner became a popular figure in New York, the city he had passed up as a player. In 1975, his final year of eligibility for Hall of Fame election by members of the Baseball Writer's Association, Ralph Kiner made it by one vote. Critics claimed that he was not a good outfielder or base runner, but surely no player ever dominated the home run charts of the National League to the degree that Ralph Kiner did.

RALPH McPHERRAN KINER

Pittsburgh 1946–1953
Chicago (N.L.) 1953–1954
Cleveland 1955

G	AB	R	H	2B	3B	HR	RBI	Avg.
1472	5205	971	1451	216	39	369	1015	.279

Kiner reaches home after belting his forty-fifth home run in 1950. Greeting him is Gus Bell. That year Kiner hit a total of 47 homers. The year before he had hit 54, and the total of 101 is a two-year National League record.

Bill Klem (1874-1951)

The man generally regarded as the greatest umpire is Bill Klem, who worked in the National League from 1905 to 1941 before becoming chief of umpires.

William Joseph Klem was born on February 22, 1874, in Rochester, New York, of German parents. His real name was Klimm but, following the example of an uncle, he changed it to Klem in 1902.

Bill's first ambition was to be a ballplayer, but he never achieved professional status. He played first base and caught on the sandlots around Rochester, and he had trials with professional teams in Hamilton, Ontario, Springfield, Massachusetts, and Augusta, Maine, during the 1896–1897 seasons. But his small stature, 5'7½" and 157 pounds, held him back. Finally, Bill injured his arm and so gave up any hope of a baseball career, returning instead to sandlot ball.

Around 1900 he migrated to Berwick, Pennsylvania, and worked as a steelworker and bartender besides playing some semi-pro ball. The transition from player to umpire was accomplished reluctantly during this period, but it enabled Klem to become affiliated with professional baseball.

A dedicated perfectionist throughout his life, Klem approached his new profession with the determination to be the best umpire in the game. A boyhood friend, Silk O'Loughlin (an American League umpire from 1902 to 1918), advised him against an umpiring career. "It's a rotten business," O'Loughlin said, but Klem ignored the advice and took a job in 1902 in the Connecticut State League.

Umpiring in those days was done under miserable conditions. Few gentlemen entered the profession, and fans seemed to have a genuine hatred for umpires, not only at the game but off the field as well. Bottle throwing was common, and vile language was heaped on them. It was a nerve-racking business, and Klem at times let it affect him. His nerves caused a skin condition to develop which was never cleared up by medicine.

In 1903 Klem worked in the New York State League, and the following year he moved up to the American Association.

Following the 1904 season, National League president Harry Pulliam hired Bill to umpire a postseason exhibition series between Pittsburgh and Cleveland. He spoke with Klem about a National League contract for the following season for the standard $1500 salary. Ban Johnson, meanwhile, offered Klem an American League contract. Although Bill knew that American League umpires received more support from the league office than did those in the National League, he had given a verbal promise to Pulliam and so joined the National League staff in 1905.

Klem immediately set about establishing his authority. He began drawing a line with

his shoe during arguments, warning the angry player or manager "don't cross the line," or "the Rio Grande" as he later called it. Bill always considered himself a gentlemen, avoiding the physical battles which had been frequent in earlier days.

When Bill joined the league, only one umpire was assigned to work a game. By the time the number was increased to two, Bill had already earned a reputation for great ability and was therefore permanently assigned to work home plate. Not until 1921, after Klem had recorded 16 consecutive years calling balls and strikes, did he begin to rotate with his fellow umpires and work the bases.

Bill was a great innovator among umpires. He was the first to employ the use of hand signals to indicate safe, out, fair, foul, ball, and strike. He was also the first to straddle the foul lines to obtain a better look at fair and foul balls. In addition to his innovations on the field, Bill fought for better dressing room conditions for the umpires. Klem also set the precedent for National League umpires to stand a bit to the side of the catcher to obtain a better look at pitches, and he was the first to wear a whalebone chest protector beneath his coat rather than the inflated pillow protector still used in the American League.

Bill could be hot-tempered when provoked. Calling him "Catfish," a nickname he despised, was grounds for immediate ejection. The name was first used by Bill Clymer, manager of the Columbus team in the American Association in 1904. Since Klem was not particularly handsome, he was very sensitive about the name.

New York Giant manager John McGraw, who had a running feud with Klem, was the most frequent user of the nickname. McGraw protested Klem's umpiring so strongly in 1928 that Bill, believing the league would back McGraw, resigned. Three months later, he reconsidered. However, he did not miss a single game since the affair had taken place during the winter.

Bill worked his first of a record 18 World Series in 1908. He and Tom Connolly formed one umpiring crew and alternated with Hank O'Day and Jack Sheridan to provide two umpires on the field for each game. Klem also worked the World Series games of 1909, 1911–1915, 1917–1918, 1920, 1922, 1924, 1926, 1929, 1931–1932, 1934, and 1940. He was an umpire in the first All-Star game in 1933 and a later game in 1938.

Prior to the 1917 World Series, Klem led a brief strike on behalf of the umpires, turning down an offer of $400 and finally accepting $650 for each man. One year

later, he demanded and received $1000 for himself for the Series while the three other umpires were paid $650. Klem also signed the first three-year contract for an umpire that season.

In 1908 Bill was selected to umpire the pennant-deciding game between the Cubs and the Giants, necessitated by the famous "Merkle boner" play several weeks before, a decision which Klem called one of the worst rulings ever made by an umpire. It was uncommon for Bill to criticize a fellow umpire, but he felt strongly about that incident.

Prior to the big game, the Giants' team physician, Joseph M. Creamer, offered Klem $2500 to "call the close ones for the Giants." Klem reported the incident and Creamer was banned from the game for life. Klem himself was once fined $50 by Commissioner Landis after renewing an argument with Goose Goslin in a public elevator in Detroit during the 1934 World Series.

Two famous statements are attributed to Klem. The first, "I never missed one in my life," he always claimed was misinterpreted. When he made the statement, he had touched his heart and indicated, "here," meaning his intention more than his perfect record. Bill's other statement, made at a winter sports banquet, was "Baseball is more than a game to me, it's a religion."

By the late 1930s, when he was in his sixties, the league tried to get Bill to accept a pension and retire, but Klem still believed himself to be the best umpire in the league. Finally, in September 1940, he failed to get out of the way of an infield grounder at the Polo Grounds. When he came off the field, a woman said, "Are you okay, Pop?" He had been called many things in his career, but that one really hurt. Bill then agreed to leave the playing field and accept the position as chief of umpires, an office he held until his death.

Bill's most cherished nickname was one that he thought up himself—"The Old Arbitrator," words he first heard in the minor leagues and thought "distinguished."

Although slowed down and with failing sight in one eye, Klem umpired a few important games late in the 1941 season. He even worked some spring training games in 1944 at the age of 70.

Bill and his wife, Marie, settled in Miami, Florida, where Bill died on September 16, 1951. He was elected to the Hall of Fame in 1953.

(Above) Klem is behind the plate during the second game of the 1912 World Series. Harry Hooper of the Boston Red Sox bats, and Chief Meyers of the Giants catches. (Below) From left, umpires "Brick" Owens and Klem and players Eddie Collins and Hervey McClellan.

Sandy Koufax (b.1935)

The youngest player ever elected to the Hall of Fame, Sandy Koufax had a fleetingly brilliant career. For six years as a left-handed fastball pitcher for the Los Angeles Dodgers, he overpowered National League hitters. Then he quit to save his arm from permanent crippling.

Sanford Koufax was born on December 30, 1935, in Brooklyn, New York. His parents, Jack and Evelyn Braun, were divorced when Sandy was three, and the youngster took the name of his mother's second husband, Irving Koufax, a lawyer.

Sandy was a good student at Lafayette High School in Brooklyn, but he spent more time in sports than he did with his books, much to the dismay of his parents. Basketball was his chief interest, and a number of colleges scouted him. Baseball at this period only filled the time between basketball seasons. On the Brooklyn sandlots, he played first base before he found his true place on the pitcher's mound.

When Sandy finished high school in 1953, he accepted an athletic scholarship from the University of Cincinnati, a basketball power in the Midwest. In his freshman year with the Bearcats, he averaged 10 points per game. In the spring he joined the college baseball team after learning that it was scheduled to make a trip to southern California. As a Bearcat pitcher that year, Koufax struck out 51 batters in 32 innings.

Baseball scouts were already aware of Sandy's potential since it was difficult to hide on the Brooklyn sandlots. One sportswriter, Jimmy Murphy, tipped off Brooklyn Dodger scout Al Campanis about the young southpaw with the dazzling fastball. The Giants, Pirates, and Braves also pursued him. In December 1954, while he was still in college in Cincinnati, Sandy accepted the Dodgers' offer of a $6,000 salary and a $14,000 bonus for signing. Other teams had posted higher bids, the Braves reportedly offering $30,000, but Sandy's father had given Campanis a handshake agreement, and Sandy was happy to play in his hometown.

Under a rule in effect at that time, a player who received a salary and bonus totaling more than $4,000 on signing his professional contract had to remain with the major league team that signed him. So Koufax held a spot on the Brooklyn roster in 1955, never having pitched in the minor leagues. The 1955 Dodgers were still "The Boys of Summer" celebrated by Roger Kahn in his 1972 best seller. The 19-year-old Koufax was surrounded by such teammates as Jackie Robinson, Roy Campanella, Duke Snider, Pee Wee Reese, Gil Hodges, Carl Furillo, and Don Newcombe.

Because of the great talent surrounding him, Sandy spent the majority of the year on the bullpen bench. He appeared in only 12 games, 5 as a starter. He won two, lost two, struck out 30, and walked 28 in 42

Sandy Koufax joined the Dodger pitching staff in 1955 at the age of 20. It took him six years to hit his stride, but in the next six years he won an MVP award, three Cy Young awards, four strikeout titles, and five consecutive ERA titles. (Opposite page) the Koufax style.

innings. It was an unimpressive season for Sandy, but the Brooklyn Dodgers won their only World Championship that year.

The Dodgers captured the pennant again in 1956. Sandy made 16 appearances, 10 starts, and notched a 2–4 record with a 4.88 ERA for only 59 innings of work. Nothing about him yet indicated the great accomplishments to come. Sandy could throw as hard as any pitcher on the Dodger staff, but he was wild and had trouble getting the most out of his pitches.

Koufax recorded a 5–4 mark in 1957, appearing in 34 games with 104 innings pitched. That fall the Dodgers stunned the baseball world by announcing their move to Los Angeles. The Brooklyn-born left-hander left his home and headed west with the club.

In 1958, their first year in Los Angeles, the Dodgers attracted more than 1,845,000 fans to the huge Los Angeles Coliseum, but the club finished in seventh place. The poor season afforded Koufax more pitching time; he made 40 appearances, posting an 11–11 record, but also recorded a 4.47 ERA and gave up 105 walks in 159 innings.

The following year Manager Walter Alston led the Dodgers to a great comeback, and the team won the World Championship. That was the first year Koufax attracted national attention. On August 31, 1959, he struck out 18 Cub batters to tie a major league record. And on October 6, he lost a 1–0 decision in the World Series to the White Sox, allowing only five hits. His record for the year was 8–6 and his ERA 4.06.

The great promise of 1959 did not materialize in 1960. Koufax won only 8 of 21 decisions but struck out 197 batters in 175 innings. The Dodgers cut his pay after the season, and Koufax seriously considered quitting. He had words with general manager Buzzie Bavasi over his lack of opportunity, and he was frustrated by his inability to pitch as hard during games as he did on the sidelines. The problem appeared to lie in his great strength. His tenseness caused him to hold back the ball rather than let his whole body aid the delivery. On a bus ride during spring training in 1961, catcher Norm Sherry suggested that Sandy just "have some fun on the mound—throw curves and changeups!"

The advice seemed to relax Koufax. If his later success can be traced to any single moment, that was probably it. And in 1961 Koufax began one of the most brilliant six-year stints ever recorded in baseball. Installed in the regular starting rotation, Sandy won 18 while losing 13 and led the National League with 269 strikeouts.

Koufax displays four "O" balls, symbols of his record four no-hitters, on September 9, 1965. He had just pitched the fourth—a perfect game. A year later, still throwing spectacular ball, he would announce his retirement to save his arm from being permanently crippled.

In 1962 the Dodgers seemed headed for the pennant. Koufax notched a 14–7 record with a league-leading 2.54 ERA. But while he was batting against the Pirates in June, a pitch nicked his bat just above his left hand, breaking the artery that let blood to the index finger. The finger numbed and Koufax was unable to grip a baseball. He was through for the year, and the Dodgers lost the pennant in a playoff with San Francisco. No one doubted that the Koufax injury had cost Los Angeles the flag.

Koufax came back in 1963 to capture 25 of 30 decisions, collect 306 strikeouts, record a 1.88 ERA, and win two games in the World Series (he struck out 15 in the first game and won the deciding fourth game). Sandy won the Most Valuable Player award, the first of three Cy Young Awards (he won others in 1965 and 1966), the second of four strikeout titles (he won others in 1961, 1965, and 1966), and the second of five consecutive ERA titles (1962–1966).

Koufax was the toast of baseball now. Despite his shyness, he appeared on many television programs and was part of a Dodger nightclub act in Las Vegas.

But injury struck Sandy again in 1964. Early in the season, adhesions in his pitching arm tore loose, leading to the first stages of traumatic arthritis. For the remainder of his career, Koufax battled this condition with injections of cortisone and oral medications. But the condition only worsened. By late August, after having pitched his third no-hitter in three years, Koufax was forced to the sidelines

by the pain in his arm. He had won 15 of his last 16 starts. His record for the year was 19–5 and his ERA was 1.74.

In 1965, in order to rest his arthritic arm, Koufax did no throwing between starts. Nevertheless, he won 26 games, losing only 8, and led the league with a 2.04 ERA. On September 9, 1965, Sandy pitched a perfect game against Chicago, breaking the record for career no-hitters with his fourth. In the World Series against Minnesota, he won two games, including the deciding seventh game after only two days' rest. His Series ERA was 0.38 that year.

Koufax was now attracting 15,000–25,000 additional fans at each game he pitched, and his salary soared. After the 1965 season, he and righthanded pitching ace Don Drysdale held out together for larger salaries, finally signing just as the regular 1966 season opened. Koufax received $125,000. The lack of spring training seemed to hurt Drysdale, who posted only a 13–16 record for the year. But Koufax won a career high of 27 games, fanning 317 batters in the process and capturing his fifth consecutive ERA title with a 1.73 mark.

Fearful that the continued strain on his arm would lead to permanent crippling, Koufax, at the very peak of his fame, announced his retirement in November 1966. For the years 1962–1966, he had won 111 games against only 34 defeats. He had

pitched 100 complete games (33 shutouts) and struck out 1444 batters, including a record 382 in 1965 (a mark later surpassed by California's Nolan Ryan). Koufax recorded a composite ERA of 1.95 for those years; his World Series ERA stood at 0.95. Sandy also established a record by striking out 10 or more batters in 97 different games.

A bachelor throughout his stardom, Koufax in 1969 married Anne Widmark, daughter of motion picture actor Richard Widmark. The two moved to Maine, and Koufax took a job as a broadcaster for NBC at a reported $100,000 per year for 10 years. By his own admission, however, he was not a good broadcaster, and after his sixth year he yielded his position to his old teammate, Maury Wills.

In 1979 he returned to uniform for the first time since his retirement, agreeing to serve as a special pitching instructor for the Dodgers during spring training.

Koufax was elected to the Hall of Fame in 1972. At the age of 36, he was the youngest man ever elected, and only the sixth to be elected in the first year of eligibility. Baseball historians will find Koufax's lifetime record far inferior to those of other Hall of Fame pitchers. But the fans who saw him fire his great fastball past the best hitters in National League from 1961 to 1966 knew that Sandy Koufax was the best pitcher of his day.

SANFORD KOUFAX

Brooklyn 1955–1957
Los Angeles 1958–1966

G	IP	W	L	Pct.	H	R	ER	SO	W	ERA
397	2325	165	87	.655	1754	806	713	2396	817	2.76

Napoleon Lajoie (1875-1959)

The first second baseman elected to baseball's Hall of Fame was Napoleon Lajoie, a professional ballplayer for 21 years who helped bring the American League from infancy to respectability.

Napoleon Lajoie was born on September 5, 1875, in Woonsocket, Rhode Island, the youngest of eight children of French-Canadian parents. The proper pronunciation of his name was "LaJwa," but he was sometimes called "La-joy-ee" or "Laj-away." No one ever pinned a colorful nickname on him, as was common in the early days of baseball, so he was usually referred to as "Nap" or "Larry."

Reared by his mother, for his father had died when he was five, young Larry worked in the cotton mills around Woonsocket at a very young age. His interest in baseball began when he was about 10 years old. The professional baseball heroes of the day made a great impression on him. Among those he recalled idolizing were such future Hall of Famers as King Kelly, Hoss Radbourne, John Montgomery Ward, and John Clarkson.

As a catcher, first baseman, and outfielder, Larry was playing semipro ball in Rhode Island in 1895, in addition to working for a livery stable, when he was approached by Charley Marston, manager of the Fall River team in the New England League. Marston offered Lajoie $100 per month to sign with his club for the 1896 season, and the 20-year-old Napoleon jumped at the offer.

Lajoie played in 80 games for Fall River, primarily as an outfielder, and batted .429, the top mark in the league. Included were 163 hits, 94 runs scored, 34 doubles, 16 triples, and 16 home runs—an exceptionally high total for pre-1900 ball.

Despite his performance, Lajoie failed to impress a Boston scout, who reported that Nap did not appear to be a good hitter. Lajoie, did, however, impress Marston, for the Fall River manager offered him to Philadelphia when the Phillies bought Phil Geier, an outfielder. Thus after only three months of minor league baseball, Nap Lajoie was in the big leagues.

The Phillies, managed by Billy Nash, were an eighth-place club in the 12-team National League in 1896, but they featured such notable players as Dan Brouthers and Ed Delahanty. Lajoie was installed immediately at first base. Brouthers, the former first baseman, had just quit the team, and Delahanty, his temporary replacement, was delighted to return to the outfield. Nap played in 39 games for the Phillies as the 1896 season wound to a close. He distinguished himself by batting .328 with 57 hits in 39 games. It was clear that a place would have to be found for him in the Phillies lineup.

George Stallings became manager of the club in 1897, Lajoie's first full season in

the major leagues, and although the Phillies dropped to tenth place, Larry batted .363. It was a great average, but one he would better seven times.

Disputed figures from that season credit Lajoie with either 9 or 10 home runs. Some sources give him the home run championship with 10, whereas others credit Hugh Duffy of Boston with 11 four-baggers. Most baseball statistics prior to the turn of the century must be treated with caution. The important point, however, was that Lajoie was clearly established at the age of 22 as one of the better hitters in the National League.

In 1898 Lajoie switched from first base to second. Although his average slipped to .328 that year, he reached 200 hits for the first of five times and led the league with 40 doubles. Nap went on to lead the American League in doubles on four other occasions—1901 (48), 1904 (50), 1906 (49), and 1910 (51). His 650 career doubles were a record at the time of his retirement, and even today the mark has been surpassed by only four players—Tris Speaker, Stan Musial, Ty Cobb, and Honus Wagner.

Part of the reason for Lajoie's success with doubles was a bat specially designed by the J.F. Hillerich Company. The lower portion of the bat had two knobs, which enabled Lajoie to perfect his split-hands hold on the instrument. It gave Nap outstanding bat control and the ability to place the ball where he wanted it almost at will—the true art of hitting in the era before home runs were in vogue.

Lajoie spent the 1899 and 1900 seasons with the Phillies, batting .380 and .346. In 1901 the American League was born, and Connie Mack, owner and manager of the Philadelphia entry in the new league, persuaded Lajoie to jump to his club, the Athletics. Part of the incentive was salary: in the National League Nap was earning a maximum salary of $2400 per year, and Connie Mack offered him a four-year contract calling for $6000 per year. Lajoie's career average for 486 National League games was .349. The American League had obtained an authentic star.

In the 1901 campaign, Lajoie batted .422 with 145 runs scored, 229 hits, 48 doubles, and 13 home runs, all league-leading figures. The .422 average remains the highest batting average ever recorded in the American League. Rogers Hornsby holds the National League mark of .424 (in 1924 with St. Louis). But the Phillies obtained a court injunction, effective on opening day of 1902, prohibiting Lajoie from playing with any other club in Philadelphia.

Lajoie at bat. One of the game's all-time great hitters, he had a habit of drawing a line outside the batter's box for luck. For him, it seemed to work. After making his mark in the National League, Lajoie jumped to the new American League in 1901, becoming one of its first stars.

With the injunction in effect in 1902, Connie Mack saw no reason to hurt Lajoie or the rest of the American League. On June 1, Lajoie was allowed to join Cleveland so that he could play every game except those in Philadelphia.

Having been forced to sit on the sidelines until June, Larry played in only 87 games in 1902, and his average fell 56 points. However, he hit .366, which would have produced another batting title had he been to bat a sufficient number of times. In the following two seasons, Lajoie compiled batting averages of .355 and .381, both good enough to lead the league. Nap therefore could have captured four consecutive titles had he not missed two months of the 1902 season.

Along the way, Lajoie was establishing himself as the best second baseman in baseball. He led the league in fielding six times. Not considered overly fast in an era when so many ran the bases daringly, Lajoie did steal 396 bases during his career, with a high of 33 in 1898.

After his success with batting titles, and a fourth-place finish for Cleveland in 1904, Lajoie was named manager of the team for the 1905 season. He replaced Bill Armour, who had held the post for three years. Nap now had the responsibility of guiding the team's fortunes in addition to holding down second base.

Managing appeared to affect Lajoie's performance at bat, and his average dipped to .329 in 1905, his lowest mark in seven years. The team, which came to be known as the Cleveland Naps after their manager, finished fifth with a 76–78 record, 19 games behind Connie Mack's pennant-winning Athletics.

A popular Cleveland figure as player-manager, Lajoie remained at the helm until late in the 1909 season, at which time he resigned with the team in sixth place. His best finish as manager had been in 1908 when Cleveland finished a mere one-half game behind pennant-winning Detroit. It was the closest Lajoie ever came to being with a pennant winner in the major leagues.

Free of his managing burden, Lajoie batted .384 in 1910, one point behind Ty Cobb. The batting title was surrounded by controversy. Lajoie, popular with teammates and opponents, was now 35 years old, and Cobb, just starting out and only 22, was already unpopular because of his rough style of play. While Cobb sat out the final two games of the season to ensure his title, Lajoie, playing a double header on the final day of the season, collected eight hits—six of which were bunts because the St. Louis manager, Jack O'Conner, had third baseman Red Corriden play deep. The batting champion in those years received a new Chalmers car, and although Lajoie finished one point behind Cobb, the auto company gave each one a car. The bunt "scandal" highlighted the relative popularity of the two American League stars.

Lajoie's most cherished award was made by Cleveland fans on a day in his honor in 1912. The gift was an eight-foot-high horseshoe wired with 1009 silver dollars.

Lajoie continued to play for Cleveland through 1914, but his batting average had plummeted to .258 by then. Upon his release, he was signed by Connie Mack, the man who had brought Nap to the American League in 1901. In his final two years in the league, 1915 and 1916, Larry batted only .280 and .246, giving him a career average of .339. Included were 3251 hits, making him today one of only 12 players to reach the 3000 mark.

Somehow, at the age of 41, Lajoie found it in his bat in 1917 to hit a league-leading .380 with 221 hits for Toronto in the International League, a team that he directed to his only championship. In 1918 he managed Indianapolis in the American Association and batted .282.

The 1918 season marked the end of his career in baseball. Nap ran for sheriff of Cuyahoga County, Ohio, but lost the election and put politics aside. He served briefly as commissioner of the Ohio and Pennsylvania League. After a few years as a salesman for a rubber company, Larry and his wife, Myrtle, retired to Florida in 1925. He died in Daytona Beach on February 7, 1959.

In 1937 Lajoie became the sixth man elected to the Hall of Fame, following the first-year selection of Babe Ruth, Ty Cobb, Walter Johnson, Christy Mathewson, and Honus Wagner.

NAPOLEON LAJOIE

Philadelphia (N.L.) 1896–1900
Philadelphia (A.L.) 1901–1902, 1915–1916
Cleveland 1902–1914

G	AB	R	H	2B	3B	HR	RBI	Avg.
2475	9589	1503	3251	650	162	82	1599	.339

Napoleon Lajoie, framed by a gift from Cleveland fans at a day in his honor in 1912. The eight-foot-high horseshoe was wired with 1009 silver dollars. Lajoie managed Cleveland from 1905 to 1909, and with him at the helm the team had become known as the Cleveland Naps.

Kenesaw Mountain Landis (1866-1944)

Baseball's future as a professional sport was uncertain in 1920. Eight members of the Chicago White Sox had been indicted on charges of accepting bribes to fix the outcome of the 1919 World Series, which they lost to underdog Cincinnati. At that point, baseball turned to Judge Kenesaw Mountain Landis and appointed him the game's first commissioner. Never again was the integrity of baseball a matter of debate.

Landis was born on November 20, 1866, in Millville, Ohio, of Swiss ancestry. He received his colorful name in honor of Kennesaw Mountain in Georgia, where his father, Dr. Abraham Landis, had been seriously wounded during the Civil War. Why the second "n" was dropped from the spelling of Kenesaw's name is unknown.

He was the sixth of seven children. Two of his five brothers, Charles and Frederick, served in the U.S. House of Representatives. The Landis family moved to Delphi, Indiana, in 1874 and, shortly thereafter, to Logansport, Indiana, where Kenesaw assumed his first job, delivering newspapers.

"Ken" was an avid baseball fan, particularly of Mordecai Brown, star pitcher of the Cubs. He played the game himself and managed a local team at the age of 17.

His other interests included bicycle riding (at which he became a champion), work at county fairs, and the operation of a roller rink. Kenesaw did not complete his studies at Logansport High School, but he instead learned shorthand and took a job as a clerk in the South Bend, Indiana, courthouse.

Landis next moved to Cincinnati, where he took prelaw courses at the University of Cincinnati, and then obtained his law degree at Union Law School (now a part of Northwestern University). He graduated in 1891 and opened his own law practice in Chicago.

Two years later, Landis left his practice to serve as private secretary to Secretary of State Walter Q. Gresham in Washington. It was a significant post in the federal government for the 27-year-old attorney, but Gresham died in 1895 and Landis returned to his law practice in Chicago.

In 1895 Landis married Winifred Reed of Ottawa, Illinois. They had two children, Colonel Reed Graham Landis, a World War I aviator, and a daughter, Suzanne.

In March 1905, President Theodore Roosevelt appointed Landis a United States District Judge for the Northern District of Illinois. It marked the beginning of a brilliant and at times controversial career on the bench for Landis, a small, thin man with a serious nature.

Kenesaw came to national attention in 1907 when he brought John D. Rockefeller to his court and fined the Standard Oil Company the sensational sum of $29,240,000 in a freight rebate case. The decision was overturned by the U.S. Supreme Court, but Landis received wide-spread publicity for his sharp handling of Rockefeller.

Judge Kenesaw Mountain Landis was appointed baseball's first commissioner in 1920 to restore the game's reputation for integrity after a World Series betting scandal in 1919. (Opposite page) Flanked by the club chiefs, he signs the contract making him baseball's "Czar" on November 12, 1920. Landis kept the position until his death in 1944, earning the reputation of "players' commissioner."

Not all of his cases were as newsworthy, but Landis developed a reputation for the unpredictable. Once an 18-year-old messenger, entrusted to deliver $750,000 worth of government bonds, was brought before Landis and charged with stealing them. "I wish I had the power to jail the man who sent him out with the bonds," stated an understanding Landis as he set the youth free.

During World War I, Landis sentenced 94 members of the International Workers of the World to prison. The action resulted in the bombing of his office a few weeks later, but he was not present.

Kenesaw's path first crossed with that of baseball in 1915 when the Federal League brought the American and National Leagues to court in a battle for recognition. Landis cleverly withheld a decision, clearing the way for the two leagues to absorb the Feds and bring peace to the game. Landis said at the time, "Both sides may understand that any blows at this thing called baseball would be regarded by this court as a blow to a national institution." Landis often found time to attend games at both Comiskey Park and Wrigley Field in Chicago.

Then came the "Black Sox" scandal of 1919, which hit the headlines in the closing weeks of the 1920 season.

Baseball at that time was governed by the National Commission, comprised of the two league presidents and Cincinnati Reds' president Garry Herrmann. Herrmann resigned however, leaving a vacancy in the chairmanship of the commission at a most critical time. Among those mentioned for the post were former President William Howard Taft and General John Pershing. Landis was suggested under the so-called Albert Lasker plan, Lasker being a stockholder in the Cubs. The plan was actually drafted by Comiskey's attorney, Alfred Austrian.

Major league club owners went to Landis's courtroom in Chicago to offer him the $50,000-per-year position. He accepted, but on his own terms—that he be given absolute power and that he have a totally free hand. The owners agreed and Landis signed a seven-year contract, deducting part of the $50,000 since he intended to continue on the bench in addition to serving in his new job as "Commissioner" (his choice of title), or, as the sportswriters dubbed him, "Czar," of baseball.

Unlike the men who followed him in the office, Landis earned a reputation as a "player's commissioner," frequently siding with them in disputes with management.

But Kenesaw maintained a hard approach to any hint of gambling, banning the eight Black Sox players from baseball for life despite repeated pleas that their names be cleared. Landis also would not permit any club owner to have an affiliation with horse racing, making it difficult for such a well-known personality as Bing Crosby to purchase part of the Pittsburgh Pirates.

Landis's first decision involved a young player named Phil Todt, whom Branch Rickey had signed for the Cardinals. Rickey had covered up Todt's status for two years, and the youngster finally broke away and signed with the Browns. Landis awarded him to the Browns. It was the first of many times in which Landis and Rickey clashed. Kenesaw was not a supporter of the idea of a farm system which Rickey was cultivating, and at one point Landis freed hundreds of Cardinal minor leaguers by declaring them free agents.

Landis banned Babe Ruth and Bob Meusel from the first 40 games of the 1922 season after they had defied him and played in exhibition games following the 1921 World Series. Opposing Ruth and Yankee owner Jacob Ruppert required considerable courage, and it clearly established Kenesaw's power over any individual in the game.

Commissioner Landis resigned from the bench in March 1922 to devote his complete time to baseball duties. He restored his salary to $50,000, and eventually it reached $65,000. But Landis cut the figure to $40,000 during the Depression years.

Landis banned New York Giant pitcher Phil Douglas for suggesting that he would leave the club to make the Giants lose the pennant. Also banished were Giant rookie Jimmy O'Connell and coach Cozy Dolan in a bribe case.

A great controversy arose in 1927 involving Ty Cobb and Tris Speaker. Both were implicated in throwing a game in 1919 for the benefit of gamblers. American League president Ban Johnson, acting on an incriminating letter Cobb had written to pitcher Joe Wood, sought permanent banishment of the two great stars. But Landis, battling Johnson as he often did, permitted their careers to continue. Johnson's anger never subsided, and his downfall as league president followed shortly thereafter.

Another Landis antagonist was Browns' owner Phil Ball, who traditionally cast the only vote against Landis when the 16 owners would meet to debate an issue.

A famous incident involving Landis occurred during the 1934 World Series. Landis removed left fielder Joe Medwick of the Cardinals from the final game "for his own protection" when Tiger fans began pelting him with objects from the stands. Another great Cardinal star, Dizzy Dean, was forbidden by Landis to broadcast the 1944 World Series because of his bad grammar and incorrect use of the English language. Landis's 1936 declaration of pitcher Bob Feller as Cleveland property,

his release of Cardinal and Tiger farmhands in 1938 and 1940, respectively, and his banishment of Philadelphia Phillies owner William Cox in 1943 for betting on his own team's games were other notable decisions during his career.

Landis was a personality larger than his decisions. Whatever they were, the fact that one man was making them and his word was law restored any doubts fans may have had concerning the game. Kenesaw may have been dictatorial at times, and perhaps some of his decisions were overly strong, but he was a force that baseball needed at a critical time.

The white-haired Landis, a familiar figure at World Series games with his chin resting on the rail in front of him, ruled baseball for 25 years. Kenesaw maintained homes in Glencoe, Illinois, and Belleair, Florida. He was in poor health for the majority of his final nine years as commissioner, but he was nevertheless elected to a new seven-year term on November 17, 1944. Eight days later, however, he died at St. Luke's Hospital in Chicago at the age of 78.

The following month, Kenesaw Mountain Landis was voted into the Hall of Fame, where he had made the dedication speech in 1939.

Robert Granville Lemon (b. 1920)

Bob Lemon was one of the few modern players to make the conversion from hitter to pitcher, a conversion he achieved so well that he wound up winning over 200 games.

Robert Granville Lemon was born on September 22, 1920, in San Bernardino, California, the younger of two children. He was raised in the Long Beach area, where his parents Earl (an iceman) and Ruth Lemon, were known as "Ma and Pa" throughout most of the neighborhood.

Bob began playing ball while he was a student at Laurel Grammar School. He continued to develop as a ballplayer through Jefferson Junior High and into Woodrow Wilson High School, where he was a shortstop and a pitcher.

It was in this dual role that Cleveland Indians' scout Johnny Angel signed him to a $500 bonus in 1938. Lemon used the money to buy a Model-T Ford and drove to Springfield, Ohio, to begin his professional career. Lou Boudreau and Jim Hegan, who were later teammates in the major leagues, were also members of the Middle Atlantic League team, where Bob appeared in 7 games and collected four hits. He was soon moved to Oswego (Canadian–American League), where he appeared in 75 games as a shortstop and outfielder, batting .312.

Had Bob not decided to enter baseball, he would probably have been quite content as a gas station operator. He was an unpretentious man with simple tastes, and he was content with the minor league apprenticeship the Indians had arranged for him.

Lemon was back at Springfield in 1939, appearing in 80 games and hitting .293 before finishing the year with New Orleans, (Southern League), where he hit .309 in 52 games. There was nothing at this point to indicate that Bob would be anything less than successful as a hitter. At 6' and 180 pounds, the lefthanded-hitting, righthanded-throwing Lemon was just approaching his prime.

Bob spent the 1940 and 1941 seasons at Wilkes-Barre of the Eastern League. He played third base and hit .301 in the latter season, earning a late season promotion to the Indians, for whom he collected a single in four at bats.

He repeated the pattern in 1942, hitting .268 for Baltimore (International League) and getting into one game at third for the Indians at the end of the year.

World War II then interrupted Bob's career. He put in three seasons with the Navy, stationed on the West Coast and in Hawaii. In 1944 he married Jane McGee, and they had three sons.

In 1946, at the age of 25, Bob was ready for the majors. He had a good spring training, but he failed to dislodge Kenny Keltner from third base and was thus installed in

Bob Lemon was one of the best hitting pitchers in baseball, earning a career average of .284 as a pinch hitter while recording 20 victories 7 times in his career. He was a good fielding pitcher too, setting a record in 1953 by participating in 15 double plays. (Opposite page) His hurling style.

center field on opening day. He was still there on April 30 when Bob Feller no-hit the Yankees, but it was soon evident that he was having difficulty hitting major league pitching. With his average at only .180, playing-manager Lou Boudreau transferred him to the bullpen, where he spent the remainder of the season adjusting to a new job. He appeared in 32 games, 27 of them in relief, and had a 4–5 record with a 2.49 earned-run average. He seemed to have made the adjustment well, considering that his minor league pitching experience had consisted of two innings.

Except for two games in the outfield in 1947, Bob was now strictly a pitcher. And although he probably could not have remained in the majors with his bat, as a pitcher he was recognized as one of the best hitters in the game. He collected a career total of 37 home runs, many of them as a pinch-hitter, and he hit as many as 7 homers in one season (1949). As a pinch-hitter, Lemon had a .284 career mark.

Bob's experience as an infielder also stayed with him, and he became one of the best fielding pitchers in baseball. Five times he led the league in putouts and six times he was tops in assists. In 1953 he set a major league record by participating in 15 double plays.

Lemon began the 1947 season in the bullpen, but on July 31 he moved into the starting rotation and proceeded to win 10 consecutive games. He finished the season with an 11–5 record, and was ready for his first full year as a starting pitcher.

The year 1948 turned out to be a great success for both Bob and the Indians. He had a 20–14 record, and led the league in complete games and innings pitched. He hurled 10 shutouts, including a 2–0 no-hitter against the Tigers on June 30. He made the All-Star team (his first of seven consecutive selections) and was named Pitcher of the Year by *The Sporting News* (an honor that was repeated in 1950 and 1954).

Meanwhile, the Indians won the American League pennant with a playoff victory over Boston, and then went on to beat the Braves in the World Series, as Lemon won both the second and sixth games, the sixth being the final game. It was a fitting climax to a sensational season.

And Lemon, for all that, was just beginning to make his mark. He won 20 games seven times between 1948 and 1956, missing only in 1951 and 1955, although his 18 victories in 1955 tied him for the league lead. Only Walter Johnson, Lefty Grove, and Eddie Plank had previously recorded seven 20-victory campaigns in the American League.

Bob was 22–10 in 1949 and 23–11 in 1950; in the latter year he also led the

league with 170 strikeouts. He was 17–14 in 1951, but then 22–11 in 1952 and 21–15 in 1953. The Indians had good teams during those five years and their pitching staff was the toast of baseball, but the Yankees won the pennant every year. The Indians came close in 1951, but a perfect bunt by Phil Rizzuto in a late-September game found Lemon holding the ball as Joe DiMaggio raced home to beat Cleveland and send the Yanks on to the pennant. In 1952 the Yankee margin over the Tribe was only two games. In 1953 the Yanks edged the Indians by 8½.

But things were different in 1954. Lemon was 23–7, tying teammate Early Wynn for the most wins in the league. Mike Garcia added 19, Art Houtteman 15, and Bob Feller 13. The Indians won 111 games, an American League record, and topped the Yankees by 8 full games.

The New York Giants, however, swept the World Series from Cleveland in four straight, using their late-season momentum to walk over Al Lopez' team. Bob lost two of the four games in the Series, marking his final appearances on a pennant-winning club.

Lemon was 18–10 in 1955 and 20–14 in 1956, his seventh and final visit to the 20-victory circle.

Then a leg injury in 1957, followed by an elbow injury in 1958, brought Bob's career to a close. He fell to a 6–11 record in 1957, and was then 0–1 in 1958 before the Indians sent him to San Diego (Pacific Coast League), for whom he was 2–5 before calling it a career. His major league record, all with Cleveland, was 207–128 for a brilliant .618 winning percentage, a percentage topped by only 13 twentieth-century pitchers in the Hall of Fame.

Bob never had trouble landing a baseball job after his playing days were over. He moved around often, but was always in demand.

In 1959 he was a scout for the Indians, and in 1960 he was the club's pitching coach through May 7, when a managerial change forced his release and the close of his long association with Cleveland. In 1961, Gene Mauch hired him as the Philadelphia pitching coach, but he was back in the American League the following year, beginning a seven year association with the Angels.

In 1962 and 1963 he was a pitching instructor and scout for the Angels, and in 1964 he became manager of their top minor league club, Hawaii (Pacific Coast League). He finished sixth that season and in 1965 and 1966 moved on to manage Seattle (Pacific Coast League) where he finished second and then first and captured Minor League Manager of the Year honors from *The Sporting News*.

In 1967 and 1968 he was back in the majors as the Angels' pitching coach, and then in 1969 he returned to the Coast League as manager of Vancouver, finishing second.

In 1970 the Kansas City Royals, in only their second season, named Bob as pitching coach, but on June 8 he was tabbed to succeed Charlie Metro as manager. Bob finished fourth that year, but in 1971 he brought the Royals into a tie for second and earned himself the runner-up spot in Manager of the Year voting. In 1972 the club slipped back to fourth, but Bob's job was not considered in danger until a Los Angeles newspaper quoted him as saying that he was looking forward to his retirement some day, thus prompting Royals owner Ewing Kauffman to seek a man with a more youthful attitude. At age 52, Lemon was fired.

He scouted for the Royals in 1973, and was back in the Coast League in 1974 as manager of Sacramento, a last-place club in a tiny ballpark with a lot of fans and a 232-foot left-field foul line. The club belted 305 home runs that year, and Bob laughingly said he had to wear a golf glove in the dugout just to shake hands after his men circled the bases.

In 1975 he was hired as a scout by the Atlanta Braves, but upon the death in mid-season of Richmond manager Clint Courtney, Lemon took the helm and won 31 of 71 games with the International League club.

In 1976, the year of his election to the Hall of Fame (belatedly, many felt), Bob was named pitching coach of the New York Yankees, the team he had once rivaled so fiercely. A year later, he was selected to manage the Chicago White Sox. He was named Manager of the Year by United Press International for leading his team to 90 wins and a strong third place finish before a record home attendance in 1977, but in 1978, with the White Sox slipping, he was fired.

A few days later he was hired by the slumping Yankee team to replace Billy Martin. Lemon became the first replacement manager to lead a team to a pennant, piloting the Yankees to a sensational comeback which culminated in a World Series victory over the Dodgers.

ROBERT GRANVILLE LEMON

Cleveland 1946–1958

G	IP	W	L	Pct.	H	R	ER	SO	BB	ERA
460	2849	207	128	.618	2559	1185	1024	1277	1251	3.23

Bob Lemon throws a hard one. He learned to pitch after joining the Cleveland Indians in 1946 as a third baseman.

Buck Leonard (b.1907)

Known as "the black Lou Gehrig" during his years in the Negro Leagues, Buck Leonard never had the opportunity to play before major league fans. By the time blacks were admitted to the majors, Buck was too old to join them.

Walter Fenner Leonard was born on September 8, 1907, in Rocky Mount, North Carolina, which remained his lifelong home. His parents had six children, three of them boys. His father worked as a railroad fireman.

Buck was nicknamed by his brother, who could not pronounce "Buddy," his parents' pet name for Walter. Leonard attended Lincoln Elementary School in Rocky Mount and went on to graduate from high school through correspondence courses. As a youngster, he worked as a shoeshine boy to help supplement the family income.

Baseball was Buck's only sport. He played on the sandlots of Rocky Mount with the Elks and the Black Swans while working for the Atlantic Coast Railroad. When the Depression hit, Buck lost his job on the railroad. He was playing semipro ball with the Portsmouth Firefighters in Virginia in 1933 when Ben Taylor, a former first baseman with the Indianapolis club of the Negro League, signed him to play for the Baltimore Stars, whom Taylor now managed.

The Negro Leagues offered little security, but Buck direly needed a job. In his own words, "Life in Negro baseball was tough. It was tough in our Negro National League, and when you went down to the Negro Southern League, it was tougher." Salaries were low, and on the road players received 60 cents per day for expenses. Eventually, meal money reached two dollars per day, and Buck's salary eventually rose to $1000 per month, third in the league behind Satchel Paige and Josh Gibson. His peak salary was paid in 1948 when he earned $10,000, but that required playing 12 months per year and some 250 games. Like most Negro League stars, Buck spent his winters playing ball in Mexico or the Carribean.

Leonard's experience with the Baltimore team was shortlived. The club ran out of money while on a trip to New York, and it disbanded right there, leaving all the players stranded.

Buck got a job with the Brooklyn Royal Giants later that same season. Shortly thereafter, he met Smokey Joe Williams, a great Negro League pitcher who was running a Harlem bar at the time. Williams knew of Buck's prowess in the field and at bat, and he arranged for Leonard to sign with the Homestead Grays in 1934 for a salary of $125 per month. The Grays were a

prestigious team and the salary was decent. Buck spent the next 17 seasons playing first base for Homestead, forming a great 1-2 power punch for many years with the legendary Homestead catcher, Josh Gibson.

As a first baseman, Buck was considered sensational. He had a powerful throwing arm and great agility, causing some to compare him as a fielder with Hal Chase. The stocky, 5'10" 185-pounder usually hit in the high .300s, and on occasion topped the .400 mark. No accurate records were kept by the league, however, and Buck's actual records, like those of Gibson and Satchel Paige, are not available. Leonard is credited with leading the league in 1948 with a .391 batting average, and in 1945 he finished second to Gibson, hitting .375 to Josh's .393.

Buck usually batted fourth in the Grays' lineup, behind Gibson. It cut down his RBI production somewhat, but he was usually among the league leaders regardless. Gibson's many home runs had earned him the title "the black Babe Ruth," and first baseman Leonard became "the black Lou Gehrig." Buck, a lefthanded hitter and thrower, always used a Gehrig-style bat and pounded out line drives.

Buck's first experience with winter ball occurred in 1935 when he played in Puerto Rico with an American all-star team. In 1936 he played for Marianao, a Cuban League team, and then for American all-star teams in Cuba in 1938 and 1939. The winter of 1940–1941 was spent with Mayaguez, Puerto Rico.

Buck was a member of Satchel Paige's all-stars in California in the winter of 1942, teaming with Paige and Gibson and playing stars of the major leagues. But the series did not last long, for Commissioner Landis, thinking that the barnstorming games took away from the "organized nature" of major league ball, stopped the exhibitions.

Buck played in Caracas, Venezuela, with Jackie Robinson, Roy Campanella, and others in 1945 and 1949. In the winter of 1945–1946, he also barnstormed with Dan Bankhead's all-stars. It was a fast-moving, well-traveled life. A cheerful, happy person, Buck was always glad to see new sights and meet new people. He was considered a fine team man wherever he went.

Meanwhile, Leonard and Gibson were leading Homestead to the most successful record in the Negro Leagues. The Grays won championships from 1937 through

1945, and in 1948; the club lost the playoffs between the first- and second-place teams only in 1939. Buck himself was selected to play in 12 Negro League All-Star games, and he batted .273 with three home runs in those highly popular matchups.

Gibson and Leonard were particularly adept at packing Washington's Griffith Stadium, and in the early 1940s Senators' owner Clark Griffith toyed with the idea of signing the pair. He even brought the two sluggers into his office to discuss the possibility with them, but mindful of the controversy it would raise, Griffith changed his mind.

By the time Jackie Robinson was ready to enter professional baseball in 1946, Buck was 38 years old. When Bill Veeck offered him a job with the St. Louis Browns in 1952, Leonard thought that he was too old for the tough competition of the major leagues. He believed the Negro Leagues, at their best, were comparable only to Triple-A ball. In his opinion they lacked the depth that major league clubs had.

The Homestead Grays folded at the end of the 1950 season, and the Negro National League soon expired as black players now entered organized ball. Buck then went to Mexico to spend three seasons with Torreon. He played winter ball in 1951 at Obregon, Mexico, and the following three winters at Jalapa, Mexico. Buck also played briefly with the Portsmouth club in the Class B Piedmont League in 1953. In 1954 and 1955, he played for Durango in the Mexican Central League, finally retiring as a player at the age of 48.

Buck returned to Rocky Mount, where he served as a truant officer for 11 years. He also spent a year as Rocky Mount's recreation director. Buck became a director of the Rocky Mount team in the Carolina League, and he was president of Buck Leonard's Realty Agency.

In 1972 the Hall of Fame Committee on the Negro Leagues selected him for membership in the Baseball Hall of Fame. At last Buck Leonard joined the men in the Hall of Fame with whom he had never been permitted to play.

WALTER FENNER LEONARD

Negro Leagues 1933–1950
Mexican League 1951–1955

No records available.

(Top picture) First baseman Buck Leonard of the Homestead Grays tags out a base runner in Washington, D.C., in 1946. (Below) In a 1944 game, Leonard is run down between bases by Baltimore third baseman Snow and catcher Clark. The other Grays' base runner, at far left, is Josh Gibson. (Opposite page) Leonard's batting stance, front foot impatiently hovering above the ground.

Fred Lindstrom (b. 1905)

Fred Lindstrom found fame and misfortune in the major leagues before his nineteenth birthday, and then settled into a steady career which netted him a .311 career average.

Frederick Charles Lindstrom was born in Chicago, Illinois, on November 21, 1905. He was the youngest of five children born to Mary Sweeney and Fred Lindstrom, Sr., a plumbing contractor.

As a youngster, Fred was a pitcher in the public parks of Chicago and at the All Saints and Mark Sheridan Grammar Schools. Not until he entered Tilden High School did he switch to the infield. Eventually he transferred to Loyola Academy where his coach was Jake Weimer, a former major league pitcher who had broken in with the hometown Cubs back in 1903, winning 20 games in each of his first two seasons.

Jake was one of many scholastic coaches throughout the country who would at times tip off John McGraw of the Giants when a good prospect came along. Lindstrom was such a prospect, and McGraw dispatched his top scout, Dick Kinsella, to check on Freddy. The reports were sound, and Lindstrom was signed to a Giant contract upon graduation from Loyola in 1922.

He was assigned to Toledo of the American Association, where he played 18 games at third base, hitting .304. It was a fine accomplishment for a 16-year-old playing Triple-A ball.

In 1923 Fred was again at Toledo, with McGraw keeping close tabs on him. He played in 147 games and batted .270 with one home run. Some considered it a disappointing year, but considering the boy's age, McGraw was pleased. In addition, Fred was much overshadowed by the Toledo first baseman Bill Terry, who batted .377 and received a late-season call from the Giants. The sensation Terry created in spring training of 1924 took much of the pressure off Lindstrom.

Heinie Groh, the veteran star of "bottle bat" fame, was manning the third base slot on the Giants that year, and Lindstrom made the team with the idea of sitting beside McGraw in the dugout and learning about the National League. But Groh, who was enjoying a fine .290 season, tore his knee late in the year and was sidelined. The Giants were in a pennant race, and they had no other choice than to turn third base over to Lindstrom. Fred responded by collecting 20 hits in 79 at bats for a .253 average as the Giants marched on to a fourth consecutive pennant.

At 18 years and 10 months, Lindstrom thus became the youngest man ever to appear in a World Series. And not only did he appear, but by virtue of Groh's injury he was both a regular and the leadoff hitter. Forming an infield with Bill Terry, Frankie Frisch, and Travis Jackson, Freddy was anxious for the meeting with the Washing-

ton Senators. And he dazzled the fans in the fifth game when he banged out four hits in five times at bat. All the papers were aglow with accounts of the teenage wonder.

The Giants won that fifth game, but Washington tied the Series the next day, setting up the decisive seventh game in Washington on October 10. Unfortunately, it was not Fred Lindstrom's day.

The Giants led, 3–1, after seven, but in the eighth Bucky Harris hit a grounder to Lindstrom, which hit a pebble and bounced over his head for a hit, scoring the tying runs. The game was still tied after nine, and the Senators brought in the great Walter Johnson to pitch. Finally, in the twelfth inning, Giants catcher Hank Gowdy dropped a foul pop, giving Muddy Ruel a life, and then a double. That brought up Earl McNeely and he proceeded to hit another grounder to Lindstrom. The players were all convinced that a power greater than they controlled fate that afternoon, for again the ball hit a pebble, and again it went over Lindstrom's head. The Senators were World Champions—the only World Series they ever won.

Lindstrom was miserable, and in fact he was never forgotten for the unfortunate events, although on neither ball was he charged with an error. And by hitting .333 for the Series he had really made a fine impression on baseball.

In 1925 Groh was back at third and Fred served as a utility infielder, appearing in 104 games at second, short, and third, batting .287 with a dozen triples. But in 1926 it was Groh who became the utility man, with Lindstrom the third baseman. Freddy hit .302 that season with nine homers.

At 5'11" and 170 pounds, the righthanded-hitting Lindstrom could have used the Polo Grounds' short foul lines for more home runs, but he was not the sort who would swing for distance. He was a line-drive hitter who seldom went after the long ball, and although he reached a high of 22 homers in 1930, his 13-year total was only 103 and he was never regarded as a true long-ball threat.

Fred hit .306 in 1927, bringing his lifetime batting average over .300 to stay. He scored 107 runs for the Giants that year and was considered by many to be the heart of their attack. But the Giants never won another pennant during Fred's stay.

On Valentine's Day in 1928, Fred married the former Irene Kiedaisch, whom he had known since childhood. They had three sons, and Chuck, the youngest, became a catcher who appeared in one game for the

Fred Lindstrom throws the ball from third base. After several years as a star in that position, Lindstrom moved to center field where his strong throwing arm served him well.

1958 Chicago White Sox. Another son, Fred, served as the director of Chicago's Urban Renewal Program in the 1970s.

Fred enjoyed a fine season in 1928, playing 153 games and leading the league's third basemen in fielding. At bat, he topped the National League with 231 hits and batted .358, third in the league behind Rogers Hornsby and Paul Waner. His 330 total bases were second only to the Cardinals' Jim Bottomley, and he stole a career high of 15 bases. But the Giants were nosed out of the pennant by St. Louis.

Fred dropped to .319 in 1929, which was still a fine average, but he really was sensational in 1930, batting .379 in a year in which the league averaged .303. Fred's average was fifth best in the league, and his 231 hits included three games in which he collected five safeties (April 26, May 8, and July 10). It was a record which stood until 1948 when Stan Musial had four games of five hits in one season. Lindstrom hit his 22 home runs that season and drove in 106 runs, giving him a three-year record of 51 homers, 304 RBIs, and a .353 batting average.

In Philadelphia in 1931, Freddy broke his leg while he was sliding. This accident cut his season to 78 games and made his average dip to .300. Further disappointment came his way in 1932, the year in which Terry replaced McGraw as manager. Lindstrom had hoped to be considered for the job, but instead he found himself passed over and on December 12 he was traded to Pittsburgh in a three-team deal which also involved the Phillies. Thus his Giant career came to a close.

By now Freddy was seeing little action at third base, for in 1931 McGraw, feeling the need for a quality player at center field, had moved Fred to that position. Lindstrom rather enjoyed the switch, and his strong arm enabled him to gain recognition as a fine outfielder.

With the Pirates, Fred batted .310 and .290 in two seasons, the first of which almost saw Pittsburgh beat out New York for the pennant. But the 1934 Pirates were fifth, and on November 22, the day after his twenty-ninth birthday, Lindstrom was traded to the Cubs with Larry French for Babe Herman, Guy Bush, and Jim Weaver. The deal pleased Fred, for he now had the opportunity to play in his hometown. Furthermore, the Cubs had a strong team, and went on to win the 1935 pennant. Lindstrom batted .275 in the regular season and .200 in the World Series loss to Detroit.

Although he was only 30, Fred had slowed down a great deal, and the Cubs released him after the Series. He signed with the Brooklyn Dodgers on January 26, 1936, and then appeared in 26 games, batting .264 before announcing his retirement on May 18, at the age of 31. A change of heart the following winter failed to stir the Dodgers' interest.

Fred did a daily radio sports program in Chicago in 1937 and 1938 and looked after some real estate investments in northern Wisconsin. He enjoyed hunting with old friends like Dave Bancroft and Burleigh Grimes, but he welcomed the opportunity to return to organized ball in 1940 as manager of Knoxville (Southern Association). He spent two seasons there, and in 1942 his old roommate Bill Terry asked him to manage the Giants' farm club in Fort Smith (Western Association). It turned out to be his last job in professional baseball.

During World War II, Fred filled in as acting postmaster in Evanston, Illinois. When the regular postmaster returned from the war, Fred spent a year lecturing to Chicago high school students on traffic safety. His qualifications were said to stem from his reputation for good sportsmanship. In 1947, Fred was appointed baseball coach at Northwestern University, a position he held until 1960. He was named an assistant professor at the school, quite an honor for a man who had never attended college.

When his coaching was behind him, Fred was again named postmaster in Evanston, this time on a permanent basis, and he held the job until his retirement in 1972. With that, he left Chicago and moved with his wife to Port Richey, Florida, where he became a proficient golfer. A heart attack in 1975 set him back temporarily, but then he continued his daily round on the links.

The Baseball Writers Association never gave him more than seven votes in any Hall of Fame election, but in 1976 the Committee on Veterans evaluated his career and selected him for membership in the Hall.

FREDERICK CHARLES LINDSTROM

New York (N.L.) 1924–1932
Pittsburgh 1933–1934
Chicago (N.L.) 1935
Brooklyn 1936

G	AB	R	H	2B	3B	HR	RBI	Avg.
1438	5611	895	1747	301	81	103	779	.311

Ted Lyons (b. 1900)

Ted Lyons jumped directly from college into the major leagues and spent his entire 21-year career with one club, the Chicago White Sox.

Theodore Amar Lyons was born on December 28, 1900, in Lake Charles, Louisiana, of Scotch-Irish descent. His father was a cattle rancher, and Ted had two brothers and a sister. In 1902 the Lyons family moved to Vinton, Louisiana.

Ted was a second base star at Vinton High School in addition to participating in basketball. He spent a substantial part of his free time playing semipro ball. College rules were not quite so strict in those days, and the semipro experience did not hurt Ted's eligibility when he entered college.

Interested in a law career, Ted was accepted at Baylor University in 1919. He tried out for coach Frank Bridges's baseball team, but the squad was overloaded with infielders, and Bridges suggested that Lyons try his hand at pitching. The 5'11", 200-pound righthander made the team and compiled a 10–2 record as a freshman.

News from the Waco, Texas, campus traveled rapidly. Harry Davis, representing Connie Mack's Philadelphia Athletics, offered Ted full payment for his education if he would sign at once with the A's. Ted declined the offer, as well as a similar one from the Cleveland Indians.

Lyons continued to shine at Baylor. In 1921 he first tried a knuckleball after seeing a magazine photograph of Philadelphia's Ed Rommel holding one. The pitch would later be very important in Ted's career.

By the time his junior year had passed, Ted had compiled a 27–8 record for Baylor. In his senior year, the Chicago White Sox were training in Waco, and Bridges summoned the Sox catcher, Ray Schalk, to watch Lyons pitch. Local newspaper photographers thought it would make a great picture to have Schalk warm up Lyons, but it turned into more than that when Ray returned to the White Sox with a glowing report. Shortly thereafter, Charles Comiskey himself signed Lyons to a $1000 bonus and a $300-per-month contract, which included the stipulation that Ted would not be demoted to the minor leagues but rather would spend at least his first full year in the major leagues.

It was not a difficult promise for Comiskey to maintain since the White Sox were still suffering from the expulsion of eight players following the investigation of the 1919 World Series fix. For many years the Sox were unable to climb back into contention; in fact, it was not until 1959 that the team captured another pennant. Thus Lyons never pitched for a pennant winner, spending 16 of his 21 seasons with second-division clubs. That only made his pitching accomplishments all the more impressive.

Ted made his major league debut on his

first day with the White Sox, July 2, 1923. Directly out of Baylor, Lyon was attending his first major league game when acting manager Eddie Collins called him to the mound to face the St. Louis Browns. Ted retired the first three batters in his relief assignment in the losing cause. He finished his rookie season with nine appearances and a 2–1 record, although his earned-run average was an unimpressive 6.26. He also saw action in the city series against the Cubs that fall.

Employing a sneaky fastball, Ted produced a 12–11 mark in his first full season the following year, and he cut his ERA to a still-high 4.88. But in 1925, his second full season, Lyons tied for the American League lead in victories with 21 and led the league in shutouts with five. He was not overpowering on the mound (only 45 strikeouts in 263 innings), but he had mastered the art of getting batters out. In September, he came within one out of a perfect game, spoiled by a hit by Washington's Bobby Veach.

On August 21, 1926, en route to an 18–16 season, Ted pitched a no-hitter against the Red Sox.

In 1927 Ted notched what may have been his greatest season. He again tied for the league leadership in victories (posting a 22–14 record), and he topped the league with 308 innings pitched and 30 complete games in 34 starts.

Ted usually seemed able to finish the games he started. In his career, Lyons recorded 356 complete games in 484 starts. From 1937 until the end of his career, he was never once used in relief, a tribute to his consistency on the mound in starting assignments.

Ted was also a good hitter, which caused him to boast. His career batting average was .233, not bad for a pitcher, and in 1930 he hit .311. A switch-hitter, Ted managed to belt two doubles in one inning in 1935 to tie a major league record. Lyons was a good runner and fielder as well.

Not once in his career did Ted strike out 100 batters in a single season, but such hitters as Babe Ruth and Tris Speaker spoke of his abilities with respect. Because of his longevity Lyons proved to be a difficult pitcher for two great hitters from such different eras as Ty Cobb and Ted Williams.

Lyons won 22 games again in 1930, leading the league with 298 innings and 29 complete games. It was the third and last time he reached the 20-victory mark. His career total of 260 wins would doubtless have been higher had he pitched for better clubs. The lack of strong support accounts also for his failure to earn All-Star accolades, for he was selected only once (1939) and did not appear in the game.

The Ted Lyons windup. His pitching always presented a problem to batters, who seldom guessed what was coming at them. His fastball had a little extra on it, and, half way through his career, Lyons perfected an exceptional knuckle ball.

On two occasions, Ted lost 20 games in a season; he posted a 14–20 mark in 1929 and a 10–21 record in 1933. One of his most memorable pitching performances occurred on May 4, 1929, when he lost a 21-inning game to Detroit by a 6–5 score. Ted went the distance in that game, opposed for the first 20 innings by George Uhle, with Lil Stoner pitching the final inning for the victory.

During spring training in 1931, the White Sox played an unusual night exhibition game against the Giants. Letting loose a curveball to a Giant hitter, Lyons felt something pop in his right shoulder. He probably should have missed the entire 1931 season, but he struggled through it with a 4–6 record for 101 innings. Early in the year, he began serious work on the knuckleball which came to be the salvation of his career. By late-season, Lyons was ready to throw it. The pitch provided Ted with another 12 seasons out of a career that many feared was over.

True, Lyons was not the pitcher he once had been, but he was also over 30, and the White Sox were not any better. Ted recorded a 15–8 mark in 1935 and compiled a 14–6 record in both 1939 and 1942, his best victory seasons after the injury. Otherwise, Lyons was basically a crafty pitcher with a .500 percentage.

A popular, outgoing, and friendly man, Ted was a roommate of Monty Stratton in 1938, the year before Stratton lost a leg in a hunting accident. That season, Stratton and Lyons became "Sunday pitchers" as the crowd-hungry White Sox would save both men for the big attendance day, Sunday. The pair would each work only once per week. The strategy proved most effective in 1938 when the two captured 15 of 16 decisions on Sundays.

A 42-year-old bachelor when World War II broke out, Ted could easily have avoided service because of his age. But he enlisted in the Marines and saw combat in the Pacific, missing three full years of baseball (1943–1945). The White Sox told him that he could have a coaching job when he returned, but the 1942 season—when Ted was 14–6 with a league-leading 2.10 ERA—had been one of his best, and he was eager to resume his career as a player.

Returning in 1946 as the oldest player in baseball, Ted pitched in five games, compiling a 1–4 record with a 2.30 earned-run average. That wrapped up his career with a 260–230 record.

A development that occurred on May 25, 1946 probably had more to do with ending Lyon's pitching career than anything else. On that date he was named to replace Jimmie Dykes as manager of the White Sox. Ted never pitched in another game. Under Dykes, Chicago had posted a 10–20 record. Under Lyons, the club managed to win 64 and lose 60 during the remainder of the season to finish fifth.

Ted was the boss for the entire season of 1947, but the Sox finished sixth at 70–84, 27 games behind the Yankees. In 1948 Chicago finished last, winning only 51 games, and Ted was fired at the end of the season. After 26 years, Lyons was no longer under contract to the White Sox.

Ted went over to the Detroit Tigers as a coach in 1949, remaining with the club through 1953. In his last season with the Tigers, he became acting manager one day after Fred Hutchinson had been ejected from the game. Lyons thus had the opportunity to insert Al Kaline into a lineup for the first time. Like Lyons, Kaline had gone directly into the majors from school, and Al likewise spent his entire career with one club.

Ted coached for the Dodgers in 1954, after which he returned to the White Sox as a southeastern scout from 1955 to 1966. In his first year back with Chicago, Ted Lyons was elected to the Hall of Fame.

After his retirement in 1966, Ted devoted his entire time to a 760-acre rice farm in Vinton, leased by himself and his sister.

THEODORE AMAR LYONS

Chicago (A.L.) 1923–1942, 1946

G	IP	W	L	Pct.	H	R	ER	SO	BB	ERA
594	4162	260	230	.531	4489	2056	1696	1073	1121	3.67

Connie Mack (1862-1956)

Connie Mack managed the Philadelphia Athletics for 50 years, winning nine pennants. But his greatest contribution was the dignity he imparted to the game in its formative years early in this century.

He was born Cornelius McGillicuddy on December 22, 1862, in East Brookfield, Massachusetts, a town of some 300 people. He was one of seven children of Michael and Mary McGillicuddy, Irish immigrants. His father, who worked in a cotton mill, was a Union soldier in the Civil War when Connie was born. The elder McGillicuddy died when Connie was still a youth, leaving Mary to rear the family. Connie left school at the age of 16 to take a job at the Green and Twitchell Shoe Factory in East Brookfield. Work did not bother the youngster since he had first toiled at 35 cents per day in the same mill as his father when he was nine years old.

Meanwhile, Connie fell in love with baseball, which was just finding its roots in America. He became a catcher on the East Brookfield team, the Central Massachusetts champions, and bore the nickname "Slats" because of his long, lean build.

In 1883 Cap Anson brought his team to East Brookfield to play an exhibition game. Connie was fascinated by the lure of professional baseball, and one year later he was summoned to report to Meriden, a team in the Connecticut State League. A friend, William Hogan, had recommended Connie to his manager when the team was without a catcher. Connie staged a brief holdout to get a salary of $90 per month, and that year saw his name shortened to "Connie Mack" so that it would fit into newspaper box scores.

Catching was a difficult chore in the 1880s. Catchers wore no protection, stood 15 feet behind the batter, and caught the underhanded deliveries on the bounce. Connie was a favorite of the Meriden fans, who presented him with a gold watch at the end of the season for his rugged performance.

Connie jumped to Hartford in 1885, where he eventually earned $125 per month. Late in the season he appeared in one game for Newark of the Eastern League, and then returned to Hartford of the Eastern League in 1886, catching 69 games and batting .248. While never much of a hitter, Mack as a catcher helped to pioneer overhand pitching and was among the first to move under the hitter's bat when assuming his position. He also developed the pesky habit of tipping the bat if it could help prevent a hit.

Connie reached the major leagues in September 1886 when he was sold to Washington with four other players for $3500. He caught 10 games for the club and batted .361.

In 1887 Connie married William Hogan's sister, Margaret. They had three children, but she died at the age of 26, leaving Mack

a young widower with a family. Connie's mother cared for the children while he played ball. Mack eventually remarried in 1910, producing another five children with his second wife, Katherine Hallahan.

Connie spent three full seasons as a catcher for Washington. His best year was 1889 when he batted .293 and earned $2750. In 1890 Mack joined the Brotherhood of Professional Baseball Players and invested his life savings in the Buffalo club of the new Players' League. The league folded after one year, and Connie lost all his money.

Returning to the National League, he joined Pittsburgh in 1891 and remained with the club through the 1896 season. On September 3, 1894, he was appointed manager of the team but was fired after a sixth-place finish in 1896. That concluded his major league playing career as well; he showed a .251 career batting average for 695 games. A broken left ankle, incurred during a game with Boston in 1893, brought an early end to his effectiveness as an athlete.

At this point, his friend Ban Johnson, presiding over the Western League, asked Connie to manage the Milwaukee club. Mack accepted and ran the team for four seasons. When Johnson decided to turn the Western League into the American League, he awarded the Philadelphia franchise to Connie. Mack, who received a 25 percent interest in the team, obtained most of his financial backing from Benjamin F. Shibe of the Reach Sporting Goods Company. Mack thus became manager of the Philadelphia Athletics in 1901, the first season of play in the American League.

Connie set out to raid National League teams of their best players—not too difficult a feat considering the National League had a maximum salary of $2400. John McGraw, viewing the raids, tabbed the Athletics the "White Elephants" in his attempt to demean the new league, and the nickname and symbol stuck with the Athletics throughout their stay in Philadelphia and on to Kansas City. Mack's biggest catch was Napoleon Lajoie, but after one season the Pennsylvania State Supreme Court banned all Philadelphia Phillie players who had jumped to the Athletics from participating in American League games in Philadelphia. Thus Mack lost Lajoie after one year. He did manage to grab Harry Davis, Socks Seybold, Dave Fultz, Chick Fraser, Bill Bernhard, and a Gettysburg College product, Eddie Plank. His first American League club finished fourth.

Connie Mack, dressed as always in stiff white collar and dark suit, steps briskly out of the Athletics dugout to loud cheers at Yankee Stadium in 1949. In New York, as throughout the country, Mack was revered as a leading symbol of baseball's endurance. The following year, Mack's last as Athletics manager, New Yorkers honored him in their traditional way, with a ticker-tape parade.

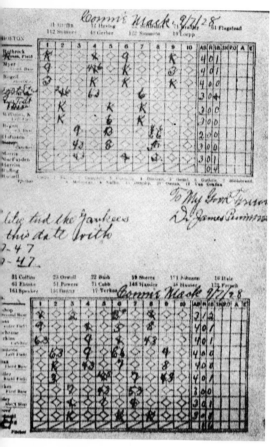

Connie Mack's scorecard for the Philadelphia-Boston game on September 8, 1928. The Athletics won and, as Mack noted on the card, tied the Yankees in the year's standings.

The Athletics played their home games in Columbia Park until the construction of Shibe Park in 1909. The latter became one of the longest-standing stadiums in baseball; in 1953 its name was changed to Connie Mack Stadium.

Connie Mack created a new image for baseball. Unlike many of his contemporaries, particularly among managers, he was kindly and softspoken, never smoked, cursed, or drank heavily. Connie was never ejected by an umpire in his entire baseball career.

Standing 6'1" and weighing 150 pounds, Mack knew that he struck an unimpressive figure in a baseball uniform, and he decided not to wear one when he became a bench manager. Mack always wore a high, stiff collar with a necktie and business suit, alternating between a straw hat and a derby. He became famous for positioning his players during a game by waving a folded scorecard.

Players always held Connie in great respect; all but the eccentric Rube Waddell addressed him as Mr. Mack. Waddell, considered unmanageable until he came under Mack's control, always called him Connie. Many players thought Mack perhaps a bit too tight with the dollar, but he generally ran his club with little capital and twice was forced to sell great players to stabilize the team's financial situation.

The Athletics captured their first pennant in 1902, a year in which no World Series was played. In 1905 Waddell and Plank won 50 games between them, and the A's notched a second pennant. The Giants won the World Series that year in five games. Connie's next two pennants came in 1910 and 1911. In these years he first boasted of his "$100,000 Infield"—composed of Stuffy McInnis, Eddie Collins, Jack Barry, and Home Run Baker. Both of those seasons produced World Series victories.

The Athletics gained pennants again in 1913 and 1914, capturing the World Championship in the former year but losing to the Braves the following season. At that point, Connie broke up his famed team to rebuild with younger, lower-paid players.

After a long, hard struggle, the A's returned to the first division in 1925, coming in second. In the interim, they had finished last for seven consecutive years (1915–1921), losing 100 or more games five times. The Athletics won pennants in 1929, 1930, and 1931, and captured World Championships in 1929 and 1930. But again hard-hit financially and in debt nearly $500,000, Connie broke up his championship unit, dispersing such stars as Al Simmons, Mickey Cochrane, Jimmie Foxx, and Lefty Grove over the ensuing four years. It broke Connie's heart to sell these great players, but it was necessary to salvage the franchise.

In 1930 the city of Philadelphia presented the $10,000 Bok Award to Connie for his great service. The award normally went to scientists or civic developers. During the 1930s, the nation began to view Connie as one of the great men of American athletics. Considered a pioneer in the development of the game, Mack was named to the Hall of Fame in 1937, the second year of elections.

The Athletics finished second in 1932 and third in 1933, but the team then settled into the second division again for the next 14 years, finishing last nine times. The last first-division team that Connie managed was the fourth-place Athletics of 1948.

Mack assumed majority control of the team in December 1940, purchasing enough stock from Shibe's widow to give himself 58 percent ownership of the team. He paid himself a handsome salary and employed his sons Roy, Earle, and Connie, Jr., as club executives.

In 1950, at the age of 87, Connie undertook his fiftieth season as Athletics' manager. No individual of such age was believed to hold an active executive position in the United States. Connie was revered and honored throughout the country, hailed with a ticker-tape parade in New York, and greeted by the President in Washington. He finally retired from the game after the 1950 season, leaving the business end of the team to his sons and the managerial reins to one of his former players, Jimmie Dykes.

The franchise did not remain long thereafter in Philadelphia. The Mack brothers battled each other for control of the club, and the team floundered on the field and at the gate. In 1953 only 362,113 fans paid to see the A's at home. After a last-place finish in 1954, the Macks sold the team to Arnold Johnson, who transferred it to Kansas City.

On October 1, 1955, Connie fell from his bed and fractured his right hip. Confined to a wheel chair thereafter he died on February 8, 1956, at his daughter's home in Germantown, Pennsylvania, at the age of 93.

Mickey Mantle (b. 1931)

The fourth Yankee superstar in the succession of Babe Ruth, Lou Gehrig, and Joe DiMaggio that made the New York team the dominant force in baseball for 40 years was Mickey Mantle.

Mickey Charles Mantle was born in Spavinaw, Oklahoma, on October 22, 1931. He was named "Mickey" after his father's favorite baseball player, Mickey Cochrane, the Hall of Fame catcher of the Philadelphia Athletics. The "Charles" came from his grandfather, a lefthanded thrower who teamed with Mickey's father, Elvin "Mutt" Mantle (a righty), to teach Mick to switch-hit as a young boy. Although he rebelled against their instruction, preferring his natural righthanded stance, he later proved to be the greatest switch-hitter of his time.

The Mantle family moved to Commerce, Oklahoma, where Elvin Mantle worked in the lead mines. Faced with the possibility of spending his life as a miner, Mickey concentrated on sports as the best avenue of escape. His father encouraged him and often traveled with him to St. Louis to see the Cardinals play.

In high school, Mickey played football and baseball. A leg injury during football practice resulted in osteomyelitis of the bone. The disease would keep Mantle out of the army during the Korean war, for which he was unfairly criticized. The disability was genuine, and he suffered from the disease throughout his career.

In 1949 Yankee scout Tom Greenwade watched Mantle belt the ball tremendous distances as he closed his high school career and played on the sandlots. Mickey was a shortstop at that time—not a very good one, but a natural star at the bat. Greenwade offered him a $1150 bonus to sign with the Yankees.

Mantle spent the 1949 season with Independence in the K-O-M (Kansas-Oklahoma-Missouri) League and batted .313 with 7 home runs in 89 games. He also committed 47 errors at shortstop.

In 1950 Mantle was moved to Joplin in the Western Association, where he batted a league-leading .383 with 26 homers, 199 hits, and 141 runs scored. Mantle was ready for the major leagues as a hitter, but his 55 errors convinced Casey Stengel, the Yankee manager, that Mickey would be better in the outfield. Joe DiMaggio had announced that 1951 would be his final season, and Stengel had Mantle in mind as Joe's successor.

Mickey opened the 1951 season in right field, adjacent to DiMaggio. His rookie season in the majors was a frustrating one. Mick struck out too often and felt his confidence fail. The press and the fans were hostile after his big buildup, and Mantle was sent to Kansas City, then a minor-league farm club in the American Association, in midseason. When he spoke dejectedly to his father about quitting, the elder Mantle barked, "Okay, if that's the kind of

stuff you're made of, come back to the lead mines with me!" Mickey returned to the minors, batted .361 in 40 games, and was back in Yankee Stadium by late August.

During the 1951 World Series, Mantle tripped over a drain in right field and was sent to the hospital for surgery on torn knee cartilage. There he shared a room with his dad, who was stricken with Hodgkin's disease and was fated to die in a few months. "Mutt" Mantle never lived to see his son achieve greatness, but he knew the boy had made it to the Yankees to stay at the age of 20.

The injury, one of many which Mantle would encounter in his career, was his most serious. Thereafter, his leg had to be heavily taped by the trainer each day. Near the end of his career, both legs were taped daily. Other injuries plagued him throughout his career, such as pulled groin muscles, pulled hamstring muscles, sprains, shoulder injuries, a bloody hip abscess, and a fracture of the foot.

After DiMaggio's retirement, Mantle moved to center field. In 1954 Mickey led the American League in runs scored, and in 1955 he won his first home run title with 37 four-baggers. All of this was but a prelude to the 1956 season, still considered by many baseball watchers to be his best. It was the year that Mickey made his first assault on Babe Ruth's single-season home run record, finishing the season with 52 and winning baseball's Triple Crown. Mantle batted .300 or better in five consecutive seasons, reaching a career high in 1957 with a .365 mark. He led the American League in batting in 1956 (.353), and in home runs in 1955 (37), 1958 (42), and 1960 (40), in addition to the 52 four-baggers in 1956. Mickey was voted the league's Most Valuable Player in 1956, 1957, and 1962; he missed the coveted honor by only a few votes in 1960 and 1961. Although a runner who could race from home to first base in 3.1 seconds, Mantle is best remembered as one of the greatest power hitters. His longest home run—in Washington in 1953—was measured at 565 feet. Twice he came within inches of being the only man ever to hit a fair ball out of Yankee Stadium. For six years (1963–1968), Mantle earned $100,-000 per year. Endorsements substantially increased his income.

Despite his rise into the ranks of superstars, Mantle was for many years unpopular with the fans, who resented the youthful aspirant to the pedestal of the great DiMaggio. His shyness manifested itself in

(At right) Eighteen-year-old Mantle bats for the Yankee farm team in Joplin, Missouri. Already, Casey Stengel was predicting to sportswriters that Mantle would become a Yankee all-time great. Said Stengel, "I believe that Mantle is our biggest prize, and that he is the number one kid ballplayer in the professional game." (Below) A mature Mantle, having fulfilled the prophesy, blasts one over the wall in 1968.

silence or outbursts of temper when fans or journalists pressed him too insistently. He was much more comfortable with his teammates, particularly his close friends Whitey Ford and Billy Martin, with whom he frequently led a roistering night life.

Mantle's popularity rose in 1961 when Casey Stengel's successor as manager, Ralph Houk, made it clear that Mickey was the team leader. A new antihero, Roger Maris, also came along. Maris, in only his fifth major league season and his second with the Yankees, and Mantle, the "M and M" boys, launched twin challenges to Ruth's record of 60 home runs. Mantle, by now used to publicity, reacted with reserve and maturity, while Maris angered the fans and became the "heavy" in the drama. Maris won the race that year, hitting a record 61 home runs, but Mantle, who belted 54, won over the fans forever. The muscular 200-pound six-footer was now cheered at every park he played in.

Perhaps it was his courageous struggle to overcome his injuries that finally endeared Mantle to the fans. On June 5, 1963, he broke his left foot on the fence in Baltimore, causing him to miss nearly two months of play. Mickey returned to the lineup on August 4 as a pinch-hitter in a 11–10 victory against the same Orioles in Yankee Stadium. The crowd greeted him with a standing ovation. Thinking only of putting his bat on the ball to avoid the embarrassment of striking out (Mantle holds the record for career strikeouts with 1710), he found the first pitch to his liking and smacked an emotion-filled home run.

Mantle's own choice as his most memorable home run was a ninth-inning, game-winning blast in the 1964 World Series off St. Louis Cardinal pitcher Barney Schultz. It was his sixteenth Series home run, breaking Babe Ruth's record (Mantle finished with 18 in Series play). The 1964 World Series was also his twelfth and last. The Yankees captured 12 pennants during Mantle's 18 years on the team.

Following the 1964 season, the Yankee dynasty fell. Mantle's great teammates were leaving. Yogi Berra was fired as manager after the 1964 World Series. Bobby Richardson, Tony Kubek, and Whitey Ford retired shortly thereafter. Elston Howard, Clete Boyer, and Maris were later traded. Mantle outlasted them all, continuing to be the class of a fading team and the biggest attraction in the league. The 16-time All-Star never hit above .300 after 1964, but he played four more seasons, making him the all-time Yankee leader in games played (2401), a remarkable achievement in view of his injuries. A .237 season batting average in his final season (1968) brought his lifetime average below .300 to the figure of .298. His home run totals in the last four years fell to 19, 23, 22, and 18.

During spring training in 1969, Mantle finally decided to quit. "I just can't hit any more," he said.

At retirement ceremonies in Yankee Stadium on June 8, 1969, Mantle was greeted by the sellout crowd with an ovation that lasted nearly 10 minutes. Mick was 37 years old, still handsome, boyish, and shy, and he was deeply moved by the emotional outpouring of the New York fans.

Mantle never really became a New Yorker. He was always the "country boy," and in retirement he returned to his home in Dallas where he had lived since 1956. With him were his wife, Merlyn, and their four sons. Rumors of financial difficulties as a consequence of poor personal management surrounded him, and his immediate business ventures after baseball—a clothing chain, a restaurant chain, and an employment agency in partnership with football star Joe Namath—all failed.

Mantle spent spring trainings with the Yankees in Fort Lauderdale as a special instructor, but he found the job somewhat unrewarding. Mickey was too shy to approach young players with unsolicited advice, and the players were too much in awe of Mantle to approach him easily. He expressed a desire to manage in the major leagues, but a vacancy in his hometown on the Texas Rangers was filled by his old friend Billy Martin.

In Dallas, Mantle played golf and did public relations work for a bank. He served as a television announcer for NBC in 1970 and earned plaudits for his charm on the air, but he left in the final month of the season to coach first base for the Yankees.

Mickey Mantle was elected to the Hall of Fame in his first year of eligibility, the seventh man to achieve that distinction. He was named on January 16, 1974, the same day as Whitey Ford.

MICKEY CHARLES MANTLE

New York (A.L.) 1951–1968

G	AB	R	H	2B	3B	HR	RBI	Avg.
2401	8102	1677	2415	344	72	536	1509	.298

Number 500 for Mantle. Elston Howard and the Yankee bat boy greet Mantle at home plate following his five-hundredth home run on May 14, 1967. Mantle hit the big one off the Orioles' Stu Miller, giving the Yanks a 6–5 win.

Heinie Manush (1901-1971)

Heinie Manush compiled a lifetime .330 batting average while playing for six major league clubs.

Henry Emmett Manush was born on July 20, 1901, in Tuscumbia, Alabama, the youngest of seven boys. Three of the boys played professional ball. Frank, the oldest, played 23 games at third base for the Philadelphia Athletics in 1908 and batted .255. Ernest played only minor league ball.

Heinie was an outstanding baseball player in high school, and he continued to develop his talents during two years at Massey Military Academy in Pulaski, Tennessee. Although his brother had brought home money for playing ball, Heinie did not foresee professional baseball in his future. He took a job as an apprentice pipefitter and traveled to Salt Lake City, Utah, to work in a refinery. There Heinie played first base for the company team; he also spent some time in Los Angeles playing in a semipro winter league.

It was during this period that Heinie was scouted and signed to his first professional contract by the Detroit Tigers. Leaving his pipefitting days behind, he was assigned to Edmonton of the Western Canada League. He never played first base there, for the club had a pretty good prospect named Babe Herman handling the position, so Heinie was converted into a left fielder.

Manush batted .321 in 83 games at Edmonton, leading the league with nine homers. However, he was not really a power hitter and never belted more than 14 home runs in the majors, collecting only 110 four-baggers for his career. Heinie actually choked up on the bat and was an outstanding line-drive hitter. At first he was strictly a pull hitter, but in later years he managed to hit to the opposite field. Four times Heinie had more than 200 hits in a single campaign, and on six occasions he hit more than 40 doubles in a season.

Both Manush and Herman were moved up to Omaha of the Western League in 1922. Herman hit .416 in 92 games but did not reach the major leagues until 1926. Manush compiled a .376 average that year, belting 245 hits in 167 games, including 44 doubles, 20 triples, and 20 home runs. Without surprise, he found himself in spring training with the Tigers in 1923.

Ty Cobb, manager and star outfielder of the Tigers, was not an easy man to break in under. Cobb did not even give Manush an opportunity to take batting practice that spring until Harry Heilmann, befriending the 21-year-old rookie, gave up his turn to let Manush hit. Once Heinie had the opportunity, he made the most of it and won a regular job in the Tiger outfield, joining future Hall of Famers Cobb and Heilmann.

The Yankees won the pennant that year, with Detroit finishing a distant second. Manush had a fine season. He batted .334 in 109 games and set a rookie record by

being hit with pitched balls 17 times. Eventually, Manush replaced Cobb in center field.

In 1924 the Tigers slipped to third place, and Manush's average fell to .289. But he came back in 1925 to bat .303. In 1926 the 24-year-old lefthanded hitter won the American League batting championship with a .378 average. Locked in a close race with Babe Ruth through much of September, Heinie collected six hits in nine at bats during a double header on the final day of the season to beat Ruth by six points. Heinie played 136 games that year and smacked 188 hits, including 14 home runs.

Heinie was on a hunting trip in Minnesota with Heilmann and George Moriarty during the winter of 1926–1927 when Moriarty was informed that he would replace Cobb as Detroit manager. Although friendly at first, Manush and Moriarty did not always see eye to eye during the 1927 season, one in which the Tigers placed fourth. Heinie hit .298, but that December he and Lu Blue were traded to the St. Louis Browns for Harry Rice, Chick Galloway, and Elam Van Gilder. It was a trade the Tigers came to regret.

In his first season with the Browns (1928), Heinie equaled his career high with a .378 average. This time, however, he failed to capture the batting championship. Goose Goslin of the Senators, playing reluctantly on the last day of the season, edged Manush by less than one point. Heinie did tie Lou Gehrig for the league lead in doubles with 47, and he led the league with 241 hits, 31 more than runnerup Gehrig. The Browns had an impressive third place showing while Detroit stumbled to sixth.

In 1929 Heinie finished third in the American League batting race with a .355 average. Again he tied for the league lead in doubles, and again he topped the 200-hit mark.

But the winter was one of discontent and bitterness between Manush and Browns' owner Phil Ball. Manush thought his salary was less than his value to the Browns, and he reported for the 1930 season only after a long hassle. After playing in 49 games, he was dealt to the Senators two days before the trading deadline, moving over with pitcher Al Crowder in exchange for Goslin, the man who had bested him for the 1928 batting race.

Manush completed the 1930 season with a .350 batting average and collected 194 hits, giving him a three-year hit total of 639. In 1931, his first full year under manager Walter Johnson, he batted .307 for the third-place Senators. The team placed

Manush swings in the style that made him an American League batting leader for more than a decade. Twice he averaged .378 for a season, once beating out Babe Ruth for the 1926 batting championship and the second time barely losing out to Goose Goslin.

third again in 1932, with Heinie hitting .342. Then in 1933, the Senators captured the American League pennant by a seven-game margin over the Yankees. Heinie's contribution was a .336 batting average, a distant second to league-leader Jimmie Foxx. Manush led the league with 221 hits and 17 triples.

In the World Series of 1933, Heinie battled his way through a mad scramble to redeem the first ball thrown out by President Franklin D. Roosevelt prior to the start of the third game. The following day Manush was called out in a close play at first base, and he argued vehemently with umpire Charlie Moran. Heinie became so incensed that he grabbed Moran's bow tie, gave it a yank, and let it snap back to Moran's throat with a thud. Heinie was immediately ejected, but he took his position in left field regardless before finally leaving. He was the first player to be tossed out of a World Series game since Ray Schalk in 1919.

Commissioner Landis, sitting with Roosevelt, fined Manush $50, but Landis informed his umpires that in the future any ejections in the World Series would have to be approved by the commissioner.

Heinie collected only two hits in 18 at bats in the 1933 World Series, his only Series appearance.

Manush's only selection to the All-Star game came in 1934, and Heinie drew a walk in the first inning off Carl Hubbell. Hubbell then proceeded to strike out Babe Ruth, Lou Gehrig, Jimmie Foxx, Al Simmons, and Joe Cronin in succession. In that 1934 season, the Senators fell to seventh, but Heinie placed third in the league with a .349 average.

After batting .273 in 1935, Manush was traded to the Red Sox for Roy Johnson and Carl Reynolds. Heinie played one year in Fenway Park, hitting .291 to close out his American League career with a .331 average.

The Red Sox released Manush on September 28, 1936. Ten weeks later he was signed as a free agent by the Brooklyn Dodgers. Heinie spent one and a half years with Brooklyn, hitting .333 in 1937 to finish among the league's top 10 hitters. In May 1938, he was released to the Pirates on

waivers, and he finished the season with Toronto in the International League, hitting .310.

Heinie returned in 1939 to play 10 games with Pittsburgh, closing out his major league career with a .330 batting average. Most of the 1939 season though was spent at Toronto. In 1940 Manush took a managing job with Rocky Mount of the Piedmont League. From 1940 through 1945, Heinie managed in the minors, always playing a few games himself, even at the age of 44. He was at the helm of Greensboro in the Piedmont League in 1941 and 1942, at Roanoke in the Piedmont League in 1943, at Scranton in the Eastern League in 1944, and at Martinsville in the Carolina League in 1945.

Heinie worked as a scout for the Boston Braves in 1946, and served as a Pirate scout in 1947 and 1948. In 1949 his wife, Betty, died, leaving him a widower with three daughters. The couple had been married in 1928.

Heinie returned to the Washington Senators in 1953 and 1954 as a coach. He also scouted for the expansion Washington Senators in 1961 and 1962, his last affiliation with baseball.

Heinie Manush was named to the Hall of Fame in 1964. In poor health during his later years, Heinie underwent a serious cataract operation in 1969. He developed cancer the same year, costing him his power of speech. He died in Sarasota, Florida, on May 12, 1971, three days before Goslin's death.

HENRY EMMETT MANUSH

Detroit 1923–1927
St. Louis (A.L.) 1928–1930
Washington 1930–1935
Boston (A.L.) 1936
Brooklyn 1937–1938
Pittsburgh 1938–1939

G	AB	R	H	2B	3B	HR	RBI	Avg.
2009	7653	1287	2524	491	160	110	1173	.330

Rabbit Maranville (1891-1954)

Many infielders in baseball history have contributed far more to their teams than their batting averages would indicate. Defense, base running, leadership, and a keen knowledge of the game are valuable assets in a player, and few men had more of these than Rabbit Maranville, a lifetime .258 hitter.

James Walter Vincent Maranville was born on November 11, 1891, in Springfield, Massachusetts, the third of five children of French-Irish parents. His father was a policeman who hoped Jimmy would grow up to be a steamfitter. In the meanwhile, Maranville played ball on the sandlots and in school as a catcher. At 5'5", he seemed to have little potential for professional baseball.

Nevertheless, later on, while Rabbit was playing in a semipro league in Springfield, Tommy Dowd, manager of the New Bedford club in the New England League, offered him $750 to spend the 1911 season on his team. Maranville accepted—but he also let Dowd talk him into buying an insurance policy from a relative for $323.

Dowd converted Maranville into a shortstop that season, but the youngster batted only .227 in 117 games. With no better offers, he returned to New Bedford in 1912, and was hitting .283 in August when John Montgomery Ward, the great nineteenth-century star and then part-owner of the Boston Braves, spotted him while on a scouting mission. At this point the Giants were also interested, but Ward outfoxed his New York scouting rival by talking down Maranville's chances because of his size. When the Giants hesitated, Ward bought him from New Bedford for $2200.

It was during his New Bedford days that Maranville acquired the nickname "Rabbit." A young girl in the stands, spotting his hippity-hoppity movements around the infield, called him Rabbit, and the nickname stuck—for which Maranville was grateful, since it replaced "Stumpy" and "Bunty" among his teammates.

Rabbit joined a rather poor club when he reported to the Braves late in 1912. They were en route to a last-place finish, 52 games out of first, with a 52–101 record. There was not a player of real note on the team, and Maranville did not excite many people either, batting .209 in 29 games.

In 1913, when George Stallings became manager of the Braves, he and Maranville hit it off right away. The team's heir apparent at shortstop was Artie Bues, who happened to be Stallings' nephew. After a good spring-training performance, Maranville went to Stallings and said, "Do I have to beat out your whole family?" That kind of spunk had a special appeal to Stallings, and Maranville became not only the regular shortstop but the sparkplug of the rebuilding Braves. He had good speed,

sure hands, a lot of range, and a strong, accurate arm. The Braves improved their ranking to fifth in 1913 and hoped for better the following year.

Maranville was ill as the 1914 season began, and the Braves had a very poor start. They found themselves in last place on July 4, and they remained there as late as July 19 before they started to move. Finally, in a historic pennant drive, the "Miracle Braves" of 1914 managed to tie for first place on August 23 and won the pennant by 10½ games over the Giants. Rabbit hit only .246, but he led the league in games played and set a record for chances handled by a shortstop with 981. It was typical of his career in that his batting average was seldom worth mentioning while his inspired play often led to victory.

The Braves continued to roll in the World Series, besting the Athletics in four games, with Rabbit hitting .308.

Rabbit was fun wherever he went. Often he traveled with a pet monkey or parrot, and his antics became legendary, if not somewhat exaggerated. Once he disguised himself in blackface and knocked on Stallings' door, posing as a telegram messenger. Stallings accepted the phony wire, but Maranville remained in the room instead of leaving. Finally, Stallings asked him what he was waiting for, and Rabbit answered, "I'm just waiting for my dime, you cheapskate."

The little guy with the big ears once swam across the Charles River in Boston just to avoid a 10-block walk to cross a bridge. Getting wet on such impulse was nothing new to him, however. In St. Louis one day he had dived into a hotel fountain fully clothed in response to a dare. Many claimed he emerged from the fountain with a goldfish in his mouth, but Rabbit claimed only to have bitten the fish.

In Philadelphia, his teammates once locked him in his twelfth-floor hotel room so they could play a quiet game of cards, but Rabbit, always daring, climbed out the window. He was never afraid of a fight, knowing that bigger men would usually hold back with him. One day in New York, after a set-to with the Giants' Jim Thorpe, the two walked off the field arm in arm.

Another time in New York, Rabbit chased a teammate down Broadway yelling "Stop! Thief!" as a startled crowd looked on. Off the field, the Braves had no rules other than keeping out of jail and showing up for games. There were times when Maranville's drinking got him locked up overnight, but, as his wife Helene said, "At least I know where he is."

(Above left) Maranville, top row second from right, with his Springfield High School teammates in 1909. (Above) He's ready to bat with an unusual "bottle bat," sawed off at the top. (Right) Boston fans honor Maranville, one of their favorites, in 1930. They showered him with gifts, including the automobile. Maranville's father (left) and in front of the car are Maranville's wife, his daughter Betty, and Rabbit, in uniform.

Infielder Maranville tags out another future Hall of Famer, Frank Frisch. Maranville switched to second base from shortstop during his days at Pittsburgh.

On the field, Rabbit was always entertaining. He could be counted on to sit on base runners sliding into second or to crawl between an umpire's legs. Fans loved his "vest-pocket catches," in which he caught pop-ups at the last second, waist high with glove up. It was a forerunner of Willie Mays' basket catch, and Rabbit even did it on the stage one winter when he played vaudeville. His theatrical career ended when he demonstrated sliding one day and slid off the stage and into the orchestra where his foot broke through a snare drum.

Rabbit stayed with Boston through the 1920 season, although he missed most of 1918 when he served as a gunner's mate on the USS *Pennsylvania* in World War I. His salary rose from $1800 to $6000 during his Boston days, but then, in a major trade, the Pittsburgh Pirates in February 1921 obtained him for three players and $15,-000. They were still searching for a replacement at shortstop for Honus Wagner who had retired in 1917.

Maranville's best years at bat were 1921 and 1922 when he hit .294 and .295. Then, in 1924, he shifted to second base when Glenn Wright arrived to play short. At second, Rabbit set a National League record for chances accepted with 933 in 1924.

Primarily a singles hitter, Rabbit hit only 28 homers in his career, and set a record of sorts in 1922 by batting 672 times without a homer.

Following the 1924 season, Maranville was traded to the Cubs with Charlie Grimm, one of his carousing partners on the Pirates. The two had helped turn the Pirates into pennant contenders.

On July 7, 1925, Rabbit was appointed manager of the Cubs and celebrated by pouring ice water over all the players sleeping in the Pullman on which they were traveling at the time. But his eccentricities were not appropriate for a manager, the Cub management decided, and on September 3, after only eight weeks on the job, he was fired. That November he was released to the Dodgers on waivers, and he spent the 1926 season recovering from a broken leg and playing only 78 games.

Sent to Rochester of the International League in 1927, Rabbit took stock of his life and decided to stop drinking. The decision changed his entire outlook and he returned to the majors a new man. The Cardinals' shortstop, Tommy Thevenow, had fractured a leg, and Branch Rickey bought Rabbit late in the 1927 season to replace him. The following season, 14 years after his first World Series, Rabbit helped the Cardinals into another one. Although they were beaten by the Yankees, Maranville repeated his earlier October performance by again hitting .308.

The Cardinals got Charlie Gelbert to play short for 1929 and sold Maranville to the Braves on December 8, 1928. Back at the scene of his earlier triumphs, Rabbit hit 284, and in July he was named manager of the team. He finished last but demanded a five-year contract to continue as manager. When the Braves refused, Rabbit returned to the players' ranks.

Rabbit remained a regular in the Boston infield through 1933 and until he was 42 years old. Then, in an exhibition game before the 1934 season, he broke a leg trying to steal home. He missed the entire year but came back in 1935 to play 23 games for Boston, which gave him a career total of 23 seasons in the National League—a record. He was second only to Honus Wagner in total games played in the league, and was one of only a handful with more than 10,000 career at bats.

Rabbit managed Elmira (New York–Penn League) in 1936, hitting .323 in 123 games for the minor league club. In 1937 and 1938 he managed Montreal of the International League, and in 1939 led Albany of the Eastern League, participating in six games at the age of 47. His final job in organized ball was as manager at Springfield (Eastern League), his hometown, in 1941.

Maranville served again in the Navy in World War II, and then worked with youth groups in New York, running a sandlot baseball program for the Hearst newspapers.

On January 5, 1954, he suffered a heart attack in Woodside, New York, and died at the age of 62. Several weeks later, he was named to the Hall of Fame.

JAMES WALTER VINCENT MARANVILLE

Boston (N.L.) 1912–1921, 1929–1935
Pittsburgh 1921–1924
Chicago (N.L) 1925
Brooklyn 1926
St. Louis (N.L.) 1927–1928

G	AB	R	H	2B	3B	HR	RBI	Avg.
2670	10078	1255	2605	380	177	28	874	.258

Rube Marquard (b. 1889)

Early in the twentieth century, the New York Giants had three great pitchers whose names began with the letter M. Christy Mathewson joined the club in 1900, Joe McGinnity in 1902, and then, in 1908, Rube Marquard arrived in a blaze of publicity.

Richard William Marquard was born on October 9, 1889, in Cleveland, Ohio. His father was the chief engineer of the city of Cleveland. There were four boys and a girl in the family, and the girl, at 6'2", was the shortest of the lot. Richard grew to be 6'3" and 180 pounds. His father had no use for baseball, and when Richard left home to play professional ball, his father told him never to return again. The two went 10 years without speaking.

As a boy, Richard became an accomplished sandlot pitcher. Because of his size he played with boys and men years older than he was. He was a big fan of the Cleveland Broncos, later the Cleveland Naps (still later the Indians), and served as batboy for the team during its postseason exhibition contests in Cleveland. One year he even pitched a game for Cleveland third baseman Billy Bradley's "Boo Gang," a postseason barnstorming team. That was in 1904 when Marquard was only 15 years old.

In 1906, a friend of Marquard's named Howard Wakefield was catching for the Waterloo team of the Iowa State League. He had his manager wire Marquard in Cleveland, offering him a tryout. Rube needed transportation money, but when Waterloo would not advance it, he hitched rides and rode freight trains for five days to reach the club. Given the opportunity to pitch against last-place Keokuk without a contract, Marquard took the opportunity and beat them 6–2. When he was still not given a contract, he felt cheated and returned to Cleveland.

When the 1907 baseball season opened, Rube was working for an ice cream company, earning $25 a week in the factory and pitching for the company baseball team. The Cleveland club offered him $100 a month to sign with them, but he had been cheated once and was already earning that much with the ice cream company. At that point, the Indianapolis club of the American Association came up with an offer of $200 a month, and Marquard accepted it. Optioned to Canton of the Central League, he pitched 40 games, had a 23–13 record, and led the league in victories.

In 1908, during spring training with Indianapolis, Marquard had the opportunity to defeat Cleveland, 2–0, in an exhibition.

That season he was 28–19, pitching 367 innings, striking out 250 batters, and leading the American Association in almost every department. The Indianapolis *Star*, reporting on the youngster's progress, compared him with another famous

lefthander, Philadelphia's Rube Waddell. It was from that point on that Marquard, also, was known as Rube. But the similarity ended there. Marquard was an intelligent, city-bred man who neither drank nor smoked and was never known to miss curfew.

On September 3, major league scouts went to Columbus to watch the sensational Marquard pitch. It was rumored that there would be a bidding war for his services after the game if he was impressive. Rube went out and pitched a no-hitter against Columbus. The bidding war resembled a horse auction. Cleveland offered Indianapolis $10,500, whereupon the Giants offered $11,000—a record price at the time, exceeding the $10,000 paid by Boston for Mike Kelly in 1887. But Kelly was a major league purchase, and $11,000 for a minor leaguer was an unprecedented sum.

As Kelly had become known as the "$10,000 Beauty" 21 years before, New York newspapers called Marquard the "$11,000 Beauty." The 18-year-old arrived heralded as the finest pitching prospect in the country. McGraw would have preferred to have kept him on the bench for awhile and broken him in slowly, but the Giant management had paid a lot for Rube and he was sent into action on September 25, 1908. The result was a five-run, six-hit showing in five innings, but it did not rattle the youth's confidence. He waved at the bleacher fans as he headed for the clubhouse, promising to be back. But in 1909 he had a poor 5–13 record for 29 games. The sportswriters tabbed Rube the "$11,000 Lemon" and the Giants wondered what had gone wrong.

Rube went through a 4–4 season in 1910, and in 1911 Giant coach Wilbert Robinson came to the rescue. Robinson worked with Rube on his curve ball and helped him perfect his three-quarter delivery. The results were gratifying, as Rube put together a 24–7 record, teaming with his roommate Christy Mathewson to pitch the Giants into the World Series. Rube led the National League with 237 strikeouts that year. Marquard lost his only decision in the 1911 World Series, as "Home Run" Baker beat him with the long ball, and he engaged in a back-and-forth debate with Mathewson in rival newspapers over the method of pitching to Baker. It did not affect their long friendship, however, and the two continued to be roommates throughout their stay together on the Giants.

Marquard had another great year in 1912. He posted a 26–11 record, winning his first 19 decisions. That tied the major-league record set by old Giant Tim Keefe

when the pitching mound was only 50 feet. As Rube correctly pointed out, the record would have been 20 under later rules, for he entered one game in relief with the Giants behind, 3–2, and they rallied to win. But the victory went to starter Jeff Tesreau.

During his 19-win streak, Rube allowed only 49 runs to his opponents while the Giants scored 139. He did not lose his first game until July 8. Then, in the World Series, he twice defeated Boston with complete-game efforts, although the Giants lost the Series, four games to three.

With 50 victories in two seasons, Marquard was a sports celebrity in New York. He made a movie that winter, with Alice Joyce and Maurice Costello, and began a vaudeville tour with his first wife, actress Blossom Seely, in which the two did a dance routine. They kept the act and the marriage for three years, but then they parted. Rube married two more times.

Rube was 23–10 in 1913, for a three-year total of 73 victories, just one less than Mathewson. Again the Giants were in the World Series, but Marquard lost his only decision.

Things turned around for Rube in 1914. He lost 12 straight and finished with a 12–22 record. His high point that year was a 21-inning victory over Babe Adams of Pittsburgh, but his difficulties contributed to the Giants' finishing 10½ games behind Boston. In 1915 Rube no-hit Brooklyn on April 15, but soon afterward fell into disfavor with McGraw and, when given the opportunity to make his own deal, sold himself to Wilbert Robinson in Brooklyn for $7500. He finished the split season with an 11–10 record.

That was the year in which Rube tried to jump to the Federal League, but when the Feds discovered he had already signed his Giant contract, they told him to forget it. The hasty signing with New York cost him a $10,000 contract, but the Federal League folded after the 1915 season.

In 1916, Marquard was 13–6 for the pennant-winning "Robins" of Brooklyn, but was beaten twice in the World Series. He was 19–12 in 1917, and 9–18 in 1918. The 1919 season might have been a better one for Brooklyn if Rube had not broken a leg and missed most of the year.

Brooklyn won another pennant in 1920. Rube's contribution was a 10–7 record, but in his fifth World Series he lost his only decision, making him 2–5 overall in Series competition. The 1920 Series was marked by Rube's arrest on a charge of speculating in World Series tickets, but after paying the fine he claimed he had only bought the tickets for a friend and was caught turning them over.

In December 1920, Rube was traded to Cincinnati for Dutch Ruether. After a 17–14 season for Cincinnati in 1921, he was traded to the Boston Braves for John Scott and Bill Kopf. He spent his last four big-league seasons in Boston, with a combined 25–39 record. In 1924 he underwent an appendectomy, and was virtually through as a big leaguer. He finished with 201 career victories.

Rube managed the Providence team in the Eastern League in 1926, pitching seven games for them as well, and in 1927 he divided the season between Baltimore (International League) and Birmingham (Southern League). He was out of baseball in 1928 but returned to manage and pitch for Jacksonville (Southeastern Association) in 1929 and 1930. In 1931 he served as an Eastern League umpire, and in 1932 he was a coach-scout and pitcher for Atlanta in the Southern Association. He closed out his career at 43 by briefly managing Wichita of the Western League in 1933.

Rube moved to Baltimore in 1930, and remained there for more than 40 years working in mutual windows at various racetracks.

In 1971, at 82, he was elected to the Hall of Fame.

RICHARD WILLIAM MARQUARD

New York (N.L.) 1908–1915
Brooklyn 1915–1920
Cincinnati 1921
Boston (N.L.) 1922–1925

G	IP	W	L	Pct.	H	R	ER	SO.	BB	ERA
536	3307	201	177	.532	3233	1443	inc.	1593	858	inc.

(Above) Rube Marquard, who tied a record with his 1912 19-game winning streak, winds up to pitch. (At left) He poses with first wife Blossom Seely, with whom he had a dance act.

Christy Mathewson (1880-1925)

At the turn of the century, baseball as a profession was generally looked upon with disdain as a game played by crude, uneducated men and was considered unfit for women to watch. No one did so much to change that image as the sensational New York Giant righthander, Christy Mathewson.

Christopher Mathewson was born on August 12, 1880, in Factoryville, Pennsylvania. He was the oldest of five children, and had a brother, Henry, who also played briefly in the major leagues.

Christy had a comfortable childhood. His mother was wealthy and his father was a gentleman farmer. By the time he entered Keystone Academy in 1894, Christy had already been pitching for three years against boys much older than he was. During his years at the academy he received $1 a game to pitch for a local team 12 miles away. In 1896 he had his first experience in a high semipro league when he was asked to substitute for a regular who had not arrived at the Scranton ballpark. He is said to have struck out 15 batters that day.

After his graduation from Keystone, Christy entered Bucknell University. There, he starred in baseball, football, and basketball, was elected class president, was a member of two literary societies and the glee club, pitched semipro ball in the summers, and met Jane Stoughton, whom he later married.

Christy left Bucknell in 1899 to sign his first professional contract—$90 a month for Taunton, Massachusetts, in the New England League. At Taunton he won five of seven decisions in 17 appearances, but, more important, he discovered, through a teammate, a method for throwing a "reverse curve," or "fadeaway" as it came to be known. (Today the pitch is called a screwball.)

Armed with the new pitch, Christy began the 1900 season with Norfolk in the Virginia League. He started 22 games by July and won 20 of them, a feat that did not pass unnoticed by the major leagues. He received offers from both the Giants and the Phillies, surveyed the pitching rosters of both clubs, and decided he would pitch more in New York. So the Giants got Mathewson for $2000, and George Davis, the new Giant manager, had himself a 6'1½" future Hall of Famer.

How Christy got his nickname "Big Six" is not known for sure, but the popular theory is that it merely had to do with his height—he was tall for his times. In all probability he was asked his height, replied "six feet," and someone probably said it was a "big six." Hence the unexplained nickname.

The Giants of 1900 were a poor team, finishing last in the National League with only 60 victories and 78 defeats. Mathewson appeared in only six games, lost all

three decisions in which he was involved, and walked 20 men in 34 innings. He had not yet perfected his control of the fadeaway.

Disappointed in his showing, the Giants decided to return Mathewson to Norfolk after the season. Subsequently, Cincinnati drafted him. The price was $100, but the Redlegs then peddled him back to the Giants in exchange for Amos Rusie, a 29-year-old pitcher who had won 241 games in 9 seasons but whose sore arm had kept him out of action since 1898. Rusie was to hurl three games for the Redlegs, lose his only decision, and never pitch again in the big leagues.

Mathewson, however, was on the threshold of greatness. Although the 1901 Giants finished seventh (the Redlegs were last), Christy won 20 games, had 5 shutouts, and struck out 215 batters. He had a no-hitter against St. Louis on July 15, the first of two in his career. (The second was against Chicago on June 13, 1905.) At the age of 21, he had arrived.

The Giants finished last in 1902. It was Christy's only losing season—he posted a 14–17 record despite eight shutouts. He also played three games at first base and four in the outfield. His new manager, John McGraw, liked to say facetiously that he "converted" Christy to a pitcher, but there was never any question about where Christy belonged.

In 1903, "Iron Man" Joe McGinnity, who had joined the club the previous summer, teamed with Mathewson to hoist the Giants from the cellar to second place. McGinnity won 31 games, Mathewson 30. Christy never dropped under 22 victories again until 1915.

Mathewson won 33 games and lost only 12 in 1904, and won his second of six strikeout titles (1903–1905, 1907–1908, 1910). The Giants finished first, but McGraw refused to meet the Red Sox in a World Series, stubbornly viewing the four-year-old American League as a minor circuit. He changed his mind, however, in 1905, when the Giants won another pennant. Mathewson led the league that year with 31 victories, losing only 9 games and pitching 9 shutouts. Connie Mack's Philadelphia Athletics were the American League champions.

The 1905 World Series opened in Philadelphia, where Mathewson stopped the A's, 3–0, on a four-hitter. Game 2, in New York, featured the shutout pitching of Chief Bender as the A's evened the series. A rainout permitted Mathewson to start the third game, back in Philadelphia, and again he pitched a four-hit shutout, winning 9–0. McGinnity won the fourth game, 1–0, and Mathewson wrapped it up in five

Mathewson, son of wealthy Pennsylvania landowners, got his early sports training at prestigious schools. (Above left) Mathewson, left, stands with a Keystone Academy football teammate. (Upper right) The interior of his room at Bucknell College, with tennis racket and sports pictures prominent in the decor. (At right) Mathewson, in shirt sleeves at right of table, defeats champions of Ohio and Indiana at checkers. (Opposite page) Mathewson delivers a "roundhouse curve" in upper picture and a fastball, below.

games with a six-hit, 2–0 victory at the Polo Grounds. He had pitched three shut-outs in the Series, allowing only 14 hits in 27 innings, with 18 strikeouts and one walk.

As is the case today, the World Series enhanced a player's reputation nationally, and Christy became a popular hero. He was reputed not to drink or smoke (although he did on occasion), and his Bucknell background made him a model for parents to point to.

Although the Giants did not return to the World Series until 1911, in the interim Christy had seasons of 22 victories (1906), 24 (1907), 37 (1908), 25 (1909), and 27 (1910). The 37 victories in 1908 are a National League record for the twentieth century. Mathewson appeared in 56 games that season, hurled 391 innings, posted 12 shutouts, lost only 11 games, and fanned 259 batters.

In 1911, with Rube Marquard having replaced McGinnity as Matty's pitching partner, the Giants won the first of three consecutive pennants. Mathewson won 26 and lost 13 that year. But in the 1911 World Series, Philadelphia defeated the Giants in six games, beating Matty twice in three decisions. In 1912, Christy won 23 games, but was again beaten twice in the World Series, which was won by Boston. In 1913, a year in which Mathewson won 25 games and went 68 consecutive innings without walking a batter, the Giants lost their third World Series in a row, with Christy splitting two decisions against Philadelphia. His 2–5 record in those three World Series belies some brilliant pitching, for his combined ERA was 1.51.

Mathewson's last big year was 1914, when he won 24 games for his twelfth consecutive season of 20-plus victories. This gave him 361 career victories, just 12 short of his lifetime total of 373, reached over the next two years. This was a National League record until it was tied by Grover Cleveland Alexander in 1929.

In 1915 Christy won only 8 games, lost 14, and had clearly lost the zip on his fastball. On July 20, 1916, he was traded to Cincinnati with Edd Roush and Bill McKechnie (both also future Hall of Famers) for player-manager Charlie "Buck" Herzog and Wade Killefer. The idea was not to give Cincinnati another pitcher—Christy pitched only one game for the Redlegs—but to provide the Reds with a new manager to succeed Herzog. Christy was immediately installed as skipper, the third Cincinnati manager that year, and the team won only 25 of the remaining 68 games and finished seventh.

Matty managed the Reds to fourth place the following year, and in 1918 they were in third place when, on August 28, Matty entered the Army at the age of 38. While in action overseas he inhaled poison gas which permanently damaged his lungs and left him with a serious cough.

Mathewson was back home in 1919, but Pat Moran had become manager of the Reds, who went on to win the World Championship. Mathewson was hired by McGraw as a coach for the Giants. He coached the Giants for three seasons, but when his cough got worse he was forced to enter the sanitorium in Saranac Lake, New York. He had tuberculosis.

But illness could not keep Mathewson away from baseball. In 1923 he accepted the presidency of the Boston Braves, a post he held until the first game of the 1925 World Series. At that time, word reached Forbes Field that Christy had died in Saranac Lake at the age of 45.

In 1936—with Ty Cobb, Honus Wagner, Babe Ruth, and Walter Johnson—Christy was in the first group of men elected to the Hall of Fame. By then, baseball was a widely accepted national pastime, and Christy had done a lot to make it so.

CHRISTOPHER MATHEWSON

New York (N.L.) 1900–1916
Cincinnati 1916

G	IP	W	L	Pct.	H	R	ER	SO	BB	ERA
635	4781	373	188	.665	4203	1613	inc.	2505	837	inc.

Joe McCarthy (1887-1978)

Joe McCarthy never played a game in the major leagues, but he became one of baseball's most successful managers. He led the New York Yankees to eight pennants and seven world championships.

Joseph Vincent McCarthy was born on April 21, 1887, in the Germantown section of Philadelphia, Pennsylvania. He was educated in Philadelphia, and played schoolboys' sandlot ball there during the time that Ed Delahanty and Elmer Flick were playing for the Phillies.

After high school, Joe enrolled in Niagara University in Buffalo, New York. He stayed for two years, then abandoned school for the promise of a professional baseball career.

Joe signed his first contract in 1907 with the Wilmington team of the Tri-State League, played a dozen games in the infield, and jumped the club to accept a better offer from the Franklin club of the outlaw Inter-State League. There, playing second, short, and third, McCarthy batted .314 in 71 games and earned a reputation as a pretty fair prospect.

He stood only 5'8½" and had a playing weight of about 170. Righthanded all the way, he was noted for his keen knowledge of the game and his aggressiveness on the field.

He was back in organized baseball in 1908, joining the Toledo club of the American Association, a high minor league. Joe did not hit much at Toledo but he became a popular little infielder who found other ways of winning games than with his bat—he spent three full seasons at Toledo and never hit over .254. In 1911, he was sold to Indianapolis of the same league, and finished the year with a .268 average, even taking a turn behind the plate as catcher.

In 1912, Joe found himself playing the infield for Wilkes-Barre of the New York State League. That was the season in which he made second base his permanent home, after having previously divided his playing time between the outfield and third base. He batted .274 for Wilkes-Barre, impressed everyone with his on-the-field leadership, and in 1913, at age 26, was named playing-manager of the team.

It was a good move for Wilkes-Barre. Joe brought the club home in second place and batted .325, his top showing as a hitter in organized ball. He played 132 games and had 164 hits, even showing some power with 36 doubles, 9 triples, and 6 home runs.

With that successful stint behind him, he was back in the International League in 1914, playing second for Buffalo. He batted against Babe Ruth in Ruth's pitching debut with Baltimore. Ruth got McCarthy out four times that day, but Joe hit .266 for the season and duplicated that figure in 1915.

Ed Barrow, president of the International

Joe McCarthy, who managed the New York Yankees to eight pennants and seven World Championships, rose through the minor league playing and managing ranks. (Opposite page) From the Yankee dugout, McCarthy sends out an array of signals, accompanied by a wide range of facial expressions.

League at the time, recommended McCarthy to the Yankees as a major league prospect. A deal was almost made when McCarthy decided to sign a contract with the Brooklyn club in the Federal League for the 1916 season. Unfortunately, the Federal League folded before the season began, and McCarthy's only shot at a major league playing job went by the boards.

Instead, Joe went to Louisville in 1916 and earned recognition as one of the top infielders in the American Association as well as one of the brightest. He remained the regular second baseman of the club through the 1919 season, and in midseason that year was appointed manager of the team.

He led the club to 39 victories in 69 games and a third-place finish, and then, in 1920, he advanced the team to second. in 1921, Joe played his final 11 games, concluding his minor league career with a lifetime .261 average. But, more noteworthy, he won his first pennant as a manager, as the Colonels compiled a 98–70 record.

Joe stayed in Louisville as manager through the 1925 season. Only once did he finish out of the first division. In 1925 the Colonels won 102 games and another pennant.

In Chicago, William Wrigley had become discontented with the way his Cubs were going. He had tried the unpredictable Rabbit Maranville as manager in 1925, but the team had finished last. Seeking a new man for 1926, Wrigley listened to the advice of John B. Foster, editor of the Spalding Baseball Guide, and approached McCarthy about the job.

Although it was a major league opportunity, McCarthy was at first hesitant. He was, after all, both popular and secure at Louisville, where he was considered the best minor league manager in the country. After a good deal of thought, however, he decided to take the gamble, and he assumed command of the Cubs.

His first bold move in 1926 was to ask waivers on Grover Cleveland Alexander, the popular pitcher. That established his control of the team, and no one ever doubted his authority. He was a master tactician, stressing the double play and forcing his pitchers to learn to field properly. His own playing career, he felt, had ended on a rundown play in 1920 when he was bowled over by a baserunner at second. When he had screamed at Jay Kirke, the first baseman who did not throw the ball, Kirke had told Joe, "You ain't looked

so good lately either." Joe never forgot it, and never let his players get too complacent.

Joe was fourth in his first two years in Chicago, third in 1928, and won the 1929 pennant after telling his boss, "Get me Rogers Hornsby and I'll win the pennant." Hornsby hit .380 and the Cubs won, but they lost to the Athletics in the World Series.

But the Cubs finished second in 1930 (Hack Wilson hit 56 homers and drove in 190 runs) and McCarthy had trouble with Hornsby all year. He felt Rogers was undermining him, and in disgust he resigned on September 24 with four games left. Hornsby succeeded him.

McCarthy brooded over the situation for several days. Meanwhile, the Yankees were looking for someone to replace Bob Shawkey for the 1931 season, and McCarthy immediately became a prime candidate. He went to Philadelphia during the 1930 World Series, met with Barrow and Jacob Ruppert, and was given a contract. His signing was announced the day after the Series ended and met with great approval among New York sportswriters.

The players, however, expressed mixed reactions. Babe Ruth had openly declared his desire for the job, and many players sided with him. Ruth and McCarthy never got along very well, and in 1935 Babe finally went to Boston.

McCarthy brought Jimmy Burke with him from Chicago as a coach, and he inherited Art Fletcher, who remained there throughout most of Joe's stay with the Yankees. Fletcher was a great help in briefing McCarthy on the Yankees and on the American League.

Joe finished second with the Yankees in 1931, while learning the league. He smashed the card table in the Yankee clubhouse and set the tone for Yankee "class" by telling his players, "You're Yankees—act like Yankees!" Suddenly the team was not only winning games but setting the standard for excellence on and off the field.

When the Yankees won the 1932 flag, Joe became the first manager to win pennants in both leagues. He was pleased that his Series opponents were the Cubs, whom the Yankees defeated in four straight games.

The Yankees then finished second for three years in a row, testing McCarthy's Irish temper, for he was never satisfied to finish any place but first. But by 1936 he had what he considered one of the game's greatest all-time clubs. The infield featured Lou Gehrig, Tony Lazzeri, Frank Crosetti, and Red Rolfe, while George Selkirk, Joe

DiMaggio, and Jake Powell played the outfield, Bill Dickey caught, and the pitching staff included Red Ruffing, Monte Pearson, and Lefty Gomez. Over the years, these men would be replaced by such stars as Phil Rizzuto, Tommy Henrich, Charlie Keller, and Joe Gordon.

From 1936 to 1939 the Yankees won four consecutive World Championships, the first time any club had ever accomplished such a feat. In those four World Series the Yankees lost only three games, and it was at that point that the expression "Yankee Dynasty" first came to be used.

McCarthy won three more pennants in 1941, 1942, and 1943, creating makeshift lineups when World War II took away his big stars. In 1943 he won his third Manager of the Year award, having also won in 1936 and 1938.

Bothered by poor health and, some said, an inability to get along with the new Yankee president, Larry MacPhail, Joe left the Yankees on May 21, 1946, complaining of a gall bladder attack. Three days later he formally resigned and was replaced by Bill Dickey. Speculation over the real reasons circulated, but McCarthy never claimed it to be anything but health, and MacPhail claimed to have pleaded with Joe to stay on.

McCarthy stayed out of baseball in 1947, but then went to Boston to manage the Red Sox for three years. He almost won the 1948 pennant, losing in a playoff to Lou Boudreau's Indians, and then he finished second in 1949. He resigned on June 22, 1950, with the club again in second place.

Joe retired with his wife, the former Elizabeth "Babe" McCave, to their home in Tonawanda, New York, outside of Buffalo. Age limited his activities of hunting, fishing, and golf, but he remained mentally alert into the 1970s and was still held in the highest esteem by almost every player who ever played for him.

In 1957, Joe was elected to the Hall of Fame. In 1976, a plaque in his honor was dedicated in Yankee Stadium on his 89th birthday. He died of pneumonia at age 90, on January 13, 1978 in Buffalo, New York.

Tommy McCarthy (1864-1922)

Tommy McCarthy, one of the "Heavenly Twins" of the Boston Beaneaters outfield in the 1890s, added several innovations to the style of play on the baseball diamond.

Thomas Francis Michael McCarthy was born on July 24, 1864, in South Boston, Massachusetts. Playing ball on the sand-lots of Boston, he was discovered by Tim Murnane, the manager of the Boston club in the Union Association, in 1884.

The Union Association was the first "rebel" league to be considered as a major league alongside the National League and the American Association. Although it operated 12 franchises, it was not particularly successful because there were not enough really good players to service three leagues. McCarthy, in fact, was the only Union Association player to make the Hall of Fame.

Tommy began the 1884 season as an outfielder, finishing as a pitcher, and losing all seven games he appeared in, allowing 73 hits in 56 innings. With that, he was taken off the mound and returned to the outfield. For the remainder of his major league career he took the mound only six more times without picking up a decision. But moving him to the outfield was an unspectacular move, for he batted only .218 in 53 games and made 13 errors.

The Boston club, owned by George Wright, finished fifth, and the league folded after one season. With the players all free agents, Tommy remained in his home town and joined the Boston Nationals. But things did not improve for him in the National League. He batted only .182 in 1885, and then .185 in eight games with the Philadelphia club in 1886. He saw minor league action that year at Providence (Eastern League) and Brockton (New England League).

Obviously in need of further seasoning, McCarthy was sent in 1887 to Oshkosh of the Northwestern League. There he seemed to find himself, for the Oshkosh club won the pennant and Tommy enjoyed a fine year, hitting .389 in 80 games. As the season drew to a close, the millionaire owner of the team surrendered the franchise, and Tommy finally returned to Philadelphia. His credentials for the season showed 18 games with Philadelphia with a .208 average and 15 stolen bases.

In 1888, McCarthy jumped to the St. Louis Browns of the American Association, managed by Charles Comiskey and operated by Chris Von der Ahe. The Browns were the leading team of the Association, having won pennants in 1885, 1886, and 1887. Their regular outfield consisted of Tip O'Neill, Curt Welch, and Hugh Nicol, but Nicol departed after the 1886 season and Welch after the 1887 season, leaving two openings. Center field went to a weak-hitting youngster named Harry Lyons in 1888, and right field was handed to Tommy McCarthy.

There was pressure on the newcomers to keep the pennant streak alive. Tommy did his share by playing in 131 games and

stealing 109 bases while hitting .276. His efforts helped Comiskey's club to a fourth straight pennant, although they lost to the Giants in 10 games (6–4) in the World Series. Tommy stole six bases in the Series but batted only .244.

The Browns dropped to second in 1889, but Tommy hit .297 and stole 59 bases in 140 games, while scoring 136 runs. Because of his size—he stood only 5'7"—the St. Louis fans called him "Little Mack" or "The Kid." Although he was short, he weighed 170 pounds.

Comiskey left the Browns for a job in the Players League in 1890, and McCarthy succeeded him as playing-manager. That experiment lasted only 26 games. With a 13–13 record as manager, Tommy stepped aside in favor of Chief Roseman and, later, Count Campau. The Browns finished the season in third place. McCarthy batted .351 that year and led the Association with 134 runs scored and 91 stolen bases.

Comiskey returned and assumed command of the Browns in 1891. In the American Association's last year. McCarthy hit .309 and the Browns finished second.

Despite the breakup of the league, Chris Von der Ahe felt he still retained rights to his players. When McCarthy went home to join the Boston Beaneaters, Von der Ahe demanded compensation for his star right fielder. The Boston owners, of course, saw no reason to pay for Tommy's contract. So Von der Ahe hired a break-and-enter specialist to break into McCarthy's room at the Laclede Hotel and take what he could get—which was $19 in cash from Tommy's pocket and a watch of equal value. Von der Ahe considered the debt paid.

Before his hometown fans in Boston, Tommy became an immediate sensation. He and center fielder Hugh Duffy became known as the "Heavenly Twins" and were the darlings of the fans. Close friends and roommates, the future Hall of Famers had a flair for entertaining the crowds. The fact that both were Irish did not hurt their popularity in Boston.

The Beaneaters, under manager Frank Selee, had won the National League pennant in 1891. Although he batted only .244 in 1892. McCarthy was outstanding on the bases, stealing 59 and scoring 116 runs. With such other fine players as King Kelly, Kid Nichols, John Clarkson, and Bobby Lowe, Boston again won the pennant.

Tommy had his best season at bat in 1893 when the pitching mound was moved back to 60'6". He hit .361 with 159 hits in 116 games, scoring 108 runs and stealing 49 bases. Again it was a championship season for Boston as Selee's team won 86 and lost only 43, with Kid Nichols winning 33 games.

That season Tommy was credited with a

Tommy McCarthy at bat. The fake bunt was one of his best batting techniques, drawing in the opposing infielders and then slugging the ball past them.

record 53 assists in the outfield. Many were the result of a specialty play he perfected—the trap. He would charge in for a line drive with a runner on first, intentionally trap him on a short bounce, and throw to second to start a double play. Years later, umpire Bill Klem credited McCarthy's play with the reason for the establishment of the infield fly rule.

In addition to his famous trap play, Tommy was one of baseball's first outstanding hit-and-run men, working the play effectively with Hugh Duffy over and over again. The two were also expert at the double steal, and McCarthy was skilled at the fake bunt, drawing the infield in and slapping the ball past them.

Another specialty of Tommy's was sign stealing. He was believed to be the first man to learn to read catchers' signals while he was standing on second base, and from there he passed them along to the batters.

Duffy and McCarthy both held out before the 1894 season, but both were in the lineup on opening day. Tommy had his last big year that season. He batted .349, hit 13 home runs, and scored more than 100 runs for the seventh consecutive year. Although Boston went through the entire season without being shut out, the team could only finish third. The Orioles that year won their first of four straight pennants.

In 1895, Tommy played 116 games and batted .291. At the end of the season the "Heavenly Twins" duo was broken up when Tommy was sold to Brooklyn, where he hit .254 for a ninth-place club. That concluded his major league career. His career average was .294.

Tommy returned to Boston and opened a combination bowling alley and saloon, known as "Duffy and McCarthy," a magical pair of names in that city. It was located on Washington Street and did quite well until the magic began to wear off.

From 1909 to 1912, Tommy served as a scout for the Cincinnati Reds. He scouted for the Boston Nationals in 1914 and 1917, and was manager at Newark in the New International League in 1918, where pitcher Ed Rommel played for him. In between, he distinguished himself by serving at various times as baseball coach for Dartmouth, Holy Cross, and Boston College.

Tommy died in Boston on August 5, 1922. He was named to the Hall of Fame in 1946.

THOMAS FRANCIS MICHAEL McCARTHY

Boston (U.A.) 1884
Boston (N.L.) 1885, 1892–1895
Philadelphia (N.L.) 1887
St. Louis (A.A.) 1888–1891
Brooklyn (N.L.) 1896

G	AB	R	H	2B	3B	HR	RBI	Avg.
1258	5055	1050	1485	194	58	43	666	.294

Joe McGinnity (1871-1929)

Joe McGinnity pitched both games of a double header five times and remained an active pitcher until he was 54 years old. His famous nickname, "Iron Man," which derived from his off-season occupation as an ironworker in his father-in-law's factory, was an appropriate one for the hardest-working pitcher in the early days of the twentieth century. His feat of winning three double headers in one month for the 1904 Giants led most people to assume the nickname was based on his durability, and in later years McGinnity himself acknowledged that his pitching was a source of the name.

Joseph Jerome McGinnity was born on March 19, 1871, in Rock Island, Illinois. Most Midwestern towns in those days had their "town team," which paid a little money to their players. Joe's first experience in organized baseball was with the semipro Rock Island team. A fastball pitcher who could strike out a lot of opponents, he came to the attention of manager John McCloskey of the Montgomery, Alabama, team in the Southern League while he was pitching in Van Buren, Arkansas. A friend of McCloskey's had seen McGinnity strike out 19 batters in a single game. When McCloskey heard about it, he said, "I don't care if they were 19 women—get me McGinnity."

Joe joined the Montgomery club in 1893 at the age of 22. After posting a 10–19 record for 31 games, he found himself the following year at Kansas City in the Western League. There he was only 8–10, striking out just 31 batters in 124 innings.

At the end of the 1894 season, Joe married Margaret Redpath, went through a period of poor health, and reflected gloomily on his two years in the minor leagues. Professional baseball did not seem to be his calling.

So Joe left the game and opened a saloon in Illinois. To advertise the establishment he pitched semipro ball, working on an underhand delivery that produced a tantalizing but tricky upcurve—a pitch he came to call "Old Sal." This turned out to be his ticket back into professional ball, for while hurling in Krebs, Oklahoma, he again came to the attention of scouts. In 1898 he was back in the minor leagues, resuming his career with Peoria of the Western Association.

At Peoria, he had a 10–3 record in 16 games. On June 26 he won a 21-inning game, going all the way. A few days later the league folded. However, on the strength of his fine showing with Peoria, the Baltimore Orioles of the 12-team National League signed him for 1899. The Orioles were managed by John McGraw at the time.

Joe had a brilliant season for the third-place Orioles that year. He won 28 games

(including 4 shutouts) for an all-time rookie record. When the National League consolidated to eight teams for the 1900 season, the 28-year-old pitcher was transferred to Brooklyn.

Working under manager Ned Hanlon that year, McGinnity led the Superbas to a first-place finish with a 29–9 record, tops in the National League. His 45 mound appearances also led the league. In all, Joe would lead his league seven times in games pitched, and in 1903 he set a twentieth-century National League record with 48 starts in a single season.

The first record Joe set in baseball was not one to boast about. He hit 41 batters during the 1900 season, a record that still stands. Joe was having a problem with his control, not yet having perfected the slow underhand curve, but no one doubted his ability to work hard. He sparked Brooklyn's pennant drive by winning 5 games in 11 days late in September, the Superbas edging the Pirates by 4½ games for the pennant. (There was no World Series that year.)

For his efforts, at the end of the season McGinnity received a rare cash bonus of $700. It was a handsome sum, for his yearly salary was only $1800.

As the 1901 season approached, Joe jumped to the Baltimore franchise of the new American League, joining McGraw. Technically, he was the first American League player, for his was the first contract signing announced by the league.

The 5'11", 206-pound righthander pitched in 48 games for the American League Orioles in 1901, posting a 26–21 record. He worked 378 innings, and allowed all-time record totals of 219 runs and 401 hits. But Baltimore finished fifth, and in 1902 it dropped to last place. McGinnity had a 13–10 record through July, when he and McGraw jumped back to the National League, joining the New York Giants. McGraw was made Giant manager, and he took his pitching ace McGinnity, his star catcher Roger Bresnahan, and several other players with him to give the Giants the nucleus of a fine team.

A pleasant man in general, Joe had one notable fight during his career. It was in 1902 while he was still with Baltimore. In the course of an argument with umpire Tom Connolly, Joe stomped on Connolly's shoes and spat in his face. The result was a fine and suspension from league president Ban Johnson, a strong supporter of his umpires. That was one of the incidents that persuaded the hot-tempered McGraw to leave the American League.

For the Giants, McGraw not only used

McGinnity's windup, in the days when he and Mathewson were the New York Giants' M and M boys, each of them winning over 30 games per season.

McGinnity on the mound, where he was 8–8, but also in the outfield and at second base occasionally, for Joe was not a bad hitter and he ran the bases well. He was also noted as a fine fielding pitcher, despite his stocky build.

In 1903, Joe's first full season with the Giants, the team jumped from last to second, with McGinnity showing a 31–20 record for 434 innings pitched (a modern National League record), while his pitching partner Christy Mathewson was 30–13. The two were the best one-two punch in the league. In 1904, Joe upped his record to 35–8 as the Giants won 106 games and the National League pennant. Included for Joe were a 14-game winning streak, a league-leading 9 shutouts, and 408 innings of work.

The high spot of these first two full years with the Giants, when he won 66 games, came in August 1903 when Joe three times won both ends of a double header. On August 1, he twice beat Boston, 4–1 and 5–2. On August 8, he stopped Brooklyn 6–1 and 4–3, with Oscar Jones losing both games. And on August 31, he twice beat Philadelphia, winning 4–1 and 9–2. The feat is the most remembered achievement of his career.

In 1905 Joe was 21–15 and appeared in his only World Series, the famous Series in which each of the five games between the Giants and the Athletics was a shutout. Mathewson won three of the games, as the Giants won the World Championship. Joe lost the second game, 3–0, but came back to win the fourth game, beating Eddie Plank, 1–0, on a five-hitter.

McGinnity led the National League in victories for the fifth and last time in 1906, posting a 27–12 record with 45 games, 37 starts, and 32 complete games. In his career, he completed 314 of 381 starts.

Joe was 18–18 in 1907, a year in which the Giants finished fourth. By that time, Mathewson was clearly the No. 1 man on McGraw's pitching staff. In 1908, Joe hurled only 186 innings and had an 11–7 record. He figured prominently in the famous "Merkle Boner" game on September 23, 1908. In the confusion that followed the sudden ending to the game. McGinnity, who had been coaching at third base, threw the ball into the stands to put it out of play. Chicago's Johnny Evers came up with another ball, tagged second base to retire Merkle, and eventually the Giants lost the pennant.

Following the 1908 season, with his place on the Giant staff no longer significant and with young Rube Marquard coming along to fill his shoes, Joe requested his release to accept a managing job at Newark in the Eastern League. Thus his major-league career, which lasted only 10 seasons, came to an end when he was 38 years old.

But there was still a lot of power in Joe's arm, and his easy delivery permitted him to continue pitching for 17 more seasons, most of them as a playing-manager. He managed Newark through 1912, the year the Eastern League became the International League, then switched to Tacoma of the Northwestern League from 1913 to 1915. He managed Butte of the Northwestern League in 1916 and part of 1917. In each of his first two seasons at Newark he pitched more than 400 innings, posting records of 29–16 and 30–19. His 1913 season at Tacoma saw him hurl a league-leading 68 games and 436 innings for a 22–19 record.

In 1918 he pitched briefly at Vancouver of the Pacific Coast–International League, and then left professional ball for three years to manage independent teams. He returned in 1922 as a pitcher for Danville (Three-I League), and in midseason got a job managing Dubuque of the Mississippi Valley League. He managed that club through 1923, sat out the 1924 season, and in 1925 was part owner and manager of Dubuque, pitching 15 games with a 6–6 record at the age of 54.

Wilbert Robinson brought him back to Brooklyn as a first base coach in 1926, but it was not a happy year for Joe. The players did not respect the overweight former star, and he left after one season. Failing to catch on with a team in the Midwest, he finally returned to Brooklyn in 1927 to live with his daughter, his wife having died in 1925. He served as an assistant baseball coach at Williams College before cancer claimed his life on November 14, 1929, in Brooklyn.

Joe was elected to the Hall of Fame in 1946.

JOSEPH JEROME McGINNITY

Baltimore (N.L.) 1899
Brooklyn (N.L.) 1900
Baltimore (A.L.) 1901–1902
New York (N.L.) 1902–1908

G	IP	W	L	Pct.	H	R	ER	SO	BB	ERA
467	3455	247	145	.630	3236	1442	inc.	1064	803	inc.

John McGraw (1873-1934)

An outstanding infielder for the Baltimore Orioles of the 1890s, John McGraw became the most highly regarded manager in National League history, piloting the New York Giants from 1902 to 1932.

John Joseph McGraw was born on April 7, 1873, in Truxton, New York, a small town in the center of the state. His widower father, John McGraw, Sr., was an Irish-born Civil War veteran who settled in Truxton in 1871 with an infant girl. He got a job as a railroad maintenance man, and a year later married Ellen Comerfort. They had eight children of their own, the first of whom was John.

Little John, or Jack as he was then called, began playing baseball when he was seven. He earned some money doing farm chores for a neighbor, attended the Union Free School, and battled his father over the merits of playing baseball.

In 1885 a diphtheria epidemic claimed the lives of his mother, two sisters, and two brothers within a matter of weeks. Needing to make more money, John took over the local delivery route of the Elmira *Telegram* and worked on the railroad, selling candy in the cars. He continued to read up on baseball and became an expert on the rules and a fine pitcher for his school team. None of this was of any value to his father, who severely beat him one day after young John had broken a neighbor's window during a game. The beating drove John out of the house and he moved in with a neighbor. By agreement with his father, he continued to live in the neighbor's home.

John was first noticed by adults when he pitched for the Truxton Grays, the local town team. He was able to throw a curve ball, a relatively unfamiliar skill at the time, and despite his lack of size he was a quality hitter. In addition, no one knew as much about baseball rules as John did.

In 1890, Bert Kenney, who had headed the town team, organized the Olean club in the New York–Penn League. The club had only an 11-man roster, but John got off badly and was benched. He left the team shortly before it disbanded entirely and joined the Wellsville team in the Western New York League, batting .365 in 24 games and taking the mound on occasion.

After the 1890 season he was invited on a trip to Cuba to play with a group of high minor league all-stars. On the way home many of the club members stopped in Ocala, Florida, and played an exhibition game against the Cleveland Spiders of the National League. Cleveland won the game, 9–6, but McGraw played an impressive shortstop and was signed to play for Cedar Rapids in 1891.

John played 85 games in the Illinois–Iowa League in 1891 before Rockford

manager and major league scout Bill Gleason tipped off the Baltimore Orioles to John's abilities. On August 26, 1891, he reported to the Orioles and began a 42-year major league career.

The Orioles, managed by Billy Barnie, were then in the American Association. John played 31 games and hit .245 as the league finished its final season. In 1892 it merged into an expanded, 12-team National League, and Ned Hanlon took over as manager of the Orioles early in the season.

The club was last that year, but Hanlon began to build it up. He started with McGraw and catcher Wilbert Robinson and added outfielder Joe Kelley, second baseman Kid Gleason, shortstop Hughey Jennings (moving McGraw to third), and outfielder Willie Keeler. By 1894 the Orioles were champions of the league and McGraw was their sparkplug. John fielded his position brilliantly and personally devised many plays previously untried in baseball. He and Keeler perfected the hit-and-run play. The Orioles won pennants in 1894, 1895, and 1896, and won the Temple Cup playoff series in 1896 and 1897. McGraw topped .300 for nine consecutive years, batting as high as .374 (1895).

He and his close friend Jennings enrolled at St. Bonaventure College in the winter of 1893–1894 in exchange for performing coaching duties. Although only 5'7", McGraw had also developed a reputation as a scrapper—and nothing got him into a fight faster than having someone call him by the hated nickname "Muggsy."

In 1899 Ned Hanlon and many of the Orioles moved to Brooklyn and won the pennant for the Brooklyn Superbas. McGraw, who owned a café in Baltimore in partnership with Wilbert Robinson, remained behind and was appointed manager of the 1899 Orioles. He finished fourth with an 86–62 record while hitting .390 in 118 games. In 1900, he and Robinson were sold to the St. Louis club, but after one season there he jumped to the American League, accepting Ban Johnson's offer to manage the Orioles.

Johnson, founder and president of the league, greatly admired McGraw's spirit, and as a popular figure in Baltimore McGraw was a good choice to lead the new team. But McGraw and Johnson soon grew apart. While Johnson backed his umpires to the hilt, McGraw continued to fight them, both verbally and, at times, physically. He could not stand Johnson's support of the umpires against him, and in disgust he accepted the offer of New York

(Above) The Alleghany Baseball Club of St. Bonaventure's, with McGraw in the rear row, far right, and fellow Hall of Famer, Hugh Jennings, opposite him at far left. (Far left) Player McGraw bats. He topped .300 for nine consecutive years as an Oriole in the 1890s.

Giant manager John McGraw and his pet margay. He took it not only to games but also to parties and banquets, delighting his hosts less than the fans in the ball park.

Giants' owner Andrew Freedman to manage the Giants, and left for New York in July 1902.

McGraw had advanced $7000 of his own money to help pay Oriole debts. In exchange for the loan, he was granted his release by the Orioles to pave the way for his trip to New York. With him went Joe McGinnity, Roger Bresnahan, Jack Cronin, and Dan McGann.

Reporting to Freedman's office, McGraw looked at the 23-man roster and promptly crossed off 11 names. "I can finish last just as easily with 12 men as with 23," he said, and Freedman was immediately impressed by his thrift. And last was exactly where McGraw did finish with the lackluster Giants.

But in 1903, his first full season, he finished second. Christy Mathewson, who was to become McGraw's favorite, developed into a big winner, and Joe McGinnity won 31 games. In 1904 McGraw won his first of 10 pennants but refused to meet the Red Sox in a World Series. He changed his mind in 1905 and captured his first World Championship (he won two others), beating Connie Mack's Athletics as Mathewson hurled three World Series shutouts.

The Giants did not win another pennant until 1911, but McGraw usually had them in contention every year and they became the best-known team in baseball. He came close to winning in 1908, but in a crucial game Fred Merkle failed to touch second base and the Giants lost the replay of the game with Chicago after finishing the regular season in a first-place tie with the Cubs. The "Merkle Boner" play became famous, but the compassionate McGraw defended young Merkle and gave him a raise the following year.

By then, John was general manager as well as manager, although the title did not actually exist. But "The Little Napoleon" was clearly the boss of the club. He could be softhearted too, however, as he showed by employing many former friends as coaches or Polo Grounds employees. He wept when Christy Mathewson and Ross Youngs died at early ages. But he could still be tough, as he was so often with his team captains. Frankie Frisch walked out in 1926 when he had taken enough abuse from McGraw. Bill Terry and McGraw did not speak for two years.

Among the Hall-of-Famers who played for McGraw were Mathewson, McGinnity,

Youngs, Frisch, Hornsby, Terry, Marquard, Bresnahan, Kelly, Bancroft, Stengel, Roush, Ott, Grimes, and Hubbell. Although he worked his team hard, and had men cursing at him behind his back, few who played for him ever doubted that he was the best baseball man in the business. "Mr. McGraw" was without peer in his league during his 30 years with the Giants.

He won pennants in 1911, 1912, 1913, and 1917, but lost all four World Series. He became the first twentieth-century manager to win four pennants in a row (1921–1924), winning World Championships from the Yankees in 1921 and 1922. In 28 full seasons with the Giants he finished out of the first division only twice.

John had married Blanche Sindall in January 1902. The two lived comfortably in New Rochelle, New York, during his years with the Giants.

By the early 1930s McGraw's health was failing and his nerves were edgier than usual. His umpire-baiting became more frequent, and he battled with the league president and with his players. Although the Giants finished second in 1931, McGraw was not speaking to Terry and players called him an "old man" behind his back.

He was frequently absent early in the 1932 season. Then, suddenly, he called Terry into his office on June 3, 1932, and gave him the job as manager.

McGraw would not have been welcome in Terry's office, and he never returned to the clubhouse. But he still held stock in the club and he visited the Giants' downtown offices frequently. His only public appearance in baseball after his retirement as Giants' manager was to manage the first National League All-Star team in 1933.

Ill with prostate cancer and uremic poisoning, McGraw died on February 25, 1934, in New Rochelle. He was elected to the Hall of Fame in 1937.

JOHN JOSEPH McGRAW

Baltimore (A.A.) 1891
Baltimore (N.L.) 1892–1899
St. Louis (N.L.) 1900
Baltimore (A.L.) 1901–1902
New York (N.L.) 1902–1906

G	AB	R	H	2B	3B	HR	RBI	Avg.
1082	3919	1019	1307	124	71	12	462	.334

Bill McKechnie (1887-1965)

Bill McKechnie was not only a fine gentleman but was one of the game's most successful managers. He won pennants with three different National League clubs—a record. He also got great seasons out of teams without much talent. Once he was voted Manager of the Year with a second-division club that finished only six games over .500.

William Boyd McKechnie was born in Wilkinsburg, Pennsylvania, on August 7, 1887. Both his parents had emigrated from Scotland. Bill was raised in a religious home and adopted most of the traits of his parents—he was soft-spoken, clean living, and did not drink. For more than 25 years he was a member of the Wilkinsburg Methodist Church choir.

Bill never went to college but he was bright and quick to learn. At 18 he signed his first contract, joining the Washington, Pennsylvania, club in the Pennsylvania-Ohio-Maryland League. He stayed there for a year and a half, hitting very little but fielding adequately. Late in 1907 the Pittsburgh Pirates purchased him when they were short of infielders, and Bill got into three games—one at second, and two at third—collecting one single and one run batted in. Fred Clarke was the Pirates manager, but it was Honus Wagner who told Bill how to play the different hitters and what to expect from the pitchers.

However, the weak-hitting McKechnie failed to make the team in 1908 and was instead farmed out to Canton of the Ohio–Pennsylvania League. There, the 5'10", 180-pound switch-hitter played 118 games and batted .283. In 1909 he had another good year, batting .274 in 132 games for Wheeling in the Central League. That would have been a good season to be with the Pirates, for they won the pennant, but Bill did not make it back to Pittsburgh until 1910 when he spent the entire season in a utility role, playing 60 games and batting .217.

He had a decent shot in 1911, going to bat 321 times, but he hit only .227 and could not break into the regular lineup with any consistency. He opened the 1912 season with Pittsburgh, but after playing in 24 games and hitting .247 he was sent to St. Paul of the American Association.

It was obvious that Bill was never going to be a great hitter, but he was a capable infielder and a most pleasant man. He finished the 1912 season at St. Paul, hitting .234, and opened the 1913 season there, although he was by then the property of the Boston Braves, who had drafted him the previous fall.

Bill played one game for the 1913 Braves, then was claimed on waivers by the New York Yankees, playing their first season in the Polo Grounds under manager Frank Chance.

Bill's value as a player was clearly demonstrated with the Yankees. Although

McKechnie batted only .134 for 44 games, Chance surprised New York sportswriters at the end of the season by naming McKechnie "one of my most valuable players." Chance liked Bill's knowledge of the game and found him to be the only man on the club with whom he could discuss baseball.

The tribute was nice, but it was not enough to keep Bill in New York. He jumped to the Federal League in 1914, spending the season as regular third baseman for the pennant-winning Indianapolis club, where he batted .305. That said something about the league.

Indianapolis was not in the Federal League in 1915, so Bill joined the Newark club, owned by oilman Harry Sinclair. Sinclair bought the Indianapolis club in March 1915 and transferred it to Newark. On June 18, McKechnie was named to replace Bill Phillips as manager. He was only 27 years old but he did a good job, winning 54 of 99 games to finish fifth. Edd Roush was one of his players.

Since the Federal League had folded at the close of the season, Bill was signed by the New York Giants along with Roush. On July 20, he, Roush, and Christy Mathewson (three future Hall of Famers) were traded to Cincinnati for Buck Herzog and Wade Killefer.

"Deacon Bill," as he was called because of his religious background, hit .256 in 1916 and .254 with the Reds in 1917. In March 1918 he was sold to Pittsburgh again, this time playing 126 games and batting .255. He gave up baseball in 1919 but came back in 1920 to bat .218 with the Pirates, and then finished his active playing career with Minneapolis of the American Association in 1921, batting .321 in 156 games. Bill's lifetime major league batting average was .234 with 5 home runs and 127 stolen bases.

With the end of McKechnie's playing career came the beginning of a great managerial career. His first assignment was with the Pirates, for whom he was initially hired as a coach. But on July 15, 1922, he replaced George Gibson as manager with the club in sixth place. He wound up with a 47–26 record, lifting the team to fourth.

Bill was third the next two years, and then in 1925 led the team to its first pennant since 1909. He had really done a job rebuilding the club. His greatest success was the permanent move of Pie Traynor to third base. When faced with the problem of

McKechnie on the field. As a player, before his notable success as a manager with several teams, McKechnie was a good infielder and baseball expert, but a fairly weak hitter.

wild players who caroused all night, such as Rabbit Maranville, McKechnie simply roomed with them to keep an eye on them.

His 1925 club was typical of his four pennant winners. There were few stars, but most players had good seasons. As hitters he had Max Carey, Traynor, Kiki Cuyler, George Grantham, and Glenn Wright, but Bill admitted he was never much of a hitting coach anyway. Pitching was his forte, and he got excellent seasons out of Lee Meadows and Ray Kremer to help the Pirates win.

Down three games to one in the 1925 World Series, McKechnie brought his club back to defeat the Washington Senators for the World Championship.

The 1926 season was not a happy one for McKechnie. Fred Clarke had been named assistant manager and vice president, and dissension rode with the club. Late in the year, captain Max Carey called a meeting of all players to choose between Clarke and McKechnie. By a vote of 18–6 the players picked Clarke, but owner Barney Dreyfuss backed his manager and discarded the troublemaking players. McKechnie, however, departed after the season.

In 1927 he was a coach under Bob O'Farrell in St. Louis. Branch Rickey, the Cardinals' general manager, liked Bill's religious background. In 1928 O'Farrell was gone and McKechnie was named manager. He promptly led the Cards to the pennant, coping with Grover Cleveland Alexander's problems while making good pitchers out of Wee Willie Sherdel and Flint Rhem.

When the Yankees won four straight in the 1928 World Series, owner Sam Breadon humiliated McKechnie by shipping him off to manage Rochester of the International League and bringing up Billy Southworth to run the Cards. But after 88 games Breadon admitted his mistake and switched the two men again. The Cards finished fourth in 1929.

McKechnie could have remained with St. Louis, but he was offered a three-year contract by the Boston Braves and Breadon permitted him to take it. As it was, Bill almost left baseball that winter anyway, for he ran for tax collector in Wilkinsburg and would have quit baseball had he won the election. He lost.

Bill did not win any pennants with the Braves, but he took a hopelessly bad club and lifted it year by year. By 1933 he had the club in fourth place with an 83–71 record. It was considered a tremendous achievement.

In 1935 Judge Emil Fuchs, the Braves' owner, resigned, and Bill was named president pro tem of the club until Bob Quinn was hired. But it was a tough year with the unmanageable Babe Ruth on the roster. Two years later Bill made 20-game winners out of two rookies who were in their thirties, Lou Fette and Jim Turner, the club finished a surprisingly good fifth, and Bill was named Manager of the Year for his efforts.

In 1938 Warren Giles took over as general manager of the Cincinnati Reds and proceeded to lure his old friend from Rochester, McKechnie, to the Reds. Bill resigned from Boston and took the Cincinnati job at $25,000 a year. He finished fourth in 1938 and then won back-to-back pennants in 1939 and 1940, making big winners out of pitchers Paul Derringer, Bucky Walters, and Johnny Vander Meer. The 1940 club won 100 games and beat Detroit in the World Series.

Bill remained with the Reds through the 1946 season, but when postwar fans found his conservative brand of percentage baseball a little too dull, Giles regretfully had to let his close friend go.

In 1947 Bill Veeck hired McKechnie as a $45,000-a-year coach to assist young Lou Boudreau, and the Deacon stayed there for three years, finally retiring from baseball after the 1949 season.

In 1953 Bill moved to Bradenton, Florida, and did well with oil and land investments. His wife, the former Beryl Bien, died in 1957 after 46 years of marriage. They had two sons and two daughters, and Bill, Jr., eventually rose to become president of the Pacific Coast League.

In 1962, Bill was named to the Hall of Fame. He died in Bradenton on October 29, 1965, at the age of 78.

WILLIAM BOYD McKECHNIE

Pittsburgh 1907, 1910–1912, 1918, 1920
Boston (N.L.) 1913
New York (A.L.) 1913
Indianapolis (F.L.) 1914
Newark (F.L.) 1915
New York (N.L.) 1916
Cincinnati 1916–1917

G	AB	R	H	2B	3B	HR	RBI	Avg.
546	1822	163	427	40	22	5	180	.234

Joe Medwick (1911-1975)

A lifetime .324 hitter, Joe Medwick was the strong man of the St. Louis Cardinals' "Gas House Gang" of the 1930s.

Joseph Michael Medwick was born on November 24, 1911, in Carteret, New Jersey, of Hungarian parents. Athletic from an early age, he learned golf, handball, tennis, skating, and ping pong, in addition to starring at Carteret High School in baseball, football, and basketball. He was a third baseman and outfielder on the diamond, a halfback in football, and a forward in basketball. Football was perhaps his best sport, and at one point he hoped to attend Notre Dame.

After high school Medwick played semi-pro ball. In 1929 he had a chance to sign a professional contract with Newark of the International League, managed by Tris Speaker. But Medwick, a hardheaded, aggressive youngster, was kept waiting half an hour to see the management and stormed out of the Newark offices in a huff.

Medwick was playing sandlot ball back home when he was scouted by the Cardinals' Charlie (Pop) Kelchner in 1930. The Cardinals, under Branch Rickey, had an extensive scouting and minor league system and were able to find prospects even as far from St. Louis as Carteret. Medwick signed a contract with St. Louis and was assigned to Scottsdale of the Middle Atlantic League, where he played under the name of Mickey King in an effort to protect his amateur standing in case he had a chance to go to Notre Dame.

But after a season at Scottsdale, Joe left his football aspirations behind. He played in 75 games and batted .419 with 22 homers and 100 runs batted in. Suddenly, at 18, he was one of the hottest properties in baseball.

The Cardinals moved Joe up to Houston for the 1931 season. He led the Texas League in home runs (19), runs batted in (126), and games played (161), while batting .305. Chick Hafey was still occupying Joe's future position in the Cardinal outfield, and Hafey had led the National League in hitting in 1931, so Medwick, still only 20, started the 1932 season back in Houston.

He played 139 games there and batted .354 with 26 homers and 111 RBIs. By September he was in St. Louis. Hafey had been traded to Cincinnati in April and Joe moved into the left field job. He batted .349 in the season's last 26 games.

Joe was an aggressive, competitive fellow who easily fit into the Gas House Gang style of play. Sometimes his temper got the better of him. In ensuing years he got into fights with teammates Tex Carlton, Rip Collins, and Ed Heusser, which caused

some problems in the Cardinals' clubhouse. Once, back home at a Carteret–Perth Amboy football game, he got into a fight with an usher and was sued for $10,000.

In 1933, Joe's first full season with St. Louis, Frankie Frisch replaced Gabby Street as manager and the Cardinals finished fifth. Joe hit .306. It was the first of 10 consecutive seasons in which he batted .300 or better.

Joe had a big season in 1934, and the Cardinals won the pennant. He hit .319, led the league with 18 triples, and had 18 homers, 40 doubles, and 106 runs batted in. For the next six years Joe reached or topped the 40 mark in doubles each time. The 1934 season also earned him his first of 10 All-Star game selections, and he responded with a three-run homer off Lefty Gomez in the third inning.

The colorful Gas House Gang—whose name came into widespread use in 1935—included Medwick, Frisch, Collins, Leo Durocher, Pepper Martin, Dizzy and Paul Dean, and Ernie Orsatti. Martin, Medwick, and the Dean brothers teamed up to form the "Mudcatters," a musical combo which entertained teammates all season on the washboard, kazoo, whiskey jug, and musical saw.

Medwick had been known as "Ducky Wucky" since his Houston days when a girl fan had commented that he walked like a duck. Joe naturally preferred the nickname "Muscles," but his teammates and the St. Louis fans insisted on calling him Ducky Medwick.

During the 1934 World Series, Medwick figured in one of baseball's most unforgettable incidents. In the seventh and deciding game, played at Navin Field in Detroit, Joe recorded his eleventh hit of the Series in the seventh inning, a triple. He slid hard into third baseman Marv Owen, after Owen had faked him out with a phantom tag. Although the play was a tough one, no harm was done to either player and the umpires ignored the matter.

When the Cardinals' inning ended, Medwick returned to his left field position only to be greeted by a shower of fruit, newspapers, and bottles from the frustrated and angry Tiger fans, whose heroes were losing the game, 11–0. Medwick made light of the matter, picking up the fruit and playing catch with Martin and Orsatti, but the more he did so, the more debris the fans hurled, until the situation became dangerous. Commissioner Landis, watching the game, called Medwick and manager Frisch over to his box, discussed the situation with them, and ordered Medwick out of the game for his own protection. Since it was the seventh inning of an 11–0 game, Joe did not protest much. He wound up hitting .379 for the Series.

Joe really came alive with the bat in 1935, hitting .353. In 1936 he batted .351, setting a National League record by hitting 64 doubles and tying a league record by getting 10 consecutive hits. He also led the league with 138 RBIs, the first of a record-tying three consecutive years in which he would lead the league. Only Rogers Hornsby (1920–1922) had ever managed three in a row.

In 1937, Joe had one of the finest seasons ever recorded in the National League. He led the league in games, at bats, runs, hits, doubles, batting average, and runs batted in, and he tied Mel Ott for the lead in home runs with 31. Joe actually hit 32 that year, but one was canceled in a forfeit. He had 10 triples, the only batting department in which he did not lead, as he batted .374 and drove in 154 runs. He also led the league's outfielders in fielding percentage. Joe was an easy choice for the Most Valuable Player award that season. The next spring he held out until he got a $20,000 contract.

Medwick hit .322 in 1938 and again led the league in RBIs and in doubles.

Joe was noted as a bad ball hitter with great power, but the power fell off to 14 homers in 1939, a year in which some accused the 5'10", 178-pounder of playing more for himself than for the team. Just before the trading deadline in 1940, Joe was dealt to the Brooklyn Dodgers. Larry MacPhail paid $125,000 plus four players for Medwick and pitcher Curt Davis.

Six days after the trade, Joe was playing for Brooklyn against his former Cardinal teammates when pitcher Bob Bowman hit him on the head with a fastball, knocking him out and precipitating a major fight on the field. The Dodgers went so far as to demand that the New York District Attorney investigate, but the matter never went past National League president Ford Frick, who ruled it an accident. Medwick suffered a concussion, but he was back in action soon afterward. However, from then on he was always considered somewhat gun-shy at the plate.

He hit .301 in 1940 and .318 in 1941, a championship season for the Dodgers. He hit 18 home runs that year, his last time in double figures. In the 1941 World Series he batted .235.

Joe hit .300 in 1942 and .272 in 48 games for the 1943 Dodgers before he was sold across town to the Giants on July 6. Playing some first base for the first time, Joe wound up the year with a .278 mark, his first time under .300 since he began his professional career.

He came back in 1944 to hit .337 for New York, third in the league behind Dixie Walker and Stan Musial. It was really his last great batting feat, for in 1945 he was

traded to the Braves with Ewald Pyle for Clyde Kluttz, and then released by the Braves prior to spring training of 1946. The St. Louis Browns signed him for spring training but released him before the season began, and he sat idle until the Dodgers gave him another contract on June 28. He played 41 games for Brooklyn and hit .312, but did not have a home run until August 4, when he hit the 200th of his career.

The Dodgers released him after the 1946 season and he was signed by the Yankees. He spent spring training with them in St. Petersburg in 1947, but he failed to make the club. Upon his release he was signed again by the Cardinals, as an old hero coming home.

Joe hit .307 in 75 games for the Cards in 1947, and played 20 games with them in 1948, hitting .211 to conclude his major-league career. He returned to Houston, where a candy bar had once been named "Ducky Wucky" after him, and batted .276.

In 1949 he managed Miami Beach in the Florida International League, playing 106 games and hitting .323. In 1951 he was player-manager at Raleigh (Carolina League), and in 1952 player-manager at Tampa (Florida International League).

Joe and his wife Isabelle, whom he had married during the 1936 season, settled in St. Louis, from where he ran a small insurance business and actively campaigned for election to the Hall of Fame.

He returned to the Cardinals in 1966 as their minor league hitting instructor, and two years later he achieved his Hall of Fame goal, overcoming the handicap of his unpopularity among sportswriters.

Joe was in St. Petersburg, Florida, assisting the Cardinals with spring training, when he died of a heart attack on March 21, 1975, at the age of 63.

JOSEPH MICHAEL MEDWICK

St. Louis (N.L.) 1932–1940, 1947–1948
Brooklyn 1940–1943, 1946
New York (N.L.) 1943–1945
Boston (N.L.) 1945

G	AB	R	H	2B	3B	HR	RBI	Avg.
1984	7635	1198	2471	540	113	205	1383	.324

(At left) Tigers encircle Medwick after a set-to between Medwick and Tiger third baseman Marv Owen in the final game of the 1934 World Series. Medwick had slid hard into Owen, spikes flying. After the incident, Detroit fans threw bottles at Medwick, and (at right) Commissioner Landis decides to remove Medwick from the game. The Cards won. (Above) Medwick at bat: It was a foul ball.

Stan Musial (b.1920)

When Stan Musial retired from baseball in 1963 after 22 years in the majors, he left behind more than 50 major and National League records. Ten years after his retirement, a market research company found his name still ranked first among athletes when consumers were asked whose endorsement of a product they would most trust.

Stanley Frank Musial was born on November 21, 1920, in the coal mining town of Donora, Pennsylvania. His father, Lukasz Musial, was a Polish-speaking immigrant, and his mother, Mary, was a New Yorker. Stan, christened Stanislaus, was the fifth of six children, with four older sisters and a younger brother. He became Stanley when he entered school.

Inspired by a neighbor, a former minor-league player named Joe Barboa, Stan first dreamed of becoming a baseball player when he was eight. He began pitching for neighborhood teams, served as batboy for an adult team, and one day, when given the opportunity to pitch, struck out 13 men in 6 innings. Playing against boys his own age, Stan was the outstanding athlete of the community. He played American Legion and high school ball.

At 17, still a junior in high school, Stan tried out at nearby Monessen where the St. Louis Cardinals had a farm team. Stan's father wanted him to accept a basketball scholarship from the University of Pittsburgh, but baseball was too much on Stan's mind. In later years he deeply regretted not having first gone to college and he always urged young people to go.

Stan made a favorable impression at the Monessen tryout but did not hear from the Cardinals until the following spring. In the interim, Pie Traynor, the Pirate manager, offered Stan a contract, but since he had signed a letter of agreement with St. Louis the previous year, Stan decided to wait for the Cardinals to make an offer.

It came shortly thereafter, and in 1938 Stan signed his first professional contract, reporting to Williamson in the Mountain State League as a pitcher as soon as his high school term was completed. He won six games, lost six, had a 4.66 earned-run average, and a .258 batting average. The following season he let his girl friend Lillian Labash pick up his diploma, for he had already returned to Williamson to post a 9–2 record and a .352 batting average. In November, on Stan's nineteenth birthday, he and Lillian were married. They had four children.

The first child was born in 1940 when Stan and Lillian were living in the home of his manager, Dickie Kerr, at Daytona Beach (Florida State League). Kerr's fondness for the Musials and his generosity in a time of need were never forgotten. Years later, Stan quietly bought a home for the Kerrs in Houston.

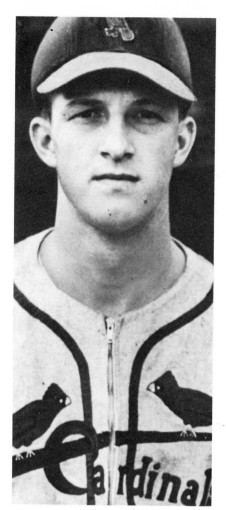

Stan Musial started professional ball as a pitcher, a career cut short by an army injury. Moved to the outfield, he won seven National League batting championships and chalked up a lifetime total of 3630 hits, second only to Ty Cobb. (Opposite page) The powerful Musial swing.

Kerr recognized Stan's skills with the bat and used him in the outfield in 57 games in 1940 on days when he was not pitching his way to an 18–5 record. But he was bothered by wildness, and did not seem pointed toward the big leagues as a pitcher.

Late in the 1940 season Stan fell on his throwing arm in the outfield and seriously injured it. When he reported in 1941 the arm was dead and he was through as a pitcher. Ollie Vanek, Stan's first professional manager and now the manager of Springfield (Western Association), agreed to take Stan as an outfielder for the 1941 season. The result was a .379 batting average with 26 home runs in just 87 games. Despite a career total of 475 major league homers, that was the only home run title ever won by Musial.

In midseason of 1941 Stan was advanced to Rochester of the International League, where he hit .326 in 54 games. By the end of the season he had joined the Cardinals. He played in 12 games for St. Louis to close out the season, pounding out 20 hits for a .426 average.

In 1942 Stan stepped into the regular lineup of the championship-bound Cardinals. During the next 22 years (with the exception of 1945 when he was in military service) he set major league records for most seasons of 100 or more games, most extra base hits, most total bases, and most home runs in a double header (5). Among his National League records were games played, consecutive games played (later broken by Billy Williams), times at bat, runs, hits, doubles, runs batted in, most years with 100 or more RBIs, and most years leading outfielders in fielding.

Many of his National League records were later broken by Hank Aaron, but when Stan quit only Ty Cobb had a better overall collection of lifetime credentials.

The 1942 Cardinals won 106 games under manager Billy Southworth, and Stan batted .315 with 10 homers and 72 runs batted in. This was the first of three consecutive Cardinal pennants with each club winning more than 100 games. In 1943, Stan won his first of seven batting championships, hitting .357 with league-leading figures in games, hits, doubles, and triples. In his sophomore season he won his first of three Most Valuable Player awards.

In the Cardinals' third straight pennant year, 1944, Stan hit .347 and led the league in hits and doubles. (He led the National League in hits six times and in doubles eight times.) His home run production soared when he altered his batting stance into an odd, hump-backed position from the left side of the plate, with the bat held straight up.

Stan was in the Navy in 1945, playing service ball at home and in the Pacific, but

he returned to the Cardinals in 1946 to find himself a featured member of another pennant-winning club. He won both his second batting crown (.365) and his second Most Valuable Player award, leading the league in runs, hits (228), doubles, and triples. In four full seasons Stan had played on four pennant winners, but 1946 was the last pennant the Cards would win during Stan's career. His batting average for 23 World Series games was only .256.

That 1946 season earned Musial the nickname of "Stan the Man." It was given to him in Brooklyn, for it was there that he enjoyed his greatest success, compiling a lifetime .356 batting average in Ebbets Field.

Stan moved to first base in 1946, dividing the remainder of his career between first and the outfield. He is the only man ever to play 1000 games at each position. After hitting .312 in 1947, he came back in 1948 to record his finest year—a .376 average, with 39 homers, and league-leading figures in RBIs (131), runs (135), hits (230), doubles (46), and triples (18). Again bat control was Stan's strong point, despite a reputation as a power hitter. Stan never struck out more than 46 times in any season.

The 1948 season led to Stan's third MVP award, and although his awards and pennants were behind him, he remained one of the great stars of baseball throughout the 1950s. He opened the decade with three consecutive batting titles (.346 in 1950, .355 in 1951, and .336 in 1952). Stan played in 24 All-Star Games with 6 homers and a .317 average, and won the 1955 game at Milwaukee with a twelfth-inning home run.

At times Stan held out for more money, but he was generally cooperative. He had played for $13,500 in 1946, turned down a big offer to jump to Mexico, and finally climbed to $31,000 in 1947. By 1958, the year in which he recorded his 3000th hit, his salary was up to $100,000, making him only the third man to reach that figure. (Joe DiMaggio and Hank Greenberg had preceded him, and Ted Williams also made it that year.)

A durable athlete, Stan played 895 consecutive games between April 15, 1952 and August 22, 1957.

In 1959 Stan fell below .300 for the first time in his career, batting only .255 and convincing many that he had lost his skills. But he continued his difficult training methods throughout the winter months as though he were still 22 years old and improved his average to .275 in 1960 and .288 in 1961. Then, in 1962, the 41-year-old grandfather batted .330 for the sixth-place Cardinals to finish third in the league in hitting. He announced his retirement following the 1963 season and was honored in every park in the league. His lifetime total of 3630 hits was second only to Ty Cobb's, and his .331 lifetime average was bettered only by Ted Williams among post-World War II players.

Following his retirement, Stan was appointed a vice-president of the Cardinals. In 1967, a pennant-winning season for the club, he served as general manager but gave up the position at the end of the year and became senior vice-president. A bronze statue of Musial was later erected outside the Cardinals' new park.

In 1969, his first year of eligibility, Stan was elected to the Hall of Fame by the sportswriters who had come to appreciate him as not only the best hitter of his era in the National League but as one of the finest gentlemen ever to play professional sports.

STANLEY FRANK MUSIAL

St. Louis (N.L.) 1941–1963

G	AB	R	H	2B	3B	HR	RBI	Avg.
3026	10972	1949	3630	725	177	475	1951	.331

"Stan the Man" Musial catches one just for fun. He got his famous nickname from Brooklyn fans, who groaned when he got up to bat in Ebbets Field, where his lifetime batting average was .356. His overall average was .331, the second highest in post-World War II baseball.

Kid Nichols (1869-1953)

Kid Nichols's lifetime victory total is exceeded only by those of Cy Young, Walter Johnson, Grover Alexander, Christy Mathewson, and Warren Spahn. But because the slight righthander won most of his games in the nineteenth century, baseball fans have generally forgotten his name.

Charles Augustus Nichols was born on September 14, 1869, in Madison, Wisconsin. His family moved to Kansas City, Missouri, in 1884, and Nichols gained most of his early baseball experience on the Kansas City sandlots.

Unlike many promising players who were scouted or recommended to professional clubs, Nichols had to act on his own behalf to get a contract. In 1886 he applied for a job as a pitcher with the Kansas City team in the National League, a major league club with only a 30–91 record that year. Although the team had no players of note, Nichols was turned down, and instead joined an amateur team, the Blue Avenue Club of Kansas City.

He pitched well there, but at only 5'9'' and 145 pounds he was not considered much of a prospect. In 1887, when he again applied to Kansas City for a job, he was again turned down. This time Kansas City was in the Western League, a minor circuit.

But in June, Kansas City finally gave Nichols a job when the club was in need of pitching. Immediately displaying the strong arm they thought he lacked, Nichols registered a 21–11 record in just two-thirds of a season.

Nichols began the 1888 campaign with Memphis of the Southern League, but after pitching 15 games he spent the remainder of the season back in Kansas City, then in the Western Association.

His first big break came in 1889 when he landed with the Omaha team in the Western Association. There his manager, Frank Selee, used him in 48 games, and he responded with 36 victories and 12 defeats. He struck out 357 batters and walked only 92.

Hired to manage the Boston Beaneaters of the National League in 1890, Selee urged the club to sign Nichols as well. Nichols was scouted late in the year by Bill Conant and purchased from Omaha for $3000.

Slight of build and youthful in appearance, Nichols was given the nickname "Kid" by his new teammates. The gentlemanly righthander retained the nickname throughout his life.

Nichols's game was based on speed and control. He had no breaking pitch and used a change of pace only on occasion. He was an overhand pitcher who employed no windup, since he found that it interfered with his control.

He also had one of the strongest arms ever owned by a pitcher. In his 12 years with Boston he pitched more than 400 innings five times, and more than 300 innings in all but one season. He was relieved only 25 times in the 502 games he started for Boston. His career total of 530 complete games ranks fourth on the all-time list. He holds the record for most 300-inning seasons with 12, and also the record for most 30-victory seasons with 7.

In 1890, his rookie year, Nichols led the Beaneaters with 27 wins, surpassing John Clarkson as the leader of the pitching staff. Boston was only fifth that year, but in 1891 the club jumped to the top of the standings, beating Cap Anson's White Stockings by 3½ games. Nichols was 30–17 with 213 strikeouts and only 96 walks in 423 innings. It was his first of seven consecutive seasons of 30 victories or more.

In 1892, Kid was 35–16, his top victory total. He pitched 454 innings, had 49 complete games, and at one point late in the year pitched three complete game victories on three consecutive days in three different cities.

There was a post-season playoff that year between the first and second half champions, Cleveland and Boston. In the opening game of the series one of baseball's most memorable pitching duels was staged, with Nichols opposing Cy Young. The two hurled an 11-inning scoreless tie. Boston went on to win the next five games to gain the championship.

The Beaneaters were first again in 1893 with Nichols posting a 33–13 record. He had a decision in every game he appeared in. During his career, which covered 582 games, he failed to gain a decision only 20 times.

Baseball was a rough sport for both players and fans in those days. Locked in a close pennant race with Pittsburgh in September 1893, Nichols beat the Pirates in Pittsburgh, 7–3, then found himself both mobbed and stoned by angry fans after the game. Only a fierce whipping of the horses on his carriage enabled him to make a getaway, but he claimed to have been struck at least a dozen times by the rioting fans.

Boston finished third, tied for fifth, and fourth in the next three seasons while Nichols had records of 32–13, 30–14, and 30–15. In the latter year, he led the league in victories for the first time. In 1897 the Beaneaters again finished first, this time finding themselves in the Temple Cup series against the great Baltimore Orioles.

Nichols, who had pitched 358 innings with a 30–11 record during the regular season, won the first game of the Temple

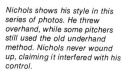
Nichols shows his style in this series of photos. He threw overhand, while some pitchers still used the old underhand method. Nichols never wound up, claiming it interfered with his control.

Cup series, 13–12, but lasted only six innings. Claiming that his arm was at last somewhat sore, he elected to rest it until the next season. Baltimore went on to win four straight for the Cup.

The winter's rest served Nichols well, for Boston won the pennant again in 1898, and "Nervy Nick" had a 29–12 record, leading the league in victories for the third consecutive year. He had gotten the "Nervy Nick" name the previous year when he beat the Orioles two out of three late in the season to clinch the pennant for Boston.

Kid was earning the maximum National League salary at the time, $2400, but he held out for more money as the 1899 season approached. At last, the management gave him a $235 bonus for winning the 1898 pennant. Still not satisfied, Nichols took the money and went back to work.

He spent three more seasons in Boston, winning 21 and losing 17 in 1899, then going 13–15 and 18–15 in his final two seasons.

In 1902 he bought a part interest in the Kansas City team of the Western League, the team that had once shunned him. As a pitcher and manager he was 27–7 in 1902 and 21–12 in 1903. The following year he was given the job as manager of the St. Louis Cardinals.

Nichols also pitched for the Cardinals, posting a 21–13 record, but aside from first baseman Jake Beckley and pitcher Jack Taylor, he was the only talented player on the team. The Cardinals finished fifth.

Returning as player and manager in 1905 with virtually the same club, Nichols did not get off to a good start, and the Cardinals won only 19 of their first 48 games before he was replaced as manager in mid-June. Nichols himself was battling an attack of pleurisy, and his own record as a pitcher was limited to 1–5. But the final blow was a dispute with management over one of his duties.

It was the practice of visiting clubs to assign a pitcher not working that day to watch the gates, count the tickets, and make sure the visitors got the correct share of the receipts. Nichols had done this for years while pitching for Boston. He recalled counting 30,000 tickets at the Polo Grounds in New York one day, and said it was "tougher than pitching nine innings."

When the Cardinal management asked him to be the ticket counter, he protested the additional duty. His illness, the team's showing, and the dispute, led to his release in July.

Nichols soon signed with Hugh Duffy's Philadelphia Phillies and was 10–6 in 17 games for the remainder of the year. In 1906 he returned to the Phillies and had an 0–1 record when a bad back forced him to the sidelines. His pitching career, covering 360 victories, was over. He was 36 years old.

Kid returned to Kansas City and bought into a bowling alley. He coached for several years at Missouri Valley College in Marshall, Missouri. He also coached amateur clubs in the Kansas City area for many years. Among his pupils was Casey Stengel.

Nichols played golf and bowled, becoming quite adept at the latter sport. He won the Kansas City bowling championship in 1933 at the age of 64. He was still bowling when he was in his 70s.

In 1949, somewhat late, many felt, he was named to the Hall of Fame. Three years later he was bothered by a severe neck ailment, and on April 11, 1953, he died in Kansas City at the age of 83.

CHARLES AUGUSTUS NICHOLS

Boston (N.L.) 1890–1901
St. Louis (N.L.) 1904–1905
Philadelphia (N.L.) 1905–1906

G	IP	W	L	Pct.	H	R	ER	SO	BB	ERA
582	5067	360	202	.641	4854	inc.	inc.	1866	1245	inc.

Jim O'Rourke (1852-1919)

"Orator" Jim O'Rourke was an eloquent player and club official who began playing baseball in 1866 and completed his career 48 years later.

James Henry O'Rourke was born in East Bridgeport, Connecticut, on August 24, 1852. He was the son of a poor farmer who died when Jim was still quite young, leaving his mother to manage the farm along with Jim and his younger brother, John. John was later a teammate of Jim's on the Boston Red Stockings (1880) and played for the New York Metropolitans in 1883, recording a lifetime .295 average for 230 games.

Jim first began playing baseball in 1866 with the Bridgeport Unions, an amateur team. He was somewhat bowlegged, stood only 5'8", and weighed a stocky 185 pounds during his career. He was never outstanding defensively at any one position, but from an early age he was a good hitter.

Jim had to schedule his playing time around his farm chores for his mother depended on the two boys to work the farm. In 1867 he found time to join the Mansfields of Middletown, an outstanding amateur team that also featured Tim Murnane. In 1872 the Mansfields turned professional, joining the year-old National Association, baseball's first major league. The manager of the club, Ben Douglas, went to the O'Rourke farm to sign Jim, but could only get him by providing a farm worker to take his place at home. Once that was accomplished, Jim was off to play professional ball.

He played particularly well that season when facing Harry Wright's Boston Red Stockings. When Mansfield disbanded after the 1872 season, Wright recruited Jim for the champion Red Stockings.

In 1873 he played in 57 of the club's 59 games and hit .347, helping the club to another championship. The Red Stockings went on to win in 1874 and 1875 as well, with Jim getting increased playing time. Harry Wright also made a fine opposite-field hitter out of the righthanded-hitting O'Rourke.

When the National League was formed in 1876 to replace the National Association, Jim remained in Boston to play for the first Boston team in that league. In fact, he had the distinction of getting the first hit in National League history, a clean line-drive single to left.

Jim was a proud man of keen intelligence. When he first came to Boston, at a time of discrimination against the Irish, Wright asked him if he would mind playing under the name of "Rourke." "I'd rather die than give up part of my father's name," he answered. And so it was always O'Rourke.

With Jim batting .351 and playing center

field, Boston won the pennant in 1877.

While playing in Boston, Jim took advantage of his off seasons to attend Yale Law School. He received a law degree and eventually opened his own law practice. As a ball player, he was fairly well paid for the period, and he managed to save his money and put it into wise land investments. With his wife and eight children (seven of them daughters) he expanded the family farm in Bridgeport and became a leading citizen of the small Connecticut city. Still, he remained popular with his teammates.

Jim was furious over a provision in his contract in 1878 that called for a $20 deduction from his salary to pay for his uniform. When he refused to sign it, the fans raised the money to outfit him. But in 1879, Jim and Boston manager-shortstop George Wright went to the Providence Grays and helped them to the 1879 National League pennant. Jim hit .351 that year.

Jim returned to the Red Stockings in 1880, when he tied for the National League lead in home runs with six and batted .282 for the sixth-place Boston club. That year he became close friends with English boxing champion Patsey Shepard, who tried to get him to leave baseball for a career in the ring. Jim, however, declined.

In 1881, Jim transferred his loyalties to the Buffalo club of the National League, where he was named manager. He had an impressive array of players on that team, including Dan Brouthers, Pud Galvin, Hardie Richardson, and Deacon White, but they finished third. Jim brought them home in a third place tie in 1882, fifth in 1883, and third in 1884, when he won the National League batting championship with a .350 average.

O'Rourke's nickname "Orator Jim" dates from this period and derived from his astonishing vocabulary and verbosity. Once, while replying to a player's request for a raise in salary, Jim said, "I'm sorry, but the exigencies of the occasion and the condition of our exchequer will not permit anything of the sort at this period of our existence. Subsequent developments in the field of finance may remove the present gloom and we may emerge into a condition where we may see fit to reply in the affirmative to your exceedingly modest request." That was Jim O'Rourke.

In 1885, Jim Mutrie became manager of the New York Giants and invited O'Rourke

Jim O'Rourke, who made the first hit in the history of the National League. It was a line drive single to the left for Boston at the start of the 1876 season. O'Rourke combined baseball with studying law at Yale.

to join his club. Playing with men like Tim Keefe, Mickey Welch, Roger Connor, Buck Ewing, and John Montgomery Ward (another lawyer), Jim hit .300. Despite his lack of speed, he tied for the league lead with 15 triples.

Jim was as popular in New York as he had been in Boston, and he enjoyed the off days on Sunday when he could travel up to his growing farm in Bridgeport to see that all was going well. His baseball career certainly flourished for he helped the Giants to their first two pennants in 1888 and 1889. Jim hit .274 and .321 in those two seasons, playing mostly left field as Ewing handled the catching.

In 1890, Jim was among the many stars who deserted the National League for the Players' League. He played for Ewing on the New York team and hit a career high .367, third in the league. But when the league died after one season he returned to the Giants for the 1891 and 1892 seasons.

Jim completed his major league playing career with a .306 average for the National League's Washington Senators in 1893. His career mark was .314.

In 1894, Orator Jim tried his hand at umpiring in the National League, but he found the work thankless and not to his style. At that point he returned home to Bridgeport, where he became active in baseball organization and government.

"Uncle Jeems," as he was now called, founded the Victor League in Connecticut and managed the Bridgeport Victors in 1895 and 1896. All games were played on a field carved out of his own farm.

After the 1896 season Jim founded the Connecticut League, serving as the first secretary and treasurer. He was the manager of the Bridgeport club, and at one point his only son, James Stephen O'Rourke, was one of his players.

Jim was by no means an inactive member of the league. He remained in good shape and continued to catch most of the games for Bridgeport. He batted as high as .358 in 1900, at the age of 48. And four years later John McGraw of the Giants recruited Jim to catch a full game, as the Giants marched to the 1904 pennant. At age 52, Jim stepped behind the plate to handle Joe McGinnity and had one hit in four appearances. The Giants won the game and the pennant.

He continued to manage Bridgeport through the 1908 season, although his playing ended in 1907. But even with the end of his professional career, he continued to play for his Elks Lodge team.

Active in politics, Jim was a fire commissioner in Bridgeport and a member of the paving and sewer commission. He remained an influential figure in baseball, serving on the Board of Arbitration for the minor leagues and, later, on the board of directors of the National League.

In 1902 he hired Bill Klem as a Connecticut League umpire, and sent him on to become the major leagues' leading umpire.

In 1909, O'Rourke sold the Bridgeport club and devoted most of his remaining years to his law practice. He died of pneumonia on January 8, 1919, at the age of 66.

In 1945, Jim O'Rourke was named to the Hall of Fame.

JAMES HENRY O'ROURKE

Mansfield (N.A.) 1872
Boston (N.A.) 1873–1875
Boston (N.L.) 1876–1878, 1880
Providence (N.L.) 1879
Buffalo (N.L.) 1881–1884
New York (N.L.) 1885–1889, 1891–1892, 1904
New York (P.L.) 1890
Washington (N.L.) 1893

G	AB	R	H	2B	3B	HR	RBI	Avg.
1750	7365	1425	2314	385	139	49	inc.	.314

Mel Ott (1909-1958)

The first man in National League history to hit 500 home runs was only 5'9" and weighed 170 pounds. But for 22 years Melvin Thomas Ott was one of the most feared hitters in baseball.

Mel Ott was born on March 2, 1909, in Gretna, Louisiana. His father and uncle were semipro players. At Gretna High School, Mel was a catcher on the school team and also played football and basketball.

In 1925, when he was only 16, Mel tried out with the New Orleans club in the Southern Association but was turned down because he was too small and too young. While his high school battery mate, Les Ruprich, was given a New Orleans contract, Mel was told to try a semipro outfit in Patterson, Louisiana.

Mel took the advice, joined the Patterson team, and established a warm relationship with the club's millionaire owner, Harry Williams. Williams paid Mel $150 a month to play about 14 games. When New Orleans changed its mind about Mel a few weeks later, Mel's loyalty to Williams kept him in Patterson.

In August, Williams arranged for Ott to go to New York and look up John McGraw for a tryout with the New York Giants. McGraw trusted Williams's advice, but he was only mildly interested in Ott when he saw how small the young catcher was. Mel worked out for a few days in the Polo Grounds, soon finding his batting range and poking balls over the fence with its convenient 257-foot right field foul line.

It was hard not to notice Mel at bat. Aside from his power, he had a unique batting style. With his feet planted wide apart in the lefthanded batting box, he would approach a pitch by raising his right leg in the air, dropping it quickly, and lashing out at the ball. The entire stride was only a few inches.

McGraw was now impressed by Ott's hitting, and although Mel was only 16 years old the Giant manager decided to keep him on the major league club rather than risk having a minor league manager alter the batting stance.

Mel did not appear in any games in 1925, but he was a big leaguer at 16, and he sat close to McGraw on the Giant bench, learning all about National League pitchers. Only Christy Mathewson and Ross Youngs had found places in McGraw's heart as Ott did. Although McGraw would never admit to playing favorites, Mel clearly became one.

McGraw's first decision regarding Mel was to move him to right field. Mel was not big enough to catch, but he had the speed other positions demanded. He learned to play right field very well, and even in later years when his eyesight was slipping he could still get a great jump on a ball by relying on his keen instincts.

Ross Youngs was the Giants' right fielder in 1926, and Mel, as his backup man, appeared in 35 games that year at the age of 17, hitting .383 in 60 times at bat.

He increased his playing time to 82 games in 1927, batting .282 and hitting an inside-the-park home run. It was his first of 511 National League home runs, a league record which stood until the late 1960s when Willie Mays, Hank Aaron, Ernie Banks, and Ed Mathews all broke it.

Mel also set National League records for runs batted in and runs scored, but these, too, were later broken, first by Stan Musial and then by Hank Aaron. Such is the nature of records, for Ott himself had broken many of Honus Wagner's career marks. The one National League record set by Ott that still stands is for bases on balls, something he managed 1708 times, including 10 seasons of 100 or more.

Mel's first season of regular play was 1928, when he appeared in 124 games and batted .322 with 18 home runs. It marked the first of 10 seasons as a regular in which Ott would hit .300, leaving a lifetime average of .304.

His power more than doubled in 1929 when he belted 42 home runs and drove in 151 runs, both career highs, although neither figure led the league.

In 1930 Ott hit .349 and in 1931 he had a .292 average. By midseason of 1932, McGraw was gone, never having managed Ott in a World Series. Bill Terry became the new Giant manager. Mel shared his first of six home run titles that year, belting 38 to tie Chuck Klein for the honor.

The Giants won the 1933 pennant for Terry, although Mel batted only .283 with 23 home runs. In the World Series against Washington, however, he batted .389, going 4 for 4 in his first Series game, and winning the fifth and deciding game with a tenth-inning home run off Jack Russell.

Mel had married in 1930, and he and his wife Mickey lived in the Greenwich Village section of New York City with their two daughters. Only once did he work during the winter—when he took a job in a clothing store after his rookie year. Otherwise, Mel never knew any business but baseball.

Entering his ninth big-league season at the age of 25, Mel batted .326 and shared the home run crown with Rip Collins, each hitting 35. He also won his only RBI title in 1934, driving in 135 runs. The following season Terry asked Ott to try third base, and Mel played there from time to time in his career, including regular stints in 1937 and 1938. He batted .322 in 1935, and .328 in 1936 as the Giants won another pennant, with Mel gaining another home run title (33). In the World Series loss to the Yankees, Mel hit .304.

In 1937, Ott hit 31 homers, tying Joe Medwick for the league lead, and played third base in the World Series, again won by the Yankees. His .200 mark in that Series gave him a .295 showing for the three World Series in which he played.

Mel won still another home run crown in 1938 with 36, and his 116 RBIs gave him nine seasons of 100 RBIs or better, the first eight (1929–1936) having come consecutively. The Giants, however, had become a .500 club under Terry, and were out of the pennant races now. So in 1942 Giant owner Horace Stoneham replaced Terry with Ott, now a 33-year old veteran. Stoneham admitted that "Mel's the favorite player of both my wife and daughter—I could never fire him."

Mel's first season as manager saw the Giants, who had been 74–79 in 1941, achieve an 85–67 record, good for third place in the first of the war years. Mel's 30 home runs netted a final home run title, and he batted .295, leading the league with 118 runs scored.

But in 1943 the Giants crumbled to last place, winning only 55 games. Mel himself dropped to .234 with only 18 home runs. The 1944 Giants finished fifth (Mel hit .288), and the 1945 Giants stayed there, as Mel hit .308 in his final season as a regular.

The war was over in 1946, and major-league rosters were back at full strength. Mel limited himself to 68 times at bat that season, and had only five hits for an .074 average. Included was his 511th and last home run, but again the Giants finished in the cellar.

Struggling along as manager, Mel rallied the team a bit in 1947, gaining a fourth-place finish. The Giants' Johnny Mize won the RBI crown and shared the homer title that year. But the archrival Brooklyn Dodgers won the pennant, and that did not help the Giants' box office at all.

Mel made his final four pinch-hitting appearances in 1947, failed each time, and ended his playing career.

In 1948 the Giants again got off to a bad start. They were 27–38 on July 16 when Stoneham made the difficult decision to fire Ott and replace him with former Dodger manager Leo Durocher. Leo's famous "nice guys finish last" statement had been directed at Ott several years before, and many felt that was part of the reason for Ott's limited success as a manager—he had simply been too nice.

As a valued member of the Giants' organization, Mel was given the job of assisting Carl Hubbell with the farm system. He received credit for developing the batting style of Bobby Thomson, but by the time Thomson hit his famous 1951 home run to win the pennant Ott had moved on. Seeking to return to the big leagues as a manager, Mel went to Oakland in the Pacific Coast League that year. Casey Stengel had managed Oakland before going to the Yankees.

During the 1951 season Mel became a Hall-of-Famer. He managed Oakland that year and the next, but when no major league offers came he retired from the game.

Mel made some money in a contracting business back home in Metairie, Louisiana, a suburb of New Orleans. He returned to baseball as a broadcaster, first working as an announcer for the "Game of the Day" radio program and then spending three seasons on the Detroit Tigers' radio network.

On November 14, 1958, he and his wife were involved in an automobile accident near Bay St. Louis, Mississippi. The driver of the other car that foggy night was killed, and both Mel and his wife were seriously injured. Mel was transferred to a hospital in New Orleans where a valiant effort was made to save his life. But on November 21, at the age of 49, Mel Ott died.

MELVIN THOMAS OTT

New York (N.L.) 1926–1947

G	AB	R	H	2B	3B	HR	RBI	Avg.
2730	9456	1859	2876	488	72	511	1860	.304

Mel Ott's style of play: (Opposite page) Ott gets ready to slug the ball in the unique way that got him 511 homers. He would raise his right leg in the air, then drop it quickly and lash out at the ball. (This page, left) He streaks back into the outfield for a long fly ball. (Near left) Ott in the outfield, awaiting the fate of the pitch.

Satchel Paige (b.1906)

Satchel Paige was not only one of the longest-lasting, most highly accomplished pitchers in baseball history, he was undoubtedly one of the game's great showmen. He packed ballparks throughout the country both before and after reaching the major leagues, something he did not achieve until he was 42 years old.

According to a Mobile, Alabama, birth certificate, he was born, LeRoy Robert Page on July 7, 1906. John Page, his father, was a gardener, and Lula, his mother, a domestic. According to Satchel, they changed the spelling of the family name to Paige "to sound more high tone."

Satchel's age was always a great mystery, for many doubted that anyone of his supposed years could still pitch effectively enough to stick in the American League. And showman that he was, Satch always kept them guessing. But he finally did reveal the existence of the birth certificate.

Satchel was the seventh of 11 children in a poor family. He briefly attended school at the W. H. Council elementary school, and at the age of 10 was a pitcher for the school team. But much of his childhood was spent getting into trouble—playing hookey, fighting, and in general being a problem.

When he was only seven, his mother got him a job toting satchels at the local depot, and that is how he got his nickname. When he was eight, he practiced throwing rocks at targets and became quite accomplished at it.

A theft of some small toys from a Mobile store caused Paige to be committed to the Industrial School for Negro Children at Mount Meigs, Alabama, in July 1918. The five and a half years he spent in the reformatory "made a man out of me." He played ball, participated in the choir and band, and got a sound education.

In December 1923 he was released and returned home to Mobile. His older brother, Wilson, was playing for a local semipro team, the Mobile Tigers, and in 1924 he got Satchel a job as a $1-a-game pitcher. Paige's record that summer was something like 30–1, but as a semipro pitcher he had no loyalty to any club and went wherever the money was. That was somewhat typical of his professional career too, and he was often accused of jumping teams whenever a better offer came along.

In 1926 he signed his first professional contract, joining the Chattanooga Black Lookouts in the Negro Southern League for $50 a month. While most black ballplayers simply accepted the Negro leagues as a fact of life, Paige, from the start, was bitter over the lack of opportunity to play in the major leagues. Full of confidence, he was outraged at the idea that he would never be able to pitch to Babe Ruth.

Satchel Paige dominated Negro baseball in the late 1930s and early 1940s. He probably won more games than any other pitcher in history. He drew huge crowds wherever he played, and when he finally entered the majors as a 42-year-old rookie, he filled the stands. (Opposite) Paige draws back to fire his legendary fastball for the Kansas City Monarchs.

Satchel was strictly a fastball pitcher when he began. He was tall and thin and used a windmill delivery. He called his fastball his "bee ball" and outclassed most of the hitters in the Negro Southern League.

In 1928 he was given a $275-a-month contract by the Birmingham Black Barons. The Birmingham manager, Bill Gatewood, worked to perfect Satchel's skills and made him into something of a gate attraction. There were even times when Gatewood rented Paige to other clubs for a day or two.

Sold to the Nashville Elite Giants late in 1929, Paige began to play baseball 12 months a year. Although his earnings in baseball became better than those of any other black player, he was always on the move, pitching as many as 200 games a season. He spent winters in the Caribbean, summers in the States, and always carried two suitcases—one full and one empty, to bring back any gifts he might accumulate.

After spending the winter of 1929–1930 pitching in Cuba, Satch returned to Nashville for the 1930 season. The Elite Giants operated out of Cleveland part of that season.

His first great fame followed the 1930 season, when he was hired by the Baltimore Black Sox to pitch against a barnstorming team led by Babe Ruth. Paige never faced Ruth on the tour because Babe was in the lineup only on Satch's off days, but Satch had an outstanding series, striking out 22 batters in one game against a team that included Hack Wilson and Babe Herman.

Early in 1931 the Elite Giants folded and Paige caught on with Gus Greenlee's Pittsburgh Crawfords for $250 a month. There his battery mate was the great Josh Gibson. There, also, after he defeated archrival Homestead in his debut, Satch had his salary raised to $700 a month. Greenlee advertised his club heavily as it traveled the country, claiming in his ads that "Josh Gibson will hit two home runs and Satchel Paige will strike out the first nine batters!" There were times when he was proved correct.

Satch's heaviest schedule came in the early 1930s. He traveled to the West Coast and Hawaii, pitched in Canada, Venezuela, Cuba, and the Dominican Republic. Frequently he faced big leaguers in the winter exhibition matches, and he always did well. He seldom lost in those days when his "bee ball" was at its best. Paige was thus the first to make good money in the Negro circuit.

Off the field, Paige enjoyed trap-shooting, billiards, and china and antique collecting. He married Janet Howard on October 26, 1934, with entertainer Bill "Bojangles" Robinson as his best man. But the long separations were difficult on the marriage, and the two were finally divorced in 1943. On October 12, 1947, Paige married

Lahoma Brown, his longtime girl friend. They had six children.

Late in 1934, Paige and Greenlee fought over salary, and Satchel jumped the club for an integrated team in Bismarck, North Dakota. But conditions were even more difficult there than they had been in the South, and when Satch could not get a place to live, he sought another change.

In the fall of 1934–1935, Satchel toured the country against the Dizzy Dean All-Stars and won four of the six games. Dean thought Paige was as good as any pitcher he had ever seen, including himself.

For jumping the Pittsburgh club in 1934, Satchel was banned by the Negro Leagues in 1935. He spent the year barnstorming and won the Most Valuable Player award in the first National Baseball Congress semipro tournament in Wichita. That winter, the Satchel Paige All-Stars faced the Dick Bartell All-Stars in a series in Oakland, California.

The ban was lifted on Paige in 1936, and he rejoined the Pittsburgh Crawfords. But the following year he accepted a $30,000 offer to pitch in the Dominican Republic. Satch did not last through the season, however; the political pressures of the Trujillo government scared him back to Pittsburgh. But he jumped again, this time to Mexico, and for Greenlee this was the last straw. Greenlee traded him to the Newark Eagles, and Paige never bothered to report.

A sore arm in 1938 seemed to spell the end of his career, but J. L. Wilkinson and Tom Baird, owners of the Kansas City Monarchs, rescued him and gave him a job. He learned to throw breaking pitches, and gradually his arm returned to form. He reached his greatest fame with the Monarchs, where his salary went as high as $22,000 a year. Paige spent nine full seasons with the Monarchs, during which time his club won five pennants, and he pitched three or four times a week. In 1943 he developed his "hesitation pitch," later ruled illegal by the major leagues. He registered for the Army in World War II but was not taken, so instead he pitched exhibitions and visited Army hospitals. In 1946 his owners in Kansas City bought him a two-seater plane called *The Satchel Paige* to help him on his barnstorming schedule.

Paige faced the Bob Feller All-Stars on the West Coast in the winter of 1947 and, at age 41, made an impressive showing. Jackie Robinson, a former teammate on the Monarchs, had reached the major leagues that year, and other black players were being signed ahead of Paige. He knew his age was the reason, but he still felt he could pitch in the big leagues and thought he deserved an opportunity.

(Far left) Paige, with Cecil Travis and Dizzy Dean, center, enjoying a break in one of the exhibition games pitting major leaguers against Negro leaguers. (Above) Bill Veeck, owner of the St. Louis Browns, welcomes Paige back to the big leagues in 1951.

Bill Veeck, dynamic owner of the Indians, came to Paige's rescue. A showman in his own right, Veeck signed Satchel in July 1948 as the fifth black in the major leagues, and the first black pitcher in the American League. At 42, he was also the oldest rookie in baseball history, signing right on his birthday after working out for manager Lou Boudreau. In an act of generosity, Veeck paid Baird and Wilkinson $5000 for Paige.

Paige worked two shutout innings of relief of Bob Lemon on July 9, and then made three starts in Cleveland which attracted over 200,000 fans to Municipal Stadium. His second start was a shutout. He finished the year with a 6–1 record and a 2.48 ERA. It was the first year of his life in which accurate statistics were kept. He then worked briefly in relief against the Braves in the 1948 World Series without a decision.

Trim and in top condition, Paige paid close attention to a set of rules he established for himself, including "avoid running at all times, go easy on the vices, and avoid fried foods." But teeth and stomach problems caused him to have a bad year in 1949, and with Veeck's departure he was released after the season. He spent 1950 back on the barnstorming trail with the Chicago American Giants.

Veeck employed him again in 1951, signing him in July for the St. Louis Browns. The bullpen was outfitted with a rocking chair just for Satch. He was 3–4 that season, but in 1952 he was the league's top relief pitcher with a 12–10 record and 10 saves. He made the All-Star team in both 1952 and 1953, when he saved another 11 games. When Veeck left St. Louis and the team moved to Baltimore, Paige was again released, virtually ending his major league career.

He continued to barnstorm, drawing top exhibition crowds wherever he appeared. He rejoined the Monarchs, strictly a road team, in 1955, and a year later Veeck, then with the Miami club of the International League, signed him again. Paige was 11–4 with a 1.86 ERA in 1956, and stayed with Miami through 1958. Now sporting eyeglasses, he appeared in a 1957 motion picture with Robert Mitchum and Julie London, *The Wonderful Country,* but continued to earn his living by pitching. In 1961 he pitched briefly for Portland of the Pacific Coast League, and Charles Finley hired him to pitch three innings against the Red Sox in the uniform of the Kansas City Athletics on September 25, 1965. At the age of 59 he was the oldest man to appear in a major league game, and his three innings were scoreless. His last pitching appearance in organized ball was a two inning stint for the Peninsula club of the Carolina League in 1966.

Paige, who lived in Kansas City, was at times a deputy sheriff, and in 1968 ran unsuccessfully for the Missouri legislature. The Atlanta Braves signed him that year as a coach, giving him the necessary 158 days he needed to qualify for a pension.

Paige was the first man elected to the Hall of Fame by the Committee on Negro Leagues formed in 1971. He called the day of induction the "proudest of my life." As an elder statesman of the game he still did occasional barnstorming and continued to live by his best-known rule, "Don't look back . . . something might be gaining on you."

LEROY ROBERT PAIGE

Negro Leagues 1926–1947
Cleveland 1948–1949
St. Louis (A.L.) 1951–1953
Kansas City 1965

G	IP	W	L	Pct.	H	R	ER	SO	BB	ERA
179	463	28	31	.475	429	191	174	290	183	3.38

Major league totals only

Herb Pennock (1894-1948)

Herb Pennock pitched for 22 seasons in the major leagues without the aid of a blazing fastball. Control and a knowledge of hitters were his principal tools.

Herbet Jefferis Pennock was born on February 10, 1894, in Kennett Square, Pennsylvania, about 25 miles from Philadelphia. Later known as "The Squire of Kennett Square," Herb came from Quaker parents and lived in Kennett Square all his life.

Herb's grandfather was an inventor of road-building machinery, and the Pennock family became wealthy selling the inventions. His parents were able to retire to farming when Herb and his brother George were both still young.

Pennock began playing ball in elementary school, and enrolled at the Friends' School of West Town, Pennsylvania, a Quaker-run institution. He then transferred to Cedar Croft, a prep school just outside Philadelphia that had a baseball team. There he played first base while his brother pitched—until the day George quit the team and Herb replaced him on the mound.

Although Herb was only 16 years old, Connie Mack arranged for him to pitch semipro ball during summer vacations. Pitching in Atlantic City, with Connie's son Earle as his catcher, Herb attracted attention with an exceptional performance against a top-rated Negro League team. In 1912, still hoping to attend the University of Pennsylvania, he transferred to Wenonah Military Academy. But when Connie Mack offered him a contract, he decided to launch a professional baseball career.

Although he never did get to college, Herb was always considered one of the game's intellectuals, and the reputation led to major executive positions once his playing career was over.

As an 18-year-old, Herb joined the Athletics in 1912 with no minor league experience. The team then boasted such future Hall-of-Famers as Eddie Collins, Home Run Baker, Eddie Plank, and Chief Bender. Collins and Pennock formed a strong friendship, and years later Herb's daughter Jane married Eddie Collins, Jr.

Bender took a quick liking to Pennock and taught him to throw a screwball. Screwballs, curves, and off-speed deliveries were to be the keys to Pennock's success. He seldom threw more than 10 fastballs per game, using the pitch only to keep hitters off stride. He also threw either overhand or sidearm. Few batters ever felt comfortable facing the lanky six-foot, 165-pound pitcher.

Pennock pitched only 50 innings in 1912, winning one game and losing two. He saw even less action the following year,

a pennant season for the Athletics. He worked 33 innings in 1913 with a 2–1 record, and did not appear in the World Series.

In 1914 he won 11 and lost 4 as the A's again won the pennant. This time he pitched three shutout innings in the Series loss to the Braves. But he had a falling out with Connie Mack in 1915, reportedly failing to follow the manager's pitching instructions. He was sold to Boston in June, and the following month farmed out to Providence, for whom he was 6–4. Connie Mack was later to call the move one of his great errors, but the two never discussed any of the difficulties between them and came to speak highly of each other.

Pennock opened the 1916 season with Boston, but after nine appearances he was sent to Buffalo in the International League, where he started 15 games and had a 7–6 record and a 1.67 ERA. In 1917 he returned to Boston and was never in the minors again. That year he was 5–5, with Babe Ruth winning 24 and Carl Mays 22.

Herb spent the 1918 season in the Navy. He received great attention back home when he pitched an exhibition game against an Army team before the King and Queen of England outside of London.

Returning to the Red Sox in 1919, Herb moved into the regular rotation at last, winning 16 games, losing 8, and posting a 2.71 ERA. In 1920 both Ruth and Mays were traded to the Yankees and Herb took up some of the slack, pitching 242 innings with a 16–13 record. He spent two more years in Boston, going 12–14 in 1921 and 10–17 in 1922. At age 29, his career mark was only 76–72, and no one at this point considered him one of the game's greats.

On January 30, 1923, Herb was traded to the Yankees for outfielder Camp Skinner, infielder Norm McMillan, pitcher George Murray, and cash. The Yankees were making many successful trades with the financially hard-pressed Red Sox, and this would be just another that would help launch the Yankee dynasty of the 1920s.

Herb was an immediate hit in the first year of Yankee Stadium, winning 19 of 25 decisions for a league-leading .760 percentage. He won two games in the World Series and, along with Waite Hoyt, Bob Shawkey, Joe Bush, Wilcy Moore, George Pipgras, and Urban Shocker, formed the pitching staff that would complement the Yankees' "Murderers' Row" batting order.

Herb Pennock lets fly his unpredictable pitches. He hurled screwballs, curves, and off-speed deliveries, with an occasional fastball as a surprise. Switching from sidearm to overhand style also kept batters off guard.

In 1924 he won 21 and lost 9, and in 1925 he led the league with 277 innings pitched while posting a 16–17 record.

Already wealthy, Pennock owned a 33-acre fox ranch in Kennett Square, where he lived with his wife Esther. His foxes were worth some $45,000 and he was winning blue ribbons breeding them. A single pelt brought him as much as $700. It took a raise to $20,000 from the Yankees to keep him in the game.

Pennock was a key member of the 1926 Yankees, winning 23, losing 11, and walking only 43 batters in 266 innings. He was now in the finest form of his career, helped by an understanding manager, Miller Huggins. Pennock was unable to sleep on trains, and Huggins always scheduled his starts on days when the team did not travel.

He won two more games in the 1926 World Series, and then had a 19–8 record for the famed 1927 Yanks. In the 1927 Series he started the third game and retired the first 22 batters, the closest any man had come to a Series no-hitter up to that point.

The victory gave him a lifetime 5–0 Series record with a 1.95 ERA for 55 1/3

innings. A sore arm kept him out of the 1928 Series after a 17–6 regular season.

He remained a Yankee through 1933, but was no longer as effective as before. He slipped to 9–11 in 1929, then to 11–7 (1930), 11–6 (1931), 9–5 (1932), and 7–4 (1933).

Released by the Yankees in January 1934, Pennock was signed by his old Red Sox team. It was too late to give Boston his best, but he did post a 2–0 record and a 3.05 ERA for 30 appearances in 1934, the final year of his playing career. The 22 big-league seasons tied the pitching record of Sam Jones, and it stood until Early Wynn passed them both many years later.

His old friend Eddie Collins, general manager of the Red Sox, gave Herb a job as president of the Charlotte (Piedmont League) club in 1935. He returned to Boston as a coach from 1936 to 1940, and from 1941 to 1943 he served as supervisor of the Red Sox farm system.

When Bob Carpenter bought the Philadelphia Phillies late in 1943, he summoned Herb from the Red Sox to be his general manager. Herb was new to the National

League, but certainly not to Philadelphia, where he had begun his professional career.

As vice-president and general manager of the Phillies, Herb spent a lot of money to build up the team. The Phillies had not won a pennant since 1915 but Herb invested wisely in signing such pitching prospects as Robin Roberts and Curt Simmons. The Phillie fans had shown great patience over the years, and Pennock worked long hours to rebuild the club for them.

On January 30, 1948, while attending a National League meeting at a New York hotel, Herb was stricken with a cerebral hemorrhage and died at 53.

A month later, on February 28, his election to the Hall of Fame was announced by the baseball writers. And in 1950, as a final tribute to his dedication in his final years, the Phillies won the National League pennant.

HERBERT JEFFERIS PENNOCK

Philadelphia (A.L.) 1912–1915
Boston (A.L.) 1915–1922, 1934
New York (A.L.) 1923–1933

G	IP	W	L	Pct.	H	R	ER	SO	BB	ERA
617	3558	240	162	.597	3900	1699	1403	1227	916	3.60

Eddie Plank (1875-1926)

One of the first great pitchers employed by Connie Mack was Philadelphia Athletics lefthander Eddie Plank who reached the majors with no minor league experience and won 20 or more games 8 times in his 17-season career.

Edward Stewart Plank was born on a farm in Gettysburg, Pennsylvania, on August 31, 1875. The boy sometimes amused himself by hurling stones at birds perched on fences. But he had no organized baseball experience when he enrolled at Gettysburg College at the age of 21.

The Gettysburg baseball coach was Frank Foreman, who had pitched for 9 teams in 11 seasons between 1884 and 1902 with a 99–93 record. Frank had a younger brother nicknamed "Brownie" who pitched for Connie Mack briefly in Pittsburgh but whose behavior was so eccentric that Connie traded him the following year, his last in the majors.

Frank Foreman talked Plank into trying out for the varsity baseball team, and both soon discovered that Eddie had a flair for pitching. He became one of the best in the state, although admittedly he was older than other college students.

One student pitcher he never managed to beat was Bucknell star Christy Mathewson, who usually seemed also to get the better of Plank when the two met in later World Series games.

Eddie was a good student at Gettysburg, enjoying success both athletically and academically. He graduated in 1901, at which time Foreman called Connie Mack and touted him on Plank's abilities. Foreman knew Connie through his brother, and the relationship turned out to be a beneficial one for Mack, who was just starting out with his Philadelphia A's.

Although Plank was nearly 26 years old, Connie thought "the boy showed promise," and he signed him for the 1901 season, the American League's first as a major league.

Foreman had another pitcher at Gettysburg, George "Sassafras" Winter, whom he sent to the Boston Red Sox. It was quite a contribution for a small college to make, as Winter won 16 games for Boston that year, and Plank won 17 for Philadelphia, pitching 262 innings.

It was not common for a college man to enter professional baseball in those days, and the presence of Plank and Mathewson added a great deal of respectability to the game.

The sleek, expressionless Plank stood 5'11½" and weighed 175 pounds. He was always in good physical condition and never had a weight problem. Nor did he ever complain of overwork.

Eddie was not a trick pitcher. Having learned the game at a late age, he relied strictly on a fastball and a curve and he

often came sidearm to offer a difficult, crossfire delivery.

He became noted for his long delays on the pitching mound. He would tug at his cap, kick his spikes, look at the runners, pick up the resin bag, step off the mound, and start again. It was exasperating to opponents, umpires, and fans, but his slow, deliberate style was frustrating enough to get the hitters off stride.

Eddie also talked to himself a great deal on the mound. His voice had a distinct, nasal quality and those near him could hear him say "nine to go" or "eight to go" as the game moved into its final innings. Sportswriters found him totally humorless and far too studious to be playing "only a game." He was a loner on road trips and remained a bachelor until after his playing career had ended.

In the winters he returned to the family farm in Gettysburg and served as a tour guide at the Gettysburg battlefield. Few tourists knew that their guide was Eddie Plank of the Philadelphia Athletics.

The Athletics won the pennant in 1902, a year in which no World Series was played. Plank had a 20–15 record, his first of eight 20-win seasons. He struck out 110 batters, marking the first of a record 14 consecutive years in which he would fan 100 or more.

He had unusually good control, and among pitchers with 4000 or more innings pitched he walked fewer men than anyone in American League history (984). He recorded the most victories and the most defeats of any lefthander in American League history, as well as the most shutouts (64).

Plank was 23–16 in 1903, the Athletics finishing second. In 1904 he won 26 games, matching his career high. He also struck out 209 batters that season, fourth in the league.

The Athletics won the 1905 pennant by two games over Chicago, Plank contributing a 25–12 record. That year he had his first opportunity to pitch in a World Series, and was beaten twice by the Giants. The opening game pitted him against his old Bucknell opponent, Christy Mathewson, who beat him, 3–0. Joe McGinnity beat him, 1–0, in the fourth game of a Series decided completely by shutouts. Plank was to lose five World Series games in his career, four of them via shutouts. He won two games. His career World Series ERA was 1.15.

Plank failed to reach 20 victories in 1906 but his 19–6 record represented the top winning percentage in the league.

In 1907 the Athletics and the Tigers battled down to the wire for the pennant. Late in the season both Jack Coombs and Chief

Eddie Plank's methodical approach to pitching shows in his intense expression above. Scorning tricks, he employed a fastball and a curve. He won more games and threw more shutouts than any other lefthanded pitcher in American League history.

Bender were nursing sore arms, and all Connie Mack had to turn to were Plank, Jimmy Dygert, and the unpredictable Rube Waddell. He managed to get by with the three-man pitching staff, overworking them out of necessity.

On Friday, September 27, the Tigers' Wild Bill Donovan beat Plank, 5–4, to put Detroit mere percentage points ahead of Philadelphia. Saturday's game was rained out, and, with no games permitted in Pennsylvania on Sunday, a double header was scheduled for Monday afternoon. Dygert started the first game and was relieved early by Waddell. Plank had to come in for the ninth inning. The Tigers had come from behind off Waddell to tie the score, and the game wound up going 17 innings, with Plank and Donovan, who hurled the route for Detroit, matching zeroes on the scoreboard. Eventually darkness prevailed and the game ended in a 9–9 tie. The Tigers left town, still percentage points ahead, and never relinquished the lead. Plank wound up 24–16 for the season, but Detroit won the pennant.

Eddie was 14–16 in 1908 and 19–19 in 1909. Then the Athletics came back to win the 1910 pennant, with Plank 16–10 for the regular season. He did not appear in the World Series; Connie Mack used only Coombs and Bender.

In 1911, Eddie was 22–8 with six shutouts, and split a pair of decisions in the World Series. He beat Rube Marquard of the Giants with a five-hitter in the second game, but then lost in relief in the fifth game on a sacrifice fly by Fred Merkle in the tenth inning.

Plank was 26–6 in 1912 when the A's finished third. They were back in the World Series again in 1913. Eddie, who was 18–10 in the regular season, split another pair of decisions in the Series. Mathewson beat him again in the second game, this time 3–0, and then he finally beat the great Giant righthander with what many thought was the finest game of Eddie's career. It was a two-hit, 3–1 victory in the fifth and final game to give the A's the World Championship. A single by Matty and a single by catcher Larry McLean were the only Giant hits.

Eddie hurled for his sixth pennant winner in 1914 when he compiled a 15–7 regular-season record, but he lost another heart-breaker in the World Series, this one a 1–0 setback to Boston's Miracle Braves.

Connie Mack did not have the money to meet the promises of the new Federal League after the 1914 season. The Feds had already been in operation for a year and Connie had held onto his players, but

he could not hold them any longer. He tried to sell Plank to the Yankees, but the Yanks knew Eddie was bound for the Feds. Connie finally gave Plank his release rather than have him jump, and he also released Coombs and Bender.

Plank landed with the St. Louis Terriers, managed by Fielder Jones. They were the second place team that season, and Eddie led the league with a 2.01 earned-run average. He won 21, lost 11. The victories, which counted in his major league totals, helped him become the winningest lefthander in baseball until Warren Spahn came along.

When the Federal League folded after the 1915 season, Eddie remained in St. Louis, catching on with the Browns. He pitched for them for two years, winning 16 games the first season. His final season, 1917, produced a 1.79 ERA at age 42 despite the 5–6 record.

On January 21, 1918, he was traded with Del Pratt and $15,000 to the Yankees for Les Nunamaker, Fritz Maisel, Nick Cullop, Urban Shocker, and Joe Gedeon, but Eddie felt he had pitched enough and never reported. Instead, he went home to Gettysburg, continuing to work on his farm and pitching some semipro ball in the Bethlehem Steel League. He was so good in that league that manager Miller Huggins of the Yankees continued to try to get him to report to New York, but Eddie refused to yield to the offers.

Plank suffered a stroke on February 22, 1926, and two days later died in Gettysburg at the age of 50.

In 1946 Plank was elected to the Hall of Fame. Not until 1962 did Spahn pass him for most victories by a lefthander.

EDWARD STEWART PLANK

Philadelphia (A.L.) 1901–1914
St. Louis (F.L.) 1915
St. Louis (A.L.) 1916–1917

G	IP	W	L	Pct.	H	R	ER	SO	BB	ERA
623	4503	326	192	.629	3892	1545	inc.	2257	1042	inc.

Old Hoss Radbourn (1853-1897)

No one has ever matched Old Hoss Radbourn's record of 60 victories in one season. Radbourn's Hall of Fame plaque says he was the "greatest of all nineteenth century pitchers."

Charles Gardner Radbourn was born in Rochester, New York, on December 9, 1853. While he was still a baby, the Radbourns moved to Bloomington, Illinois, where eventually there were 18 children in the family. A younger brother, George, pitched briefly for Detroit in 1883.

Throughout Charley's career, his name was generally spelled Radbourne, but in 1942 a surviving sister corrected the long-standing error for the sake of official records.

Charley grew up learning to play baseball on the corner lots of Bloomington. He pitched for town teams, and once posed as a college student and played the outfield for Illinois Wesleyan. This gave rise to a general belief that he was a college graduate, but in fact his education ended with the seventh grade.

Radbourn was known from an early age for a quick temper and a fiery disposition. This was perhaps due to the problems of competing for attention in a family of 20. In any event, Charley left home around 1876 to take a job as a railroad brakeman for the Indiana-Bloomington-Western Railroad.

In 1878, Radbourn signed a contract with the Peoria Reds, an independent professional team. Strictly an outfielder in those days, Charley batted .289 in 28 games and was observed in action by Ted Sullivan, owner of the Dubuque franchise of the Northwest League. Sullivan, in partnership, had started the league that very season as one of the first minor leagues in the country. One of his star players was Charles Comiskey, later the owner of the Chicago White Sox.

Ted saw in Radbourn a potentially outstanding athlete. Although Charley was only 5'9" and weighed 168 pounds, he had a strong arm and seemed devoted to the game. Sullivan contacted him about joining the Dubuque club for the 1879 season and Radbourn said he would like to make $75 a month, $20 more than Peoria had paid him. Considering this a bargain, Sullivan quickly got his signature, with Charley's father serving as a witness.

Unfortunately for the Northwest League, the Dubuque Rabbits were too good. They ran away with the pennant, and by August all the other clubs had lost interest and the league folded. Radbourn, who had shut out Rockford, 8–0, in his first game, went on to hit .387 as a right fielder and to compile an impressive though unrecorded won-lost mark as a pitcher. For the remainder of the season, Sullivan took his Rabbits on tour throughout the Midwest.

In 1880, Radbourn found himself in the major leagues. Signed by the Buffalo club of the National League as a right fielder, he made his debut on May 5 against Cleveland. Charley distinguished himself by collecting one hit in four times at bat and by being the only man in the Buffalo lineup who did not make an error. The club made 17 in all and lost the game, 22–3.

Several days later, after playing six games and hitting .143, Charley developed a sore arm and was released. He returned to Bloomington with no intention of resuming his baseball career and became an apprentice butcher.

In 1881, the Providence Grays, in their fourth year of competition in the National League, attempted to enlist Radbourn's services. Sullivan had recommended Charley as a "change" pitcher, meaning a right fielder who could take an occasional turn on the pitching plate. But Radbourn did not even answer the telegrams from Providence. Finally, a boyhood friend, Bill Hunter, returned a wire, accepted a $750-per-season offer, and told Radbourn to get on his way.

On May 5, 1881, Charley outpitched Boston star Tommy Bond, 4–2, for his first major league victory. Alternating pitching duties with John Montgomery Ward, Charley finished the season with a 25–11 record.

Radbourn never altered his pitching style throughout his career, although rules changes would have permitted it. He was considered to be the first man to use the curve ball effectively and was noted for outstanding control and speed. He always pitched underhand, even after the rules permitted overhand pitching in 1884. The pitching distance during most of Radbourn's career was 50 feet, and batters could request high or low pitches.

In 1882, Radbourn batted .239 as a part-time outfielder and posted a 31–19 record as a pitcher for the Grays, then managed by Harry Wright. On August 17 of that season the Grays faced Frank Bancroft's Detroit Club in Providence. Ward was locked in a scoreless pitching duel with Stump Weidman for a full 17 innings when, in the top of the eighteenth, Radbourn belted a home run to give the Grays a 1–0 victory. The fans went berserk with ecstasy. Newspapers described the interest in the game as being "as though fans were awaiting the outcome of a presidential election."

In 1883, Radbourn led the National League with a 49–25 record, accounting for all but nine of the Grays' victories. On July 25 that year, he hurled a no-hitter against Cleveland. (Radbourn also pitched seven one-hitters during his career.) His 1883 salary of $2000 was increased to $3000 for the following season.

Charley Radbourne, who stars in some of the most glorious tales of the early days of baseball. In an 1882 game, he played the outfield in a 17-inning, 0-0 tie, and then belted a home run to win the game 1-0.

No baseball scholar can recall the year 1884 without thinking of Radbourn. First, he turned down an attractive offer from the Union Association, a third major league. But on joining Providence, he found himself involved all spring in a continuous conflict with the club's other pitcher, Charles Sweeney. Sweeney had a way of inciting arguments by demeaning Radbourn, and Radbourn of course was no angel either. He had by now developed a reputation for frequenting saloons and bawdy houses.

On July 16, 1884, his problems came to a climax. Sweeney was annoying him, his arm hurt, he felt the umpires were making bad calls, and his teammates were making too many errors. In disgust, he lobbed the ball up to the plate without any effort and lost the game, 5–2. Frank Bancroft, now managing Providence, suspended him at once without pay.

During Radbourn's suspension, Sweeney got drunk, was also suspended, and jumped the club, joining the St. Louis team of the Union Association. (Sweeney later wound up in San Quentin prison for murder.) Suddenly Providence was without a pitcher, and the players appealed to Bancroft to talk Radbourn into returning.

Charley consented, with the understanding that he would be given his release at the end of the year and that he would be given additional money at once to pitch every remaining game. Providence was battling for its first pennant, and Radbourn had a difficult assignment. But he met the challenge in record-breaking fashion. He pitched every game on the schedule between July 23 and September 24, until he could not even raise his arm to comb his hair. He won 18 consecutive games, lost a 2–0 decision, and then won 8 more. By the time the 27-game streak was over, Radbourn had a 60–12 record with 11 shutouts, 679 innings, and 411 strikeouts. Then, in the "World Series" against New York, he won all three games, 6–0, 3–1, and 11–2.

It was during that season that he first became "Old Hoss." He would warm up in the outfield and finally announce, "Old Hoss is ready." From then on, it was "Old Hoss Radbourn."

Given the opportunity to get his release, Radbourn instead accepted a $2000 raise for 1885. He never again approached his 1884 record, but he did win 20 or more games five more times. His 1885 record was 26–20, despite a line drive to his chin in midseason.

In 1886, the Grays disbanded and Hoss moved to Boston. He spent four years with the Red Stockings, while John Clarkson passed him as the leader of the pitching staff. In 1890 he jumped to the Players' League and had a 27–12 record for the Boston team. He returned to the National League with Cincinnati in 1891 and was 12–12 for 25 games. Weakened by paresis and syphilis, he ended his baseball career that year.

Radbourn returned to Bloomington with his wife and stepson and opened a poolroom. On April 13, 1894, as the result of a hunting accident in which part of his face was blown off, he suffered the loss of an eye, loss of speech, and partial paralysis. It was a morose and reclusive Old Hoss Radbourn who spent his final days in the back room of his pool hall, ashamed to be seen in public.

He died on February 5, 1897, at the age of 43. In 1939 he was elected to the Hall of Fame.

CHARLES GARDNER RADBOURN

Buffalo (N.L.) 1880
Providence (N.L.) 1881–1885
Boston (N.L.) 1886–1889
Boston (P.L.) 1890
Cincinnati (N.L.) 1891

G	IP	W	L	Pct.	H	R	ER	SO	BB	ERA
517	4543	308	191	.617	4500	2300	inc.	1746	856	inc.

Sam Rice (1890-1974)

Sam Rice, who compiled a lifetime .322 batting average during a 19-season career in the nation's capital, was a member of all three pennant-winning Washington Senators teams.

Edgar Charles Rice was born on February 20, 1890. Not until he was a professional baseball player did people begin calling him Sam, and that came about when a sportswriter forgot his real name.

Rice was born on a small farm in Morocco, Indiana, but he enjoyed simply telling people he was from Morocco and leaving the rest to their imaginations. When he was still quite young, his family moved to a larger farm in Watseka, Illinois, and that remained home to Rice for much of his early adult life.

His first baseball experience was as a pitcher. He starred for his town team in Watseka in 1910 and 1911. But baseball was not Sam's only interest or occupation. He had worked on the family farm, worked in the wheat fields of the Dakotas, and labored in a whiskey-bottling plant in Louisville. From there he went to Norfolk, Virginia, and in 1913, enlisted in the Navy, where he was stationed aboard the U.S.S. *Hampshire.*

As a sailor, Sam participated in the American occupation of Veracruz, Mexico, in 1914. As bullets buzzed past him, Sam doubtless gave at least a little thought to trying his hand at professional baseball.

He pitched for the ship's baseball team, and when the *Hampshire* was docked off Virginia he was scouted by the Petersburg club of the Virginia League. As soon as Sam was through with the Navy, he signed with Petersburg and compiled a 9–2 record in 15 appearances to close out the 1914 season.

He was back at Petersburg in 1915, pitching 29 games and working 233 innings with an 11–12 record. Early that season, Washington Senators' owner Clark Griffith loaned $600 to the Petersburg owner to help him meet expenses. By the middle of the season it was obvious that the failing club would not be able to repay the money.

"But I've got a fine young pitcher who might interest you," Griffith was wired. "Name is Rice."

Griffith accepted Sam and canceled the debt. Joining the fourth place Senators, Rice found himself on the same pitching staff with Walter Johnson. Sam won his only decision in four mound appearances that year. He was primarily a fastball pitcher and his strong arm would later serve him well in the outfield.

Sam was 26 years old as the 1916 season opened. He began as a righthanded pitcher with an 0–1 record in five games.

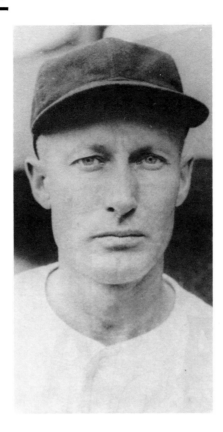

But as a lefthand hitter, he looked impressive. Infielder Eddie Foster urged Sam to switch to the outfield, but Griffith was short of righthanders and needed Sam on the mound.

One day against Detroit, Sam's pitching opponent, George Dauss (a .189 hitter), belted a triple to center. Sam walked off the mound and said, "Gimme an outfielder's glove." He borrowed the trainer's knife and cut the metal toe plate off his shoe. For all practical purposes, his pitching days were over.

Griffith began to use Sam as a pinch-hitter, but during the second half of the season Rice became a fixture in the Washington outfield. He was one of those quiet, reserved men who seemed to show up every day and do a big job in an unspectacular manner. Sam never quarreled with umpires and never said much to anyone. He batted over .300 for 14 seasons and let that do his speaking for him.

Replacing Turney Barber in the outfield, Sam celebrated his first game with a single and double in three plate appearances. Playing regularly, he continued to develop his batting eye, and finished the 1916 season with a spurt of 20 hits in 55 at bats for a .299 season's average.

In 1917, his first year of regular play, he appeared in 155 games and batted .302. Sam was a slender 5'10" and usually weighed around 155. He hit only 34 home runs in his career, but he was an exceptionally good doubles hitter. The 1917 season was the first in which Sam had a chance to show off his baserunning speed, for which he gained the nickname "Man o' War," after the famous race horse. Sam stole 351 bases in his career, with a league-leading 63 in 1920.

Sam returned to the service in 1918 during World War I, but this time he went into the Army. He was stationed at Fort Terry, Connecticut, and was able to draw passes to play for the Senators in one series in Boston and for a six-day stretch in June. Sam managed to appear in seven games and hit .348.

Back in baseball in 1919, he led the American League with 141 games played and batted .321. In 1920, the year he led in stolen bases, he collected 211 hits and batted .336, also leading the league's outfielders in putouts.

Meanwhile, the Senators were not making much noise in the pennant races. Johnson was the star pitcher and Rice the star hitter, but otherwise the team was rather lackluster. Sam hit .330 in 1921, .295 in 1922, and .316 in 1923, tying for the league lead with 18 triples.

Not until 1924 did the Senators win their first American League pennant. Sam's contribution was a 31-game hitting streak

319

and a .334 batting average. He led the league with 216 hits and 646 at bats. It was one of eight seasons in which Sam topped 600 at bats, a difficult chore in preexpansion days.

Part of the reason for his many official at bats was the infrequency of his walks. But he was even more remarkable in strikeouts, for during his career he fanned fewer than 20 times in each of 10 full seasons. In 1929, he had 616 at bats and struck out only 9 times. For his career, he struck out only 275 times in 9269 at bats, or once every 337 times up.

Playing in the 1924 World Series, Sam had only six singles and one run batted in against the Giants, hitting .207. But Washington won the Series, capturing the only World Championship in its history.

The team won the pennant again in 1925, with Rice batting .350 and setting an American League record with 182 singles. He had 227 hits in all.

In the 1925 World Series, Sam hit .364 with a record 12 hits, a mark that stood for 39 years until broken by Bobby Richardson. But it was in the field that Sam became part of one of the most controversial plays of all time.

In the eighth inning of the third game, with Washington winning, 4–3, Pittsburgh's Earl Smith belted a long fly to center. Rice went back to the temporary bleachers, jumped, and toppled into the stands. For almost 15 seconds he and the ball were hidden, but finally he emerged, holding the ball aloft. Umpire Cy Rigler ruled the ball caught, and a tremendous argument ensued, with Pirates' owner Barney Dreyfuss running onto the field to take part in the protest.

Judge Landis conferred with Rice, and all Sam said was, "The umpire said I caught it." Some 1600 fans voluntarily sent letters telling what "really happened," but they disagreed nearly 50–50. During his lifetime, Sam never answered the question of what "really happened." Instead he always repeated, "The umpire said I caught it," for he enjoyed the long-running controversy.

Rice was earning about $18,000 a year at that point, an excellent salary of which only about $1000 went to taxes. He continued his fine playing, leading the league in

hits and at bats in 1926 and going over 200 hits again in both 1928 and 1930. But it was not until 1933 that the Senators won another pennant, their last, and by then Sam was 43 years old and only a part-time player. For the first time since 1918 he failed to play in 100 games, but he still batted .294 for the season. In the World Series he got a pinch-hit single in the second game, marking his final appearance in a Senator uniform.

Given his release by Washington in January 1934, Rice signed with Cleveland, playing 97 games of the 1934 season and hitting .293. But at 44 he recognized that his reflexes were slipping, and he retired at the end of the season only 13 hits short of 3000.

After his retirement Rice settled on a chicken farm in Ashton, Maryland, where he spent most of his remaining years. Many thought his 1963 election to the Hall of Fame was late in coming, and Sam tended to agree, stating, "It's fine, but I can't say I'm too thrilled."

In 1965, he presented a sealed letter to the Hall of Fame with "the true story of what happened on that catch in the 1925 World Series." The letter was not to be opened until after his death.

Sam died on October 13, 1974, in Silver Springs, Maryland, two months after his final visit to Cooperstown at the age of 84. His wife and daughter approved the opening of the letter a few weeks later. In the letter Sam went into great detail about the play, described the "deathgrip" he had on the ball, and stated, "At no time did I lose possession of the ball."

EDGAR CHARLES RICE

Washington 1915–1933
Cleveland 1934

G	AB	R	H	2B	3B	HR	RBI	Avg.
2404	9269	1515	2987	497	184	34	1077	.322

(Above) Rounding the bases like "Man o' War," which is what the fans called him, is Sam Rice, whose 63 stolen bases led the American League in 1920. (At left) Rice, a lifetime .322 batter, follows through on his swing.

Branch Rickey (1881-1965)

Branch Rickey rose from the players ranks to become one of the most significant executives in baseball history. He established the modern farm system and brought black players back into organized baseball.

Wesley Branch Rickey was born on December 20, 1881, in Lucasville, Ohio, the son of strict, fundamentalist, Methodist parents. He recalled that his boyhood punishments consisted of listening to his mother pray for God's forgiveness for "not doing my duty as a mother."

Branch completed elementary school and taught himself Latin and higher mathematics. He took a job as a country schoolteacher near Lucasville, earning $35 a month. Accepting a partial scholarship to attend Ohio Wesleyan, he earned money for college by playing minor league ball at Terre Haute (Central League) and LeMars (Iowa-South Dakota League). At college he captained the baseball team, participated in basketball and football, and also served as athletic director.

Upon graduation, he returned to minor league ball, catching 41 games for Dallas (Texas League) in 1904 and hitting .261. Late in August he was sold to the Cincinnati Reds, but after appearing in a few exhibition games he was dropped by the club when, respecting his mother's wishes, he refused to play ball on Sundays.

Rickey returned to Allegheny College for further undergraduate courses. Early in 1905 the Dallas club sold his contract to the Chicago White Sox, who in turn sold it immediately to the St. Louis Browns. Rickey reported in June after his college chores were finished and played in one big-league game before being returned to Dallas, where he hit .295 in 37 games. In 1906, he earned a second bachelor's degree from Allegheny, then spent a full season with the Browns, hitting .284 and collecting two home runs in one game against the New York Highlanders. He married Jane Moulton the same year.

The Highlanders obtained Branch in a 1907 trade, but it was not a good year for the 5'9", 175-pound receiver. He batted only .182, and on June 28 he permitted 13 Washington runners to steal bases, a major league record.

Rickey returned to school, this time Ohio State University, where he studied law. The end of his baseball career was hastened by a bout with tuberculosis which sent him for recovery to Saranac Lake, New York. Undoubtedly his career was also hindered by his refusal to play Sunday ball. Although he later became the originator of the standard Sunday doubleheader and made a great deal of money off Sunday baseball, he always respected his mother's wishes and never personally attended a Sunday game.

Recovered from his bout with tuberculosis, he entered the University of Michigan in the fall of 1909 and coached the college baseball teams in 1910 and 1911. Receiving his law degree in 1911, he went to Boise, Idaho, where he set up a law practice. But he soon became discouraged when a client told him to "get the hell out of here" and returned to Michigan as baseball coach in 1912.

In 1913, Robert Lee Hedges, owner of the Browns, offered Rickey the opportunity to become his assistant at $7500 a year while also coaching at Michigan. At Michigan Branch coached young George Sisler. In 1915 he represented George in a legal battle to get his signature on a Browns contract.

Rickey took over as St. Louis manager on September 6, 1913. He did not have an easy rapport with the players. A man who had toured the country in 1909 lecturing in favor of prohibition could not be "one of the boys" on the Browns' fun-loving team.

The Browns finished fifth in 1914 and sixth in 1915. Late that year Phil Ball had become owner of the team, and he decided to relieve Rickey of his managerial duties. Rickey, however, was already signed for the 1916 season, and Ball gave him a job totally lacking in responsibility, calling him "vice-president and business manager."

Ball was delighted to let Rickey move to the Cardinals in 1917. Branch at once became the highest-paid executive in the game, earning $15,000 a year. When he joined the Cardinals, the team was $175,000 in debt. Rickey gradually brought about significant changes that turned the fortunes of the team around.

In 1913, Branch had helped introduce Ladies' Days with the Browns, but he popularized the idea with the Cardinals and helped raise the caliber of fans attending games in St. Louis. He also established "Knot Hole Gangs," letting youngsters in free to establish their baseball interest. Smoking and profanity by the youngsters were banned, and adult supervision was required.

In spring training, he introduced such innovations as batting cages, blackboard drills, and sliding pits. In 1927 he authorized the first radio broadcasts of major league baseball games. But by far his most significant contribution with the Cardinals was his development of the farm system.

In 1919 he bought a 50 percent interest in the Fort Smith, Arkansas, team. Soon after, he bought a 15 percent interest in the Texas League's Houston franchise, and then added Syracuse of the International League. The Cardinals had been unable to sign players because wealthier clubs outbid them, but by setting up a chain of farm teams the Cardinals became competitive with richer teams. By 1941, they had 32 minor league affiliates and between 600 and 700 players, many signed directly out of Cardinal tryouts and many suggested to Branch by his friends on the nation's college campuses.

After a brief stint in the Chemical Warfare Service during World War I, Rickey managed the Cardinals from 1919 to 1925. He had little success, finishing no higher than third in 1921, when Rogers Hornsby led the National League with a .397 average. Branch refused to manage on Sundays, letting a coach handle the job.

On May 30, 1925, Cardinal owner Sam Breadon fired Rickey and replaced him with Hornsby. Rickey reluctantly returned to the Cards' front office, becoming vice-president and business manager through the 1942 season. The Cardinals won pennants in 1926, 1928, 1930, 1931, 1934, and 1942. Rickey's farm system produced Dizzy Dean and other stars. Later, Rickey's trade of the sore-armed Dean to Chicago for two players and $185,000 was hailed as a brilliant move.

When he was fired as manager, Branch sold his stock in the Cardinals to Breadon and Hornsby for $250,000. After the 1942 season, he and Breadon parted ways, Rickey moving to Brooklyn to become president and general manager of the Dodgers.

Fans did not view Rickey as a genius when he first came to Brooklyn, for he sold such stars as Joe Medwick and Eddie Stanky. But as he had done in St. Louis, he built a strong farm system for the Dodgers, and left them with the nucleus of the team that would win five pennants in the 1950s.

Rickey remained with the Dodgers through 1950, winning pennants in 1947 and 1949, and eventually purchasing the club with Walter O'Malley and John L. Smith. But his most historic move was in 1946 when he signed Jackie Robinson out of the Negro Leagues and assigned him to Montreal.

Rickey had operated the Brooklyn Brown Dodgers in the United States League in 1945 and had always felt strongly about integrating organized baseball. For his bold project, Rickey needed a man who could handle himself off the field as well as on, become accepted by the press, the fans, and the players, and withstand the abuse that would surely be aimed at him. He found this man in the well-spoken, well-educated, extraordinary athlete, Jackie Robinson. Rickey handled the situation well, urging black leaders to avoid "Jackie Robinson Days" and other fanfare that would put needless pressure on Robinson. The move was a huge success and permanently changed the major leagues.

Branch became vice-president and general manager of the Pirates in 1951, after selling his Dodger stock for $1 million. In 1956 the cigar-smoking, teetotaling, bow-tied Rickey became chairman of the board of directors of the Pirates.

Leaving the Pirates in 1959, Rickey busied himself organizing the Continental League, a prospective third major league that planned to put franchises in New York, Buffalo, Toronto, Minneapolis–St. Paul, Houston, Dallas–Fort Worth, Atlanta, and Denver. The league never got off the ground, but it did bring about the expansion of the two established leagues with

the creation of the New York Mets, Los Angeles Angels, Houston Colt 45s (later named the Astros), and the new Washington Senators to replace the team that became the Minnesota Twins.

Nicknamed "The Mahatma," the brilliant and quotable Rickey had once been urged to enter politics. In 1941, Republican leaders assured him of the nomination for governor of Missouri but he decided to remain in baseball.

Rickey returned to the Cardinals in 1963 as special advisor to president Gussie Busch and remained until his resignation in October, 1964. He managed to rouse some controversy even in his final baseball job by publicly voicing the opinion that Stan Musial should retire.

On November 13, 1965, he was making an acceptance speech following his induction into the Missouri Sports Hall of Fame when he collapsed with a heart attack. On December 9, he died in Columbia, Missouri.

Rickey was elected to the Hall of Fame in 1967.

WESLEY BRANCH RICKEY

St. Louis (A.L.) 1905–1906, 1914
New York (A.L.) 1907

G	AB	R	H	2B	3B	HR	RBI	Avg.
119	343	38	82	9	6	3	39	.239

Brooklyn Dodger president Branch Rickey (right) watches closely as Jackie Robinson signs one of baseball's most momentous contracts in 1947. To integrate baseball, Rickey had to quell a mutiny on his own team, and Robinson had to face taunts from players and fans alike.

Eppa Rixey (1891-1963)

Until Warren Spahn came along, Eppa Rixey was the winningest lefthanded pitcher in baseball. He spent a record 21 seasons pitching in the National League, dividing his time between Philadelphia and Cincinnati.

Eppa Rixey was born of well-to-do parents on May 3, 1891, in Culpeper, Virginia. As a boy he was generally known as Junior, but when he reached the big leagues, Cincinnati sportswriter William Phelon called him Eppa Jeptha, a nickname which made as much sense as his given name, at least as far as he was concerned.

Eppa grew to be 6'5" and weighed 210 pounds, making him one of the largest players in the game. He was slow afoot and not a very good hitter, but he could pitch and he concentrated on that art.

Enrolled in the University of Virginia in 1909 as a chemistry major, Eppa came under the coaching of Charles "Cy" Rigler, who also happened to be a National League umpire. After three years at Virginia, Rigler arranged for the big youngster to sign a contract with the Philadelphia Phillies, for which Rigler received $2000. When this news came out, other National League clubs banded together to prohibit umpires from serving in scouting capabilities for any team.

With no minor league experience, Eppa in 1912 joined Red Dooin's Phillie pitching staff, which included Grover Cleveland Alexander. He had a fine rookie season, appearing in 23 games, splitting 20 decisions, and compiling a 2.50 earned-run average, 31 points lower than Alexander's.

He received permission from the Phillies to report late in 1913 so he could complete his studies at the University of Virginia. Joining the team in May, he managed to pitch in 35 games and had a 9–5 record.

From the start, Eppa was not a strikeout pitcher. He much preferred to fool the hitters, and was often behind in the count. Still, he seldom walked anyone. His career highs in strikeouts and walks were 134 and 74, respectively, both set in 1916.

The 1914 season, his third with the Phillies, should have been a big one, considering the experience he had picked up. But Rixey could not get untracked. He finished the year with only two victories, losing 11 times and running up a 4.37 ERA.

The Phillies were only sixth in 1914, and at season's end Dooin was fired and Pat Moran hired to replace him. The move proved to be a good one as far as Rixey was concerned, for Moran took a quick liking to Eppa, both personally and professionally, and used him effectively in 1915. For the season, Eppa was only 11–12, but he had a 2.39 earned-run average as the Phillies won their first National League

pennant. Alexander, with a 31–10 record and a 1.22 ERA, was the big man on the pitching staff.

Hoping to get into the World Series, Rixey got the call in the third inning of the fifth game before his home-town fans. He worked six and two-thirds innings that day, allowing four hits and three runs, two of them earned. Two home runs off the bat of Harry Hooper bounced into the centerfield stands in Philadelphia. (There was no ground-rule double rule at the time). Rixey was tagged with the 5–4 loss as the Series ended 4–1 in favor of the Boston Red Sox.

Although Rixey had many better seasons in later years, he never again pitched in a World Series.

The Phillies dropped to second in 1916, but Pat Moran got a lot out of Rixey. Eppa won 22 games, lost only 10, and had a 1.85 earned-run average, third in the league behind Alexander and Rube Marquard. Only three of his victories were shutouts, and the low ERA therefore was based on consistently fine pitching all season.

The 1917 season was not a pleasant one for Eppa, for although the Phillies were again second, Rixey was 16–21, tying for the league lead in defeats. Running up a lot of defeats became a mark of Eppa's durability; his 251 career losses are an all-time record for lefthanders.

During World War I, Eppa served in a chemical warfare unit overseas. He was not mustered out of the Army until late May of 1919 and thus was delayed in rejoining the Phillies. The club finished in last place that year, Pat Moran having moved over to the pennant-winning Cincinnati Redlegs. Eppa's contribution upon returning was a 6–12 record for 23 appearances.

As the 1920 season progressed, Philadelphia owner William Baker was determined to trade Eppa, who did not do much to help his own cause. He had an 11–22 record, leading the National League in defeats again. Just before spring training in 1921, Eppa was traded to Cincinnati for pitcher Jimmy Ring and outfielder Earle "Greasy" Neale.

The trade delighted Rixey. He knew he had worn out his welcome in Philadelphia, and in Cincinnati he was reunited with the man to whom he credited most of his success, Pat Moran. In 1921 he led the Reds with a 19–18 record, and then in 1922 he lifted the club all the way to second with his finest season in the majors. He won 25 games to lead the National League, lost only 13, and worked a league-leading 313 innings.

The Reds were second again in 1923, and again Eppa won 20 games, this time going 20–15 with a 2.80 earned-run average, second in the league to teammate

Dolph Luque. His salary for 1924 was upped to $12,000, making him second only to Edd Roush on the club. And the big, personable gentleman was enjoying great popularity in Cincinnati. He settled there and married Dorothy Meyers in 1924.

Eppa was only 15–14 in 1924, but he was third in earned run average and was recognized as one of the finest pitchers in the National League. In 1925 he bounced back to win another 21 games, only one behind Dazzy Vance's league-leading total, and he was again second to Luque in earned run average. That made three consecutive seasons in which he had been in the top three in ERA in the National League.

Rixey never reached the 20-victory mark again, but few pitchers ever managed to make it four times as he did. And in his crafty way, without the benefit of a good fastball, he continued to be a highly competent pitcher for eight more years.

Rixey's next big year was 1928, when he had a 19–18 record. The Boston Braves that season, had erected new stands in right field, known as the "Jury Box," to make it easier for left handers to hit home runs. The first day Cincinnati played in Boston, Reds pitcher Ray Kolp homered into the Jury Box. The second day, Reds pitcher Pete Donohue homered into the same spot. When Rixey, a righthanded batter and a lifetime .191 hitter with only two previous career homers, proceeded to hit one into the Jury Box in the third game, the temporary seats came down.

Eppa's last season in double figures in victories was 1929, when he had a 10–13 record for the seventh-place Reds. At 38, many thought he might be through, but Eppa claimed he felt as good as he ever did and continued to report to spring training.

He pitched 164 innings in 1930, the first time since 1919 he had been under 200, and his record was only 9–13. He was 4–7 in 1931 and 5–5 in 1932. Still, he had great confidence in himself, and was quite upset when his manager, Donie Bush, used him primarily against Pittsburgh in 1933. Pittsburgh always seemed to be an easy match for Rixey, and he notched a 6–3 record and 3.16 ERA at the age of 42. But Eppa wanted to pitch more than the 94 innings he toiled in 1933, and during the winter he

went to the club's new general manager, Larry MacPhail, to voice his opinion.

MacPhail told him the matter was entirely up to the manager, and as the situation did not seem as though it would change, Rixey retired.

He had been building up a small insurance business in the Cincinnati area during his later years with the Reds, and now he devoted his full efforts to making it one of the most successful agencies in the area.

In 1959, Milwaukee's Warren Spahn passed Rixey in career victories, the most ever for a lefthander. Rixey commented, "I'm glad Warren did it. If he hadn't broken my record, no one would have known I'd set it."

It was true that he was not very well remembered outside of Cincinnati, but in January 1963 his election to the Hall of Fame revived memories of him. One month later, on February 28, he died in Cincinnati at the age of 71.

In 1969, Cincinnati fans voted him the greatest lefthanded pitcher in the Reds' history.

EPPA RIXEY

Philadelphia (N.L.) 1912–1920
Cincinnati 1921–1933

G	IP	W	L	Pct.	H	R	ER	SO	BB	ERA
692	4494	266	251	.515	4633	1986	1572	1350	1082	3.15

6'5" Eppa Rixey, lefthanded superpitcher of the 1920s. He had some interesting thoughts on batters, wondering why they looked for a fastball in a 2–1 or 3–1 situation and were always surprised when it did not come

Robin Roberts (b. 1926)

Robin Roberts was a master of control who, during the 1950s, recorded six consecutive 20-victory seasons for the Philadelphia Phillies.

Robin Evan Roberts was born on September 30, 1926, one of five children of Tom and Sarah Roberts, English immigrants who came to America in 1921. Tom Roberts was a Welsh miner who began working the mines when he was 11, but when a prolonged strike threatened to starve his family he set out for America with his wife and two children and settled in Springfield, Illinois, where Robin and two other children were born. His oldest son, Tom, Jr., was killed in World War II.

Robin attended the East Pleasant Hill Grade School, where a teacher, C. B. Lindsay, fostered his interest in athletics. In 1935, pitching-immortal Grover Cleveland Alexander spoke at a school sports banquet and captured Robin's imagination with tales of the big leagues, although Roberts' hero was not a pitcher, but Yankee star Lou Gehrig.

Robin went on to Springfield High School without showing much athletic ability, but when he transferred to Lamphier High his sports prowess began to emerge. Basketball was his best sport, and colleges were soon showing interest in the handsome forward.

In 1944 Robin qualified for the Air Force cadet program and was soon assigned to Wichita Falls, Texas, for basic training. At the same time he received an offer of a basketball scholarship from Michigan State University, and upon his discharge from the Air Force on November 1, 1945, Robin enrolled in college. Eventually he received a Bachelor of Science degree in physical education from Michigan State.

At first basketball was Robin's best sport, but eventually baseball coach John Kobs recruited him and turned him from an infielder, which he was initially, into a pitcher. As a collegian Robin hurled a pair of no-hitters, including one against archrival University of Michigan. Beginning in 1946 the Michigan coach, Ray Fisher, put Robin in a summer league in Vermont so that he could develop his pitching at a more competitive level.

In 1948, Philadelphia Phillies' scout Jack Rossiter observed Roberts carefully, and the Phillies became one of several clubs to bid for his services. At 6'1" and 201 pounds, the strong righthander was offered contracts by the Braves, Yankees, Red Sox, and Tigers, but when Phillie scout Chuck Ward raised the bonus offer from $10,000 to $25,000 within three days, Robin signed. He used the money to buy a new home for his parents, and reported to Wilmington of the Inter-State League.

Robin was obviously far too advanced for the low-classification farm team. He started 11 games and had a 9–1 record, leading the league in both won-lost per-

centage and earned run average (2.06). On June 17, 1948, he was called up by the Phillies. He made his first start the next day, losing a 2–0 decision to Pittsburgh despite a 5-hitter. But his next time out he beat Cincinnati, 3–2, for the first of 286 career victories. Robin, showing a lot of poise at 22, wound up 7–9 that first year with a 3.18 ERA.

The 1949 season was one of improvement for the Phillies, who were in their first full year under the management of Eddie Sawyer. The club advanced from sixth to third and began to take on the look of a pennant-contending team. Robin was 15–15 that year, despite the development of an ulcer.

On December 26, 1949, Robin married Mary Ann Kalnes, a schoolteacher. They had four sons.

If the Phillies had a year to remember, it would have to have been 1950. They were called the "Whiz Kids" that season because of the combination of their youth and maturity. The infield consisted of Eddie Waitkus, Mike Goliat, Granny Hamner, and Willie Jones. Del Ennis, Richie Ashburn, and Dick Sisler were in the outfield, and Andy Seminick was the regular catcher. Robin headed a pitching staff that also included his roommate and neighbor, Curt Simmons, and the top relief pitcher in the game, Jim Konstanty, the MVP award winner that season.

It was a thrilling pennant race that went right down to the final game in Ebbets Field between Philadelphia and Brooklyn. Richie Ashburn's throw kept Phillie hopes alive as the game went to the tenth inning; then Roberts led off with a single, and came home on a dramatic three-run homer by Dick Sisler (son of Hall of Famer George Sisler). The 4–1 Phillie victory, clinching the pennant, was Robin's twentieth win of the year (he lost 11), and it marked the first Phillie flag in 35 years.

Robin had hurled three of the final five games of the season, which made Konstanty a surprise starter in the first game of the World Series against the Yankees. Robin started the second game and lost 2–1 in 10 innings on a home run by Joe DiMaggio. He relieved Konstanty in the fourth game for one scoreless inning, but the Yankees wrapped it up in four straight, and that was the final Series appearance for Roberts.

The 1950 season not only made a star out of Roberts, but it kicked off a string of great successes. Although the Phillies failed to win another pennant, Robin was 21–15 in 1951, 28–7 in 1952, 23–16 in 1953, 23–15 in 1954, and 23–14 in 1955. From 1952 to 1955 he led the National League in victories every year (tying Warren Spahn in

By stopping the action at each stage of his windup and pitch, the camera catches the sizzling style of Robin Roberts. The upper picture series was taken in 1950, the year the Phillies' "Whiz Kids" won a pennant and Roberts kicked off a string of successes that was to last throughout the decade, even when the team slumped badly. (Below) A closeup of Robert's grip on the ball.

1953). In each of the five years (1951 to 1955) he led the league in innings pitched, topping 300 each time, and in 1953 he reached a high of 347 with a league-leading 33 complete games. Altogether, Robin led the league in complete games five times (1952 to 1956).

In 1952 his 28–7 record threatened to make him the first National Leaguer since Dizzy Dean (1934) to win 30 games, and he was named the Major League Player of the Year by *The Sporting News,* an honor which was repeated in 1955. He was also selected to seven National League All-Star teams, hurling in five of the games without a decision. He was one of the best-known players in baseball, and all before he reached his thirtieth birthday.

If Robin did have one problem, it was only the result of his fine control. Never did he walk more than 77 batters in a season, while he topped 100 strikeouts 14 times and led the league twice. But he was a frequent victim of home runs, and his career total of 502 is a major league record. He led the league in home runs permitted four times, and set a record by yielding 46 in 1956.

Robin was the pride of the Phillies during the 1950s, whether they were a good team, as they were early in the decade, or a bad one, as they became. Thirteen times during his career he was named the opening-day pitcher.

Roberts worked hard at the end of 1955 to bring the Phillies to a .500 season under Mayo Smith, but he felt that overwork caused him to lose the good wrist snap in his right arm. Although he was 19–18 in 1956, he felt a difference, and never again was he a 20-victory pitcher. In 1957 he fell to a 10–22 record with a 4.07 earned-run average.

In 1958 he rallied to a 17–14 showing, but by his own admission he was a frequent contributor to Phillie failures. After

1959 and 1960 showings of 15–17 and 12–16, in 1961 he fell to an embarrassing 1–10 record with a 5.85 earned-run average. At age 35, many felt certain that he was through, and on October 16, 1961, his Phillie career ended with his sale to the New York Yankees.

In 1962 Robin trained with the Yankees in Fort Lauderdale and went north with the team, but he failed to make a single appearance. On April 30 the Yankees elected to retain rookie Jim Bouton and handed Robin his release. On May 21 Roberts signed with the Baltimore Orioles, and the move proved to be a good one. He spent three and a half years in Baltimore and regained his touch as a steady, dependable pitcher. He was 42–36 during his stay with the Orioles, and 14–13 and 13–7 seasons in 1963 and 1964 showed that he was still a quality hurler.

Robin drew his Oriole release on July 31, 1965, and signed with the Houston Astros a few days later, marking his return to the National League. And he did well for the Astros, winning five of seven decisions and recording a 1.89 ERA.

In July of 1966, Houston released him and the Chicago Cubs picked him up. He won his final game in the major leagues that September, and then agreed to go to the minors for the 1967 season. At the age of 40, Robin was 5–3 for Reading (Eastern League) with a fine 2.48 earned run average. He was prepared to continue playing, and there were indications that the Orioles were again interested in him, but an elbow operation at the end of the season put an end to his career.

Bright and well-spoken, Robin was often involved in improving benefits for the players, and he had become an officer of the Players Association. He was perhaps the

most influential man in selecting Marvin Miller to head the association in 1966. Roberts recognized the need to take the decision-making powers out of the players' hands and to put them in those of experienced union leaders. The entry of Miller into baseball, although providing anything but a calming effect, nevertheless brought dynamic changes to the salaries and benefits of all players.

Following his retirement Robin entered the security investment business, which frequently brought him to New York from his home in Fort Washington, Pennsylvania. In 1974 he became part owner of a minor league hockey team in Philadelphia, but he sold his interest after one year. In 1975 he returned to the Phillies as a radio broadcaster for selected home games.

Robin was elected to the Hall of Fame in 1976 and was, ironically, the first Phillie so honored since Grover Cleveland Alexander, that guest speaker back at a Springfield school sports banquet so many years before.

ROBIN EVAN ROBERTS

Philadelphia (N.L.) 1948–1961
Baltimore 1962–1965
Houston 1965–1966
Chicago (N.L.) 1966

G	IP	W	L	Pct.	H	R	ER	SO	BB	ERA
676	4689	286	245	.539	4582	1962	1774	2357	902	3.40

Jackie Robinson (1919-1972)

No figure in the history of professional baseball made a greater impact on the game than did Jackie Robinson, star infielder for 10 seasons with the Brooklyn Dodgers and the first black player in the major leagues in this century. An exciting and controversial player, Robinson displayed exceptional strength of character in pioneering the historic breaking of baseball's "color line."

Born in Cairo, Georgia, on January 31, 1919, Jack Roosevelt Robinson was the youngest of five children. In 1920, having been deserted by her husband, Jackie's mother took the five children to Pasadena, California, where she worked as a maid for $8 a week.

Jackie grew up on Pepper Street, a neighborhood composed of blacks, Mexicans, and Japanese. An older sister, Willie Mae, had a great hand in raising him, although she was only two years older. Like many other slum children, Jackie and his friends were drifting into trouble when a man named Carl Anderson came to town and organized sports teams in the neighborhood. The influence of sports on his own life convinced Jackie of their value in preventing juvenile delinquency. For this reason he devoted much of his adult life to the encouragement of sports programs for city youths.

It was Jackie's older brother, Mack, who was the sports star of the neighborhood. Mack participated in the 1936 Olympics in Berlin, finishing second to Jesse Owens in the 200 meters. Following in Mack's footsteps was not easy, but Jackie had great speed and agility and eventually he starred in four sports.

Not an exceptional student, Jackie got a partial scholarship to the University of California at Los Angeles after beginning at Pasadena Junior College. At UCLA in the late 1930s Jackie first began to attract national attention. He was UCLA's only four-sport letterman. In track he broke the Pacific Coast Conference broad-jump record. He was the league's leading scorer in basketball. In football as a running back he led the nation in rushing, averaging 12 yards a carry. And in baseball, his first love, he began to put together his own aggressive style of play.

Despite his mother's protests, and the objections of his much-admired Methodist minister, the Rev. Karl Downs, Jackie quit school short of his degree when his athletic eligibility ended after four years and took a job as an assistant athletic director in the National Youth Administration. In 1941 he began his professional sports career by playing football for the Los Angeles Bulldogs. With the close of the football season came the Japanese attack on Pearl Harbor, and in a few months Jackie found himself in Officer Candidate School in Kansas. Because of chipped bones in his ankle, he never served over-

seas, but he was discharged in November 1944, as a first lieutenant.

Once out of the service, Jackie took a job as basketball coach at Samuel Houston College in Austin, Texas, a black school. But at the urging of a service buddy, he wrote to Tom Baird, co-owner of the Kansas City Monarchs in the Negro American League, asking for a tryout, and the Monarchs signed him as a shortstop for $400 a month.

For the Monarchs in 1945 Jackie batted around .345 (accurate records were not kept), but the highlight of the season was certainly his meeting with Branch Rickey, president and general manager of the Brooklyn Dodgers, on August 28, 1945.

Rickey had determined to challenge baseball's unwritten ban of black players. His aim was twofold—to rectify a basic injustice and to get the pick of black players for the Dodgers. Although not considered the best player in the Negro Leagues, and certainly not as well known as Satchel Paige or Monte Irvin, Jackie was considered by scouts and Rickey himself to be the best choice for the difficult task.

Rickey told Robinson that the only way he could win acceptance would be to let his skills do his talking. As a lone figure in a highly publicized struggle, he would be subjected to ugly racial insults and would feel like fighting back. But, Rickey told him, he would have to turn the other cheek and let his abilities answer for him.

Robinson was not at all sure he could make it. The civil rights struggle in America had hardly begun in 1946. No black player had appeared in the major leagues since 1888. But at least baseball was taking the initiative, not waiting for external forces to compel integration. Jackie resolved to do his part.

Rickey urged Jackie to marry his girl friend Rachel, for he would need the strong support of a wife, and they married on February 10, 1946.

Jackie was assigned to Montreal in the International League for the 1946 season, and, converted from short to second base, led the league in batting with a .349 average. Although he was almost 28 years old, his talents were very much in demand by the Dodgers, and during spring training in 1947 Jackie was promoted to the Brooklyn roster. On opening day, with the Dodgers facing the Boston Braves, baseball's color line was broken. Jackie was at first base for Brooklyn.

Rickey's warnings to Robinson had been correct. Some of his Dodger teammates demanded to be traded, although Pee Wee Reese and Eddie Stanky offered friendship and support. In St. Louis, the Cardinals threatened to strike if Jackie played; they backed down under stern

(Upper left) Jackie Robinson playing basketball for UCLA. But football was his favorite college sport. (Center picture) He circles right end against the University of Washington on November 23, 1940. (Upper right) Robinson with the Kansas City Monarchs in 1945. (Below) Robinson, now a Dodger superstar, steals home safely under lunging Cub catcher, Johnny Pramesa, in Ebbets Field on May 12, 1952. Umpire is Augie Guglielmo.

orders from league president Ford Frick. There was an ugly incident of bench jockeying and racial attacks in Philadelphia. A highly emotional man by nature, Jackie managed to go through the entire season without fighting back. A generation later he was criticized for that attitude by young blacks, but at the time, and considering the task before him, Rickey's strategy made sense, and the results were positive.

Jackie won the Rookie of the Year Award in 1947, the first year it was presented, after batting .297 with 12 homers in 151 games. He led the league with 29 stolen bases, his first of two stolen base titles. The Dodgers, managed by Burt Shotton, captured the pennant.

In 1948 Robinson replaced Stanky at second base and batted .296. He enjoyed his finest season in 1949, winning the Most Valuable Player Award in the National League by hitting .342 with 203 hits, 38 doubles, 12 triples, 16 homers, 124 runs batted in, and 122 runs scored. His .342 average and his 37 stolen bases led the league. It was the first of six straight seasons in which he batted over .300.

The Dodgers were back in the World Series in 1949, only to be beaten again by the Yankees, as they would be in five of the six World Series in which Jackie played.

Robinson played only one game—in 1953—at shortstop in his major-league career. The versatile righthanded hitter, who stood 5′11½″ and weighed between 190 and 230 during his career, played 197 games at first, 751 at second, 256 at third, and 152 in the outfield. Wherever he played, he was a vital part of a great Brooklyn lineup that included Duke Snider, Gil Hodges, Roy Campanella, Reese, Carl Furillo, and Billy Cox.

The Dodgers lost the 1950 pennant by two games to Philadelphia despite late season heroics by Jackie. In 1951 they had a 13½-game lead over the Giants as late as mid-August, but saw the lead die as the Giants got hot. The Giants could have won the pennant on the last day of the regular season if the Phillies had beaten Brooklyn, but Robinson hit a two-run homer in the fourteenth inning to win that game and tie up the race. The home run was all the more exciting in that Jackie had been knocked unconscious earlier in the game while making a play at third base. The Dodgers and Giants went into a three-game playoff, which the Giants won on another dramatic home run—Bobby Thomson's last-of-the-ninth blow in the third game.

The Dodgers returned to the World Series in 1952 and 1953, losing both times. By 1955, when they won their first World Championship, Jackie had been reduced to 105 games and had batted .256. He hit only .182 in the World Series, though he grabbed the headlines with a steal of home. He was completing only his ninth

year in the majors, but he was nearly 37 years old.

In 1956, Jackie batted .275 with 10 homers. He was clearly slowing down, but it was still a shocked baseball world which read on December 13, 1956, that Jackie had been traded to the archrival New York Giants for Dick Littlefield and $35,000.

Jackie knew his career was about over. He wanted to spend more time with his wife and three children. On January 5, 1957, just 23 days after the trade, Jackie announced his retirement in a magazine article, angering the press, the Giants, and the Dodgers. But Jackie was very much his own man, and the trade was negated.

Out of baseball, Jackie worked for a restaurant chain in New York. As the years went on, he became a major spokesman in the civil rights movement. The family moved to Stamford, Connecticut, and Jackie became involved in politics, working for New York Governor Nelson Rockefeller. He worked for a bank, wrote newspaper columns, and did frequent television and radio work, including baseball announcing for ABC television on the Game of the Week. But he became bitter over the lack of blacks in baseball's front offices and as managers and began to avoid baseball gatherings.

Personal problems beset him. Jackie, Jr., was a drug addict upon his return from Vietnam, and when he had the addiction beaten and was working in a rehabilitation center he was killed in an auto accident. Jackie himself suffered from diabetes, and he had a mild heart attack in 1968. He walked with a cane and his sight was failing.

In 1962, his first year of eligibility, Jackie Robinson was elected to the Baseball Hall of Fame. The Dodgers subsequently retired his number—42. But he continued to be outspoken about baseball's lack of progress in racial integration off the field. At the opening game of the 1972 World Series he made a rare appearance to be honored by the sport that he helped to revolutionize.

Several weeks later, on October 24, Jackie died at the age of 53. He had told a television interviewer, while reviewing the tragic events of his later years, that he had had a "wonderful life." Whether he really believed it, only he knew. But his life had certainly been purposeful, and his contribution to baseball is measured not so much by the words on his plaque in the Hall of Fame as by the black players who have followed there. Jackie Robinson led the way.

JACK ROOSEVELT ROBINSON

Brooklyn 1947–1956

G	AB	R	H	2B	3B	HR	RBI	Avg.
1382	4877	947	1518	273	54	137	734	.311

Jackie Robinson jogs home to a handshake from St. Louis Cardinal star Stan Musial, after Robinson hit a home run for the National League in the first inning of the 1952 All-Star game.

Wilbert Robinson (1864-1934)

Once a star catcher for the World Champion Baltimore Orioles, plump, absent-minded "Uncle Robbie" achieved enormous popularity as manager of the rag-tag Brooklyn "Robins" during the 1920s.

Wilbert Robinson was born on June 2, 1864, in Hudson, Massachusetts. His father was a butcher and fish dealer. As a boy, Wilbert helped out by hawking fish through the streets of Hudson and Bolton.

Robinson broke into organized baseball in 1885 with the Haverhill club in the New England League, playing 73 games and batting .269. The following season he joined the Philadelphia Athletics of the American Association, a major league, and became the club's regular catcher.

Catching was a difficult art in those days, for no shin guards were worn and only the thinnest of gloves. So despite a .205 rookie batting average, Wilbert was recognized as a good addition to the team because of his catching abilities.

Philadelphia fans took a quick liking to Robbie, who was 5'8½" and about 170 pounds when he began. (Years later, as Brooklyn manager, he weighed more than 250.) He was known as Billy Robinson, or Billy Fish, for his previous occupation.

Robinson remained with the Athletics into the 1890 season, although the club never finished higher than third. His best season was 1887, when he hit .286. Late in the 1890 season he was transferred to the Baltimore Orioles, who had been moved from Brooklyn.

The 1890 Orioles finished in last place. But in 1891, the final year of the American Association, the Orioles finished third, and were one of the teams incorporated into the National League for the 1892 season.

Robbie hit .271 in 1892, but Baltimore finished last in the 12-team league. Ned Hanlon took over as manager early that season, and the fortunes of the franchise began to improve rapidly in the following year. John McGraw and Joe Kelley were added to the regular lineup, Robbie hit .338, and the club advanced to eighth.

Then, in 1894, Dan Brouthers, Willie Keeler, and Hughey Jennings came aboard, and the Orioles won the pennant with an 89–39 record. It was the first of four straight years in which Baltimore participated in the Temple Cup "World Series." The club won the cup twice in these four years. It was recognized as the best team of the nineteenth century.

Robinson hit as high as .354 in 1896, the year he had a finger amputated after an injury. He is still in the record books today for his 7-for-7 game against St. Louis on June 10, 1892, when he drove in 11 runs.

Robinson and McGraw became close friends as well as business partners in Baltimore. Robbie was captain of the team, and McGraw sort of the field leader. The two opened a café in Baltimore known as

The Diamond, and it did a good business.

McGraw became manager of the Orioles in 1899, but early in 1900 the franchise was disbanded as the National League reduced from 12 clubs to 8, and most of the Oriole players were transferred to Brooklyn. McGraw and Robinson, however, were sold to St. Louis along with second baseman Billy Keister for $15,000. They spent the 1900 season playing for Patsy Tebeau's Cardinals.

Eager to get back to their café, and with McGraw promised a managing job, McGraw and Robbie jumped to the American League in 1901 to join the new Baltimore franchise. Robbie, bothered by a broken finger, was only a backup catcher to Roger Bresnahan and often a peacemaker in the many battles McGraw had with umpires. In July of 1902 the irascible McGraw quit the Orioles and joined the New York Giants. Robinson finished the season as the Baltimore manager, winning 22 games and losing 54. The club finished last.

The Oriole franchise was transferred to New York in 1903, but Robbie remained in Baltimore, running the café and serving as manager of the Baltimore club in the Eastern League in 1903 and part of 1904. In the next few years his affiliation with the game was slight. Sometimes he coached for Jack Dunn with the Orioles, but mostly he looked after the business.

In 1911, McGraw summoned Robinson to New York to serve as his pitching coach. The move proved a brilliant one, for Robbie turned the career of Rube Marquard around and made him a big winner. He was also a great help in the development of Jeff Tesreau.

Robinson remained with McGraw through the 1913 season. But the two began to quarrel late that year. In the World Series they battled repeatedly over strategy and the use of signs. They split after the season and remained bitter rivals for the rest of their careers.

The Brooklyn Dodgers were seeking a new manager in 1914, and their first choice was Hughey Jennings. Robinson was at first hired as a coach, but when Jennings proved unavailable, Robbie was named manager—to the delight of the Brooklyn fans.

Before the 1914 season was through, Robinson had become "Uncle Robbie" and the team had become known as the Brooklyn Robins. His contract was torn up in June, and a new, three-year pact was written. The club finished only fifth, but attendance soared, and Robbie helped build it with his colorful personality.

On the field he was fiery and profane,

but his rotund body made him seem comical. He had a tendency to be absent-minded, and his team seemed to follow suit, developing a reputation for unpredictability.

Once Robbie told his players he was establishing a "Bonehead Club," with fines for every player who made a dumb play on the field. That day he handed the umpires the wrong lineup and became the first member of the club.

As a stunt, he offered to catch a baseball dropped from an airplane during spring training of 1915. Ruth Law, the famous aviatrix, was the pilot, and was to drop the ball. But she forgot the baseball and dropped a grapefruit instead. Robbie fell to the ground, thinking he had been struck by a lethal weapon.

Robbie and his wife, "Ma," became favorites in Brooklyn. The fans seemed to adore his warm and simple approach to life. In 1916 they really loved him, for he led the Robins to the National League pennant.

In 1918, Colonel Huston of the Yankees wanted Robinson to manage his club, but Colonel Ruppert, co-owner of the Yankees, overruled him and hired Miller Huggins. It was a compliment to Robbie's growing reputation and enhanced his popularity in Brooklyn.

Robbie's next pennant came in 1920, when he happily beat McGraw's Giants by

seven games. His club, a surprise winner, featured Zack Wheat and Burleigh Grimes but lost the World Series to the Indians. Robbie never managed a World Championship club.

He almost won another pennant in 1924, losing to McGraw by a game and a half. The following spring, Brooklyn owner Charles Ebbets died, and a short time thereafter the acting president, Ed McKeever, also died. The directors elected Robinson president of the club, with Zack Wheat chosen as acting manager. The arrangement did not work well, and Robbie returned to the dugout in a matter of weeks, causing confusion all around. This was not unusual for the Robins, however, who were known as the Daffiness Boys. Babe Herman and Dazzy Vance were two of the more notable "flakes" on his teams.

Robinson retained the titles of president and manager through the 1929 season, but as early as 1926 he and director Steve McKeever battled. Only the Ebbets heirs kept Robinson around, and eventually Robbie and McKeever did not even speak.

Robbie staged a good pennant chase in 1930, finishing fourth but only six games out of first. In 1931 he was again fourth, and at the end of the season, tired of arguing with management and disappointed over the 11 seasons without a pennant, he resigned. Most writers reported that he had been forced out.

His record as a manager was 1397–1395, reflecting a good job with generally mediocre teams. His 18 years as manager in Brooklyn represented a Dodger record which lasted until Walter Alston broke it.

Robbie and "Ma" retired to their hunting lodge in Georgia in 1932. The following year Robbie became owner and manager of the Atlanta club in the Southern Association. In 1934 he gave up the managerial reins, serving only as president. On August 8 of that year he died in Atlanta at the age of 70.

Robinson was named to the Hall of Fame in 1945.

WILBERT ROBINSON

Philadelphia (A.A.) 1886–1890
Baltimore (A.A.) 1890–1891
Baltimore (N.L.) 1890–1899
St. Louis (N.L.) 1900
Baltimore (A.L.) 1901–1902

G	AB	R	H	2B	3B	HR	RBI	Avg.
1316	4942	632	1386	210	54	17	219	.280

(Far left) Wilbert Robinson, star catcher of the Baltimore Orioles, before he became "Uncle Robbie," beloved manager of the Brooklyn Robins. Whenever his baseball fortunes looked bleak, Robbie always had butchering, his family trade, to turn back to until a new baseball job turned up.

Edd Roush (b.1893)

Edd Roush was considered the finest center fielder in the National League during the 1920s, and one of the best Cincinnati Redleg players of all time.

Edd J. Roush and his twin brother Fred were born on May 8, 1893, in Oakland City, Indiana. Edd never knew the reason for the odd spelling of his first name but he did know that he had been given only a middle initial to please his uncles, James and Joseph. His father, William C. Roush, had been a semipro ballplayer in the 1880s.

Edd began playing ball seriously around 1909, when the regular center fielder of the amateur Oakland City Walk-Overs failed to show up for a game. In 1910 he became a regular member of the Walk-Overs and became noted for an ability to throw with either hand. Roush, a natural lefthander, denied that an injury forced him to throw righthanded temporarily. The truth was that, as an amateur, he had trouble finding a glove to fit his right hand and so was forced to use lefthanded gloves. When he turned professional and was able to afford the proper equipment he always threw with his stronger arm, the left one.

Edd quit the Walk-Overs in 1911 when he discovered he wasn't receiving the same $5 a game the other players were. Traveling to Princeton, Indiana, by horse and buggy, he joined the local team there and became a big drawing card whenever the two rival clubs met. That year he entered pro ball with Henderson (Kitty League), batting .222 in ten games. In 1912 he signed a professional contract with the Evansville team in the Kitty League, a club about 30 miles from Oakland City. Edd reported there as a second baseman and batted .284 in 41 games.

In 1913 the Evansville team moved into the Central League, and Edd moved to the outfield, batting .317 in 89 games. Late in the season he was sold to the Chicago White Sox, and made his major league debut in August as a teammate of Ed Cicotte, Buck Weaver, Ray Schalk, and Ed Walsh. Roush played two games in the outfield, pinch-hit four times, and pinch-ran three times. With 1 hit in 10 at bats, he was optioned to Lincoln (Western League) in September. That was the extent of his American League career.

In 1914, the Indianapolis club of the newly formed Federal League offered Edd $225 a month—double his Lincoln salary—to jump to that team. While the Federal League managed to grab some of the established stars of the American and National Leagues, few young players developed there. Edd turned out to be the best of the players who began their careers in the Federal League.

Roush hit .333 for Indianapolis in 1914, and his club won the first Federal League pennant. In 1915 the franchise folded, and he was transferred to Newark, where he batted .298 in 145 games.

The Federal League folded after the 1915 season, permitting open bidding for its players. Roush was one of the few with little previous major league experience who seemed to be in demand. Germany Schaefer, the veteran player and "baseball clown," had played at Newark and strongly recommended Roush to New York Giants manager John McGraw. McGraw was interested, but he had an even greater interest in the league's leading hitter, center fielder Benny Kauff of Brooklyn. He signed Kauff for $35,000 and Roush for $7500. All the Roush money went to the Newark owner, Harry Sinclair; since the Federal League had folded, Roush thought this was unfair.

The welcome mat was not out for Edd in New York. He resented McGraw's short temper and tough discipline. A stubborn, independent fellow, Roush saw no place for himself in the Giant picture, for Kauff played the same position he did and the Giants' investment in Kauff was far greater.

Edd played only 39 games for the Giants with a .188 batting average before being traded to Cincinnati with Christy Mathewson and Bill McKechnie for Buck Herzog and Wade Killefer on July 20, 1916. Mathewson, of course, was the big name in the deal; the greatest of all Giant pitchers, he was moving on to become manager of the Redlegs, replacing Herzog. Killefer, the Redlegs' center fielder, was immediately replaced by Roush.

Edd hit .267 for the season, but staged a holdout the following spring, demanding $5000 instead of the offered $4500. Holdouts became an annual affair for the 5'11", 175-pound lefthander. They usually got him a little more money than the club had intended, and they gave him more time to hunt quail and rabbits near his Oakland City home. Roush hated spring training. He felt he needed no more than 10 days to get in shape, sometimes less. The monotony of playing games that did not count was something he constantly sought to avoid.

In 1917, his first season as a full-time regular in the National League, Edd batted .341 to lead the league. He beat Rogers Hornsby by 14 points and quickly became a much-talked-about player.

As a hitter, Edd was unpredictable. He could hit to all fields and was always changing his stance. He used a 48-ounce bat, the heaviest in the league. He had a special fondness for triples, and ran his total into double digits 11 times, including a league-leading 21 in 1924.

In the field, Roush was recognized as probably the finest defensive center fielder in the National League, rivaled only by Tris Speaker in the American League. He would race far back to the flagpole in Redland Field to make circus catches. If he had a weakness, it was in handling ground balls. And if there was anything that kept him out of a game, it was a recurring problem with charley horses.

In 1918, Mathewson's last year as Redleg manager, Edd hit .333 to finish two points behind Zack Wheat for the batting title. But in 1919 he repeated his championship with a .321 mark, as the Reds won the National League pennant and the eight-game World Series against the notorious Chicago "Black Sox," the team accused of fixing the Series. Roush hit .214 in the Series. Later, manager Pat Moran called a clubhouse meeting to ask if anyone had heard of a fix. Roush had, but had dismissed the talk as folly.

The Reds never won another pennant during Edd's years there, but they finished second in 1922, a year in which Edd held out until August. They were second again in 1923 as Edd hit .351 (fourth in the league), but in 1924 they dropped to fourth. That season Edd had his first of two 27-game hitting streaks (the other was in 1927), and he batted .348, fifth in the National League.

After a .339 season in 1925, Edd and the Reds had a disappointing year in 1926. The team was in the pennant race until the final few days, when Roush made two costly errors in a series at Boston. The usually dependable outfielder even dropped a routine fly ball hit by the Braves' Les Mann, leading to a Redleg loss and elimination from the pennant race. Cincinnati finished two games behind the Cardinals, and Edd did not even show up for the final game of the season.

In January, 1927, Edd's Redleg days ended with a trade to the Giants for George Kelly and cash. The thought of returning to McGraw was unpleasant to Roush, and he battled long and hard before signing a three-year, $70,000 contract in 1927. McGraw agreed not to publicly reprimand Roush if he made a bad play.

Edd hit .304 in his first season back in New York. Illness limited him to 46 games in 1928; he batted .252, breaking a streak of 11 straight .300 seasons. In 1929 he hit .324.

Edd's contract with the Giants ran out after the 1929 season. When the Giants sought to cut him to $15,000 for 1930, he remained at home in Oakland City and sat out the entire season. Not once during the year were the two parties in touch with each other.

Two players had previously sat out full seasons over contract disputes, both of them early-day Giants (Mike Donlin and Amos Rusie). But Roush was, and remains, the biggest name ever to sit out a full year.

Edd obtained his release from New York in March 1931 and signed again with his beloved Reds, whose fans had come to adore him. He finished his career in 1931 by playing in 101 games and batting .271 for Cincinnati.

The only other job Edd ever had in baseball was a 1938 coaching position for the Reds, but his baseball earnings and wise stock investments permitted him to move to Florida with his wife Essie, and to travel around the state at will for many years in a trailer. In 1952, he bought a home in Bradenton and was a frequent visitor at spring training games.

Maintaining his home in Oakland City, Edd served eight years on the school board, four years on the town board, and managed a cemetery for many years until he suffered a stroke in 1971. He still divided his year between Oakland City and Bradenton.

Edd Roush was elected to the Hall of Fame in 1962.

EDD J. ROUSH

Chicago (A.L.) 1913
Indianapolis (F.L.) 1914
Newark (F.L.) 1915
New York (N.L.) 1916, 1927–1929
Cincinnati 1916–1926, 1931

G	AB	R	H	2B	3B	HR	RBI	Avg.
1748	6646	1001	2158	311	168	63	882	.325

Edd Roush bunting (above) and catching an easy one at center field for the Giants (below). One of the best fielders in the game during the 1920s, Roush often skipped spring training and held out for more pay. He bounced around the leagues but played his best ball for Cincinnati.

Red Ruffing (b.1905)

Red Ruffing won more games than any Yankee pitcher until Whitey Ford came along.

Charles Herbert Ruffing, known to baseball fans as Red but to friends and players as Charley, was born on May 3, 1905, in Granville, Illinois. He grew up playing sandlot ball and following the progress of the White Sox and Cubs, the major league teams nearest his home.

At the age of 15, Charley left school to join his father in the coal mines of Nokomis, Illinois. The senior Ruffing was a veteran of the mines, and a good athlete in his own right. As manager of the company's baseball team, he put his son at first base and in the outfield, making use of his good bat.

Red matured fast. He grew to be 6'1½" and weighed over 200 pounds. Work in the mines strengthened his arms and he was noted as a great power hitter. But in 1921 a mining accident cost Red four toes on his left foot. The loss took away a great deal of his athletic ability, particularly in running, and he did not touch a baseball for nearly a year.

Finally, in 1922, he turned to pitching. Hesitant at first, he soon found that his handicap did not affect his pitching ability at all. He pitched for the mining team, and also worked for a semipro club near Nokomis for $15 a game.

In 1923 he signed his first professional contract, with the Danville club of the Three-I League. He proved at once that he had a strong arm, for he worked in 39 games and 239 innings, compiling a 12–16 record. He had a good fastball and a fair curve, no trick pitches, and fairly good control. The Boston Red Sox were sufficiently impressed to purchase his contract from Danville at the end of the season for $4000.

Ruffing trained with the Red Sox in 1924 and made the club. However, he was used sparingly; he appeared in only eight games, six of them in relief, without a decision, and was farmed to Dover of the Eastern Shore League in July to work on his curve.

At Dover, Red pitched in 15 games and had a 4–7 record. But he struck out 72 and walked only 23. The next spring he was back with the Red Sox.

The Red Sox club that Red joined in 1925 was still trying to get over the poor deals it had been making with the Yankees. Many of its fine players had been dealt or sold to New York in an effort to get the club on its feet financially. The biggest name of all, of course, was Babe Ruth. Boston would never live that one down.

But the Sox had also supplied the Yankees with pitchers like Carl Mays, Sam Jones, Herb Pennock, Waite Hoyt, and Joe

Bush. Lee Fohl was the manager of the Red Sox in 1925, but he did not have much of a club to work with. Ruffing easily made the starting rotation as there really was not a stopper on the staff. Red's nine victories were second only to Ted Wingfield's 12, but he lost 18 games and had a 5.02 earned-run average. The club lost 105 games and finished last, 21 games behind the seventh-place Yankees.

In 1926 the Yankees moved to first. Boston remained last, and this time lost 107 games. Fifteen of the defeats were charged to Ruffing, who won only six games and had a 4.39 earned-run average.

Red continued to have difficulty winning in 1927, running up a 5–13 record. In 1928 he stumbled to a 10–25 mark, leading the league in losses. He did chalk up a decent 3.89 ERA, however, and people were beginning to appreciate his basic pitching ability, despite the poor team backing him up.

Usually Red was the best hitter in the lineup when he pitched. He was certainly one of the best hitting pitchers of all time, compiling a lifetime .269 average with 36 homers and 273 runs batted in. Eight times he batted over .300, with a high of .364 in 1930. He had as many as five home runs in one season (1936), and was used as a pinch-hitter almost 250 times in his career. Had the mining injury not forced his conversion to the mound, he almost certainly would have been a major league star with the bat.

In 1929 Red again led the league in defeats. His record was 9–22 with a 4.87 earned run average. Twelve of the losses were consecutive. But the mighty Yankees saw something in Ruffing that they admired and wanted. Their only problem was whether they could steal yet another pitcher away from the Red Sox, considering the way the Boston fans were howling.

When Red got off to an 0–3 start for Boston in 1930, Bob Shawkey, managing and Yanks, finally, on May 6, persuaded Jacob Ruppert and Ed Barrow to swing the deal. On that day the Yankees traded outfielder Cedric Durst and $50,000 to Boston for Ruffing. It was, as usual for the Yankees, a great steal. Durst had never played 100 games in any season and, as it turned out, the 1930 season was his last in the majors. He finished his seven year career with a .244 mark and 15 home runs. Ruffing accomplished a great deal more.

Red's career record at Boston had been 39–96. But everything turned around for him when he joined the mighty Yankees. In his first season, he was 15–5 for New York. In 1931 he was 16–14, but then in 1932, a pennant-winning year for the Yanks, he was 18–7, second only to Lefty Gomez on the staff in victories.

That was the year Red first learned to throw a changeup. On one of the first times he used it he beat Washington, 1–0,

Red Ruffing fires a pitch. Although it kept him from being a batting star, a mine injury that cost him four toes on his left foot did not stop him from balancing on that foot to throw.

with 10 strikeouts. And he hit a home run for the game's only run.

Red appeared in his first World Series in 1932, facing the Chicago Cubs in the opening game and beating them, 12–6; three of their runs were unearned. It was the first of seven World Series victories for Red, who lost only twice in ten series starts.

In 1933, just when things seemed to be on the upswing, Red's record fell to a disappointing 9–14. Still, he worked his usual 235 innings, and that in itself was a great boost to the pitching staff. Between 1928 and 1940, Red never pitched fewer than 222 innings in a season. He seldom missed a start, and from 1936 until the end of his career he never pitched in relief. The 241 consecutive starting assignments stood as a league record until a later Yankee right-hander, Mel Stottlemyre, broke it in 1973.

Red was 19–11 in 1934, and 16–11 in 1935. In neither season did the Yankees win the pennant, but in 1936 they did and Red had his first 20-victory year. He was 20–12 in the regular season, and then 0–1 in the Series, losing to Carl Hubbell in the opening game.

In 1937, Red was 20–7, and he beat the Giants in the Series. In 1938, he led the league with a 21–7 record, also led in shut-outs, and beat the Cubs twice in the Series, winning the first game, 3–1, and the fourth and final game, 8–3.

Then in 1939 Red was 21–7 again, and defeated Cincinnati, 2–1, in the World Series opener. For the four consecutive World Championship Yankee teams, Red had compiled a regular season record of 82–33, and a 4–1 record in the World Series. "Break up the Yankees!" was the cry of the other teams in baseball, and if they had been able to do so they might have had to start with Ruffing.

At this point Red was the complete professional. While teammate Lefty Gomez was an unassuming, easy-going man, Red was a proud, rugged competitor who commanded respect on and off the field. He was an imposing-looking man, very well read and well spoken, and something of a symbol of Yankee success.

The Yanks did not win in 1940, and Red was only 15–12 for the season. In 1941 he was 15–6, and in 1942 he had a 14–7

record. He won a game in the 1941 World Series, and was 1–1 in the 1942 Series.

In 1942 he was 37 years old and married, but despite all that and the loss of the four toes the Army found him fit for World War II. Charley was inducted on December 29, 1942. Not until June 5, 1945 was he released, and by then he was 40 years old. He rejoined the Yankees on July 16, appeared in 11 games for the remainder of the season, and had a 7–3 record with a 2.90 earned-run average—the lowest of his career.

In 1946 he got off to a 5–1 record with a 1.77 ERA, but he broke his ankle after eight appearances and that finished him for the year. On September 20 the Yankees released him.

The White Sox signed Red in December 1946, but he appeared in only nine games with them in 1947, posting a 3–5 record before reinjuring his knee and calling it quits.

His long career had established major league records for most runs and most earned runs allowed, but Red could also be proud of his 273–225 record after such a poor start in Boston.

Ruffing scouted for the White Sox in 1948 and managed Muskegon of the Central League in 1949. In 1950 he was manager of Daytona Beach (Florida State League), finishing second. From 1951 until June 1959 he scouted for the Cleveland Indians, and he and his wife, Pauline, settled in the Cleveland area. He was a New York Mets scout in 1961, and the Mets' first pitching coach in 1962.

In 1967, he was elected to the Hall of Fame. He suffered a stroke in September, 1973 which left him confined to a wheel-chair, but still sound of mind, and an annual visitor to Hall of Fame ceremonies.

CHARLES HERBERT RUFFING

Boston (A.L.) 1924–1930
New York (A.L.) 1930–1946
Chicago (A.L.) 1947

G	IP	W	L	Pct.	H	R	ER	SO	BB	ERA
624	4342	273	225	.548	4294	2117	1833	1987	1541	3.80

Babe Ruth (1895-1948)

Until Babe Ruth began hitting home runs as no one ever had before, baseball was an artful succession of base hits, leading to one run at a time. Ruth's barrage of power transformed the game, making it possible to destroy an opponent with one mighty swing of the bat. In personality and style, as well as in hitting and pitching, Babe Ruth was the most dynamic figure in baseball history.

George Herman Ruth was born on February 6, 1895, in Baltimore, Maryland. His birthplace, now a landmark, was merely a small apartment. He was not the product of a stable household, and as a child he was left more or less on his own. His mother died when he was 16, and his father, a saloon operator, was shot to death in front of his bar when Babe was 24. Neither had devoted much time to George, and he was generally considered an orphan. When he was eight, he was placed in St. Mary's Industrial School, a reform school for incorrigible boys. He remained at St. Mary's until he entered professional baseball at age 19.

George was introduced to baseball at St. Mary's by Brother Matthias, the first adult he learned to trust. Brother Matthias enlisted Ruth as a lefthanded catcher and first baseman for the school's team, and later urged Jack Dunn, owner of the Baltimore Orioles (International League), to give Ruth a look.

Dunn was impressed by the strong, roundfaced youth and agreed to adopt him as legal guardian and give him a job. So Ruth joined the Orioles, where Dunn converted him to a pitcher and quickly sold him to the Boston Red Sox. The Red Sox used him twice and then optioned him to Providence, also in the International League. For the two minor league clubs Babe had a 22–9 record in 1914, making him the league's leading pitcher.

George received the nickname "Babe" because of his youth. In later years fans called him "The Bambino" or "The Sultan of Swat." Teammates sometimes called him "Jidge," a New England pronunciation for George, but opponents teased him with such less-pleasant names as "Baboon" and "Monkey." His odd build lent itself to these taunts, for he was barrel-shaped and awkward looking. He stood 6'2" and weighed 215 pounds, at times rising to 265 pounds. Most of this weight was in his belly. When he struck out, as he did often, his thick body wound his thin legs up like a corkscrew. But although he had a strange build for an athlete he was a graceful outfielder and a fine base runner—123 lifetime stolen bases.

At the end of the 1914 season, when he was 19 years old, the Red Sox recalled Babe. He won two games for them and never returned to the minor leagues.

In 1915, Ruth found himself a member of a pennant-winning pitching staff that

included Rube Foster, Ernie Shore, Joe Wood, Dutch Leonard, and Carl Mays. Ruth distinguished himself by winning 18 games against only 8 defeats. As a hitter, the big lefthander socked the first four home runs of his career—the first of 714, a total that stood as the top lifetime total until surpassed by Hank Aaron in 1974. Ruth's home runs, hit in 8399 official times at bat, gave him an average of one home run every 11.7 times at bat, the top frequency ever recorded. His career at bat total was limited by a record 2056 bases on balls.

Ruth did not appear on the mound in the 1915 World Series, although he did pinch-hit once. In 1916 he became the leader of the Red Sox pitching staff with a 23–12 record and a league-leading 1.75 earned-run average. He started the second game of the World Series that year and pitched a route-going 14-inning, 2–1 victory over Brooklyn's Sherry Smith. It remains the longest Series game on record. Ruth allowed only six hits and three walks.

Boston slipped to second place in 1917, but Ruth won 24, lost 13, and had a 2.02 ERA. His hitting was getting better, and although he was still strictly a pitcher, he batted .325. He got some valuable batting pointers from Chicago's Shoeless Joe Jackson, who taught Ruth his batting stance. Ed Barrow, Ruth's manager at the time (later his general manager in New York), saw the advantage of having Babe play the outfield on off days. In 1918 Ruth appeared in 59 games in the outfield and in 13 at first base.

Ruth was 13–7 as a pitcher in 1918 and batted .300 with 11 home runs to tie Tilly Walker of Philadelphia for the league lead. It was his first of 12 home run titles.

Babe's last big moment as a pitcher came in the 1918 World Series when he set a record by extending his string of consecutive scoreless innings in Series competition to 29⅔, a record that stood until Whitey Ford broke it in 1961. Ruth's overall pitching record in World Series competition was 3–0, with a 0.87 ERA.

In 1919, his final year as a pitcher, Ruth had a 9–5 record and a 2.97 ERA. In later years Babe pitched five games for the Yankees, always as an attendance booster at the end of a season, and he won all five, giving him a career pitching mark of 94–46, a .671 percentage with a 2.28 ERA.

After the 1919 season the financially desperate Red Sox sold Ruth to the Yankees. This became the most noted deal in the history of the game, for it helped to launch the great New York Yankee dynasty—and Boston did not win another pennant until 1946.

The complicated sale was valued at over $400,000. In an agreement signed on December 26, 1919, Jacob Ruppert and his partner, Colonel Tillinghast L'Hommedieu Huston, agreed to pay Boston's Harry Frazee $25,000 in cash and three promissory notes of $25,000 each plus interest. In addition, Ruppert and Huston agreed to lend Frazee $300,000 and to hold the mortgage on Fenway Park.

Not only did the Red Sox make money on the deal, but Ruth himself did well. Although he was not well educated, and was noted as a spendthrift with lavish tastes in his lustful pursuit of pleasure, Ruth could be shrewd at contract time. He negotiated a two-year pact for $41,000 for 1920–1921, and eventually earned $80,000 during Depression years—worth over $300,000 by today's standards. Informed once that he was making more than the President of the United States, Ruth replied, "Hell, I had a better year than he did."

He probably did, for every year seemed to be better for Ruth in New York. After hitting a record 29 home runs in 1919 for Boston, he belted 54 in his first season with the Yankees, along with a .376 batting average. His slugging percentage that year was .847, a major league record, and one point better than his 1921 showing when he again broke the home run record, this time hitting 59 with 170 runs batted in. Adding to the magnitude of his home run feats was the fact that the year he hit 54 the entire American League had only 369, and except for the Yankees, no club hit more than 50.

Ruth played on his first of seven Yankee pennant winners in 1921, the year of the first Yankee World Series. He was at his best in these October showdowns. He set a record with 15 Series homers (since broken by Mickey Mantle), batted .625 in the 1928 Series, hit four home runs in the 1926 Series, and hit his famous, if somewhat questionable, "called shot home run" in the 1932 Series at Wrigley Field, Chicago.

Ruth and legend went together. He was beloved by children and had a deep affection for them, signing autographs endlessly, visiting hospital wards, promising home runs, and spreading happiness with his great personality wherever he went. He had no memory for names, and everyone was "Kid" or "Doc." His off-field life befitted his "Sultan" nickname, for he indulged an enormous capacity for food, drink, women, and the fast life.

His first wife, Helen, died in a fire in 1929. They were legally separated at the time, but had a daughter. Soon after he married Claire Hodgson, a New York showgirl who helped somewhat to slow down his fast-paced life.

That's George Herman Ruth, standing left (above) with catcher's mitt and mask, with his teammates at St. Mary's Industrial School, Baltimore, Maryland. Placed in the reform school at the age of eight, Ruth learned there to trust adults and to play baseball. He stayed there until he was 19, when Brother Matthias helped him into professional ball. (At right) Ruth as a lefthanded pitcher for the Boston Red Sox.

Ruth slams a long one (at right)
and (the upper sequence, taken
from motion picture film)
connects and takes off around
the bases, doffing his cap to fans
as he goes. Ruth's 29 home runs
in 1919 shifted him forever from
a pitching career. His salary rose
from $4000 in 1914 to $80,000 in
the Depression. He spent it
recklessly, but he was the
country's greatest hero.

Among Babe's many feuds with his manager, Miller Huggins, was one that developed over a 1925 "stomach ache" that caused him to miss more than 50 games and bat only .290. Huggins fined him $5000 that year and the two developed a strong mutual dislike. The Yankees finished seventh in 1925, the only bad season they had during the Ruth era.

From its opening in 1923 Yankee Stadium was known as "The House that Ruth Built" because of the vastly increased gate receipts that Ruth brought to the Yankees and for the odd field dimensions, tailored to Babe's power. Ruth hit the first home run in the new park. Dramatic home runs were his style, and he also hit the first All-Star Game homer in 1933.

In 1927 Ruth hit 60 home runs to break his own record; that mark stood for 34 years until Roger Maris hit 61 in 1961 in a schedule that was eight games longer. In all, Ruth topped the 50-homer mark four times, was a six-time RBI champ, an eight-time runs-scored champ, and the 1924 batting champion at .378 (although his career high was .393 in 1923 with 205 hits and 170 walks).

He led the American League in slugging percentage 13 times, and set a record by scoring 177 runs in 1921. On 72 occasions he hit two or more home runs in a game. He was the league's Most Valuable Player in 1923, and whenever the appropriate polls were taken he was usually found to have been voted the game's greatest player of all time, beating out the unpopular Ty Cobb.

By 1934 Ruth had slipped to a .288 average with 22 home runs. He wanted to manage the Yankees, but since, according to the Yankee ownership, he had difficulty in managing even his own affairs, no offer was forthcoming. He was, however, offered the managerial job with the Yankees' Newark farm club, but he turned it down and was released to the Boston Braves on February 26, 1935.

With Boston, Babe served as a vice-president and assistant manager as well as player. He played the last 28 games of his career with the Braves that year, hitting only .181 but enjoying a final bit of drama when he hit his last three home runs all in one game—on May 25, 1935, in Forbes Field, Pittsburgh. A few days later, he called it a career.

Frustrated by his inability to get a managing job, he accepted a coaching position with the Dodgers in 1938, but that was his only baseball job after his playing career. He toured Japan and Europe and became an international celebrity. In 1936 he was one of five players elected in the first Hall of Fame balloting.

During his last years Ruth lived in a New York apartment and enjoyed his accumulated wealth. He played himself in the movie *Pride of the Yankees*, based on Lou Gehrig's life. (He had made another movie, *Goin' Home,* early in his career.) His famed uniform, No. 3, was retired by the Yankees and hung in a special Babe Ruth Room in the National Baseball Hall of Fame and Museum. His name was included in most American history textbooks.

Finally stricken with throat cancer, Ruth made a moving farewell appearance at Yankee Stadium on June 13, 1948. He died on August 16. Thousands passed his body as it lay in state in the lobby of Yankee Stadium. He was buried in Westchester County and remained the game's most memorable figure years after his death.

GEORGE HERMAN RUTH

Boston (A.L.) 1914–1919
New York (A.L.) 1920–1934
Boston (N.L.) 1935

G	AB	R	H	2B	3B	HR	RBI	Avg.
2503	8399	2174	2873	506	136	714	2204	.342

G	IP	W	L	Pct.	H	R	ER	SO	BB	ERA
163	1221	94	46	.671	974	400	309	488	441	2.28

Despite their loyalties to various sports superstars of today, the kids still flock to the special Babe Ruth Room in the National Baseball Hall of Fame and Museum to study the Ruth memorabilia and line up to hear his voice on a recorded message. Ruth loved kids and would sign autographs endlessly, visit hospital wards, promise home runs, and generally spread cheer with his sunny personality.

Ray Schalk (1892-1970)

Ray Schalk stood only 5'7" and weighed 155 pounds, but for 17 years with the Chicago White Sox he proved that a small man could be a success as a catcher.

Raymond William Schalk was born on August 12, 1892, in Harvel, Illinois, but always claimed nearby Litchfield as his home town. His parents were German immigrants who had met and married in the United States.

Ray left high school in 1910 and went to Brooklyn, New York, to train as a linotype operator. His father was pleased to see the boy learning a profession, but Ray returned home after 10 weeks when he discovered that his $7-a-week salary would remain unchanged during a four-year apprenticeship.

Back in Litchfield, he helped out on the family farm and played semipro ball for $3 a game. In 1911 a nearby minor league team, Taylorville (Illinois–Missouri League), needed a catcher and offered Ray $65 a month. He gladly accepted the offer, and at a lightweight 135 pounds became the team's regular catcher.

Not big enough to block home plate from charging base runners, Ray developed a style of spinning the runners around him with his shinguards. Stocky and durable, he remained remarkably injury-free throughout his career.

Ray hit .398 for Taylorville in 1911, impressing observers with his good bat. But that aspect of Ray's game was misleading, for it was the only time Ray ever batted over .300, and his lifetime .253 average included only 12 big-league home runs.

Advancing to Milwaukee (American Association) late in 1911, Ray batted .237. He began the 1912 season with the Brewers, catching 80 games through early August. On August 10 he was purchased by the Chicago White Sox for four minor league players representing a total value of some $17,000.

Ray arrived in Chicago on August 11 and headed for Comiskey Park, the beautiful two-year-old stadium that was home to the White Sox. That day's game was the first major league game Ray had ever seen, and he was immediately pressed into action.

Charles Comiskey took a look at the little catcher and was skeptical of his potential. Pitching star Ed Walsh, nearing the end of his career, was equally doubtful, but when he warmed up his spitball on the sidelines with Schalk early in the afternoon, he was at once impressed. From that point on, Walsh always used Schalk as his catcher.

Ray made his debut that day by catching Doc White in a 9–6 loss to the Philadelphia Athletics. Schalk had one hit, a single, in three times at bat.

Almost from the day he reported, Schalk was known by the nickname "Cracker."

There were several versions of the origin of the name, and Ray himself did not know which was correct.

Catching for the White Sox in those days required the ability to handle almost any kind of pitch known to the game—spitballs, shine balls, emory balls, knucklers, curves, etc. Over the years, Ray's fingers were broken many times. He was a wizard at calling a game, and is believed to have been the first catcher to regularly back up throws at first and third bases. During his career he recorded putouts at each of the four bases. He also shares a record with Bill Dickey for recording three assists in one inning, and was one of the best at nailing Ty Cobb in base-stealing attempts.

Ray caught 23 games to close out the 1912 season, batting .286, but making 14 errors for a poor .917 fielding percentage. But he was getting the feel of the league, as catchers must do to call a good game, and beginning with 1913 he rolled up some of the game's most impressive catching statistics. Eight times he led the league's receivers in fielding percentage (a major league record), nine times he led in putouts (a major league record), twice he led in assists, and he recorded a career total of 1810 assists from behind the plate (another major league record).

Ray was the catcher in 4 no-hit games— Jim Scott's 10-inning loss to Washington in 1914, Joe Benz's win over Cleveland 17 days later, Ed Cicotte's no-hitter against St. Louis in 1917, and Charlie Robertson's perfect game over Detroit on April 30, 1922, the last perfect game in the major leagues until Don Larsen's World Series gem 34 years later.

Ray batted .244 in his first season as a regular (1913). Twelve times, including 11 straight years from 1913 to 1923, he caught more than 100 games a season. In 1920 he performed the amazing feat of catching 151 of the 154 games on the White Sox schedule.

The White Sox won the pennant in 1917, when manager Pants Rowland led the team to 100 victories and a nine-game edge over Boston. Although Ray hit only .226 that year, he was an excellent hit-and-run man and drove in 53 runs with a lot of big hits. Unusually fast for a catcher, Schalk also helped the club on the basepaths. He stole as many as 30 bases in one season (1916) and had a career total of 176. No catcher has ever stolen as many in one year.

In the 1917 World Series, Urban (Red) Faber won three games for the White Sox, who defeated the Giants, four games to two, for the World Championship. The Faber-Schalk battery became the most famous in White Sox history. The two remained close friends throughout

Schalk's life, and both eventually gained admittance to the Hall of Fame.

The White Sox fell to sixth in 1918, but in 1919 they assembled one of their best clubs and won another pennant. The infield had Chick Gandil, Eddie Collins, Swede Risberg, and Buck Weaver; the outfield had Joe Jackson, Happy Felsch, and Nemo Leibold. The leading pitchers were Faber, Cicotte, Lefty Williams, and Dickie Kerr.

But the great team lost the World Series in eight games to the underdog Cincinnati Redlegs, and details of a fix later came to light. As a result, eight men on the "Black Sox" were suspended from the game for life for their association with gamblers in allegedly throwing the Series. The eight were Jackson, Felsch, Gandil, Weaver, Risbert, Cicotte, Williams, and utility man Fred McMullin.

The news was especially startling to those who were innocent. Schalk, as the catcher, was presumed to know something was wrong when Cicotte and Williams repeatedly threw pitches other than those called for.

But the Cracker never talked much about the Series, in which he batted .304. Even to friends he seldom said more than "We'd have won the Series despite the gamblers if Faber had been able to pitch." Red had missed the Series with a sore arm. Schalk even turned down a magazine offer of $40,000 to tell his side of the Black Sox scandal.

That was the last Series the White Sox were in until 1959. But Schalk continued to do a steady, high-grade job year after year as the White Sox catcher.

Following a fifth-place finish under manager Eddie Collins in 1926, Comiskey asked Schalk to take the managing job. It was not easy for the popular little guy suddenly to become manager of his teammates, and he could not improve on the club's fifth-place standing in 1927. He

appeared in only 16 games that year and hit .231, turning over the regular catching job to Harry McCurdy.

When the 1928 White Sox won only 32 of their first 74 games, Comiskey asked Schalk for his resignation early in July. Ray was reluctant to give up the $25,000-a-year job, but at last he announced his departure on July 4. He had hoped to remain with the club as a backup catcher for $15,000, but when Comiskey offered only $6000 Schalk announced his retirement. This was the only falling out he ever had with Comiskey, but they patched things up a few years later and Ray remained a big White Sox supporter.

In 1929 Ray got a job as player-coach for John McGraw in New York, serving on occasion as acting manager of the Giants. He participated in his last five major league games that year.

His major league career behind him, Ray scouted briefly for the Cubs, then managed Buffalo of the International League from 1932 to 1937. He spent the next two seasons managing Indianapolis (American Association), then moved to the Milwaukee job in 1940 for one season. In 1950 he returned to Buffalo for one last fling as a minor league manager.

Settled in Chicago with his wife, Lavina, and their two children, Ray opened a successful bowling alley and operated it for several years before selling it at a profit. He then became assistant baseball coach at Purdue University, where he helped to develop Bill Skowron as a player. Although Ray had never graduated from high school, the popular Schalk was awarded an honorary degree from Purdue during his career there.

He enjoyed golf and bowling, and remained close to baseball as a fan. At the opening game of the 1959 World Series, Faber delivered the ceremonial first ball to Schalk.

In 1955 Ray was named to the Hall of Fame, and in 1969 he was selected as the greatest catcher in White Sox history. A year later, on May 19, he died in Chicago after a long bout with cancer.

RAYMOND WILLIAM SCHALK

Chicago (A.L.) 1912–1928
New York (N.L.) 1929

G	AB	R	H	2B	3B	HR	RBI	Avg.
1760	5306	579	1345	199	48	12	596	.253

Movie footage shows angry White Sox catcher Ray Schalk during the 1919 World Series. He yelled obscenities at pitchers Cicotte and Williams, who were later suspended for throwing the Series.

Al Simmons (1903-1956)

One of the great hitting stars of Connie Mack's Philadelphia Athletic champions of 1929–1931 was Al Simmons, a barrel-chested righthanded hitter who played in the major leagues for 20 years.

Aloysius Harry Szymanski was born on May 22, 1903, in Milwaukee, Wisconsin, the son of Polish immigrants. He later changed and shortened the name to Simmons, which he had seen on a billboard advertising a hardware company.

As a youth Al was totally dedicated to baseball. He practiced the game for hours on end on Milwaukee's South Side, and although he briefly attended Stevens Point Teachers College as a football player, his first love remained baseball.

A boyhood hero of Al's, New York Giant catcher Roger Bresnahan, was managing at Toledo, and Al wrote him a letter requesting a tryout but he never received a reply. So he turned instead to semipro ball, and while he was playing for Juneau, Wisconsin, in the Lake Shore League, he hit an inside-the-park home run to defeat the strong Milwaukee amateur team. This brought him to the attention of the Milwaukee Brewers of the American Association, with whom he signed his first professional contract in 1922 at the age of 19.

Always full of confidence, Al reported to the Milwaukee training base in Caruthersville, Missouri, for spring training, but found himself farmed out to Aberdeen of the Dakota League shortly thereafter. He batted .365 in 99 games there, prompting a recall, and after hitting .360 in 144 games at Shreveport (Texas League) in 1923 he bounced back to his home-town team late in the season to hit .398 in 24 games for the Brewers.

By 1924 Al was ready for the big leagues. Connie Mack, the manager and part owner of the Athletics, paid somewhere between $40,000 and $70,000 for Simmons's contract. As a rookie left fielder, Al played in every game and batted .308 with eight homers and 102 runs batted in.

Al came to the big leagues with the peculiar habit of striding with his left foot pointed toward third base rather than toward the pitcher, in the traditional straight movement. It did not seem to bother Al's power or balance, for his weight was still properly directed, but the unusual style earned him the nickname "Bucketfoot Al."

Simmons had a sensational sophomore season in 1925. He led the league with 253 hits, just four short of the major league record set by George Sisler in 1920. He had 43 doubles, 12 triples, and 24 home runs; he scored 122 times and drove in 129 runs. His .384 average was third in the league behind Harry Heilmann's .393 and Tris Speaker's .389. Simmons's outstand-

ing year helped the Athletics to a second-place finish.

By 1926, Simmons was one of the established hitting stars of the American League. He batted .343 that year with 19 homers and 109 RBIs, and followed that in 1927 by hitting .392 in a season cut short by a groin injury. Heilmann won the batting title, however, with a .398 mark. Simmons had 108 RBIs in 106 games in 1927, an outstanding pace.

Al was a gifted leftfielder with a strong throwing arm. Although 6' and 210 pounds, he was able to cover a lot of ground. In 1928, despite illness, the presence on the same team of Simmons, Ty Cobb, and Tris Speaker caused a sensation. Simmons, although a veteran himself, was a great admirer of Cobb, and sought him out often during the year for batting advice. Philadelphia finished second in 1928, as Simmons hit .351, fourth in the league.

In 1929 the Athletics won their first of three consecutive pennants. Al, Jimmie Foxx, Mickey Cochrane, Bing Miller, and Mule Haas offered a devastating attack in the A's lineup. Al's contribution was a .365 season with 34 home runs and a league-leading 157 runs batted in. He was voted the Most Valuable Player in the American League.

In the 1929 World Series, won by Philadelphia in five games over the Cubs, Al batted .300, hit two homers, and was a key participant in the biggest inning in Series history. That was the seventh inning of the fourth game. The Cubs were leading, 8–0, when Al opened the Athletics' home half with a home run and, later in that inning, singled as the A's scored 10 runs to win the game and turn the Series around.

The Athletics made it a second successive pennant in 1930, a great hitters' year all around. Simmons emerged as the league's top batter with a .381 average, edging Lou Gehrig by two points. He also led the league with 152 runs scored, and in the 1930 World Series, won by Philadelphia in six games over the Cardinals, Al batted .364 with another two home runs.

Simmons held out in 1931, missing the entire spring training period and not signing until hours before the opening-day game. But he hit a home run his first time up and went on to win his second successive batting championship, this time with a .390 average, 17 points higher than runner-up Babe Ruth. Al was really earning the $100,000, spread over three seasons, that he had won in his contract battle.

The Athletics won their third consecutive pennant in 1931. Although they lost the World Series in seven games to St. Louis, Al hit .333 with two homers and eight RBIs in the seven games.

Philadelphia slipped to second place in 1932, with Al hitting .322 despite a league-leading 216 hits. At this point Connie Mack

Al Simmons, Philadelphia Athletics superstar from his 1924 rookie season until 1932, when Connie Mack was forced to trade away his best players to keep the team from going under financially. In 1921, the story goes, Simmons wrote to Mack saying he would come to Philadelphia for the price of the train ride. But Mack did not send the fare, and Simmons worked his way up through the minors, only to be purchased by the Athletics for something between $40,000 and $70,000.

began trading away his great stars. Simmons, Jimmie Dykes, and Mule Haas were sent to the Chicago White Sox for $150,000 as soon as the season ended. Simmons had not fallen out of favor with Connie Mack—in fact, Mack always regarded him very highly. But the White Sox were better able to pay Al's salary. It was a move that Simmons regretted but understood.

Al's biggest years, it developed, were behind him in Philadelphia. In 1930 he had reached highs of 36 home runs and 165 RBIs, and the .322 average in 1932 was the lowest he had hit since his rookie season of 1924. The rest of his career would be well traveled, not as sensational, but still full of highly competitive showings.

In 1933, Al batted .331 with 14 homers and 119 RBIs for the White Sox, followed by a .344 showing in 1934. He drove in over 100 runs for the eleventh consecutive season that year; in those 11 years he had never fallen below .308 or 102 RBIs. Six times he had reached or topped 200 hits, and on another occasion he had 199.

But in 1935 he fell to .267 with 16 homers and 79 runs batted in. Dykes, his onetime teammate and now his manager, received cash offers from both the Yankees and the Tigers for Al's contract. Dykes left the choice up to Simmons, and Al decided to go to Detroit where he could play for another old teammate, Mickey Cochrane.

Simmons was joining a club that had just won two successive pennants, but although he batted .327 in 1936 the team finished second. On April 4, 1937, he was sold to the Washington Senators for a mere $15,000. Many felt he was nearing

the end of the line when he hit .279 in 1937, but he came back in 1938 to hit .302 with 21 home runs for the Senators.

After the 1938 season he was off again, this time sold to the Boston Braves, his first National League team. He was hitting .282 for the Braves when the pennant-bound Cincinnati Reds purchased him on August 31, just in time to make him eligible for World Series play. Al got into nine games down the stretch for the Reds, hit only .143, and then had one hit in four times at bat in the Series.

Released by Cincinnati after the Series, Al rejoined the Athletics in 1940 as a player-coach. He hit .309 in 37 games that year, then .125 in 9 games in 1941. He served strictly as third base coach for the A's in 1942 and was given his release following that season to become an active player again, this time with the Red Sox during the war-shortage season of 1943.

In 40 games for Boston, 40-year-old Al batted only .203 and hit the last of his 307 big-league home runs. The Red Sox released him after the season and he returned to the Philadelphia A's, for whom he served as a coach through the 1949 campaign. In 1944 he made his final appearances as a player, getting three hits in six at bats, but falling 73 hits short of the magic 3000 total.

Al's last job in the big leagues was as a coach for the Cleveland Indians in 1950, and briefly in 1951. He had become a lonely man since a divorce from his wife, the former Doris Reader, and had taken to heavy drinking. In 1953 he was elected to the Hall of Fame on the strength of a .334 lifetime batting average. The following year he got a job directing a sandlot baseball program in New York City.

By 1956 his health had declined. He was hospitalized for phlebitis. On May 26 he collapsed and died in Milwaukee, at the age of 53.

ALOYSIUS HARRY SIMMONS

Philadelphia (A.L.) 1924–1932, 1940–1941, 1944
Chicago (A.L.) 1933–1935
Detroit 1936
Washington 1937–1938
Boston (N.L.) 1939
Cincinnati 1939
Boston (A.L.) 1943

G	AB	R	H	2B	3B	HR	RBI	Avg.
2215	8761	1507	2927	539	149	307	1827	.334

George Sisler (1893-1973)

George Sisler entered professional baseball amid bitter controversy, but no one could quarrel with his record as one of the best hitters of all time.

George Harold Sisler was born on March 24, 1893, in Nimisila, Ohio. Both his parents were graduates of Hiram College. His father, Cassius, supervised a coal mine, and his uncle was the mayor of Akron.

George moved to Akron when he was 14 so he could play on the Akron High School baseball team, since Nimisila did not have a school team. While he was pitching for Akron High, he signed a professional contract with the local team in the Ohio–Pennsylvania League. The Akron contract was effective upon his graduation, but when that day came, George, at his father's urging, decided to enroll at the University of Michigan.

He had received no money from the Akron club, but the club officers considered him their property even while he was a student at Michigan. As his reputation spread throughout the country as the best college player around, Akron transferred his contract to its parent team, Columbus. In turn, Columbus sold the contract to the Pittsburgh Pirates, and owner Barney Dreyfuss listed George's name on his club's roster.

George's coach at Michigan, Branch Rickey, also served as a scout for the St. Louis Browns of the American League. As George entered his senior year, Rickey represented his interests in attempting to void the Pittsburgh contract, which had been signed when Sisler was still a minor and without parental consent. George and his father wrote letters attesting to this, and the matter went before the National Commission, composed of the two league presidents and one club owner, Cincinnati's Garry Herrmann. (This commission predated the office of the Commissioner of Baseball.)

After much controversy and bitterness on all sides, the Commission decided that the contract was indeed void. Dreyfuss, furious, seldom spoke to Herrmann again. And when all the dust had settled, Sisler signed with the Browns, now managed by his college coach, Rickey. The contract was for $400 a month with a $5000 bonus.

The bond between Sisler and Rickey lasted until Rickey's death in 1965. George always referred to Rickey as "the coach."

And so Sisler was already a celebrity when he took the mound in 1915 to begin pitching for the Browns. He worked in 15 games that season, and had a 4–4 record and a 2.83 earned-run average. He also batted .285 in 81 games, which included some time at first and in the outfield.

Rickey recognized Sisler's batting potential, despite the slim frame of only 5'10½" and 170 pounds. He converted Sisler into a first baseman. Not only did

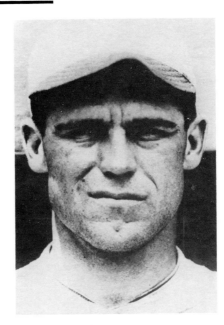

George adjust well to the new position, but he went on to lead American League first basemen in assists six times.

Unfortunately for Sisler, the St. Louis Browns offered little in the way of a supporting cast; he was the only outstanding player on the club in his early years in St. Louis. The Browns' cross-town rivals, the Cardinals, came up with Rogers Hornsby at the same time, and the two competed for local headlines as they led their respective clubs. Hornsby, however, was blessed with better clubs, found himself in World Series spotlights, and became a bigger name. Sisler never appeared in a World Series.

In 1916, George's first year as the team's regular first baseman, he batted .305 in 151 games. He pitched in three games, but never again took the mound except for an occasional stint in season finales to draw fans. His lifetime ERA was a neat 2.13 for 22 pitching appearances.

It was in 1917, a seventh-place season for the Browns, that Sisler enjoyed his first great year at bat. He hit .353 with 190 hits that year, and followed up with a .341 season in 1918.

The lefthanded-hitting Sisler, whose squint made him always appear to smile on the field, won his first assist championship in 1919, ranging far off the base to earn recognition as the finest fielding first baseman since Hal Chase. In addition, he batted .352, third in the league behind Ty Cobb and Bobby Veach, both of Detroit.

Beginning with 1920, George put together three of the finest consecutive seasons ever recorded by a hitter. Although the Browns were only fourth that year, Sisler led the league with a .407 average. He led the league also in games (154), at bats (631), assists (140), and hits (257), a major league record. In the last category were 49 doubles, 18 triples, and 19 home runs—a distant second to Babe Ruth's 54 that year, but still a very high total for the era. Sisler also scored 137 runs, drove in 122, stole 42 bases, and went hitless in only 23 games in the entire season.

In 1921 the Browns, under Lee Fohl, edged their way to third place as George hit .371, fourth in the league, and had 216 hits in 138 games. The Browns came their closest to a pennant during Sisler's era in 1922 when they went down to the wire in an exciting race with the Yankees, eventually losing by just one game. Although George considered his 1920 season to have been a better one, he set a league record (later broken by Joe DiMaggio) in 1922 with a 41-game hitting streak and batted a sensational .420. He led the league with 18 triples, 134 runs, 246 hits, and 125 assists, earning himself the Most Valuable Player award. He struck out only

14 times all season and stole a career high of 51 bases. His three-year hit total was 719.

Possessor of an incredible batting eye, George fanned only 327 times in 15 seasons. But George and his famed batting eye were kept out of the entire 1923 campaign when he developed poisonous sinusitis, which caused double vision. He never felt he was the same hitter again.

George returned to baseball in 1924, accepting a $25,000 contract as player-manager of the Browns even though he felt that he was not ready for the dual responsibility. That season the club finished fourth with Sisler hitting .305. He managed the team for two more seasons, finishing third and seventh and batting .345 and .289. At his own suggestion, he turned over the managing job to Dan Howley in 1927 and limited himself to first base play. He batted .327 that year.

Then, in a surprise deal, the Browns sold Sisler to Washington for $25,000. It was a small amount, considering a $200,000 offer once refused by the Browns. Obviously, his eyesight was in great question, and he was not the player he once had been.

After appearing in only 20 games for the Senators, Sisler was sold again, on May 27, 1928, to the Boston Braves for only $7500. Playing in a new league, George batted .340 in 118 games. He remained with the Braves through the 1930 season, hitting .326 and .309 in the remaining two years. His American League career average had

been .344, and his National League mark was .326 for a .340 total, a level reached by only 15 players in the game's history.

In 1931 George went to the minor leagues for the first time, joining Rochester of the International League. He played 159 games there as a 38-year-old first baseman and batted .303. In 1932 he managed Shreveport-Tyler in the Texas League and participated in 70 games, batting .287.

George then left professional baseball for 10 seasons. He lent his name to a St. Louis printing company and a sporting goods firm. He operated softball parks and began installing lights long before night baseball was introduced to the major leagues. He also served as commissioner of the National Baseball Congress, a nationwide semipro organization.

Sisler and his wife, Kathleen, whom he had met at the University of Michigan, had a daughter and three sons. All three boys went on to play professional baseball. George, Jr., was a minor league player and executive who eventually became president of the International League. Dick played for the Cardinals, Phillies, and Reds, hitting a dramatic pennant-winning home run for the 1950 Phillies. He went on to manage the Cincinnati Reds. Dave pitched for four teams in the major leagues between 1956 and 1962, winning 38 games and losing 44.

In 1939, the fourth year of voting, George was elected to the Hall of Fame. He returned to organized ball in 1943 as a scout for Branch Rickey's Brooklyn Dodgers, serving there through 1950. When Rickey moved to Pittsburgh, George transferred, too, and worked for the Pirates from 1951 until his death.

In poor health during his final years, Sisler died on March 26, 1973, in Richmond Heights, Missouri, a St. Louis suburb.

GEORGE HAROLD SISLER

St. Louis (A.L.) 1915–1927
Washington 1928
Boston (N.L.) 1928–1930

G	AB	R	H	2B	3B	HR	RBI	Avg.
2055	8267	1284	2812	425	165	100	1180	.340

George Sisler at first base (above), where he led the American League in assists six times, and batting, where he shone in 1922 with a .420 average. Actually, Sisler started professional baseball as a pitcher and in 1915 outpitched Walter Johnson 2–1.

Warren Spahn (b. 1921)

Most pitching records involving longevity and endurance were established in the early days of baseball. Pitching staffs were small, men pitched 400 or more innings a season, and the ball was not as lively as now. That is why the feats of Warren Spahn, a modern pitcher who chalked up more victories than any lefthander in the history of baseball, are so remarkable.

Born on April 23, 1921, in Buffalo, New York, Warren Edward Spahn was named after President Warren G. Harding and his own father, Edward Spahn, an amateur ballplayer who trained his son to become a professional.

Skinny as a boy and remaining so into his manhood, Warren was originally a first baseman. At the age of nine, he joined the Lake City Athletic Club in Buffalo, where he donned a uniform for the first time. By the time he was 12 years old, he was serving as batboy and occasionally playing first base for the local Junior American Legion team. Three years later Warren was playing in three leagues, and in one of the leagues he was a teammate of his father.

It was in high school that Warren turned to pitching. Unable to beat out the team's first baseman, he went to work on what would become a famous pitching delivery. The bony frame, perched on the pitching rubber, would wind up, reel back, kick the right leg high in the air, and bring the left arm whipping overhead with the baseball. Not especially noted for his speed, Spahn became a master of control and "artistry"—setting up hitters and working the corners of the plate. He was never afraid to add a new pitch to his assortment.

In 1940 scout Billy Myers of the Boston Braves watched Warren pitch and offered him a contract with Bradford in the Pony League. Although only 19 years old, Warren showed considerable poise in the Class D League, posting a 2.73 earned run average and a 5–4 won-lost mark in 66 innings.

Advanced to Evansville in the Three-I League the following year, Warren tore the league apart, winning 19 of 25 decisions, leading the league with a 1.83 earned run average, and firing 193 strikeouts in 212 innings.

Spahn went to spring training with the Braves in 1942 and relieved in two games during April. But he failed to impress manager Casey Stengel. Admitting it to be one of the greatest mistakes in his long baseball career, Stengel passed Spahn over because he doubted his courage. "I asked him to throw at a hitter, and he wouldn't," related Stengel. "I wrote him off as a result." Casey would laugh about it years later, after he had been elected to the Hall of Fame for his managerial genius with the New York Yankees.

Warren was returned to the minors, where he won 17 and lost 12 for Hartford in the Eastern League while compiling a 1.96

earned run average. Clearly ready for the majors, he returned to Boston late that season, starting two games with no decisions.

While on the threshold of a major league career in 1943, Warren was drafted into the army. He spent three years in the service, earning a Purple Heart and a citation for bravery in the collapse of a bridge at Remagen, on the Rhine River, when he helped save many American lives during a German bombing attack.

The three years overseas postponed Spahn's first major league victory until he was 25 years old—a fact which makes his career total of 363 triumphs all the more remarkable. Joining the Braves in 1946, Warren won eight games and lost five, with a 2.93 ERA in 24 appearances. Billy Southworth was the team's manager at the time, with Johnny Sain the top pitcher on the staff. The club finished fourth behind St. Louis, Brooklyn, and Chicago.

By 1947 Spahn was ready for his first big year in the major leagues. He was married now, having wed Lorene Southard the previous August. With the Braves moving up to third place, Spahn won 21 games for the first of 13 seasons in the 20-victory class. He lost only 10 decisions and captured his first of three earned run average titles with a 2.33 showing, 14 points better than runnerup Ewell Blackwell of the Reds.

Curiously, it was in 1948, one of the few years in which he did not win 20 games, that Spahn achieved national prominence. His mound mark was only 15–12, mediocre by his standards. But the Boston Braves captured the pennant, largely with only two pitchers—Spahn and Johnny Sain, who posted a 24–15 record. Late that season Boston fans coined the expression "Spahn and Sain and pray for rain." Actually, with 15 victories, Spahn recorded only two more triumphs than Bill Voiselle, and four more than Vern Bickford, the Braves' two "rainout" pitchers. But Spahn and Sain were the big men.

In the World Series that fall, Cleveland, led by player-manager Lou Boudreau, captured the World Championship four games to two. Spahn lost the second game to Bob Lemon, but he won the fifth game in relief of Nelson Potter. Warren also worked in relief in the sixth and deciding game, but he did not receive the loss. It was unusual for Spahn to pitch in relief. He did it only 66 times between 1942 and 1963, and only 85 times in 750 mound appearances.

The Braves failed to repeat as pennant winners in 1949, dropping under .500, but

Spahn compiled a 21–14 record, the first of eight seasons in which he either led the National League in victories or tied for the lead.

What followed in Boston were good years for Spahn but declining years for the Braves. In 1950 Spahn won 21 but the club again finished fourth. In 1951 he posted 22 victories, and the team placed fourth once more. In 1952, although Spahn recorded only a 14–19 mark, he won his fourth consecutive strikeout title. The Braves fell to seventh that season, drawing only 281,278 fans. It was apparent that the welcome mat was no longer out in Boston for the National League.

In 1953 the Braves became the first modern team to shift cities, moving to Milwaukee. There was little outcry over the Braves' move, and their reception in Milwaukee was outstanding. In the first year in Wisconsin, the team drew 1,826,397 fans and then proceeded to pass the two million mark for four consecutive years.

That first year in Milwaukee, Spahn won a career high of 23 games, losing only seven and leading the league with a 2.10 ERA. The Braves finished an exciting second and began to put together the club that was headed for pennants. Joe Adcock, Lew Burdette, Johnny Logan, Eddie Mathews, Del Crandall, and Billy Bruton had joined Spahn by 1953, and the following year Hank Aaron came along.

In 1954 the Braves finished third, and Warren posted a 21–12 record. Spahn won 17 in 1955 as the Braves moved up to second place behind Brooklyn. The standings of the two clubs were repeated the following year, with Brooklyn edging Milwaukee by just one game. Spahn won 20 games and Burdette 19 during the season.

In 1957 Spahn gained the Cy Young Award as the best pitcher in baseball, notching 21 victories and losing only 11 with a 2.69 ERA. The Braves electrified the city of Milwaukee by winning the pennant by eight games; they then defeated the mighty Yankees in seven games, with Burdette winning three Series games and Spahn the other.

The Braves repeated as pennant winners in 1958 as Spahn won 22 and Burdette 20. The World Series, however, went to the Yankees, who stormed back after having been down three games to one.

Spahn posted 21 victories the following year. The Braves lost the pennant playoff with the Los Angeles Dodgers, two games to none. That was the end of Spahn's World Series career; he compiled a 4–3 record in eight Series games overall.

With their pennants behind them, the Braves continued to be led by the ageless Spahn. Winning 20 games became a habit for the bony lefthander with the hook nose. He compiled 20 or more victories for six successive years between 1956 and 1961. His two no-hitters in the major leagues were hurled in 1960 and 1961. Spahn was 40

years old in 1961, just a bit younger than Cy Young when Young became the oldest man to notch a no-hitter. In 1961 Spahn also won his third ERA title, although his 3.01 average was rather high to lead the league.

When Spahn slipped to 18 victories in 1962, some thought it might be the beginning of the end. But Warren came back in 1963—at the age of 42—to win 23 and lose only 7 with a 2.60 ERA. Thus his sudden fall from glory in 1964 stunned many who thought he could go on forever. Spahn won only six and lost 13 for the Braves that year with a 5.28 earned-run average—very embarrassing for a man of his stature. But rather than call it quits, he was determined to pursue the National League record of 373 victories (held by Christy Mathewson and Grover Cleveland Alexander) and possibly to seek the 400 mark.

The Braves, thinking of their move to Atlanta and Spahn's $80,000 salary, sold Warren in November 1964 to the lowly New York Mets as a pitcher and coach. But he failed to return to form that year and was released on July 19. Signed by the Giants three days later, Warren struggled through the season with a 7–16 record for a career total of 363 wins. His career total of 750 mound appearances, sixth on the all-time list, included 665 complete games, the fourth highest total.

Spahn's fans would have been happier if he had quit while still on top, for he had certainly dimmed his image by hanging on. Nor did Warren enhance his status in 1966 when he pitched three games for the Mexico City Tigers.

Off the playing field at last, Warren could devote more time to his 2800-acre ranch in Hartshorne, Oklahoma. But his knees, on which he had surgery three times during his playing days, were giving him trouble.

With many bone chips in his knees, he wound up in a wheelchair and saw his weight drop from 183 to 160 pounds. An operation in 1969 saved him from a life in a wheelchair.

Spahn managed Tulsa in the Pacific Coast League (later the American Association) from 1967 to 1971. He pitched three more games for Tulsa in 1967, delaying for still another year his election to the Hall of Fame—which finally came in his first year of eligibility, 1973. Warren spent 1972 and 1973 as a pitching coach for the Cleveland Indians, his first appearance in an American League uniform. The Indians, however, changed their coaching staff for 1974, leaving Spahn out of baseball for the first time since 1940, with the exception of the war years.

For several seasons starting in 1975, Spahn spent brief periods of time in Japan tutoring the Hiroshima team, and worked each fall with young prospects of the San Diego Padres in the Arizona Instructional League. In 1979 he became minor league pitching instructor for the California Angels.

It was unfortunate that Spahn prolonged his brilliant career past his prime, but during his heyday—a period of 17 years in which he failed to win 20 games only four times—he was unquestionably the best pitcher of his era. Statistically, Warren was the winningest lefthander of all time.

WARREN EDWARD SPAHN

Boston (N.L.) 1942–1952
Milwaukee 1953–1964
New York (N.L.) 1965
San Francisco 1965

G	IP	W	L	Pct.	H	R	ER	SO	BB	ERA
750	5246	363	245	.597	4830	2016	1798	2583	1434	3.08

(At left) Warren Spahn, baseball's winningest lefthanded pitcher, makes his acting debut in a war scene for television in 1963. In a game against the New York Mets that same year, Milwaukee Braves' pitcher Spahn shows his sweeping overhand pitch (the sequence below). The game was his eighteenth victory of the season, a year in which Spahn, at age 42, won 23 and lost only 7.

Albert Spalding (1850-1915)

Albert Goodwill Spalding was one of the better pitchers in the days before the birth of the National League, but he left the ranks of active players to become a successful club official and the head of a large sporting goods firm.

The son of prosperous farmers, Spalding was born on September 2, 1850, in Byron, Illinois. His father died when Albert was nine, leaving the mother to rear the family. Albert took a $3-per-week job as a grocery boy, attended school, and played as much baseball as he could.

Baseball was just taking hold as a popular sport when Spalding was growing up. Many of the rules were created as the games were played, with each town playing a slightly different contest than the next.

In the fall of 1865, Albert's youthful team challenged the local adult team to a game. Albert pitched, allowed only two runs (run production was generally quite high in those days), and the youngsters defeated the adults.

Observing the game was a group of players from the Forest City team of Rockford, Illinois, and they quickly enlisted Spalding and a teammate, Ross Barnes (who later played for Boston). They would leave school each day to play with Forest City. At the age of 16, Al was playing his first game and pitching in what would have been called semipro ball.

In 1867 George Wright, playing for the Washington Nationals, led his team into Rockford as part of a western tour. Spalding beat the Nationals, 29–23 (a more typical score), handing Washington its only defeat on the tour. With the victory under his belt, Al was offered $40 per week to transfer to Chicago and pitch for a team called the Excelsiors. The salary, a high one, included work as a bill clerk in a Chicago grocery, but the grocer went bankrupt and the whole deal fell through.

Rather than leave Chicago, Al went to work for an uncle in the insurance business. But the agency failed and Spalding returned home.

His mother sought to have him complete his education, but Al gave up his schooling one year before graduation to rejoin Forest City. Few records were compiled, but it is known that the 1869 Forest City club had a 20–4 record, with all the losses coming at the hands of the undefeated Cincinnati Red Stockings, baseball's first professional team. In 1870 the Forest Citys toured the East. Spalding pitched almost every game, and the club compiled a 13–3–1 record.

In 1871 the National Association, baseball's first major league, was formed. Harry Wright, operator of the Boston franchise, visited Rockford on a recruiting mission

Al Spalding pitched the Chicago White Stockings' first victory in the new National League and had a 43–13 record as Chicago took the first pennant. He became a club executive, sporting goods magnate, and sports publisher. He organized international baseball jaunts: in England his tour drew little attention until the players accepted a challenge to play cricket. (Opposite page) An older Spalding demonstrates techniques described in his books, one of which is shown at right.

and offered Spalding $1500 per year to sign with his club. Al took the offer and became a professional.

Spalding posted a 20–10 record in 1871, and Boston finished third. From 1872 to 1875, Boston won the pennant each year, with Spalding the star pitcher. The team's overall record for the four seasons was 205–50, including a 71–8 mark in 1875. Wright named Spalding team captain that year.

After the Boston team toured Canada in 1872, Spalding conceived the idea of a tour of England. In the winter of 1872–1873, he journeyed to England to make arrangements, and on February 27, 1874, he participated in the first baseball game played in Britain. The tour was set for the summer of 1874, and Spalding led a group of 22 players, with Harry Wright as manager. The Red Stockings played the Philadelphia Athletics in the exhibitions. The British were hospitable and polite but not enthused by the game.

In November 1875, Al married Josie Keith of Brockton, Massachusetts. Several months later, William Hulbert became president of the Chicago franchise of a new league, and he offered Spalding $4000 to join his club as manager, captain, and pitcher. Hulbert also signed Ross Barnes, Cal McVey, and Deacon White from the Boston club.

Spalding and Hulbert drafted the constitution for the new league, which Hulbert named the National League. Spalding insisted that gambling and alcohol be barred from the ballparks.

The first National League game was played on April 22, 1876, in Philadelphia. Three days later, Chicago played its first game with Spalding pitching a 4–0 victory over Louisville. Al recorded a 47–13 mark in 1876, and the White Stockings captured the first National League pennant. But by 1877, most pitchers were throwing curveballs, something Al never mastered. Spalding soon retired as a player to devote himself to business.

In 1876 Al and his younger brother, J. Walter Spalding, opened a sporting goods store at 118 Randolph Street in Chicago. The firm sold uniforms to the teams, different colored caps for each player (an early means of identifying players), and standardized baseballs. Two years later, the Spalding baseballs were "officially" adopted, with Spalding paying the league one dollar per dozen to ensure him of this vital advertising.

In 1877 the Spalding brothers entered the publishing business, producing their first official *Baseball Guide*. The Spalding guide was edited for many years by Henry Chadwick, and it represented the official source for the history of the game. Spalding also published scores of other books and pamphlets on many sports.

Although baseball equipment remained its chief line, the Spalding Company produced equipment for most other sports as well. Branches opened throughout the country. In 1885 Spalding purchased a half-interest in the Philadelphia firm of A. J. Reach and Company, and in 1891, he bought an interest in Boston's Wright and Ditson. By 1901, Spalding's company was producing baseballs for both the American and National Leagues. The company did so through 1976, after which Rawlings signed to manufacture the official baseball.

After his retirement as a player, Spalding remained with the White Stockings as an advisor. When Hulbert died in 1882, Spalding became president of the team. During the 1880s, Chicago won five pennants and Spalding distinguished himself as a shrewd executive. In 1887 he sold King Kelly to Boston for a record $10,000, and a year later he did the same with John Clarkson.

Following the 1888 season, Spalding organized a world tour, taking 20 players, George Wright as an umpire, and several newspapermen to Hawaii, New Zealand, Australia, Ceylon, Egypt, Italy, France, and England. The group returned home on April 6, 1889, in time for the new National League season. While in London, Spalding opened a new branch of his firm. Back in America, he began to import bicycles and golf clubs. Al also began to sell basketballs, making him the first in America to deal with the sports of golf and basketball.

After helping negotiate an end to the Players' League rebellion of 1890, Spalding resigned as president of the Chicago club but remained the principal stockholder. He became involved in real estate, founded the Chicago Athletic Club, and helped plan the 1893 Chicago World's Fair.

In 1899 Al's wife died following an appendicitis operation. A year later, he married Mrs. Elizabeth Mayer, a widow with two children, and they moved to an estate in Point Loma, California. The same year, Spalding was a large exhibitor at the Second Olympic Games in Paris.

Spalding adopted Mrs. Mayer's two children and gave the youngest his own name. A nephew, also named Albert Spalding, became a famed concert violinist.

Although he was seldom involved with baseball after 1891, Spalding helped negotiate a peace settlement between the American and National Leagues in 1903. At a National League meeting, he gave an impassioned speech urging the ouster of Giant owner Andrew Freedman in the interest of breaking up syndicate ownership in baseball.

Returning to California, Spalding became an enthusiastic horseman and motorist, and a member of the San Diego Road Commission. In 1905 he instituted a special commission to investigate the origin of baseball. The commission found the sport to be of American origin, with only Chadwick arguing for British ancestry. In 1911 Spalding wrote and published *America's National Game,* the first history of baseball.

Spalding was a candidate for the Republican nomination for U.S. Senator in 1910, won the primary, but lost the election in the California state legislature.

Two strokes in later years weakened Spalding badly. On September 9, 1915, he died in Point Loma at the age of 65. His sporting goods empire perpetuated his name long after his death. In 1939 Albert Spalding was elected to the Hall of Fame.

ALBERT GOODWILL SPALDING

Boston (N.A.) 1871–1875
Chicago (N.L.) 1876–1877

G	IP	W	L	Pct.	H	R	ER	SO	BB	ERA
409	inc.	262	68	.794	inc.	inc.	inc.	inc.	inc.	inc.

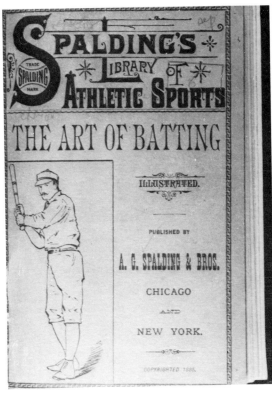

Tris Speaker (1888-1958)

Tris Speaker, holder of a .344 lifetime batting average is generally considered to have revolutionized center field play.

Tristram Speaker was born on April 4, 1888, in Hubbard City, Texas. His father died when he was 10 years old, leaving his mother, Jennie, to rear a large family. Mrs. Speaker was never enthusiastic about Tris's entry into professional baseball. She thought that the trading and selling of players by club owners was demeaning.

Tris was a natural righthander, but he broke his arm while horseback riding as a youngster and so learned to bat and throw lefthanded. He played both baseball and football in high school but concentrated on baseball at the Fort Worth Polytechnic Institute.

During his sophomore year, Tris was scouted by the owner of the Cleburne team in the North Texas League. Tris was a pitcher in those days, but he also impressed observers with his bat. Speaker signed a $50-per-month contract with Cleburne and was immediately placed in the starting rotation by manager Benny Shelton. He lost his first decision, 2–1, on Shelton's error at first base.

Speaker pitched a total of seven games for Cleburne, the last of which resulted in a 22-run pasting. During that game one ball was hit so hard that it broke the cheekbone of the Cleburne right fielder. That finished Speaker's pitching career. He volunteered to replace the right fielder and never left the outfield after that.

In 1907 the players of the Cleburne club were transferred to Houston in the Texas League. There Tris led all hitters with a .314 average in 118 games. His outfield play, on which he worked hard, became not only outstanding but unique. His secret consisted of playing an extremely shallow center field. He developed a great knack for racing back for a ball, seldom permitting one to go over his head. Speed and the ability to determine the destination of a ball at the moment of impact with the bat made him a sensation.

Moreover, his shallow location made him virtually a fifth infielder. Frequently he ran in to cover second base. As a major leaguer, Speaker often would take pickoff throws from pitchers, catching base runners completely by surprise. On one occasion he even acted as the middle man on a double play, the play going from second baseman to center fielder to first baseman. Twice within an 11-day stretch in 1918, Tris caught fast line drives and raced in to step on second for unassisted double plays.

Assists, infrequent for outfielders, were numerous for Speaker. Four times he led American League outfielders in assists, reaching or topping the 30 mark four times. In his first full season with Boston in 1909, he tied the American League record of 35 assists, a mark that still stands. A true artist at his position, Tris became one of

the first players to test wind direction by tossing some outfield grass in the air before a pitch.

The St. Louis Browns had first shot at acquiring Tris from Houston, but when they displayed little interest the Red Sox purchased him for $800. He played in seven games for Boston in 1907, but collected only three hits for a .158 average. The Red Sox did not send Speaker a contract for the 1908 compaign.

Tris reported to the New York Giants' training camp in 1908, but John McGraw failed to offer him a job. Speaker then went to the Red Sox camp, but Boston left him behind in Little Rock, Arkansas, as payment for the use of their field during spring training. That was probably the sort of treatment Jennie Speaker had in mind.

At Little Rock that year, Tris topped the Southern League with a .350 average and was again sold to Boston at the end of the season. This time he batted .220 in 31 games. Invited to train with the Red Sox in 1909, Speaker made the club as the regular center fielder.

Tris hit .309 for Boston that year and remained over the .300 mark for 10 consecutive seasons, 18 in all. In 1910 the Red Sox finished fourth, as Tris batted .340. Tris, Harry Hooper, and Duffy Lewis comprised one of the best outfield units ever assembled. The Red Sox finished fifth in 1911, but they won the 1912 pennant under manager Jake Stahl, with Speaker capturing the league's Most Valuable Player award. He batted .383, had 136 runs scored, 222 hits, 53 doubles, 13 triples, 9 home runs, and 98 runs batted in. The .383 average was only good enough for third place in the league standings behind Ty Cobb and Joe Jackson. Throughout his career, Tris usually found himself falling just short of Cobb in the batting race.

In the 1912 World Series, won by Boston over the Giants, Tris led the Red Sox with a .300 batting average.

Although Speaker batted .365 and .338 in the following two seasons, the Red Sox were unable to repeat as league champions. But Boston did capture another pennant in 1915, with Babe Ruth starring on the mound and Speaker in the outfield. Tris batted .322 for the regular season and .294 in the World Series.

At this point in his career, Tris was earning $18,000 per year. It was a good salary, due in part to his strong negotiating ability, and warranted in part by Boston's fear that Speaker might jump to the rival Federal League. But when the Federal League folded in 1916, Joe Lannin, the Red Sox owner, decided to cut Speaker to a $9000

(Upper left) The earliest picture of Tris Speaker, standing second from left in a group of church thespians. (Above and at left) Speaker doing what he did best—playing ball. Connie Mack described him this way: "Tris was everywhere in the outfield; he could grab a ball up against the fence and net a ball off his shoes directly behind second base. The instant a batter hit a ball, Tris could gauge the spot where it was headed. He could sprint with his back to the stand, and the ball would generally land in his hands, so accurate was his judgment of speed and distance."

(Above) Tris Speaker with his mother, Jennie. She had discouraged him from playing pro ball. (Below) Speaker in an exhibition rodeo performance.

figure. A long holdout developed. Speaker played in exhibition games that spring only on a per-game salary to help attendance.

Finally, as the season approached, Speaker was traded to Cleveland. He was not only disappointed, but he also demanded $10,000 of the purchase price, which totaled $50,000 in addition to pitcher Sam Jones and infielder Fred Thomas. When Tris threatened to leave the game and return home to Texas, the Red Sox gave him the money and he agreed to report to Cleveland.

In his first year with the Indians, Speaker batted .386 to win the league title, breaking a streak of nine successive crowns for Cobb. Speaker also led the league in hits and doubles. Doubles were his specialty, for he led the league in that category eight times and wound up with the all-time record of 793 two-baggers.

Although Speaker played well in his first years with the Indians, the team did not challenge for the pennant. On July 19, 1919, Tris was named to replace Lee Fohl as Indian manager. Serving in the dual role of player-manager, he brought the club home second in 1919. But his batting average dropped to .296, his only season below the .300 mark between 1909 and 1927.

But 1920 was a big year for Cleveland. Tris came back to hit .388, and the Indians edged Chicago by two games for the pennant. The season was marked by the death of Indian shortstop Ray Chapman, who was hit by a pitch thrown by the Yankees' Carl Mays. It was the only death ever to occur on the field in the history of major league baseball.

In the exciting World Series victory over Brooklyn that October, second baseman Bill Wambsganss of the Indians performed that rarest of baseball feats, an unassisted triple play.

The Indians were unable to capture another pennant under Speaker, but Tris continued to play well. In 1923 he tied Babe Ruth for the league RBI title with 130. Then on December 2, 1926, he suddenly and without explanation resigned from the Indians.

Several weeks later it developed that Hub Leonard, a rival pitcher, had named Speaker and Cobb as having arranged to fix a game between the Indians and Tigers in 1919. Cobb's release as player-manager of Detroit after the 1926 season also raised speculation that the charge was true.

After much newspaper coverage and statements by the league president and Commissioner Landis, the two great stars were found innocent of any wrongdoing. Still, their clubs had made them free agents. Cobb went to Philadelphia and Speaker, "The Gray Eagle," signed with Washington.

Tris batted .327 in 141 games for the Senators at the age of 39, but his salary was too much for Washington to handle, and he was released at the season's end. Speaker signed with Philadelphia on February 5, 1928, joining Cobb in the Athletics' outfield. There, in his final major league season, Tris played 64 games and batted .267.

In 1929 and 1930, Speaker managed Newark of the International League and also saw a little playing time. He quit in 1931 to take a radio announcing job in Chicago. Two years later Tris and two partners (including comedian Joe E. Brown) purchased the minor league Kansas City Blues. It was not a good investment, however, and Speaker sold his interest to return to baseball broadcasting in Cleveland. He maintained a side interest in a liquor business and represented a steel company.

Retired to Florida with his wife, whom he had married in 1925, Tris was a frequent banquet speaker and a fine goodwill ambassador for baseball. In 1937, the second year of elections, Tris Speaker was named to the Hall of Fame. His 3515 career hits placed him second to Cobb at the time of his retirement, and his .344 average ranks him fifth on the all-time list.

Speaker suffered a fracture of the skull in a fall while living in Florida, and his health deteriorated after he was struck by a heart attack in 1954. On December 8, 1958, Tris suffered a second coronary and died at Lake Whitney, Texas.

TRISTRAM SPEAKER

Boston (A.L.) 1907–1915
Cleveland 1916–1926
Washington 1927
Philadelphia (A.L.) 1928

G	AB	R	H	2B	3B	HR	RBI	Avg.
2789	10208	1881	3515	793	224	115	1559	.344

Casey Stengel (1889-1975)

The long career of Casey Stengel as player and manager extended from the days of Christy Mathewson to those of Tom Seaver. By the time he retired, Casey was one of the most beloved personalities on the American scene.

Charles Dillon Stengel was born on July 30, 1889, in Kansas City, Missouri. (There is some confusion over the year, some sources claiming 1890. Stengel didn't know for sure.) His father was of German blood and his mother was of Irish extraction. The nickname "Casey," given him when he reached the major leagues, was derived from the initials of his hometown. As a star in baseball, football, and basketball for Central High School in Kansas City, Stengel was more commonly known as "Dutch."

Dutch had a brother and a sister; it was his older brother Grant who taught him to play baseball.

After high school graduation, Stengel enrolled at Western Dental College in Kansas City, intent on overcoming the handicap of being a lefthanded dentist. Although it came to be believed that he quit in frustration, since all dental equipment was manufactured for right-handed individuals, the truth was that Stengel accepted an offer to play professional baseball as a means of earning money to continue his schooling. But once he signed that first contract in 1910, with Kankakee of the Northern Association, Stengel was lost to dentistry.

His entry into professional baseball was not marked by great success. The very league he began in disbanded in July 1910, leaving no record of any of Stengel's statistics. He transferred to Maysville in the Blue Grass League, finishing the season with a .223 average in 69 games.

In 1911 Stengel joined Aurora of the Wisconsin-Illinois League, and he led all hitters with a .352 average. For the following season, he moved to Montgomery in the Southern League and batted .290. That was the year Brooklyn scout Larry Sutton happened upon Stengel and purchased him for $300.

Casey made his major league debut on September 17, 1912, collecting four hits in four at bats and playing flawlessly in the outfield. He finished the season with a .316 average in 17 games under manager Bill Dahlen.

Stengel became a regular in the outfield in 1913, hitting .272 against the likes of Christy Mathewson, Grover Cleveland Alexander, Rube Marquard, and others. The Dodgers finished sixth that year.

Wilbert Robinson took over as manager in 1914 and gave the Brooklyn club an entirely new look. The team came to be known as the Robins and the Daffyness Boys. Stengel, a great favorite of Robinson's, hit .316 in 1914 but fell to .237 in 1915.

The Robins won the 1916 National League pennant, with Casey contributing a

.279 average and played all three outfield positions. In the 1916 World Series loss to Boston, Casey led all Brooklyn hitters with a .364 batting average.

Casey's last season in Brooklyn was 1917, during which he hit .257 and led all National League outfielders with 30 assists. On January 9, 1918, he was traded to Pittsburgh in a five-player deal that brought Burleigh Grimes to the Robins.

Expecting a warm greeting upon returning to Ebbets Field with the Pirates the following year, he received instead a chorus of boos from the Brooklyn fans. So the next day, Casey hid a sparrow in his cap, and when the fans booed, he gallantly bowed, tipped the cap, and let the sparrow fly out. The story is typical of one of baseball's great—if often unintentional—comedians.

Casey's Pirate career was short and uneventful. He played in only 39 games in 1918, then enlisted in the navy for the remainder of the war. Returning in 1919, Stengel was hitting .293 after 89 games when the Pirates traded him to Philadelphia in August. When the Phillies attempted to cut his salary, he refused to report and sat out the remainder of the season.

Casey played for the Phillies in 1920, hitting .292, and for half of the 1921 season before being traded to the Giants for players valued at some $75,000. Although he and John McGraw respected one another, McGraw's practice of using private detectives to trail his players at night bothered Casey. "I didn't resent the detectives so much," he recalled, "as having one detective assigned to Irish Meusel and myself. I thought I deserved my own!"

Casey helped the Giants to capture pennants in 1922 and 1923. In the 1923 World Series, he hit the first Series home run in Yankee Stadium. It was a ninth-inning, inside-the-park homer that won the game, 5–4, and he lost his shoe running the bases. He homered again in the seventh inning of the third game, which the Giants won, 1–0. His .417 Series average in 1923 gave him a career Series mark of .393 for 12 games.

One month later, however, Casey was traded again, this time to the Boston Braves. He completed his major league playing career there in 1925 with a .284 lifetime average and 60 home runs.

The Braves made Stengel president and manager of their Worcester (Eastern League) franchise, and it was there that Casey first met George M. Weiss, who was running the New Haven club. The two would later form a great management team.

Casey continued to play while managing, first at Worcester and then at Toledo

of the American Association from 1926 to 1931. His move from Worcester was brought about when Stengel, the president, wrote his own release as manager and then resigned as president. He won a pennant with his 1927 Toledo team.

Casey returned to coach for Brooklyn in 1932 and 1933, and he then succeeded Max Carey as Dodger manager in 1934. He lasted three seasons there, finishing sixth, fifth, and seventh, before Burleigh Grimes replaced him with a year still to go on his contract. Casey always liked to say that he was paid not to manage in 1937.

Stengel returned to Boston in 1938, and his six-year stay as manager of the Braves produced six second-division finishes. At one point, when a taxicab broke one of his legs in an accident, he was sidelined for two months, and a Boston sportswriter suggested giving the cab driver the award as "The Man Who Did Most for Baseball in Boston in 1938."

In 1942 Casey cut rookie Warren Spahn early in the season when the tall lefty failed

to throw at the hitters as Stengel had ordered. He later admitted that it was one of his greatest misjudgments of a player.

Casey was hired to manage Milwaukee in the American Association in 1944 while the club's owner, Bill Veeck, was away in the service. Upon hearing the news, Veeck was outraged, claiming Casey was little more than a clown. Despite a first-place finish in 1945, Stengel was dismissed when Veeck returned home.

Subsequently, George Weiss, then running the Yankees' minor league system, hired Casey to manage Kansas City of the American Association. He finished seventh and moved on to Oakland of the Pacific Coast League for the 1946–1948 seasons, climaxing his tenure with a pennant in his last year. Stengel had now won Triple-A titles in three cities, but he was still generally considered a well-traveled funnyman, and far from a genius.

But Weiss made Stengel the surprise choice to succeed Bucky Harris as Yankee manager in 1949, handing him the top managerial position in baseball. Casey inherited a great team but succeeded in impressing his own identity on it, thus

establishing himself as one of the game's great managers.

Casey captured World Championships in his first five Yankee seasons. His club finished second in 1954 despite winning 103 games. Then Casey led the Yanks to four more pennants (and two World Championships), a third-place finish in 1959, and another flag in 1960. In 12 seasons as their manager, Stengel brought the Yankees 10 pennants and 7 World Championships.

Naturally, he had great players. Included among them were Joe DiMaggio, Mickey Mantle, Yogi Berra, Whitey Ford, Allie Reynolds, Vic Raschi, Ed Lopat, Roger Maris, Elston Howard, Bill Skowron, Joe Collins, Johnny Mize, Gene Woodling, Hank Bauer, Tommy Henrich, Gil McDougald, Billy Martin, Phil Rizzuto, Bobby Brown, Joe Page, and Bob Turley. Casey was a master at platooning his talent and of getting big years from as many players as possible,

even if it meant hurting their pride by not playing them every day.

Casey was voted Manager of the Year in 1949, 1953, and 1958. He considered the 1949 pennant, won despite numerous injuries to his team, his most satisfying.

Casey was always a master showman, and at his best with "my writers," as he called the loving press corps that covered the Yankees. Casey provided them with his own brand of doubletalk which came to be known as Stengelese. The incomprehensible flow of language astonished the nation when he testified in his own inimitable way before the Senate Anti-Monopoly Committee investigating baseball in 1958.

At the end of the 1960 World Series, won by Pittsburgh on a ninth-inning home run by Bill Mazeroski in the seventh game, both Stengel and Weiss were dismissed by the Yankees. Their age was given as the reason, but Stengel shocked a press conference by stating, "I was told my services would not be desired any longer with this ball club. I had not much of an argument."

Casey sat out the 1961 season, tending to his duties as a director of the Valley National Bank at his hometown of Glendale, California. He and his wife, Edna, had become quite wealthy, and Stengel could easily have retired to a quiet life. But Casey missed the limelight, and when Weiss became president of the Mets in 1962, he brought Stengel back to New York to manage the new National League franchise. Although his teams were terrible, finishing last and setting all sorts of futility records, Casey's love affair with the media and the fans helped to establish the Mets as a great gate attraction.

On July 23, 1967, a year after his installation in the Hall of Fame, Casey fell and broke his hip. His formal retirement was announced on August 30, but he continued to be listed as a vice president of the Mets.

The rubber-faced master of platoon baseball—who once said, "People think I was born looking this old . . . I was young once"—left a great impact on baseball in one of the longest careers ever recorded. Casey Stengel died of cancer on September 29, 1975, at the age of 85.

CHARLES DILLON STENGEL

Brooklyn 1912–1917
Pittsburgh 1918–1919
Philadelphia (N.L.) 1920–1921
New York (N.L.) 1921–1923
Boston (N.L.) 1924–1925

G	AB	R	H	2B	3B	HR	RBI	Avg.
1277	4288	575	1219	182	89	60	518	.284

The many "faces" of Casey Stengel. (Above, from far left opposite page) Stengel playing for the Pirates, taking a whack at tennis, hamming it up with a harp at a convention, and being forcibly restrained at home plate by laughing umpires in 1949. The furious Yankee manager "thought the umps had gone nuts," but they kept him there until a cake arrived to mark his fifty-eighth birthday. (At left) A thoughtful Stengel watches batting practice.

Bill Terry (b. 1898)

When it came to baseball, Bill Terry was all business—hard working and competitive. His approach to the game was devoid of fun, but he was a talented first baseman and one of only two National Leaguers to record a .400 batting average in this century.

William Harold Terry was born on October 30, 1898, in Atlanta, Georgia. The year has frequently been questioned since ballplayers often understate their ages to heighten management's interest in them in later years, but Terry's birth certificate confirms 1898 as his year of birth.

Boyhood for Bill Terry did not last very long. His parents were separated, and his education ended at the age of 13. Bill began to support himself that year, and by the age of 15 he was doing heavy work in the Atlanta railroad yards. Hunger was a part of Bill's early life. Seeking to stabilize his fortunes, he married Virginia Snead in November 1916, when he had just turned 18.

A pitcher for local teams, Bill was invited by the St. Louis Browns to attend a spring training session in St. Petersburg as early as 1914. But the informal invitation was never followed up with specific reporting instructions, and the Browns and Bill never got together.

But the following season, Bill did sign a professional contract, agreeing to pitch for Newnan of the Georgia-Alabama League. There, the 16-year-old lefty pitched eight games, winning seven and hurling a no-hitter.

In 1916 Terry posted an 11–8 record with Newnan before being sold in August to Shreveport of the Texas League. He won six of eight decisions with Shreveport that season and notched a 14–11 mark in 1917. But in his travels he found a way to earn more money. He left professional baseball in 1918 and took a job with the Standard Oil Company in Memphis, primarily to pitch for the company's semipro team but meanwhile learning enough about the oil business to make himself wealthy in later years through wise investments. He and his wife settled in Memphis, and they remained residents there for much of their lives.

Terry spent four years with the semipro club. In 1922 he was scouted by John McGraw, manager of the New York Giants. McGraw had received a tip on Bill from Tom Watkins, owner of the Memphis team of the Southern Association. Watkins knew that he could never afford to pay Terry, so he recommended him to McGraw.

McGraw liked what he saw—not Terry the pitcher, but Terry the lefthanded hitter. But Bill was not dazzled by the prospect of a contract from the Giants. He saw to it that the offer made it worth his while to leave his semipro outfit. When McGraw eventually came across with $5000, Terry committed himself.

Back in organized ball at the age of 23,

Terry was optioned to Toledo of the American Association, where he pitched in 26 games with a 9–9 record in addition to learning to play first base and hitting .336 with 14 homers.

At Toledo in 1923, Terry hit .377 with 15 home runs in 109 games. Deciding that Bill was ready to play first base in the big leagues, McGraw called him up to the Giants at the end of the 1923 season. Bill appeared in three games and watched his club play the Yankees in the first World Series in Yankee Stadium.

Bill was not quite ready for regular duty in 1924, as McGraw saw it, since George Kelly, himself a future Hall of Famer, was manning the position. Terry and McGraw, who would often clash, battled over this matter. Terry batted only 163 times that year, hitting .239 with 5 homers and 24 runs batted in. But Bill came alive in the World Series, battering Washington Senator pitching for a .429 average. In one game Bucky Harris intentionally switched pitchers to keep Terry out of the lineup.

In 1925 Kelly was moved to second base to allow Terry a slot in the regular lineup. Bill responded with a .319 average and 11 home runs. The following year Terry batted .289 in 98 games.

The 6'11½" 200-pounder really found his stride in 1927, batting .326 with 20 home runs and 121 RBIs, the fifth highest total in the league. It was the first of six consecutive seasons in which Bill would drive in more than 100 runs, the first of six straight years in which he scored 100 runs, and the first of ten successive campaigns in which he topped the .300 mark.

Terry repeated his .326 showing in 1928, and he then posted the league's fourth highest figure in 1929 with a .372 average. This was the period of twentieth-century baseball when hitters were enjoying their highest averages. In 1930, when National League players hit a combined .303, Bill led the way with a sensational .401 mark. Only Rogers Hornsby (1922, 1924, 1925) had topped the .400 mark in the National League since the turn of the century. No other National Leaguer has accomplished the feat since 1930.

Terry accomplished his feat with 254 hits, tying Lefty O'Doul's National League record and missing George Sisler's major league mark by only three. Terry's great statistical showing for the year included 139 runs, 129 RBIs, 39 doubles, 15 triples, and 23 home runs. Despite a third-place finish by the Giants, Bill was an easy Most Valuable Player winner.

In 1931 Terry narrowly missed repeating as batting champ, as the Cardinals' Chick Hafey edged him by a fraction of a point,

both being credited with .349 averages. Terry led the league with 20 triples that year, and he tied Chuck Klein for the lead in runs scored with 121.

McGraw and Terry went through the entire 1931 season without speaking to each other. Both were strong-willed, and Terry had begun to feel that McGraw, who had not won a pennant since 1924, was not the leader he once was. Hidden feelings finally erupted one day when McGraw berated Terry in a clubhouse meeting. Bill, in a rare act toward the manager, shouted back at McGraw, and for a year and a half the two men did not speak.

Finally, on June 3, 1932, McGraw called Terry into his office and offered him the chance to succeed him as manager. It was a move which showed great character on McGraw's part. Terry immediately took the job. McGraw moved into the front office but had virtually no authority.

The Giants compiled a 17–23 record when Terry took over, and the club finished in sixth place with a 72–82 mark. Terry left no doubt, however, as to who was boss. McGraw seldom ventured into the clubhouse. Terry also took steps that year to establish the Giants' farm system under his own direction.

Terry remained the club's first baseman, completing a streak of three consecutive years in which he did not miss a game, and batted .350 with a career high of 28 home runs in his first season as manager. In 1933 Terry showed that he could achieve excellence as a manager as well as a player. He led the Giants to a pennant in his first

full year at the helm, contributing a .322 season of his own. In the World Series against Washington, Terry hit .273 as the Giants downed the Senators in five games for the world championship.

Bill hit .354 in 1934, second in the league behind Paul Waner, but the Giants finished two games behind St. Louis. The following season they slipped to third place despite a .341 showing from Bill in his final season as a regular.

By 1936 Terry's knees troubled him, and he saw only limited duty. Ignoring a doctor's advice, Bill remained active all year, played 79 games, and hit .310. The Giants captured the pennant, and Terry batted .240 in the six-game World Series loss to the Yankees. After the Series, he quit as an active player.

With Mel Ott and Carl Hubbell the top attractions, Terry led the Giants to another pennant in 1937. But again the Yankees won the World Series, this time in five games.

The Giants finished third in 1938, fifth in 1939, sixth in 1940, and fifth in 1941. Some thought that Terry had lost his ability to motivate. Whatever the reason for the Giants' decline, Terry stepped down after the 1941 season in favor of Ott. He spent one season as the club's farm director before leaving the game for good.

After his retirement from baseball, Terry prospered with a Memphis automobile agency. He turned down managing jobs with the Dodgers and the Redlegs, returning to baseball only briefly in the mid-1950s as president of the South Atlantic League.

Perhaps because of his inability to get along with sportswriters, Terry waited 18 years for induction into the Hall of Fame. He was finally elected in 1954. Bill returned many times to Cooperstown after his election, smiling for photographers and enjoying the company of his former teammates and opponents. But if the years had mellowed him, Terry would not admit it, at least not for the press.

WILLIAM HAROLD TERRY

New York (N.L.) 1923–1936

G	AB	R	H	2B	3B	HR	RBI	Avg.
1721	6428	1120	2193	373	112	154	1078	.341

(Above) Bill Terry was a pitcher before John McGraw had him moved to first base to take advantage of his bat. Terry hit over .300 in 10 consecutive seasons with a high of .401 in 1930.

Sam Thompson (1860-1922)

Big Sam Thompson was a great home-run hitter in the nineteenth century, but the art of power hitting was unappreciated at the time and Sam was soon forgotten. The 1896 *Spalding Baseball Guide* classified Sam as one of the "rutty class of slugging batsman, who think of nothing else when they go to the bat but that of gaining the applause of the 'groundlings' by the novice's hit to the outfield for a 'homer,' one of the least difficult hits known to batting in baseball, as it needs only muscle and not brains to make it."

Samuel Luther Thompson was born on March 5, 1860, in Danville, Indiana, the fifth of 11 children. Four boys preceded Sam—Lawrence, Arthur, Nathan, and Cyrus. Nathan was a farmer, Cy a druggist, and Lawrence and Arthur followed their father into the carpenter's trade. Sam too was headed on that path, training as a cabinetmaker, but his chief interest was the town baseball team.

In 1883, when Sam was already 23 years old, a scout came to Danville looking for Cy Thompson, reportedly a fine player himself. Cy was a better hitter than his younger brother, but he lacked Sam's power. However, that was considered an asset, for a home run generally meant a lost ball and the end of the game.

Cy was flattered by the scout's interest, but he was already 26 years old and established as a druggist. He recommended Sam, and the scout traveled 12 miles to find Sam and his father doing carpentry work in Stinesville. The scout persuaded Sam to come down from the roof on which he was working and talk. An offer of $2.50 per game was made, which Sam considered a good deal. Although his father advised him against professional baseball, Sam accepted the offer and joined the nearby Evansville club of the Northwest League, played in five games before the club folded, and hit .391 in 23 times at bat.

Dan O'Leary, manager of the Indianapolis club of the Western League, signed Thompson for the 1885 season. Sam got off to a fast start, hitting .316 in 30 games. It was not long before he found himself a member of the Detroit Wolverines of the National League, thus making his major league debut at the age of 25.

Sam played his first game for Detroit on July 2, 1885. When Gene Moriarity crashed into the outfield wall that day and was knocked unconscious, Thompson was sent to right field. He collected a hit and a run in two times at bat.

In his first week in the majors, Sam had 11 hits in 26 at bats for a .423 average. The regular right field job was his from then on. He wound up leading the club with a .303 average as Detroit finished sixth in the eight-team league.

Sam's first full season was 1886, and Detroit had assembled an impressive array of talent during the winter months. In addition to Thompson, the team now included Dan Brouthers, Deacon White, Ned Hanlon, and Hardie Richardson. The club finished only two and one-half games behind Cap Anson's pennant-winning Chicago White Stockings. Sam hit .310 and belted eight home runs.

Thompson had an unusual batting stance, but he derived great strength from it. A lefthanded hitter, he would crouch quite low at the plate with his weight planted on his left foot. When the pitch was released, he would pop out of the crouch to lash out at the ball. Sam came to be regarded as one of the hardest hitters in the game. As fielders wore very small gloves, they would frequently feel the sting of even a ground ball by Thompson.

Sam was a sensation in 1887, a season in which Detroit captured the pennant. Walks counted as hits that year, and Sam was credited with 32 walks in batting .406. He collected 29 doubles, 23 triples, 11 homers, and 166 runs batted in, leading the league in triples and RBIs. Runs batted in were not actually compiled at the time, the figure being determined in later years. Had they been tallied when Sam was playing, fans would have appreciated his remarkable run production. Thompson drove in 1299 men in 1405 games, a percentage higher than any man who ever played major league baseball.

In the 15-game "World Series" against the St. Louis Browns that fall, Sam collected 19 hits. Detroit was the victor, 10 games to 5. In the eighth game, Sam became the second man to hit two home runs in one Series game. The feat was not duplicated until 1917, when the Giants' Benny Kauff did it against the White Sox. Sam saved the seventh game of the Series with a circus catch.

Sam was famous for one innovation as an outfielder—the one-bounce throw to home to catch runners trying to score. Sam's decision to avoid the cutoff man and throw directly to the plate resulted in as many as 32 assists in one season for him.

At 6'2" and 207 pounds, Sam stood out on the field. He was not noted for speed, but he stole 235 bases in his career with a season high of 33.

A sore throwing arm put Sam on the sidelines in 1888 from July 6 until the end of the season, except for a five-game comeback attempt in early August. For the season, Sam played in only 55 games and batted .282. Much of the Detroit club was dispersed at that point, and Sam was sold to the Philadelphia Phillies for the 1889 season.

Those who thought Thompson was through were in for quite a surprise. Sam went on to play 10 years in Philadelphia, topping the .300 figure in seven of those seasons and reaching the .400 mark for a second time, making him one of only eight players who have ever performed the feat more than once.

Harry Wright was the Philadelphia manager in Sam's first season there, and the Phils finished fourth with a 63–64 record. Sam batted .296 and belted 20 home runs, a career high and a sensational total for the period. Only four times previously, all in 1884, had the mark been surpassed.

Big Sam led the league in home runs twice, but he reached double figures six times and posted a career total of 128. That stood as a National League record until Rogers Hornsby hit no. 129 in 1924.

In 1890 Sam's home run output dropped to four, but he raised his batting average to .313 as the Phillies climbed to third. One year later, Ed Delahanty joined Sam and Billy Hamilton and the Phillie outfield of Delahanty-Hamilton-Thompson was the best in baseball at the time. All three players were eventually installed in the Hall of Fame.

Sam hit .296 in 1891 and .304 in 1892. In 1893 he batted .377, second only to Hamilton in the league. But that was only a prelude to a fabulous 1894 season, when four Philadelphia outfielders hit over .400 combined. It was one of the most amazing statistics in baseball history. Thompson hit .404, Hamilton .399, Delahanty .400, and reserve outfielder Tuck Turner compiled a .416 average in 339 at bats. Despite the heavy hitting (the team average was .349), the Phillies finished fourth again; they had little pitching.

Sam had still another big year in 1895, hitting .394 with league-leading figures in home runs (18), triples (22), and the unofficial RBI category (165). In 1896, his last full season, Thompson batted .306 with 12 homers and 100 RBIs.

Sam was on the Phillie roster in 1897, but a bad back forced him to the sidelines after only three games, and he was out for the remainder of the season. He tried again in 1898 but the same backache forced him to the sidelines in mid-May, after he had batted .365 in 14 games.

Sam returned to his home in Detroit and began to sell real estate. He also was appointed a United States deputy marshall and served as a court bailiff for many years. He kept active and in good physical condition by playing semipro ball in Detroit. In 1906, when the Tigers were plagued by injuries, manager Bill Armour signed Thompson to a contract, and at the age of 46, he replaced Sam Crawford in the outfield and batted .226 in eight games. Thus Sam was a teammate of Ty Cobb during Cobb's first full season.

Sam died in Detroit on November 7, 1922, and faded into baseball obscurity. When the Committee on Veterans named him to the Hall of Fame in 1974, even students of the game were hard pressed to remember Sam, the National League's leading home run hitter of the nineteenth century.

SAMUEL LUTHER THOMPSON

Detroit (N.L.) 1885–1888
Philadelphia (N.L.) 1889–1898
Detroit (A.L.) 1906

G	AB	R	H	2B	3B	HR	RBI	Avg.
1405	6004	1259	2016	326	146	128	1299	.336

Big Sam Thompson, who used to dazzle fans with his slugging in the nineteenth century. Although the fans loved his home runs, the so-called experts of baseball berated them, sneering that the homer required only strength, no skill. It was many years later that his power hitting was translated into runs brought in and his name went into the record books with 1299 RBIs in 1405 games.

Joe Tinker (1880-1948)

Joe Tinker, of the Chicago Cubs' Tinker-to-Evers-to-Chance double-play combination, was only a .264 lifetime hitter but a sparkplug of four Cub championship teams.

Joseph Bert Tinker was born on July 27, 1880, in the small town of Muscotah, Kansas. Before his nineteenth birthday, he signed his first contract with a semipro club in nearby Coffeyville.

Joe stood only 5'9" and weighed less than 135 pounds at the time, but he was adept at shortstop and covered considerable ground. In 1900 he was sent to Denver of the Western League, where he batted .219. Tinker finished the season in the Montana State League, hitting .322 in 57 games for Great Falls–Helena. With the exception of one season in the major leagues, his performance with Great Falls–Helena was the only time Joe batted higher than .300.

In 1901 Tinker played shortstop and third base for Portland in the Pacific Northwest League, batted .290 with 37 stolen bases, and led the league in chances and fielding percentage.

Frank Selee, the old Boston manager, had taken over the Cubs in 1902. Chicago had finished sixth in 1901, and Selee was determined to rebuild the team. One of his first moves was the purchase of Tinker from Portland. Joe opened the season at third base but was shifted to shortstop in midyear. Selee made two other notable moves with his infield that season. He moved his catcher, Frank Chance, to first base, replacing him behind the plate with Johnny Kling; and in September Selee picked up little Johnny Evers from Troy and positioned him at second base, replacing the veteran Bobby Lowe.

On September 13, 1902, the trio of Tinker at short, Evers at second, and Chance at first appeared in the lineup together for the first time. Tinker and Evers participated in a double play that day, and two days later Tinker, Evers, and Chance turned their first double play.

Double plays were not recorded until 1919, and consequently there are no official statistics on how many these men actually made. Their total was undoubtedly small in comparison to today's figures since baseball then featured so many bunting and hit-and-run plays that opportunities for double plays were less frequent. But Tinker, Evers, and Chance became the best-known double-play combination in the National League, although unofficial statistics, compiled years later by a Chicago sportswriter, gave them credit for only 54 double plays as a trio between 1906 and 1909.

The Cubs finished fifth in 1902, with Joe hitting .273 as a rookie. In 1903 Chicago advanced to third. The infield had learned to work together, and Joe batted .291. Tinker committed an incredible 140 errors

in his first two seasons, but Selee saw something in Joe's abilities and stayed with him. Meanwhile, Tinker increased his weight to 175 pounds, filling out into a solidly built man.

The Cubs moved up to second place in 1904 despite a .221 year from Tinker. In 1905 Chance succeeded Selee as manager and the club won 92 games. Joe batted .247, and his salary for the 1906 season was increased to $1500 per year.

On September 13, 1905, the Cubs played an exhibition game in Bedford, Indiana. Tinker and Evers—the heart of the Cub infield, the fine hit-and-run men, and the double play partners—exchanged angry words. Evers took a cab to the park, leaving Tinker and others stranded at the hotel. During the game, the pair actually got into a fistfight at second base. The fight was quickly broken up, but the men did not speak to each other for nearly three years thereafter.

Despite the silence of two star players, Chicago captured the 1906 pennant with a record of 116–36, finishing 20 games ahead of the second-place Giants. Tinker hit .233 and topped the league's shortstops in fielding percentage for the first time. For his career, Joe led five times in all, a National League record equaled only by Hughey Jennings before Tinker and by Eddie Miller after him.

Joe batted only .167 in the 1906 World Series, but he had a chance to better that performance in 1907 when the Cubs won another pennant. This time, Joe hit .221 in the regular season and .154 in the Series. Obviously, it was not hit hitting that made him popular in Chicago.

Curiously, there was one man who Tinker did hit consistently, and that was Christy Mathewson, the great Giant pitcher. Joe never knew the reason for his success against Matty, but in 1908, for example, he hit .421 against him. On September 23, 1908, the Cubs played the Giants in New York to decide the National League pennant. Tinker belted a big triple off Mathewson to lead the Cubs to a 4–2 victory and their third consecutive pennant.

In the World Series against Detroit, Joe further startled the fans by belting a home run off Bill Donovan in the eighth inning of the second game to break a scoreless tie. It was the first World Series home run since the initial Series in 1903.

The Cubs finished second in 1909 but were victors in 1910. During July of that year, Tinker, Evers, and Chance were immortalized in "Baseball's Sad Lexicon," an eight-line poem penned by Franklin P. Adams in the New York *Evening Mail*. Adams wrote,

> These are the saddest of possible words,
>   Tinker to Evers to Chance
> Trio of Bear Cubs and fleeter than birds,

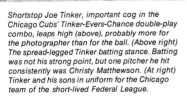

Shortstop Joe Tinker, important cog in the Chicago Cubs' Tinker-Evers-Chance double-play combo, leaps high (above), probably more for the photographer than for the ball. (Above right) The spread-legged Tinker batting stance. Batting was not his strong point, but one pitcher he hit consistently was Christy Matthewson. (At right) Tinker and his sons in uniform for the Chicago team of the short-lived Federal League.

Joe Tinker Day in Cincinnati, where the fans paid tribute, although his one year there as player-manager in 1913 was marked by constant battles between Tinker and the front office.

Tinker to Evers to Chance
Thoughtlessly pricking our gonfalon bubble,
Making a Giant hit into a double
Words that are weighty with nothing but trouble—
Tinker to Evers to Chance.

The poem made the trio famous throughout the country. Tinker capitalized on his popularity to begin a highly successful vaudeville career. Many baseball players spent their winters on the stage, but Tinker played to rave reviews and almost quit baseball for the stage in 1913.

Meanwhile, Joe starred in the Chicago infield. In 1910 he became the first man to steal home twice in one game. He hit .288 that year, and the stocky righthanded hitter was among the most popular players in the league.

Tinker remained with the Cubs through the 1912 season, after which he was traded to Cincinnati to become player-manager of the Reds. The transaction, completed in December 1912, sent Tinker, Grover Lowdermilk, and Harry Chapman to the Reds for Bert Humphries, Pete Knisely, Red Corriden, Art Phelan, and Mike Mitchell.

Things were not pleasant for Joe in Cincinnati. Although he batted .317, third highest average in the National League, the team finished seventh, and the new manager argued all year with owner Garry Herrmann. Herrmann would give Tinker no say in trades, and he sent a front-office representative on each trip to keep an eye on the club. When 1914 promised no improvement, Joe resigned as manager.

Cincinnati tried to trade Tinker to Brooklyn in December 1913, but the Dodgers wanted to pay Joe only $7500. Furthermore, although the purchase price of $25,000 was supposed to include $10,000 for Tinker, the Reds wanted additional players in the deal. As the parties haggled, Tinker decided to jump to the new Federal League. He joined the Chicago Whales as manager, the first player of note to jump to the new league. His move persuaded others to follow, including his old Cub teammate, Mordecai Brown.

The Whales moved into a new park, built by owner Charles F. Weeghman; today, that park, somewhat remodeled, is Wrigley Field. When the Federal League folded, Weeghman bought the Cubs, hired Tinker as manager, and moved the Cubs into the new stadium.

Under Tinker the Whales finished second in the pennant race in 1914 and first in 1915. Joe batted .259 the first year and then virtually terminated his active playing career in 1915 with only 69 at bats.

When the Federal League folded, Joe returned to the Cubs, received the managing job, and brought his club home in fifth place while playing his last seven major league games. For his career, Tinker batted only .264 with 29 home runs in 1642 games. William Wrigley, a stockholder, took a more active interest in the club beginning in 1917. Tinker was then let go as manager, replaced by Fred Mitchell.

Joe became manager and president of the Columbus team in the American Association in 1917 and 1918. He served as club president in 1919 and 1920. Then Tinker, his wife, three sons, and a daughter settled in Orlando, Florida, where Joe developed real estate and made a fortune. He built Tinker Field, a fine little park, and leased it to the Reds for spring training for many years.

In 1921 Tinker bought the Orlando club in the Florida State League and became its manager. He was a vice president of the club in 1923.

The Depression wiped out much of Joe's fortune, and he finally invested in a billiard parlor and bar. He even worked as a boiler inspector to help make ends meet.

Tinker's health declined in later years as he developed diabetes and a heart condition. While scouting for the Cubs, he was elected to the Hall of Fame in 1946 along with Evers and Chance.

Early in 1948, Joe came to national attention again when his left leg was amputated. Thousands of old fans sent cards to him. But on July 27, his sixty-eighth birthday, Joe Tinker died in Orlando.

JOSEPH BERT TINKER

Chicago (N.L.) 1902–1912, 1916
Cincinnati 1913
Chicago (F.L.) 1914–1915

G	AB	R	H	2B	3B	HR	RBI	Avg.
1642	5936	716	1565	238	106	29	783	.264

Pie Traynor (1899-1972)

Pie Traynor combined an outstanding glove with a .320 lifetime batting average to earn wide acclaim as the greatest third baseman in baseball history. The only other third basemen in the Hall of Fame are Jimmy Collins and Home Run Baker (John McGraw was elected primarily as a manager). Among modern players, Brooks Robinson is generally included among the finest to have played that position, but no one can match Traynor's statistics, compiled over a 17-year career with the Pittsburgh Pirates.

Harold Joseph Traynor was born on November 11, 1899, in Framingham, Massachusetts. His father, a printer, claimed to have hung the nickname "Pie" on his eight-year-old son when the boy came home covered with dirt. The senior Traynor used a printing expression in proclaiming, "You look like pied type!" Pie later said he felt the nickname may have come from a boyhood fondness for pies.

Traynor's interest in baseball was formed very early in life, and he recalled catching a hardball game—without a mask—at the age of six. His recollection included the loss of his two front teeth.

By the time he was 12 years old, Pie would walk three miles to Boston to work as an office boy. The walking habit never left him, and he became famous for it, frequently hiking from his team's hotels to the ballparks.

Traynor attempted to enlist in World War I. When he was rejected because of being under age, he assisted the war effort by loading freight cars.

When he was 18 years old and playing sandlot ball in Somerville, a Boston Braves' scout urged him to see manager George Stallings of the Braves for a tryout. This delighted Pie, but the shy youth was turned away by Stallings when he showed up on the field without an appointment.

Two years later Pie was scouted by both the Athletics and the Red Sox, the latter being his favorite team. When the Portsmouth club of the Virginia League offered him a contract, Red Sox manager Ed Barrow urged Pie to take it.

Playing shortstop for Portsmouth, Pie hit .270 in 104 games, prompting Barrow to make the club an offer for Traynor's services. But it was too late for the Red Sox. Acting on the advice of scout Tom McNamara, Pittsburgh Pirate owner Barney Dreyfuss paid Portsmouth $10,000—a large sum at the time—for Traynor's contract. Pie reported to the Pirates at the end of the 1920 season, played 17 games at shortstop, and batted .212. Neither at bat nor in the field did he make a good impression. His 12 errors at short hardly helped Pirate fans forget the recently retired Honus Wagner.

The following winter, Pittsburgh traded for Rabbit Maranville and optioned Tray-

nor to Birmingham of the Southern Association. He played 131 games there, batted .336, and was again called up at the end of the season. He played six games, hit .263, and made a costly error at third base.

Maranville was shifted to second, Clyde Barnhardt installed at third, and Traynor positioned at short as the 1922 season opened. But when Bill McKechnie replaced George Gibson as Pirate manager late in June, Barnhardt was returned to the outfield, Maranville was moved back to short, and Traynor was given the third base job. It was the turning point of Pie's career.

Traynor developed a style at third unmatched in his day. He was sensational at covering the line, and seldom would a ball be hit past him. Pie fielded bunts expertly, had a great throwing arm, and could range far to his left. permitting shortstop Glenn Wright (Maranville's successor) to cover even more territory. The Pirates thus had one of the best left sides of an infield in major league history.

Later in his career, when his speed had left him, Traynor developed an even greater instinct and a broader knowledge of hitters, enabling him to compensate for his slowness and remain the best third baseman in baseball.

In his first season as a regular, 1922, Pie batted .282 with 4 home runs and 81 runs batted in. Never a power hitter (his career high of 12 homers was accomplished in 1923), Pie compiled a total of only 58 major league home runs. But he topped the .300 mark 10 times. The first such season was 1923, which he considered to be his finest.

That year Traynor tied for the league lead in triples with 19, collected 208 hits, scored 108 runs, and drove in 101. In addition to a batting average of .338, Traynor played in all but one of the Pirates' games.

The following year Pie hit .294, but in 1925 he rebounded to bat .320 with 114 runs scored, 106 RBIs, and some brilliant fielding that helped the Pirates win the National League pennant. The Pirates had a combined .307 batting average that year, 24 points higher than the runnerup Giants of John McGraw. McGraw in fact was a great admirer of Traynor, calling him "the greatest team player in baseball." Joining Pie over the .300 mark on the Pirates were George Grantham, Glenn Wright, Kiki Cuyler, Max Carey, Clyde Barnhart, and Earl Smith.

The Pirates beat the Washington Senators in the 1925 World Series, with the righthanded-hitting Traynor batting .346 and reaching Walter Johnson for a home run in the opening game.

Traynor batted .317 in 1926, but the team fell to third place. In 1927 Lloyd Waner joined brother Paul on the team, and the Pirates captured another pennant. Traynor hit .342 with 106 RBIs that year, but he batted only .200 in the four-game World Series loss to the Yankees.

That was Pie's final World Series. The Pirates came close in 1938 when Traynor was managing the team, but they never entered the winners' circle again during his stay with Pittsburgh.

The 6'½", 175-pound Trayner remained a model of consistency at third base in Forbes Field. In the three years following the 1927 pennant, he batted .337, .356, and .366, topping the 100 RBI mark each time. He surpassed 100 RBIs seven times in all.

Pie never became rich playing baseball, for his top salary was $14,000, and a substantial part of his earnings were wiped out in the stock-market crash of 1929. But Traynor was a wise, conservative man who remained a bachelor until he was 32. Then he married Eva Helmer, a switchboard operator in a Cincinnati hotel. The couple had no children.

Pie batted .298 in 1931, but the Pirates had become a sub-.500 club under manager Jewel Ens. In 1932 Ens was replaced by George Gibson, the man who had originally tried to make Pie a shortstop. Traynor batted .329 in 1932 as the club finished second. He then hit .304 in 1933, playing in every game of the season, while Pittsburgh again finished second.

In 1934 the Pirates believed that they really had a shot at the pennant. But the club got off to a 27–24 start, Gibson was

fired, and Traynor was named player-manager.

Only 34, and now managing his teammates and friends, Pie failed to work any miracles. Paul Waner won a batting title, but the team under Pie compiled a 47–52 record and finished fifth. Traynor hit .309 but suffered an injury to his throwing arm while sliding home in a game against Philadelphia. The injury virtually brought his playing career to a halt.

Pie played in only 57 games in 1935, letting Tommy Thevenow replace him as the regular third baseman. In 1936 Traynor was strictly a bench manager, not appearing at all as a player. In 1937 he played in five games. During those three seasons, Pittsburgh finished fourth, fourth, and third.

The year of greatest disappointment to Traynor was 1938, when Gabby Hartnett's twilight home run late in September brought the Cubs a pennant over the Pirates. It was a season in which future Hall of Famers managed seven of the eight National League teams—Hartnett (Cubs), Traynor (Pirates), Bill Terry (Giants), Bill McKechnie (Redlegs), Casey Stengel (Braves), Burleigh Grimes (Dodgers), and Frankie Frisch (Cardinals).

Pie's final season as Pirate manager was 1939, and the club finished sixth. Frisch

replaced Traynor at the end ot the season. Traynor was only 40 years old, but his career as player and manager was now behind him.

Too much a part of Pirate history to be cast aside, Pie was made a Pittsburgh scout, a position he held until his death. He often conducted tryouts for the Pirates, served as a spring-training instructor, and always remained in good physical condition.

Living in Cincinnati after his managing stint, Traynor returned to Pittsburgh in 1944 for a one-year job as radio announcer on KOV. The station found his New England accent appealing and made him sports director. He remained on the air until 1966.

In 1948 Pie Traynor was elected to the Hall of Fame, and in 1969 he was selected as the game's greatest third baseman in a poll of sportswriters conducted during baseball's centennial season.

Pie Traynor died on March 16, 1972, in Pittsburgh—the city that adored him on the playing field and the city which he called home for nearly 50 years.

HAROLD JOSEPH TRAYNOR

Pittsburgh 1920–1935, 1937

G	AB	R	H	2B	3B	HR	RBI	Avg.
1941	7559	1183	2416	371	164	58	1273	.320

A collage of the great Pie Traynor, selected history's best third baseman by sportswriters during baseball's centennial. Ed Barrow, who scouted Traynor in 1920, remembered: "I looked out and watched him. He looked like a real ballplayer, even though he seemed to be all arms and legs and did have feet like violin cases. He also had big hands and scooped up every ball hit at him and fired it over to first base."

Dazzy Vance (1891-1961)

Dazzy Vance spent 10 years in the minor leagues before winning his first major league game at the age of 31. He then went on to record a pitching career worthy of the Hall of Fame.

Actually, everyone thought Dazzy was 29 when he came up, but as he finally admitted in later years, he was born on March 4, 1891—not 1893 as most record books claimed. There was also confusion over his real name. He claimed to be Arthur Charles Vance, as his Hall of Fame plaque reads, but a family Bible disclosed that he was actually born Clarence Arthur Vance in Orient, Iowa, of Scotch-Irish parents. But keeping people guessing was just part of this good-natured man's way of life.

A. C. "Dazzy" Vance, as he signed his autograph, moved with his family to Hastings, Nebraska, when he was five. Shortly thereafter, an uncle bestowed the nickname Dazzy on him when young Vance mimicked a cowboy-entertainer who pronounced "Daisy" as "Dazzy." The name stuck, and it later served as an appropriate moniker for a man who threw with "dazzling" speed.

The young farmboy played ball for a nearby town team in Cowles in addition to pitching for his high school team in Hastings. In 1912, at the age of 21, Dazzy signed a professional contract with Superior in the Nebraska League for $100 per month.

Vance, who stood 6'1" and weighed between 200 and 215 pounds during his career, broke in with an 11–15 record in 1912. Dazzy had an almost identical record with Superior in 1913, going 11–14, but he really hit it big in 1914 with a 17–4 mark for his hometown Hastings club in the same league. That earned Vance a promotion to the St. Joseph team in the Western League in August, and he recorded a 9–8 mark with a 2.96 earned-run average there.

The Pittsburgh Pirates gave Dazzy a chance in 1915, but after walking five men and allowing two runs in three innings, he was returned to St. Joseph for an eventful year.

Dazzy's large frame caused managers to believe he had greater strength than he actually possessed. At St. Joe, Vance was pressed into 39 starts and 264 innings, winning 17, losing 15, and in one stretch pitching five complete games within seven days. Finally, his arm began to ache, and he went to his family doctor in Hastings to have it examined. To neither's surprise, Dazzy had a sore arm, with rest prescribed as the only cure. "How much rest?" asked Vance. "About five years," said the doctor.

With little education and no other professional skills, Dazzy could not afford to give up the game. He was purchased by the Yankees as the 1915 season drew to a close, but his record was 0–3 in eight games with 16 walks in 28 innings. Vance would have to begin his career once again

in the minor leagues, learning to throw breaking pitches, working on his control, and hoping his arm would work itself out.

Dazzy continued to travel through the minor leagues. At one point later in his career, he bet his manager, Wilbert Robinson, that there was not a clubhouse in America which he could enter without knowing at least three players.

Perfecting his curveball and style of pitching, Dazzy spent the next few years with Columbus, Toledo, Memphis, Rochester, Sacramento, and briefly again with the Yankess in 1918. His only double-digit entry in the victory column was a 10–18 season at Sacramento in 1919.

In 1920 Dazzy reported to Memphis of the Southern Association and later was transferred to New Orleans. By 1921 he had began to rediscover his fastball. He worked in a strict rotation, pitching every fifth day; the plan helped to restore strength in his arm. Not only had his fastball returned, but it was one of the best in baseball. Vance posted a 21–11 record in 1921, and at the end of the season he was purchased by the Brooklyn Dodgers, or Robins, as they were then called.

There was a certain irony in the sale. The best pitcher on New Orleans was another righthander, Tom Phillips. Since the Cleveland Indians held a working agreement with New Orleans, they had first pick of a pitcher and selected Phillips. Larry Sutton, the Dodger scout, recommended Vance to owner Charles Ebbets, along with Dazzy's catcher, Hank DeBerry, who was 29 years old. Ebbets would have preferred Phillips, but he received Vance and DeBerry for $10,000, and the two old rookies went on to become a long-standing, first-rate battery for Brooklyn. Phillips never won a game for Cleveland.

Vance joined a lackluster 1922 Dodger team that finished sixth under Wilbert Robinson. He joined Dutch Ruether, Leon Cadore, and Burleigh Grimes in the starting rotation and posted an 18–12 record, leading the league with 134 strikeouts. It was the first of seven consecutive seasons in which Vance would top the league in strikeouts—a record for most consecutive years leading the league and for most years, period. And he accomplished the feat in his first seven seasons!

Strikeouts became the name of Vance's game. His long arms, which enabled him to span 83 inches, would flail widly as he kicked his left leg high into the air, lashing great effort into every pitch. DeBerry claimed he threw a very light ball despite the great speed, making him easy to handle. Vance was also famous for a tattered undershirt sleeve beneath his uniform, which became a trademark of sorts. It

helped in his total deception of hitters, but when umpires challenged the legality of the torn shirt, Dazzy would plead that he needed his lucky shirt to get by. The unwashed, ripped shirt, damaged by his own razor blade, remained a part of his uniform.

Dazzy reached a high of 262 strikeouts in 1924, the year in which he compiled a 28–6 record with a 2.16 earned-run average for a Brooklyn team that lost the pennant to the Giants by the narrow margin of one and one-half games. By leading the league in victories, strikeouts, and ERA, Dazzy earned the Most Valuable Player Award in the National League, beating out Rogers Hornsby, who had batted .424.

Three times in his career, Vance struck out 15 batters in a game, once each in 1924, 1926, and 1928. In 1924 he struck out seven consecutive hitters. In 1925 he struck out 17 batters in a 10-inning game. That was also the year in which Dazzy no-hit Philadelphia, 10–1, on September 13. Left fielder Jimmy Johnson's double error led to the Phillies' only run.

Five days before the no-hitter, Vance had pitched a one-hitter against the Phillies, facing only 27 batters while beating them, 1–0. Phillie manager Art Fletcher bet Vance that he could not duplicate the feat. Needless to say, Dazzy won the bet.

The Brooklyn teams of the 1920s became known as the "Daffyness Boys." They were unpredictable, colorful, and seldom good. Their only serious run at a pennant occurred in 1924. But in 1925, when Vance compiled a 22–9 mark, the Dodgers slipped to sixth place. As one of the biggest gate attractions in the league, Vance earned more money than any pitcher in the National League. In 1925 he held out with Burleigh Grimes until March 10, then signed a three-year contract for $47,500. In 1928 his salary jumped to $20,000 per year, and in 1929 he reached his peak of $25,000.

Dazzy could always keep fans and players laughing. He established the Oh-for-Four Club in the Dodger clubhouse for batters who had gone hitless in four at bats for the day.

In a famous incident on the bases in 1926, Babe Herman lined a bases-loaded drive off the wall. One run scored, and Vance, the man on second, hesitated after going past third and returned to the base. Chick Fewster, the runner on first, landed at third as well, as did Herman, running at full speed. Three Dodgers on the same base! It could only have happened in Brooklyn.

Vance was especially tough when dueling the up-and-coming Carl Hubbell of New York. He beat Carl seven consecutive times before Hubbell finally won in 1932, the last time they ever faced each other.

A bad case of boils caused Vance to slip to a 9–10 record in 1926, but in 1927 he

posted a 16–15 mark. In 1928 he won 20 for the last time, sporting a 22–10 record and leading the league with a 2.09 ERA. Dazzy captured his third and last ERA crown two years later with a 2.61 mark.

On February 9, 1933, Dazzy was traded to St. Louis with Gordon Slade for Jake Flowers and Owen Carroll. No longer able to buzz the fastball past hitters, Dazzy got by on a sweeping curve, posting a 6–2 record for the Cardinals. In February 1934, he was sold to the Redlegs, but the Cardinals received him back on waivers on June 25.

At long last, Dazzy was on a pennant winner. His one and one-third innings of relief in the 1934 World Series, with three strikeouts and no runs, was a highlight of his career.

Vance was released the following April and spent 1935 back home with Brooklyn, winning three and losing two. Then, at the age of 44, with 197 lifetime victories, he retired.

Dazzy and his wife, Edyth, settled in Homosassa Springs, Florida, on acreage purchased by the Vances in 1927. He became the town's most famous citizen and opened a hunting-fishing lodge, selling his own driftwood carvings in the adjoining gift shop. Vance lost money in the 1929 stock-market crash, and gasoline rationing during World War II hurt his lodge business, but he generally lived well and enjoyed the leisure pastimes of hunting, fishing, and golf. He helped to organize the Homosassa Springs Chamber of Commerce and served as its chairman. Vance also managed the Homosassa Wild Cats, a team of "semi-amateurs."

Each winter Dazzy would welcome old teammates en route to their Florida training bases. The personable redhead was one of the most popular figures in the game even in retirement, and he certainly had many former teammates.

In 1955 Dazzy Vance was elected to the Hall of Fame. On February 16, 1961, he died in his sleep of a heart attack at his Florida home.

ARTHUR CHARLES VANCE

Pittsburgh 1915
New York (A.L.) 1915, 1918
Brooklyn 1922–1932, 1935
St. Louis (N.L.) 1933–1934
Cincinnati 1934

G	IP	W	L	Pct.	H	R	ER	SO	BB	ERA
442	2967	197	140	.585	2809	1246	1068	2045	840	3.24

St. Louis Cards' pitcher Dazzy Vance (at right above) chats in 1933 with former Brooklyn Robins' teammate, Babe Herman of the Chicago Cubs. (Below) Vance's 1924 MVP award. (Opposite page) Vance fires one for Cincinnati, late in his career.

Rube Waddell (1876-1914)

Rube Waddell was eccentric, unpredictable, unmanageable, and the biggest drawing card in the early days of the American League. He was also the best lefthanded pitcher in baseball during his brief term with the Philadelphia Athletics.

Born of poor farm parents on October 13, 1876, in Bradford, Pennsylvania, George Edward Waddell was known as Eddie to his friends. He received little in the way of an education. At the age of three he ran away from home and slept in a firehouse. His fascination with firemen stayed with him throughout his life. When Waddell became a professional pitcher, he always wore a red shirt under his uniform, frequently participated in fire-fighting exploits, and occasionally left games to follow fire engines.

Rube worked on his parents' farm, building great strength in his arms by plowing fields. He developed his pitching skill by throwing stones at flying crows. At the age of 18, he began to pitch for the Butler, Pennsylvania, town team. Although younger than most of his teammates, and never too reliable about showing up for games, Rube was clearly the best player on the club.

In 1896 a traveling salesman named Wesley Baker saw Waddell pitch in Prospect, Pennsylvania, and recommended him to the Franklin team, a high-ranking, semipro outfit. When Waddell arrived in Franklin, catcher Jack Nelson greeted him with, "All right, Rube, let's see what you can do." The nickname stuck, and although Waddell resented strangers using the name, he eventually recognized its appeal to fans.

Waddell was sensational at Franklin, and at the end of the season he was hired to pitch for the Homestead Athletic Club in a series against Duquesne County. He pitched and won all four games, receiving $100 for his efforts—and a $500 offer from Fred Clarke, manager of the National League's Louisville franchise.

Reaching Louisville at two in the morning, Rube awakened his new manager and informed him of his arrival. It was the beginning of a bad relationship between Rube and Clarke, who was a strong disciplinarian. Waddell was about the least likely man to accept discipline. After he had pitched only two games for Louisville in 1897, Clarke fined him $50 for his excessive drinking. After the incident, Rube jumped the club.

In 1898 Waddell was sent to Detroit, a minor league team in the Western League. There he pitched in nine games, split eight decisions, and left to work for Chatham, a Canadian semipro club. While a sensation with Chatham, Waddell was lured back to the United States in 1899 to pitch for Columbus, a franchise in the Western League that was shifted to Grand Rapids early in the season. Rube won 26 and lost

Rube Waddell, after a flamboyant but unsteady fling in the majors, was tracked down in Punxsutawney, Pennsylvania, by Connie Mack in 1900. Waddell challenged him, "Who the hell are you?" but went on to pitch brilliantly for Mack in the style shown on the opposite page. He once pitched a 17-inning game, hit a triple, struck out the last three batters, and did handstands to the bench. Then he won the second game of the doubleheader 1–0.

only 8; several of his victories were against Connie Mack's Milwaukee team. Mack made a mental note to remember Waddell.

Louisville bought Rube again at the end of the 1899 season, and he won seven of nine decisions for Clarke. In 1900 Barney Dreyfuss moved the team to Pittsburgh, along with many of his great players, including Waddell and Honus Wagner.

Rube and Clarke were still unable to get along. Waddell skipped games whenever he pleased, often just taking the afternoon off to go fishing. Sometimes he would dally outside the ballpark to play with young fans. He compiled a 9–11 record for Pittsburgh in 1900, but after many fines he jumped the club again early in July and headed for Punxsutawney, Pennsylvania, where Connie Mack tracked him down.

Mack asked Barney Dreyfuss if he would object to giving up the rights to Waddell. Dreyfuss did not mind a bit, and Mack took a train to Punxsutawney, paid off Waddell's debts, and brought Rube back to Milwaukee, where Mack was managing in the American League's first season.

Waddell was a big gate attraction from the start. Connie Mack knew a crowd pleaser when he saw one, and he never inhibited Waddell's style. Rube won 10 and lost 3 for Milwaukee in 1900, including a double header victory over Chicago in which the first game lasted 17 innings.

The double victory having brought Waddell national attention, Dreyfuss wired Connie Mack that he wanted Waddell back. (The American League, was a minor league that year.) Mack played it squarely and agreed since no official transaction had ever moved Rube from Pittsburgh. But Waddell was less willing to return. Pittsburgh catcher Chief Zimmer was sent to Milwaukee to bring Waddell back. With offers of fishing equipment and new clothing, Zimmer persuaded Waddell to return to Pittsburgh early in September.

The third attempt by Clarke to manage Waddell also failed, and Rube was traded early in May 1901 to Chicago. For Pittsburgh and Chicago that year, he posted a combined 13–16 record. Rube participated in a post-season west coast exhibition series that made him a big favorite of Los Angeles fans, and he spent the first part of the 1902 season in the Pacific Coast League, notching a 12–7 record. Again interested in him, Connie Mack sent two Pinkerton detectives to Los Angeles to bring Waddell to Philadelphia, now Mack's home base. Waddell then settled down in Philadelphia in 1902 to begin the most stable and satisfying period of his life.

Rube won 23 and lost only 7 in that partial season of 1902 with the Athletics.

He teamed up with his catcher, Ossie Schreckengost, to form a zany bond of friendship. Once Ossie saved Rube from suicide when he tried to drown himself in Jacksonville, Florida, over an unrequited love affair. The only time they ever seriously differed concerned Waddell's habit of eating animal crackers in bed. In those days, players shared the same bed for economic reasons when on the road, and "Schreck" had it written into Waddell's contract that he was forbidden to eat the crackers in bed.

Waddell struck out 210 and walked only 67 in 1902. In Detroit one day, he motioned his three outfielders to sit down just behind the infield while he struck out the side.

Rube did not generally pull that sort of stunt in regular season games, but he often delighted exhibition crowds with such theatrics. He once threatened to quit baseball and pursue a career in vaudeville. One year he appeared in a play called "The Stain of Guilt," with New York Giants' player Bugs Raymond.

After the 1902 season, Rube put his 6'2" frame, weighing 196 pounds, to work for Connie Mack's Philadelphia professional football team, but that career was short-lived, as was the team.

Rube was as wild as ever off the field. He wrestled alligators professionally, rocked team busses, tended bar, and generally showed little sense of responsibility. Whatever money he earned was always spent, even though his top baseball salary was only $3000. Rube married three times and went to jail frequently for missing alimony payments.

But on the mound, Waddell remained in a class by himself. Between 1902 and 1908, Rube struck out more than 200 batters each season, a major league record. For five of those years (1902–1906), he led the major leagues in strikeouts, topping only the American League in 1907. Twice in that span he surpassed the 300 mark with figures of 301 in 1903 and 349 in 1904 (generally listed as 343). Bob Feller fanned 348 batters in 1946 and was given credit for breaking Waddell's record, but the title remained in question until Sandy Koufax passed them both with 382 in 1965.

Rube posted a 21–16 record in 1903, and a 25–19 mark in 1904. His best season was 1905, in which he compiled a 26–11 record despite missing the final four weeks of the season and the World Series. Rube had injured his arm during a victory celebration when teammate Andy Coakley fell on him during a fight for possession of a straw hat. Some accused Waddell of conspiring with gamblers to miss the World Series, but the change was unsubstantiated.

The high point of Waddell's 1905 season was a classic, 20-inning, 4–2 complete-game victory over Cy Young on July 4, which made Rube a household name around the country. He often managed to get free drinks by presenting bartenders with "the actual baseball" with which he had beaten Young. The "actual baseball" was displayed in scores of barroom windows around the country.

Waddell began to slow down after the 1907 season, and Connie Mack reached the end of his patience with him. He sold "the best lefthander I ever saw" to the St. Louis Browns for $5000. With the Browns in 1908, Rube struck out 16 of his former Philadelphia teammates to set a single-game record that stood for many years.

Rube pitched for the Browns into the 1910 season. Released to Newark, he compiled a 5–3 record, and then he was purchased by Minneapolis for the 1911–1912 seasons. Waddell met with success in 1911, posting a 20–17 mark.

Early in 1912, Rube became a hero of sorts when he stood shoulder deep in icy water while placing sacks of sand on embankments to help save the town of Hickman, Kentucky, from a flood. He caught a severe cold from which he never really recovered.

Rube pitched for Virginia of the Northern League in 1913, completing his career with a 3–9 record. Joe Cantillon, owner of the Minneapolis team, then paid for Rube to enter a sanatorium in San Antonio. His weight fell to nearly 100 pounds, and he was sinking fast as his former teammates came to see him. Despite his wild life, Rube was a lovable character who added considerable color to the early days of the American League.

On April 1, 1914, Waddell died of tuberculosis. He was buried in San Antonio under a simple wooden marker. Later, Harry Benson, president of the San Antonio club, discovered the unattended grave and, with the help of John McGraw and Connie Mack, collected money for a proper granite marker.

In 1946 Rube Waddell was elected to the Hall of Fame.

GEORGE EDWARD WADDELL

Louisville (N.L.) 1897, 1899
Pittsburgh (N.L.) 1900, 1901
Chicago (N.L.) 1901
Philadelphia (A.L.) 1902–1907
St. Louis (A.L.) 1908–1910

G	IP	W	L	Pct.	H	R	ER	SO	BB	ERA
407	2958	191	142	.574	2480	1079	inc.	2310	771	inc.

Honus Wagner (1874-1955)

Although he retired as a player in 1917, Honus Wagner is still considered by baseball experts to have been the finest shortstop ever to play the game. For many years he was considered the best player in the history of the National League, an argument for which he can still score many points.

John Peter Wagner was born on February 24, 1874, in Mansfield, Pennsylvania, a town known today as Carnegie. He was one of the nine children of Bavarian immigrants. In the German community in which he was reared, John was more commonly referred to as Johannes, which resulted in the nickname "Hans." "Hans" turned to "Honus" when Wagner became established as a baseball player.

Wagner's father was a coal miner, and Honus himself began work in the mines at the age of 12. His wages were $3.50 per week, which he increased by turning to semipro ball in his late teens.

Fortunately (and it was uncommon in that era), Wagner's father became a baseball fan, and he was pleased when Honus was offered a professional contract in 1895. An older brother, Albert, had preceeded Honus as a minor league player. He played 74 games in the major leagues in 1898, batting .224 for Washington and .237 for Brooklyn. But brother Honus was far more talented.

Honus's contract brought him a salary of $35 per week and placed him in Steubenville in the Inter-State League. The records show that he batted .402 in 44 games.

Wagner also played briefly that year at Mansfield in the Ohio State League and with Adrian in the Michigan State League. He then closed the 1895 season with 65 games for Warren in the Iron-Oil League. It was a well-traveled season for the 21-year-old player.

After the 1895 season, Edward Grant Barrow, just 27 years old and breaking into baseball as the owner of the Paterson, New Jersey, team in the Atlantic League, purchased Wagner from Warren. Just as Wagner was embarking on a brilliant career on the playing field, Barrow was beginning a dynamic career in the front office that eventually led to his election to the Hall of Fame. Barrow gained most of his fame by steering the development of the New York Yankee dynasty in the 1920s and 1930s.

Wagner proved to be Barrow's first major purchase. Barrow removed the strong-armed righthander from any further pitching assignments and placed him virtually full-time in the infield. Wagner's oversized hands gave him great fielding prowess in an era of tiny mitts. His hands were not the only distinctive feature of his

physique. Wagner stood 5'11" and weighed 200 pounds. Much of his weight was concentrated in his massive chest; his legs were bowed and his arms very long. Honus gave the impression of considerable strength, and indeed he displayed it at bat in the dead-ball era when home runs were not the measure of a man's power.

Wagner played 109 games for Barrow in 1896, collecting 145 hits for a .349 average. He was doing even better the following season, batting .379 after 74 games, when Barrow sold him to Louisville in the National League. At age 23, Wagner had reached the major leagues, beating his older brother by a full season.

Although Louisville was a poor team in 1897, finishing eleventh in a 12-club league, Wagner batted .344. Only player-manager, Fred Clarke, had a higher average on the team. Wagner played 61 games, almost all in the outfield; the shortstop position was manned by Bob Stafford, a .278 hitter.

In 1898 Claude Ritchey became the Louisville shortstop, and Wagner played 148 games, primarily at first and third. (Not until his final season, 1917, did Honus play in fewer than 100 games.) His batting average was .305, his lowest average for the next 15 years, and he tied for second in home runs in the National League with 10.

Louisville still floundered in the second division in 1899, but Wagner had a big season, hitting .359 in 144 games. In 1900 Honus stole 38 bases, tying for the fifth highest mark in the league. Wagner went on to lead the National League in stolen bases five times—1901 (49), 1902 (42), 1904 (53), 1907 (61), and 1908 (53). His 720 career thefts ranks fifth on baseball's all-time list of modern players.

As the twentieth century dawned, Louisville dropped out of the National League, as did Baltimore, Washington, and Cleveland. The latter three were placed in the new American League a year later, and Louisville forever withdrew from major league baseball. Fifteen Louisville players, including Wagner and manager Clarke, were transferred to Pittsburgh.

At Pittsburgh in 1900 Wagner won his first of eight National League batting titles, hitting .381 while leading the league in doubles (45) and triples (22). During his career, Wagner won three titles in triples and eight doubles championships. He still ranks fifth in doubles and third in triples on the all-time listing of major leaguers, with 651 and 252, respectively.

With the addition of the Louisville players, Pittsburgh finished second in 1900, just four and one-half games behind Brooklyn. And in 1901, with Wagner batting .353 as an all-purpose player and leading the league with 49 stolen bases, the

"Hans" Wagner stands third from left (above) with the 1896 Paterson, New Jersey, team. Seated in civvies is team owner Ed Barrow, who described discovering Wagner: "I found him betting all comers that he could throw a rock farther than any other man in the crowd. He would easily throw a rock a hundred yards. . . . I signed him on the spot for $430 a week . . . and he quickly proved himself to be the greatest slugger of all time." (Left) Wagner's slugging style.

Pirates finished first. This was two years before the first modern World Series, since the established National League rejected a post-season playoff with the year-old American League. Thus Wagner's accomplishments netted him only the maximum salary for the season—$2400.

Money was not all-important to Honus, however, as he demonstrated several years later when Clark Griffith of the New York Highlanders offered him $20,000 to jump to the American League. Loyal to Pittsburgh, Wagner rejected the offer. Honus never earned more than $10,000 per year, his salary from 1909 to 1917.

Not that Wagner was indifferent to money. He achieved his $10,000 salary only by threatening to quit after the 1908 season. But once he reached that figure, which he thought to be fair and sufficient, he never bargained again. Honus always said that he would play for the same amount as the previous year.

In 1903 Wagner finally settled at shortstop as Wid Conroy jumped to the Highlanders. The season produced a second batting championship for Honus—at .355—and a place in the first World Series, in which Pittsburgh met Boston. Wagner batted only .222 in the eight-game Series, and Pittsburgh suffered an embarrassing loss to the upstart Red Sox, thus bringing about parity between the American and the established National League. Wagner was eager to redeem himself and the league in another World Series, but that would be six years away.

Wagner repeated his batting crown in 1904 with a .349 average, but he finished second to Cy Seymour's .377 in 1905 with "only" a .363 figure. The lost crown interrupted a streak of consecutive batting titles (1902–1904, 1906–1909). He captured the crown each year from 1906 to 1909 with averages of .339, .350, .354, and .339.

With the passage of years, Wagner achieved the status of an authentic folk hero. Honus was a model of clean living and good sportsmanship. Because of his disdain for smoking, he even had a baseball-card portrait of himself that was distributed with cigarettes withdrawn from the market. (He did allow himself an occasional cigar in later years, however.) That card has become the most-prized baseball picture of all time, and it is valued by collectors at about $1500 today.

The most celebrated matchup of the day occurred in the 1909 World Series, in which Pittsburgh faced Detroit, and the good-natured Wagner met the ruthless Ty Cobb. Wagner was considered the best player in the National League; Cobb, although only 22 years old, was the terror of the Americans. The brash Cobb taunted Wagner during the Series, calling him "Krauthead" and threatening to slide in spikes up when stealing second base. Wagner, always a gentlemen, merely said, "I'll be waiting." The pre-Series publicity was not unlike the buildup of a heavyweight boxing match.

The Series belonged to Wagner and the Pirates, who captured the World Championship in seven games. Cobb stole only two bases, with Wagner badly cutting Ty's lip with a hard tag at second base. Cobb batted .231, while Wagner hit .333 and swiped six bases, a record for a single Series that stood until 1967 when Lou Brock stole seven for St. Louis. (Brock also swiped seven bases in 1968.)

The 1909 Series marked the first and only confrontation between Wagner and Cobb, and for years fans debated whether Wagner or Cobb was the best player in baseball. Later the comparison was shifted to Babe Ruth and Cobb, with Wagner recognized as merely the best shortstop. But many baseball insiders, including Barrow and John McGraw, always thought that Wagner was the best all-around player in the game.

Wagner continued to play consistently outstanding baseball with Pittsburgh, winning the first three RBI titles recorded in the National League (1907–1909) and showing little sign of slowing down. At the age of 37, he won his eighth and last batting title, hitting .334. But by 1914, arthritis began to affect his legs and Honus was no longer beating out infield hits. He hit an even .300 in 1913, but batted only .252 in 1914. Wagner followed that with averages of .274 in 1915 and .287 in 1916, as he approached his final season as a player.

Fred Clarke's last year as Pirate manager was 1915. His replacement, Jim Callahan, brought the team home sixth in 1916, and Pittsburgh had won only 20 of 60 games in 1917 when he was dismissed. Pirate owner Barney Dreyfuss then named Wagner as manager. Honus was having his troubles at bat again, destined to play only 74 games and bat .265 in his final year. But Wagner's taste was not for managing. He ran the club for just five games, won one, and happily handed over the reins to Hugo Bezdek.

Out of baseball now, leaving behind him a National League record of 3430 hits, (later broken by Stan Musial), Wagner, with his wife, Bessie, and two daughters, settled in Carnegie. He was basketball and baseball coach at Carnegie Tech for a short time, served as sergeant-at-arms in the Pennsylvania State Legislature, and ventured with Pie Traynor in a sporting goods store that failed.

In 1933, at the age of 59, he was summoned back to a Pirate uniform as a coach—a position he filled with good humor and distinction until he became strictly a dugout figure at the age of 77. In 1936, along with Cobb, Ruth, Walter Johnson, and Christy Mathewson, Wagner was in the first group of players elected to the Hall of Fame.

Honus Wagner died on December 6, 1955, in Carnegie. At the time of his death, he was still the National League's all-time leader in games played, times at bat, hits, singles, doubles, and triples.

In 1955 a massive statue of Wagner was dedicated in Schenley Park, near Forbes Field, Pittsburgh, where he had played from its opening in 1909 until his retirement. At baseball's centennial celebration in 1969, Wagner was voted the greatest Pirate of all time by the Pittsburgh fans.

JOHN PETER WAGNER

Louisville 1897–1899
Pittsburgh 1900–1917

G	AB	R	H	2B	3B	HR	RBI	Avg.
2785	10427	1740	3430	651	252	101	inc.	.329

The Hans Wagner basketball team with Wagner himself standing at the far right. When Wagner retired from baseball in 1917, after a very short and unsatisfying fling at managing, Wagner and his wife settled in his home town of Carnegie, Pennsylvania, and for a while he took on the dual job of basketball and baseball coach at Carnegie Tech.

Bobby Wallace (1874-1960)

Bobby Wallace was the first American League shortstop inducted into the Hall of Fame. Although he couldn't rival Honus Wagner as a hitter, it was fashionable at the time to call him the American League's counterpart at short.

Roderick John Wallace was born of Scotch descent on November 4, 1874, in Pittsburgh, Pennsylvania. The family moved to Millvale, Pennsylvania, when Bobby was still quite young, and it was there that he began playing baseball. Games were played on corner lots since the local school prohibited playing on its field because too many windows were being broken.

As he grew, Bobby took a job in his brother-in-law's feed store in Millvale, and he developed great strength in his arms by lifting 100-pound sacks of corn and oats. Wallace only grew to be 5'8" and weighed 170 pounds, but no one ever questioned his strength.

Well known in western Pennsylvania as a pitcher with a good fastball and curve, Bobby was invited in 1893 to pitch for the Wilkinsburg amateur team. Later that season, the Clarion Eagles, an independent club, offered Bobby $25 and transportation expenses to pitch for them against their arch-rival, Franklin. Bobby lost the game, but he so impressed the Franklin team that they asked him to join the club for the 1894 season. They paid him $45 per month plus living expenses, but the club folded in July.

Later that season, Bobby went to Pittsburgh where the National League club was being managed by a rookie pilot, Connie Mack. Wallace told Connie that he was a good pitcher, but Connie dismissed the 19-year-old righthander as too small. Wallace never let Connie forget the mistake throughout their long careers.

A Cleveland scout, John Stovick, who was quite familiar with players from western Pennsylvania, recommended Bobby to Cleveland manager Pat Tebeau. Tebeau signed Wallace to a contract on September 13, 1894. Two days later, he started against the Boston Red Stockings of Hugh Duffy and Tommy McCarthy, and was beaten, 7–2. Wallace allowed 12 hits in the rain-shortened, six-inning game.

Wallace pitched four games and posted a 2–1 record as the 1894 season drew to a close. As a regular member of Tebeau's pitching staff in 1895, he completed 21 of 30 games, worked 222 innings, and compiled a 12–13 record. In 1896 Bobby notched a 10–7 mark for the Spiders, and Cleveland met the great Baltimore Orioles in the Temple Cup Series. The Orioles swept the Series in four games, with Bobby losing one of them.

If Wallace stood out on the pitching mound, it was not so much for his pitching as for his fielding. He once knocked out manager Tebeau, who was playing first base, when he surprised him with a throw. Tebeau had hollered "Throw to second!"

But Bobby, not hearing the call, landed one right in Tebeau's stomach.

Bobby batted .216 and .231 in his two full seasons as a pitcher. When the 1897 season opened, Tebeau calmly told him, "You're on third."

Without any experience, Bobby took over the hot corner. He had a strong arm that was never bothered by soreness. Wallace adjusted well to the position, and he surprised even Tebeau by batting .339 for the season.

It was one of only three seasons in which Bobby topped the .300 mark, and his lifetime average was only .267. But infielders did not have to be exceptional hitters if they were adept in the field, and Bobby certainly was.

At third, Bobby had to be tough to handle the hard-sliding base runners. He had a particularly long-running rivalry with Bobby Clarke of Louisville and Pittsburgh. The rivalry extended to the entire team, and one day the full Cleveland club was hauled into court in Louisville, in their uniforms, charged with inciting to riot.

In 1899 Frank de Haas Robison moved his Cleveland team to St. Louis. Attendance had been poor in Cleveland, and prospects appeared better in a new territory. Tebeau, still the manager, made another maneuver with Wallace on June 6. He moved him to shortstop to replace the aging Ed McKean.

Wallace immediately found a home at short. The position let him take advantage of his great mobility and show off his strong throwing arm. Bobby invented the scoop-and-toss play needed to nail fast runners on slow-hit balls. He went on to tie a major league record for most seasons spent at shortstop.

Bobby hit .302 in that first year in St. Louis, and by 1900 he had lifted his salary to the National League maximum of $2400. In 1902 the St. Louis Browns offered Wallace a sensational contract to jump across town into the new American League. It called for a $6500 advance and a five-year, $32,500 contract with a provision stating that he could not be traded without his consent. Wallace gave Robison the opportunity to match the offer. When Robison called it absurd, Wallace joined the American League as one of its highest-salaried players.

St. Louis's National League fans would go out to see the Browns play and shout "Bobby, come home!" But it was to no avail. As Honus Wagner emerged as the best shortstop in the National League, Wallace established his fame in the American League. Although the Browns seldom challenged for the pennant, Bobby always made sure that the team was not ignored.

In 1908 his game-saving play on the next-to-last day of the season cost the Cleveland Naps a pennant. It was just a typical play for Bobby, but he chose a good time to make it.

In 1910 Ty Cobb and Napoleon Lajoie battled down to the final day for the league's batting championship and the Chalmers automobile that went with it. Lajoie, by far the more popular among players, was given an advantage when Browns manager Jack O'Connor ordered third baseman Red Corriden to play deep and permit Lajoie to bunt for hits. Nevertheless, Cobb wound up the winner, but the manuever embarrassed the Browns' management enough to fire O'Connor after the season.

The job was offered to Wallace, who accepted it reluctantly. Bobby was not a particularly good manager, nor did he have much talent available. The Browns finished last in 1911, and the club was also mired in last place again in 1912 when Wallace was happily relieved on June 1.

In 1913 a broken hand cost Wallace his regular job for the first time. New manager Branch Rickey, who was busily signing college players, inserted the University of Michigan's John Lavan at short.

Wallace attempted to recapture the job in 1914, but he was badly burned in an accident and played only 26 games all year. Bobby started the 1915 season with the Browns, but he left on June 1 to try his hand as an American League umpire.

Working with Billy Evans, Bobby found umpiring not to his liking. He stuck it out through August 1, 1916. Wallace then returned to the Browns to play 14 games, mostly as a defensive replacement for Lavan.

In 1917 Wallace was given another opportunity to manage, with Wichita of the Western League. But he lost the job in June and returned to St. Louis, this time to play for the Cardinals. He was with the Cardinals again in 1918, finishing his major league career after 25 seasons.

Bobby managed Muskogee of the Southwestern League in 1921, and he scouted for the Chicago Cubs in 1924. Two years later, the Cincinnati Reds made him a coach under Jack Hendricks, and in 1927 he was shifted to scouting duties.

Bobby remained on the Reds' payroll as a scout for 34 years. The only interruption occurred late in September 1937: Charlie Dressen was fired as manager and Bobby was hired to finish out the season. But the players had given up by the time Wallace assumed the reins, and the club captured only 5 of 25 games under his direction.

Residing in Redondo Beach, California, Bobby devoted his free time to billiards and golf. Long after he was able to scout actively, Wallace remained on the Reds' scouting staff with the title chief of scouts. In 1953 Bobby Wallace was elected to the Hall of Fame.

Bobby died in Torrance, California, on November 3, 1960, one day before his eighty-sixth birthday.

RODERICK JOHN WALLACE

Cleveland (N.L.) 1894–1898
St. Louis (N.L.) 1899–1901, 1917–1918
St. Louis (A.L.) 1902–1916

G	AB	R	H	2B	3B	HR	RBI	Avg.
2369	8629	1056	2308	395	149	36	1121	.267

Bobby Wallace, star infielder for the St. Louis Browns, was one of the American League's highest paid players in 1905, earning $8500. He was one of the greatest fielding shortstops ever to play the game.

Ed Walsh (1881-1959)

One of the early spitball pitchers, Ed Walsh was also one of the most successful. Much of his success can be attributed to hard work; in fact, in one season he hurled a record 464 innings.

Edward Augustin Walsh was born in Plains, Pennsylvania, on May 14, 1881. As a young man he worked in the local coal mines and pitched for the company team. Walsh was strictly a fastball pitcher in those days. In 1902, after a brief period at the University of Pennsylvania, Ed signed with the Wilkes-Barre club of the Pennsylvania State League.

When a miners' strike riddled the economy of Wilkes-Barre and took the majority of the fans away from the game, the league folded. Walsh's catcher, Frank Burke, tipped off C. J. Danaher, a stockholder in the Meriden club of the Connecticut League, about Ed. Danaher then wired an offer of $125 per month to the Walsh home in Plains. It was more money than the handsome young Irishman had ever seen, but he demanded $150 and got it. Off he went to Meriden.

Ed finished out the 1902 season with a 15-5 record in 21 games for Meriden, and he returned the following year to post an 11-10 mark in 23 games. A few clubs scouted him, but no offers came until late in July when Newark of the Eastern League purchased him. There, he concluded the 1903 season with a 9-5 record and an impressive strikeout-walk ratio of 77-28. His fine showing led the Chicago White Sox to draft him.

During spring training with the White Sox in 1904, Ed learned to throw the spitball from his roommate, Elmer Stricklett. But Walsh did not attempt to throw the pitch in a regular season game until he felt he had mastered it—it would be another two years.

In his rookie season, 1904, Walsh was merely another face on the White Sox pitching staff. He received little opportunity to work and finished with a 6-3 record. Early in the season, Fielder Jones replaced Jim Callahan as manager, and the White Sox finished third.

Ed did not pitch much more in 1905, posting an 8-3 record, but he continued to improve his skills and developed an outstanding pickoff move for a righthanded pitcher. Walsh had some trouble in the field, but two years later he set major league records for chances handled and assists by a pitcher in a single season.

On September 26, 1905, Ed had his first opportunity to demonstrate his rubber arm. He pitched and won both ends of a doubleheader in Boston, 10-5 and 3-1. It was the first of two such performances during his career.

By 1906, Ed was ready to turn his spitball loose. It was a good one, breaking sharply down to hitters. Ed was a big reason that the White Sox, those "Hitless Wonders of

1906," were able to edge the New York Highlanders for their first American League pennant. Walsh posted a 17-13 record, including a league-leading 10 shutouts. The White Sox batted only .230 for the season with six home runs, but their pitching and fielding kept them in the race. They even managed to beat the Cubs in the World Series. Walsh won the third game with a 12-strikeout, two-hit shutout, 3-0, and stopped the Cubs in the fifth game, 8-6, with relief help.

Big Ed did not really reach his peak until 1907 even though he never pitched for another pennant winner in a career that lasted through 1917. Walsh was now the leader of the White Sox pitching staff, and he had replaced New York's Jack Chesbro as the best spitballer in the league. Ed kept tablets made from the bark of slippery elm in his mouth, mixing them with chewing gum to provide the substance with which he moistened the baseball. He would hold his glove in front of his face when he loaded up the ball, sometimes spitting on it, sometimes not. Only the Philadelphia Athletics—probably the A's second-base star Eddie Collins—seemed to notice that Ed's cap moved slightly when he actually spit. The Athletics were the only team that consistently gave Walsh trouble.

In 1907 Ed worked 419 innings in a league-leading 56 games for a 24-18 record. He struck out 207 and walked only 85. Chicago fans took particular delight in his infrequent relief appearances, for Ed would saunter in from the bullpen with a cocky, confident walk that really excited the crowd. He became a great favorite of Chicago fans.

Off the field, Eddie was a flashy dresser and a dapper gentleman, always ready to burst into song. He would grab some teammates and serenade hotel guests long into the night when the White Sox were on the road.

The 1908 season was one of the most memorable of Walsh's career. He appeared in 66 of his team's 156 games that season, setting a modern major league record of 464 innings pitched. With a 40-15 record, he fell only one victory short of Chesbro's all-time record. Ed struck out 269 batters and walked only 56, while leading the league with a dozen shutouts.

The 1908 season saw a great four-team pennant race, with Detroit, Cleveland, St. Louis, and Chicago all battling down the stretch. In September, Ed worked seven times in the final nine games of the season, winning four of five decisions—

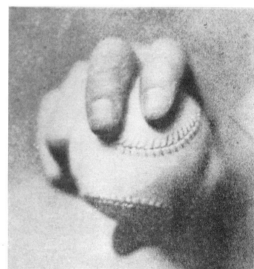

(Above) A collage of Ed Walsh, Chicago White Sox' successful spitball hurler. In the center, the camera captures Walsh from many angles as he works his deceptive spitball. (At right) The closeups show how he gripped the ball. As held in the picture at near right, the ball would break "out"—toward the batter's right. The ball at far right would break straight down.

including a double-header sweep of the Red Sox on September 29 in which Boston scored only one run and collected only one walk. Ed's only defeat in that stretch was a 1–0 setback to Cleveland when Addie Joss pitched a perfect game. The next day, Walsh came into the game in a relief assignment with the bases loaded and struck out Napoleon Lajoie on a called third strike. Walsh rated that his finest moment.

The Tigers won the pennant in their final game of the season, and Chicago finished third. The Sox had hit only three home runs during the entire season, one of them by Walsh himself.

Charles Comiskey, never noted for his generosity, was so moved by Ed's season that he gave him a $3500 bonus, doubling his current salary. That was the peak of Walsh's earnings in baseball.

In 1907 and 1908, Ed had pitched 883 innings in 122 appearances. In his own words, "This being regarded as a star pitcher is a harder job than being a coal miner!"

When Walsh pitched "only" 230 innings in 1909. some thought that the overwork of the previous two seasons had begun to take its toll on Ed. His record was 15–11, a far cry from the 40–15 of the previous year, but again he led the league with eight shutouts.

In 1910 Walsh led the league with 45 appearances, working 370 innings for an 18–20 record. The White Sox finished sixth that season. Then in 1911 Ed silenced all doubters by working 56 games and 369 innings; he struck out 255 and posted a 27–18 record. Included was the only no-hitter of his career, a 5–0 victory over Boston on August 27.

For a man who always appeared to be in poor health, Ed still pitched an awesome number of innings in 1912 at the age of 31. That season he worked 393 innings in 62 games, both league-leading figures, and again he won 27 games, losing 17.

Overwork finally caught up with Ed in 1913 and his arm went bad. He appeared in only 16 games, worked 98 innings, and compiled an 8–3 record. Never again was he the pitcher who had crammed 168 victories into just seven seasons.

Ed remained with Chicago for three more seasons, seeing only limited action and winning five additional games. As the White Sox were preparing for their 1917 pennant-winning season, Walsh was sent to the Boston Braves, and he ended his American League career with a 195–125

record. He pitched in only four games for George Stallings's Braves, losing his only decision. Ed then remained out of baseball until 1919 when he appeared in four games for the Milwaukee Brewers of the American Association.

In 1920, the year spitballs were banned, Ed managed the Bridgeport club in the Eastern league and took the mound three times for a 1–1 record. His next appearance in baseball came late in 1922 when American League President Ban Johnson got him a job as an umpire to keep the great star, with his magnificent physical presence, active in the league. Ed was assigned to work with the league's top umpire, Billy Evans, but after a few weeks on the job Walsh called it quits.

"It's a strange business," he said. "All jeers and no cheers. You can have it."

Walsh coached for the White Sox from 1923 to 1925, and he served as baseball coach at Notre Dame in 1926. From 1928 to 1930 Ed was back in Chicago, coaching for the White Sox before leaving baseball forever.

Moving with his family to Cheshire, Connecticut, Ed worked for many years at the water plant in Meriden. Two of his sons pursued baseball careers. Bob had a tryout with the Yankees but never made it, and Ed, Jr., spent four seasons with the White Sox (1928–1932, including years when his father coached), and compiled an 11–24 won-lost record. Ed, Jr., died in 1937.

Ed Walsh was elected to the Hall of Fame in 1946, and he was always a welcome guest at Hall of Fame gatherings. His erect posture and youthful approach to life remained with him into the 1950s. Cancer finally claimed Ed Walsh on May 26, 1959, three years after he had settled in Pompano Beach, Florida.

EDWARD AUGUSTIN WALSH

Chicago (A.L.) 1904–1916
Boston (N.L.) 1917

G	IP	W	L	Pct.	H	R	ER	SO	BB	ERA
431	2968	195	126	.607	2335	882	inc.	1731	620	inc.

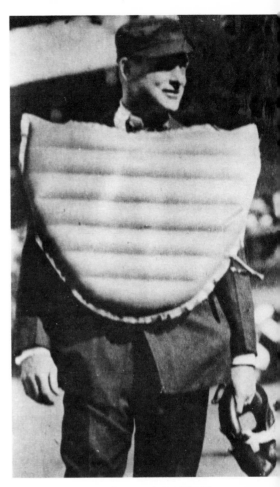

In a new role as umpire, Ed Walsh steps back onto the American League playing fields. But Walsh was to find umpiring "all jeers and no cheers" and to leave after only a few weeks.

Lloyd Waner (b.1906)

Lloyd Waner and his older brother Paul provided the Pittsburgh Pirates with one of baseball's greatest brother acts over a 14-year period.

Lloyd James Waner was born on March 16, 1906, in Harrah, Oklahoma. His brother Paul was three years older. A third brother, the oldest, played amateur ball and became an accountant. There were also two sisters in the family.

All five Waner children attended the one-room Dewey District School. It was a two and one-half mile walk from the Waner farm, and the boys played catch and talked baseball as they took the daily hike. Their parents hoped that all three boys would graduate from college, but Paul left East Central State Teachers' College in Ada, Oklahoma, to play professional ball. Lloyd came within one semester of graduation from the same school, but after making it in the major leagues, he "forgot to finish."

Following in Paul's footsteps, Lloyd signed with the San Francisco Seals of the Pacific Coast League in 1925. Paul, a teammate, led the league with a .401 average that season, but Lloyd could not get started. He played 31 games and hit .250 with one run batted in. Generally, Lloyd was only a late-inning replacement.

Paul went to the Pirates in 1926 and Lloyd returned to San Francisco. But after collecting only four hits in six games, he was cut loose and became a free agent.

Paul, on his way to a .336 rookie season, spoke in his brother's behalf to Pirate owner Barney Dreyfuss, claiming that Lloyd was every bit as good a player as he. Dreyfuss chanced the cost of a railroad ticket to take a personal look at the youngest brother, and he agreed to sign him. Lloyd was assigned to Columbia of the South Atlantic League, where he hit .345 in 121 games.

His performance with Columbia brought Lloyd an invitation to attend spring training with the Pirates in 1927 at Paso Robles, California. Lloyd reported at 5'7" and 145 pounds, causing team physician Dr. William Marks to remark, "He'll never make it through a season with a build like that."

But Lloyd, who never grew much bigger, made it through quite a few seasons. He finally reached 5'8½" and 150 pounds, slightly smaller than Paul.

The new Waner was the sensation of the Pirates' spring camp of 1927. Lloyd was the best hitter there, and he impressed manager Donie Bush to the extent that he was given the leftfield job, replacing the established veteran Clyde Barnhart. Midway into the 1927 season, Bush decided to bench Kiki Cuyler. He moved Lloyd to center, stationed Barnhart in left, and kept Paul in right.

Lloyd played on opening day of 1927. In his first time up, batting second, he beat out a drag bunt for a base hit. Paul

followed with a two-run double and the Waner act was underway. For 14 seasons, Paul and Lloyd remained teammates.

Early in the season, the nicknames "Big Poison" and "Little Poison" were given to the Waner brothers. According to Lloyd, the nicknames had nothing to do with their abilities at bat, although it certainly seemed appropriate to opposing pitchers. Rather, while they were playing at the Polo Grounds one day, a newspaperman with a Brooklyn accent referred to them as "big person and little person." Another writer overheard the accented description, and papers the next day proclaimed them as poison to Giant pitching.

Lloyd had a sensational rookie season. He batted .355 and led the league with 133 runs scored. He collected a rookie record of 223 hits, 198 of which were singles. That set a modern National League record for singles, only four short of Willie Keeler's 1898 record. In all, Lloyd led the National League in singles four times—1927, 1928, 1929, and 1931.

With Paul topping the league with a .380 average, the Waners led the Pirates to the 1927 pennant. It was the only pennant winner either played for. Although the Yankees won four consecutive games in the World Series, the Waners distinguished themselves. Lloyd led the Pirates with a .400 Series average, pounding out six hits in 15 at-bats, and Paul hit .333.

After the Series, the brothers went on the vaudeville stage, earning more money there than they did playing baseball. The pair set attendance records in New York, Pittsburgh, St. Louis, Los Angeles, and San Francisco. After sixteen weeks, Dreyfuss ordered them to report to spring training.

As a leadoff hitter, Lloyd was one of the best in the league. He did not have much power and was not a big run producer, but he had a sharp batting eye, made good contact with the ball, and could hit behind runners and bunt. Lloyd boasts one of the best strikeout records in baseball history, fanning only 173 times in 18 major league seasons. His high for any year was 23 (his rookie year), and in only one other season did he strike out more than 20 times. In 1933 Lloyd struck out eight times in 500 at bats. In 1941 he went 77 consecutive games—his entire season—without a strikeout.

Lloyd was considered the fastest man in the league in getting from home to first. Although he stole only 67 bases in his career (14 of them in 1927), he was superb at racing from first to third on base hits.

Lloyd was a much quieter man than his brother, who was famous for keeping late

Lloyd, left, and Paul Waner, sensational brother act for the Pirates from 1927 to 1941. The Waners paced the Pirates to a pennant in 1927, Lloyd's rookie year. While Paul topped the league with a .380 batting average, Lloyd batted .400 in the World Series.

hours. The younger Waner preferred to retire early. After the two had roomed together for several years, they split up as roommates although they always remained personally close.

Lloyd collected 221 hits and compiled a .335 average in 1928. The following season he pounded out 234 hits for a .353 batting average. That gave him 678 hits in his first three major league seasons. The younger Waner was established as a National League star.

Illness forced Lloyd to miss almost all of the first half of the 1930 season. Returning to action late in June, he batted .362 in 68 games. The league had a combined .303 average that year.

In 1931 the Pirates finished fifth, but Lloyd led the National League with 214 hits and batted .314. His sixth consecutive .300 season occurred in 1932 when he batted .333. In all, Lloyd topped the .300 mark 11 times.

The Pirates made runs for the pennant in 1932, 1933, and 1938, finishing second each time. Waner continued to be a dependable leadoff hitter, but as a team the Pirates always seemed to fall short. After two seasons below the .300 mark (1933–1934), Lloyd bounced back to top .300 each year from 1935 to 1938, including a .330 performance in 1937. Although Paul was picked for four National League All-Star teams, Lloyd was chosen only once but did not get to play.

Lloyd's playing time fell to 72 games in 1940, and he batted only .259. He spent spring training with the Pirates in 1941, but after three regular-season games he was dealt to the Boston Braves for pitcher Nick Strincevich. Lloyd played 19 games for Casey Stengel's Braves, then was traded to Cincinnati on June 12 for pitcher John Hutchings. For the three teams, Lloyd played 77 games without a strikeout while hitting .292.

Released by the Reds on October 8, 1941, Lloyd was signed by the Philadelphia Phillies on December 4. At the age of 36, he played 101 games for the Phils during the player-shortage season of 1942 and batted .261. On March 8, 1943, Lloyd and Al Glossop were traded to the Brooklyn Dodgers for Babe Dahlgren, but Lloyd announced his retirement instead.

With the war continuing to thin rosters, Lloyd had a change of heart in 1944 and rejoined the Dodgers. They released him after 15 games, and his former team, the Pirates, signed him on the following day. He received a hero's welcome on his return to the baseball-hungry town. Used almost exclusively as a pinch-hitter, Lloyd batted .321 in 1944 and .263 in 1945. After the latter season, Lloyd called it a career.

The Pirates retained Lloyd's services as a scout from 1946 to 1949. His only other job in baseball was a scouting assignment for the Orioles in 1955.

In 1950 Lloyd took a job as a field clerk with the city government of Oklahoma City. He remained in this position until 1967, at which time he was forced to retire.

That year "Little Poison" joined his brother in the Hall of Fame. Paul had been elected in 1952 and had died in 1965. George and Harry Wright are the only other brothers enshrined in Cooperstown.

LLOYD JAMES WANER

Pittsburgh 1927–1941, 1944–1945
Boston (N.L.) 1941
Cincinnati 1941
Philadelphia (N.L.) 1942
Brooklyn 1944

G	AB	R	H	2B	3B	HR	RBI	Avg.
1993	7772	1201	2459	281	118	28	598	.316

Paul Waner (1903-1965)

Paul Waner was the older of two Waner brothers who starred for the Pittsburgh Pirates and went on to reach the Hall of Fame. The fraction of an inch difference between Paul and Lloyd Waner was enough to earn Paul the nickname "Big Poison," while Lloyd (three years younger) became "Little Poison."

Paul Glee Waner was born on April 16, 1903, in Harrah, Oklahoma, where his father was a prosperous farmer. His first experience in baseball was as a pitcher on local independent teams. The lefthander reportedly won 19 consecutive games while spending days off the mound as an outfielder or first baseman.

As a pitcher for East Central State Teachers' College in Ada, Oklahoma, Paul caught the eye of Dick Williams, a scout for the highly regarded San Francisco Seals of the Pacific Coast League. Williams watched Waner pitch 10 games, returned to the coast, and offered Paul a contract through the mail.

Paul's father, however, wanted his son to complete college. Paul himself had given thought to a career in law. But the offer was flattering and intriguing, and Paul replied that he wanted $500 per month. To his father he promised that if he did not make good, he would return to school.

The Seals approved the $500, and Paul took the train to San Francisco. He was just turning 20.

On the first day of spring training, Paul was pitching in an intrasquad game when something popped in his arm. The arm remained sore for several days, and Paul figured that his pitching career was over before it had begun. To pass the time until his anticipated release, he had three major leaguers (who were working out with the Seals before reporting South for their own training periods) hit fly balls to him in the outfield. The trio—Willie Kamm, Lew Fonseca, and Jimmy O'Connell—suggested that Paul take his turn in the batting cage. When Waner began to belt hard line drives, manager Jack Miller decided to find a place in the San Francisco outfield for Paul.

In his rookie season as a professional, Paul hit .369 in 112 games. He determined to stick with baseball and leave college to little brother Lloyd. But two years later Lloyd followed Paul to San Francisco, and eventually to Pittsburgh.

In 1924 Paul batted .365 for the Seals. In the following season, Paul increased his average to a league-leading .401, which included 280 hits in the expanded 174-game season. Waner hit 75 doubles and scored 167 runs. At the end of the year, the Pirates bought him and shortstop Hal Rhyne from San Francisco for a reported $100,000 and three players.

In his rookie National League season, 1926, Paul batted .336 with a league-leading 22 triples for manager Bill McKechnie. Waner's tiny frame (his top weight was 153) always limited his home run production, but he became a pesky line-drive hitter who reached the 200-hit mark eight times, equaling Willie Keeler's all-time National League record. On August 26 of that season, Paul collected six hits in six times at bat, a feat never before performed by a rookie.

Following the Pirates' third-place finish in 1926, Paul urged the club to buy his brother Lloyd. The two joined forces in the Pittsburgh outfield in 1927, lasting as a combination until 1940. Paul generally played right field and batted second or third, while Lloyd was the center fielder and leadoff man.

In 1927, under manager Donie Bush, the Pirates won the National League pennant by one and one-half games over the Cardinals. Paul, playing only his second season in the league, won the Most Valuable Player award and finished 19 points ahead of Rogers Hornsby with a .380 batting average to top the league. He was also the league's title holder in triples with 17, runs batted in with 131, and hits with 237 while playing every game of the schedule.

The Yankees of 1927 were a legendary team, and they easily swept the Pirates in four games in the World Series, although Paul batted .333 and Lloyd .400. It was the only World Series in which the brothers ever appeared.

Paul batted .370 in 1928, finishing second to Hornsby, but he led the league with 50 doubles and 142 runs scored. Three times in his career, Paul belted 50 or more doubles, and his career total of 603 placed him fifth on the all-time list at the time of his retirement.

The 1929 season saw Paul record 100 runs batted in and a career high of 15 home runs, along with 200 hits and a .336 batting average. Paul seemed to be at his best with two strikes on him. Normally, the pitcher is considered to have an edge in such a situation, but Paul's marvelous bat control permitted him to foul off pitch after pitch while he waited for the one he wanted. Paul never struck out more than 34 times in any season. His 376 career strikeouts meant that he fanned on the average of once every 25 times at bat.

In 1930, a year in which National League players hit a collective .303, Paul batted .368 with 217 hits. He reached 62 doubles in 1932, and in 1933, when the Pirates had their second successive second-place finish, Paul batted .309, topping the .300 mark for the eighth consecutive season.

Paul Waner, big brother of the famous Waner team. He won the 1927 MVP award and captured three batting titles. He reached the 200 hit mark eight times. After retiring from play, he became an excellent batting instructor.

"Big Poison" enjoyed his own brand of late-night poison. Noted as a night person, Paul drank often; some felt the liquor diminished his abilities. But one year, when manager Pie Traynor limited him to beer, Paul's average dropped to .240, and Pie started to buy him drinks. His average climbed and no one ever halted his social habits again.

Traynor became player-manager of the Pirates in 1934. Although the club fell to fifth, Paul captured his second batting crown that year, hitting .362 and leading the league in runs (122) and hits (217). After batting .321 in 1935, he won his third and last batting title in 1936 with a .373 average; of his 218 hits that season only five were home runs.

Paul remained with the Pirates through the 1940 season. Only in 1938 did the team come close to winning another pennant, but a late-season home run by the Cubs' Gabby Hartnett buried the Pirate chances. Paul batted only .290 in 89 games for the 1940 Pirates and was released on December 10. A month and a half later, the Brooklyn Dodgers signed him. But Paul played in only 11 games for Brooklyn in 1941, drawing his release on May 11. On May 24, the Boston Braves signed him, and he concluded the season with a combined .258 average.

Under ordinary conditions, that might have signaled the end of Paul's career. But World War II was thinning out big league rosters and the 39-year-old Waner was asked to stay on with the Braves, then managed by Casey Stengel. Paul was seeking 3000 career hits. That, not the money, was his incentive for staying. His top salary in the major leagues was $18,500.

On June 19, 1942, Paul cracked a clean single for his 3000th career hit. It came against his old teammates, the Pirates, and made him only the seventh player in baseball history to have accomplished the feat.

Paul hit .258 in 1942, was again released after the season, and again signed by Brooklyn. He played for the Dodgers in 1943 and 1944, then was released for the fourth time.

But Paul was not through yet. The Yankees signed him late in September 1944. He pinch-hit seven times and collected one single and one RBI. That marked his final major league hit. The following year, although training with the Yankees, Paul was released again on May 3 after drawing a walk in his only plate appearance. His career average was .333 and he had collected 3152 hits.

After working briefly for the U.S.O. in 1945, Paul was named manager of the Miami team in the Florida International League in 1946. As a first baseman and pinch-hitter there, he batted .325. But Paul left the game after that and moved to Sarasota, Florida. There he improved his golf game, went through two divorces, and learned of his election to the Hall of Fame in 1952.

Recognized as an expert on hitting, Paul was hired by the Milwaukee Braves as a batting instructor in 1957. The Braves, bound for a World Championship, found him a capable instructor. He worked with Hank Aaron, Eddie Mathews, Del Crandall, Billy Bruton, and others.

Paul authored a booklet on hitting that many players read. It was especially popular in the early 1960s, when several players attributed their new-found batting success to Waner's booklet. Basically, his theory was to face the pitcher with both eyes and to cut down on the ball.

Paul served as a hitting instructor for the Cardinals in 1958 and 1959, and also for the Phillies from 1960 until he died on August 29, 1965, in Sarasota at the age of 62.

PAUL GLEE WANER

Pittsburgh 1926–1940
Brooklyn 1941, 1943–1944
Boston (N.L.) 1941–1942
New York (A.L.) 1944–1945

G	AB	R	H	2B	3B	HR	RBI	Avg.
2549	9459	1626	3152	603	190	112	1309	.333

George Weiss (1894-1972)

When Jacob Ruppert decided that the New York Yankees should have a farm system, he called on George Weiss to direct it. Weiss went on to become one of the most successful baseball executives the game has ever known.

George Martin Weiss was born on June 23, 1894, in New Haven, Connecticut. He was the son of middle-class German grocers, although he preferred to think of his father as a "fancy grocer." Weiss did not have an athletic build but was short and plump, and in personality he was quiet and shy.

Unable to participate in his favorite spectator sport, baseball, George became manager of his high school team in New Haven during his senior year, 1912. The team won the state championship, and Weiss received a letter. Among the team's stars were third baseman Joe Dugan and future Harvard football greats Eddie Mahan and Charley Brickley.

In 1914, while attending Yale University, Weiss organized a semipro team known as the New Haven Colonials. To compete for an audience with the New Haven professional minor league club, Weiss had the club play Sunday baseball, which the professionals were forbidden to do by a local ordinance. Weiss was director, secretary, and manager of his team, and he promoted such stunts as the importation of a Chinese team and a "Bloomer Girls" team. George would lure major league stars away from their teams on Sundays, attracting such men as Ty Cobb to play for the Colonials. Cobb insisted on $350 for his first appearance, but Weiss handed him $800. Thereafter, he had Cobb's services whenever the Tigers had an off-day in either Boston or New York.

Whenever possible, Weiss would arrange for his club to play major league clubs in exhibitions. In April 1915, his team faced the Yankees at the Polo Grounds. Three days after Boston won the 1916 World Series, Weiss' team played the Red Sox, with Babe Ruth at first base for the Sox.

In 1919 the owners of the New Haven professional team gave up competing with Weiss and sold him the Eastern League club for $5000. George borrowed the money and made his first entry into professional ball as the head of the Eastern League franchise.

A new stadium was built in New Haven in 1920, and it was named Weiss Stadium. By then George was in the second of 10 seasons at the helm his team, which finished out of the first division only once. Three of his clubs—the 1920, 1922, and 1928 entries—won pennants.

On December 9, 1923, Weiss was almost killed in a train wreck that claimed the life

of Wild Bill Donovan, his drawing-room companion and manager of New Haven. They were on route to the annual baseball meeting in Chicago at the time when the train was wrecked near Erie, Pennsylvania.

In October 1928, Jack Dunn, owner of the International League's Baltimore Orioles, died in a fall from a horse. Shortly thereafter, Weiss was invited to take control of this prestigious minor league club as vice president and general manager, but he continued to retain ownership of the New Haven club. In three seasons with the Orioles, during which the team never won fewer than 90 games, Weiss sold eight players to the majors. Vince Barton was sold to the Cubs for the sensational sum of $40,000; the eight players together brought the Orioles $242,000. The player sales managed to keep the team running during the Depression.

Weiss instituted "ladies days" in Baltimore, which he promoted to a limited degree. His feeling then, and always, was that winning baseball would draw fans on its own.

That was the kind of thinking that appealed to Jake Ruppert, owner of the Yankees. Ruppert telephoned Weiss early in 1932 and offered him the position of farm director. The Cardinals' farm system had proved successful, and Ruppert was eager to develop one for the Yankees. Ed Barrow, who would be Weiss' immediate boss, was not particularly enthusiastic about the idea and thought that Weiss would undermine his control. Despite the coolness between them, the two respected each other's abilities, and the Yankee farm system became one of the most successful in baseball history.

At one point, the system had 21 teams, with Newark, New Jersey, at the top of the ladder. Weiss had responsibilities on the major league level, but the establishment of a strong Newark team was his first priority.

In 1936 Weiss was instrumental in the purchase of Joe DiMaggio from San Francisco after many thought an injury had made Joe a poor risk. Weiss convinced Ruppert to send five Newark players and $25,000 to the Pacific Coast League club for DiMaggio.

With Joe McCarthy assuming the managerial reins in 1931, the Yankees captured pennants in 1932, 1936, 1937, 1938, 1939, 1941, 1942, and 1943. In 1946 with McCarthy in poor health, Weiss first suggested Casey Stengel as his successor, but Bucky Harris eventually got the job.

Following the Yankee World Series victory in 1947, Larry MacPhail, a part-owner of the team, fired Weiss in a celebrated battle during the Series party. The next day, Dan Topping and Del Webb bought out MacPhail and rehired Weiss with the new title of general manager.

After the Yankees finished third in 1948, Bucky Harris was dismissed. Weiss engineered the arrangement to bring Stengel to town as his replacement. The move was widely criticized since Stengel had met with little managerial success in the past and had acquired a reputation as a clown. But the Stengel-Weiss team quickly silenced the critics by capturing an unprecedented five consecutive World Championships during Casey's first five seasons as manager (1949–1953). The team then won 103 games while finishing second in 1954, took four more pennants from 1955 to 1958, came in third in 1959, and captured the flag again in 1960.

Weiss was a master dealer in those days, picking up many veteran players and getting great service from them. The players said that putting on the Yankee uniform added new life to their careers. The farm system continued to flourish, with Yogi Berra, Whitey Ford, and Mickey Mantle coming up through the ranks. In 1954 Weiss engineered a 17-player trade with Baltimore that brought Bob Turley and Don Larsen to the Yankees.

Weiss was the only man to win four Executive of the Year Awards given by *The Sporting News.* He received the award in 1950, 1951, 1952, and 1960.

Weiss was 66 years old and had been in professional baseball for 42 seasons when the Stengel-Weiss era ended for the Yankees. First, Casey was fired. Two weeks later, on November 3, 1960, Weiss resigned to accept an advisory position with the club at half-pay. He refused to acknowledge that he had been "kicked upstairs," but it was clear that his power was gone. The Yankees installed Ralph Houk as manager and Roy Hamey as general manager. The club promptly won three more pennants in their first three years.

Weiss did not remain out of New York baseball for long. In March 1961, he was hired as the first president of the New York Mets, an expansion team scheduled to begin play in 1962.

In October 1961, Weiss hired Stengel to manage the Mets. The reunited duo, while unsuccessful in winning games, established a prosperous franchise that set a National League attendance record in New York with the opening of Shea Stadium in 1964.

Weiss, considered shy, sensitive, sentimental, and proud, exercised a stock option with the Mets in 1965 that gave him a voting interest in the club. Although he had become a vice president with the Yankees before leaving them, he had never achieved the executive security and status which he enjoyed with the Mets.

On November 14, 1966, Weiss retired from active duty with the Mets, one year after a broken hip had put Stengel on the sidelines for good. Weiss returned to his Greenwich, Connecticut home, enjoyed an occasional golf game, spent more time with his wife Hazel, and followed the horses. He stayed out of the public eye, living up to his reputation as "Lonesome George," a nickname he greatly disliked.

In 1971 George Weiss was named to the Baseball Hall of Fame by the Committee on Veterans. He died on August 13, 1972, in a nursing home in Greenwich at the age of 78.

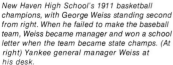

New Haven High School's 1911 basketball champions, with George Weiss standing second from right. When he failed to make the baseball team, Weiss became manager and won a school letter when the team became state champs. (At right) Yankee general manager Weiss at his desk.

Mickey Welch (1859-1941)

"Smiling Mickey" Welch was one of the great pitchers of the nineteenth century, pouring 308 victories into only 13 National League seasons.

Michael Francis Welch was born on July 4, 1859, in Brooklyn, New York, seventeen years before the birth of the National League. Baseball was virtually unknown as a professional sport in America during Mickey's childhood, but it was growing in popularity as a street game. Mickey played the sport on the streets of Brooklyn until 1877 when he traveled up the Hudson River to Poughkeepsie to join a professional team known as the Volunteers. His salary was $45 per month.

In 1878 Welch pitched for Auburn in the National Association, a minor league, and in 1879 he hurled for Holyoke in the same league. No records exist of Mickey's performances in those three seasons, in which the mound was only 45 feet from home, and all pitching was done under-handed.

In 1880 Mickey joined the Troy Haymakers of the National League to begin his major league career. There he teamed with Tim Keefe, another righthander, and the pair handled the bulk of the pitching in the 83-game schedule. Welch worked 65 of the 83 games, completed all 64 starts, and posted a 34–30 record for 574 innings pitched—a sensational total even for those days. Baseball was not a free-swinging game in that era, and despite the high total of innings, Mickey struck out only 115 batters while walking 80.

At 5'7" and 140 pounds, Mickey was not overpowering, but he had a good curveball, a change of pace, and a screwball that predated those of Christy Mathewson and Carl Hubbell. Possibly he was the originator of the pitch.

The pitching distance was moved back to 50 feet in 1881, then to 60'6" (its present distance) in 1894. Welch never pitched from the latter distance.

In 1881 the Troy team finished fifth in the National League with a 39–45 record. Mickey's contribution to the total was a 21–18 mark, with Keefe winning the 18 other games and losing 27. Mickey trimmed his innings-pitched total that season to 362, but he did complete all of his 40 starts, giving him 104 consecutive complete games. The streak ended at 105 following his first appearance in 1882.

The 1882 season was another disappointing one for Troy, as the Haymakers finished seventh in the eight-team league with a 35–48 record. Welch compiled a 14–16 record with five shutouts—tops in the league—and 282 innings pitched.

Then in 1883, John B. Day, owner of the original New York Mets of the American Association, purchased the Troy club and moved the franchise, with most of the players, into New York to share the Polo

Grounds with the Mets. This was the original Polo Grounds, located at Fifth Avenue and 110th Street at the northern boundary of Central Park. They were, in fact, grounds on which polo was played, and when the Mets folded and the Giants moved uptown, the name followed the club into the new park.

Welch received the honor of pitching the first game in the Polo Grounds for the New York team. (They were called the Maroons in those days. Two years later, manager Jim Mutrie proclaimed, "My big fellows, my giants!" after a victory, and the name stuck.) The premier season for the soon-to-be "Giants" resulted in a sixth-place finish. Welch, who posted a 25–23 record, and John Montgomery Ward handled most of the remaining pitching. Mickey also played 38 games in the outfield and batted .234, hitting 3 of the Giants' 25 home runs.

As the 1884 season approached, Mickey decided that he was being overworked. The streak of 105 complete games, and the feat of having pitched two consecutive complete-game victories against Cleveland in 1881, had earned him the reputation of a rubber-armed pitcher with no limit. Welch demanded that a clause be written into his contract prohibiting the manager from pitching him more than every other day. The clause remained in Mickey's contract until his retirement.

The Giants got their money's worth from Welch that season. Mickey started 65 games, completed 62, and compiled a 39–21 record. By now he had found the knack of striking men out, as demonstrated by his 349 whiffs in 1884, but he also led the league with 141 walks. On August 28 that season, Mickey struck out the first nine Cleveland batters he faced; no pitcher since has fanned more than the first six.

In the mid-1880s, Welch was nicknamed "Smiling Mickey" as a result of a crooked smile characterized in *Puck* and the *New York Journal* by cartoonist R.V. Munkitrict. The nickname suited his easygoing nature, one which never became upset if a teammate committed an error.

When asked the secret of his pitching success, Mickey attributed it to drinking beer. He prepared a little poem for sportswriters covering the Giants that read:

> Pure elixer of malt and hops
> Beats all the drugs and all the drops.

In 1885 the Giants finished second to Cap Anson's Chicago entry, and Mickey enjoyed his finest season. He won 44 games, lost only 11, started and completed 55 games, struck out 256 batters, and worked 496 innings. Although earned run averages were not computed at the time, box scores indicate that his ERA for the

"Smiling Mickey" Welch, one of the first to hurl a screwball and one of 14 pitchers to win 300 games. He credited his success to beer drinking, rhapsodizing: "Pure elixir of malt and hops, Beats all the drugs and all the drops."

season probably would have been under 1.70. During the season, Mickey ran off a streak of 17 consecutive victories.

The Giants finished third in 1886 as Welch won 33 and lost 22, leading the league in walks for the third straight season. In 1887 Tim Keefe, reunited with his old pitching partner, passed Mickey as the ace of the staff. Welch had a 22–15 record for the season.

The Giants finished first in 1888, with Welch winning 26 games and losing 19. A post-season playoff was arranged between the Giants and the St. Louis Browns, Charles Comiskey's American Association champions. The Giants captured what amounted to a World Series, taking 6 of the 10 games. Welch split two decisions in the competition.

The following year the Giants repeated their pennant finish, with Welch posting a 27–12 record. Facing Brooklyn in the post-season playoff, Welch lost his only decision, but the Giants repeated as champions.

Tim Keefe jumped to the Players' League in 1890, joining many other stars in a show of unity against the club owners. But Welch remained with the Giants, becoming the team's senior member. The Giants, however, finished sixth, and Welch compiled only a 17–13 record. In 1891 Mickey started only 15 games and was 6–9. After one game in 1892, he was sent to Troy, then a Giant farm team in the Eastern League. Mickey then concluded his active pitching career at the age of 33 with a 16–14 record.

In 12 seasons, Mickey won 308 games (some publications list his total as 309 or 311). He is one of only 14 pitchers in baseball history to have won 300 or more games.

Following his retirement from baseball, Mickey, his wife, and daughter moved to Holyoke, Massachusetts, where he served for many years as a steward in the Elks Club. In 1912 he returned to New York and was hired by the Giants as a watcher at the bleacher entrance of the Polo Grounds, where he was popular with the older fans.

Asked to pick his all-time team by a reporter in 1941, shortly before his death, Welch named only Frankie Frisch (second base) and Carl Hubbell (pitcher) among modern players. The other players mentioned were all of his era, headed by the catcher from his days with Troy, Buck Ewing. Not even Honus Wagner, in Welch's opinion, was as good a shortstop as Ed Williamson, a .267 hitter between 1878 and 1890.

While visiting a grandson in Nashua, New Hampshire, Mickey became ill. He died on July 30, 1941 at nearby Concord, New Hampshire.

Welch had been generally forgotten by the baseball world when the Committee on Veterans decided to put him into the Hall of Fame with the other 300-game winners in 1973.

MICHAEL FRANCIS WELCH

Troy (N.L.) 1880–1882
New York (N.L.) 1883–1892

G	IP	W	L	Pct.	H	R	ER	SO	BB	ERA
565	4784	308	209	.594	4648	2508	inc.	1841	1305	inc.

Zach Wheat (1888-1972)

Zack Wheat was the first great star of the Brooklyn Dodgers, and he spent 18 years in left field as one of the most popular players Brooklyn ever knew.

Of English and Irish descent, and also part Cherokee Indian, Zachariah Davis Wheat was born on May 23, 1888, in Hamilton, Missouri. He always claimed that his name was Zachary, but the birth records show otherwise. His parents had recently moved from Kentucky to Missouri, where his father became a cattle dealer.

A brother, McKinley ("Mack") Davis Wheat, five years younger than Zack, spent seven seasons in the major leagues. The first five were as a teammate of Zack's in Brooklyn, and the 1920 and 1921 seasons were spent with the Phillies. Mack was a catcher and a .204 lifetime hitter.

When his father died in 1905, Zack took a job as a semipro baseball player in Enterprise, Kansas, sending money home to his widowed mother. In 1907 he signed with Fort Worth of the Texas League and appeared in six games near the close of the season. The following year, he played for Shreveport of the Texas League, where manager Dale Gear helped him considerably as a hitter.

Zack stood 5'10" and weighed 170 pounds. While a lefthanded batter with fair power for his day, Zack was noted primarily as a line-drive hitter. In addition to his good speed in going from home to first, he was considered exceptionally quick racing from first to third on base hits. As an outfielder, Zack possessed good range, fine judgment, and an accurate throwing arm. He was, in short, an all-round professional baseball player.

Zack hit .268 at Shreveport and advanced to Mobile of the Southern Association in 1909. At the time, the Brooklyn Superbas, playing in Washington Park, were an unimpressive club still looking for their first pennant. Unable to come up with any promising young talent, owner Charles Ebbets hired former minor league umpire Larry Sutton as a scout and told him, "Go get me some players!"

Traveling in the South, Sutton received a tip from George Solomon, a New York traveling salesman stationed in Mobile. Solomon had watched Wheat play at Mobile and thought he could make the grade in the majors. Sutton went to see him play, wired a recommendation to Ebbets, and Brooklyn purchased him at the close of the Southern Association season for $1200.

Wheat reported to Brooklyn after a .246 showing with Mobile. Hearing this, Ebbets was suddenly skeptical about the purchase. But Wheat immediately moved into leftfield, replacing Wally Clement. In the final 26 games of the 1909 season, Zack batted .304 with 31 hits. He did not leave his outfield post until 1927.

Wheat was a quiet, gentlemanly man who was devoted to his family and always on his best behavior. He was never ejected by an umpire in his entire career. A pleasant man to deal with (even during salary negotiations with Ebbets), Wheat actually loaned Ebbets money on at least two occasions to help bail his boss out of financial difficulties.

In his first full season with Brooklyn, Wheat batted .284 with 36 doubles, the third highest figure in the league. The fans took a quick liking to Zack, and he would banter back and forth with the left field bleacher patrons between innings. Even advertisers were quick to recognize his popularity; one company's billboard read: "Zack Wheat caught 400 flies last season—Tanglewood Fly Paper caught 10 million."

The Superbas finished sixth in 1910, seventh in 1911 and 1912, and sixth again in 1913. Obviously, Wheat could not carry the team himself, but for those four years he batted .284, .287, .305, and .301. Zack topped the .300 mark 14 times in all during his career.

Brooklyn's fortunes began to turn in 1914 when Wilbert Robinson was named manager. "Uncle Robby," the old Oriole star, led the team to a fifth-place finish in his maiden season, as Zack batter .319 and led the league's outfielders in putouts. He tied for third in the National League batting race, as the Brooklyn club, now known as the "Robins," topped the league in hitting.

The Federal League was making mass raids on American and National League stars between 1914 and 1915, but Ebbets kept Wheat and other Robins loyal. Ebbets personally traveled to Wheat's Missouri farm to sign Zack to a contract and keep him from jumping.

In 1915 Zack's batting average fell to .258. He collected only 32 extra-base hits for the season. But Robinson brought the team up to third place, only 10 games out of first, and Zack was a fine contributor on the bases and in the field.

Brooklyn finally captured the pennant in 1916. The club compiled a 94–60 record, finishing two and one-half games ahead of defending champion Philadelphia. The team again led the league in hitting, while the club's pitching staff captured the ERA title. Wheat batted .312, fifth in the league, and rolled off a 29-game hitting streak late in the year, an all-time Dodger record. The streak was finally stopped late in September by Cincinnati's Fred Toney.

Brooklyn met the Red Sox in the World Series. Wheat, batting cleanup as usual,

(Above) Brooklyn star Zach Wheat gets tagged
out by his brother Mack, the Phillies catcher.
(Below) Zach, who batted over .300 14 times in
his career, swings with a slashing cut, but hits a
low foul back toward catcher James Archer.

Zach Wheat streaks back for a hard line drive. One advertiser recognized Wheat's fielding ability with the slogan: "Zach Wheat caught 1400 flies last season—Tanglewood Fly Paper caught 10 million."

hit .211 in the five-game Series loss. Zack went 0–5 in the 14-inning, 2–1 loss to Babe Ruth in the second game.

Following the 1916 season, Zack became a serious holdout for the first time. He kept returning unsigned contracts to Ebbets from his farm. Even a personal visit by the Brooklyn president failed to result in agreement with the terms. With spring training already begun, Wheat finally received a telegram, signed by C.H. Ebbets, telling him to report at once.

Ebbets was surprised and happy to see his star. But when Wheat produced the telegram, Ebbets claimed to know nothing about it. After a brief shouting match, the two adjourned to a private room from which they emerged in agreement over terms. The telegram had been sent by sportswriter Abe Yager, who was covering the team and creating his own story.

Zack, also known as "Buck Wheat" during his career, matched his 1916 performance by again hitting .312 in 1917, but Brooklyn dropped all the way to seventh place that year. In 1918 Wheat engaged in a close batting race with Cincinnati's Edd Roush. In the season's closing days, Zack pulled ahead to win the National League batting title with a .335 mark. Roush hit .333. It was the last Brooklyn batting championship until Lefty O'Doul captured the crown in 1932.

Wheat played only 105 games that season, but he recorded enough at bats to qualify. Zack infrequently walked or struck out. He was a good low-ball hitter who liked to whip his heavy black bat against as many pitches as he could reach.

Brooklyn still floundered in 1919 as Zack dipped to a .297 average. But in 1920 the Superbas won the pennant by seven games. Zack's .328 average was fourth in the league and tops on the club. Although Cleveland captured the World Championship in seven games, Zack had a fine Series, hitting .333 with seven singles and two doubles. It was the last World Series Brooklyn would play for 21 years.

Wheat continued his fine hitting in the years that followed, ensuring a lifetime .317 batting average. He batted .320 in 1921 and .335 in 1922. Brooklyn was now competing with Babe Ruth's Yankees for the New York sports fans attention. In 1923, the year that Yankee Stadium opened, Zack kept many fans home in Brooklyn by batting .375 in 98 games even though the club played less than .500 ball.

Zack batted .375 again in 1924 while playing 141 games, but all he could do was finish second in the league, 49 points

behind Rogers Hornsby's record-setting .424 mark.

In April 1925, Charles Ebbets died. In a peculiar turn of events, Ed McKeever, the acting president upon Ebbets' death, caught pneumonia at the funeral and died a week later. With the club leaderless, Wilbert Robinson became acting president and appointed Wheat acting manager. But Robinson insisted on sitting next to the dugout and making suggestions. When the club continued to lose, he moved back into the dugout and began directing the team, without saying a word to Wheat. No one knew who was in charge, least of all Zack, but by the end of the season Wheat was merely the left fielder. He hit .359 amid the confusion.

Some accused Wheat of not hustling in 1926, when he was 38 years old. Zack batted .290 for Brooklyn, and at the end of the season the most popular of Flatbush stars was given his release. Connie Mack signed him in January 1927, and Zack spent his final major league season batting .324 in 88 games for the Philadelphia Athletics.

In 1928 Wheat hit .309 for Minneapolis of the American Association and then hung up his spikes for good. He was considered a leading candidate to succeed Robinson as Brooklyn manager in 1932, but the job went to Max Carey.

Wheat and Cotton Tierney, an old teammate, opened a bowling alley in Kansas City, and Zack also served on the Kansas City police force. An automobile accident fractured his skull, wrist, and ribs, keeping him in a hospital for five months. Recovered, Zack moved his family to Sunrise Beach, Missouri, where he operated a hunting and fishing resort. During World War II, he worked in a war plant in Wichita.

Zack Wheat was named to the Hall of Fame in 1959. He died on March 11, 1972, in Sedalia, Missouri, at the age of 83.

ZACHARIAH DAVIS WHEAT

Brooklyn 1909–1926
Philadelphia (A.L.) 1927

G	AB	R	H	2B	3B	HR	RBI	Avg.
2406	9106	1289	2884	476	172	132	1265	.317

Ted Williams (b.1918)

Ted Williams was the finest student of hitting in modern baseball, as his six batting titles, including one at the age of 40, attest. Ted was quick-tempered, arrogant, opinionated, and independent, but he was without peer among hitters during his career in the American League.

Theodore Samuel Williams was born in San Diego, California, on August 30, 1918. His parents were seldom together; his mother devoted herself to work for the Salvation Army and left Ted primarily on his own as a youngster. He learned to play baseball on the San Diego playgrounds and then later at Herbert Hoover High School. His instructors and coaches during that period, Rod Luscomb and Wes Caldwell, helped Ted to perfect his great hitting skills.

Tall and thin upon entering professional baseball, Ted was first called "The Splendid Splinter," but he filled out to 6'4" and 200 pounds during his career.

At the age of 17, Ted signed a contract with the San Diego Padres of the Pacific Coast League, a high classification for a player just starting out. His salary was $150 per month, and he batted .271 with no home runs in 42 games. Returning to the Padres in 1937, Ted batted .291 with 23 homers and 98 runs batted in for 138 games. The Boston Red Sox general manager, Eddie Collins, the one-time Philadelphia and Chicago star, went to San Diego to buy Bobby Doerr, the Padres' second baseman, but after seeing Ted, he decided to purchase both of them.

Ted received a $1000 bonus for signing with Boston. In addition to the bonus, he signed a two-year contract for $7500.

The Red Sox outfield in 1938 featured Doc Cramer, Joe Vosmik, and Ben Chapman, a trio of .300 hitters. After spring training with the parent club, Ted was farmed to Minneapolis of the American Association. He had been in training long enough to strike up a lifelong friendship with a Boston clubhouse man, Johnny Orlando, who pinned the nickname "Kid" on Ted.

Young and reckless, Williams was not a favorite of Minneapolis manager Donie Bush. Nevertheless, Ted hit .366 to lead the league, clubbing 43 homers and driving home 142 runners, both also league-leading figures.

Ted opened the 1939 season as the Boston right fielder. He eventually moved to left field, his position through 1960. Williams was never considered an exceptional defensive player, but he had good baseball sense, knew where to position himself for different hitters, and became adept at playing balls off the high left field wall in Fenway Park.

Hitting was Ted's life, however, and he devoted hours to mastering it, treating it as

though it were a science. Years after his retirement Williams published a book on hitting, offering such pointers as "Never give the pitcher an edge." and "For the first two strikes, wait for a pitch right in the power portion of the strike zone. If you have patience, you'll get your pitch."

Patience became one of Ted's chief attributes as a hitter. He received 2018 walks in his career, second only to Babe Ruth. This contrasted with a mere 709 total strikeouts. Only three times did Williams fan more than 50 times in a season.

As a rookie in 1939, Ted batted .327 with 31 home runs and a league-leading 145 runs batted in. The following season he increased his average to .344 (his lifetime average). Ted made the 1940 All-Star team, his first of 18 All-Star appearances. In the 1941 game, he hit a three-run homer with two out in the ninth inning for a dramatic 7–5 American League victory, and in 1946 he belted two homers and two singles in four trips for five runs batted in. His lifetime All-Star average was .304.

Ted's most sensational season was 1941, even though he was only 23 years old and still developing his talents. He batted .406 that year, becoming the last man to reach the .400 mark and the first since 1930. In the American League, the feat had not been performed since Harry Heilmann accomplished it in 1923.

The .406 mark was attained in a dramatic style. Ted was batting .400 with a doubleheader scheduled for the final day of the season, and manager Joe Cronin offered him the opportunity to sit it out and protect his average. Instead, Williams played, collected six hits in eight at bats, and finished at .406.

In the Most Valuable Player voting, however, Joe DiMaggio, who had hit safely in 56 consecutive games that season, edged Williams for the honor. Ted accepted that defeat well, but in subsequent years he became somewhat bitter at being passed over for the award. Williams thought it was due to his poor relationship with the press in general. His contention was highlighted in 1947 when he won the Triple Crown but saw the MVP award go again to DiMaggio. One Boston writer left Ted completely off the ballot.

Ted also missed the MVP award in 1942, when he again captured the Triple Crown with a .356 average, 36 homers, and 137 RBIs. Joe Gordon of the Yankees received the MVP trophy that year.

Ted's attitude toward fans was not always polite. When they booed him in Fenway Park early in his career, Williams vowed never to tip his cap to them after a home run. Even when he hit one in his last time at bat before retiring, he did not

relent. There were occasional incidents with fans involving obscene gestures and spitting. And it was virtually impossible to get Ted to attend a dinner in his honor or on behalf of the club. Only a charity affair on behalf of the Jimmy Fund in Boston would ever make him appear in public, and even then he would refuse to wear a necktie—another Williams trademark.

As he neared his fiftieth birthday, twice divorced and three times married, Ted had a son. The boy, John Henry, was a great source of pride to Ted, who was not otherwise sentimental. Williams always assumed a rather hard-nosed approach to politics and world affairs, subjects which he did not hesitate to speak out on.

Ted lost three years from his playing career between 1943 and 1945 when he served as a Marine pilot; he saw no combat. In 1952 his Marine reserve unit was called up for duty in the Korean war, and Ted missed most of two additional seasons. This time he did see combat duty. The nearly five years removed from his career made a significiant dent in his lifetime statistics.

Returning from World War II in 1946, Ted encountered the "Williams Shift," invented by Cleveland manager Lou Boudreau. The shift involved the placement of three infielders on the second base side of the diamond to counter Ted's pulling ability as a lefthanded hitter. Rather than change his style, Ted challenged the shift, succeeded, and earned his first MVP award. The 1946 Red Sox captured the pennant—Ted's only championship team—but Williams hit a disappointing .200 in the World Series without an extra-base hit.

Following the triple-crown season of 1947, Ted won his fourth batting crown in 1948 with a .369 average. In 1949 he notched the MVP award again, leading the league in five categories including home runs with 43.

In the 1950 All-Star game in Chicago, Ted fractured his left elbow while crashing into the outfield wall in the first inning. Although Williams played the remainder of the game, he required surgery and was limited to only 89 games that season.

In 1951 Ted batted .318. After nearly two years in Korea, Williams returned late in

Ted Williams in his first and last years as a professional baseball player. (At left) As a 17-year-old with the San Diego Padres, when he learned the joys of paychecks and train rides. (Below) In 1960, he slugs a homer against the Senators.

(Above) Williams' smashed plane marked another episode in an eventful career during the Korean War. (Center) Captain Williams in the cockpit as a Marine pilot. Two stints in the Marines took a total of five years out of his playing career. (Below) Always a fighter, Manager Williams argues a point with the umpires in 1972.

the 1953 season to play 37 games and bat .407 with 13 homers and a .901 slugging average.

Ted's batting heroics continued throughout the 1950s, climaxed by consecutive batting titles in 1957 and 1958 when he was 39 and 40 years old. At the age of 39, Williams clubbed 38 homers and missed reaching the .400 mark by only five hits over the course of the season. He hit .388 that year. The MVP award, however, went to Mickey Mantle.

At the age of 40, Ted became the oldest player to capture a batting championship with a figure of .328 in 1958.

A neck injury in 1959 caused him to slip to .254, the first time he had fallen under .317. But Williams came back in 1960 to bat .316. He hit an emotion-packed home run on his final time at bat in the big leagues before a hometown crowd in Boston.

Ted's last homer gave him a total of 521, third highest figure in the game's history at the time of his retirement despite his five years in the service. He set major league records for consecutive seasons leading in runs (5) and walks (6). In 1957 Ted received a record 33 intentional walks. Twice during that season he belted three home runs in one game. Ted also managed to hit four consecutive homers over a span of three games. Williams led the league in total bases six times and in slugging percentage nine times. He earned a top salary of $125,000 per year, bearing the distinction of the second American Leaguer (after DiMaggio) to reach the $100,000 mark.

After closing out his playing career, Ted declined managing offers, preferring to live quietly in Florida and devote himself to fishing. His only outside interests were the Jimmy Fund in Boston and promotional work for Sears Roebuck sporting goods.

In 1966, Ted's first year of eligibility, the baseball writers with whom he had battled over the years voted him into the Hall of Fame.

In 1969, after eight seasons away from the game except for holding a title of vice president of the Red Sox, Ted was persuaded to manage the Washington Senators by the principal owner, Robert Short, in exchange for a hefty salary and a piece of the club. Ted worked hard and was named Manager of the Year for a fourth place finish. He managed the club for three more seasons, moving with the team to Texas in 1972, but he never did as well as that first campaign. His patience for managing wore thin, and he returned to Florida to fish, but in 1978 he was persuaded to return to the Red Sox as a spring training batting instructor.

THEODORE SAMUEL WILLIAMS

Boston (A.L.) 1939–1960

G	AB	R	H	2B	3B	HR	RBI	Avg.
2292	7706	1798	2654	525	71	521	1839	.344

George Wright (1847-1937)

George Wright starred for baseball's first professional team, the Cincinnati Red Stockings, who went undefeated during the 1869 season. He was the first baseball pioneer elected to the Hall of Fame.

George Wright was born at 110th Street and Third Avenue in the Harlem section of New York City on January 28, 1847. In 1836, his parents had come to America from Sheffield, England, bring along George's older brother, Harry. A third brother, Sam, was born in 1848.

George's father had been a cricket player of note in England, and he continued to play in the United States as a member of the St. George Cricket Club of Hoboken, New Jersey. All three sons played cricket in addition to experimenting with baseball in its earliest form. Sam was perhaps the best of the boys at cricket; in baseball, he played only 45 games at shortstop in a brief major league career.

Harry was more of an organizer, and he eventually founded the first professional team. But George, 12 years younger than Harry, always seemed to steal the spotlight. He was a dashing young man with great athletic ability.

George's first experience in organized baseball came in 1864 when he played for the Gothams of New York. The team followed Alexander Cartwright's basic rules, and it did quite well.

In 1865 George played for the Philadelphia Olympics, but he was back with the Gothams in 1866. During this period George played every position, as there were only 9 or 10 men on a full roster. But he was particularly adept at shortstop, which became his principal position.

George first reached a measure of local fame late in 1866 when he joined the Morrisania Union team in the Bronx. His growing reputation brought him an offer from the Washington Nationals for the 1867 season.

The Nationals were allegedly amateurs, but it is questionable if George would have gone as far away as Washington unless he had received some form of monetary inducement. All players on the team were listed in a program along with their "government occupation." George was listed as a clerk, with a business address of 238 Pennsylvania Avenue—a public park.

Surviving statistics show that George played in 29 games for Washington and scored 182 runs, which must have been an outstanding feat. But in 1868 he rejoined the Morrisania team and there established a reputation as the best player in the East.

At this point, brother Harry formed the nation's first truly professional team, the Cincinnati Red Stockings. George, having been chosen to the nation's first all-star team in 1868 by writer Henry Chadwick,

George Wright served on the Centennial Committee that helped plan the National Baseball Hall of Fame. He had been a star for the National Association's greatest team, the Boston Red Stockings, which won the pennant in four of the league's five years. (Opposite page) Wright in Boston uniform and adorning the club's record book.

was induced by his brother to go to Cincinnati to play for the Red Stockings.

George at once became the highest-paid player on the team. His salary was listed as $1400, and Harry's was figured at $1200. Although this was a widely publicized list, proving the professionalism of the team, George later claimed that he was paid $1800 and Harry $2000.

The Red Stockings easily defeated every opponent they faced that year since most teams west of the Appalachians were just learning the game. The team compiled a 57–0 record in 1869, and George's batting average has been computed as .629 for the 57 games.

In 1870 the Red Stockings continued their winning ways, running the streak to 130 victories before losing on June 14 to the Atlantics of Brooklyn in extra innings.

George proved to be an outstanding shortstop. Like everyone else, he played without a glove and delighted the fans by snaring hard-hit line drives. His strong arm enabled him to play a deep shortstop, and he became the first player to cover second base when the second baseman was otherwise occupied on a play.

George also invented the trap play for setting up double plays. Later, the infield fly rule was passed to prevent this maneuver. The Red Stockings broke up after the 1870 season, and the Wright brothers went to Boston to form a new entry in the National Association, the first major league. Harry was the manager, and George the shortstop and most popular player on the team. Young fans would say, "I'd rather be Wright than President," and good crowds turned out to watch the games.

Philadelphia captured the first National Association pennant. Boston, which scored more runs and collected more hits than any club, finished third.

But Boston won the championship each of the next four seasons. The team seemed to get better each season, and by 1875, the final year of the National Association, the team compiled a 71–8 record. George, hitting against underhand pitching with no curveballs, batted .409, .336, .378, .345, and .337 during the five years of National Association play.

George stood 5'9½" and his playing weight was listed at 150 pounds. He had dark wavy hair and a bushy mustache. His dashing image helped him to establish a thriving sporting goods business in Boston.

In 1872 George and Henry Ditson opened Wright and Ditson Sporting Goods, the largest such firm in New England. The store sold "Cigars and Base Balls" and later introduced the first tennis and golf equipment in the area. In later years, the firm was bought out by Albert Spalding of Chicago.

In 1876 the National League was formed, replacing the National Association. Chicago, managed by Spalding, had the best team, but Harry Wright moved his Boston club into the new league. With 29-year-old George as the shortstop, Boston managed to finish in fourth place behind Chicago, St. Louis, and Hartford. The Boston program that year listed George's occupation as "engraver."

George was the first batter in National League history, for he led off the April 22 game at Philadelphia and grounded to shortstop.

The Boston Red Stockings won the pennant in 1877, but by then George had fallen off badly as a hitter. He was unable to adjust to curveball and overhand pitching, and the once-proud .300 hitter now batted only .255. After Boston repeated its pennant effort in 1878, giving Harry and George six championship teams in seven years, George jumped to the Providence Grays in 1879 to serve as shortstop and manager.

Playing against his brother in a hotly contested pennant race, George brought the Grays home in first place, beating Harry's Red Stockings by five games.

When Jim Bullock became Providence manager in 1880, George returned to Boston, played seven games, and batted .172. In 1881 he appeared in one game and collected one hit in four at bats. In 1882 Harry shifted over to manage Providence, and George joined him to play 45 games, but he batted only .162.

George left baseball at that point to devote most of his time to his sporting goods business. He also helped rear a family of two daughters and two sons. The two boys, Beals and Irving, were both outstanding tennis players, with Beals competing in the 1905 Davis Cup matches.

George was also a pioneer in golf. He played the first match in New England, which may also have been the first in America.

In 1884 George backed the new Union Association, a third major league created to compete with the National League and the American Association. George bought the Boston franchise and arranged for the league to use only baseballs manufactured by Wright and Ditson. Unfortunately, the Union Association lasted only one season.

George accompanied the Philadelphia Athletics and the Boston Red Stockings in 1874 on a tour of England. The Americans first demonstrated baseball to the British and then proceeded to defeat them at cricket. In 1888 Albert Spalding organized a grand world tour, taking his Chicago White Stockings and a group of All-Stars. George accompanied the group as umpire.

George lived to be 90 years old. Long a consultant on the game, he served on the Centennial Committee that helped lay plans for the National Baseball Hall of Fame in Cooperstown.

In 1937 George Wright was elected to the Hall of Fame, beating his brother Harry by 16 years. George died in Boston on August 31, 1937.

GEORGE WRIGHT

Boston (N.A.) 1871–1875
Boston (N.L.) 1876–1878, 1880–1881
Providence (N.L.) 1879, 1882

G	AB	R	H	2B	3B	HR	RBI	Avg.
577	2848	inc.	858	inc.	inc.	inc.	inc.	.301

RECORD OF THE
oston Base Ball Club,
SINCE ITS ORGANIZATION,

WITH A SKETCH OF ALL ITS PLAYERS.
For 1871, '72, '73 and '74.
AND OTHER ITEMS OF INTEREST.

BY
GEORGE WRIGHT, B.B.B.C.

Harry Wright (1835-1895)

Harry Wright managed baseball's first professional team, the Cincinnati Red Stockings, and later the Boston, Providence, and Philadelphia teams in the young National League.

William Henry Wright was born on January 10, 1835 in Sheffield, England. His father, a professional cricket player, moved the family in 1836 to New York City, where he continued to play cricket with the St. George Cricket Club in Hoboken, New Jersey. Two more sons were born to the Wright family in America—George in 1847, and Sam one year later.

Harry, too, became a member of the St. George Cricket Club. He was recognized early as one of the outstanding cricket players in America. As the matches were played in Hoboken, it was not surprising that he should encounter the Knickerbocker Base Ball Club, the team formed by Alexander Cartwright that played at Elysian Fields in Hoboken.

Harry earned his living as a jeweler, but he was already more interested in sports. In 1858 he joined the Knickerbockers as an outfielder. All teams were of amateur status at the time, although some made money on the side. In 1863 Harry staged a "benefit game" and charged 25 cents admission. His ledger shows that he earned $29.65 from the game.

Harry was a well-built 160-pounder of great imagination and ambition. As an athlete, he was considered above average. But he excelled at organization and instruction, and in August 1865, he accepted a position as cricket instructor at the Union Cricket Club in Cincinnati, Ohio. His salary was $1200 per year.

The following July, Harry organized the Cincinnati Red Stockings Base Ball team, an amateur club made up of local athletes. He was elected captain, and as the veteran player on the team he was also the best. In 1867 Harry was reported to have hit seven home runs in a single game at Newport, Kentucky.

Harry soon abandoned cricket and concentrated all his interests on the Red Stockings. By 1869, he was prepared to make them the nation's first professional team.

Harry recruited the finest baseball players in the East for his club. His first choice was his younger brother George, who was playing for the Morrisania club in New York. George was paid $1400 to play for the Red Stockings, and Harry, the center fielder and manager, paid himself $1200. Pitcher Asa Brainard earned $1100, third baseman Fred Waterman received $1000, and the other players—second baseman Charles Sweasy, first baseman Charles Gould, catcher Douglas Allison, left fielder Andrew Leonard, and right fielder Calvin McVey—all made $800. Substitute Richard Hurley was paid $600.

Naturally, the Red Stockings were at

once the best baseball team in the country. To prove the point, Harry took his team—outfitted in knickerbocker pants and long socks—throughout the country in 1869, winning 57 consecutive games for an undefeated season. Harry played the outfield and took a few turns on the mound, demonstrating an excellent "slow ball" which was one of the first changeups ever thrown in a game.

In 1870, after running their winning streak to 130 games, the Red Stockings lost to the Atlantics of Brooklyn, 8–7, in 11 innings. The loss took the spark out of the club since they were no longer an "undefeated" attraction.

After breaking up the Red Stockings, Harry in 1871 helped form the first major league, the National Association. He and his brother George joined the Boston club, with Harry becoming its manager. In a bitter rivalry with Philadelphia in 1871, the Association's first season, the Athletics finished first and Boston third. But after that showing Boston never again lost a National Association pennant. They captured the next four, climaxed by a 71–8 season in 1875. From their rivals' fans came cries of "Break up Wright's Red Stockings!"

As a manager, Harry was very much a gentleman. He neither berated his players nor argued with umpires. Still he had good business sense. Harry opposed the playing of Sunday baseball on religious grounds, but he also realized that Sunday games took away from the weekday crowds. Happy to offer free advice to anyone seeking to establish a baseball team, he profited by representing a turnstile company and a ball manufacturer. Harry even patented a scorecard, which was sold at all Boston home games. He also accepted payment from newspapers to file stories with them on his team's games.

Sportswriter Henry Chadwick called Harry "The Father of Professional Baseball," and Wright returned the compliment by labeling Chadwick "The Father of Baseball." Chadwick, however, criticized the National Association as "questionable in its honesty." Harry resented the criticism.

Harry continued to play a game or two every year in order to keep in shape. Following the 1874 season, he accompanied Albert Spalding on a baseball tour of his native England, engaging in baseball and cricket matches.

When the National Association folded after the 1875 season, Harry was appointed secretary at the meeting that launched the new National League. Nathaniel T. Apollonio was granted the Boston franchise,

and Harry was named manager. George remained with him as shortstop.

Chicago took the first National League pennant, but Boston captured the championship in both 1877 and 1878, giving Harry six pennants in seven years. His well-disciplined team including Deacon White, Jim O'Rourke, and his brother. Harry would have his nine starters march to first base at the start of each home game, and then break off in a run toward their respective positions.

In 1882 Harry and George Wright transferred to the Providence Grays, the team of Hoss Radbourn and John Montgomery Ward. Harry led the club to a second-place finish in 1882, a third-place showing in 1883, and then resigned his post.

Harry signed a unique contract to manage the Philadelphia club in 1884. It called for Wright to receive one-quarter of the profits. If there were no profits, he would earn nothing.

Philadelphia compiled only a 39–73 record in 1884, but somehow the team finished sixth in the eight-club National League. Philadelphia netted $6028, paying Harry $1507. In 1885 Harry brought the team over the .500 mark for a third place finish behind Cap Anson's Cubs and Jim Mutrie's Giants. His skills as a manager were never so apparent as they were that season.

Harry led the club to a second-place finish in 1887, his highest standing with the Phillies. Within a few years, he added such great hitters as Sam Thompson, Billy Hamilton, and Ed Delahanty, but he never had enough pitching to go all the way. Harry retired as a manager following the 1893 season. The league created the position of chief of umpires for him, and Harry served in this post in 1894 and 1895.

Immediately after the 1895 season, Harry became ill. He died in Atlantic City, New Jersey, on October 3, and his memory soon faded. George Wright, the more dynamic and colorful of the two brothers, was elected to the Hall of Fame in 1937. Not until 1953 was Harry Wright so honored.

Harry Wright, one of the most important managers of nineteenth century baseball, in uniform for Boston (upper left), which he led to four National Association pennants. His National League Boston team later won two pennants. Baseball's traditional uniform is based on Wright's design, with which he outfitted his 1869 Cincinnati Red Stockings, baseball's first pro team. (At left and above) His meticulously kept records of expenses and players.

Early Wynn (b.1920)

At the age of 43, Early Wynn became the fourteenth pitcher to record 300 career victories. He did it with the determination and hard work that characterized his long major league career.

Early was born on November 6, 1920, in Hartford, Alabama, the state's peanut-producing center. His father, of American Indian ancestry, was an auto mechanic and a semipro player of note in Hartford. Early's parents were divorced when he was in his teens, and times were difficult when the Depression hit the South. During his after-school time, Early worked for 10 cents an hour lifting 500-pound bales of cotton.

At Hartford High School, Early first went out for football as a halfback but broke a leg during a game. Upon recovery he switched to baseball and became team captain, clean-up hitter, shortstop, and star pitcher. Following his sophomore year, Early was invited to a Washington Senator baseball school in Sanford, Florida. He made a favorable impression as a pitcher on Washington scout Clyde Milan, and when he was offered $100 per month to sign, Early quit school after his junior year and entered the ranks of the professionals.

At Sanford, a Florida State League team, the 17-year-old righthander won 16 games, lost 11, and pitched 235 innings. In 1938 Early moved to Charlotte of the Piedmont League and posted a 10–11 record. He remained with Charlotte in 1939, lost a no-hitter, 2–1, when his club committed five errors, and compiled a 15–14 mark. During the year, he married a local girl, Mabel Allman; the couple had a son, Joe Early. Two years later, Mabel was driving a baby sitter home when her car was struck by a bus, killing her and leaving Early a 21-year-old widower with an infant son.

In the meantime, Early had gained his first taste of the major leagues, joining the Senators at the end of the 1939 season. He appeared in three games and lost his only two decisions. The 1939 appearances, and his retirement in 1963, made Early one of only three men—the others were Ted Williams and Mickey Vernon—whose careers spanned the four decades of the 1930s, 1940s, 1950s, and 1960s.

In 1940, however, Early was back at Charlotte, pitching mostly in relief and earning a promotion in 1941 to Springfield of the Eastern League. When his wife died that year, Early, struggling along on a minor league salary, moved in with his mother and sister.

When the Senators sought to move Wynn to another minor league club late in 1941, Commissioner Landis voided the move and the Senators were forced to bring him up or sell him to another organization. Not wishing to lose him completely, the Senators brought Early up in September 1941. Wynn never again returned to the minor leagues.

Early Wynn, durable righthander, had his best season in 1959 at the age of 39, when his 22–10 record paced the Chicago White Sox to its first pennant since the infamous 1919 "Black Sox" days. (Opposite page) Wynn, playing for Cleveland in 1957, fires one to the plate in a shutout victory against the Yanks.

Early recorded a 3–1 mark in September 1941. In 1942 he worked 190 innings for the seventh-place Senators, posting a 10–16 record with a 5.12 earned-run average. The 16 losses were not the most he ever experienced in one season, but Early never mastered the art of being a good loser. It was not uncommon to see a chair fly across the clubhouse after a particularly tough loss.

Wynn's reputation on the mound was just as mean. Brushback pitches were a part of his game, and he always kept the hitters honest. The long-running joke for Wynn was that "He'd throw at his own mother," to which Early replied, "She was a helluva curveball hitter."

"Gus" (a nickname derived simply because "he looked like a Gus") did not throw a curve when he first came up, getting by on a fastball and knuckleball. Not until his eighth big league season did Wynn add a curve to his arsenal.

It was in 1943, a talent-short year because of World War II, that Early first became a recognized star. He posted an 18–12 record that season, leading the Senators to a surprising second-place finish. But in 1944 Washington fell to last place, and Wynn led the league with 17 defeats while winning only eight.

In September 1944, Early joined the army and also married Lorraine Follin. He completed his military service in 1945, missing the entire season, but returned to a stable home life and a bright future.

Wynn compiled an 8–5 record in 17 games for the 1946 Senators, but he came back to notch a 17–15 mark in 1947 when the Senators won only 64 games. Early was earning $20,000 per year at this point.

The 1948 season was a disappointing one for Early. He won only 8 games, lost 19, and registered a 5.82 earned run average.

His relatively high salary and the bad season had diminished Early's value. On December 14, 1948, Wynn and Mickey Vernon were traded to the Indians for Joe Haynes, Ed Klieman, and Eddie Robinson. It was one of the best trades the Cleveland Indians ever made.

In Cleveland, Wynn joined a pitching staff that included Bob Lemon, Bob Feller, and Mike Garcia. Pitching coach Mel Harder taught Early to throw a curve. Wynn compiled only an 11–7 mark in his first season as an Indian, but in 1950 he led the American League with a 3.20 earned run average and posted an 18–8 record, second only to Lemon on the Cleveland staff. In 1951 Early reached the 20-victory circle for the first time in addition to leading the

league with 274 innings pitched. And in 1952, he recorded a 23–12 mark with a 2.90 ERA.

Wynn also led the American League with 132 walks in 1952. His career total of 1775 base on balls is the highest figure in major league history.

The Indians captured the 1954 pennant with a league record of 111 victories. Early notched 23 wins, tying Lemon for the league lead. Al Lopez, his manager, would always turn to Wynn for the big game, and the 6′ 235-pounder was usually at his best then. From 1955 to 1957, Wynn's records were 17–11, 20–9, and 14–17.

In 1955 Early began to write a newspaper column for the Cleveland *News.* He never employed a ghost writer and never hesitated to criticize umpires, official scorers, or even his own general manager, Hank Greenberg. The job was one of many Early had outside of baseball, dating back to his early off-seasons when he worked as a truckdriver, a short-order cook, and a clothing salesman.

The column, not a popular one with the Cleveland management, lasted three years—until Wynn and Al Smith were traded to the Chicago White Sox on December 4, 1957 for Minnie Minoso and Fred Hatfield. Early's new White Sox contract prohibited him from writing a newspaper column, with the club agreeing to compensate him for the loss of income. Wynn agreed, for he had been donating the money to the Elks Club Building Fund in his home town of Nokomis, Florida, anyway.

With the White Sox, Wynn's manager once again was Al Lopez. Despite Chicago's second place finish in 1958, Wynn contributed only a 14–16 record.

But the next year, 1959—when Early was 39 years old—was Wynn's best. He had a 22–10 record to lead the league, hurled 256 innings (also tops in the league), and notched a 3.16 ERA. The White Sox captured their first pennant since the scandal-ridden 1919 "Black Sox" days, and Wynn was voted the Cy Young Award as the best pitcher in the majors. He won one and lost one in the 1959 World Series loss to Los Angeles.

The 1959 season left Wynn 29 victories short of 300, and as he entered his fourth decade in baseball he announced that his goal would be 300 wins. Early knocked off 13 victories that year, and he was on the way to a good season in 1961 when his elbow began to bother him, knocking him off the active list on August 10. His 8–2 record for the year gave him 292 career wins. The injury turned out to be gout, which caused a sore pitching elbow, right hand, and knee. The goal of 300 victories seemed beyond Wynn's grasp.

Eliminating meat from his diet and relying on a high slider and a knuckleball, Early set out in 1962 to gain his last eight victories. His record for the season was 7–15. Repeatedly he failed to notch that last, elusive victory. The White Sox stuck by him, but finally they handed him his release on November 20, 1962. All Early could do was wait at home and hope some club would call. He kept his arm loose by working out at a local gym, but his weight was up, giving him a portly, less-mean appearance on the mound.

Finally, the call came. The Cleveland Indians, his old club, signed him on June 21, 1963, when they needed pitching help.

Early began his twenty-third major league season as the oldest player in the league. He lost his first two attempts at No. 300, but on July 13 he went five innings against Kansas City and the Indians hung on to win, 7–4, for Early's three hundredth and final victory. He remained with the club to the end of the season but did not add to his total. His 23 seasons as a pitcher equaled a record set by Jack Quinn between 1909 and 1933 in three major leagues.

Early served as pitching coach for the Indians from 1964 to 1966. He then shifted to the Minnesota Twins in a similar capacity from 1967 to 1969. In 1970 and 1971, Early was a major league scout for the Twins. In 1972, the year of his election to the Hall of Fame, Early managed Orlando in the Florida State League while enjoying life at home in Nokomis. He became a radio broadcaster for the Toronto Blue Jays in 1977.

EARLY WYNN

Washington 1939, 1941–1948
Cleveland 1949–1957, 1963
Chicago (A.L.) 1958–1962

G	IP	W	L	Pct.	H	R	ER	SO	BB	ERA
691	4566	300	244	.551	4291	2037	1796	2334	1775	3.54

Early Wynn hurls the first pitch of the 1959 World Series between the Chicago White Sox and the Los Angeles Dodgers. The Dodger batter, Jim Gilliam, lets it go for a called strike. The catcher is Sherm Lollar, the umpire Bill Summers. Gilliam eventually grounded out to short. Wynn, Cy Young Award winner that year, won one and lost one as the Dodgers took the championship.

Cy Young (1867-1955)

Every year the top pitcher in each major league, as selected by members of the Baseball Writers' Association, receives an award named after the winningest pitcher in baseball history—Cy Young. The award was instituted in 1956, 45 years after Young's retirement. Had it been awarded at the time he pitched, Young would doubtless have won it many times.

Denton True Young was born on March 29, 1867, in Gilmore, Ohio, about 50 miles from Canton. "Dent" spent his first 23 years working on his family's farm, rising to a salary of $10 per month plus his keep. Baseball was his only outside interest.

In 1890 the manager of the Canton club in the Tri-State League offered Young $40 per month to pitch for his team. Young's parents hesitated to give up their son to a baseball career, but when the bid was raised to $60 per month, they consented.

Warming up in Canton by throwing a ball against a board fence in the outfield, Young did enough damage to six planks to cause someone to remark, "It looks like a cyclone hit the fence." A sportswriter picked up the phrase, and Young became known as "Cy."

In his first professional season at Canton, Young established the pattern for the remainder of his career. He was a workhorse pitcher, hurling 260 innings during his first campaign. He also demonstrated superb control, striking out 201 batters while walking only 33. His ratio of strikeouts to walks generally was excellent throughout his career. Although Cy threw a good fastball and developed an excellent curve, his hallmark was always control.

After he had posted a 15–15 record for Canton, Young's contract was sold to the Cleveland Spiders of the National League. The purchase figure, according to Young, was $250, but it was long believed that the price had been a new suit of clothes for the Canton owner. Whatever the price, it was a great bargain for Cleveland.

Young's rookie season in the National League found him in the company of such baseball pioneers as Cap Anson, John Montgomery Ward, and Kid Nichols. Cy made his debut against Anson's Chicago team in August 1890, and he allowed only three hits in gaining his first of 511 career victories. In the last seven weeks of the season, Young pitched in 17 games for Cleveland and compiled a 9–7 record.

In 1891, his first full season in the National League, Cy won 27 of 47 decisions, pitched 430 innings, and made 46 starts. It was the first of 14 consecutive seasons (16 in all) in which Young scored 20 or more victories. In five of those seasons, Cy topped the 30 mark, and for his 22-year career, he averaged 23 victories per season.

Work was the name of Young's game. In an era when pitching staffs were half of today's size, Cy usually pitched after just

two days rest and frequently after only one. He never had a sore arm, but he sometimes admitted to its being "tired." In the winters, Cy kept in shape by swinging an ax and working on his farm. Young stood 6'2" and weighed nearly 210 pounds for most of his career.

Young notched his first season of better than 30 victories in 1892 when he posted a 36–11 record with nine shutouts in 455 innings of work. The pitching mound in those days was a flat, square area 50 feet from home, where a barehanded catcher awaited each pitch. Fielders also played barehanded. Young himself did not wear a glove until 1897.

Cy won 32 games in 1893 to give him a two-year total of 68 victories against only 27 losses. He added 25 victories in 1894, the last year in which he walked more than 100 batters. From then on his control became sensational, reaching a peak in 1904 when he struck out 203 and walked only 28 in 380 innings.

The 1895 season was the first in which Young participated in a postseason championship, the Temple Cup Series, a forerunner of the World Series. Pitching against Baltimore in a best-of-seven contest between the two top teams in the National League, Young notched three complete game wins over the Orioles in the five-game Cleveland victory. Cy allowed only seven runs in the three games.

Young continued his winning ways for three more years with Cleveland, pitching his first of three no-hitters in 1897 (defeating Cincinnati, 6–0). But attendance in Cleveland was poor. Frank Robison therefore transferred his best players to the St. Louis club, which he also owned, and disbanded the Spiders. Young pitched two seasons for St. Louis, winning 46, losing 33, and earning the ceiling salary in the league, $2400 per year.

With the birth of the American League in 1901, Young was lured by the promise of a $3000 contract with the Boston Red Sox. Now 33 years old, Young was preparing to embark on a new career with a new league. But his St. Louis owner, Robison, did not see it that way. He predicted an early demise for both Young and the league.

Instead, the league caught on. As its first pitching star Young led the circuit in victories in each of its first three seasons, winning 33, 32, and 28, while losing 10 each season.

In 1903 the first modern World Series was played. The National League entry, Pittsburgh, was heavily favored to defeat the American League champions, the Red

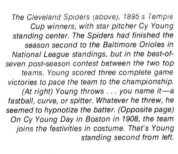

The Cleveland Spiders (above), 1895 s Temple Cup winners, with star pitcher Cy Young standing center. The Spiders had finished the season second to the Baltimore Orioles in National League standings, but in the best-of-seven post-season contest between the two top teams, Young scored three complete game victories to pace the team to the championship. (At right) Young throws . . . you name it—a fastball, curve, or spitter. Whatever he threw, he seemed to hypnotize the batter. (Opposite page) On Cy Young Day in Boston in 1908, the team joins the festivities in costume. That's Young standing second from left.

Sox. The Pirates captured three of the first four games. But Boston swept the following four games, with Young winning two of them. Boston's 5–3 World Series victory brought the American League into parity with the senior circuit.

Though he relinquished the league victory title in 1904 to Jack Chesbro, who won a record 41 games, Young topped the league with 10 shutouts while posting 26 victories. He also pitched what is considered to be the finest game of his career—a 3–0 perfect game against Philadelphia on May 5. He struck out 8 batters, retired 9 men on ground balls, and induced 10 batters to lift short popups. Not a single man reached base.

In 1905 Young slipped to 18 victories, his first season below the 20 mark since he began to play professional baseball. Furthermore, Cy lost 19 games that year, falling below the .500 mark for the first time. Things were no better in 1906, with Young winning only 13 games while leading the league with 21 defeats. It was the most defeats pinned on Young since he had lost 22 games in 1894, but his victory total that season had been 25. Although Young owns the most victories in baseball history, he also sustained the most defeats, 313.

At the age of 40, with his better days apparently behind him, Young rebounded to 20-victory form with Boston, winning 22, losing only 15, and pitching 6 shutouts. The following year, at the age of 41, Cy pitched his third career no-hitter, stopping the New York Highlanders, 8–0, on June 20. Not until Sandy Koufax performed the feat nearly 60 years later did anyone ever pitch more than three no-hitters.

Cy's last year with Boston, 1908, is remembered for a thrilling "Cy Young Day" at the Boston park on Huntington Avenue. With a crowd of some 20,000 on hand, Young received cash gifts of close to $7500, a great bounty considering his salary from baseball never reached $5000. He even received gifts from the league's umpires and opposing players—evidence of the great respect in which he was held.

In 1909 Young was sold to Cleveland for $12,500, and at the age of 42 he gave the Indians a 19–15 year and 295 innings of work. But in 1910 Cy posted a 7–10 mark, and after compiling a 3–4 record in 1911, he was released in August. Signing with Boston in the National League, he started 11 games, notched a 4–5 record, and retired the following spring before the 1912 campaign began.

In 22 seasons in the major leagues, Young won 511 games—289 in the National League and 222 in the American. Walter Johnson, runnerup to Young in career victories, posted only 416. Cy's 906 appearances on the mound represented a record that stood until broken in 1968 by relief pitcher Hoyt Wilhelm, but no hurler has come close to his 7377 innings pitched.

With his playing days behind him, Young retired to his farm near Peoli, Ohio, with his wife, Robba. After her death in 1933, Cy moved in with friends, the John Benedums, and worked on their farm until he was past 80.

While not active in baseball, Young followed the sport avidly and was a frequent guest at Old Timers' reunions. It was a source of dismay that he was passed up in the first Hall of Fame election in 1936, but he received his due the following year and was present at the Hall of Fame dedication ceremonies in 1939.

Cy Young died near Peoli on November 4, 1955. Shortly thereafter, Commissioner Ford Frick created a most valuable pitcher award in Cy's name. It is a fitting remembrance for the man who won more games than any pitcher in baseball history. Cy will probably hold that distinction for a long time to come, if not forever.

DENTON TRUE YOUNG

Cleveland (N.L.) 1890–1898
St. Louis (N.L.) 1899–1900
Boston (A.L.) 1901–1908
Cleveland (A.L.) 1909–1911
Boston (N.L.) 1911

G	IP	W	L	Pct.	H	R	ER	SO	BB	ERA
906	7377	511	313	.620	7078	3168	inc.	2819	1209	inc.

Ross Youngs (1897-1927)

Ross Youngs seldom had his name spelled correctly during his career, but he was unmistakable when he donned the Giant uniform and took his place in right field. Had his career not been cut short by a premature death, Ross might have proved to be one of the best outfielders in baseball history.

Ross Middlebrook Youngs was born in Shiner, Texas, on April 10, 1897. Most people neglected to use the "s" at the end of his surname, and he went through his career being called "Young."

While Ross was still a child, the Youngs family moved from Shiner to San Antonio. At West Texas Military Academy, Ross played little baseball, concentrating on football and track. His reputation as an outstanding halfback brought him dozens of college offers, but he turned them all down to pursue his primary interest, professional baseball.

In 1914, at the age of 17, Ross joined the Austin club of the Texas League late in the season. He batted only .097 in 10 games and then was released.

Ross stood only 5'8", and at his peak he weighed about 162 pounds. But he was stocky and well-built, with a strong back and powerful muscles, and demonstrated a great throwing arm.

Youngs opened the 1915 season with Brenham of the Mid-Texas League, but the league folded on June 19 and no records were compiled. Off he went to Waxahachie of the Central Texas League, but that league disbanded late in July.

Signed in 1916 by Sherman of the Western Association, Ross played mostly the infield (second, short, and third). A switch-hitter at that point in his career, Ross led the league with a .362 batting average, 103 runs, and 195 hits. But his 71 errors proved that he was miscast for handling ground balls.

While Ross was at Sherman, John McGraw, manager of the Giants, received a tip on him. Scout Dick Kinsella was then sent to Texas to observe Youngs. Kinsella was at once impressed, and on August 14 the Giants bought Ross for a reported $2000. He was told to finish the season at Sherman.

Ross would have preferred to go to the Detroit Tigers, who also expressed an interest. He thought that he had a greater chance of breaking into the Tiger lineup, but McGraw took one look at Youngs in spring training of 1917 and converted him into an outfielder.

Ross made a fine impression on everyone at the first major league training camp in Marlin, Texas. He was nicknamed "Pep," and he was more commonly called Pep Young (or Youngs) than Ross for the duration of his career.

There was no room on the Giant roster for Pep in 1917, and McGraw thought that

he would profit from a year's experience in the outfield. He took Rochester manager Mickey Doolan aside and said, "I'm giving you one of the greatest players I've ever seen. If anything happens to him, I'm holding you responsible."

Ross hit .356 in 140 games for the Red Wings in 1917. He was then recalled by McGraw and appeared in seven late-season games.

In 1918 the Giants' regular right fielder, Dave Robertson, quit baseball and thereby opened a place for Ross. In his rookie season of 1918, the young outfielder concentrated on hitting only from the left side on McGraw's orders and batted .302. He also learned to play the difficult right-field walls in the Polo Grounds, quickly gaining popularity among the fans for his hustle, desire, and "pep."

In 1919 Ross got off so fast at bat that by the end of May, while he was hitting over .400, fans started to call him "Ty Cobb, Jr." McGraw seemed to have a special fondness for the likeable Texan, and by the end of the year, Ross had batted .311, had led the league with 31 doubles, and had topped all outfielders with 23 assists. His strong arm was now the terror of the National League, and Ross was already considered to be the best right fielder in the league.

In 1920 the Giants finished second for the third consecutive year. Ross batted .351, again led the league in assists, and placed second to Rogers Hornsby in the batting race. His 204 hits tied for second behind Hornsby.

The Giants captured their first of four successive pennants in 1921. Ross was a big man in the attack, batting .327 and driving in 102 runs despite hitting only three home runs. Batting cleanup in the World Series against the Yankees, Youngs hit .280. In the third game, Ross belted a double and a triple in two at bats during an eight-run seventh inning for the Giants. The Giants won the Series.

For the pennant-winning Giants of 1922, Ross hit .331 and threw out 28 runners from right field to again lead the league in assists. He then had a fine World Series, batting .375 against Yankee pitching while Babe Ruth, his opposite number in right field, hit only .118. Asked if he would trade Youngs for Ruth, McGraw answered, "I would never make that deal."

McGraw treated Youngs like everyone else, but there was no mistaking his special feeling for the young man. It manifested itself in later years when McGraw had only two photographs hanging in his Polo Grounds office—one of Christy Mathewson and the other of Ross Youngs.

Ernie Ba...

Ernie Banks spent 1...
go Cubs and was the...
in virtually every bat...
a career total of 511 h...
Eddie Mathews for...
time list, but it was...
more than anything,...
the game's most be...

Ernest Banks was...
1931 in Dallas, Texa...
children born to Edd...
nights for a wholesa...
er from whom he in...
look on life. Ernie a...
Washington High Sc...
he participated in ba...
ketball, and track. H...
glove for $2.98, and...
deal of time playing...
YMCA teams. It was...
that Ernie was spott...
Amarillo Colts, a Neg...
the age of 17, he join...
played some semipr...
Robinson All-Stars...
was signed by Tom...
Monarchs, a strong...
Leagues. The travel...
years, and Ernie con...
Baird talked him int...
encouraging him wi...
league scouts comi...

Drafted by the Ar...
years overseas. He r...
the Cleveland India...
Dodgers while he w...
returning, received...
Monarch manager,...
rejoined Kansas Cit...

Tom Gordon, ge...
Macon team in the...
expressed an intere...
would not think of s...
major league club. V...
to Chicago, and it w...
Cubs would purcha...
Dickey and shortstc...
each. The date was...
Ernie was in the big...
having played in the...

On September 14...
first pitch of his first...
the left-field bleach...
few days later came...
lowed shortly there...
run.

Banks played 424...
record playing strea...
career. The righthan...
weighed 180 pound...
but he had exceptic...
which produced mc...
had expected from...

FRATS WIN FROM ENGINEER TEAM IN LAST 45 SECONDS

ROSS YOUNGS FLASHES THIRTY-FIVE YARDS THROUGH ARMY FOR TOUCHDOWN.

CONTEST IS SPECTACULAR

His Sensational Run Wins for Frat Team

—Smith Photo.

ROSS YOUNGS.

Youngs in the last forty-five seconds of play tore around and through the Engineers for the touchdown that won the game for the Mu Nu Sigmas. His punting, however, was just as important a factor, for it not only saved the team from defeat, but it kept the ball down in the army territory. He averaged more than fifty yards on his punts. He has been elected captain of the 1916 West Texas Military Academy team, with which he has starred for two years. He is the youngest member of the Mu Nu Sigma fraternity here.

Ross Youngs could have made it big as a football player, as the newspaper clipping (at left) shows, but all he ever really wanted to do was play baseball. As a Giant star (above), he more than fulfilled that wish.

In 1923 Ross led the league with 121 runs scored, collected 200 hits, and batted .336. In the World Series, the first ever played in Yankee Stadium, Youngs batted .348 and hit a home run off Bob Shawkey.

Ross enjoyed his finest year at bat in 1924, hitting .356 (third in the league) with a career high of 10 home runs. But the year was clouded for him by the mention of his name in a bribery scandal. The Giants' Jimmy O'Connell had offered a bribe to Philadelphia's Heinie Sand, asking Heinie "not to play too hard against the Giants" in hopes that it would produce a pennant. The offer became known, and Commissioner Landis banned O'Connell from baseball for life. In testifying, however, O'Connell named Frankie Frisch, George Kelly, and Ross Youngs as having participated in the conversation and having witnessed the offer. The commissioner called in all three of them, satisfied himself that they had played no part in the bribe offer, and did not press the issue.

The Giants lost the 1924 World Series to Washington. Ross hit only .185, giving him a career Series mark of .286.

The 1925 Giants slipped to second place, and Ross's average dropped to .264, the first time he had ever hit below .300. McGraw noticed that Ross did not appear well, but Ross left after the season with his wife and baby girl to visit Europe.

When Youngs returned for spring training in 1926, McGraw ordered him to be checked by physicians. They discovered that Ross was suffering from a serious kidney disorder, Bright's disease.

McGraw, who had wept when Mathewson died in 1925, at once hired a male nurse to accompany Ross wherever the Giants went in 1926, just as he had hired a keeper for wild Phil Douglas a few years earlier. Ross laughed and called the nurse "my keeper." His spirits remained high, and he raised his batting average to .306 while playing 95 games in the Giants' outfield and helping to teach young Mel Ott the finer points of right field.

Finally, too ill to continue, Ross had to leave the club. He returned home to San Antonio and was bedridden for the entire 1927 season. His weight dropped to under 120 pounds. On October 22, 1927, Ross died in San Antonio at the age of 30.

Owner of a lifetime .322 batting average, Ross Youngs was selected for the Hall of Fame in 1972.

ROSS MIDDLEBROOK YOUNGS

New York (N.L.) 1917–1926

G	AB	R	H	2B	3B	HR	RBI	Avg.
1211	4627	812	1491	236	93	42	596	.322

Had the Cubs been a better team, Ernie might have retired earlier. But he, Billy Williams, and Ron Santo were really the only consistent punch in the lineup, even after Ernie's big years were behind him. In 1967 he was made a player-coach, but a year later staged a comeback of sorts by belting 32 home runs. In 1969 the Cubs under Leo Durocher made a genuine run at the Eastern Division title, only to be swept away by the New York Mets. It was Ernie's last year as a regular, and the year in which Cubs fans voted him the "Greatest Cub Ever."

Ernie was a part-time player in 1970 and 1971, before calling it a career. He remained in the Cub organization after his playing days, serving in a variety of capacities. He was a major league coach, a minor league batting instructor, and involved in group sales. In December 1977, he was named to the Cubs' Board of Directors. Perhaps more than any other player of his era, he seemed to "go with the franchise."

As great a player as he had been, it was his smiling face and "beautiful day for a ballgame" attitude that made him a favorite of fans everywhere.

In 1977, Ernie Banks became only the eighth player to be elected to the Hall of Fame in his first year of eligibility.

ERNEST BANKS

Chicago (N.L.) 1953–1971

G	AB	R	H	2B	3B	HR	RBI	Avg.
2528	9421	1305	2583	407	90	512	1636	.274

Chicago Cubs slugger Ernie Banks, the opposing catcher, and the umpire watch the flight of a long ball before Banks sets off around the bases. (Left) Banks crosses home plate for his 500th home run in a 1970 game against the Braves. Umpire Tony Venzon has a new ball ready to flip to Braves catcher Bob Tillman.

Martin Dihigo (1905-1971)

Martin Dihigo stands unique among baseball stars. While some were pitchers who became hitters, and some went the other way, no one—not even Babe Ruth—managed to do both over a long period of time with such great results. But Dihigo was a dark-skinned Cuban, and was unable to participate in the major leagues. His career then is recorded by only fragmentary statistics, pieced together by historians, and recalled with awe by those who saw him play.

Dihigo was born on May 24, 1905 in Havana, Cuba. Cuba was always a great sports country, and was among the first of the Latin American nations to learn baseball. Mike Gonzalez and Dolph Luque were among the early Cuban stars who made their way into the majors, but they were light skinned, and did not feel the unwritten ban.

Dihigo's professional career can be traced to January 21, 1923, when he was sent up to pinch-hit for the Havana Reds in the Cuban Winter League. The 17-year old righthanded hitter batted for a pitcher named Chicho Hernandez, and stayed in the game as his replacement, losing 8-5 to Marianao. He played baseball for more than 30 additional years.

A former Cuban umpire, Eustaquio Pedroso, got Martin a permit to go to the United States that year to join the Eastern Colored League. He signed with the Cuban Stars, a team made up mostly of American Negroes, and operated by Alex Pompez. Dihigo spent most of the season at first base, although he did play a bit at second, and took the mound on occasion.

Records, although sketchy, show that Dihigo batted only .198 that year for the Cuban Stars, and that back home in Havana he hit only .143. In 1924, he hit about .275 in Havana and only .229 in the States. Still, he was not yet 20, and was just feeling his way around.

Dihigo played for the Cuban Stars through the 1927 season, blossoming into a powerful .300 hitter and becoming adept at all the infield and outfield positions. His 6'1" frame filled out to 190 pounds. He led the Eastern Colored League in home runs in 1926 and tied for the lead in 1927. He continued to play for Havana in the winters, remaining with them through the 1928-29 season. Here, he was able to approach a .400 season at bat, and on the mound was developing into a hard thrower.

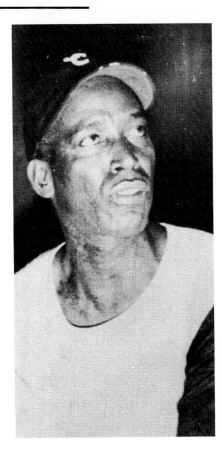

In 1928, Dihigo played for the Homestead Grays, and in 1929 for the Hilldale Club of Philadelphia. He is credited there with hitting .386, belting 18 homers and stealing 21 bases in some 65 games, while winning four of six decisions on the mound.

As a pitcher, the hard throwing righty saw much more action south of the border than he did in the United States. In the Negro Leagues, his lifetime record is said to be 11-6, whereas in Cuba it was 115-60, and in Mexico, 119-57.

Martin was also a star in Venezuela, where he played from 1931–1934. In Cuba in this period, he was a member of the Almendares club, pitching and playing the outfield.

Martin did not return to the States until 1935, for his first of two seasons with the New York Cubans of the Negro National League. In the first of those years, he hit .372 in league games, and starred in the East-West All-Star Game. He started that game in center field, batted third in the lineup, and finished the game pitching in relief.

After the 1936 season, Martin tried his hand in the Dominican Republic. He played 25 games there and hit .351 before moving over to Mexico, where he based his summer season every year until 1944. In the winters, it was always back home to Cuba, where he played for Santa Clara (1935–36), Marianao (1936–38), Havana (1938–39), Cienfuegos (1939–40), and Havana (1940–45). Although he never lost his reputation as a great hitter, the existing statistics from Cuban Winter League baseball point towards a lifetime average of slightly under .300 for his many years in the league. It was as a pitcher that his reputation grew in his homeland.

Martin's final venture into the United States came in 1945, when he managed the New York Cubans to a championship. Playing briefly, he made the All-Star team, but batted only .204 and had a 1-2 record on the mound.

In 1946, the Dodgers signed Jackie Robinson and the color line was broken. But Dihigo was already 41 years old and it was too late for him to make his move. His

Martin Dihigo watches the play from the dugout. In the Negro Leagues and in Mexico and his native Cuba, he was an awesome batter and a formidable pitcher.

career turned to Mexico, where he managed and played for Veracruz as late as the 1957 season.

In Mexico, Dihigo pitched the first no-hitter in Mexican League history, after earlier hurling one in Venezuela, and another in Puerto Rico.

When the Castro government made travel difficult in the late 1950s and early 1960s, Martin retired from baseball for good, and settled in Cienfuegos, the town in which he concluded his Cuban Winter League play in 1947. He married a woman from Cruces and had one son, Martin, Jr. A national hero, Dihigo was named Minister of Sports in Cuba. He was named to both the Cuban and Mexican Halls of Fame.

But his inability to leave Cuba made him virtually unknown to a whole new generation of Americans. People like Monte Irvin and Roy Campanella, who had considered Dihigo among the best they ever saw, kept his name alive in the States.

Dihigo died on May 20, 1971 in Cienfuegos, Cuba, just before his 66th birthday. He was named to the Hall of Fame in 1977 on the basis of his achievements in the Negro Leagues.

MARTIN DIHIGO

Negro Leagues, 1923–1931, 1935–1936, 1945

No records available.

John Henry Lloyd (1884-1965)

"Pop" Lloyd was one of the first great stars of the Negro Leagues, and a shortstop so adept he came to be known as the "Black Wagner." The legendary Honus Wagner, turned the compliment around, saying "It's a privilege to have been compared to him."

John Henry Lloyd was born on April 15, 1884, with the place of birth variously listed as Palatka, Jacksonville or Gainsville, Florida. His father died while he was an infant, and when his mother remarried Lloyd was raised by his grandmother. As a youngster he completed his education with the seventh grade, worked as a delivery boy, and played ball. In his teens he took a job as a porter for the Southern Express Company in Jacksonville, and worked in a store. He played semipro ball for a team known as the Young Receivers, and in 1905, at the age of 21, he joined a fast semipro outfit in Georgia, the Macon Acmes, as a catcher.

The following year he entered the ranks of professional baseball, joining a team known as the Cuban X-Giants. None of the players were Cuban; all were American Negroes like Lloyd. In his very first game, John beat the Wilmington Giants with a tenth inning double. He was on his way.

There was not a great deal of stability to the Negro Leagues, players tending to go from club to club in search of the best money. Lloyd was no different. He played out of a love of baseball, but the conditions were rough, and he was always seeking the better deal. It was not uncommon to see John play a 12-month schedule, heading for warmer climates south of the border once the American season ended.

In 1907, John headed north and joined the Philadelphia Giants. There, his manager, Sol White, switched him from second base to shortstop to take advantage of his long arms, big hands, and outstanding range. The move was a brilliant one, for Lloyd developed into one of the best shortstops in baseball history.

Lloyd spent three seasons with Philadelphia, and, in the winter, played for the Havana Reds. After the 1910 season, he played for the Almendares club in Cuba in a 12-game exhibition series against the American League champion Detroit Tigers. Detroit managed to win only seven of the games. Lloyd hit .500 in the series, while Ty Cobb batted .370. The Cubans called John "El Cuchara"—the Shovel.

In 1911, John went to New York, where he starred with the Lincoln Giants. This team, operated by Jess and Rod McMahon, played their games in Harlem at 136th Street and Fifth Avenue, and attracted great crowds. In one of the few seasons in which statistics were compiled, John was reported to have batted .475 with 112 hits in 62 games.

It was with Lincoln that Lloyd had an opportunity to play some exhibitions against John McGraw's Giants in 1913. That was the year his team won the first championship of the Negro Leagues, besting Rube Foster's Chicago club six games to four. McGraw was so favorably impressed with Lloyd that he toyed with the idea of bringing John into the National League. But the idea came and went, and baseball was not integrated until Jackie Robinson signed with the Dodgers in 1946.

Lloyd teamed up with the great Rube Foster in 1914, heading for Chicago to play for the American Giants. This was a reunion of sorts, as Lloyd had spent part of the 1910 season with Foster on the Leland Giants. Now, returning at age 30, he was at the peak of his career. The 5'11", 180 pound righthander was already considered one of the greats of the game.

Lloyd played in Chicago into 1918, also holding a job that year in the Army Quartermasters depot. Then his first opportunity to manage developed, and he left Foster to join the Brooklyn Royal Giants as player-manager. This became the pattern for the remainder of his career. He continued to play, while developing the reputation of a fine manager in the Connie Mack tradition—patient and paternal. John didn't drink and didn't smoke, save for an occasional cigar. In later years, men like Mack, McGraw, and Hughey Jennings all rated Lloyd as among the best players in baseball history.

In 1919, Lloyd was playing manager of the Bacharach Giants. In 1921 he led the Columbus Buckeyes, and in 1923, he managed the Philadelphia Hilldale club, while compiling an average estimated at .415. The following year, he was back with the Bacharachs, leading the league with a .444 average for 41 league games.

Lloyd continued his professional career as a player and manager until 1931, when he was 47 years old. By then, he had shifted to first base, but he could still hit with authority. He earned his pay in those years from the Royal Giants, the Buckeyes, the Bacharachs, Hilldale, and Lincoln.

With his retirement in 1931, John settled in Atlantic City, New Jersey. He didn't marry until 1944, when he and Nan Moore were wed. They had no children.

Lloyd became a janitor in the Atlantic City post office, and in the mid-30s became school janitor at the Indiana Avenue School. There he became a great favorite of the youngsters, who called him by his baseball nickname, "Pop," and he was appointed commissioner of the Atlantic City Little Leagues. He continued to play semipro ball until he was 58 years old, holding down first base for the Johnson Stars and the Farley Stars. In 1949, a large city park was named in his honor.

It was not until *Esquire* magazine did a story on Lloyd in 1938, comparing him to Babe Ruth, that he received wide attention among white baseball fans.

Lloyd died on March 19, 1965 in Atlantic City at the age of 80.

JOHN HENRY LLOYD

Negro Leagues, 1905–1931

No records available.

John Henry Lloyd in 1918 when he joined the Brooklyn Royal Giants as player-manager. A shortstop until then, Lloyd often placed himself at first base, and, according to available figures, maintained a .400 batting average.

Al Lopez (b. 1908)

Al Lopez seemingly made a career out of finishing second to his friend Casey Stengel, but the ledger shows him to be the 10th winningest manager in history, and the player who caught more games in the major leagues than anyone.

Alfonso Raymond Lopez was born in Tampa, Florida on August 20, 1908. Both his parents were born in Spain, and although Al never had a trace of a Castilian accent, he came to be known as "The Señor" among baseball people.

Al's father worked in a cigar factory in Ybor City, Florida, and Al himself would join in when on vacation from school. It was in school and on the sandlots that his coach Frank McKenna developed Al's interest in baseball, and Al never had any ambition other than to be a player.

He was only 16 years old when the opportunity arrived. The Washington Senators, preparing for what would be their championship season of 1925, were training in Tampa. Manager Bucky Harris needed an extra catcher one day for his pitching staff, and spotted Al in the stands with a rather inexpensive mitt. He recruited Lopez to help out, and Al put on catching gear and warmed up Walter Johnson. It was quite a thrill, but the Senators gave him a day's wages and sent him on his way.

Several weeks later, Al signed a contract with the Tampa club in the Florida State League, and his baseball career was underway. He spent two years with Tampa and then moved up to Jacksonville (Southeastern League) in 1927. There, he had an opportunity to participate in a game against the Brooklyn Dodgers (or "Robins," as they were called, after manager Wilbert Robinson). The great Dazzy Vance was the pitcher, and Lopez came through with a double and a triple. Robinson was greatly impressed with the right-handed hitter, and promptly purchased his contract for $10,000, a large sum at the time.

Lopez was assigned to Macon for the 1928 season, but managed to appear in three games for the Dodgers at the end of the year. They were the first of 1,918 games behind the plate for Lopez, a record for catchers.

In 1929, Al hit .327 for Atlanta and was at last ready for the major leagues. At 5'11" and 165 pounds, he was not a giant of a man, but he was a strong, aggressive player, who managed to stay relatively injury free throughout his career.

Al had a splendid rookie season in 1930, batting .309 in 128 games. It was the first of three seasons in which he topped the .300 mark, en route to a lifetime batting average of .261. Al was not a power hitter, managing only 52 homers over his 19 seasons, but he was by no means an easy out.

Lopez stayed with the Dodgers through the 1935 season. He caught over 100 games every year, including a high of 137 in 1934. That year he was behind the plate late in the season as the Dodgers bested the Giants to spoil New York's pennant hopes in favor of the Cardinals. In 1933 he tied a record by pulling off an unassisted double play. He played for Robinson, Max Carey, and Casey Stengel during his Dodger years, and Stengel finally dealt him to Boston in 1935 with Tony Cuccinello, Ray Benge, and Bobby Reis for Ed Brandt and Randy Moore. By 1938, Stengel had come over to manage the Braves, and two years later, he traded Al again, this time to Pittsburgh for Ray Berres and $4000. Lopez' friendships in the game were long lasting, however—he and Stengel, who were later rival managers in the American League, were always close. And Cuccinello became a loyal coach for Lopez for many years.

Lopez remained with the Pirates through the 1946 season. In 1941, he caught 114 games without a passed ball. But by 1945, he was no longer a full-time player. In 1947 he was traded to Cleveland for Gene Woodling, finishing up his playing career by catching in 57 games and hitting .262.

Now 39 years old, Lopez was not interested in remaining a part-time player. Bill Veeck, owner of the Indians, came close to naming Lopez the Tribe's manager for 1948, but public pressure made him stay with Lou Boudreau. The Indians won the pennant, and Lopez took over the managing job at Indianapolis of the American Association. He spent three seasons there, finishing first, second, and second. Whereas Al never played with a pennant winner in his 19 seasons as a catcher, he was now embarking on a managing career which would find him a perennial contender.

After the 1950 season, Cleveland general manager Hank Greenberg hired him to succeed Boudreau at last. Al won 93 games and brought the Indians home second in 1951. He was second in 1952 and 1953 as well, trailing Stengel's Yankees each time. Finally, he broke through in 1954, winning a record 111 games. The Indians were led by a pitching staff featuring Bob Lemon, Early Wynn, Mike Garcia, Art Houtteman, and Bob Feller, plus hitters Bobby Avila, Al Rosen, and Larry Doby. Despite the sensational season, the Giants swept the Indians in four straight in the 1954 World Series.

The year away from the game did not seem to bother Amos a bit. He had a 29-8 record in 1897, for the best winning percentage in the league. The Giants, seventh in 1896, were third in 1897. Rusie pitched 300 innings in 1898, posting a 20-10 record for his eighth consecutive season of 20 or more wins, and for a lifetime total of 241.

Following the 1898 season, Freedman attempted to cut Rusie's pay from $3000 to $2000, and to include fine provisions of $100 per offense. Rusie, feeling he was being humiliated, sat out the 1899 season.

He seemed to have settled his differences in 1900 and reported to spring training, but marital problems found him following his estranged wife to Muncie, Indiana, and leaving his career behind him. He was remarried to his first wife several months after a divorce.

In 1901 the Cincinnati Reds still found Rusie an attractive hurler, and decided to trade a rookie pitcher they had drafted from the Giants just a few months before. His name was Christy Mathewson, and while he went on to win 373 games for the Giants, Rusie was 0-1 in three games for the Reds before giving up.

He moved west to Seattle and labored for 10 years as a steamfitter in a paper mill and eventually became foreman. In 1921 John McGraw brought him back to New York for a time as a security officer at the Polo Grounds, but Rusie had developed a prosperous chicken farm in Seattle and left baseball for good. The depression of the 1930s ruined his business, and in 1934, a serious automobile accident left him with a concussion and in bad health for the rest of his life. He died in Seattle on December 6, 1942—two months after his wife—at the age of 71. He was survived by one daughter.

AMOS WILSON RUSIE

Indianapolis 1889
New York (N.L.) 1890–98
Cincinnati 1901

G	IP	W	L	PCT.	H	R	ER	SO	BB	ERA
412	2410	241	158	.604	3177	1908	inc.	1953	1637	inc.

After pitching one season (1899) for Indianapolis, Amos Rusie went to New York where he gained fame on the mound and notoriety in a salary dispute.

Joe Sewell (b. 1898)

In 14 seasons in the majors, Joe Sewell went to bat 7,132 times and struck out only 113 times. (A 1923 strikeout wrongly charged against him has set his record at 114 in some sources.)

Joseph Wheeler Sewell was born in Titus, Alabama on October 9, 1898, the son of a physician. He was the oldest of three brothers who reached the big leagues. Luke Sewell, two years younger, was a catcher for 20 years in the American League (1921–1942). From 1921–1930, he was a teammate of Joe's on the Cleveland Indians, and was later a major league manager with the Browns and the Reds. A third brother, Tommy, was an infielder who appeared in one game with the Cubs in 1927. He was eight years Joe's junior.

Alabama was always home to Joe, who went to the public schools in Titus, and then to the University of Alabama. There, his coach and mentor was Xen Scott, a famous football coach, who also had good connections in professional baseball. It was on his recommendation that the 5'7" shortstop found himself in pro ball in 1920 upon leaving school.

Joe spent spring training of 1920 with the Cleveland Indians, but didn't make much of an impression on manager Tris Speaker. The lefthanded-hitting infielder weighed only 155 pounds, and failed to distinguish himself in his first training camp. He was optioned to New Orleans and spent the year adjusting to daily baseball games and long bus rides.

Meanwhile, the Indians were seeking their first American League pennant. Their hopes were set back tragically in August when Ray Chapman, their fine shortstop, was struck in the head by a pitch delivered by the Yankees' Carl Mays. Chapman died the next day—the only player ever killed in a major league game.

The Indians' only replacement for Chapman, was Harry Lunte, who was batting only .197 when he hurt his leg on Labor Day. Desperate now, Cleveland owner Jim Dunn suggested Sewell to Speaker. Tris remembered Joe as quite raw and not ready for the major leagues, but when he learned that Joe was hitting .289 at New Orleans, he decided to give the young player a shot at the job.

To get Sewell, Dunn paid New Orleans $6000 and forfeited his club's rights to all optioned New Orleans players.

Speaker advised Sewell just to "get a piece of the ball," and sent Joe out into a pennant race. The 21-year old Alabamian responded with a single and a triple in his first game and went on to bat .329 in the remaining 22 games of the season, as the Indians won their first flag.

As Joe had arrived after September 1, special permission was needed from the Dodgers for him to appear in the World Series. The permission was granted, and Joe played in every game, as the Indians won the World Championship. He batted only .174 and made six errors however.

Joe had no competition for the shortstop job in 1921. He played in 154 games and batted .318, driving home 91 runs. Unfortunately, the Indians failed to repeat as pennant winners, as the Yankees began their dynasty that season. But Joe settled down as a quality hitter for the Indians, and a durable performer. From September 13, 1922 until April 30, 1930, he played in 1,103 consecutive games, a major league record later broken by Everett Scott and then by Lou Gehrig. It is still the fourth longest streak in baseball history, with Billy Williams the only other player to pass it.

Joe hit over .300 ten times in his 14-year career and twice batted in over 100 runs (1923–1924). But it was his incredible ability to put "Black Betsy," his 40 ounce bat, on the ball, that made him famous. In 1925, 1929, and 1933 he struck out only four times each season, going to bat 608 times in 1925, 578 times in 1929, and 524 times in 1933. In only four seasons did he reach double figures in strikeouts, with a high of 20 in 1922. With 7,132 lifetime at bats, he averaged a strikeout once every 62 times at bat, or approximately once every 14 games.

Joe had his finest season in 1923, when he batted .353 with 41 doubles, 10 triples and 4 home runs. He was never a power hitter, connecting for only 49 homers in his career, 19 of them as a Yankee.

In the field, Joe was less steady. He made 111 errors in 1923–1924, leading the league with 59 in the latter season. By 1928, he was shifted to third base, where he managed to lead the league in assists.

Joe was an 11-year veteran at the age of 32 when the 1930 season ended, and in January, 1931, he was released by the Indians. The emphasis in baseball was now on the long ball, and although Joe had batted .289 in 1930, he hadn't hit any home runs. As irony would have it, he was picked up by the team hitting the most home runs of all—the New York Yankees, ready to embark on their first season under manager Joe McCarthy.

Joe was positioned at third base in 1931, finding himself a teammate of Babe Ruth, Lou Gehrig, Bill Dickey, Earle Combs, Lefty Gomez, Red Ruffing; and Herb Pennock, all future Hall of Famers. Joe hit .302 that year as the Yankees finished second, and then in 1932, he found himself in another World Series. His contribution that year was a .272 average with a career high of 11 home runs. In the four game series sweep of the Cubs, Joe batted .333.

His final year as an active player came in 1933, as he batted .273 to give himself a career mark of .312. The Yankees released him after the season along with Pennock, and Joe's playing days were over. He stayed with McCarthy as a coach in 1934 and 1935, and then left baseball and took his family back to Alabama. In 1953, he returned to baseball as a scout, serving eleven years with the Indians and one with the Mets. Bear Bryant then made Joe baseball coach at his alma mater, the University of Alabama, and he lead his team to the 1968 Southeastern Conference title. After six years he retired to become a public relations representative for a milk distributor in his home of Tuscaloosa. He and his wife raised two sons who became doctors, and a daughter who married one.

JOSEPH WHEELER SEWELL

Cleveland 1920–30
New York (A.L.) 1931–33

G	AB	R	H	2B	3B	HR	RBI	Avg.
1903	7132	1141	2226	436	68	49	1051	.312

The swing that always connected: Joe Sewell, who batted .312 in his career with the Indians and the Yanks, had the lowest strikeout record in the majors.

1978 Inductees

Addie Joss (1880-1911)

Addie Joss was one of the first great pitchers in the American League, but his untimely death at the age of 31 prevented full appreciation of his talents by baseball fans.

He was born on April 12, 1880, in Juneau, Wisconsin, and named Adrian Joss. During his career, he was frequently listed as Adrian C. Joss, probably after Adrian C. Anson, the famous nineteenth-century star, but in fact he had no middle name or initial.

Born into a large family, he was sent by his widowed mother to live with her sister to ease some of the burden. But Addie still lived in Juneau and attended public school there. He was a good student and quite athletic as well. He seemed to take to pitching at a tender age, and was a star with his school teams throughout high school. Tall for his age (he grew to be 6'3" and weighed 185 pounds), he was nevertheless well coordinated.

Following high school, he enrolled in Sacred Heart Academy in Watertown, Wisconsin, where his pitching was recognized throughout the state. He played semipro ball in both Juneau and Sheboygan, and attended some classes at the University of Wisconsin.

A peddler observed Joss in action and recommended him to Bob Gilks, manager of the Toledo team in the Inter-State League. Gilks paid the peddler $25 for the tip and signed Joss to a contract. Addie was a fast hit for the Toledo club, which was owned by Charles J. Strobel. He won 19 games, including a one-hitter, a pair of two-hitters, and 2 four-hitters. He was charged with 16 defeats, but under the watchful eyes of Strobel and Gilks, he matured into a first-rate performer.

In 1901 Toledo moved into the Western Association, and Joss remained with the team and made Toledo his home for the rest of his life. He had a 25–11 record that season and was pursued by major league clubs.

In March 1902, he joined the Cleveland franchise of the young American League, a team managed by Bill Armour. The transfer was held in dispute since Toledo claimed to maintain rights to him, and Brooklyn, under Charles Ebbets, also claimed to have an agreement with Joss. The two major leagues were still feuding, and there seemed to be no hope that the Cleveland-Brooklyn dispute could be resolved. But Cleveland eventually paid Toledo $500 to assure ownership rights. In later years, when Joss reached stardom, writers would return to the $500 figure and report that "he couldn't be bought for $25,000 today."

Addie made his debut on April 26, 1902, in St. Louis and proceeded to fire a one-hit shutout against the Browns. The only

safety for the losers was a hit to right by Jesse Burkett that Zaza Harvey claimed to have caught.

Addie struck out four of the first six batters he faced, en route to his first of a league-leading five shutouts. Cleveland finished only two games above .500 for the 1902 season, but Joss developed into the team's top pitcher, winning 16 games (some sources say 17), and losing 13. He flirted with a second no-hitter on May 4 against Detroit, when he had one out in the ninth inning before Bill Bradley made an error at third base. Two singles followed to spoil the rookie's effort.

Addie was one of the few college-educated men in baseball, but he was a "regular guy," and fit in well with his teammates. He even joined three of them in forming a singing quartet, which toured vaudeville stages in off-seasons.

Joss also occupied his off-seasons as a sportswriter, contributing baseball columns to his local paper in Toledo, as well as an occasional story for *The Sporting News.* He was a charter member of the National Baseball Writers Association, and obviously a favorite of the writers who covered Cleveland baseball.

Addie married and had two children. He became active in the Masons, reaching the 32d degree, and was a member of the Mystic Shrine.

On the mound, the lanky righthander was very deceptive. He threw hard but also had a variety of breaking pitches. In pitching, he rotated in a complete pivot, swinging his arm quickly with a sidearm, almost catapult, motion.

In an era when pitchers were important for their fielding abilities, Joss was recognized as one of the better fielding pitchers. He was especially strong handling bunts, and led the league in fielding percentage in 1904.

He was also all business and a fast worker on the mound. In 1903 he locked into a duel with Philadelphia's Rube Waddell, losing 2–1 in 14 innings, the game lasting only two hours and 10 minutes.

The 1903 season saw Joss compile an 18–13 record (some sources say 19–13), as Cleveland moved up to third place.

Although earned run averages were not compiled until the 1920s, it was possible to go back in the records and determine them. So while no one was actually aware of it, Joss had a league-leading 1.59 ERA in 1904 to go with a 14–9 record. By the time his career was over, he would have a 1.88 ERA, second only to Ed Walsh.

As a college-bred player, Addie was part of a small minority in the early days of the American League, but he was personable and well liked by teammates. His delivery, illustrated here, tended to be sidearm, a manner difficult to control, but very effective once mastered.

Durability was Addie's game. He completed 60 of his first 61 major league starts, missing only on August 1, 1902, when he left the game in the fifth inning with a twisted knee. In all, he started 261 games and completed 235 of them. Excluding errors, he allowed an average of only 8.73 runners per nine innings, the best proportion ever compiled. And while he was striking out 926 batters, he walked only 370 in 2336 innings.

Teammate Napolean Lajoie became Cleveland's manager in 1905 and the team became known as the Naps. Joss headed the pitching staff and won 20 games for the first of four consecutive seasons.

In 1906 he was 21–9 for the third place Naps, and then in 1907 he led the league with 27 victories, losing only 10, and compiling a 1.83 ERA. Still, the Naps failed to challenge for the pennant.

The potential for a serious run existed in 1908, however, and Joss made everyone aware of it early. He pitched and won 5 of Cleveland's first 9 games—then 8 of 13 and 9 of 15. In his first nine starts, he walked only four batters, and he won 9 of his first 10 outings. The season developed into a four-team race between Detroit, Cleveland, St. Louis, and Chicago, with the Browns dropping out first.

On October 2, in front of a big crowd in Cleveland, Joss locked horns with the ace of the White Sox staff, Ed Walsh. Walsh was on his way to a 40-victory season and was in his prime, but Joss was to be a 24–12 pitcher that year and the matchup was well publicized.

Walsh, as expected, was brilliant. He allowed only four hits while striking out 15, and the only run he permitted was on a wild pitch.

Joss, meanwhile, was striking out only three, but he got Chicago to hit ground balls all afternoon, resulting in 16 putouts for his first baseman. In the end, Joss had hurled a perfect game—only the fourth in history, and the second for the American League. (The first in the majors was by John Richmond of Worcester in 1880. Richmond later taught high school math to Joss's son in Toledo.)

The day after the perfect game, however, Walsh beat Cleveland and knocked them out of the pennant race, as Detroit finished first. It was the closest Joss ever came to playing for a pennant winner.

Cy Young became a teammate of Joss in 1909, and Addie, with a 14–13 record, was no longer the ace of the staff. But pitching on opening day in Chicago, on April 20, 1910, he again no-hit the White Sox, this time allowing two walks, and it appeared that he was back on his form. But later that year he hurt his elbow in Philadelphia, and was able to compile only a 5–5 record for the season.

Considering his value to the club, Cleveland hired a trainer just to work with Addie during the off-season in Toledo. The trainer stayed with him into spring training of 1911, and Addie reported that he felt good.

Spring training was drawing to a close, and he had already been named to pitch on opening day. But on April 3 in Chattanooga, he fainted and was taken to a hospital. He rejoined his teammates that night and joked about his "baby act" to get out of work.

But by the time the club reached Cincinnati, he knew something was wrong. He told Charles Somers, the Cleveland owner, that he felt like going home to Toledo, and permission was granted. There, physicians first diagnosed his trouble as pleurisy, complicated by water on the chest and symptoms of brain trouble. Within a few days, he was dead. Tubercular meningitis was determined to be the cause.

His funeral was to be in Toledo on opening day, and his teammates refused to play in order to attend. Newspapers reported that they "went on strike" against management's wishes, but the game was later rescheduled. Player-turned-evangelist Billy Sunday presided over the funeral, and the baseball world was in shock.

On July 24, 1911, a benefit was held in Cleveland between a team of American League All-Stars and Joss's teammates. Nearly $13,000 was raised for his widow and two children.

Hall of Fame entry requirements called for participation in 10 seasons of major league baseball. Joss, missing his opening-day assignment in 1911, had only nine, and this technicality kept him out of the Hall until the rule was waived by the newly expanded Veterans' Committee in 1978.

ADRIAN JOSS

Cleveland 1902–1910

G	IP	W	L	Pct	H	R	ER	SO	BB	ERA
287	2336	160	97	.623	1895	inc.	487	926	370	1.88

Larry MacPhail (1890-1975)

Larry MacPhail was a flamboyant baseball executive who combined showmanship with great business acumen to find success with three major league clubs.

Leland Stanford MacPhail was born on February 3, 1890, in Cass City, Michigan, to Curtis William MacPhail and the former Katherine McMurtrie. His grandfather was an immigrant from Scotland. He had a half brother, Herman, from his father's first marriage.

His father started with a general store in Cass City, but a good sense of finance soon took him into the field of banking, and eventually he owned a chain of 21 small banks in Michigan. The family would move frequently throughout the state as each branch was established. Larry was graduated from Ludington High School and attended Staunton Military Academy, where he was an outstanding student and athlete, participating in baseball and football.

At 16 he passed the entrance examination for the Naval Academy in Annapolis, but his parents advised him to delay such schooling until he was older. Instead, he enrolled in Beloit College and began to study law, while also playing baseball and football.

He transferred to the University of Michigan in 1907 and then to Georgetown University, from which he received a law degree in 1910, attending school at night while stringing for the Washington *Herald* as a sportswriter and performing secretarial duties for the United States Senate. He was only 20 years old when he got his degree in law, and he soon moved to Chicago to join a law firm, passing up a consular appointment to a small French seaport.

In Chicago he met and married Inez Francis Thompson and within six months became a partner in another law firm. One of his clients was the Rich Tool Company, and he soon left his law practice to be their sales manager.

After a year, MacPhail became president of Huddleston-Cooper Company, a large Nashville department store, where he met former U.S. Senator Luke Lea. With the outbreak of World War I, Lea and MacPhail formed a volunteer artillery regiment, and MacPhail enlisted as a private. By the time he was sent overseas in February 1918, he had risen to captain.

His most memorable war experience was an abortive attempt to kidnap the Kaiser in the Netherlands. Lea and MacPhail got inside the castle where the Kaiser was residing, but save for an ashtray MacPhail managed to grab, the mission was a failure.

Discharged in April 1919, MacPhail found a partner and established the Standard Corporation, in Columbus, Ohio, a glass-manufacturing company. In 1923, he became the Ohio distributor for Overland and Wills St. Claire automobiles, sold his interest, and entered real estate, building a medical office building in Columbus. He also worked on improving his golf game, and was a semifinalist in the Ohio amateur competition in 1928.

Baseball was still a strong interest of his, as well as officiating in Big Ten football games. And in 1930, he had his first opportunity to enter pro baseball—purchasing the Columbus franchise in the American Association for $100,000, with the help of local backers.

Searching for a connection with a major league club, MacPhail was introduced to Branch Rickey of the Cardinals, and promptly sold Columbus to Rickey for a profit, retaining the club presidency.

MacPhail operated the Columbus team on a higher level than big league operators were used to observing. He clashed with Rickey over the Cardinals' right to players during the season. He put his farm team on an airplane for a road trip—something even major league teams were avoiding.

MacPhail made Columbus a financial success after many poor seasons. He drew great crowds, and instituted a playoff system for the minor leagues. He started a Knothole Gang for young fans, hired a 100-piece band, turned down the league presidency, continued football officiating, fired two managers, and built a pennant winner in 1933, his final year in Columbus. It was a stormy but successful tenure.

MacPhail's 1933 season actually ended in June, when the Cardinals had had enough of his lavish operation. But by that time, Larry had gotten wind of an attempt to sell the Cincinnati Reds, a financially starved team. MacPhail convinced the Cincinnati banks that he was the man to save the franchise. He talked Powell Crosley, Jr., a local refrigerator and radio manufacturer, into purchasing the Reds and installing him as general manager. By the time the 1934 season opened, the new regime was in power, with MacPhail calling the shots.

MacPhail's most memorable contribution to baseball came in 1935, when he installed lights in Crosley Field. He had done so in Columbus in 1932, and now received league approval to play seven night games a year. The first major league night game was played on May 24, 1935, and MacPhail got President Franklin D. Roosevelt to throw the switch from the White House to illuminate the field.

MacPhail painted his ballpark orange, hired girls as ushers, sponsored firework displays, hired bands, and put his team in the air for a flight to Chicago. He brought Red Barber to Cincinnati to handle radio broadcasts of the Reds.

Although Cincinnati didn't improve greatly in the standings, their finances improved and attendance soared. He brought in Chuck Dressen as manager, and began to build a club that would eventually win pennants in 1939 and 1940.

But MacPhail didn't last long enough to taste victory. An outspoken and volatile sort, he clashed with Crosley over assuming stock in the club, and by the end of the 1936 season, he was gone.

Claiming that baseball was too aggravating for him, he returned to Michigan where he joined his father and brother in an investment business. But after only a year, baseball called him back. Again, it was a club in financial trouble, and again, MacPhail was the man to visit the banks and get support. Branch Rickey recommended him to the Brooklyn Trust Company, with the Dodgers $500,000 in debt, and MacPhail was named club president.

Persuading the bank to advance him additional money, MacPhail purchased Dolph Camilli from the Phillies and began to renovate Ebbets Field. He imported Red Barber and began the first broadcasts of baseball in New York. He devised a pressroom for the writers, introduced night baseball to Brooklyn (with Johnny Vander Meer of the Reds hurling his second consecutive no-hitter on the premier occasion), obtained Pee Wee Reese, Pete Reiser, Joe Medwick, Dixie Walker, Whitlow Wyatt, and Billy Herman, hired the fiery Leo Durocher as manager, and won a pennant in 1941. He was named Executive of the Year by *The Sporting News* in 1939.

MacPhail left the Dodgers in 1942 to reenter the service, this time as a colonel in World War II, serving as a special assistant to the Undersecretary of War in Washington.

In 1945, he joined with Dan Topping and Del Webb to purchase the New York Yankees from the estate of Jacob Ruppert. He clashed with manager Joe McCarthy, as he so often had with Durocher, and McCarthy quit in 1946, allowing MacPhail to bring Bucky Harris in to manage.

He brought night baseball to Yankee Stadium, opened the first stadium dining room, began Old Timers' Day as an annual feature, and saw the Yankees win the 1947 pennant.

But while the club was celebrating that flag, MacPhail fought with his co-owners and general manager George Weiss at the victory celebration, and Topping and Webb bought him out the next day. He had retired from baseball, but he went out a winner.

MacPhail retired to a 930-acre estate in Bel Air, Maryland, including the Maryland Golf and Country Club that he built. He raised Black Angus cattle and thoroughbred racehorses on his Glenangus Farms. He served briefly as president of Bowie Race Track, and often attended Oriole games.

Among the innovations he brought to baseball were the groundwork for a player pension fund, spring training allowances, and moving expenses. He was considered the man most influential in bringing Happy Chandler to the commissioner's office.

His son Lee was a top executive with the Orioles and Yankees and became President of the American League in 1974. His other son, Bill, served as president of CBS sports. One of his two daughters became the Research Chief for *Life* magazine.

He died on October 1, 1975 (the day after Casey Stengel died), in Miami, Florida, at the age of 85, and was buried at his birthplace of Cass City, Michigan.

He was elected to the Hall of Fame in 1978.

(Top) *Behind the promotional schemes and innovations MacPhail brought to baseball was a hard-working front-office boss who spent long hours at his desk. His frequent disputes with employees, best exemplified by his firing of George Weiss as Yankee general manager in 1946, were often the result of his bombastic, quick-to-action manner.* (Bottom) *MacPhail meets with Grantland Rice, the dean of American sportswriters, in the hospitality suite, prior to the 1947 World Series. A week later, Larry retired from baseball. Ernest Heyn, editor of* Sport Magazine, *is in the center.*

Eddie Mathews (b.1931)

Eddie Mathews and teammate Hank Aaron combined to become the most prolific home run-hitting teammates in baseball history, surpassing the feats of even Babe Ruth and Lou Gehrig. And although Aaron eventually emerged as the all-time home run king, it was Mathews who captured the glamor in the early years of the duo, rivaling Mickey Mantle for national attention.

Edwin Lee Mathews, Jr., was born on October 13, 1931, seven days before Mantle, in Texarkana, Texas. His father, Ed, Sr., was a one-time semipro ballplayer in the Dallas area; his mother was the former Eloise Hess. Eddie was an only child.

When he was four, the Mathews family moved to Santa Barbara, California, where the senior Ed became a Western Union wire chief and covered that city's California League games. Both of Eddie's parents encouraged his interest in sports, and he remembers his mother pitching to him while his father shagged fly balls. The family spent a good deal of time with relatives, so that despite having no siblings, Ed was frequently surrounded by sports-minded cousins.

Eddie attended the Harding Grammar School, La Cumbre Junior High School, and Santa Barbara High School, where he starred as halfback for the football team. Baseball, however, was his principal interest, and since he was not scholastically inclined, he had little interest in pursuing a college football scholarship.

He first began to attract the attention of pro baseball scouts while playing the infield for the American Legion team in Santa Barbara. His infield work left a lot to be desired, but he was a remarkable power hitter, with a well-developed, muscular body despite his youth.

Johnny Moore, a former big leaguer and a scout for the Boston Braves, paid the most attention to Eddie, and befriended the Mathews family. These were, of course, the days before the draft system, and a scout's ingenuity could still pay off in recruiting talent.

Fifteen scouts were wooing Mathews, and the Pirates were reportedly prepared to offer as much as $30,000 for his signature. But Moore leveled with Eddie, advising him that he was really a raw talent and would need seasoning in the minors to become a major leaguer. A bonus of over $6000 would require, at that time, a move to the majors after only one season in the minors. Moore impressed the Mathews family with his honest appraisal of the situation, and also pointed out the vulnerability of the Braves at third base, where Bob Elliott seemed to be coming to the end of the line.

Graduation night coincided with the senior prom at Santa Barbara, and Moore cleverly sent a corsage to Mathews's date. While other scouts waited for the dance to end and the midnight deadline to pass, which would make Eddie eligible to sign a pro contract, Moore hustled Mathews, his date, and his parents out of the building and over to the Barbara Hotel, where he signed a $6000 contract, broken into bonus and salary to protect him from the one-year-and-up rule.

Ed was flown to Chicago where he put on a Braves' uniform and worked out with the team for a few days. His power impressed everyone. He joined the High Point–Thomasville team of the North Carolina State League, and immediately showed everyone why he was so highly regarded. In 63 games, he batted .363 with 17 homers, 62 runs, and 56 runs batted in. He had a .683 slugging percentage.

For 1950, Eddie was assigned to the Atlanta Crackers of the Southern League, where he hit 32 home runs and drove in 106, batting .286. His third base play was still considered suspect.

Following the 1950 season, Eddie enlisted in the Navy. But after a few months, his father became ill with tuberculosis, and Mathews received a dependency discharge as the sole support of his mother. The discharge, in the summer of 1951, permitted Eddie to return to Atlanta, where he appeared in 37 games and drove in 29 runs. Clearly, he was to be a potent run producer.

At the end of the 1951 season, Mathews was moved up to the Milwaukee Brewers of the American Association, the Braves' top farm club. He collected three hits in nine at bats and would never again play in the minors.

During spring training in 1952, two things helped speed Mathews's move to the majors. The first happened in the Braves' own camp, where Billy Jurges worked with Mathews and helped him develop greater confidence at third base.

Mathews and Hank Aaron may be looking in opposite directions here, but they generally shared the same view of a baseball —soaring over the fence for a home run. As teammates, they combined for 863 home runs in 13 seasons, more than even Babe Ruth and Lou Gehrig managed together.

Mathews can claim the unusual distinction of playing for the same team, the Braves, in three different home cities. Before Milwaukee and Atlanta, the Braves were based in Boston, and rookie Mathews, posing for this 1952 photo, wore a "B" on his cap.

A seasoned and wiser Mathews sported a mustache as Atlanta manager in 1974, but found modern players difficult to work with during his brief tenure in command.

The second happened in the Giants' spring camp, where Monte Irvin broke his ankle sliding into a base. Desperate for a replacement, the Giants acquired Elliott from the Braves, and Mathews was handed his job.

Already developed to a handsome 6'1" and 195 pounds, the powerful lefthand hitter moved right into the Boston Braves' lineup and played 145 games, batting .242. His salary was $8000 for the season, and with 25 home runs he tied for fourth in the league in that category. On September 27, he became the first rookie to ever hit three home runs in a single game.

However, he also set a rookie record with 115 strikeouts, tops in the National League, and it was obvious that he would need additional polish. That polish would come not in Boston, but in Milwaukee, where the Braves announced they were moving for the 1953 season.

Milwaukee fans greeted with great enthusiasm the Braves, especially the young bachelor Mathews, a hero among the ladies. And he was nothing short of sensational in 1953, belting 47 home runs to lead the National League at the age of 21. He hit 30 home runs on the road that year, a league record, and tied with Duke Snider for the league's top slugging percentage, .627. The 47 home runs set a

Braves' record, which was tied in 1971 by Aaron, when the team was in Atlanta and Mathews was a coach.

The 1953 season was also the first of nine in a row, a league record, in which Mathews would hit 30 or more home runs.

By 1954, Aaron had joined the team, and the Braves were building toward respectability. Mathews, "the National League's Mickey Mantle," was frequently admired for his long home runs and great run production. He would drive in over 100 runs five times, and score more than 100 eight times.

Together, Mathews and Aaron would hit 863 home runs as teammates between 1954 and 1966, a combined average of 64 a year. With the additions of Del Crandall, Billy Bruton, Joe Adcock, Johnny Logan, and Red Schoendienst to the lineup, the Braves were becoming a pennant contender, and the pitching staff, led by Warren Spahn and Lew Burdette, was first-rate. In 1957, it all fell together for the Braves. They won the National League pennant and then defeated the Yankees in a thrilling seven-game World Series. In that series, Mathews won the fourth game with a tenth inning home run, and nailed the final line drive in the ninth inning of the seventh game to wrap up the World Championship.

The Braves won the 1958 pennant, but this time lost the Series to the Yankees in seven. In 1959, Mathews won his second home run title, blasting 46, but the Braves lost the pennant in a playoff to the Dodgers, and never challenged again during Mathews's career.

In 1962, Mathews's home run production dropped under 30 for the first time in 10 years, and any talk of his breaking Babe Ruth's record was transferred to Aaron. In 1965, he rebounded to hit 32 home runs with 95 RBIs, his last big year.

Following the 1965 season, during which he was named captain of the Braves, the team moved again, this time to Atlanta, where Mathews had played minor league ball. He thus became the only man to play for the same team in three home cities.

Mathews batted .250 with 16 home runs in the first year in Atlanta, and when the season was over, he was traded to the Houston Astros where he would be converted to first base. As a third baseman, Eddie would wind up playing more games than any other National Leaguer (2154), and he tied Pie Traynor and Stan Hack for the league record of 16 seasons at third.

On July 22, 1967, Eddie was off again, this time to the Detroit Tigers. He was glad of the change—the Astros were a young club, while the Tigers had more veterans like himself.

Although now only a part-time player, Mathews was a popular addition to Detroit,

and in 1968, he was a key contributor off the bench as the Tigers marched toward a World Championship. Mathews missed some three months due to removal of a spinal disc, but he was activated in time to be eligible for the World Series. It was his first series in 10 years, and he wound up with a .200 batting average for his three Series.

A member of 12 All-Star teams, Eddie had only two hits in All-Star competition, but they were both home runs, coming in the 1959 and 1960 games.

Mathews retired following the 1968 season with 512 home runs, a total later tied by Ernie Banks for tenth on the all-time list. He was sixth at the time of his retirement. Forty-nine times in his career he belted two or more homers in a game, a total topped by only five players. He was also third, behind Mantle and Willie Mays, in career strikeouts with 1487, and eleventh in career walks with 1444.

Eddie became a representative of a sporting goods company in 1969 and 1970, and then returned to Atlanta as a coach in 1971. On August 7, 1972, he was named manager of the Braves, replacing Lum Harris. In 1973, his only full season as Atlanta manager, he finished fifth out of six in the Western Division with a 76–85 record. He was fired on July 22, 1974, and although taken by surprise, he later reflected that he found it difficult to manage modern players.

At times sullen and aloof early in his career, he was more outgoing as the years went on and was always a fan favorite. He was married twice, the second time to a daughter of St. Louis Cardinal owner Gussie Busch.

Mathews scouted for the Braves for the remainder of 1974 and all of 1975. He was out of baseball in 1976, and was a scout for the Milwaukee Brewers in 1977 and 1978. Mathews became a special assignment scout and hitting instructor for the Texas Rangers in 1979. It was during the 1978 season that he was elected to the Hall of Fame.

EDWIN LEE MATHEWS

Boston (N.L.) 1952
Milwaukee (N.L.) 1953–1965
Atlanta 1966
Houston 1967
Detroit 1967–1968

G	AB	R	H	2B	3B	HR	RBI	Avg.
2391	8537	1509	2315	354	72	512	1453	.271

1979 Inductees

Warren Giles (1896-1979)

Under the presidency of Warren Giles, who served longer than any of his 11 predecessors, the National League rose to competitive greatness, dominating All Star competition and achieving record growth. Giles saw to it that the league was considered first-class.

Warren Crandall Giles was born on May 28, 1896, in the small town of Tiskilwa, Illinois. He was the only son among five children born to William Giles, a painting contractor, and the former Isabella Slattery.

When Warren was four, the family moved to Moline, Illinois, where his interest in sports began to grow. Although he would eventually grow to a rotund 185 pounds at 5'8'', Warren was athletic as a youngster. He participated in all sports at Moline High School, and when he transferred to Staunton (Virginia) Military Academy, he played football, basketball, and baseball, serving as a second baseman on the baseball team. Larry MacPhail had attended Staunton a few years earlier.

After being graduated from Staunton, Giles enrolled in Washington and Lee University. But in April 1917, with funds running short and a world war developing, Warren dropped out and enlisted in officers' training camp at Fort Sheridan, near Chicago. World War I soon found him serving with the Seventeenth Provisional Training Regiment in France, where he was wounded in combat while leading a mortar platoon. His service complete, he returned to New York as a first lieutenant in 1919.

Faced at this point with little idea as to his future plans, Warren went to work for his father in Moline. One day his old baseball coach from high school asked him to intercede in a matter involving the local professional team, a member of the Three-I-League. It seemed that Moline's franchise also had a pro football team, and the high school wished to borrow the uniforms for an alumni game. Giles was asked to make the simple request.

Visiting with the club president, Warren found himself offering advice on the operation of the baseball team. The team's owner took to Giles, invited him to a stockholders' meeting, and before Giles knew it, he was elected club president. It was 1919, and the start of a half century of service to professional baseball.

Although Warren was unsalaried and still on his father's payroll, he devoted long hours to the running of the club. One of his first acts was to hire Earle Mack, son of Connie Mack, as manager.

Moline moved up into the first division in 1920, and then won the Three-I-League pennant in 1921. Although they failed in 1922, they had a strong team, and Giles's father urged him to either stay in the contracting business or seek a full career in baseball. Warren decided that baseball was his calling, but he needed a job that paid a salary. He contacted the league president, Al Tearney, who arranged for him to meet with the Minneapolis Millers of the American Association. He got his first paying job as business manager of the Millers' farm club of St. Joseph, Missouri. (In those days, the top Triple-A teams had their own farm clubs.)

After a third-place finish in 1923, Giles took the bold step of purchasing the St. Joseph team from Minneapolis. Among the players assigned to St. Joseph for the 1924 season was a St. Louis Cardinal prospect named Taylor Douthit.

Because of an oversight, the Cardinals left Douthit unprotected, and the player now belonged to Giles. Warren received several offers from major league teams for his contract, but recognizing the error made by the Cardinals' Branch Rickey, Giles telephoned and told Rickey, "The player is still yours."

Rickey never forgot Giles's integrity and generosity. In March 1926, he asked Giles to take over the Cardinals' top farm team in Syracuse, New York. Two years later, the franchise was shifted to Rochester, where the Red Wings promptly won four consecutive International League pennants and two Junior World Series, enhancing Giles's reputation and making Rochester one of the best minor league operations in organized baseball.

On October 29, 1932, Giles married Jane Skinner, the daughter of the mayor of Moline, and the great-granddaughter of John Deere, founder of the farm tool company. It was her second marriage, and she brought a daughter, Jean, into it. Warren and Jane had a son of their own, Bill, who became a baseball executive with Houston and Philadelphia. Jane died at the age of 39 in 1943 of a cerebral hemorrhage, and Warren never remarried.

Giles served as president of the Rochester Red Wings until September 1936. During his tenure there, he hired Gabe Paul to work with the team, and Paul eventually went with Giles into the major leagues.

When the International League president, Charles Knapp, died in 1936, Giles was elected to fill out his unexpired term while still running the Rochester team.

In August 1936, Giles signed a new, five-year contract with the Cardinals to continue running the Red Wings. Two weeks later, Powell Crosley offered him the vice-presidency of the Cincinnati Reds, a team $700,000 in debt and seeking a replacement for the departing Larry MacPhail.

Giles received permission from Rickey and the Cardinals to make the move, and within two years, the Reds jumped from the cellar to fourth place. Giles was named Executive of the Year for 1938 by *The Sporting News.* That year he brought up his Rochester manager, Bill McKechnie, to take over the club.

The Reds then captured the National League pennants in 1939 and 1940. As vice-president and general manager, Giles was hailed as one of the outstanding baseball executives in the country. In 1946, he was named president of the Reds.

In 1951, baseball owners were seeking a new commissioner to succeed Happy Chandler. The balloting soon came down to a struggle between National League President Ford Frick, and Giles. Warren came very close to winning the election, and might have made it, but after 17 ballots he saw that a compromise would be best for the game. He withdrew in favor of Frick, with the understanding that he would succeed Frick as league president. This peacemaking gesture received great attention.

Warren set up his offices in Cincinnati, taking over Chandler's old offices, while Frick, in New York, used his old league office as the new commissioner's office.

When Warren assumed office, the American League was still basking in the glory of the power-hitting days of Ruth, Gehrig, Greenberg, Foxx, and DiMaggio. In the eyes of the fans, it was the superior league, and in fact, it had won 12 of the first 17 All-Star games. While that did not necessarily indicate supremacy, baseball's All-Star battles were the most prestigious of any pro sport, and the public paid a great deal of attention to them.

When Giles entered the National League, it was beginning to feel the impact of gaining on its rival by signing black and Latin stars. The idea of the National League becoming superior was important to Giles. In his first year, he sent telegrams to every National League manager, urging them to beat American League teams in spring exhibitions. He hired a public relations man, and frequently sent out releases putting the National League in a favorable light. He always arranged for a National League team to arrive in a city first during World Series time so that it would receive greater attention. And he really concentrated on winning All-Star games—to the tune of 17 wins and a tie in 23 games during his administration.

The three best hitters of his tenure, Willie Mays, Hank Aaron, and Roberto Clemente, underscored the role played by blacks and Latins in the National League's growth.

Giles was a strong foe of interleague play, thinking that his league simply did not need it. He oversaw the expansion of the league in 1962, bringing in Houston and the Mets, and in 1969, when San Diego and Montreal joined. Montreal was the first Canadian team to enter major league baseball. Attendance boomed during Warren's presidency, going from 7.2 million in 1951 to 15.1 million in 1969.

Giles would not blanch at fining an umpire on occasion, and rather than appoint a supervisor of umpires, he handled that himself, occasionally dealing with the inevitable salary disputes of his staff. He claimed that his most difficult decision was the battle between Juan Mar-

Warren was a handsome doughboy in 1917, attending officers' training camp at Fort Sheridan, near Chicago, prior to duty in World War I.

ichal and John Roseboro in 1965, when Marichal clubbed the Dodger catcher with his bat. Giles suspended Marichal for three pitching turns and fined him $1750, which many felt was too light a penalty.

Even his son Bill, serving as publicity chief in Houston, came under his criticism for mocking opponents and umpires with the big Astrodome scoreboard. Warren had to reprimand him publicly.

In the long run, Giles's administration was marked by the increased prestige and expansion of the league to the West Coast in 1958 when the Dodgers and Giants relocated.

Giles was succeeded by Chub Feeney, and was named president emeritus for the balance of his life. He never missed a winter meeting, and was a great booster of the league well past his retirement.

Warren Giles died at the age of 82 on February 7, 1979, in Cincinnati. He could have been named to the Hall of Fame during his life, but he served on the Veterans' Committee and always urged them to select someone else. He was finally named by that committee a month after his passing.

The duties of a league president are both ceremonial and business-oriented. In the photo (above), Warren presents the 1955 MVP award to Brooklyn's Roy Campanella, as Commissioner Ford Frick (center) looks on. All three are in the Hall of Fame. (Below) Giles presides over a meeting in his Cincinnati offices.

Willie Mays (b. 1931)

Very few players have ever enjoyed the reputation of being "complete players"—men who could hit for power, hit for average, steal bases, field and throw brilliantly. Willie Mays was one of the few who earned such a reputation, and he came to be considered one of the best modern athletes in America.

Willie Howard Mays, Jr., was born on May 6, 1931, in Westfield, Alabama, a suburb of Birmingham. His father, William, worked in a steel mill and played some semipro ball, and his mother, Ann, was a high school track star. A grandfather, Walter Mays, had pitched for his town team in Tuscaloosa.

Because his parents were divorced before he entered elementary school, Willie spent a good part of his youth living with his Aunt Sarah in Fairfield, Alabama. When his mother remarried, he found himself with 10 half brothers and half sisters.

It was Willie's father who first started the youngster on his way to a baseball career. By the time Willie was six, the two played ball together, and at 14, Willie was pitching for his father's steel mill team.

At Fairfield Industrial High School, Willie was a three-sport star. He was the leading basketball scorer in the county, and was a star quarterback, fullback, and kicker in football. But baseball was his primary interest, and Joe DiMaggio his hero. With the steel mill team, Willie was playing with men twice his age—and he was a star among them!

At the age of 17, Willie was taken by his father to see Lorenzo Piper Davis, the manager of the Birmingham Black Barons of the Negro National League. These were the dying days of the Negro Leagues, since organized baseball had begun to sign the great Negro League stars two years before. But the league still contained some fine players, a chance for valuable experience, and in Mays's case, a chance to earn some money playing ball in his own hometown.

Davis insisted that Mays finish high school, which he did, after which he signed a contract with the Barons calling for $300 a season. Willie did not immediately achieve stardom. He failed to hit .300 in 1948, his first season, and a Dodger scout, Wid Mathews, reported that he "can't hit the curve."

He was, after all, still only 17 years old. The Barons won the championship in 1948, and in 1949, Willie raised his average to a reported .316. In 1950 he did even better, getting off to a fine start, with reports indicating an average of about .350. Statistics were never kept very well in the Negro Leagues.

Early in that 1950 season, the New York Giants sent scouts Ed Montague and Bill Harris to Birmingham, on a tip from another scout, Alex Pompez, to observe first baseman Alonzo Perry. They couldn't help but be impressed with the sleek and speedy Mays, who had already grown to his 5'11" height and 187-pound weight. Within a few days, Montague returned and

offered the Barons $10,000 for Willie, with a $6000 bonus going directly to Mays himself. The Giants outbid the Boston Braves and Chicago White Sox, and the deal was accepted.

Mays was sent to the Giants' Trenton, New Jersey, farm club in the Inter-State League to finish the 1950 season. He was to earn $250 a month, and it would be the first time he ever faced white competition. His manager was Bill McKechnie, Jr., son of the Hall-of-Famer, and despite an 0-for-22 debut, Mays wound up hitting .353 in 81 games, leading the league with 17 assists from his center-field position.

Baseball people were all aware of this rising star now, but Willie trained at the Giants' minor league camp in 1951, and started the season with Minneapolis, their top farm team in the American Association. There he appeared in the team's first 35 games and collected 71 hits—29 for extra bases, with 30 runs batted in and a phenomenal .477 batting average.

The Giants were off to a mediocre start (17–19), and manager Leo Durocher put out the call for Willie. Mays got the news but was scared to report. It took a lot of persuasion to convince him he was ready for the major leagues, and he reported to the Giants on May 25, 1951. Doubtless because of his nervous state, he went hitless in his first 12 at bats, hit a home run in the Polo Grounds off Warren Spahn, and then went hitless in his next 13 trips. The 1-for-26 debut saw his average at .039, and he was in tears in the Giants' clubhouse. Durocher told him to put his worries aside, that he would be in center field as long as Leo managed, and to just relax.

A father-son relationship developed between Durocher and Mays and never faded. None of the future managers Mays ever played for could measure up to Durocher in Willie's eyes. Mays became a key member, at the age of 20, of the 1951 Giants, a team that was 13 games behind Brooklyn on August 11, but that rallied to tie for first at the end of the season, and to go on to win an exciting three-game play-off, when Bobby Thomson hit "the shot heard round the world," to win the pennant (Mays was the on-deck hitter).

For the regular season, Mays wound up hitting .274 with 20 home runs, and was voted the National League's Rookie of the Year. It was the same season in which Mickey Mantle debuted for the Yankees, the Giants' World Series opponents, and the Yankees defeated their cross-river rivals in six games, with Willie collecting only 4 singles in 22 at bats.

Mays never had much success in World Series play, batting only .239 in his four World Series and failing to hit a home run in 71 at bats.

Willie got off to a slow start in 1952, and he was drafted into the Army on May 28 and assigned to Fort Eustis, Virginia, where he spent the next 22 months. He had a rather easy tour of duty, mostly playing ball, and he and the Army were later subjected to some criticism for it.

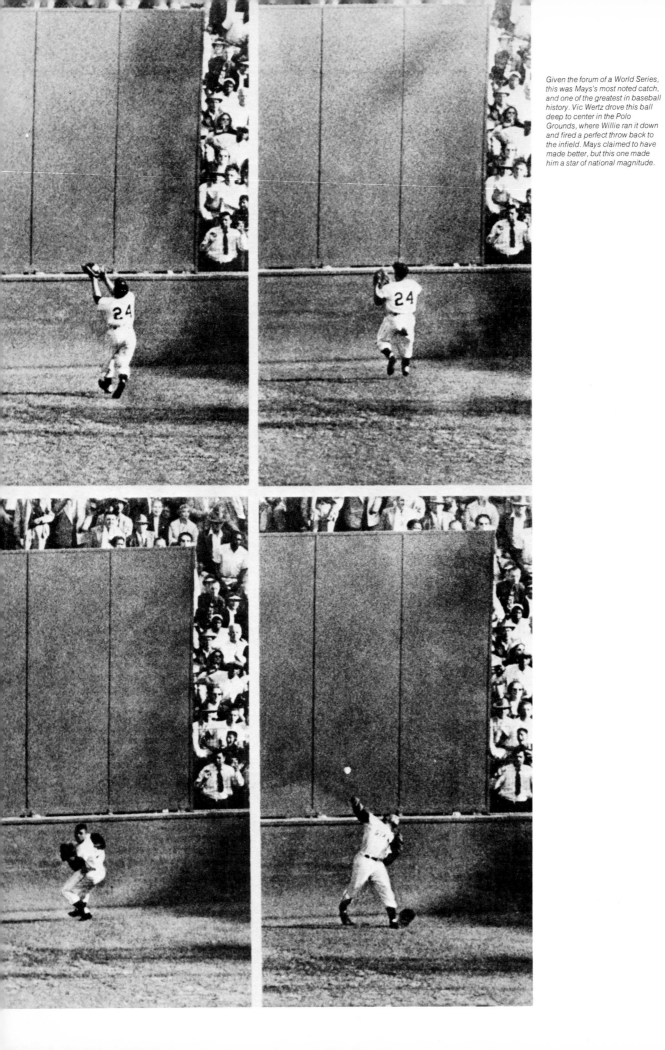

Given the forum of a World Series, this was Mays's most noted catch, and one of the greatest in baseball history. Vic Wertz drove this ball deep to center in the Polo Grounds, where Willie ran it down and fired a perfect throw back to the infield. Mays claimed to have made better, but this one made him a star of national magnitude.

In the army, Willie picked up a "basket catch," grabbing fly balls at waist level with glove up. It became part of the Mays style—the cap flying off his head, the daring base-running, the graceful manner. Later Mays became the first player to taper his uniform into a form-fitting style, paving the way for fashion on the field.

He didn't often play stickball on the streets of Harlem outside the Polo Grounds—perhaps only a handful of times—but the photographers duly recorded the event, and it became another trademark. New York fans loved him, and even those whose loyalties were with the Yankees, who had Mantle, or the Dodgers, who had Duke Snider, appreciated his greatness. It was in New York that he became the "Say-Hey Kid," after his expression for people whose names he didn't remember.

Returning to the Giants in 1954, Mays batted .345 to win his only batting title, and he also hit 41 home runs and drove in 110. The Giants won another pennant, and in the first game of the World Series, Willie made what may be the most famous catch in baseball history—a thrilling, back-to-home-plate grab of a tremendous drive off the bat of Vic Wertz, followed by a great throw to hold the runners in place.

By his own admission, it was not his greatest catch—he made plenty of great ones—but it was certainly the one that received the most attention from a national audience.

In 1954, when Mays won the Most Valuable Player Award and the Hickock Belt as Athlete of the Year, his stardom was assured. He played winter ball that year for the first and only time, saw his salary for 1955 go to $40,000, and knew he was on his way.

He won his first of four home run titles in 1955, belting 51, with a career high of 127 RBIs. In 1957, he hit 20 triples to lead the league, but at the end of the year, the Giants joined the Dodgers in moving west, bound for San Francisco. Mays's career in New York lasted only five full seasons, but his legend was never forgotten.

In San Francisco, he lost none of his skills, but his popularity didn't carry over. Here, he was competing with the memories of native heroes Joe DiMaggio and Lefty O'Doul—and even with young Giant stars such as Orlando Cepeda and Willie McCovey. He was never appreciated as much in San Francisco as he was in New York, and his returns with the Giants to play the Mets, starting in 1962, were always hailed with great enthusiasm.

The records and statistics began to mount up for Mays. He played relatively injury-free, save for a couple of blackouts in 1962 and 1963, diagnosed as exhaustion. The Giants won the 1962 pennant in a playoff with the Dodgers, with Mays a late-season playoff hero, finishing with a league-leading 49 home runs. His annual

(Top) Winner of the National League batting title and MVP award for 1954, Mays posed with some of the "spoils" at the start of the 1955 season. He won a second MVP honor in 1965 with San Francisco. (Bottom) Mays took physical conditioning very seriously, and although he was considered to have "natural talent," he never allowed himself to get out of shape. Here he's at work building his powerful forearms and shoulders during his early New York Giants' days.

Mays set a fashion trend in the early 1960s, when he became the first player to have his uniform made into a custom-fitted, tight look. The perfect fit seemed to match the perfect swing. Jerry Grote is the catcher for the Mets, with Jim Ray Hart in the on-deck circle.

salary went over the $100,000 level in 1963. In 1965, he hit a high of 52 homers and won his second MVP award.

He had married the twice-divorced Marghuerite Wendelle Kenny Chapman in 1956 and adopted her daughter. The couple then had a son of their own, but by 1962 the marriage had failed. Willie remarried in 1971, wedding San Francisco social worker Mae Louise Allen.

His closest friend among players was his first Giant roommate, Monte Irvin, but he was well liked by all players. In 1964 he became the first black player ever to be named team captain. He earned great respect as a peacemaker during the brutal bat-wielding fight between teammate Juan Marichal and the Dodgers's John Roseboro in 1965.

The idea of anyone catching Babe Ruth's home-run record of 714 was once unthinkable, but Willie was headed for the all-time National League mark of 511 held by Mel Ott, and he broke that in 1966. He eventually became the second man to reach 600 home runs, and set other National League marks that were later bettered by Hank Aaron. He wound up with 660 career home runs.

A perennial standout at the All-Star game, Willie was the MVP in the game twice (1963 and 1968), and tied a record by appearing in 24 of the games. He also had the most at bats, runs, and hits in All-Star play.

As a league leader, Mays topped the National League in the following departments—runs (twice); hits, walks, and bat-

ting average (once each); triples (three times); home runs (four times); stolen bases (four times); total bases (three times); and slugging percentage (five times).

He won 11 Gold Gloves for his play in the outfield, and was named Player of the Decade by *The Sporting News* in 1969. At the time of his retirement, he enjoyed the following ranks on the all-time charts: games (third), at bats (fourth), runs (third), hits (seventh), home runs (third), and RBIs (seventh).

In 1961, Willie hit four home runs in a single game. In 1965, he hit 17 home runs in one month (August), a National League record. He achieved his 3000th hit in 1970. He became the first man with 300 home runs and 300 stolen bases for a career, and twice he had at least 30 homers and 30 stolen bases in the same season. On 63 occasions he hit two or more home runs in a game, and 10 times he surpassed 100 RBIs in a season. He enjoyed 12 consecutive seasons of 100 or more runs scored, and set major league records for career putouts and total chances in the outfield.

Realizing that the Giants would be financially unable to care for Willie upon his retirement, owner Horace Stoneham stunned baseball on May 11, 1972, when he traded Willie back to New York—this time to the Mets—for rookie pitcher Charlie Williams and $50,000 in cash. Earlier in Willie's career Stoneham had turned down offers reported as high as $1,000,000 for Mays.

Mays made his Mets' debut on May 14, 1972, against the Giants—and hit a fifth-inning home run to break a 4–4 tie. While he was no longer the young star he had been when he first played in New York, the local fans loved his every move, and he

played for the Mets for two seasons, earning $150,000 a year, and finding himself a member of the 1973 National League champions in his final year.

True to their arrangement, the Mets made Willie a coach following his retirement, not requiring that he make every road trip. There was some early dispute as to whether he was in uniform often enough, but it was worked out in short order. Mays made all his Old Timers' Day appearances in a Met, rather than a Giant uniform, underscoring the way the Mets had "taken care of him" in the end.

In October 1979 Mays accepted an offer to become special assistant to the president of the Park Place Hotel in Atlantic City, New Jersey. It was a 10-year contract worth more than $1 million, but it forced Mays to leave the Mets when Commissioner Bowie Kuhn ruled that a baseball employee could not also be an employee of a gambling casino.

The great number 24, one of the finest righthanded hitters who ever lived, was elected to the Hall of Fame in his first year on the ballot, 1979.

WILLIE HOWARD MAYS

New York (N.L.) 1951–1957
San Francisco 1958–1972
New York (N.L.) 1972–1973

G	AB	R	H	2B	3B	HR	RBI	Avg.
2992	10881	2062	3283	523	140	660	1903	.302

Hack Wilson (1900-1948)

Hack Wilson was, for about six years, one of the premier sluggers in the history of the National League.

His father was Robert Wilson, and his mother, Jennie Caldwell, delivered him when she was only 16 years old. They were never married, and he was thus born as Lewis Caldwell on April 26, 1900, in Ellwood City, Pennsylvania. When Lew's mother died seven years later, the youngster went to live with his father and became Lewis Robert Wilson.

The senior Wilson was an iron mill worker, and Lew was raised for several years largely by a neighbor, Connie Wardman, a former minor league baseball player and a sponsor of local amateur teams. Wardman, very strict, had a strong influence on Lewis, who had become a behavior problem in school.

Lewis took well to baseball, and by age 10 was as good as boys much older. It was in that year that he and his father moved 350 miles east to Chester, Pennsylvania, where his father got a job in a forge shop.

By the age of 16, Lewis still hadn't completed the sixth grade, and he left school to go to work. He worked at various assignments in a print shop, a locomotive factory, and a silk factory, always managing to find some time for baseball. He developed great bulk in his upper body, and although he stood only 5'6" as an adult, he weighed a solid 195 pounds, much of it in his barrel chest and massive arms.

He played for all the local amateur teams, such as the Leipersville Field Club, the Good Will Fire Company, the Chester Athletic Club, the American Steel team, and finally, the Viscose Silk team, representing his employer. By the time he was 17, Lew was living on his own, although he maintained a good relationship with his father.

Wilson continued playing for local teams into 1921, dreaming of being discovered by a scout and reaching the big leagues. Information about this right-handed strongboy was passed along to Lewis Thompson, the president of the Martinsburg, West Virginia, team in the Blue Ridge League. Thompson signed Wilson, and his first step toward the major leagues had been taken.

Signed as a catcher, which seemed to best suit his stocky build, Wilson made a memorable debut. He reached base his first time at bat, but broke his leg sliding home and was out of action until July 11.

The broken leg in his first professional game was significant. In the first place, it helped to end his catching career, for when he returned, he found the stress on his leg difficult behind the plate. Furthermore, while hospitalized, he met a woman 10 years his senior, Virginia Riddleburger. He and Virginia were married in August 1923, and Wilson lived in Martinsburg until 1941. His only child, Robert, was born there in 1925.

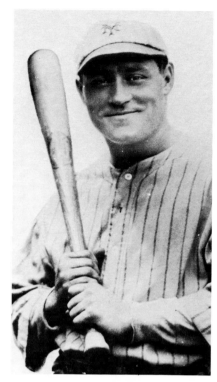

Hack as a 24-year-old rookie in 1924, the year he picked up his nickname and took over in center field for the Giants.

Returning to action, Wilson managed to appear in 30 games during the 1921 season, batting an impressive .356 with five home runs. It wasn't much of a trial though, so he was back with the Martinsburg club again in 1922, and he enjoyed a longer and more productive year, belting 30 home runs in only 84 games, with a .366 batting average. The 30 home runs set a league record, Wilson moved to the outfield, and his team won the pennant. In Martinsburg, where baseball was a happy part of his life, he was affectionately dubbed "Stouts" Wilson.

Wilson was sold to Portsmouth of the Virginia League for the 1923 season, and he was once again devastating. In 115 games, he drove in 101 runs, batted .388, and hit 19 home runs to win the league's triple crown. He also clobbered 37 doubles and 15 triples; he had clearly outgrown minor league baseball.

New York Giants' manager John McGraw saw Wilson play while on a scouting mission to Portsmouth, and he purchased Lew and a young pitching prospect for $11,000. The pair joined the Giants in Chicago on September 15, the same day that Bill Terry came up from Toledo. Wilson didn't appear in a game until September 27, when he made an error that cost New York two runs. He never did become much of an outfielder, but he had arrived in the big leagues.

Wilson became a regular in center field for the Giants in 1924 and earned his nickname, Hack, that same year. He was named after the Cubs' Hack Miller, who was built somewhat like Wilson, and who had been named for a noted Russian wrestler of the period, George Hackenschmidt.

Wilson was sensational in 1924, hoisting his batting average to a robust .373 by July 12. But a late-season ankle injury slowed him down and caused his average to fall to .295 at season's end. He had 10 home runs and played all seven games of the 1924 World Series, which the Giants lost to Washington. Hack hit .233 in the Series.

His slump continued into the 1925 season. Although he hit two home runs in one inning on July 1, he had hit only .239 by late July and was demoted to Toledo. There he regained his touch, batting .343 in 55 games, but the Giants failed to protect him after the season, and he was drafted by the Cubs for $5000.

Joe McCarthy joined the Cubs as manager in 1926; he had managed against Wilson while at Louisville. It was his recommendation that brougbt Hack back into the big leagues for the most glorious period of his life.

Wilson seemed perfect for Chicago. A free-wheeling, night-life sort of fellow, quick to anger and brawl, and well acquainted with all the speakeasies the Windy City had to offer, Wilson soon emerged as something of a folk hero.

He led the National League with 21 home runs in 1926, driving in 109 runs and batting .321. A year later, he drove in 129, missing the RBI title by only 2, while hitting .318 and smacking 30 homers, tying Cy Williams of the Phillies for the league lead.

Hack's assault on enemy pitchers continued in 1928, as he batted .313 with 31 homers and 120 runs batted in, sharing his third home run crown with Jim Bottomley.

The 1929 Cubs were pennant winners at last, as Hack was teamed with such outstanding players as Rogers Hornsby, Kiki Cuyler, Gabby Hartnett, Charlie Grimm, and Riggs Stephenson. Wilson contributed a batting average of .345 with 39 homers and a league-leading 159 runs batted in, which set a new National League record. In the World Series, Hack batted .471, but the Cubs lost to the Athletics in five games. In the fourth game, Chicago had an 8–0 lead after six innings, but Philadelphia rallied for 10 runs in the seventh, aided by a costly error by Wilson in center.

The 1930 season would be Wilson's finest, and one of the finest ever enjoyed by any player. The entire league was doing some great hitting, and the league batting average for the year was .303. Seventeen men bettered the 100 RBI mark, but none shone so brightly as Wilson, who by the end of August had broken Chuck Klein's league record set the year before, of 43 homers, and his own league RBI mark. In August, Wilson hit 13 home runs and drove in 53 runs in 31 games. Although the Cubs would not repeat their pennant and McCarthy would not finish out the season as manager, Wilson had a terrific September and wound up with 56 home runs and 190 runs batted in. The home run total set a National League record, and the RBI total set a major league record that most people feel will stand forever.

The fans loved to watch Wilson at bat. With his odd size and tremendous power, he was unique among players in his day, and like Babe Ruth in the American League, his mighty swing could result in either a long home run or an embarrassing miss.

Hack finished the year with a .356 batting average, 146 runs scored, 208 hits, and a .723 slugging percentage.

Hornsby became manager of the Cubs in 1931, and Wilson never took to his style. He followed his terrific year with an incredible dive, batting just .261 with 13 homers and 61 RBIs. He was making $33,000 a year, but Hornsby suspended him on September 6 for the remainder of the season, and it cost him some $3500 in salary. The suspension was over a fight involving two sportswriters and pitcher Pat Malone. Wilson was apparently a bystander who refused to break up the brawl, and it was the last straw in a bad relationship with Hornsby.

His six years with the Cubs were over. In December he was traded with Art Teachout to St. Louis for Burleigh Grimes; but when Branch Rickey mailed Hack a contract for only $7500, Wilson refused to play for the Cardinals. A month later he was traded to Brooklyn, where he received a contract worth $16,500.

Had there been such a thing as "Comeback of the Year" for 1932, Wilson would have won it. He finished fifth in both homers (23) and RBIs (123), and batted .297 for the Dodgers. But it was his last taste of glory.

One afternoon in Philadelphia that year, Hack was somewhat hung over, and spent much of the game fielding line drives off the right field wall. At last, Casey Stengel, the Brooklyn manager, strode to the mound to remove his pitcher, "Boom Boom" Beck. In anger, Beck spun and whipped the ball towards the outfield. Hack had been resting during the pitching change, but hearing the sound of the ball hitting the wall, he spun and chased it down, firing a perfect strike to second base. Stengel called it his finest play of the season.

In 1934 he started slowly with the Dodgers and in August was released and signed by the Phillies. He hit a combined .267 with nine homers for the two clubs in 74 games and was through with major league baseball.

Hack got a job with the Albany team of the International League in 1935, batted just .263 with three homers, and was assigned to Portland, Oregon, in June. Portland was too far away for Hack's taste, and he announced his retirement from pro ball. He wound up with a .307 career average and was sixth on the all-time home run list with 244 at the time of his retirement.

The remainder of his life was sad and aimless. He played semipro ball in Martinsburg, and opened a bar, serving as both bartender and best customer. His reputation as a brawler continued.

His partner bought him out in 1937, and in 1938, he was divorced, losing his house and what little money he had left. He married Hazel Miller that same year, and they moved to McKeesport, Pennsylvania, where he continued to find odd jobs, usu-ally as a greeter in bars. He still played some semipro ball and was occasionally in demand for a personal appearance.

His first wife died in 1940, and he returned to Martinsburg for the funeral and remained there for a time. He was later spotted in Chicago, doing odd jobs and living in boarding houses behind saloons.

He moved to Baltimore in 1941 and lived there for the rest of his life, having little contact with his son, and his second wife eventually left him too. By 1947, he had decided to stop drinking, but his once powerful body was already damaged, and he died at the age of 48 on November 11, 1948, of pulmonary edema. He was buried in Martinsburg, where the local Elks Club donated a handsome marker for his grave. Joe McCarthy led a memorial service for him.

His reputation for drinking and his relatively brief reign of greatness kept him out of the Hall of Fame for many years, but at last, in 1979, the Veterans' Committee selected him for induction.

LEWIS ROBERT WILSON

New York (N.L.) 1923–1925
Chicago (N.L.) 1926–1931
Brooklyn 1932–1934
Philadelphia (N.L.) 1934

G	AB	R	H	2B	3B	HR	RBI	Avg.
1348	4760	884	1461	266	67	244	1062	.307

Hack in a moment of repose in Wrigley Field. Despite the serious expression, he was always "one of the boys," and lived life to its fullest during his glory years, however brief they were.